PHILIP LARKIN
A Writer's Life

Andrew Motion was born in 1952 and educated at University College, Oxford. He is the author of the biographies *The Lamberts* and *Keats*, of critical studies of Philip Larkin and Edward Thomas, and of seven collections of poetry, and he has been the recipient of the John Llewellyn Rhys Prize, the Somerset Maugham Award and the Dylan Thomas Award. He lives in London with his wife and their three children.

PHILIP LARKIN

A Writer's Life

ANDREW MOTION

faber and faber

First published in 1993
by Faber and Faber Limited
3 Queen Square London WC1N 3AU
This paperback edition first published 1994

Photoset by Parker Typesetting Service, Leicester
Printed in England
by Clays Ltd, St Ives plc

A CIP record for this book
is available from the British Library

ISBN 0–571–17065–X

10 9 8 7 6 5 4 3 2

CONTENTS

ILLUSTRATIONS

ACKNOWLEDGEMENTS

Monica Jones, who was Philip Larkin's confidante and companion for nearly forty years, has helped me more than anyone else while I have been writing this book. She has been unfailingly generous, candid and hospitable. I am deeply in her debt, and so is everyone who cares about Larkin's writing.

Sir Kingsley Amis, Maeve Brennan, Winifred Dawson (née Arnott), Judy Egerton, Betty Mackereth, Charles Monteith, Ruth Siverns (née Bowman), Jim Sutton, and (with Monica Jones) my co-literary executor of the Larkin Estate, Anthony Thwaite, have also been exceptionally helpful. They have given many hours of their time, endured my interrogations, patiently reconstructed the past, and granted me permission to quote material in their possession. I am very grateful to them all.

My friends Alan Hollinghurst, Robert McCrum, Blake Morrison, Christopher Reid – who is also my editor – and Marion Shaw read the book in its penultimate draft, and made many valuable suggestions. Marion Shaw deserves a special word of thanks. On my many visits to Hull over the past several years she has listened to me, fed me and lent me her guest room. I owe her a great deal.

I owe even more to my wife, Jan Dalley. She has always asked the right questions, and her insights have always deepened my understanding. Without her, this book would have been much less than it is.

Larkin liked to give the impression that he lived an invariably quiet life, but while he had a small number of close friends he had a very large number of acquaintances and professional colleagues. An even larger number of people – some of whom only knew the work, not the man – have also been drawn into the orbit of this book. They have all been extremely encouraging and forthcoming – sharing their memories of Larkin, their thoughts about him, and letting me read their letters from him. For their kindness, conversation, advice, practical help and permission to quote I am pleased to acknowledge:

Simon Adams, Martin Amis, Peter Antrobus.

Phil Bacon, Christopher Baker, Jill Balcon, Donald Bancroft, Jonathan Barker, Julian Barnes, Max Barnett, Joan Barton, Molly Bateman, Ida Beck, J. C. Beckett, Margaret Bell, Sir Isaiah Berlin, the estate of Sir John Betjeman, the estate of Elizabeth Bishop, Stella Bishop, Bronwen Biswas, Robin Biswas, Caroline Blackwood, B. C. Bloomfield, James Booth, Michael Bowen, Alan Bower, Father Francis Bown, Harrison Boyle, Eric Bracewell, Malcolm Bradbury, Dennis Bradley, Melvyn Bragg, E. B. Bramwell, Ray Brett, Frieda Brown, Philip Brown, Sir Mervyn Brown,

Ivory Buchan, Bohdan Buciak, Campbell Burnap.

Donald Campbell, Raymond Cass, Roy Castle, Lady Elizabeth Cavendish, Harry Chambers, John Chapple, Maurice B. Cloud, George Cole, Philip Collins, Robert Conquest, R. J. Cooper, John Cotton, C. B. Cox, Tom Cusack.

Alec Dalgarno, Barbara Dalgarno, Timothy d'Arch Smith, the late Dan Davin, Eddie Dawes, the estate of C. Day-Lewis, Peter Dickinson, Edward du Cann, Peter du Sautoy, Janet Duffin, Douglas Dunn.

Robert Eborall, Margaret Elliot, D. J. Enright, Babette Evans, Matthew Evans, Barbara Everett, Jane Exall.

Jane Feaver, David Fielding, Jack Flint, Tony Flynn, Alan Fowlie, Ian Frazer, John Frazer, Paddy Frazer, John Fuller.

Patrick Garland, David Gerard, Dennis Gibbs, Robert Giroux, John Gloster, Rosemary Goad, Fay Godwin, Martin Goff, Livia Gollancz, Daisy Goodwin, Tom Graham, M. Grant Cormack, Arthur Green, Richard Griffiths, Miriam Gross, Lizzie Grossman.

John Hall, Kathleen Hall, Michael Hamburger, Ian Hamilton, Pamela Hanley, Elsie Harris, George Hartley, Jean Hartley, R. Haynes, Rev. P. N. Hayward, Seamus Heaney, Mark Hearne, John Heath-Stubbs, Anthony Hedges, Catherine Hewitt, S. Hewitt, Frances Hill, Martin Hill, Bevis Hillier, Peter Hoare, Harry Hoff, Hazel Holt, Geoff Hook, Noel Hughes, Ted Hughes, Arthur Humphries.

Norman Iles.

Robert Jackson, Anne James, K. H. Jeffrey, the late Sir Brynmor Jones, Mary Judd.

Pat Kavanagh, Mary Kelly, R. C. Kennedy, John Kenyon, Dick Kidner, Lady Hilary Kilmarnock, the late Terence Kilmartin, L. W. Kilroe, Ann Kind, L. W. Kingsland.

Sonia Lane, Ethel Leake, Peter Levi, Frank Liddiard, Solly Lipshitz, Edna Longley, Michael Longley, Graham Lord, the estate of Robert Lowell.

Basil McIvor, Jill McIvor, Lachlan Mackinnon, Henry Mackle, Charles Madge, Elizabeth Madill, Bill Manhire, Alison Mansbridge, Alan Marshall, George Martin, Tom Maschler, Frank Mattison, Oscar Mellor, Michael Meyer, A. L. Miller, Karl Miller, Donald Mitchell, Brenda Moon, Michael Moorey, Joanna Motion, Ian Mowat, Jamie Muir, Richard Murphy.

The late J. Norton Smith.

Philip Oakes, V. W. Oates, Humphrey Ocean, Martyn Offord, Charles Osborne.

Graham Parkes, Rosemary Parry, Tom Paulin, Virginia Peace, Robert Philips, Jimmy Piggott, Harold Pinter, Alan Plater, Graham Poots, Ted Poots, Henri Poulet, Anthony Powell, Neil Powell, S. L. Powsey, Judith Priestman.

Jonathan Raban, F. W. Ratcliffe, Dilys Rees, the late Garnet Rees, Wilf Richardson, Sheila Richter, Christopher Ricks, John Riggott, Layton Ring, Ernest Roe, Alan Ross, Janice Rossen, Sheila Rossiter, A. L. Rowse, Don Roy, Hilary Rubenstein, W. G. Runciman, Nick Russel, Bill Ryder.

A Writer's Life

Dale Salwak, John Saville, Penelope Scott Stokes, Garry Sergeant, John Shakespeare, Sebastian Shakespeare, Michael Sharp, the late Roger Sharrock, Fiona Shaw, Peter Sheldon, H. J. Shepheard, Brian Shepley, Michael Shere, M. Shirley, J. B. Simmons, Jack Simmons, Frank Smith, Andrew Snell, the late John Sparrow, Sir Stephen Spender, D. J. Spooner, Nora Stooke, Colin Strang, Joan Sutcliffe, Leslie Sykes, Julian Symons.

Daphne Tagg, Ted Tarling, Brian Tate, Arthur Tattersall, Anne Taylor, Brian Taylor, Patrick Taylor-Martin, Arthur Terry, James Thompson, Ann Thwaite, David Timms, Pamela Todd, James Toll, A. J. Tolley, Charles Townsend.

James Vitty, Steve Voce.

John Wain, Geoffrey Walker, Philip Walker, Bob Wallis, Bill Warley, Gwen Watkins, Barbara Watson, David Watson, J. R. Watson, Rob Watt, Peter Way, John Wells, Geoff Weston, W. G. Wheeler, John White, David Whittle, John Widowson, Jimmy Wilcox, A. N. Wilson, Bruce Woodcock.

Nicholas Zurbrugge.

I am also grateful to the following companies, institutions and organizations: the Librarian and staff of the Queen's University Library, Belfast; the staff of the Modern Manuscript and John Johnson Reading Room, the Bodleian Library, Oxford; the staff of the Department of Manuscripts, the British Library; Faber and Faber, for permission to quote from material in their archive; the Librarian and staff of the Brynmor Jones Library, the University of Hull, for permission to quote from material held in their Philip Larkin Archive (I am especially grateful to the Archivist, Brian Dyson, and to Larkin's successor as Librarian, Ian Mowat); the College Secretary and the Archivist, Malcolm Vale, at St John's College, Oxford; the Headmaster and staff of King Henry VIII School, Coventry – especially Geoff Vent; the Librarian and staff at the University of Leicester Library; Sidney F. Huttner, the Curator of the Special Collections at McFarlin Library, the University of Tulsa, for permission to quote from letters from Larkin to Patsy Strang and Richard Murphy and the Librarian at Vassar College, Poughkeepsie, for permission to quote from material held in their Elizabeth Bishop archive.

I am very happy to thank the Leverhulme Foundation, which generously awarded me a Fellowship in 1990–91.

Acknowledgement is also due to: Faber and Faber for permission to quote from poems by Philip Larkin originally published in *The Whitsun Weddings* and *High Windows*, and extracts from previously uncollected poems first published in

Collected Poems, ed. Anthony Thwaite (1988), and also for extracts from *Jill*, *A Girl in Winter*, *All What Jazz*, and *Required Writing*. Quotations from 'Lines on a Young Lady's Photograph Album', 'Wedding Wind', 'Coming', 'Next, Please', 'Going', 'Wants', 'Born Yesterday', 'No Road', 'Church Going', 'Toads', 'Poetry of Departures', 'Deceptions', 'I Remember, I Remember', 'Absences', 'Arrivals, Departures', and 'At Grass' are reprinted from *The Less Deceived* by permission of The Marvell Press, London.

Quotations from *The Oxford Book of Twentieth Century English Verse* are reprinted by permission of the Oxford University Press.

Excerpts from *High Windows*, copyright © 1974 by Philip Larkin, excerpts from *Collected Poems*, copyright © 1988, 1989 by the Estate of Philip Larkin, and excerpts from *Required Writing*, copyright © 1985 by Philip Larkin, are reprinted by permission of Farrar, Straus and Giroux, Inc., New York.

Excerpts from *Jill* and *A Girl in Winter*, both copyright © 1976 by Philip Larkin, published in the United States by the Overlook Press, are reprinted by permission of the Overlook Press, Woodstock, USA.

Excerpts from *The Oxford Book of Twentieth Century English Verse* are reprinted by permission of the Oxford University Press, New York.

Quotations from the unpublished letters of Robert Lowell are used with the permission of the Lowell Estate, copyright © 1992 by Caroline Lowell, Harriet Lowell and Sheridan Lowell.

I also acknowledge the use of extracts from the following published sources:

Kingsley Amis, *Lucky Jim* (Penguin, 1961)
——, *Memoirs* (Penguin, 1992)
B. C. Bloomfield, *Philip Larkin, A Bibliography: 1933–1976* (Faber, 1979)
James Booth, *Philip Larkin: Writer* (Harvester Press, Hemel Hempstead, 1992)
Malcolm Bradbury, *Eating People Is Wrong* (Arrow, 1978)
Humphrey Carpenter, *W. H. Auden: A Biography* (George Allen & Unwin, 1981)
Timothy d'Arch Smith, *R. A. Caton and the Fortune Press* (Bertram Rota Publishing, 1983)
The Modern Academic Library: Essays in Memory of Philip Larkin, ed. Brian Dyson (The Library Association, 1989)
Richard Griffiths, *Fellow Travellers of the Right* (Oxford, 1983)
Philip Larkin 1922–1985: A Tribute, ed. George Hartley (The Marvell Press, London, 1988)
Jean Hartley, *Philip Larkin, The Marvell Press and Me* (Carcanet, 1989)
Hazel Holt, *A Lot to Ask: A Life of Barbara Pym* (Macmillan, 1990)
Winifred Holtby, *South Riding* (Virago, 1988)
Blake Morrison, *The Movement* (Oxford, 1986)
Tom Paulin, *Minotaur* (Faber, 1992)
Jonathan Raban, *Coasting* (Picador, 1987)

Harry Ritchie, *Success Stories* (Faber, 1988)
Philip Larkin: The Man and his Work, ed. Dale Salwak (Macmillan, 1989)
Larkin at Sixty, ed. Anthony Thwaite (Faber, 1982)

Every effort has been made to trace all copyright holders, but if any have been inadvertently overlooked, the publishers will be pleased to make the necessary arrangements at the first opportunity.

Unless otherwise stated, photographs in this book are © the Estate of Philip Larkin: I gratefully acknowledge permission to reproduce them. For helping me unearth them, and for providing other pictures, I am grateful to Monica Jones – and also to Maeve Brennan, Robert Conquest, Winifred Dawson (née Arnott), Judy Egerton, Colin Gunner, Jean Hartley, Charles Monteith, Arthur Terry and D. H. Whiffen.

I am also pleased to acknowledge the following: Roland Wheeler-Osman and the University of Hull Photographic and Copy Service for the pictures of 32 Pearson Park and 105 Newland Park; the University of Hull Photographic and Copy Service for their pictures of the Library staff, the Hull University campus, Betty Mackereth, and the draft page of 'Dockery and Son'; Faber and Faber for the picture of Charles Monteith; Jane Bown for the portrait of Philip Larkin with John Betjeman; and Christopher Barker and Carcanet Press for the portrait taken of Philip Larkin in the Brynmor Jones Library in 1984.

INTRODUCTION

In 1976 I went to teach English at the University of Hull, where Philip Larkin had been the Librarian for twenty-one years. I spent my first few weeks trying not to meet him. His fame was formidable; his shyness was notorious; he was deaf and probably wouldn't be able to hear me; he was known to distrust academics and their students ('the dutiful mob that signs on each September'[1]).

When we were eventually introduced – in the university staff bar one lunchtime – he was disarmingly courteous. Taller than I had expected, heavier, dark-suited, he seemed stern but at the same time amiable, withdrawn but forthright, rigorous but sometimes extravagantly funny. By the end of term our meetings had fallen into a pattern: lunch once or twice a week in the staff bar, occasional evenings together. It remained the same until I left Hull in 1980, except that when my wife and I moved from a flat to a house in 1977 Larkin came to us more often than we went to him.[2] After 1980 we wrote to each other regularly but only saw each other from time to time – either in Oxford, where I lived, or in London. At no time during the nine years of our friendship did we discuss his biography. He did not ask me to write this book.

What he did ask – in the summer of 1983, when he was thinking about making his second will – was that I should join his long-time companion Monica Jones and friend Anthony Thwaite as one of his literary executors. 'There won't be anything difficult for you to do,' he told me. 'When I see the Grim Reaper coming up the path to my front door I'm going to the bottom of the garden, like Thomas Hardy, and I'll have a bonfire of all the things I don't want anyone to see. Now let's change the subject. This is like talking to the person who'll be washing my corpse.'[3]

As things turned out there were several months between Larkin's first sighting of the Grim Reaper and his death, but the bonfire was never made. The thirty-odd thick volumes of his diary, which he had kept on and off since his schooldays, the eight manuscript books in which he drafted his poems, and the large mass of his unpublished papers and letters lay undisturbed in his house when he was carried out of it for the last time.

Why? Monica Jones thinks that Larkin wanted to ignore his approaching death: to have lit the fire would have been to concede that he had no hope of recovery. This is perfectly likely, but it doesn't provide the whole answer. Larkin's final indecision was the last in a series that shaped his life. He had dictated the terms of his existence with great authority but was always loath to commit himself absolutely to any one or other course of action. He had become renowned for keeping things to himself, yet he also had a compulsion to reveal and share them. Although there had been plenty of time for him to dispose of his private papers himself, it was Monica who arranged for the diaries to be fed into the university's shredding machine shortly after his death. (Only a few pages were spared – torn out by Larkin during the mid 1970s when he was considering editing his diaries for publication.)

The rest of his papers survived, but so precariously that his executors took legal advice before deciding what to do next. They showed a copy of his will to a Queen's Counsel for a professional opinion, feeling that the contradictory line Larkin had taken in conversation was matched by ambiguities in the text. In the first clause of the seventh paragraph Larkin had given 'to my Trustees [Monica Jones and his solicitor Terence Wheldon] all my published and unpublished work, together with all manuscripts and letters ... with full right subject to the provisions of the following sub-clauses to publish any such unpublished works ...' In the next clause he seemed to change his mind: 'I direct that all unpublished writings and diaries and texts and manuscripts in any form whether or not published at the date of my death and in my possession at the date of my death shall be destroyed unread.' Then again, in yet another clause in this paragraph, he had instructed his trustees to consult his literary executors 'in all matters concerned with the publication of my unpublished manuscripts'. As a journalist subsequently reporting on the will put it: 'In three breaths Larkin gave his trustees the power to publish his unpublished work, instructed them to destroy it, and told them to discuss the matter with the literary executors.'[4]

In due course the Queen's Counsel declared the will 'repugnant' (legalese for contradictory). Once this opinion had been given the executors had the chance to argue for the destruction or preservation of everything – everything, that is, except the diaries, which had by then already been disposed of, following a specific request Larkin had made to Monica on his deathbed. He had given no such specific instructions about his other papers, and the executors unanimously decided to preserve them – partly because of their presumed literary importance, and partly because the executors felt (as Larkin himself had said in a talk on the value of preserving contemporary literary manuscripts) that 'Unpublished work, unfinished work, even notes towards unwritten work, all contribute to our knowledge of a writer's intentions.'[5] To prove that he meant what he said, Larkin had donated during his lifetime one of his own poetry manuscript books to the British Library. The bulk of his other papers now form part of the Philip Larkin Archive in the library he built, and which he ran for the last thirty years of his life – the library where his diaries were shredded.

When the row about the will died down, and the executors could see what had been saved, it led to a dramatic development in our understanding of Larkin's practice as a poet. The costive craftsman – almost as celebrated for the long intervals between his books as for the books themselves – wrote far more than anyone had suspected, at least until his last decade. After Anthony Thwaite had edited and published the *Collected Poems* in 1988 most readers were astonished to find it running to more than 300 pages. Readers of this book will be surprised by the extent of Larkin's other kinds of writing: by the huge spread of his letters (which includes the correspondences with Monica Jones and Maeve Brennan that are only sketched in Thwaite's *Selected Letters*, and the previously unpublished correspondence with his father and mother); by the large number of drafts he made of his two complete and two incomplete novels; by the frequency (once again at the beginning rather than the end of his life) with which he produced essays, poems, stories, short plays and reviews of books and jazz records; by the existence of two full-length, facetious, would-be lesbian romances written in the early 1940s under the pseudonym Brunette Coleman.

Larkin also bound up, at the end of every five years in the library, a 'great fat volume' of Library Committee minutes which, although 'not the same as a volume of poetry' were, as he said, 'very good minutes'.[6] In addition, he brought home from his office – and began doing so at an early age – the scrupulous habits of a good librarian. He kept a large number of his incoming letters, sorting them into shoe-boxes on which he inked the initials of the correspondent. He preserved memorabilia of all sorts – his parents' jam recipes, for instance, and the telegrams sent to him when he was awarded his degree at Oxford. In cupboards in his various flats, and eventually in the windowless lumber-room at the top of the stairs in his last house in Hull, he kept his whole life in perfect order.

During his adolescence Larkin had decided he was 'a genius'.[7] At the same time, judging by his secretive but thorough self-preservation, he accepted that he would be written about. In this, as in virtually everything else, he felt divided. His powerful self-esteem was matched by an equally virulent self-disparagement. Bernard Shaw, whom he admired, gave him a model for this, saying that he (Shaw) was 'not at all interesting biographically. I have never killed anybody. Nothing very unusual has happened to me.'[8] Time and again Larkin made a similar point. He said in his poem 'Coming' that his childhood was 'a forgotten boredom'. His undergraduate days were spent at an Oxford profoundly unlike that of 'Michael Fane and his fine bindings, or Charles Ryder and his plover's eggs'.[9] His 'very ordinary'[10] adult life was spent toiling dully in far-flung, unglamorous towns where – as he says in 'Here', 'only salesmen and relations come'.

In case all this didn't deter potential Boswells, Larkin liked to scoff at many of the basic tenets of biography itself. He derided its willingness to rely for psychological insights on formative childhood experiences. 'Whenever I read an autobiography,' he said, 'I tend to start halfway through, when the chap's grown up and it becomes interesting.'[11] In the same way, he repudiated the idea that writers might evolve in response to what happened to them in adult life. 'Only mediocrities develop,' he was fond of saying, quoting Oscar Wilde.

On the face of it, these feelings are best summarized by Larkin's poem 'Posterity', where 'my biographer' – the insultingly named Jake Balokowsky – abuses his 'old fart' subject in a way which appears to rebound entirely to his own discredit:

> 'What's he like?
> Christ, I just told you. Oh, you know the thing,
> That crummy textbook stuff from Freshman Psych,
> Not out of kicks or something happening –
> One of those old-type *natural* fouled-up guys.'

This seems straightforward. Larkin's life is neither sufficiently strange nor complex to interest Balokowsky much; writing it is merely a way of improving career prospects. But even here – and it's a qualification which runs beneath all Larkin's pronouncements about biography – difficulties arise. After 'Posterity' had been published Larkin told the poet Richard Murphy:

I'm sorry if Jake Balokowsky seemed an unfair portrait. As you see, the idea of the poem was imagining the ironical situation in which one's posthumous reputation was entrusted to somebody as utterly unlike oneself as could be. It was only after the poem had been published that I saw that Jake, wanting to do one thing but having to do something else, was really not so unlike me, and indeed had probably unconsciously been drawn to my work for this reason, which explains his bitter resentment of it.[12]

'Posterity' opens by seeming hostile to Balokowsky and ends by showing him sympathy – just as Larkin's lumber-room library, where everything stayed hidden, was also the place where everything would eventually be discovered. The poem encapsulates the whole range of paradoxes which made up Larkin's attitude to publicity. The soul of shy modesty was also a self-promoter; the man admired for avoiding bright lights was continually tempted to step into them; the 'Hermit of Hull' was his readers' friend, winning their trust and warm affection by telling them a good deal about himself.

In one obvious respect these contradictions make things easier for Larkin's biographer. They leave in their wake a large amount of material to be mulled over, and they encourage the hope that Larkin might have recorded even his most intimate moments. Yet in another respect they make him difficult to write about. By trapping him between opposing impulses they stopped him leading a life much diversified by event. His story contains only a modest number of love affairs, almost no foreign travel, no games of Russian Roulette, no shark-fishing expeditions.

Such things make a person a 'good subject' for a biography, and where they do not exist some readers, let alone some biographers, get jumpy. There is no need. Larkin lived a much more dramatic and intense life than he let on, though it was performed on an inner stage rather than before the wide world. This is the fascination of Larkin's story. Carefully shielded from surprises, his work grew in private, where the longing for calm and solitude was always a prey to the exhilarating disruption of strong feeling. To follow his development is to have our sense of his achievement sharply increased. In his lifetime he was acclaimed as the greatest poet of his generation – someone who spoke for the disillusion of the post-war years and for the value of conserving traditions, and who finally received most of his honours under a Conservative government whose leader, Mrs Thatcher, he 'adored'. After his death, it's clear that his writing transcends his time rather than merely encapsulating it: he is one of the great poets of the century.

Larkin's devotion to 'that lifted rough-tongued bell/(Art, if you like)' challenges the idea of himself as a writer that he liked to promote. By implication, it also conflicts with our sense of him as someone who never ruffled the tranquil surface of the backwaters in which he lived. He was a selfish man much given to showing love and kindness. He was a steadily deepening reactionary who was often suddenly tolerant. He was devoted to the here-and-now, but he never lost his longing for release into what 'High Windows' calls 'the deep blue air, that shows/Nothing, and is nowhere, and is endless'.

It is part of his poems' strength to speak directly to most people who come across them. He makes each of us feel he is 'our' poet, in a way that Eliot, for instance, does not – and each of us creates a highly personal version of his character to accompany his work. Pointing out that he was contradictory doesn't pose much of a threat to these versions. It's more disturbing, however, to say that many of Larkin's inner conflicts evolved in ways his work can only hint at. When he found his authentic voice in the late 1940s, the beautiful flowers of his poetry were already growing on long stalks out of pretty dismal ground. Describing this ground must necessarily alter the image of Larkin that he prepared so carefully for his readers. With half his mind – the half that asked for his unpublished papers to be destroyed – he never wanted this change to take place. With the other half – the half that left the papers to be preserved – he understood that the relationship he had created between 'high' art and 'ordinary' existence was a remarkable one, which deserved to be made public.

This book is the story of that relationship. The friends he made, the jobs he took, the habits he formed, the places he lived in, the people he loved – all were chosen so that he could concentrate on his writing, which is what mattered to him most. In the strictest sense, his was a writer's life.

A WRITER'S LIFE

ONE

There's a Philip Larkin who works as a 'Hurley Manufacturer' in Moyleen, Co. Galway. Another runs a fish and chip shop in Fermanagh.[1] With or without 'Philip' attached, the name Larkin is general all over Ireland, and at various times of his life – especially during his five years in Belfast (1950–55) – it was widely believed that Philip Larkin the writer came from that country. George Fraser, for instance, possibly remembering James Larkin (1876–1947), the well-known Irish nationalist and leader of the Irish TGWU, featured him in the anthology *Springtime* (1953) as a 'Northern Ireland regional poet'.[2] The Public Orator who presented him with an honorary Doctorate of Letters at the New University of Ulster in 1983 made a similar assumption, learnedly observing that 'according to Edward MacLysaght in his *Surnames of Ireland* [the name Larkin] is equivalent to Lorcain, from Lorc, an old name denoting rough or fierce'.[3]

Larkin himself spurned his remote relations. The idea of an extended past was as unappealing to him as the thought of a future filled by a wife and children. The few references he does make to his ancestors are always of the most vaguely anecdotal kind. 'Have just heard Handel's *Largo* and thought of Grandad,' he told his mother with typical abruptness in one letter; 'how much of a descendant of him I feel sometimes, with his bald head and solitary ecstasies!'[4] And again, elsewhere: 'I certainly agree with Grandad that the song of a blackbird is one of the most thrilling things one is likely to hear in a day's march.'[5] Larkin's pleas for independence are far more numerous than such remarks about family connections. In this, however, as in much else, he couldn't help showing a traceable characteristic. His father Sydney 'is like me', he told his mother Eva in his early twenties. 'He could walk past a whole row of his exhumed ancestors and never notice anything untoward.'[6]

It suited Larkin to accuse Sydney of taking no interest in his relations; it showed that they were both free spirits, full of choices and chances. Yet in fact Sydney and his brother Alfred spent a certain amount of time clambering in the family tree, and managed to establish its overall shape. They discovered that, far from being Irish, their branch of the Larkins came

3

from Kent and had nothing to do with Lorc. 'When surnames were first assumed in the Middle Ages,' Sydney wrote, 'LARKIN appears as that of a rascal who had the audacity to carry on his coining operations in Newgate Prison. It is said to be a pet form of the Christian name "Lawrence" and so the word "Larrikin" is probably a corruption.'[7]

In spite of Sydney's best efforts, the ancient history of the family remained obscure. But while it is bare of detail, it conveys a strong sense of fixity. The Larkins lived for many years in the same Midlands place, doing the same work in the same house, marrying in the same church and being buried in the same graveyard. They spoke with the voice of middle England,[8] suffering history as the area around them changed from Langland's 'field full of folk' into a force of the Industrial Revolution. Their stability – if Sydney and his son's feelings are anything to go by – generated a sense of nationhood which was strong but unsentimental. 'There is not much to be proud of in being English,'[9] Larkin was apt to say, yet he was always quick to adopt and defend what he reckoned to be its best qualities: realism, pragmatism, modesty. He may not have bothered much with the names and dates of his relations, but he commemorated their values in many things he wrote.

Sydney Larkin's family make their first appearance in public records during the eighteenth century, in the cathedral city of Lichfield, Staffordshire. Edmund Larkin (1720–1802), Philip's great-great-great-grandfather, inherited a tailoring business at 49 Tamworth Street, just round the corner from where Samuel Johnson was born in 1709. With his wife Sara, Edmund had two sons – John (1757–1843) and Edmund junior (1759–1839). John in due course also became a tailor, and when he died the business went to William (1809–90) – one of his four sons and three daughters – and then to another Edmund, born in 1843 and one of William's six sons and three daughters. By this time, the family had set up a number of sidelines around Tamworth Street, including coach-making and shoe-making. But while trade prospered (when William died in 1890 he left a personal estate of just under £2,000), the passing generations brought their inevitable changes. Ernest Larkin, Edmund's son, sold the family business in the early years of this century and moved to London. His six brothers – Edward, Alfred, Cecil, George, Henry and Philip's father Sydney – eventually turned to other kinds of employment. The old order vanished. The tailor's, a cramped building on the curving road below St Michael's church on Green Hill, was divided into two – a turf accountant and a barber. Now it is a bric-à-brac shop.

Larkin's mother's family was more peripatetic, and cannot be traced back as far as his father's. Born on 10 January 1886, Eva Emilie was the elder child of William James Day – born in 1859 – and Emilie Archer, who was five years his junior. Her only brother Arthur was born in 1888. Eva spent her childhood in Epping, Essex, where her father was a First Class Excise Officer, and in 1914 when war broke out they moved to Leigh in Lancashire, so that he could take up a job administering dependent allowances – pensions and so on. When Eva left Leigh Grammar School she briefly considered becoming a librarian, then like her brother took up teaching for a short while. She was bookish but eager, efficient but self-doubting, practical but easily deterred by anxieties. Details of planning and administration rattled her; she was alarmed by newness; she was scared almost into hysterics by thunderstorms.

Her parents protected her as best they could, making sure their routines were orderly. Eva grew into a quietly spoken young woman, dark-haired, thin-faced and rather studious-looking, obviously intelligent but nervous. The humdrum rhythm of her days – her work, her respectable home, the annual family holiday in a coastal resort – was organized so that her life held few surprises.

The rhythm broke by chance. Holidaying in Rhyl on the north coast of Wales during the summer of 1906 (when she was twenty), she ran out of the rain on 6 August into a hut overlooking the sea. A young man already standing inside asked, 'Will you shelter here?' She replied, 'I can't think of a reason not to'[10] – and began reading a book. The young man was only a little taller than her, and had a 'serious, rather bad-tempered face, a poisoner's thin lips and a heavy moustache'.[11] He interrupted her reading to introduce himself as Sydney Larkin and was, he explained, on a cycling holiday. He would be staying in Rhyl only for another three days. Before those days were over, Eva had got engaged to him.

Her decision was not so impetuous – and therefore uncharacteristic – as it seems. Sydney had explained that he was at the beginning of his career and could not afford to think of marriage just yet. (The wedding eventually took place five years later, on 5 October 1911.) Meanwhile, he said, they should stay in touch by letter and visit each other whenever they could. Eva, mousy and unfamiliar with the world, was impressed by Sydney's startling mixture of dynamism and prudence. Her parents assumed the engagement would come to nothing. Her son, long after they had been proved wrong, commemorated their meeting in 'To the Sea'. The poem describes successive generations of seaside holiday-makers – 'the uncertain children, frilled in white/And grasping at enormous air' and the 'rigid old' – before reaching back to the time:

> when, happy at being on my own,
> I searched the sand for Famous Cricketers,
> Or, farther back, my parents, listeners
> To the same seaside quack, first became known.

In years to come, Sydney Larkin would say that he had initially been attracted to Eva because she responded to his advances by reading a book. He had always set great store by intelligence – even as a boy in Lichfield. Born on 25 April 1884, the youngest of Edmund's seven sons, he had been encouraged by his mother Catherine to believe that native wit was more valuable than inherited privilege. His six brothers felt the same, and variously became clerks or teachers. (One of them, Alfred, managed to arouse Larkin's curiosity by making an impressive collection of antique glass and china which he kept prominently displayed in his house near Lichfield Cathedral.) None, though, was as successful as Sydney or departed so far from his origins. At Lichfield Grammar School he was a star pupil, and later at King Edward VI High School in Birmingham (to which he travelled daily by train) he passed the Cambridge Junior Local Examination with first class honours. He was a dogmatic, intense and prickly boy, clear in debate, unable to suffer fools, devoutly agnostic, and passionate in his convictions.

Although Sydney's greatest gifts were for mathematics he was an avid reader of the classics and contemporary literature. He bought new novels by Wells and Bennett, new plays by Shaw, and new books by Hardy (whom he especially revered) as they were published. He was a stickler for precision and correctness, and seemed bracingly rigorous to some, a disciplinarian to others. (He would later amuse his son by saying that Kingsley Amis's 'lack of grasp of will/shall precludes his having a future as a writer'.[12])

When Sydney left school in 1902 he was taken on as a junior by T. H. Clare, the City Treasurer of Birmingham, in whose offices he had sometimes worked during the holidays. It marked the beginning of the end of his old Larkin world. The modest routines of Lichfield, where as a child he and his brothers had slept two in a bed, were left behind for ever. In England's second city the opportunities for self-advancement seemed boundless.

Philip Larkin 'always associated' the next part of his father's life with 'the young whey-faced provincials of Arnold Bennett'; he imagined they were years 'marked by his characteristic and lonely individuality: he was secretary of a chess club, he went for long cycle rides, he studied for examinations and passed them easily, he economized – for in those Edwardian days money made sense. If you wanted something you could not afford, you saved until you could afford it.'[13] Most of these examinations were taken at the University of Birmingham where, after two years with Clare, Sydney applied to study accountancy under Professor L. R. Dicksee. When his three-year course ended in 1907 he returned to City Hall and was quickly promoted – reaching the position of Chief Audit Accountant in 1911, the same year as his wedding.

Two years later Sydney was appointed Assistant Borough Accountant in Doncaster, in the West Riding of Yorkshire, and the family settled in the town with their infant daughter Catherine (Kitty). Sydney decided Eva should not have any more children until he had been promoted yet again, and Eva complied with his ruling. Sydney went from strength to strength. 'I was able to effect considerable improvements in the accountancy system [in Doncaster],' he later boasted, 'and, by means of clauses inserted at my suggestion in the Doncaster Corporation Act of 1915, to bring up to date the methods of dealing with short term loans and to bring into effect a consolidated collection of taxes.'[14] By 1919, when he was thirty-five, he felt he had outgrown the job, and started looking round for another and larger one. He applied to Nottingham and was rejected, then to Coventry, where the post of Deputy Treasurer had fallen vacant. The city, as well as the position, appealed to him. It was near enough to Lichfield to seem part of his middle England homeland, yet far enough away to demonstrate his independence. It was a place with a long and distinguished history (and, since 1918, a cathedral), and a thriving industrial present. Its prosperity was largely due to the Daimler motor car factory, which had been opened in 1896. Over the years a large number of other manufacturing industries (ranging from bicycles to aeroplanes) had grown up around it, employing many thousands of people. In 1901 the city's population had been 70,000. By the early 1920s it had more than doubled. By the middle of the century it had grown to 350,000, making it one of the fastest-growing towns in England.

Sydney was duly appointed Deputy Treasurer. Three years later he got what he wanted: the chance to apply for the post of Treasurer itself, when the incumbent, Harry Lord, retired. In his application, describing his time as Deputy, Sydney said:

The period of my service at Coventry has been one of more than usual activity on the part of the Corporation, and there can be few problems in municipal finance with which I have not had to deal ... Since 1920 Coventry Corporation has promoted seven local Acts and the city's financial legislation has for many years been in advance of the rest of the country.[15]

As soon as Sydney knew he was going to be Treasurer, he told Eva the time was right for them to have another child. Their daughter was nearly ten years old and settled at Barrs Hill School, and their home at 2 Poultney Road – a three-bedroom house in the suburb of Radford – was suitably large and comfortable. (It was a council house; Sydney's employers had arranged for him to live there during the acute housing shortage after the war.) Although the plaster on the walls had still been wet when they moved in, Sydney had soon organized everything in the house before handing over its day-to-day running to Eva. This included buying a picture called *Love's Idyll*, which showed two lovers embracing and which shocked his in-laws. They thought him 'very modern' in spite of his evident fastidiousness, and 'very broad-minded because the house was full of books by D. H. Lawrence, Bennett, and Mary Webb'.[16]

Sydney and Eva wanted a boy, and on 9 August 1922, on a night with a full moon, they got their wish: he was nearly a month late, weighed almost ten pounds, and had luxuriant black hair. Eva wanted to call him Anthony but Sydney overruled her, arguing for Philip and Sydney. In the end they compromised on Philip Arthur – Philip after the Renaissance poet Philip Sidney, Arthur after Eva's brother – and early in September he was christened in Coventry Cathedral. It was a mark of Sydney's pleasure in having a son that he suspended his disbelief in Christianity for the day. 'Really, Philip could do no wrong in his father's eyes,' says Kitty. 'Or his mother's. They worshipped him ... [And] I helped my parents a great deal in looking after [him] from the day he was born – taking him out in the pram or push-chair and later being with him while my parents were away at conferences ... I usually put him to bed and sang him to sleep while I was doing my homework – rather difficult.'[17]

Larkin was pampered and indulged all through his earliest years, yet he never deviated from the view that his childhood was a 'forgotten boredom'. (He was pleased to remember that 'one of my mother's stories about me as a baby is how she could never keep me amused – every fresh thing put into my hands lasted me only a few minutes, then the wail began again.'[18]) Expanding on his notorious phrase towards the end of his life, he said, 'Children are often bored, I think. They don't control their destinies, and they don't do what they want or live where they want. This isn't to say I didn't have nice friends I visited and played with and so on, or that my parents weren't perfectly kind to me, but when I read accounts of other people's childhoods they always seem more lurid and exciting than mine was. It seemed to have a fairly insulated quality that looking back on I can't quite account for.'[19]

Some of the reasons for this 'insulation' aren't hard to find. Even as a very small child, Larkin's eyesight was weak; his 'long back and comparatively short legs'[20] made him ungainly; and by the age of four he had started to stammer badly. 'It was,' he said, 'on words beginning with vowels rather than consonants . . . There was no obvious reason for it: no left-handedness or physical accidents. If I had some deep traumatic experience I've forgotten it. This went on up to the age of thirty-five or so, after which the impediment slowly faded away, only to return when I am tired or confronted with a "stammering situation" – post offices, for instance.'[21]

'A stammer can be grown out of,' Larkin believed, 'if it has arisen simply from self-consciousness and shyness.'[22] On one of the first – and last – occasions that he discussed these feelings with his father, Sydney reacted in a way which indicated what their main source might be. 'I remember,' Larkin said, 'when I was quite young, telling my father I was shy, and he said very crushingly, "You don't know what shyness is," implying that he'd been more shy.'[23] This memory, passed off as a casual slight, summarizes much of what Larkin meant when he disparaged his first, formative years. In the first decade of their marriage, his parents hadn't stopped loving each other, but their feelings had gone musty. Sydney's quick temper, imperious intellect and hurrying manner were steadily intensified by Eva's docility. He needed her to be placid, he demanded that she be the home-maker (even when it meant denying the intelligence that had drawn him to her in the first place), but with part of himself he also despised her for it. Later in life Larkin would describe how he came to consciousness with the sound of them 'Bickering stupidly at home/My fault, their fault'.[24] There was very little outspoken anger, but the sense that it was always just about to begin – an atmosphere of clenched irritation which curdled the whole experience of childhood. 'I hated everybody when I was a child,' he said, 'or thought I did. When I grew up, I realized that what I hated was children.'[25]

TWO

When Larkin was five years old Sydney moved the family from the suburbs of Coventry to a larger, detached house close to the city centre – 1 Manor Road. Standing at the heart of a compact residential district, the new home had a name as well as a number (Penvorn – a wonky conflation of the names of its builder, Percy Vernon Venables) and was, Larkin said, 'quite respectable'. Glossing this, he defined the middle-class assumptions that Sydney now took for granted: they had 'a succession of maids [the one who stayed longest was called Betty] and that sort of thing, as one did before the war. It was all very normal.'[1]

Normal, but slightly forbidding. With its three storeys rising behind a six-foot hedge, its front gate overhung by trees, its dark-painted window-frames and bristling mixture of brick and pebble-dash, Penvorn looked like a suburban version of Thomas Hardy's Max Gate. It was this house (eventually demolished to make way for a ring road in the 1960s) rather than Poultney Road which Larkin remembered as his family home, and which became the main focus for his early memories. It was the place where his 'forgotten boredom' became acute.

Although he would soon make a few intense friendships, his parents ensured that he spent a great deal of his childhood alone. 'I think [they] were not very sociable,' he said, putting it mildly. 'My mother because she was too simple; she just liked living in the house and doing the house and so on. My father because he was somewhat anti-social ... Nor did we seem to have many relations. We [had] relations but they were all some way away. They weren't in Coventry. There weren't constant visits from them or anything like that.'[2] Larkin's earliest childhood acquaintances confirm this. 'I thought [his house] was somewhat gloomy,' one says, 'and Mr Larkin somewhat distant and unapproachable.'[3] Another describes Eva as 'like Mrs Gummidge, always wringing her hands and crying into the tea-pot'.[4] A third calls the atmosphere 'colourless' and 'awkward'.[5] Elsie Harris, Sydney's secretary in City Hall for many years and a regular visitor to Penvorn, remembers that Sydney sometimes upset his wife by flirting with women in his office – 'an occasional cuddle, not missing an opportunity to put an arm round a secretary'.[6] She says that while 'Mrs Larkin was a pleasant, unobtrusive person', Sydney 'was very much the male chauvinist. He thought that women were of little account, their only functions to be decorative and to wait on men. He rarely spoke of his daughter but often spoke of Philip, of whom I think he was really proud.'[7]

In the years before Larkin went to school, his mother became more anxious, his father more 'nihilistic'[8] and crushing. Yet while Sydney was quick to scorn his fellows, he also accepted that he had to find ways of getting on with them. He joined the local chess club. He gave papers to the Literary and Philosophical Society (including one on Hardy). He gained a reputation as an accomplished after-dinner speaker. Colleagues in the town may not have found him easy, but they agreed with Elsie Harris that 'on the intellectual level he was good'.[9] It was the same in Penvorn. No matter how exasperating Sydney found his wife and daughter, he paid for them (and eventually Philip) to hear and watch things he reckoned would do them good: Shakespeare at Stratford, music in Coventry, books every-where. He was, Elsie Harris remembers, 'fascinated with the origins of words and their meaning. He often used to get me to look up things in the dictionary – for my sake, I mean. And I'm sure it was the same with the children, when they were old enough. He imbued everyone with his own enthusiasm, which was his aim of course.'[10]

Fearsome and hard-driving, Sydney turned himself into a figure of considerable authority. In one respect he also became an embarrassment. 'I think,' Larkin later said, '[my father] described himself as a Conservative Anarchist, but what that means I don't know.'[11] In fact he knew all too well. During the 1920s Sydney's politics gradually swung to the right, and by the end of the decade he was 'an active and impenitent admirer'[12] of Germany's post-war recovery. Eventually, in the 1930s, he praised Hitler for his role in achieving this, and it was rumoured around Coventry that Sydney was 'a member of [the neo-Nazi organization] The Link'.[13] When it seemed likely that this charge would be made public (in *Larkin at Sixty*, a collection of essays which appeared in 1982) Larkin was horrified. He sifted through Sydney's papers, and was relieved to find nothing which supported the accusation.

The Link was never a large outfit. Founded by Admiral Sir Barry Domvile in June 1937 as a means of promoting Anglo-German friendship, and associated closely with the *Anglo-German Review*, its clientele 'were mainly ordinary people in ordinary towns, who had little influence'.[14] By the end of 1937 it had grown quickly and established four branches – in

Chelsea, Southend, west London and Birmingham – where members ranged from 'the most innocent of provincial pro-Germanists to convinced pro-Nazis of a fairly disquieting kind'.[15] Early in 1939, on the eve of war, it grew still larger by affiliating itself to the Anglo-German Brotherhood, but when war actually broke out it shrivelled at once. It was declared a proscribed organization and disbanded.

Even if Sydney hesitated to join The Link he was certainly sympathetic to many of its principles. Throughout the 1920s he made no secret of his respect for the efficiency of the National Socialists, often recommending them to his son.[16] During the 1930s his enthusiasm would quicken dramatically. He entered into correspondence with H. G. H. (Hjalmar) Schacht, Hitler's Minister of Economics from 1934 to 1937, and the man widely credited with bringing German inflation under control. He visited Germany regularly. He frequently expressed his 'admiration'[17] for its recent successes.

While denying that Sydney was part of a specific organization, Larkin admitted that his father was 'the sort of person that democracy didn't suit'.[18] There was an innocent side to this: Sydney admired Germany for its technical advances and its 'office methods'.[19] But there were more sinister aspects as well. 'According to Philip,' says John Kenyon, a drinking companion of Larkin's and formerly Professor of History at Hull, Sydney 'had been an ardent follower of the Nazis and attended several Nuremberg rallies during the 1930s; he even had a statue of Hitler on the mantelpiece [at home] which at the touch of a button leapt into a Nazi salute.'[20] Sydney's Deputy Treasurer in Coventry, Alan Marshall, reluctantly confirms this. As late as 1939, Sydney had Nazi regalia decorating his office in City Hall, and when war was declared he was ordered by the Town Clerk to remove it. 'Sydney took the point,' Marshall says, 'but continued to express his admiration for Germany. He wasn't very good at realizing what impression he was making, or he didn't care.'[21] He didn't even change his tune when Coventry was blitzed in November 1940. Instead, he congratulated himself on his foresight in having ordered one thousand cardboard coffins the previous year, and continued to praise 'efficient German administration' while disparaging Churchill – who had, he thought, 'the face of a criminal in the dock'.[22]

As a young child Larkin wouldn't have understood the intricacies and implications of his father's politics, but as a way of establishing the mood in Manor Road their importance can't easily be exaggerated. Sydney Larkin was generous to his son, and often indulged him, but nevertheless strutted through his early life with a singular arrogance. He was intolerant to the point of perversity, contemptuous of women, careless of other people's feelings or fates, yet at the same time excitingly intellectual, inspirationally quick-witted, and (at least in the matter of books) unpredictably catholic in his tastes. Everything Larkin disliked or feared in his father was matched by something he found impressive or enviable.

Far from being 'forgotten', the 'boredom' of Larkin's first few years stayed with him for ever. To be the adored only son, to have a comfortable house full of good books, and to have annual holidays (in places such as Bigbury-on-Sea, Folkestone, and Caton Bay near Filey in Yorkshire) could not compensate for the 'drab'[23] marriage of his parents, the 'intimidating'[24] atmosphere of their home, and the web of disapproval that Sydney had woven round it. The effect was to drive Larkin in on himself even before he had discovered the alternative world of school – let alone the wider reaches of Coventry and beyond. Visitors to Manor Road remember a large-faced, long-haired child haunting its gloomy rooms in silence, or hanging around the adults with awkward reverence until told he could disappear to his bedroom. Even in this sanctuary he was vulnerable. No matter how much he protested that he was happiest poring over the *Magnet*, talking to his toys (a teddy bear, a dog called Rags, and a rabbit, which eventually met its end falling into a bowl of mint sauce[25]), collecting pennies and cigarette cards, or playing with his Hornby train set, the adult world kept demanding that he come downstairs and join in.

As the first half of Larkin's childhood dripped away, the mixture of feelings he had for his family gradually thickened. By early adolescence – stimulated by the desire to seem superior and separate – it had turned into rage. 'Please believe me,' he told his first important friend, 'when I say that half my days are spent in black, surging, twitching, boiling HATE!!!'[26] By adulthood it had modulated into controlled but bitter resentment, a feeling which surfaces time and again in an unpublished fragment he wrote during the 1950s. Apparently the beginning of a much longer but never completed piece of autobiography, it shows how – at the very beginning of his life – his parents formed the cramped but creative shape of his mature personality:

When I try to tune into my childhood, the dominant emotions I pick up are, overwhelmingly, fear and boredom. Although I have an elder sister, the ... difference in our ages made me feel for practical purposes an only child, and I suppose those feelings are characteristic.

As I picture him, my father was intensely shy, inhibited not robust, devoid of careless sensual instincts (though not of humour), and I don't think he did well to choose a wife of the same pattern. The only point where they differed was that while my father's brain was dominating, active and keen, my mother was made to trust and follow, and in that respect they were well suited, at any rate at first.

What kind of home did they create . . .? I should say it was dull, pot-bound, and slightly mad. By the time I knew it, my father worked all day and shut himself away reading in the evening, or else gardened. My mother constantly toiled at 'running the house', a task that was always beyond her, even with the aid of the resident maid and daily help. My sister, whose qualities of literal-mindedness and fantasy-spinning had infuriated my father until he made her life a misery, did not have many friends and endured, I should say, a pallid existence until she took up art, and even then day classes at Midland Art School did not lead to the excitements they should have. I don't think my father liked working or gardening, I don't think my mother liked keeping house, I don't think my sister liked living at home. Yet they all seemed powerless to do anything about it. There was a curious tense boredom about the house; it was not a bad house, but the furniture was uninteresting, except for my father's books. It was not a house where anyone called unexpectedly, for my father had no friends – at least, I couldn't name anyone who was a friend as I understand the word.

However, the trouble wasn't the house but the individuals in it. My mother, as time went on, began increasingly to complain of her dreary life, her inability to run the house, and the approach of war. I suppose her age had something to do with it, but the monotonous whining monologue she treated my father to before breakfast, and all of us at mealtimes, resentful, self-pitying, full of funk and suspicion, must have remained in my mind as something I mustn't *under any circumstances* risk encountering again. Once she sprang up from the table announcing her intention to commit suicide. I never left the house without the sense of walking into a cooler, cleaner, saner and pleasanter atmosphere, and, if I had not made friends outside, life would have been scarcely tolerable.

My father's state of mind at this time cannot have been cheerful. His wife had made home a place where he simply had to shut his mouth and bear it as best he could. His first child, my sister, he thought little better than a mental defective, who was showing regrettably few signs of marrying and clearing out. Second child, myself, lived in a private world, disregarding what awkward overtures he could make, and was handicapped by an embarrassing stammer . . . Nonetheless, I think the situation was technically his fault. His personality had imposed that taut ungenerous defeated pattern of life on the family, and it was only to be expected that it would make them miserable and that their misery would react on him. And despite the fact that my mother grew to be such an obsessive snivelling pest, I think if my father had handled her properly she would have done much better.

I remember once saying to him that, after all, I supposed he had had a successful life. His humourless yap of laughter left no doubt as to what he thought on the subject. It would be somewhat absurd of me to regret his marriage, but I could never see why he needed a wife. He liked his own company best and gloried in his ability to look after himself, and his clumsiness in human relations must have made him an unsatisfactory husband, which in turn must have put a certain strain on him. Certainly the marriage left me with two convictions: that human beings should not live together, and that children should be taken from their parents at an early age.[27]

THREE

'I would rather leave a child on the steps of an orphanage than send one to public school.'[1] According to his daughter, Sydney's views on education were as dogmatic as his opinions about everything else. But while he was arrogant he wasn't a snob, and having risen unaided through various levels of society himself, he didn't believe things should be any easier for his son. The boys-only grammar school within walking distance of Manor Road – King Henry VIII School, or KHS as everyone called it – was where he decided Philip should go. Founded in 1545, it had transferred from its original position in the town to its present hill-top site in 1885. It had a junior as well as a senior section, and this created a sense of stability that appealed to Sydney. When he first took his son to meet the headmaster in September 1930, walking towards his study under the tall central red-brick tower, he was told, 'Philip won't come out this way again until he's a prefect.'[2]

Larkin would later insist that his schooldays were almost completely uneventful, largely to make them conform to the adult life he projected in his poems. He was, he told everyone, 'unsuccessful', urging them to remember that he 'was very short-sighted and . . . also that I stammered, so that classes were just me sitting with bated breath dreading lest I be called upon to say something'.[3] As far as his academic performance was concerned, at least until he reached the sixth form, his description is accurate enough. Studious rather than sparkling, he tried hard to seem ordinary. Away from his teachers he created a different impression. While remaining shy he was strongly opinionated – and also proud, confident, and contemptuous of those set in authority over him. Just because he tended to lie low during school hours, it didn't mean he was passive. On his own behalf, he was remarkably energetic: resourceful with his day-dreams, his solitary games, and his independent reading. For the first two-thirds of his time at KHS it was these things, not his work, that occupied most of his attention.

Within days of putting on the green uniform and joining the junior school, the eight-year-old Larkin had discovered that these secluded pleasures could make him 'happy'.[4] Judging by a short memoir he wrote several years later, 'Not the Place's Fault', the daily ten-minute walk from Manor Road to the huddle of Victorian classrooms was also something to enjoy:

Coming up the short – somehow rather unofficial – road that joins Warwick Road by the Station Hotel took me past the line of station horses in their carts outside the goods office. When I went back at lunchtime they were wearing their nosebags, and on my return at a quarter to two there was a scatter of chaff on the ground where they had stood. I liked this corner best at summer teatime, when in addition to the man selling the *Midland Daily Telegraph* there was frequently a white Eldorado box-tricycle that sold lime-green or strawberry-pink ices at a penny each. Beside the paper-seller was a cigarette machine, which gave ten cigarettes for sixpence and twenty for a shilling ... One of my fantasies was to unlock it and rifle the packets for cigarette cards. I sometimes think the slight scholarly stoop in my bearing today was acquired by looking for cigarette cards in Coventry gutters. There seemed to be a 'Famous Cricketers' series every summer then.[5]

Although he was reluctant to admit it, Larkin remained happy at the junior school until he left in 1933, when he was eleven. He was pleased to escape the stuffily protective atmosphere of home, and relieved to find very little being asked of him in class. 'We were just little boys in short trousers under one or two women,' he said; '– dame teachers [their names were Miss Atkinson and Miss Saunders] – not doing very much.'[6] In such a context, and in spite of his stammer, he found it easy to make friends, spending most of his time with Colin Gunner, 'an ebullient chap of classical scrum-half stockiness',[7] and James (Jim) Sutton, the son of a successful local builder. He included them in his games, invited them home to play with his Hornby train set, and introduced them to snooker and billiards on the child's-size table Sydney had bought for him. (Before long Sutton had abolished Kitty's nickname for Philip, 'Apey', and replaced it with 'Snooker'.) Encouraged by these two, and especially by Gunner, Larkin began to gain a reputation as an ingenious and slightly mischievous child. When he entered the senior school, his teachers knew not to believe that the shyness he showed in class was the sum of his whole personality.

KHS expected a good deal of its older pupils. Noel ('Josh') Hughes, who first met Larkin when they arrived together in the senior school, remembers, 'It was a very literary school, in an industrial town far removed from being an oppressed area, but having enormous cyclical employment in the motor trade. It was a local school, with no boarders and everyone coming from nearby, yet a remarkably fine one: the headmaster insisted that all the teachers had to have first-class degrees from Oxford or Cambridge.'[8] One of these teachers, Arthur Tattersall, 'a great inspirer of our youthful energies',[9] agrees:

KHS was a worthy and respectable school, not in the highest flight of day schools like Manchester Grammar School, but high up in the second division, with a long tradition. Coventry, relatively prosperous in earlier times through its weaving industry, and later from motor manufacturing, was lucky in having two good boys' grammar schools – KHS and Bablake – both semi-independent, drawing their pupils from local middle-class and professional families, with a growing admixture of working-class youngsters whose families could afford to pay fees or were keen enough to encourage their sons to work for scholarships.[10]

In the early 1930s, to cope with the school's rapidly expanding size (there were some 250 boys attending in 1930, nearly 500 in 1939), a new form structure had been devised. In their first year pupils were divided alphabetically, but subsequently the division was made according to ability, with the top stream having 'L' after their class number to show they were studying Latin, and the second stream having 'NL' to signify 'Non-Latin'. Such boys as went on from the school to university came from the 'L' stream.[11]

This streaming system, like almost everything else about the school's organization, had been the idea of the headmaster, A. A. C. Burton (inevitably known as 'Monty'). He had been appointed in 1931 after an early career teaching in Lancashire, and remained in charge for eighteen years, restoring finances which on arrival he had found shaky, and enormously improving standards. His educational beliefs were simple and strongly held:

At a speech day in 1938 he told parents: 'I hold that what a boy learns at school matters little; but the attitude he there acquires to work is of paramount importance.' He consistently commended hard work to the boys, but it must be hard work intelligently applied. He liked variety in education, but he reserved a special place for Latin, whether because it was his own pet subject, or because most people

17

found it hard, or for some less obvious reason. He showed, by his own vigorous example, that there was no necessary cleavage between academic and practical efficiency.[12]

At first sight there was little about Burton to indicate rigour, or even competence. 'He did not suggest,' one of his surviving staff says:

either in manner or appearance the Oxford scholar or the headmaster of a grammar school of repute. When I arrived for my interview, for instance, I was met by a large red-faced man with twinkling eyes and a friendly grin, dressed in a very off-duty suit and a bashed-in greasy old trilby hat. It took me a minute or two to realize that this was not the groundsman or even the caretaker. He looked like a jovial farmer . . . His house formed part of the school building and he had intruded on the playing fields to extend his patch of arable. His favourite form of punishment was to bring a boy back to school on a Saturday morning to weed the vegetable bed or plant lettuce in the greenhouse.[13]

Although Burton dramatically improved the size and standing of KHS he had few friends among the staff. 'His unpleasant characteristics stuck out more than his good ones,'[14] Arthur Tattersall remembers, and another former master says, 'He reminded me of a boa constrictor in his dealings with miscreants and his beatings were cruel. I felt sick all day after the first I witnessed.'[15] Pupils, too, walked in fear of him. Jim Sutton found him 'awesome',[16] and Larkin referred to him as 'the resident thug'.[17]

To start with, it looked as though Larkin and Burton wouldn't have much to do with each other. After his year in Form II, where the division of boys was purely alphabetical, Larkin was moved into Form III to join the 'slow learners'.[18] By 1935 he was in the 'élite' stream again, studying Latin among his other subjects and beginning to distinguish himself. 'After the minor débâcle of Lower III,' Noel Hughes remembers, 'it was quite a coup for Philip to take the second prize in his next form. Thereafter he always took some sort of prize; for three years for his contributions to the school magazine, and in his final year a special prize for General Knowledge.'[19]

As Larkin's self-confidence grew, his manner and looks began to alter. The mole-like, fuzzy-haired child, peering apprehensively through small round glasses, was now nearly six feet tall, thin, gangling, and openly seeking attention. He grew his hair long, Brylcreeming it, parting it in the middle, and combing it 'very assiduously'.[20] He began to take an interest in painting, and enjoyed his weekly art classes, where he showed a natural ability for drawing. (When Larkin eventually left KHS it crossed Sydney's mind that he should send his son to art school. Nothing came of the idea.

In later life the only surviving signs of Larkin's early enthusiasm were the skilful, fluent cartoons with which he often decorated his letters and notebooks.) To suit these new artistic allegiances, he began wearing boldly patterned sports coats and grey flannel trousers and – at the weekends – flashy bow ties. His friends thought it merely turned him from looking like a swot into a natty swot. It wasn't the effect Larkin intended, and as he moved up through the school he modified his appearance carefully. Term by term, he cast off the dullness of Manor Road and took on the bright colours he associated not only with painters but with the Romantic and *fin de siècle* writers he had begun to read. If no suitable models came to mind among writers he turned to musicians instead. Before reaching the sixth form he had started to promenade round Coventry wearing 'a green . . . jacket with a red tie which was envied greatly. He also had yellow knitted gloves which were considered *de rigueur* particularly when worn with the hacking mac he also sported. He wore brogue shoes when no one else had heard of them.'[21]

Although Sydney financed this exoticism, it was Larkin's contemporaries at school who were responsible for the change in him. Previously, while recognizing that 'friends are necessary: you cannot howl to yourself',[22] he had been forced to share the aloof life of his parents. His youth and shyness made anything else impossible. Girls had been especially difficult. At 'the age of five' he had 'conceived a violent passion for a little girl named Mary who had "lovely pussy gloves" (gloves with fur on the back)' and 'tried to make advances to her' – only to be 'violently repelled'.[23] The embarrassment lasted for years, festering in solitude. His sister's friends were too old for him to feel that he could belong in their world. There were no girls at his school or in his friends' families. He got used to living without them, slowly learning to look on 'sexual recreation as a socially remote thing, like baccarat or clog dancing'.[24]

Boys weren't much better. Apart from Gunner and Sutton, and the sons of two neighbours in St Patrick's Road – Tom Wilson and Peter Snape (who would later be killed in the war) – his only regular companion had been 'a gentle, slightly older boy' called Arthur, who lived round the corner in Stoney Road and shared his interest in devising elaborate card and board games. In Arthur, Larkin felt, he 'recognized for the first time the power to create and sustain private worlds. I can remember now his distress when our games did not tally with his imagined anticipation of them.'[25]

Once Larkin was safely installed in the senior school, he realized that not all his pleasure need be so nervously private. Jim Sutton, in particular, helped him to change his mind. Although Sutton was an intense boy, already nurturing ambitions to be a painter (in June 1938 he would move to Coventry Municipal Art School and subsequently go to the Slade), he was also open-hearted and enthusiastic. At his home in Beechwood Avenue on the other side of town, in a house constructed by his builder father, Sutton lived in an atmosphere of cheerful exuberance which was far removed from the moodiness of Manor Road. Larkin started to go there whenever he could, later recalling it as a place 'with a tennis court and a sunk ornamental pond and two garages . . .':

It was not really a big house, but it was the first I had known where people could be completely out of earshot of each other indoors, and which had a spare room or two that could be given over to a Hornby layout or a miniature battlefield that need not be cleared up at the end of the day. The careless benevolence that produced Chelsea buns and Corona at eleven, and ignored the broken window and excoriated furniture, seemed to be eloquent of a higher, richer way of living. The family were natural hosts.[26]

Sutton understood how much he meant to Larkin. 'Philip grew very fond of my father Ernest and my mother Dorothy,' he says, 'and liked the atmosphere in our house. It's true, we had quite a lot of parties where we'd drink a lot, and get in lots of local people. At his home [in Manor Road] things were always rather frightening. Sydney Larkin was frightening. He disapproved of a lot of Philip's would-be friends, but he approved of me for some reason. He was a terribly strong character – confident and dominating – and he used to ask us the sort of questions that children don't like.'[27] In spite or because of these differences between their backgrounds, Sutton was impressed by Larkin. Even though they had known each other for several years, by the time they arrived at the senior school he found him 'somehow odd, with his bad stammer, thick specs, Brylcreemed hair, long body, short legs. But I had no impulse to rag him. Something about him compelled respect. He was no softy, and he had presence. I think in the [senior section of the] school we felt slight hostility to him at first – he wanted nothing to do with wrestling and so on, but he won us over gradually while we shared common pleasures.'[28]

None of these pleasures was remarkable, but Larkin plunged into them eagerly. As soon as he was allowed out unchaperoned he became fanatical about visiting the local cinema, the Imperial (known as 'The Barn') – initially to see Laurel and Hardy, later to gorge on whatever was showing:

Major Barbara (which he saw three times), *Love on the Dole*, *The Marx Brothers Go West*, *The Hurricane*, *Prison without Bars*, *Contraband* and *The Doctor's Dilemma*. Equally keenly, he swapped and shared books, especially Billy Bunter stories. ('[Bunter's] roars and squeaks of anguish were constantly imitated then and for years after,' says Sutton; 'Philip seemed to identify with Bunter up to a point.'[29]) All in all, it constituted what Larkin called a 'sedentary' life, but a busy one – and 'when all else failed', and there were no friends to visit, 'he would cycle out into the country to look at churches', then come back to Manor Road in the evening to crouch on the floor and devote himself to 'games of all kinds':[30] spin-cricket, crossword puzzles, marbles.

Sutton and Larkin grew steadily closer as they moved up through the senior school. Tiring of their childish reading, they turned to weightier matters, Larkin discovering D. H. Lawrence and Sutton 'retaliating with Cézanne'.[31] More important still, they began to listen to jazz. Sutton heard it first, blasting from the wireless in his free-and-easy home, and 'moved Philip in the same direction',[32] whereupon the interest immediately became an obsession. Sydney – in this as in other respects – proved surprisingly difficult to offend. He paid for his son to take out a subscription to the magazine *Down Beat* and bought him 'an elementary drum kit' on which Larkin 'battered away contentedly, spending less time on the rudiments than in improvising an accompaniment to records'.[33] Not satisfied with drums alone, Larkin also longed for 'absolute mastery of what Walt Whitman called the key'd cornet',[34] and when in due course he began making visits with Sutton to the local Hippodrome to hear bands, or bought records with pocket-money, those were the instruments to which they listened most intently.

Previously, Larkin had heard only dance music (with his friend Arthur he had already tried to reproduce its sound using 'a kazoo, a battery of toffee tins, lids, pens and a hair-brush'[35]). Now he and Sutton sought out bands playing anglicized jazz – Jack Payne, Harry Roy, Billy Cotton, Nat Gonella and Teddy Foster. When they discovered American jazz proper their world was transformed. Performers like Louis Armstrong, Pee Wee Russell, Bix Beiderbecke and Sidney Bechet excited them more deeply than anything they had heard before, and Larkin listened to their records, enthused about them and analysed them for hour after hour. When he and Sutton were apart he carried on their discussions by letter, speaking in the same exhilarated language they used when they were together. Writing to Sutton from Manor Road in 1939, for instance, Larkin reported on

Armstrong's 'Dallas Blues', saying that 'Louis' break on horn serv[es] the double purpose of drawing the attention of the listener to the soloist and enabling the saxophonist to change from clarinet to saxophone in roughly three and a half secs, leading up to the perfect last chorus on trumpet (Blues playing personified) and the unfortunate ending'.[36]

The lyrics as well as the music of jazz attracted Larkin. 'Anyone living in the thirties,' he said later, 'particularly if they were fond of jazz, learned a great many lyrics of the dance bands of the day, and these were sometimes quite sophisticated if not really poetic. They rhymed and scanned, and I remember a good many of them to this day. They made up a kind of popular poetry that was quite affecting.'[37] Sometimes he wondered whether these lyrics had not influenced his own poems directly, helping to create his 'assumption that a poem is something that rhymes and scans'.[38] It is impossible to answer the question precisely, but it intriguingly suggests that what began as an appetite for subversion (the jazz) led to an endorsement of orthodoxy (in his own formal poems).

As soon as Sutton had shown him the way, Larkin became the shaping spirit of their new addiction. Sutton didn't mind this. 'Jim wasn't bossy,' a mutual friend remembers. 'He was very definite, and had qualities Philip would have liked to have. He looked nice, you know, in that wiry sort of way, and Philip was very conscious of his own plain damn ugliness – galumphing was a favourite word of his. I think he was half in love with Jim.'[39] If he was, nothing was ever said openly, although Larkin always admitted that by the time Sutton left KHS in 1939 his influence had been decisive. He was the first person to encourage Larkin to connect his solitary 'dream world' with the world at large.

Writing, Sutton thought, was the best bet. Larkin was slow to agree. In the junior school he had showed no special aptitude for English, and his first year in the senior school had been equally unremarkable. In Form III, however, while waiting to rejoin his true peers, he began to make a mark. Sutton urged him to write stories for the *Coventrian*, the school magazine. Larkin decided to try, and shortly before leaving Form III he sent the magazine a half-page of prose called 'Getting up in the Morning'. It was accepted. Years later he admitted that the whole exercise had been motivated by his desire for 'social reward':

What I was going to be praised and rewarded for – if anything – was writing. It certainly wasn't going to be languages or science, both of which we started that year, nor sport, for which advancing age, with its shortening sight and stiffening joints and increasing physical fastidiousness was rapidly unfitting me, nor was I going to do anything requiring confidence and a speaking voice. On the other hand, I was getting used to hearing my essays read out in class, and to coming top in English examinations by unarguable margins. Words were my element, though I no more understood them, in the parts of speech or philological senses, than a seal understands the water it lives in.[40]

'Getting up in the Morning' is a brief, conventional complaint about first light and having to go to work – a grumble far removed from the ferocity of one of his last poems, 'Aubade', which is set at the same time of day. It was a tentative step towards the high mountain of art, but Sutton encouraged him nonetheless. Larkin spent occasional evenings pounding out stories on his father's typewriter, he quickened the pace of his reading, he tried to match Sutton's views about painters with opinions about writers. Nothing he produced seemed exceptional to him or his teachers.

Not that his teachers saw much of what he wrote. Sutton's support was one thing; the curiosity of the rest of the school was a more embarrassing prospect. Shrinking from the good opinion of those in authority, he continued to try to seem ordinary. Noel Hughes, for instance, remembers him sitting 'over to my left, his large head slumped forward more, I suspect, to avoid catching a master's eye than the better to read a book'.[41] Colin Gunner got the same impression – and did all he could to endorse it. Dynamic, irreverent, 'always buzzing around passing notes',[42] Gunner was already renowned as a rebel. Sydney Larkin 'disliked'[43] him, the school distrusted him, but to Larkin he was 'a small agile boy with a face like a nut . . . whose home background, if not richer than mine, was at least more sophisticated: his parents had a car'.[44]

It is easy to see the combined appeal of these friends. The suave, intelligent and good-looking Hughes, and the supportive Sutton, steered Larkin towards maturity; the 'scrum-half' Gunner sniped at them mockingly. He was openly scathing about Manor Road ('if you put a speck on the floor there you felt you were spitting at the altar'[45]) and sceptical about all other conventions. 'We spent many detentions together, me and Philip,' he said later, 'and many weekends. We used to meet every Saturday morning . . . and go and do something. It was with Philip that I had my first beer.'[46] Larkin relished this bad influence, since Gunner kept him 'in fits'[47] and encouraged the feeling that to be seriously interested in something didn't necessarily involve being pompous about it. It was a role in Larkin's life which would eventually be played by a far more famous contemporary. Gunner was, Larkin said, 'a kind of pre-Kingsley [Amis]'.[48] Hughes, who also knew Amis at Oxford, agrees. Gunner's 'unfailing optimism', he says, 'was sufficient to compensate for our morose anxieties. But he was most remarkable for his unbounded imagination. Though without Kingsley Amis's talent for imitating sickly combustion engines, he played at school the role Kingsley would play at St John's: he could rescue our spirits from the blackest pit.'[49]

Gunner left KHS without reaching the sixth form (he worked for six years in the Coventry motor trade, then joined the Irish Brigade), but during his time there he had a hand in most of the things that brightened Larkin's life. He organized a 'cribbing syndicate'[50] to help Larkin with his Latin 'unseens'; once he nailed a musical box to the floor of a classroom so the master could not easily remove it when it began playing. 'We liked to get the masters so mad,' Hughes remembers, 'that they'd rush down into the class and bang someone on the head with a book. These rags would be concentrated written programmes – the first thing to do was bang the desk-top, then drop books, then ask a silly question.'[51] Larkin, gawky and stammering, was not an obvious ringleader, yet he was much admired for his ideas and planning – for the sarcastic rhymes he composed about the teachers, and for his skill in not taking the rap.

His friend Philip Antrobus, like Gunner, thinks that one escapade illustrates this better than all the others. It became known as 'The Mystery of the Dart in the Hall Ceiling':

On two consecutive mornings the first period after prayers was physics. This necessitated going from the hall back to the form room, collecting the necessary books, and returning via the hall to the physics lab, which was situated at the end of a long corridor. This hall had a vaulted wooden ceiling, and Colin Gunner was the possessor of a dart which he had adapted, by means of improvised flights, from a school pen. Going back through the hall on our way to the physics lab, Philip urged Colin to try his luck – which he did – and the thing stuck in the ceiling for all to see. After prayers the following morning, the headmaster's eyes wandered slowly yet deliberately upwards towards the offending missile, and having finally 'homed in' on the seeming enigma, he inquired, 'Have we an archer in our midst? Let him run up now, or I shall punish the whole school.' As no one wished to claim ownership, further interest was shelved and the school was dismissed. Philip and I made our way to the physics lab, this time minus Colin . . . [who] had gone to the head's study to institute his prerogative. For his honesty, the head presented Colin with a physics exercise book – a thick, cardboard-covered volume – and acquainted him with the fact that 'by this time next week, you will have filled this book from cover to cover on "Darts".' I realize that it was Colin who played the major role of the quasi-hero in this little anecdote, but it was principally Philip who had been, as it were, the spearhead of the movement.[52]

When it came to playing more legitimate games, in the Memorial Park a mile away from the school, Larkin showed the same appetite for rebellion, and the same wish to save his skin. During summer terms, when the pupils played cricket, he was a wicket-keeper, so that he didn't have to run about much. In winter terms, which brought rugby, it was harder to lead the quiet life, especially since his size meant he was useful in the line-out and scrum. By the time he was sixteen he could no longer avoid being chosen for the Second XV, but the record of his achievements is disappointing. 'Larkin, P. A. Forward', says the school magazine: 'Has considerable ability, and his height and weight ought to make him very useful ... Needs to play with far more vigour and abandon, and in the scrums to hollow his back, so as to get in a real shove.'[53]

Jazzing or japing, working or playing, the impression Larkin made during his first three years in the senior school remains the same. He was keen to save himself undue trouble. His self-esteem was sometimes high enough for him to sound haughty, and at other times low enough to make him impenetrably withdrawn. He was shy, yet could dramatize his own and other people's lives – usually to raise a laugh. He wanted to challenge the status quo, but at the same time to stay on the right side of the law. He was solitary but had a capacity for deep friendship. He enjoyed being pampered at home yet was glad to escape it. These are all attitudes which appear in more complicated forms in his mature work, but in the early writing he did at school they are non-existent. The first few pieces he wrote for the *Coventrian*, like 'Getting up in the Morning', and his unpublished yarns about treasure hunts or 'Vampire Island', are so consistently banal that it is hard to see why Sutton ever believed literature might be their author's salvation.

Larkin himself remained doubtful. At the end of his pocket diary for 1936, the year in which he finished the first half of his senior school career, he recorded day by day an unbroken run of complaints: 'pretty awful week', 'bloody day', 'grumpy growly day', 'awful day', 'tough day', 'pretty awful day'. 'However,' he says, ending December with a brief review, 'I must go on trying.'[54]

FOUR

Larkin's diary for 1936 gives no sign of it, but 'trying' was now likely to do him more good than before. This was partly because his promotion from Form III (NL) to the higher stream of pupils this autumn meant that he started to keep more stimulating company. He was also helped by a slight but important change at home. The older he became the more interest his father took in him. 'Pop more affectionate now, Mop more gloomy,'[1] he noted at the end of the year.

In the summer of 1936 Sydney had tried to build on this new sympathy by taking his son with him on a visit to Germany, to the resorts of Königswinter and Wernigerode. The following year they repeated the experiment, this time staying in Kreuznach – and in all Larkin's subsequent accounts the two trips tend to get jumbled together. The idea was that Sydney would combine some of his 'business' interests with a few days' sight-seeing, but as far as Philip was concerned the whole process soon became a kind of torture. The main reason, he always insisted later, was that he couldn't speak the language (he didn't begin learning German at school until 1938). 'I found it petrifying,' he said, 'not being able to speak to anyone or read anything ... My father liked the jolly singing in beer cellars, three-four time to accordion – Schiffer Klavier, did they call them? Think of that for someone who was just buying their first Count Basie records.'[2] Kingsley Amis remembers a similar story that Larkin told him in Oxford. 'In Germany, with his father, they put him in the front of the bus they were travelling on, next to the driver, who asked a question which Philip thought meant, "Have you been to Germany before?" "No," he said, and the driver didn't seem to like that, and didn't talk to him for the rest of the day. He found out later that what the driver had said was, "Do you like Germany?" '[3]

In years to come, Larkin would suggest that these two trips created the loathing of abroad for which he became notorious. 'I think [they] sowed the seed of my hatred of abroad,'[4] he once said – and again, more humorously but no less seriously, 'I wouldn't mind seeing China if I could come back the same day. I hate being abroad.'[5] There is no denying the authenticity of these feelings, but they are nevertheless surprising. At least, they are surprising if we believe Larkin when he says they were produced entirely by a few days of linguistic bafflement, and if we realize that two years later (in April 1939) he was still able to enjoy a ten-day school trip to Brussels, Antwerp and the Ardennes, thinking it 'the best and jolliest holiday'[6] he had ever spent.

Clearly, to understand the reasons for his xenophobia we have to look elsewhere. We have to wonder how disturbed Larkin felt being in Germany during the late 1930s with someone of his father's extreme political views. He says nothing of how his friends reacted when he returned home; he is silent about his father's reputation in Coventry; he makes no attempt to understand his unhappiness as a disguised or displaced sense of shame. Yet to a degree that is what it was. By the end of his second trip to Germany, 'abroad' was connected with feelings of embarrassment at best, humiliation at worst – feelings which as the years went by he simplified and hardened into 'hatred'. In one sense the experience hurt him deeply, increasing his awkwardness and driving him even further into himself. In another respect it made him more robust, encouraging him to slam the door through which he had recently walked from childhood into adolescence. In his year at school between the two visits to Germany, and particularly in the aftermath of the second, he became much more self-possessed. By the end of 1937, when he was fifteen, he had joined the school debating society and play-reading group; he had started to take part (backstage) in the annual school play; he had begun writing regular letters to the school magazine about anything that amused or irritated him (the amount of time devoted to gymnastics, for instance); and he had affected an interest in politics – briefly forming with Sutton and Antrobus a facetious anti-Marxist trinity, supporting Franco's cause in the Spanish Civil War.

He was more confident at home, too. Sydney gave him free run of his library, and his appetite for books grew enormously. 'Thanks to my father,' he wrote later:

our house contained not only the principal works of most main English writers in some form or other (admittedly there were exceptions, like Dickens), but also nearly-complete collections of authors my father favoured – Hardy, Bennett, Wilde, Butler and Shaw, and later on Lawrence, Huxley and Katherine Mansfield. Not till I was much older did I realize that most boys of my age were brought up to regard Galsworthy and Chesterton as the apex of modern literature, and to think of Somerset Maugham as 'a bit hot'. I was therefore lucky. Knowing what its effect would be on me, my father concealed the existence of the Central Public Library as long as he could, but in the end the secret broke and nearly every evening I set off down Friars Road with books to exchange.[7]

Once it had been discovered, the library proved irresistible:

I rapidly became what in those days was an especially irritating kind of borrower, who brought back in the evening the books he had borrowed in the morning and read in the afternoon. This was the old Coventry Central Library, nestling at the foot of the unbombed cathedral, filled with tall antiquated bookcases (blind-stamped 'Coventry Central Libraries' after the fashion of the time), with my ex-schoolfellow Ginger Thompson ... at the counter to stamp the books you chose, and the Golden Cross nearby where (in sixth-form days at least) they could be examined at leisure. This was my first experience of the addictive excitement a large open-access public library generates. The sense of imminent discovery, the impulse to start twenty books at once, the decades-old marginal addenda ('surely the problem of free will ...'), not to mention their several atmospheres: the silence of wet artesian-winter nights, the holiday-fattened shelves of summer afternoons.[8]

Sydney shaped Larkin's taste skilfully, leading him away from J. C. Powys and towards Llewelyn and T. F., towards James Joyce with no expectation that he would enjoy him, and towards poets who would remain favourites all his life: Hardy, Christina Rossetti and A. E. Housman. In late 1939, when Larkin discovered T. S. Eliot, W. H. Auden, Edward Upward and Christopher Isherwood, Sydney also encouraged him – continuing, as he had always done, to make reading seem an independent activity, only tenuously linked to schoolwork. This suited Larkin well, since he 'did not much like'[9] his English master, M. T. Mason, and wanted to keep his discoveries to himself. He succeeded. Mason, like the other teachers, reckoned that Larkin was merely 'a quiet studious youth, easy to teach',[10] and when his place was taken by L. W. 'Joey' Kingsland in 1938 the impression remained the same. Kingsland remembers that Larkin 'seemed either very shy, or, more probably, very reluctant to admit any closer relationship than that of the classroom'.[11]

As with his reading, so with his writing. Egged on by friends like Sutton and supported more sedately by his father, Larkin in 1936 and 1937 began to produce things for reasons other than 'social reward'. 'What did I write?' he wondered to himself in his fragment of autobiography:

To answer this I must mention Colin Gunner. Without being in the accepted sense literary, Colin, perhaps more than anyone I have known before or after, possessed a literary imagination. Together we got to work on reality and imposed fantasy after fantasy upon our dreary day-school life, until not only had I no time for anything else but I hardly believed anything else existed. If a master separated us, or clapped us in detention, it was plainly only because we had discovered that the repellent-looking dwarf who stumped the town wearing a black cricket cap was in fact his father, or that he eked out his living by selling out-of-date newspapers. (A favourite dodge was to rush alongside a stationary railway train shouting 'General mobilization! Europe on brink of war! Paper!' and then vanish, leaving a trainload of puzzled readers with the *Daily Mail* for, say, August 2nd 1914) . . . Colin read as much as I did and remembered it as vividly: certain sentences even now seem to me instinct with his talent: 'Half a sovereign if you run him down, coachee!' is one of them.

In essence they were fantasies of revenge upon our schoolmasters, mixed with fantasies of brutality too good-natured and free of sexual flavouring to be called sadistic, but at the same time of suspiciously illiberal tendencies.[12]

It's clear from these memories that much of Larkin's writing at KHS was a form of revolt – but a secret revolt, to be shared with only one or two close allies. It created an excitement which swept him headlong into his last two years as a schoolboy. As he said later, he 'wrote ceaselessly'.[13] The 'earliest pieces' were 'little sketches and short stories written around real people' (his dentist, for instance). Then came an abstract for a play about revolutionary schoolboys called 'With Shining Morning Face'. Then came several diatribes against various things, such as education and Christianity (though his agnosticism did not prevent him from also writing a verse drama for Holy Week in 1939, called 'Behind the Façade'). Then came 'the most incompetent rigmarole called *Death Underwater*, complete with a Chinese detective who solved the mystery in the last chapter'. This was soon followed by *Death in Swingham*, which was 'nearly a full-length novel, and was about a great saxophonist who is poisoned'.[14]

By the summer of 1938 this fountain of creativity was jetting up poems as well as stories – 'poetry of a descriptive kind, about trees and the sky and seasons', and also mildly erotic, yearning poetry full of schoolboy crushes. 'Through the winter of 1938–9,' he said, 'I continued to write poems, all very much of the same kind, faintly influenced by Keats and Aldous Huxley, until in the spring I broke into freer verse when I re-fell in love with someone. The poems became much more personal and more frequent, for I remained in love during the whole summer, though not with the same person.'[15] Larkin left no clues about the identity of those he became infatuated with – it is much more likely that they were boys than girls since, as he repeatedly said, he hardly knew any girls. He did, however, leave plenty of poetic evidence of his strong feelings. Some emerges in 'Winter Nocturne', written in December 1938, which was published in the *Coventrian* and now appears as the earliest poem in the *Collected Poems*. Yet more exists in the previously unpublished 'Butterflies':

> Side-stepping, fluttering, quick-flicking,
> Dropping like dots under the blue sky,
> Skipping white under the sultry pall
> Of green summer trees . . .
> Darling, when in the evening
> I am alone in the land,
> When the low sweep of the sun-warmed country
> Returns to me like a forgotten dream,
> I could wish that we had been here as they.

On the manuscript of this poem Larkin later added, 'written variously on a cycle tour [with his father in the summer of 1939, after they had returned from a brief family holiday in Jersey], not very good'. Later still, he put, 'Pretty bloody actually. ANUS.'[16] Other pieces from the same period were also abused when he returned to them a few years afterwards. 'Case of the fart being greater than the hole,' he scribbled on one, and on others, 'bloody awful', 'this is a lot of shit', 'there is not a line of this shitty thing that is free from the most execrable vulgarity or BAD TASTE!!! Balls. Shit all. Cunt. Arsehole.' He was just as ruthless about his prose. No sooner had he finished *Death in Swingham* than he embarked on another novel, *Present Laughter* (the story of 'a boy who went to public school just for the one summer term, but on account of his extraordinary beauty completely and farcically wrecked the place'[17]), pursued it for 25,000 words, then immediately burnt it.

Larkin's teachers knew nothing of this. As far as they were concerned, he remained above averagely good at classroom English, and undistinguished in all his other subjects. In his report for March 1937 the headmaster Burton wrote, 'not very pleasing except in English', and in December he warned, 'His literary subjects are very good, but he must work to strengthen weak subjects. Uneven and unlikely to pass School Certificate unless he devotes himself to the task of mastering certain uncongenial subjects.' When Larkin actually took his School Certificate the following year – during the summer of 1938 – it turned out that Burton had been right to feel worried. Larkin got an 'A' grade in English Language and a 'C' in English Literature and History, but only scraped through in his other subjects, with grades which included a 'D' in Latin and an 'E' (the lowest grade) in French, Physics and Chemistry. Not even winning the Senior Prize for contributions to the *Coventrian* and acting as assistant to its editor, Noel Hughes, could eradicate his family's and the school's disappointment – or their anxiety about his future.

They didn't have to fret for long. Embarrassed by his poor performance, and liberated from subjects he found difficult and boring, Larkin rallied as soon as he reached the sixth form. Throughout 1939 his reports speak of 'improvements', and even though he still did 'not much like' his English teacher he worked hard, widening his reading to include Verlaine and Lamartine as well as Auden and Eliot, and changing the mood and style of his own poems accordingly. 'Pseudo-Keats babble'[18] gave way to imitations of Auden and Eliot, and included a short series of lyrics about a Sweeney-esque character called Stanley:

> The dull whole of the drawing room
> Is crucified with crystal nails,
> Dresden shepherdesses smirk
> As Stanley practises his scales.[19]

Flaunting these new, sophisticated influences, Larkin began to change his image in the school. Instead of pranking or lurking, he became serious and urgent. One of his contemporaries remembers him 'often stopping people in a school corridor or the bicycle sheds and asking where [the] term's contribution [to the *Coventrian*] was. [He was] always with an old folder stuffed with pages of poems, short stories and articles.'[20] Such enthusiasm, combined with his now consistently good form work, impressed his teachers, and by the end of his first year in the sixth form his English master Kingsland was recommending that Larkin apply to read English at university. In the normal run of events, the school would have urged him to stay on for an extra year, so that he might have a decent crack at a scholarship, and thereby save his family some money. But as war approached, 'normal' events were thrown into disarray, and Burton advised Sydney Larkin that his son would do best to forgo the extra year and the possible scholarship, and apply at once. Sydney did not object. Burton's plan meant he would have to stump up, but he at least had the security of knowing that the fees would all be paid before he retired.

The question of where Larkin should go was more simply answered. Virtually from its foundation his school had been linked to St John's College, Oxford, at which two closed scholarship places were reserved for

KHS boys. Because the Larkin family had no connections with another college – or even university – everyone agreed that St John's was the obvious place for him to apply. He caught the train down to Oxford on 11 March 1940, stayed at the college for the next three days while he took the exams, and by the end of the month knew that he had passed: he would go up in October.

Four months later he had more exams to take – this time it was his Higher School Certificate – and he was again successful. He won a Distinction in English and in History. The boy who had been merely 'good at English' was on his way to being exceptional. The shy stammerer, veering between mischief and solitude, had discovered his intellect. The fantasist who 'got to work upon . . . dreary school life' was turning into a fastidious craftsman, drafting yet another novel. 'It is planned for 100,000 words to be cut down considerably and is very advanced and modern,' he announced to Sutton. 'I shall try to have it published by the Hogarth Press but probably I shall outgrow it quickly. Broadly speaking it is my fourth novel.'[21] He was eighteen.

As Larkin prepared to say goodbye to his friends at KHS he knew that his plans might be derailed by the war. Because of his visits to Germany, and because of his father's interests and beliefs, he had seen it coming more clearly than most of his contemporaries – but rather than taking a special interest in its development, he felt unwilling or unable to compete with Sydney's opinions. In a letter written soon after hostilities had begun, he reminded Sutton of the mood in Manor Road by sending him a cartoon entitled 'Portrait of the Author and Family'. It shows the young, bespectacled Larkin with a gigantic exclamation mark over his head, blushing as he listens to his father waving a newspaper headlined 'WAR' and saying in a speech-bubble: 'The British government have started this war . . . Hitler had done all he could for peace . . . Well, all I hope is that we get smashed to Hades . . . our army is useless. ARP? Ha, Ha! This is the end of civilization . . . after all, man has to be superseded sooner or later . . . we're only a stage in the earth's development . . . very unimportant stage too . . .' In her speech-bubble, Eva – who is knitting – replies, 'Oh, do you think so? I wonder what we ought to have for lunch tomorrow . . . don't scrape the floor like that Philip, remember I have to do all the work . . . well, I hope Hitler falls on a banana skin . . . by the way I only washed four shirts today.'[22]

Larkin showed a similar attitude to his family in other letters written during 1939. He mocked his father but never actually disagreed with him

– never sympathizing with the suffering of others, and sometimes even making a few mildly anti-Semitic and pro-German remarks of his own. He remained the same throughout the entire conflict. 'I think Fascism is a bad thing – I *think* it is,'[23] he told Sutton in 1942, only reluctantly conceding that 'the German system is, from all accounts, much more evil than last time'.[24] Even by 1945 nothing had changed. As the war drew to a close he told Sutton, 'There is a lot in the paper today about what Russia, America, Russia, England, Russia, America and Russia are going to do with Germany . . . I haven't bothered to read it.'[25] Similarly, Hiroshima gets only a passing reference and he 'can't be bothered to read about'[26] the conference at Yalta in the papers. Except as something likely to cause him a good deal of personal inconvenience, the war might not have existed.

In these narrow terms, however, it affected him profoundly. During the winter of 1939 and spring of 1940 his school grew strange to him. 'What with the advent of fire-watching at [KHS],' one contemporary recalls, 'local ARP duties for some senior boys, the call-up of staff and the new threat over us all of being marshalled into the forces, the whole of school took on a different aspect.'[27] As Larkin began his last term he accepted that leaving Coventry would, to an exceptional degree, cut him off from his past – and to prove the point he wrote a 'Last Will and Testament' with Noel Hughes, which they published in the *Coventrian*. The poem leans heavily on 'Their Last Will and Testament,' written by Auden and Louis MacNeice, and published in *Letters from Iceland* (1937); it is a series of bequests to friends and colleagues – relentlessly light-hearted, yet unavoidably elegiac:

> our corporeal remains we give
> Unto the Science Sixth – demonstrative
> Of physical fitness – for minute dissection;
>
> Trusting that they will generously forgive
> Any trifling lapses from perfection,
> And give our viscera their close attention.

Later in the summer, Larkin continued the process begun in this poem. At home in Manor Road he methodically collected all the poems, plays, stories, novels and essays he had written, destroyed those he didn't like, and 'select[ed] and retain[ed] a few from the best of the manuscripts'.[28] The surviving prose he typed up and locked in a tin trunk. The surviving poems he 'sewed up' into little booklets. It was a procedure he had first adopted in

September 1939 and March 1940, when compiling a small collection of Eliotic pieces (including a two-page free-verse drama called 'The Ships at Mylae'), and which lasted, on and off, until July 1942. By then he had made seven collections: two (following Auden's example) called simply *Poems*, and also *Seven Poems*, *The Village of the Heart* (Auden again), *Further Poems*, *Nine O'Clock Jump*, and *The Seventh Collection*. For one of the volumes called *Poems* (August 1940) he wrote a Foreword. 'This collection,' he said, 'was made with no deliberation at all, many poems being printed within a few days of their being written. In consequence there is much work that is silly, private, careless or just ordinarily bad here ... The keynotes of this collection are Carelessness (equals spontaneity) and Platitudinousness (equals simplicity). The qualities in parenthesis are what I aimed at. On the other hand I like most of the poems here.'[29]

Eventually Larkin would judge these booklets as harshly as his earlier work. 'Bollocks' he wrote in the margin of one, and in others 'more shit', 'this is a lot of cunt', and 'another bucket of shit'. At the time of making them he felt more tolerant. Before the summer was over he even liked some of the poems enough to make a selection of four and send them to the *Listener*, with a request that they be considered for publication. 'Three I thought were very good and one I put in to make the others seem even better,'[30] he said later – and to his 'amazement' it was the fourth, the Audenesque sonnet 'Ultimatum', that was accepted by the magazine's literary editor, J. R. Ackerley. The poem was eventually published on 28 November 1940, during Larkin's first term at St John's. He couldn't have asked for a more auspicious start to his career as an undergraduate writer, or for a better means of announcing his ambitions to his peers.

Half-buried under its literary borrowings, 'Ultimatum' contains images and ideas which were to remain important to Larkin throughout his life. 'The ship' in the third line appears again in 'The North Ship', in 'Poetry of Departures', in 'Next, Please', and in 'How Distant'; 'docks' and 'seagulls' return in several of the poems he wrote in Belfast and Hull. Now as later these images create a land- and sea-scape in which the longing to escape clashes against the need to stay put:

> But we must build our walls, for what we are
> Necessitates it, and we must construct
> The ship to navigate behind them, there.
> Hopeless to ignore, helpless instruct
> For any term of time beyond the years

That warn us of the need for emigration:
Exploded the ancient saying: Life is yours.

For on our island is no railway station,
There are no tickets for the Vale of Peace,
No docks where trading ships and seagulls pass.

Remember stories you read when a boy
– The shipwrecked sailor gaining safety by
His knife, treetrunk, and lianas – for now
You must escape, or perish saying no.

Although Larkin's tone would change greatly during the next several years, his themes remained strikingly consistent. While still a schoolboy he squared up to the themes of isolation, evanescence and choice which were to dominate much of his later work. Furthermore, he began to wonder what chance he had of controlling his own destiny when he knew that he was bound to die – bound to hear the wind 'blowing over the graves/Of faded summers' in 'Winter Nocturne', and to see the seasons passing in 'Fragment from May' and 'Summer Nocturne'. At this stage, his anxieties are insisted upon rather than re-created, and the treatment seems static and monotonous. Larkin realized this himself, and did what he could to dramatize his small stock of personal experiences. But the most vital one – the experience of childhood coming to an end – resisted his best efforts. He couldn't grasp it. It shaded off too quickly into an unknown future. 'What was the rock my gliding childhood struck,' he asks in 'Nothing significant was really said', without being able to give an answer. 'Choose what you can,' he urges a friend in 'After-Dinner Remarks', but has to admit that he must 'remain/As neuter' himself.

By the end of his writing life Larkin had produced a poetic universe so unified that it became in certain respects a threat to his talent. It stopped him re-inventing himself when his original sources of creative energy dried up. To start with, though, his almost instant possession of a complete set of attitudes allowed him to feel that he was bound to find his true voice before long. In an imaginary world made up of ships, shores and high attic windows, he watched the power of individual choice being challenged by death and fortified by comedy. In the real world of Manor Road he saw himself as someone both dependent upon and dragged down by his whining mother and autocratic father.

FIVE

'Oxford terrified me' was Larkin's usual line about his time as an undergraduate. 'Public schoolboys terrified me. The dons terrified me. So did the scouts.'[1] His novel *Jill* supports his claim. The hero John Kemp is pale with fear as he travels down in the train from his Midlands home to begin his first term – he even eats his sandwiches in the lavatory rather than suffer the scrutiny of his fellow-passengers, and once he reaches his college he is immediately and hopelessly out of his depth. Although Larkin said that readers should not identify him too closely with Kemp, the fictional and real-life characters are nevertheless obviously linked. Larkin wanted us to believe that Oxford continued his experience of childhood by other means. Until he arrived there, life had been largely 'boredom'; now 'boredom' was shadowed by 'fear'.

This second self-portrait is as over-simplified as the first. In spite of his continuing shyness, Larkin quickly established himself in St John's as an opinionated and even flamboyant personality. Within a matter of days he was holding forth in the Junior Common Room 'Suggestions Book', complaining about having to pay for college stationery and making pseudonymous attacks on people who offended him. (One of these attacks prompted the reply: 'This book is for suggestions, not for the very boring *self-advertisement* of the more cosmopolitan elements of the JCR.'[2]) His contemporaries only had to look at him to see that he was apparently brimming with self-confidence. 'Philip often sported a bow tie and . . . green cords and a waistcoat,' one remembers. 'With his large glasses, his high forehead and attractive low stutter, he was unmistakable, the sort of person who was not only witty in himself, but the cause of wit in other men.'[3] Others recall his thick black hair flopping forward, the slouch-brimmed hat he sometimes wore, the cerise trousers he boasted were the only pair of such a colour in Oxford (he wore them on the recommendation – 'wear red trousers' – given by Lawrence in *Lady Chatterley's Lover*), and his ostentatious pipe-smoking (later he would abandon this in favour of cigarettes, which he continued to smoke in moderation throughout his life).

Such gaudiness was not all it seemed. No matter how bravely Larkin sailed into his new world, he soon lost his nerve when called upon to be decisive, or to deal with those he reckoned his social superiors. The opposite sex was even more daunting. Hitherto, as we've seen, he had almost never come into contact with girls. 'It now seems strange to me,' he would say later, 'that all the time I lived in Coventry I never knew any girls, but it did not at the time ... None of my friends knew any either ... Perhaps strangest of all was that no girls so to speak appeared on the threshold of my life as a natural part of growing up, like beer and cigarettes, as novels say they do.'[4] Eva, dithering and socially inept, had not actually banned girls from the house – she had simply kept them out along with the rest of the world. Sydney had excluded them more deliberately. Politely exasperated by his wife, and making no secret of his opinion that she was a second-class citizen, he had passed on to his son a set of opinions about women which mingled uncertainty with dislike. Beneath a hard surface of ignorance, Larkin's ordinary teenage sexual feelings had struggled vainly for release, turning back on themselves with the shudders of physical disgust which appear in one or two of his early stories, and at moments in his schoolboy poems.

Sutton, among others, realized that Oxford was bound to aggravate these difficulties. In Coventry he had merely thought that 'Philip with his scathing tongue wasn't as impressed by women as he should be' – but now, 'when I questioned him about it he said, "Never underestimate the strength of my feeling."'[5] During his first term, Larkin tried to solve the problem by avoiding women altogether. When he arrived in his rooms on 9 October 1940, four days before term began and eight before enrolling in the Bodleian Library (where his name followed 'Iris Murdoch, Somerville College' in the register), his instinct was to seek out his former school-friends and stick to them. Sutton, whom he had expected to be at the Slade in London, was a near neighbour. (All Slade students had been moved to Oxford – to the Ashmolean – for the duration of the war.) Until Sutton joined the 14th Field Ambulance in April 1941 for what turned out to be a six-year stint – four in Egypt and two in Italy – he and Larkin saw each other regularly. Noel Hughes was even closer. He had come up from KHS to St John's on one of its reserved scholarships, and was sharing Larkin's rooms. They did most of their early exploring in a pack, joining other friends from Coventry such as Ernest Roe at Exeter College and Frank Smith at Hertford.

The Oxford they discovered was much reduced by the war. This autumn there were 'no more than sixty [undergraduates in St John's] overall,'[6] most of whom were taking truncated 'war degrees' before joining the services, and several college buildings had been requisitioned by the Ministry of Food. It was, literally and metaphorically, a life on rations. Larkin loftily wrote to Sutton the following spring:

The enormous impact of war has given Oxford a fundamental shock, so that its axis has been shaken from the Radcliffe Camera to Carfax. Army lorries thunder down Cornmarket Street in an endless procession, past queueing shoppers and shops quickly altering their standards of judgement. Away in the depths . . . of university quadrangles, I gain the impression of being at the end of an epoch. Will the axis ever return to its normal position?[7]

As Larkin tried to settle down, the war constantly pulled him awry. At night, he told his father, he was soon involved in 'a scheme of firewatching with Balliol and Trinity. Eight undergraduates (in John's anyway) are on duty . . . and if an alert takes place one goes up into the tower and the other stands ready to run messages. After half an hour they change places.'[8] (He wrote more plainly to Sutton: 'Firewatching is all right provided you sit alone in the Lodge and don't bugger about up the tower.'[9]) By day he was required to train for one and a half days each week with the Student Training Corps, debate the course of the war endlessly with those around him, and regret that nothing he did was 'really representative' of the life he had expected. 'All the young dons,' he later complained, 'had gone off either to the forces or to the ministries or to the whatever. There was not a great deal of scope for personal development in the sense of high living along the *Brideshead* lines . . . You couldn't even have meals in your own rooms. You had one bottle of wine a term from the buttery – that was your lot . . . You didn't have marvellously furnished rooms because you were all doubled up.'[10]

These peculiarities, combined with the uncertainties of being in a new place, made Larkin's first term tense and misshapen. All the same, he tried to seem as much a man-about-university as he did a man-about-college. He joined several societies, he struck up many acquaintances, he tried his hand at ventures which might or might not come to good. With his contemporary Alan Ross, for instance, who would later become well known as a writer and editor of the *London Magazine*, he took part in a game of hockey against Worcester College. ('It must be the only time I have ever played,' he said; 'I found the sticks dangerous.'[11]) He took up squash. He went to the theatre and cinema a great deal. He listened to jazz. He dodged the Proctors in pubs. He occasionally attended political meetings organized by the Labour Club in their social room in the High

Street – more for the company than anything else.

When Larkin reported back to his 'dear fambly' he tended to make no mention of these things. He concentrated, instead, on seeming diligent and embattled. 'I find it very difficult to work here,' he says in one of his first letters home. '*Very* difficult. Either the work's too hard or it's too dull ... My year here are all, as far as I can see, perfectly ordinary people. Added to this, their public school accent renders them incapable of saying anything original or amusing. No intelligent man uses the public school accent for the simple reason that one simply *cannot* say intelligent things in it. That is a *fact*.'[12] No matter how genuinely disappointed Larkin felt with this 'dullness', his refusal to be impressed forms part of a request for his father's approval. We can see it more clearly in the break-down of the 'sort of day I generally spend' that he sent to Sydney:

After being woken unofficially (by clatter of fire irons etc.) at 7 a.m. and officially at 7.30 a.m. we have a bath and breakfast. This is all over by 8.30 a.m. and between this time and 9 I write letters (sometimes). At 9 I start work, after going to the college library to get books, and work on and off through the morning. Sometimes I go to lectures (suitably gowned and plus an intelligent look) but they are often dull. Lunch is at 1.05 and is generally one cold course and as much bread and cheese as you can get your hands on. In the afternoons I take my umbrella for a walk around the bookshops or go to a cinema or buy something for tea. Most people play games but I feel very lazy up here. Then at 4 we have tea (milk ordered daily – half a pint: tea and sugar provided by the college at the beginning of term) and this extends till nearly 6. Jim [Sutton] generally drops in from the Slade for tea – although he has tea at his place later – and then we read or work till dinner at 7.15 p.m. After dinner we work till bed at about 10.30. Further diversions are tutorials on Fridays at 12 p.m., the English Club once per week, and an occasional visit to somebody else's room for coffee or something.[13]

Among his friends, Larkin had less need to seek approval by seeming put-upon. With Sutton, in particular, he openly 'enjoyed himself'[14] during his first few weeks – and when their joint adventuring was eventually interrupted by Sutton's departure for the war, Larkin continued to revel in their friendship by writing long and regular letters. Over the years, these were to build into an extraordinary correspondence – intimate, spontaneous, vital and showing a passionate interest in jazz, literature and (on Sutton's side) painting. Sutton, abroad and in uniform, never allowed their dialogue to slacken; Larkin, at home and in mufti, made sure it was conducted in language that would have made a soldier proud. 'I have a drumming sensation at the back of my skull,' he said shortly before Sutton left Oxford. '... Balls and anus! Lookahere, you, write, write and keep on writing. I'm the trapped miner you're feeding through a tube, see?'[15]

Even before Sutton's departure, Larkin decided that the 'social game' of asking people more or less indiscriminately into his rooms for 'sausage rolls and cream buns, with a cigarette thrown in for good measure' was 'too hard to keep up'.[16] A more organized pattern of friendships began to emerge. Soon after arriving in college, he became part of what one contemporary, Nick Russel, calls 'an unofficial club' which 'consisted of probably a dozen or so like-minded [jazz-fancying] undergraduates [who] didn't buy records much but enjoyed a get-together late at night in someone's rooms: ... Jimmy Willcox, David Williams, Mervyn Brown, the medical student Philip Brown – "little Philip" to distinguish him from big Philip – Graham Parkes and Edward du Cann'.[17] Other friends, in due course, included Frank Dixon in Magdalen College and Dick Kidner 'with his spotted, spectacled face and serious inferiority complex'[18] in Christ Church.

One other member of this 'club' was Larkin's first tutorial partner, Norman Iles, a former pupil of Bristol Grammar School. Impatient and contemptuous, Iles was notorious within days of arriving in St John's. Larkin immediately took to him, remembering him later as 'a large pallid-faced stranger with a rich Bristolian accent, whose preposterous skirling laugh was always ready to salute his own outrages'.[19] Because he had 'little use for self- or any other kind of discipline',[20] and was often to be found 'plucking disconsolately at a dry loaf and drinking milkless tea'[21] in his rooms after missing a lecture (let alone a meal), Iles became for Larkin a model of unconventionality. As he did so, he took on the role previously played by Colin Gunner. Larkin used Iles as a 'means of weighing up my general character and assumptions. Any action or even word implying respect for qualities such as punctuality, prudence, thrift or respectability called forth a snarling roar like that of a Metro Goldwyn Mayer lion and an accusation of bourgeoisisme; ostentatious courtesy produced a falsetto celestial effect; ostentatious sensibility the recommendation to "write a poem about it".'[22]

Iles's bolshiness and boastfulness were bound to lose their charm in due course. ('He compares himself favourably to Lawrence,' Larkin once said; ' – this seriously frightens me.'[23]) Before this happened, however, he had a considerable influence. He increased Larkin's self-esteem, eased his shyness, reinforced his attempts to seem a disaffected wit, and encouraged him to seem unconventionally 'natty'.[24] More important still, he scorned anything pretentious in whatever Larkin said or wrote. For the duration of their close friendship (most of Larkin's first year), and during the correspondence which followed, he goaded Larkin into fulfilling his talent by bombarding him with pre-emptive ironies and sarcasms.

Without Iles the disruptions of the war sometimes seemed crushingly tiresome; with him, they seemed part of universal and hilarious chaos. Larkin found this comforting, even if it didn't stop him worrying about being called up. Like most of his contemporaries, he assumed that he would be able to complete only a year's study before joining the services. But there was always a chance that the conscription age would suddenly be lowered. Then he might be called up even sooner. He might be killed. England, as Sydney kept insisting, might lose the war. After his first few weeks of tutorials and lectures, it was no longer accurate for Larkin to describe his days to his parents as 'dull' or 'difficult'. Pointless would have been nearer the mark.

This helps to explain why Larkin began university by objecting to his work so thoroughly. His course of studies was a far cry from the one which exists at Oxford today – it was strongly biased towards philology, and ended with the writers of the 1820s. The only bright spots in his week, he told Sydney and Eva, were 'Edmund Blunden [on the Lake Poets] and Lord David Cecil [on the Romantics]: for the rest I'm trying to comprehend just why the quarto *Othello* is different from the folio *Othello* and how and where and who's responsible for it.'[25] Other lecturers got similarly short shrift, among them J. R. R. Tolkien on Anglo-Saxon poetry, Nevill Coghill on Chaucer and Shakespeare, C. S. Lewis on Medieval and Renaissance literature, and Charles Williams on Milton. According to Kingsley Amis, whom Larkin did not meet until early the following spring, Larkin took Iles's advice and simply cut most of the 'group stuff' he should have attended. 'He didn't go to lectures much,' Amis says. 'Not even Lewis, who was marvellous. Not Tolkien, either, but then he was an appalling lecturer. He spoke unclearly and slurred the important words, and then he'd write them on the blackboard but keep standing between them and us, then wipe them off before he turned round.'[26]

Tutorials couldn't be avoided so easily, and Larkin had as little patience with these as with lectures. In later life he was apt to refer to them (and especially to those he attended with Iles) as a 'farrago',[27] even though he liked the Senior English Fellow at St John's, Gavin Bone. According to

Amis, Bone was 'a very nice, very tolerant man'[28] – he was the son of Muirhead Bone, an official war artist during the First World War – but no amount of personal sympathy could draw Larkin to Bone's special subject, which was Anglo-Saxon poetry. 'Nobody,' says Amis, 'had a good word to say for "Beowulf", or "The Wanderer", "The Dream of the Rood", "The Battle of Maldon". Philip had less than none. If ever a man spoke for his generation it was when mentioning some piece of what he called in a letter to me "ape's bum fodder". He said, "I can just about stand learning the filthy lingo it's written in. What gets me down is having to *admire* the bloody stuff." '[29]

Larkin felt slightly guilty about his behaviour in tutorials, especially after he discovered that Bone was ill with cancer. (Bone continued his teaching for only another year and died in 1942.) 'I cannot imagine what [he] thought of us,' he later wrote. 'Already in failing health . . . he treated us like a pair of village idiots who might if tried hard turn nasty. The highest academic compliment I received [from him] . . . was "Mr Larkin can see a point if it is explained to him." '[30] Such remarks might suggest that nothing of any value came from the contact between them. Yet in his courteous and mild-mannered way, Bone may have refined some of the views that Iles was raining down on Larkin. The Preface to Bone's post-humously published *Anglo-Saxon Poetry* (1943), for instance, outlines his belief that 'the importance of the native stock [of English poetry] has been underestimated', and at least one commentator on Larkin's work has argued that 'this [belief] encouraged [Larkin's] concern for "Englishness" . . . [and] may have helped to develop [his] respect for clarity and intelligibility'.[31]

If Larkin felt the value of Bone's arguments at the time, he gave no sign of it. Before his first term was even half over he had bracketed his tutor with the other dons he had met, and dismissed them all as boring. Bone, evidently and understandably, thought that he had discovered in Larkin just one more averagely lazy and uncommitted undergraduate, someone who did the minimum of work for his weekly essays, and only scraped through his termly Collections (exams). What he couldn't know – just as Larkin's schoolteachers hadn't known – was how enthusiastic Larkin felt about literature which had nothing to do with his set work. While dawdling in public he worked hard in private to broaden his knowledge of writers who lay outside the syllabus. The Bodleian Library's daybooks, preserving the shelfmarks of books and manuscripts ordered by readers, show that of the fifty-one entries relating to Larkin during his time as an undergraduate, the majority have nothing directly to do with his tutorials. They include Auden's *Poems* and *The Orators*, copies of *New Signatures* and the *Left Review*, Baudelaire's *Intimate Journals*, and books by Dylan Thomas, John Betjeman, William Empson, Louis MacNeice and Cyril Connolly – as well as Wilder Hobson's *American Jazz Music*.[32]

Larkin later admitted that he spent most of his time straying from the path Bone intended him to follow. 'I was on a great [George] Moore kick at that time,' he said; 'probably he was at the bottom of my style, then.'[33] If so, he was there with Lawrence. It is Lawrence, not Moore, who is mentioned most frequently in Larkin's letters to friends and family, now and for the next several years. 'You say "Lawrence is the only man I can whole-heartedly admire" [and] I agree,'[34] he told Sutton in 1941, and the following year, with youthful self-importance, 'To me, Lawrence is what Shakespeare was to Keats and all the other buggers . . . As Lawrence says, life is a question of what you thrill to. But there has been a change in English psyche. The wind is blowing "in a new direction of time", and I feel that you and I, who will be if anyone the new artists, are on to it.'[35] This 'new direction', Larkin was beginning to realize, would depend on subtlety as well as candour – the sort of approach he was learning to associate with other writers he now re-read, or read for the first time. With Henry Green and Virginia Woolf (he admired *The Waves*); with Julian Hall, whose novel of public school life *The Senior Commoner* he approved for its 'general atmosphere of not showing one's feelings in public';[36] and with Katherine Mansfield. 'I do admire her a great deal,' he told Sutton, 'and feel very close to her in some things.'[37] He believed that the value of such writers was self-evident. The danger, he thought, was that they would soon become respectable, and therefore canonical. 'There is something greater than *literature*,'[38] he told Sutton again and again, insisting that Lawrence understood this better than anyone.

Anyone except Auden and Isherwood. Although Larkin had first read them at KHS, it wasn't until he reached Oxford that he began fully to appreciate their irony and ebullient detachment (he described Isherwood's first novel, *All the Conspirators*, as being like 'life photographed'[39]). Eventually Larkin would praise Auden as 'the first "modern" poet, in that he could employ modern properties unselfconsciously'.[40] Reading him in St John's during his first term he felt:

Auden rose like a sun. It is impossible to convey the intensity of the delight felt by a . . . mind reared on 'Drake's Drum', 'Westminster Bridge' and 'Ode to a

Nightingale', when a poet is found speaking a language thrilling and beautiful, and describing things so near to everyday life that their once-removedness strikes like a strange cymbal. We entered the land, books in hand, like travellers with a guidebook . . . *Poems*, *The Orators* and *Look, Stranger!* seemed three fragments of revealed truth . . . To read *The Journal of an Airman* was like being allowed half an hour's phone conversation with God.[41]

Beauty, excitement, intensity, unaffectedness: these were the things Larkin was coming to value most. He made no attempt to explain them by theories or analysis. To do so, he believed, would be to submit to the smothering embrace of 'literature'. ('Art is awfully *wrong*, you know,'[42] he told Sutton.) Off the syllabus, unacknowledged by dons, and aimed specifically at his own generation, Auden, Isherwood, Lawrence and the rest amounted to a new kind of secret – one which combined intellectual achievement with the spirit of revolt. Their example allowed Larkin to feel that he could write without losing touch with ordinary, exhilarating reality.

SIX

Auden strengthened Larkin's resolve to become a writer; he also swamped his style. 'Ultimatum', the poem published by the *Listener* in November 1940, announced his influence to a wider public, and echoes also reverberated in the two poems Larkin began to think about during his first term, 'Out in the lane I pause' and 'New Year Poem'. 'Yet to me,' the latter echoes shamelessly,

> this decaying landscape has its uses:
> To make me remember, who am always inclined to forget,
> That there is always a changing at the root,
> And a real world in which time really passes.

Impressed by his own ventriloquial skills, Larkin soon set out to explore the jungle of undergraduate literary life. To start with, it seemed a difficult task. None of the poets who had already made a name for themselves was in his college. The most prominent were William Bell at Merton (who in

1945 would edit *Poetry from Oxford in Wartime*, which included eleven poems by Larkin), Michael Meyer at Christ Church, John Heath-Stubbs, Sidney Keyes and Drummond Allison at Queen's – and, a little later, Michael Hamburger. Larkin's first reaction to learning that they 'were the people who ran the *Cherwell* [an undergraduate magazine], and they were the people who were the literary set, and they were the people who gave Herbert Read lunch'[1] was to feel envious. His second was to disparage them, and then, of course, to be disparaged in return. Amis remembers that when *Eight Oxford Poets*, edited by Keyes and Heath-Stubbs, came out in 1941, 'Philip was not represented. It now appears that Keyes, who may have known that Philip considered him a third-rate personage, left him out with some deliberation.'[2] In later life, Larkin continued to grumble about Keyes, who was killed on active service in Tunisia in 1943. The only memory of meeting him that he chose to preserve was one in which Keyes 'was wearing a bloody silly fur hat and had smelly breath'.[3] For all that, he eventually included two of his poems in *The Oxford Book of Twentieth Century English Verse*.

Too proud, too prickly, and too unsure of himself to join the élite literary set, Larkin turned instead before term was over to the English Club. This was a society open to anyone in the university, which several times a term (weekly, if possible) invited distinguished writers to read their work. Within a short time Larkin would become Treasurer of the Club, and 'as an officer I went out to dinner with [the speakers] before the meeting and was, to some extent, responsible for entertaining them afterwards. And we met quite a lot of people one way and another,'[4] among them Stephen Spender, Vernon Watkins, R. H. Wilenski, Lord Berners ('he had one lens of his spectacles darker than the other'[5]), George Orwell and Dylan Thomas. 'I remember,' Larkin said, 'we took Dylan Thomas to the Randolph and George Orwell to the not-so-good hotel. I suppose it was my first essay in practical criticism.'[6]

These meetings with the great and famous lay a little in the future. During his first term his only recorded visit to the club was to hear Stella Gibbons, the author of *Cold Comfort Farm*. His early dealings with undergraduate magazines were just as hesitant. It wasn't until the following spring, 1941, that he sent the staff of the *Cherwell* any of his poems (one, 'Story', was accepted), or volunteered to become their college agent, soliciting material as he had done for the *Coventrian*. As term drew on, in fact, he decided to keep dark the degree if not the fact of his interest in writing, and to concentrate instead on building up new friendships by other means. By 'good steady drinking'[7] (six pints a night wasn't unusual, money and Proctors permitting). By swearing. By snazzy dressing. By irritating the authorities. By seeming witty and ridiculous – an instigator if not an exponent of practical jokes, and a gifted mimic. He was, one of his contemporaries says, 'capable of delicious drollery, never more so than when you could persuade him to "do the shoe fetishist", a finely controlled piece of delicate miming that left me ... helpless ... It featured a drab macintoshed figure loping along the pavement and glancing slyly from side to side until it reached the climactic of the shop window display, where the face suffused with wicked, gleeful ecstasy.'[8] Another remembers him as 'monstrously flippant and disrespectful', having 'no contact with the dons', and spending an inordinate amount of time trying to organize a 'college drunk' for the end of term.[9]

And listening to jazz. At the end of his first year, when the Oxford University Rhythm Club was founded, Larkin was able to go to live performances more or less whenever he wanted. (The Rhythm Club turned out to be a disappointment; it was, he told his parents, 'the nesting ground of arty Shavians, Goodmanians, jitterbugs, and other pests of jazz'.[10]) Initially he had to rely on his own and his friends' records – a haphazard way of increasing his knowledge, but one which nevertheless made him feel his musical education had taken off. 'At Oxford,' he said, 'I met people who knew more about jazz than I did, and had more records, and who could even parallel my ecstasies with their own.'[11] Larkin is unduly modest here. His surviving college friends agree that when they met for one of their 'sessions' it was usually he who knew 'more' than they did. Nick Russel, for instance, says, 'He was one of the first people I knew who was blessed with such a remarkable ear he could distinguish accurately between Johnny Dodds and Albert Nichols, say, or King Oliver and Armstrong.'[12] Mervyn Brown, who played saxophone in a university band called 'The Bandits', was also impressed, both by Larkin's memory for musical details and by his record collection. Together with other friends like Roger Frisby and Frank Dixon they trawled Acott's and Russell's (Oxford's two record shops, once separated, now joined), hunting for 'scarce deletions'.[13]

Although Larkin was – in theory – open to new influences, he stuck faithfully to the tastes he had begun to form at school. He had told Sutton in 1939:

I've come to the conclusion that there is only one kind of jazz, and that's Blues, or music based on the Blues. Formerly, I thought there were two kinds: Blues and hot music, with perhaps a section for things like the Benny Goodman hot commercials and The Chicagoans. And now I'm beginning to think that the other kind (hot music) is artificial, and although it may be weird and ghostly it can't move you in the least. So that I've come to the conclusion that the Casa Loma and the Mills Blue Rhythm and some of the Duke's records are just striving after something that isn't there, i.e. to move the listener by adopting the idiom which cannot move you in the least.[14]

When Amis arrived at St John's he found Larkin still preaching this gospel of jazz according to the emotions. Just as beauty and excitement were the qualities he was learning to value most in modern writing, so a direct appeal to strong feeling was the thing he constantly looked for in jazz. The only thing that altered was the cast list of those he thought could provide it. By 1941 he was prepared to concede that some of those he had once reckoned 'artificial' were in fact authentic. 'Our heroes,' Amis says, 'were the white Chicagoans, Count Basie's Band, Bix Beiderbecke, Sidney Bechet, Henry Allen, Fats Waller, early Armstrong, and early Ellington . . . and our heroines were Bessie Smith, Billie Holiday, Rosetta Howard . . . and Cleo Brown.'[15]

These names summarize the kind of music Larkin preferred; they can't even begin to show the intensity with which he and his friends enjoyed their music. To glimpse this, we have to turn to the rapturous letters he wrote Sutton. 'Thanks,' goes one, typically, 'for the best letter ever to arrive at Oxford with my name on the envelope! . . . I rushed out on Monday and bought "Nobody Knows The Way I Feel This Morning". Fucking, cunting, bloody good! Bechet is a great artist. As soon as he starts playing you automatically stop thinking about anything else and listen. Power and glory.'[16] In rooms after dinner, in pubs, when he should have been attending lectures or preparing for tutorials, the excitement of jazz did more than anything else to persuade Larkin that he was 'beginning to enjoy Oxford'.[17] The music was a focus for powerful feelings which were blocked in more orthodox contexts; it was the means by which his stammering shyness could be set aside; it was his most enjoyable way of feeling part of a community.

Then, suddenly and violently, his life was thrown into confusion. On 14 November 1940, at 7 in the evening, the German Luftwaffe bombed Coventry, dropping 500 tons of high explosive, killing 554 people and seriously injuring 1,000 others. Large parts of the city were obliterated. The cathedral in which Larkin had been christened was ruined. Three-quarters of the car and aeroplane plant was destroyed. Two thousand homes were made uninhabitable. It was Hitler's first blitz on an English city – something that Sydney had imagined might happen and which his family had always feared. When Larkin heard the news on the wireless in St John's he immediately turned to Noel Hughes, wondering what to do. Nothing, they decided: wait until word came from their families. But after two days, when still no news had arrived, they decided to go and see for themselves.

Larkin described what he found in *Jill*, when John Kemp returns to his home in Huddlesford to check on damage following an air raid. As he approaches the town, worrying about his parents, Kemp can think 'only of their goodness. The very things that in the past had most irritated him about them ... turned suddenly round and became emblems of their most loveable qualities.'[18] When he reaches the town centre, and discovers which streets have vanished and which have survived, distractedly taking in burnt-out shops, charred window-frames and smouldering rubbish, a sense of obligation overwhelms him:

As he went stumbling up the long hill, noticing half-bricks driven by fierce explosions into the hedges, the years reeled back and he was praying for his parents like a child and fervently. He gasped aloud that he would do anything, promise anything, if only they would be all right. Any attempts at a personal life he had made seemed merely a tangle of hypocritical selfishness: really he was theirs, dependent on them for ever.[19]

As they travelled north towards their 'home territory',[20] Larkin and Hughes could not help imagining such scenes awaiting them. They decided to hitchhike, and managed the journey in a little over two hours. The Larkin house in Manor Road, which stood a few yards away from the main south-west approach to the city, was the one they reached first. It was intact, but when they knocked at the door there was no reply. Larkin grew more frightened than ever, and for twenty minutes he and Hughes tramped the nearby streets, hoping to meet someone they knew, who would tell them what had happened. No one appeared, and when they eventually gave up and crossed over to the north-east side of the city, where Hughes lived, they were once again relieved yet disappointed. The house was standing, but empty.

Eventually Hughes found a cousin, who told him that his parents had left the area until the emergency had passed. Larkin found no one he knew, and when the time came for them to catch their lift back to Oxford, he glumly concluded that Sydney and Eva must be safely sheltering somewhere. But where? 'For at least the seven years that I had known him,'

Hughes wrote later, 'Philip lived at the same house, but at only one other house had he felt able to call for news of his missing parents. That done, he had shot his bolt ... Later, as I got to know, and to know more about, Philip's father ... I could imagine how Philip could have lived for years in a neighbourhood and yet be reared in almost total isolation from it.'[21]

When Larkin returned to St John's that evening he found a telegram from his father, one he was so pleased to receive that he never stopped to ask why it had taken such a long time to reach him. The family was safe, it said – Eva had gone to stay temporarily with Sydney's brother Alfred in Lichfield (at 33 Cherry Orchard, in a modest Victorian street on the west of the city). Sydney himself, who had been in City Hall during the raid, would be staying with his deputy, Dr Marshall, at his home in Armorial Road for a few days before joining her. The next morning Larkin wrote to tell his father he was 'tremendously relieved to know you were safe. While you had the bombings, fires, rescue parties and all the rest of the grim trappings of air raids, we merely had the unpleasant rumours, the horrific newspapers, and the lack of news.'[22]

The raids on Coventry continued into the winter. Larkin wrote to Sutton in November, 'Your house got a bollocking – as you'll have seen by now. That end of B. Avenue got the worst shitting I've seen in all the town.'[23] The following April he continued in the same vein: 'Raids of last Tuesday simply buggered our district to Hades. We were cut off by whacking great bomb craters in St P's Road (each side) and in Manor Road, and delayed action bombs in Friar's Road. Peace perfect Peace.'[24] Larkin's fears loom large behind these brave words. The November blitz frightened him badly because for the first time it made the war real, and because in threatening to destroy his past it also reminded him that he could not escape it. As its echoes died away and were replaced with the sound of other raids, he brooded on the images of destruction he had seen. The devastation continued to haunt him for many years – helping to shape his poem 'A Stone Church Damaged by a Bomb', written three years later. And in 1952, when he was living in Belfast and went to see the film *Things to Come*, he told a friend, 'The air raid set for Christmas Eve 1940 was really not a bad idea of what an air raid was like, except that there weren't enough fires and uselessly-spraying water mains. And I once saw a bank of earth in Coventry alive with tiny blue flames, like crocuses, because of a burst gas main.'[25] In his later poems, there are very few excursions into the sort of narrative that would allow him to make such direct references as these – but it's still possible to see the lasting impression that the Coventry raids made on him. The damage of 'A Stone Church Damaged by a Bomb' is assimilated into the larger ruination of 'Church Going'; the blasts around Manor Road echo underground in 'The Explosion'.

Larkin spent the last two weeks of his first term trying to pick up the threads he had woven in the first six. It was hardly long enough, and when the time came for him to go down he was sorry. 'I arrived here [33 Cherry Orchard, his Uncle Alfred's house in Lichfield] lateish on Saturday night after a sod of a journey,' he told Sutton. '. . . Makes you appreciate Oxford, you know, coming to a lonely spot like this. In fact, I feel in favour of Oxford at present.'²⁶ Cherry Orchard was a smaller house than Manor Road, and even without Sydney there (he stayed in Coventry during the week), and with Larkin given a sitting room and bedroom at a neighbour's house, the family felt crowded. Eva was still twittery after the raid, and soon got on everyone's nerves; Larkin was contemptuous of the 'coarse bluffness' of his uncle and aunt. Very soon he had reached his wits' end. 'What these fucking bastards want is some authority,' he told Sutton; '– Catholic Church would be better than nothing. Also some respect. Dirty buggers. Cunts. Shitty sods and piss pricks. Fuck 'em all. Thank God I have a room to myself where I can be quiet, can belch and fart and write to you. My uncle (when I'm reading): "What 'ave you got your nose in now?" I long to return to Oxford just to get into the company of people under the age of 40.'²⁷

Early in December, Sydney had announced that he would be taking his family back to Manor Road for Christmas. Bombs were preferable to arguments, he thought – and with Eva flapping in his wake he returned to Coventry, where Larkin sullenly sat out the rest of his vacation. At the age of eighteen, it would have been difficult for him to do anything else; he was too young and inexperienced to take charge of his own life. Yet even allowing for this, it's surprising he didn't make greater efforts to escape his family during this and subsequent vacations. Why, for instance, didn't he arrange to spend some of the time with friends? The answer takes us to the contradiction which now lay at the heart of his relationship with his parents. Much as his father daunted him, he nevertheless made him feel beholden – partly out of a sense of duty, and partly out of genuine affection. Similarly, much as his mother irritated him by being a dogsbody, he knew that his contentment depended on her remaining one. So long as she was there, he never had to make his own bed, cook his own meals or clean his shoes. Her presence left him free for his own pursuits – which included writing angry accounts of his time at home. He realized that his anger was, to a certain extent, a displacement of the frustration he felt with himself. Yet it was also a completely independent feeling, a fury at being trapped, and a fear about what sort of prediction this made for his later life. 'Isherwood is my destiny,' he told Sutton. 'Let me hug defeat like a lover.'[28]

It wasn't only rage but writing that Eva's coddling allowed – though for the time being Larkin couldn't produce any. 'I've got hours and hours to write,' he told Sutton before leaving for Oxford, 'a whole box of notepaper, and not much inclination ... I haven't written a thing since I came here. (Yes I have – I've written Fuck All.)'[29] When he picked up the booklets of poems he had made the summer before, hoping they would show him the way forward, he found that he despised them. As he finished the two poems he had started the previous term, he was dismayed by their lack of originality. 'I don't want to write anything at present,' he complained to Sutton again. 'In fact, thinking it over, I want to die. I am very impressed by this sort of unrealized deathwish of mine. Makes yer ponder ... I suppose my writing is terrible. Sod and bollocks, anyway. Not to mention cunt and fuck. Omitting bugger and shit. I think I shall start going to church.'[30]

SEVEN

Immediately after Christmas the mood lightened in Manor Road: Sydney received an OBE in the New Year's Honours list. Bolstered by this recognition, he decided that he couldn't tolerate making a life with 'the Lichfield Larkins' on a permanent basis, and began searching for a new family house. It was impossible to think they could stay much longer in Manor Road, since the centre of Coventry was still suffering heavy raids. Perhaps they should move out of the town altogether?

Larkin left his parents discussing the question and returned to St John's. Compared to family life, he found his second term even 'more enjoyable' than his first. Although he was studying Anglo-Saxon 'with the firm belief I should fail the section at the end of term',[1] he was excited by the work he had volunteered to do as agent for the *Cherwell*. There was also 'the only sign of intellectual life' in St John's, the Essay Society, which he was invited to join within a few days of his arrival. This society had a dozen members, and met regularly in the college President's rooms to discuss (or hear discussed by visiting speakers) issues to do with literature and contemporary culture. 'Dictators of Culture?' was a typical subject. There is no record in the Society's minutes of Larkin speaking from the floor, let alone giving a paper, but it is obvious from his letters home that he thought of his membership as a privilege, and revelled in the company of 'serious-minded intellectuals'.[2]

But he was still worried about his call-up – especially when, after a few days of term, he received a note from the Senior Training Corps demanding to know what size boots he took. His fears multiplied as he discovered what was happening to Sutton. In the uniform of the RASC by March, Sutton was whisked abroad by April. 'The ego's country he inherited/ From those who tended it like farmers', Larkin wrote Audenesquely in the sonnet 'Conscript', dedicated to his friend. In his letters he was more obviously apprehensive. 'Certainly I hold that the ranks would be better than the officer training unit. Next term the OTC will be a condition of residence but it's still quite on the cards that I shall be a CO. Only when I'm far away from things do I begin to think that perhaps they wouldn't be so bad. I don't think I could ever fit happily into the army.'[3]

Larkin's social politics here – his preference for 'the ranks' – indicate that by now Auden's influence was beginning to affect more than just his writing. Yet while this led him to endorse a few left-wing opinions about world affairs, it never eclipsed his father's example. 'I don't think [fascism is] third stage society,' he wrote equivocally to Sutton. 'Democracy is second stage. Therefore we must have democracy first. But then in the end we shall return to the Power and the Glory, but better and nobler. But this will take ages.'[4] When term was over, and Larkin was in direct contact with Sydney again, the conflict in his loyalties became more intense. His letters show him continuing to share some of Sydney's admiration for German efficiency, but regarding his own likely fate with dread. 'When is this invasion to start?' he asks in one of them. 'I feel the war must be over this year if Hitler does his job in his accustomed way. My only fear is he'll do it messily – gas etc. And that I will be called up to be mown down, while the real army arranges itself behind me. Cheerful thoughts.'[5] Before the vacation ended, Larkin had a dramatic chance to resolve these ambiguous feelings. On 8 April 1941 KHS was virtually destroyed in a bombing raid: of the Victorian buildings only the central tower, through which he had walked on his first visit to see the headmaster, remained standing. Yet not even this could persuade him purely and simply to denounce Germany. Some time afterwards he was still telling Sutton, 'I expect Pop will be on the lookout for a secondhand copy of Norman Baynes's edition of Hitler's speeches. I looked into them and felt the familiar sinking of heart when I saw how *right* and yet how *wrong* everything had been. The disentanglement of this epoch will be a beautiful job for someone.'[6]

Larkin had been late beginning this spring vacation – grumpily staying on in St John's to do some 'war work' in Bagley Wood, a 'generally unpleasant' sprawling copse between Oxford and the village of Radley to the south, before travelling north to his temporary address in Lichfield. (The ostensible purpose of this war work had been to plant '3,000 oak trees at a distance of 15 inches from each other. They are only baby trees of course.'[7] The reality had meant 'we don't do any work at all. Just stand about . . . and occasionally chuck sticks on fires.'[8]) Yet even a little time in Cherry Orchard was enough to make him detest life with his parents. 'Politeness is the watchword here,' he wrote to Sutton. 'I used to say, when my mother complained I had no manners, that good manners were only natural instinct. I was wrong.'[9]

By May he had escaped to Oxford again, and thrown himself more vigorously than ever into the beer-drinking, jazz-listening, non-working, all-male world he had spent the last two terms creating for himself. 'Saw a lot of Dixon and Kidner,' he wrote in one of his surviving notebooks '– and of Iles, Hughes, Parkes and Brown.' He might also have mentioned a new arrival at St John's, Kingsley Amis. On 5 May, Larkin was standing with Iles by the porter's lodge scanning the noticeboards when Iles noticed Amis's name:

'I met him at Cambridge on a schol . . . ,' Iles said. 'He's a hell of a good man.'
  'How is he?'
  'He shoots guns.'
I [Larkin] did not understand this until later in the afternoon when we were crossing the dusty first quadrangle a fair-haired young man came down staircase three and paused on the bottom step. Norman instantly pointed his right hand at him in the semblance of a pistol and uttered a short coughing bark to signify a shot – a shot not in reality, but as it would sound from a worn sound-track on Saturday afternoon in the ninepennies.
  The young man's reaction was immediate. Clutching his chest in a rictus of agony, he threw one arm up against the archway and began slowly crumpling downwards, fingers scoring the stonework. Just as he was about to collapse on the piled-up laundry . . . he righted himself and tottered over to us.

'I've been working on this,' he said as soon as introductions were completed. 'Listen. This is when you're firing in a ravine.'

We listened.

'And this is when you're firing in a ravine and the bullet ricochets off a rock.'

We listened again. Norman's appreciative laughter skirled freely: I stood silent. For the first time I felt myself in the presence of a talent greater than my own.[10]

Almost immediately, Amis was returning the compliment. Good-looking and nervously sophisticated, he felt initially that he had nothing in common with the loping, stammering Larkin. Yet within days he realized they laughed at the same things, believed in the same things, and were united in their contempt for the snobbish, public-school elements of Oxford life. They soon discovered other and more particular similarities. Amis, an only child, had been born on 16 April 1922 and brought up in the south London suburb of Norbury; his father worked as an export clerk for Colman's Mustard in Canonbury. Just as Larkin felt that in Coventry 'nothing' had happened to him, so Amis believed that he 'didn't come from a place, but from an area'.[11] Amis's parents moved three times during his childhood, each time inching their way up the social scale, and Amis himself did his bit for self-improvement by winning a scholarship to the City of London School. As a pupil he took part in debates, edited the school magazine, and was innocently mischievous in much the same way that Larkin had been at KHS – and when war broke out, he too was uprooted by the blitz: the City of London School was evacuated to Marlborough, in Wiltshire.

In such writing as Amis had produced at school, an early infatuation with the Romantics had gradually given way to an Auden-inspired modernity. A sensibility very like Larkin's had been formed in the process, one which checked lyricism with mockery, and spurned any sign of pretension. At the time of their first meeting, many of Amis's high artistic hopes were buttressed by left-wing allegiances, but otherwise there was little difference between their tastes and motivations. Their friendship grew rapidly. Amis remembers Larkin telling him that he (Amis) ' "lived in a world of the most perfectly refined pure humour" ' and added ' "in his efforts to prove he had a serious side he became insulting in his emphasis, which made him disliked by many [who nevertheless] could not appreciate the humour that he breathed like air." I think,' says Amis, 'that's the nicest thing that anyone has ever said to me.'[12]

Amis filled out the role in Larkin's life that had first been taken by Colin

Gunner, then by Norman Iles. To begin with, Larkin and Amis made Iles part of their new alliance Amis found that Iles was

> a kind of ideal bad undergraduate ... doing what he could to undermine the academic outlook by representing the university as a place where charlatans lorded it over ambitious or apathetic noodles ... [He] became the centre of a sort of circle that included Philip, me, and three or four more semi- and would-be drunks in and outside St John's. Perhaps the underlying attraction was that of the cynic or nihilist who gives others a guilty pleasure by going much further than they would have dared to go on their own. And Norman had plenty of ridicule to spare for himself. Pub-crawling was the favoured, almost the only possible, social activity, now and then too strenuous to suit me.[13]

As Larkin and Amis grew closer, their feelings for Iles faded. 'Norman's rejection of [Oxford] was total,' Larkin said. 'At first this strengthened his influence over us; but as time went on, it tended to cut him off.'[14] The same had been true of Gunner – whose friendship, like that with Iles, was all but finished off by the war. Because Gunner was already in the Irish Brigade, he and Larkin now met only occasionally. Iles, too, was soon in the army. He graduated from the OTC and according to Amis 'got a commission in the artillery and immediately stopped doing anything and went somewhere that completely hopeless officers were sent. He ended up in Poland working for a relief committee, distributing clothing for displaced persons. "Never on any occasion were we thanked," I can remember him saying. That's the sort of person he was.'[15]

Although Amis himself was often sarcastic about university life, he was never in danger of standing – like Iles – outside it altogether. The risks he ran were of a subtler kind. 'To some extent,' Larkin said, 'he suffered the familiar humorist's fate of being unable to get anyone to take him seriously,'[16] yet he realized that beneath Amis's 'rather brutal and down-to-earth deflation' lay 'a great sensitivity'.[17] Amis, in return, admired Larkin for seeming 'always the senior partner' in spite of his shyness. He was, Amis says, 'the stronger personality, always much better read, with his views very firmly fixed. I was always full of ridiculous, foolish, very young man's ideas. But he seemed to have grown up.'[18]

Amis at this time wanted his friends in St John's to believe that his most 'serious side' was 'political'. 'In those days of Help for Russia Week,' Larkin pointed out, 'when the Hammer and Sickle flew with the Union Jack in Carfax,' Amis became editor of the University Labour Club *Bulletin* ('and in this capacity printed one of my poems [in spring 1942]'[19]).

Amis – who had stood as a Communist candidate in a mock election at school and was, with Iris Murdoch, briefly a member of the student branch of the Communist Party at Oxford – has sometimes been accused of 'simply trying on political faces'[20] while an undergraduate. Larkin, certainly, was not especially impressed. As far as he was concerned, Amis was more interesting and convincing when trying on literary faces. The more ironical they were, the better they seemed to fit. 'Kingsley and I used to read other people's poems,' Larkin said later, 'and seriously planned getting a rubber stamp made – or rather two rubber stamps, one for each of us – reading "What does this mean?" and "What makes you think I care?"'[21]

Larkin had been practising this kind of mockery with Sutton for years, and enjoyed the way Amis raised the stakes. His own writing, he knew, was bound to benefit. Only recently, when producing yet another hand-sewn booklet of poems – *Chosen Poems* (April 1941) – he had shown in the Foreword that he was still prone to all kinds of pomposity:

I regard the changes that are shown throughout the style as being of interest to the psychologist if not the literary critic. They exemplify, to my mind, the natural and to some extent inevitable ossification of a 'boyish gift' with the passing of time, shown by the gradual disappearance of spontaneous verse forms and natural energy, and the accompanying de-personalization which characterizes the later poems. These latter (still speaking from the standpoint of the psychologist) are nearer the poems of a novelist than the poems of a poet.[22]

Larkin would later ridicule the idea that anyone might talk meaningfully about his 'writing at Oxford'. 'I didn't write at Oxford,'[23] he said flatly. The facts suggest otherwise. He would, occasionally, discuss work in progress with Amis, and wrote slowly but steadily. Nearly a dozen of his poems appeared in magazines during his three years as an undergraduate. He was happier to admit that he and Amis had spent a great deal of time listening to records together, sometimes in deadly earnest, sometimes prancing round the room. Sometimes, too, they spent an evening thumping on the piano in a pub off Walton Street. 'I've just battered out Philip Larkin's "Mean old kazoo and piano blues in B flat",' Larkin told Sutton one night, 'and outside it is snowing like buggery. Yes sir, like buggery. Don't like cold weather. When icicles hang from one's tool it is difficult to contemplate pure art.'[24] Amis accepted that Larkin was 'the senior partner' in jazz as in everything else they shared. 'It was impossible for anyone not to have become a jazz fan at any sort of school in the 1930s,' Amis says. 'I was a fan, but not such a one as I became under his tutelage. I had a few records, but I had started when I was twelve, then like a bloody idiot sold them. Then started again. So when I went up to Oxford I had a few by Louis Armstrong, Fats Waller, Artie Shaw, and I had a rather good gramophone (but not as good as Nick Russel's). So Philip would often come to my room for the gramophone, and took me in hand and introduced me to all these people I'd never heard of.'[25]

There were a few records they didn't agree about. Amis thought Larkin's records of Red Mackenzie and Eddie Condon's Chicagoans 'dreary'; Larkin played them 'again and again'. Larkin had a special dislike for 'records that remind[ed him] of silly old black men like Morton', which Amis admired.[26] These local disagreements were never deep, but behind them lay a larger difference of opinion, one which affected their views about literature as well as music. While Amis was excited but pragmatic in his discussions of jazz, Larkin was interested in exploring the ways in which it fed and released his unconscious. In 1943 he wrote 'a little essay'[27] explaining what he meant. 'Jazz,' he said, 'is the closest description of the unconscious we have':[28]

The decay of ritual in everything from religion to the lighting of the fire is resulting in the insulation of the unconscious which finds its daily fulfilment in such ritual ... The predicament in which the unconscious is finding itself today is reflected in the general upheaval in all the arts, and particularly in the emergence of a new art, American jazz music.

Nobody sees that the stridency of jazz is the most important thing about it, for it symbolizes the importance and urgency of its problem. The modern unconscious has chosen to symbolize its predicament of subjection through the music of a subject people; its predicament of imprisonment through the unvarying monotony of the 4/4 rhythm; its panic at the predicament through the arresting texture of the jazz tone.

Jazz is the new art of the unconscious, and is therefore improvised, for it cannot call upon consciousness to express its own divorce from consciousness.[29]

The significance of this essay lies in the way it values the depths rather than merely the surfaces of jazz. It shows Larkin was willing to see that art needs to be both immediate and profound, to have elements of obviousness as well as obscurity, and if necessary to record these things in different tones of voice. In doing so, the essay sets out many of the principles which were to govern his mature writing, in which demotic and rarefied poetic languages are brought together time and time again.

EIGHT

Even before he met Amis, Larkin knew that mentioning such things as 'the unconscious' in college would be likely to produce a chorus of Metro Goldwyn Mayer snarls. Once Amis had arrived it was out of the question – he had to settle instead for a world in which serious enthusiasms were coated with mollifying ironies, or buried altogether under layers of jokes. He did so happily enough, behaving – according to Amis – as 'an almost aggressively normal undergraduate of the non-highbrow sort, hard swearing, hard belching, etc., treating the college dons as fodder for obscene clerihews ... [and] the porter as a comic ogre'. His dislike of tutorial work grew week by week. 'We paid special attention to the Romantic poets,' Amis remembers. 'They all signed on as Bill Wordsworth and his Hot Six – Wordsworth (tmb) with "Lord" Byron (tpt), Percy Shelley (sop), Johnny Keats (alto and clt), Sam "Tea" Coleridge (pno), Jimmy Hogg (bs), Bob Southey (ds) ... Shelley was singled out for a form of travesty in which nothing was altered but much added: "Music," began one of Philip's [parodies], "when soft *silly* voices, that have been talking *piss* die,/Vibrates, like a ..."'[1] Another, longer send-up survives in a letter to Sutton. Presented as 'the latest work of the brilliant new Post-Masturbationist Poet, Shaggerybox McPhallus ... [whose] latest book of verse, "The Escaped Cock", deals almost exclusively with problems of intense spiritual value, which are yet so universal in their application as to be ensured of a wide public', it is in fact a parody of Keats's 'La Belle Dame Sans Merci':

> And this is why I shag alone
> Ere half my creeping days are done.
> The wind coughs sharply in the stove,
>   There is no sun
>
> To light my way to bed: the leaves
> Are brown upon the icy tree;
> The swallows all have left the eaves
>   Silently, silently.[2]

Where rewriting literature could not satisfy them, Larkin and Amis took to defacing it. In an essay published to commemorate Larkin's sixtieth birthday, Amis recalled coming across Larkin's comment on the St John's library copy of *The Faerie Queene*: 'At the foot of the last page of the text he had written in pencil in his unmistakable, beautiful, spacious hand':

First I thought *Troilus and Criseyde* was the most *boring* poem in English. Then I thought *Beowulf* was. Then I thought *Paradise Lost* was. Now I *know* that *The Faerie Queene* is the *dullest thing out. Blast it.*[3]

Amis tells us that he 'queried the uncharacteristically non-alcoholic language' of this, as well he might have done. A much more typical defacement was inflicted on Amis's copy of Keats's *Poems*, where beside the lines 'ethereal, flushed, and like a throbbing star/Into her dream he melted', from *The Eve of St Agnes*, Larkin wrote, 'YOU MEAN HE FUCKED HER.'[4]

There were other sorts of writerly vandalism, too. They devised a game called 'horsepissing', in which certain existing words in a text were replaced by obscenities – and in their letters to each other, now and later, versions of the same thing appeared. Whenever Larkin found himself writing a sentence which included anything risky or double-entendre-ish, he interpolated wild phonetic whoops and yelps, or a Billy Bunterish 'Aaaargh, leggo my . . . ' Similarly, it became their habit to dispense with 'love' or 'yours ever' as they signed off, and to provide instead a word or phrase about whatever happened to be preoccupying them at the time, with 'bum' stuck on the end of it. The habit lasted until Larkin died, and no one was spared: C. H. Sisson bum; Margaret Thatcher bum; *Penguin Book of Contemporary British Poetry* bum.

Amis refers to these things as 'sheer childishness',[5] and so they were, in a way. Yet it's impossible not to see in them something other than simple high spirits. In their later work, Larkin and Amis develop their undergraduate snipings into a sustained barrage against pomposity. Even more important is the way their early desecrations anticipate the structure of much of their subsequent writing, and Amis's writing in particular. Their merely 'childish' defacements create a mocking sub-text below everything that is familiar and respectable, just as *Lucky Jim* (for instance) organizes a great deal of its humour around the discrepancies between what can be said or shown in public, and what in private. Notoriously, it is the difference between public and private faces which becomes the novel's focus for comedy – the difference, that is, between Jim's university-face and his Evelyn Waugh-making, gorilla-faking, Bernard-baiting faces.

When private and public become confused, in the lecture which concludes the novel, Jim cannot keep his face straight. It is a denouement which owes a great deal to the 'hours of ingenuity'[6] Amis spent with Larkin in St John's, dreaming up ways of being disrespectful.

Larkin was confident that cynicism would stand him in better stead than the cloudy symbolism of fellow-undergraduates like Sidney Keyes. Yet he couldn't altogether deny the appeal to the subconscious which he felt when listening to jazz. And since it existed in music, why not elsewhere too? The thought might not have got very far – would certainly, in fact, have been hunted down and killed by Amis's sarcasm – had Larkin not decided to attend a course of lectures given during this summer term by John Layard. Layard, now forty years old, had been a student of modern languages and then of psychiatry at Cambridge, first under the psychologist W. H. R. Rivers, and later in analysis under Homer Lane. When he was in Berlin in 1926 recovering from a breakdown he met Auden, with whom he had a brief affair and who, although he referred to him in a poem as 'loony Layard', found him, 'with his hawk-like face and piercing eyes, a man of remarkable personality'.[7] The expositions of human psychology that Layard gave Auden (and, eventually, many other people) were a mishmash of his own beliefs, Lane's, André Gide's and D. H. Lawrence's (particularly those set out by Lawrence in the *Fantasia of the Unconscious*). Layard 'went further than Lane in declaring that the term "God" really means our physical desires, the inner law of our own nature, and that "the Devil" is in fact the conscious control of these desires'.[8] The only real sin, he believed, was obedience to the 'Devil' and disobedience to 'God' – something which orthodox education was bound to deny. When he came into Larkin's life he was teaching at New College – a slightly cranky figure, but likely to appeal to the frustrated and introspective side of Larkin's character, and also beguiling because of his association with Auden.

Amis was not impressed. 'Philip rather fell for Layard,' he admits reluctantly; ' – all that piss about the liar's quinsy.'[9] While he now wonders 'how long Philip held on to it',[10] all the signs are that for a while Layard occupied Larkin greatly, and left a mark which was never entirely eradicated. The mere fact that Layard made a direct address to the unconscious was enough to make Larkin a willing listener; that Layard also wove into his lectures a discourse on women – on their role in the world, their character and their sexuality – made him positively rapturous. 'Layard wound up the term's course with a damn fine talk,' he told Sutton before returning to Manor Road. 'Here's what he said':

The greatest revolution of our time – greater than Communism, Fascism, psychology, this war – is the fundamental change in the social position of women. He pointed out that till now contraceptives had been scarce and hard to get on a large scale, and therefore up till now women had been wholly occupied with childbearing. He pointed out the freedom of man/man's finishing with procreation in five minutes, [after which] he's free to go about organizing, discovering and so on – for the woman it takes nine months ... The solution as he saw it was that women should be the priestesses of the unconscious and help men to regain all the vision they have lost ... What women must do is – as they are in the unconscious, rubbing shoulders with all these archetypes and symbols that man so needs – is bring them up and give them to man. How this is to be done, he didn't really know.[11]

The previous winter, when Larkin first arrived at Oxford, he had become sharply aware that his ignorance of girls was remarkable. As time passed, this had started to weigh on him more heavily, especially after he began to play an active role in the English Club. According to Philip Brown, 'most of the officers of the Club were girls, and they used to lionize Philip a bit, asking him to tea and so on. It was hard to say why, since he wasn't writing very much or very well, but he was charismatic, you see. Girls wanted to find out about him.'[12] Larkin, in turn, now wanted to find out about girls, but felt incapable. His shyness quickly turned into the sneering he had learnt from his father. 'Women (university) repel me inconceivably,' he told Sutton. 'They are shits.'[13] Ever since Amis had started to keep him company, things had been both better and worse – worse because compared to his new friend he felt ugly, inept and woefully inexperienced; better because, for all his savvy, Amis conceded that everybody had difficulties with girls at some time or other. Now Layard made things even more complicated. If women really were the 'priestesses of the unconscious', as Layard said, Larkin thought they might endlessly enrich his work. How could he fulfil himself – as an artist, if not as a man – without them?

He summoned up his courage, and tried to get to know some of the girls who flattered him in the English Club, or met him in lectures. Every encounter was a disaster. Margaret Flannery, for instance, 'edged towards him but made him giggle'.[14] Hilary Allen of St Hilda's upset him by beating him at table tennis. Another girl, when he took her a bunch of flowers, alarmed him so much merely by opening the door to his knock that he was literally unable to speak to her; he thrust the flowers into her arms and fled. A fourth, when he tried to kiss her in a punt, told him, 'I'd sooner not, thanks.'[15] After this string of defeats Larkin retired hurt, sheltering behind the antagonism which had protected him in the past. 'Cunt and bugger Oxford women,'[16] he wrote to Sutton, quoting approvingly a part of the *Fantasia of the Unconscious* that Layard ignored: 'the thought of actual sex connection is usually repulsive'.[17]

In the years ahead, Larkin's hostility to women would sometimes soften but never entirely disappear. Layard had stirred up feelings which were to become a stock-in-trade: a mixture of excitement and fear, of bewilderment and the wish to dominate, of dependence and rejection. None of this would have startled Sydney, but because Larkin had the model of his family so clearly before him, he was determined not to repeat what he reckoned were his father's mistakes. The last appeal, he promised himself, would always be to the self. 'I don't,' he told Amis, 'I *don't* want to take a girl out and spend *circa* £5 when I can toss off in five minutes, free, and have the rest of the evening to myself.'[18]

If Larkin found girls so difficult, was it partly because he was really attracted to men? At school, by his own admission, he had 'fallen in love' with a number of his contemporaries, and at Oxford he broadcast his admiration for Julian Hall's novel *The Senior Commoner*, which deals directly as well as obliquely with its Etonian hero's 'not very romantic'[19] feelings for a junior boy called Murray Gawthorne ('there was something altogether immodest in [his] figure'[20]). At Oxford, too, he had dressed from his first term onwards in a way which most people in his college acknowledged to be 'camp',[21] even if it didn't always have quite the authority he intended. Noel Hughes, for example, recalled a 'hot and gloriously sunny Saturday morning [when] Philip was ... outward bound on *Cherwell* affairs. Whether to mark the errand or the splendour of the day, [he] had decided to wear beneath his jacket the top of his pyjama suit of broad matching pastel stripes. Somehow he looked more like an old man reaching back for his youth than a young blade breaking out.'[22] Dressing camply is one thing; being homosexual is another – and at least as far as the evidence of Larkin's letters goes, and the reminiscence of his friends, there's no indication that his being 'camp for art's sake' wasn't the beginning and end of it. Writing to Sutton, for instance, who at this stage was still his closest confidant, he occasionally brings in phrases from Auden or Isherwood ('Last night I slept with a haaaaaairy man') which are clearly part of a private joke, not a sign of anything more intimate. The same is true of similar remarks in letters to Amis.

Yet in a short story Larkin wrote between January and July 1941[23] a more complicated picture emerges. The story opens with three under-graduates, David, Patrick and Christopher Warner (a name he would use again in *Jill*), chatting in their Oxford college; they have all been to school together – 'Stonebridge' – and they have all evolved a distinctly camp style. ('Are you courting?' one asks at one point; 'Still waiting for the right man, my dear,' another replies.) After Patrick has left the room David and Christopher agree that they are irritated by the way he 'acts the pansy', but when we next see him we realize he more than merely 'acts' it. After a visit from David, Patrick 'walked over to the fire and noticed the other had left nearly half a cup of coffee on the arm of the sofa. He picked it up and drank it, putting his mouth where the other's had been. It was almost cold.'

The following evening, attention switches from Patrick to David. It turns out that he is keen on a girl called Elizabeth (another name re-used in *Jill*), whom he takes to a rowdy party given by Jack Tranter. There's a 'forest of bottles and glasses; on the floor beneath these were several crates of beer, and next to it was a large barrel'. Not surprisingly, everyone gets drunk; the party ends with some of the undergraduates throwing darts at photographs of naked girls, then brawling with each other. When David comes to his senses he discovers that he's in bed with Christopher. He can't remember how he got there, hastily climbs out, is sick in the grate, accidentally sets fire to a cushion and a book, then leaves his rooms in pursuit of more drink. He immediately bumps into Patrick, who becomes the focus of Larkin's interest for the final pages of the story. Incoherent, bleary, haggard with guilt, Patrick (we are left to assume, but are not told) has been with another man – presumably 'Vivian', who has been some-times mentioned but never seen – while David and Christopher have been snoring in each other's arms:

Panic-stricken, he swivelled his head from side to side, trying to shake away the darkness as an elephant might try to shake the poison arrow away from his skull. Gulfs opened beneath him as he tottered on the edge of an unmentionable collapse. Quite naturally he began to cry, shedding tears of absolute shame as he recalled the evening and his actions, the loathsome rapid servility of his hands to execute the vapid mirages of his mind. Hands swam before his eyes, grasping, touching, manipu-lating, cleverly overcoming obstacles so that the mind could gratify its absurd beliefs, half desires, and hallucinations, conspiring like vicious and unimaginative courtiers to burden further the patient and ox-like peasantry of the body . . .

Images, incidents hopped like fleas from the insanitary mass of memory: with face tilted upwards he felt chin-deep in disgust, horror and sickness. His thoughts were not original and only partly honest: even in this most sincere moment the stock figure of a mutilated boy arose from the diseased unconscious, the familiar sounds of bird and river formed the prosecuting bench of his anguish. With remembered phrases and fragments of landscape he tortured his shrinking responsible intelligence till his sensibility writhed like a boiling surface, exploding in gouts of remorse. Horror, horror. He hid his face in the darkness, feeling unworthy of warmth, of parent, sun, scenery, or friend: of his earlier self which in crude colours stood rose-lipped shadowing him like an illusion at noontide. He was foul. Foul. Foul.

The revulsion, the isolation, the reference to parents, the violation of what he calls elsewhere in the story the 'glades of self', the implied desecration of childhood – all these are themes Larkin would take up and develop in *Jill*. In both stories, they create the same half-waking, half-hallucinating state of mind. Unreal but appallingly vivid, they warn Larkin that the unconscious mind into which Layard had encouraged him to delve was capable of producing feelings and images which could violently disrupt the controlled surface of his life. Once he had written this story, Larkin seldom allowed himself such a free rein again, either in poems or prose. *Jill*, for instance, keeps the impact of the unconscious strictly monitored, and renders it respectable. Yet he knew that its narrative depended on a secret source: the novel's heterosexually inspired finale was based on an earlier, homosexually inspired story.

In one other fragment, written slightly later and preserved among his unpublished papers, Larkin returns to this theme, but investigates it with more detachment. This narrative, like the first, is spun round a group of Oxford undergraduates. Paying homage to Auden, they call themselves 'The Seven', and two of them – Edwin and Peter – decide that they are 'sexually unsatisfied and nervous' and attracted to a third, Philip. Their attraction isn't simply sexual, it's also something they work up in order to seem unconventional. Peter, at least, feels 'that there existed an awareness of an undescribable [part] of human life that he thought most important: a kind of regard for each other as humans and not as abstractions or purveyors of ideas. It was this awareness that was jokingly and half-ashamedly concealed under a common cloak of homosexuality cultivated ... as a badge of unconventionality against the rest of the college, who, they hoped, regarded [him] with shocked envy.'²⁴

The university's 'buggery business' (as one of 'The Seven' calls it) is sometimes genuinely homosexual, more often a product of pent-up heterosexual frustration, or of an ignorant fear of women which masquerades as dislike. Peter, for instance, says when he is talking about girls that he feels 'nothing but repelled disgust at their falsity and ordinariness ... He found it impossible to conceive of himself as having any kind of sexual relations with them. He was never sure whether this was his own fault or not.' At the beginning of the story, such thoughts are introduced as if they are likely to become its only theme; in the end, though, they are joined by two others. One is self-disgust (Peter, typically, describes himself as 'a mule with a perverse and all-consuming desire to be a racehorse'). The other is the social unease which reinforces their sense of physical isolation. Peter, again typically, regards 'the public school boyhood[s]' of his contemporaries as something 'from which he had always felt himself excluded'.

Both these stories, unsatisfactory in literary terms, have important things to say about Larkin's developing sexuality. Arising from the years 1941–2, they indicate that the sexual loneliness of his first year gave way during his second to a homosexual crush which was acknowledged but almost immediately repressed, then pored over with fascination and horror. Because Larkin eventually buried or denied most of the details, it's now difficult to reconstruct the episode accurately. One witness, however, does survive. Philip Brown, Larkin's contemporary in St John's, with whom he was to start sharing digs early in his second year, admits that 'Philip may have been in love with me'. Brown, a medical student, was an energetic yet fastidious young man, with an 'attractive but not conventionally pretty, crushed-up sort of face'.[25] 'I liked Philip,' he says now, 'but I certainly wasn't in love with him – I was very keen on a medical girl student, as it happens. But there were a few messy encounters between us, yes. Nothing much. Philip's sexuality was so obscured by his manner of approach and his general diffidence that frankly I would be surprised to hear that he ever had sex with anyone.'[26]

Once the feelings of guilt described in Larkin's first story had died down, they turned over the years into sympathetic curiosity. In his eventual roll-call of right-wing prejudices, he would make sure that blacks, women, children, trades unions, socialists and academics all got it in the neck, but homosexuality was almost never mentioned – or if it was mentioned, it was usually treated tolerantly. The best illustration of this occurs in a review of Jon Stallworthy's biography of Wilfred Owen (1974), where Larkin adds several biographical facts about Owen to Stallworthy's account (facts concerning Robert Graves and Robert Ross) in order to make sense of Owen's sudden development as a poet. In a letter written to

Stallworthy after the review appeared, he elaborated on what he had said in print:

I conceded I think that there is no direct evidence of practising homosexuality on Owen's part. Nevertheless, I am rather shaken by his association with (I take it) not only practising but proselytizing homosexuals: it seems to me that if he didn't like that kind of thing, he could easily have given them the brush off ... Don't forget two factors. Homosexuality in those days was at once much more of a crime than it is today (Oscar was still a memory), and at the same time much less known about. In other words, it might have been much more easy to do it, but one would have had to keep much quieter about it ... I see the relation between Owen's homosexuality and his war poems as rather resembling E. M. Forster's spell at that Indian court and *Passage to India*, or even Isherwood's time in Berlin and Sally Bowles. In other words, because one's homosexual self-realization cannot, legally, be admitted, it serves to glamorize the circumstances in which it took place. This is not to say that the resulting work of art is devalued; simply that its motivation (and who can ever be specific on such matters?) is more mixed than at first appears. The same thing, of course, could happen with heterosexual self-realization, except that self-realization is in this case less momentous, and there would be nothing against proclaiming it explicitly.[27]

'All women, without exception, *annoy* me,' Owen told his mother in 1914, indicating (among other things) that he didn't think of her as a woman. Larkin, in two undergraduate stories, was briefly led to a similar conclusion by a similar set of feelings. But when these feelings altered, and his attraction to women was rekindled, the same conclusion often returned to haunt him. It left him caught between rage and desire, cruelty and kindness, a longing for solitude and the sense that 'what will survive of us is love'. By the end of his first undergraduate year, all these paradoxical elements existed in his character – even if they were not yet in an ideally creative relationship to each other. His task, he knew, was to maintain them in a way which didn't leave him thinking it would be better to reject the world altogether. His poem 'A Writer', published in the *Cherwell* in May, made clear how badly things would turn out if he did:

> He knew, of course, no actions were rewarded,
> There were no prizes: though the eye could see
> Wide beauty in a motion or a pause,
> It need expect no lasting salary
> Beyond the bowels' momentary applause.

NINE

In June 1941, shortly before Larkin's first summer vacation started, Sydney found somewhere for the family to live outside Coventry – the house he'd been seeking since the previous autumn. Number 73 Coten End, in Warwick, was built on the same model of suburban comfort and respectability as Manor Road. It was a white-painted, early Victorian house on the main road south out of the town and had, Larkin told Sutton, 'two rooms [downstairs, besides the] kitchen and scullery, two bedrooms and two attics. Also a large cellar, a stable and a loft. It is long and tall. I sleep in one of the attics and write this in the other. Everywhere junk is piled. At my feet there are three Cassell's "Gems of Art" – Raeburn, Greuze and Rembrandt. Fuck 'em. The gospel of St John is at my elbow: the words I speak to you, they are spirit and they are life.'[1]

His family soon managed to re-create their old miseries in this new setting. 'I meet too many non-life blokes during my daily life,' Larkin complained within days of arriving. 'My father is non-life. Ditto my mother. Ditto my sister.'[2] He set about doing what he could to resist them, visiting the Shakespeare Memorial Theatre at Stratford most weekends (seeing, among other plays, *Julius Caesar*, *Twelfth Night* and *The Tempest*); reading Lawrence 'daily (like the Bible) with great devotion';[3] and visiting the cinema 'every day now, nearly',[4] to see whatever was showing: *Scarface*, *The Hurricane* and *Prison Without Bars*.[5] He also tried and failed to write a 'sodding play'[6] for his college dramatic society, and went with his parents for a fortnight's holiday near Swansea. Nothing provided more than a temporary relief. On 9 August, when he turned nineteen and became eligible for call-up, he complained of feeling trapped and helpless. In October, when he went back to St John's, he muttered desperately that he was 'in a pensive mood'.[7]

As he expected, the continuity of his life at the university had been broken. Familiar faces had disappeared, new ones had taken their place; local worries about work were jostled aside by larger fears about the course of the war, which he thought Germany was bound to win 'like a dose of salts'.[8] In November, when his call-up seemed imminent, he told Sutton:

I have been finding out that there is really no hope of my getting longer at this place than a couple of weeks. Perhaps you think I'm being a bit selfish but I just don't want to go into the Army. I want to pretend it isn't there: that there's no war on. When I do get into it, it will be a hell of a struggle of readjustment. I dare say I shall get over it in about 5 months. But they'll be a dose of hell. I wonder if Suicide is *very* easy? (Patient dragged away howling by airmen – in the Orator sense.)[9]

Sydney and Eva had indulged their son during the summer in Coten End. 'The Larkins,' a friend of the family admitted, 'believed they were better than anyone else.'[10] At Oxford, Larkin could not appeal so obviously to art over the head of ordinary life – except in his letters to Sutton. As the new term began he waged a sustained campaign of self-interest ('Fuck and bugger the war'[11]), insisting that he should be spared active service because he had his mind on higher things. If he'd been more candid, he might have added that his sense of being special had a good deal, paradoxically, to do with feeling inept and confused. As well as fearing Germany, he still retained some of his father's admiration for it: 'If there is any new life in the world today,' he wrote to Sutton, 'it is Germany. True, it's a vicious and blood-brutal affair – the new shoots are rather like bayonets. It won't suit me. By "new" life I don't mean better life, but a change, a new direction. Germany has revolted back too far, into the other extremes. But I think they have many valuable new habits.'[12]

Surrounded by so much uncertainty, Larkin struggled to renew the jaunty life he had evolved during his first year. He had mixed success. For one thing, he was no longer entitled to the room he had shared with Hughes, and took up short-term accommodation in a flat in the college President's lodgings. ('The rooms are quite comfortable,' he said, 'but directly over the President's study, so I can't play my records.'[13]) For another, the happy-go-lucky tutorials with Bone came to an end: Bone's cancer was now so far advanced that he had left the college and gone to a sanatorium (in Cheshire). Larkin was dispatched to Corpus Christi College, to be taught by 'a man called Brett [H. F. B.] Smith'.[14] His tutorial partner was Roger Sharrock (later Professor of English at Nottingham) – an older and more serious-minded companion than Iles, but not likely to make Larkin change his (non) academic ways. Brett Smith was 'nearly eighty' when he met Larkin, and 'prefer[red] talking generally to tutoring, and . . . discoursed largely on actresses, radio, the weather, etc.'[15]

Larkin kept boredom at bay by drawing his friends into a tighter circle. They called themselves 'The Seven' – a name which, as we have seen, also appears in one of Larkin's undergraduate stories. They included Larkin himself, Amis, Jimmy Willcox, Philip Brown, Nick Russel, Norman Iles and David Williams. The idea of The Seven 'arose', he said later, 'from an idea that we should form some definite group with definite ideas, set against the college authorities and all the intellectuals and scholars we disliked. As a matter of fact, after one meeting the ideas and ideals degenerated into one big supper party per week supplied by two people.'[16] Amis confirms this. 'The principal activity,' he remembers, 'was buying bottles of beer from the buttery and taking them up to someone's rooms after Hall.'[17] Although always careful to seem disorganized, The Seven did hold certain views in common. They took literature seriously (sometimes to the extent of passing round a poem one of them had written and talking about it), but wanted to make it seem part of an ordinarily hard-drinking, hard-swearing life. They had no respect for dons but no wish to challenge them openly. They wished to distance themselves from their parents' generation, but not to abandon traditional forms and beliefs. In these ways, at least, they anticipated the principles which were more coherently described by The Movement in the 1950s.

The Movement overthrew several sets of literary opinion; The Seven didn't do much more than annoy the authorities. 'We would stay in college and drink, you know,' Larkin said later, 'and play records and no doubt we got progressively noisier and noisier and then would come messages. "The Dean says less noise, sir" – and so forth. There were two confrontations that didn't do my reputation any good or anybody else's for that matter.'[18] The most serious of these involved a visit to Oxford by Colin Gunner, and required Larkin to see the Proctors in the early morning of 21 October in the Old Clarendon Building in Broad Street. Although it didn't actually involve other members of The Seven, it well illustrates the condition to which their meetings aspired. 'Fuckin' 'ell,' he wrote to Sutton immediately before seeing the Proctors. 'What a weekend. Colin [Gunner] and Josh [Noel Hughes] just didn't get on with my [other] friends and the whole affair was God's own fuck up. Added to which we went bingeing on a blind on Saturday night and when we were just embarking on stage one of blindness (riotous behaviour) the Proctors appeared and ... I got progged – the rest got away. Sodomy! This is what is technically known as the theory of buggering shite.'[19]

This kind of fooling around comes into Amis's category of 'sheer childishness', as did 'squirting the bursar'[20] during a fire practice, wandering through college draped in a sheet and pretending to be a ghost, or up-ending Amis's sofa and sticking gloves on its feet. Yet as Larkin drew nearer to the supposed date of his call-up, his japes started to seem more reckless – even slightly frenetic. 'I have a strong presentiment I shall get killed in this war,' he told Sutton; ' – not that I am resigned to it, far from it.'[21] Sometimes he tried to persuade himself that active service would be of some use to his writing by toughening him up and giving him a subject. More often he simply continued to dread it. 'We have all the hell of a way to go,' he told Sutton in November, 'both as artists and as human beings. And I sometimes don't think the army will help, except in the purely negative way of steering you clear of the war complex. Fuck and bugger the war: I realize it has really always been the thing most dreaded by me, so in a way it has always been implicit in me. Cunt all.'[22]

On 16 December, six weeks after writing this letter, Larkin was summoned for his army medical examination. He made no secret of his hopes that he would fail. The previous September, when the law had demanded that he register for service, he 'had made a special journey to St John's to do it in Oxford, because it was rumoured that they were far more lenient and understanding there to students . . . Nobody could have been expected to understand that without being a conscientious objector I did not want to join the army on moral grounds . . . I was fundamentally – like the rest of my friends – uninterested in the war.'[23] Now, as he left the medical exam, he gathered from a doctor that he wouldn't hear the results until March. Three months of anxiety lay ahead. What, he wanted to know, were his chances of failure? 'The occulist says people with more than seven diopters of myopia are graded four [i.e. failed],'[24] he told his parents. If his eyes were bad enough he would be safe.

Back in college Larkin started to worry that the examination had been too easy. He felt that he was bound to pass, and that his undergraduate life had been a waste of time. To prove the point, he sold all the books he had bought for his course work, and burnt the notes he had taken in lectures. His attendance at Brett Smith's tutorials became perfunctory, and his Early English sessions in St Peter's Hall with '[the Rev.] Houghton, a tutor I disliked from the start',[25] only showed him how little he cared for Chaucer. Langland, interestingly in view of the fact that the image of a 'field full of folk' would eventually haunt his poem 'Show Saturday', 'was much better, and I was so enthusiastic that I think [Houghton] suspected me of being a Christian'.[26]

This wish to dismantle his life was confined to areas governed by the university. Elsewhere things continued as before. Although there was no

Cherwell this term (it had closed with debts of £40), the Labour Club *Bulletin* was flourishing, and so was the English Club. In the second week of November Larkin went to hear one of the most distinguished speakers they had drawn since he became a member: Dylan Thomas. 'Hell of a fine man,' Larkin reported afterwards:

little, snubby, hopelessly pissed bloke who made hundreds of cracks and read parodies of everybody in appropriate voices. He remarked: 'I'd like to have talked about a book of poems I've been given to review, a young poet called Rupert Brooke – it's surprising how he has been influenced by Stephen Spender . . . ' There was a moment of delighted surprise, then a roar of laughter. Then he read a parody of Spender entitled 'The Parachutist' which had people rolling on the floor. He kept up this all night – parodies of everyone bar Lawrence – and finally read two of his own poems, which seem very good.[27]

The visit was a mixed blessing. On the one hand it led Larkin to 'soak'[28] in Thomas's work, and under its influence he 'quite changed [his] style of writing'.[29] Within a week he had produced the derivative sonnet 'Observation' (Amis published it in the *Bulletin* along with 'Disintegration', which the executive committee found 'morbid and unhealthy'), and for the next several years Thomas's cadences and images swirled amongst those of his other idols. On the other, the change of direction did nothing to endear Larkin to Rilke-reading, symbol-loving poets like Heath-Stubbs. Nor did it make him feel any happier about the pace of his writing. He complained repeatedly that it had slowed to a trickle since he had arrived in Oxford. The imminent publication of *Eight Oxford Poets*, in which nothing by him was included, and the news that his contemporary Alan Ross was about to publish his first collection, *Summer Thunder*, made matters worse still. 'I'm getting left,'[30] he wrote unhappily to his father shortly before the end of term.

This sense of failure grew as the vacation started. Everyone around him seemed busy (preparing for war) or productive (like, apparently, Dylan Thomas). All he did was become 'excessively convivial'.[31] He wondered to Sutton whether he should cultivate a more solitary life. Perhaps this would allow the stirrings of his unconscious to affect his writing? It was a line of thought which led him in the opposite direction to the one he would eventually take, but in his attic in Coten End he pursued it intently (showing, in the process, that he had been reading Robert Graves):

I'm against this poetry as craft business . . . Poetry (at any rate in my case) is like trying to remember a tune you've forgotten. All corrections are attempts to get

nearer the forgotten tune. A poem is written because the poet gets a sudden vision –
lasting one second or less – and he attempts to express the whole of which the
vision is a part. Or he attempts to express the vision. Blake was lucky: 'I dare not
pretend to be other than the secretary: the authors are in eternity.' And: 'I have
written this poem from immediate dictation ... even against my will.' He was
constantly in contact with the vision. Shelley in his *Defence of Poetry* points out
that even the greatest poetry is only one-tenth or less as good as what the poet
originally conceived, or felt. Lawrence had his 'daemon' which spoke through him.
So when I write:

> 'At the flicker of a letter
> Brought from smashed city under leaden sky
> In late November, at the year's sombre ending
> I at a tall window standing
> Watch the tumultuous clouds go by
> Go by field and street, college and river',

I am not trying to imitate Auden, I am juggling with sounds and associations which
will best express the original vision. It is done quite intuitively and esoterically.
That is why a poet never thinks of his reader. Why should he? The reader doesn't
come into the poem at all.[32]

Three days after writing this excited letter – which contrasts sharply
with his later statement that if poets don't keep the reader constantly in
mind they are bound to fail – Larkin had once again been overwhelmed by
the tedium of life at home. 'Warwick is very dull,' he told Sutton, 'and I
have nothing to do or say ... I sit moodily in The Crown [his local pub]
reading a good deal of the time now. Coils of shit.'[33] The following
morning, New Year's Day, everything changed again. A letter came by
special delivery, telling him that he had failed his army medical. His eyes
had been graded four; he would not be called up.

TEN

Larkin's immediate reaction to the news of his exemption was not
euphoria but 'panic'. He said later, 'I had to rush back to Oxford, re-write
all my notes, re-buy all my books and then [prepare to] do Schools [his

final exams] in another five terms ... I just think that there can't have been a great manpower shortage ... [as] I was perfectly capable of sweeping a NAAFI floor or something like that. It all seemed very odd to me.'[1]

This makes Larkin sound like a reformed character in the last half of his time at university, especially since he discovered when he arrived to begin the new term that Brett Smith had given him a distinction in the exams he had taken the previous December. In fact Larkin was reluctant to pick up the work he had recently cast aside. His new tutor was partly to blame. Rather than continuing with Brett Smith, Larkin and Sharrock were moved back into St John's to be taught by Bone's replacement, A. M. D. Hughes, who had taught at Oxford in the past. Dragged out of retirement by the war, Hughes had a 'beautiful, mellifluous, late Victorian voice' and was, according to Sharrock, 'immensely ancient and half blind'.[2] (He had been born in 1873 and was to die aged one hundred.) Larkin immediately began to take advantage of him. Since Hughes was in the habit of telling the time in tutorials by feeling the hands of a clock he kept on the mantelpiece, Larkin would silently move them forward before sitting down to begin his report on the week's work, making sure that he would not have to stay the full hour.

Hughes's modesty and enthusiasm gradually won him round. After a few weeks Larkin was telling his parents, 'I am getting to like my tutor, in as much as it is in my nature to like any tutor ... His appreciative powers make up for what he lacks intellectually – which is a pleasant change from the rest, who just don't make up for what they lack intellectually.'[3] In the university at large, he also began to stir himself. He was elected to the committee of the English Club, and in February joined the Labour Club – less for political reasons than for the chance to see more of an 'amazing' Czech woman, Chitra Rudingerova, whom he described as 'the crankiest communist I have ever met'.[4]

Elsewhere, too, his life changed and opened up. Bored with cowering in the attic above the President's study, he moved out into digs in 125 Walton Street – a small, attractive house above a tailor's and near to the Clarendon Press – which he arranged to share with Philip Brown. Because Brown was reading medicine, he was allowed to complete the full four years of his degree course: Larkin knew that he could expect a more settled life with him than with any of his other friends, all of whom were about to be called up. He also thought his barely suppressed attraction to Brown would have its advantages, at least insofar as it consoled him for his difficulties with girls and his frustrations with writing. 'I think that was it, really,' says Brown. 'We knew each other well enough to feel relaxed together, but we sort of stimulated each other too. We made each other laugh. And we both liked jazz. And drinking. This crush he might have had on me – there wasn't any serious action. Besides, I was extremely interested in girls. And so was he. He was sexual, you see, but undirected.'[5]

To start with Larkin found his new freedom an anti-climax. He soon changed his mind. Mrs Bunhill, the landlady, allowed him to behave as selfishly as he wished. 'Philip Brown and I shared a large first floor room with a piano and a wireless free,' he wrote later. 'The fires were large and I enjoyed them.'[6] To Sutton he added that the sitting room 'has three large windows. Inside it is large and filled with junk from India and China and volumes of Dickens etc.'[7] It was a place where he could concentrate on his work, and also continue his former rowdy existence. Before long he organized another 'college drunk', though when this took place it quickly got out of hand, and he was once again summoned to see the Dean. He was fined, and told he was 'not the kind of person they wanted at the college'.[8]

Now that he wasn't going into the army, Larkin could no longer claim such pranks were part of his nervousness about becoming a soldier. Yet he still felt anxious. When term was over and he had returned to Coten End he told Sutton that his worries about the war had merely given way to worries about his future as a writer:

I am extremely miserable about my writing. As you know, I am continually examining myself for signs of literary ability. This in itself is a bad thing. And there is a point of view that is always present in my mind and to which in moments of extreme gloom like this I tend to adhere. This is (1) I want to be 'a writer'. (2) The kind of writing (scribbled scratchy nonsense) I have perpetrated up till now has been entirely derivative and imitative. (3) There has been in it no 'unknown quality' such as abounds in Lawrence and all writers worth admiring. (4) It is merely a symptom of youthful onanistic egoism, of which there are far too many examples.[9]

Later in this same letter to Sutton, Larkin cites Isherwood and Auden as writers whose early work puts his own to shame, and tries unsuccessfully to cheer himself up by saying that his poems do not matter since it is prose that he really wants to write anyway. Yet as the vacation limped by, it was his lack of originality as a poet which most troubled him:

I continue shitting about Warwick, reading Eng. Lit., writing crappy poems (one per day – 'passing on to his first great creative period') and swigging beer. I find two pints a night induces a pleasant state of religious exaltation, and trundle home bawling snatches of songs, scraps of poems etc., etc. . . . The poems are either little pastoral pieces or colossal well-fused abortions made by Auden's language in Dylan T.'s construction. What a poet has to do is create a new language for himself. And more – it has to be a good one. Pound, for instance, I shit. Likewise Joyce, if you can call him a poet. But Auden, but Dylan Thomas . . . And also each poem has to be on the grand scale. Days of 'To a Skylark' are gone. Sometimes I think Auden's *Poems* is his best. The enormous monumental quality of every one. And the charade *Paid On Both Sides* – the choruses. It is in work like this that the importance of an integrated style is seen, like Teschmaker's clarinet or Pee Wee Russell.

I must get on with some fark, eh? 'And he yaf hym a sodynge gode kyk in the balles, causing hym grete dole and lamentacions, at which I hadde grate merry-ment.'[10]

No trace remains of these 'crappy poems'; whatever Larkin wrote during the spring vacation he destroyed. As soon as he returned to Oxford, though, his confidence crept back. When he heard that Ian Davie was collecting material for a Blackwell's edition of *Oxford Poetry (1942– 1943)* he decided to submit some work. (Three of his poems were eventually selected.) When he gathered that Charles Hamblett was scouting for material for an anthology The Fortune Press intended to publish called *Poetry from Oxford in Wartime*, he got in touch at once. He couldn't hide his excitement as he reported on the outcome to his parents. 'Charles Hamblett returned the story but kept the five poems,' he said, 'sending a very fulsome letter. He says they will be published . . . I don't really trust him but I suppose one is grist, etc., at this stage in the proceedings.'[11] As things turned out, and they turned out very slowly, Larkin was right not to trust The Fortune Press. Although it did more than any other small publisher to promote poetry during the difficult years of the war, many people who had any dealings with it ended up feeling unhappy. Specifically, they complained about its proprietor, R. A. (Reginald Ashley) Caton.

Long before Caton became notorious as the incompetent publisher who appears in several of Amis's novels (re-initialled 'L.S.', standing for 'Lazy Sod', and eventually killed off in *The Anti-Death League*), he was a by-word for deviousness. Alun Lewis, for instance, was already 'engaged in a furious controversy'[12] by the spring of 1941, accusing Caton of – among other things – publishing poems without bothering to read them first. This incompetence, Caton's bibliographer says, was fundamental. His 'love of travel and dislike of the telephone . . . campaigned against the very rudiments of publishing efficiency, and much of his time was taken up by the administration of numerous properties in Brighton [where he had been brought up]. He died owning ninety-one houses there, "not a bathroom among them", he used to boast.'[13]

Caton had started publishing in 1924, when he was twenty-seven, from 12 Buckingham Palace Road in London – first with a company called Fortune and Merriman (which produced only three books, one of which was Cecil Day-Lewis's *Beechen Vigil*), then with The Fortune Press. From the outset, it had been difficult to see why he bothered with poems. They made him very little money, and they also took him away from his main interest, which was pornography. A checklist of the 600-odd titles he published in the 1930s, 1940s, 1950s and (less frequently) 1960s includes such items as Oswell Blakeston's *Boys in their Ruin*, Richard Brown's *A Brute of a Boy*, Terence Greenidge's *The Magnificent: a story without a moral*, Reginald Underwood's *Bachelor's Hall*, a non-fiction title dealing with the corporal punishments meted out to women in south German prisons, and *Chastisement across the Ages*. Perhaps Caton thought poetry would throw a mantle of respectability over such things? If he did, it was largely because poets had very little chance of being published elsewhere during the war. Among those who took refuge with him for their earliest books were Larkin, Amis and Roy Fuller. And among important anthologies which appeared under his imprint were many Oxford and Cambridge collections, and the first gathering of work by 'The New Apocalypse' poets in 1939. Julian Symons, whose volume *Confusions about X* the Press brought out in 1938, later reminisced about Caton's business and appearance:

[He] . . . sat in the cellar [in Buckingham Palace Road] surrounded by stacks of his books, a tall, dirtyish, slyly smiling man with a habit of pushing his face very close to yours when making a point. Sometimes he was unshaved, often he wore no collar, and since his shirts were the old-fashioned kind fastened by studs, his collarless appearance left him looking both incomplete and slightly debauched. When met in the street he would be wearing a stiff collar, not always clean, and a shabby raincoat.[14]

It was some time before Caton met Larkin. Sheltering behind Hamblett, he remained remote but intriguing – and Larkin was content simply to know that his poems had been accepted. All other considerations, such as payment, were set aside. This was hardly surprising, since the Press's finances were chaotic. Nicholas Moore, a contributor to the first 'Apocalypse' anthology, remembered that Caton 'seemed to me at that time rather a sinister man, but I think this was probably because nobody liked him. He had a rather irritable fussy manner, mainly about money; he would have liked some from you: he didn't want to pay you any.'[15] This was putting it kindly. As Symons discovered, payment was generally non-existent, and authors were expected to buy many copies of their own books to cover the cost of producing them. 'I thought you were a man of substance,'[16] Caton told him when Symons objected. Eventually Larkin would have much the same dispiriting experience.

In the meantime, Larkin had other reasons for feeling low. As the summer term ended, his newly formed circle of friends was broken again when Amis was commissioned into the Signals. Although Amis was briefly in Oxford the following year (1943) – when Larkin told Sutton he looked 'completely false, like an advert in Austin Reed's'[17] – their friendship had to wait three years before it could be resumed. Until then Amis remained in Larkin's memory as 'a person of unbounded wit and charm',[18] someone whose combination of toughness and sensitivity he searched for in vain among his other university friends.

The vacation brought predictably little comfort, even though he and Philip Brown managed to get away for a 'very fine' fortnight in Bovra House Cottage, Port Eynon, a cottage owned by Brown's parents on the Gower Peninsula in Wales. Larkin's pleasure in the 'amazing' setting, and in 'painting all day – not impressionist but caricature,'[19] was mixed with various kinds of frustration. One was the weather, which he said in a surviving scrap of diary 'consists of a high wind and driving rain and clouds'.[20] Another, judging by the poem 'I dreamed of an out-thrust arm of land', which he later wrote about the holiday, was sexual:

> I was sleeping, and you woke me
> To walk on the chilled shore
> Of a night with no memory,
> Till your voice forsook my ear
> Till your two hands withdrew
> And I was empty of tears,
> On the edge of a bricked and streeted sea
> And a cold hill of stars.

Larkin made no mention of his feelings for Brown in letters to other friends. Turning to Sutton, for instance, he made out that his disappointments were still largely to do with writing. 'I have started . . . a novel again,' he said, 'a kind of *Lions and Sh*. . . It is better than anything I have yet done, broadly speaking, but it is nevertheless enormously insignificant. I am at present stringing incidents of my early childhood together to form the first section. But I feel my power growing. Christ . . . a few shoots should be on the move! I've also changed my poetic style, writing pompous, windy effusions of the war in the style of Stephen Spender.'[21]

Conflicting feelings continued to nag at him when he returned to Coten End in time for his twentieth birthday. Partly to resolve them, partly because he needed to earn some money to pay for his holiday, and partly to escape the 'continual strain of family life' which left him feeling 'sucked dry',[22] he cast around sourly for a distraction. He was reluctant to put himself out, but knew the Ministry of Labour had encouraged university students to do at least one month's National Service during their long vacation. When his father told him about a vacancy in the Fuel Office in City Hall, he applied.

It was his first job of any description, and he responded to it with fascinated revulsion:

The office is large, cold and melancholy. At one desk sit I. At another sits Mrs Glencross. At a third sits Derek. Derek is the office boy: he answers the phones. Mrs Glencross is a tall girl with transparent spectacles. She has the complaining Midland accent and is stupid. Our job is to reduce a Fucking Great Pile of Fuel Rationing forms into a Fucking Great Pile of Fuel Rationing forms arranged in (1) alphabetical order of streets, (2) those streets in numerical order . . . Now we are going through the forms, street by street, checking each house with the coal merchants' register, and noting any variations that occur in the merchant given on the form and the merchant who claims the house. These variations we write down on long sheets of toilet paper, which we eventually burn under the Borough Treasurer's chair. It passes the time. Mrs Glencross's hubby is in Stalag 21D, which seems to interest her. The only thing is I don't have much time to read or write.[23]

When Larkin's month in the Fuel Office was up, he went back to his old ways, 'drugging' himself 'with cigarettes, cinema and beer'[24] until term started again. His worries about his writing immediately returned. The thought that he would be 'pushed out into the world, a complete man, in *exactly one year's time*' filled him with 'terror',[25] driving him relentlessly in on himself. Reading the letters he wrote at the time, it is impossible not to be impressed by the ferocity of his misery. It is also hard not to suspect that it contains a degree of complacency. Throughout the long dull summer, with a world of diminished friendships and increased work awaiting him in his last year at Oxford, he deplored his plight but also found it comforting. Concentrating on his frustration was a way of shrinking from action. 'I'm really very sick of my own life these days,' he says in one typical outburst to Sutton. 'I feel I have got out of touch with the main way of life at present; in fact I was born out of it, and I don't feel capable of becoming an artist. I am filled with waves of self-disgust and doubt, washing and corroding my inner self away. Having read Lawrence I know what shit is, and won't write it; on the other hand, I can't write anything else. Hence the state of deadlock.'[26]

Back in St John's – he arrived a week early to act as a college firewatcher – he had less time for introspection. But his mood refused to lift, even as he installed himself again with Philip Brown in 125 Walton Street, and began looking for friends to replace those, like Amis, whom he had lost. In the unfamiliar emptiness, convinced that his feelings for Brown were leading nowhere, he began to regret even more keenly than before that women were so remote from him. At home in the vacations he simply never encountered them – his sister's contemporaries, being older than him, continued to ignore him if they were ever invited home. Sometimes, trudging round the university, he tried imagining what it would be like to escape his family altogether. Would it allow him to lead a more adventurous, fulfilled existence? However he answered the question, he knew that he needed his parents as much as he resented them – and this only increased his distress. 'There is nothing but misery to come from my home,' he told Sutton: ' – death of my father and mother etc. when it happens – and I am too weak-kneed to make any way in life. Then in the end my own death like a running wave tracks me down.'[27]

As the winter term wore on, the few girls he knew continued to thwart or embarrass him. Chitra, the Czech member of the Labour Club that he had found 'decidedly attractive', put him off by seeming 'a full-time [Communist] Party girl. She was known to interrupt kisses to say "Remember the Party comes first". In a drunken fit of bravado I asked her to tea and she came. We ate toast and marmalade, and she told me I was decadent. Nothing else happened.'[28] It was the same elsewhere; all the approaches he made to women in his last three terms were as unsuccessful as those he had made in his first six: they were 'continually depressing'[29] encounters.

The only exception was Diana Gollancz, a student at the Slade, which was still based at the Ashmolean. A year older than Larkin, and the second of the publisher Victor Gollancz's five daughters, she was 'beautiful, bright, outgoing and socially good',[30] and relaxed enough with men to let Larkin forget his shyness. Her stories of school life amused him – she had been at Dartington Hall, then at a small private school outside Gerrards Cross in Buckinghamshire – as did her 'complete lack of social conscience'.[31] She was quick but 'not academically bright',[32] committed to her work but not pretentious, flirtatious but not threatening. In effect, she appealed to him because he could treat her as an honorary man. Yet even with her, as with all the other women he knew, 'nothing happened'.

Larkin didn't merely feel he was missing out on fun. Ever since reading Lawrence, and more particularly since tangling with Layard, he had persuaded himself that 'the vision' of writing had 'got something to do with sex. I don't know what,' he admitted, 'and I don't particularly want to know. It's not surprising because obviously two creative voices would be in alliance. But the vision has a sexual quality lacking in other emotions such as pity . . . Ovid, for instance, could never write unless he was in love. Many other poets have been and are the same. I should think poetry and sex are very closely connected.'[33] According to this theory, it was also 'not surprising' that having no girls in his life should mean having no poems – and no joy and no fluency in his other work, either. The thought of his final exams made him snarl at his course work as viciously as he did at his own writing. 'We bow to each poet,' he complained, 'and learn two attitudes towards them – the wrong attitude and the right one . . . Any definite personal feeling disturbs the pattern and is therefore not to be encouraged.'[34]

Sterility at home, sterility in his social life, sterility in his work: since the world around him was so obviously disappointing, Larkin continued his long descent into self-analysis. Once again, he was encouraged by Layard, who attended the St John's Essay Society in October and gave a talk on dream symbolism entitled 'The Night Journey over the Sea'. The minutes of the meeting report that 'nearly everyone present' took part in the discussion which followed, continuing 'until a late hour, possibly the latest hour in the history of the Society'.[35] The effect this talk had on Larkin was confirmed a few days later, when he and Brown had Carl Lehmann (a friend of Brown's) to stay with them in Walton Street. 'Carl was a Jungian,' Larkin wrote later, 'and as Layard had [just] addressed the college Essay Society he fell, so to speak, on fruitful soil. [Within a short time of his arrival] we began recording our dreams . . . [and] Carl gave us indications as to how to interpret them and we began searching for problems. I don't believe [Brown] had one. I had.'[36]

Larkin left no description of what exactly he reckoned this 'problem' was, but in the ninety-five dreams he recorded over the following months (typing them up on sheets of loose paper and keeping them with his diaries) the largest concentration of images reveals a combined attraction to and revulsion from women – and from other men. A dream on 26 October, for instance, soon after the recording process began, has him entering a lavatory near the Covered Market in central Oxford: 'I started to piss, and simultaneously a man on my left started to piss across my legitimate section and with a long malformed penis. This annoyed me. After a time a woman came up on my right and also started pissing, also with a penis, but normally shaped. This surprised me.'[37] Or dream number fourteen: 'I was trying to toss off a boy with a penis like a Turkish cigarette. I had dreamt about him before that night and thought he was a Russian.'[38] Or a dream shortly before term ended: 'I seemed in the custody of four girls ... It seemed that I was going to bed with [one of them, a girl he knew slightly at Oxford]. We two went back to the first room and she lay on the floor. She was wearing a flame coloured skirt and brilliant yellow knickers. I began fucking her and she talked dreamily about copulation. After a while I stopped fucking, not feeling I was getting anywhere, and we both stood up. She maintained her dreamy indifference.'[39]

Larkin gave up writing these accounts the following January (1943), by which time he had created a detailed portrait of sexual frustration. Dreams in which he is in bed with men (friends in St John's, a 'negro') outnumber dreams in which he is trying to seduce a woman, but the world in which these encounters occur is uniformly drab and disagreeable. Nazis, black dogs, excrement and underground rooms appear time and time again, and so do the figures of parents, aloof but omnipresent. Larkin may – as he told Sutton – 'have never read a book of psychology in my life', but faced with such clear evidence about his interior state it hardly mattered. 'I can read the history of my soul in my dreams,' he said, striving to make light of his findings, 'and whoever says I can't is a fucking liar and I will see him outside, look you.'[40]

The tussle between attraction to and scorn of other people intensified throughout Larkin's life. At this early stage he couldn't gain enough distance between himself and his 'problems' to examine them clearly. He couldn't decide what form or sort of language to dress them in. Should it be prose or poetry? Should it be elaborately symbolic or rigorously austere? As term ended he thought drama might be the best thing to try – a Shavian dialogue. The result was 'The Unfinished Marriage: A Dramatic

Situation', in which Dick and Sally are marooned on their honeymoon in a remote house after a motoring accident. (The dialogue is unpublished but preserved among Larkin's papers.) In their isolation, the couple experience a rapid time acceleration, during which they glimpse the practical demands of their married life to come. We watch Dick trying to get money off his father, applying to his old school for a teaching job, and eventually (with Sally pregnant) settling in an office. Dick's death swiftly follows.

Evidently the low-spirited cogitations of Larkin's winter term had left him convinced of one thing: beyond women lay marriage, and while this might begin with excitement it inevitably ended with dullness and a sense of being trapped. His parents proved the point. 'I contain both [my mother and father],' he wrote to Sutton, 'and that . . . is the cause of my inertia, for in me they are incessantly opposed. It intrigues me to know that a thirty-year stuggle is being continued in me and in my sister too. In her it has reached a sort of conclusion – my father is winning. Pray the lord my mother is superior in me.'[41]

ELEVEN

With only two terms of his undergraduate course left, Larkin still had no idea where life was leading him. He thought his ambitions as a writer ludicrously outstripped his abilities; his degree work was always a prey to depression or proud laziness; his friends were scattered. Two terms before, his self-doubt had been licensed by the knowledge that he might at any moment be called up. Since his exemption, he had been forced to admit that much of his indecisiveness was his own creation. He was confused about sex, confused about his worth, confused about what sort of personality he had, confused about the war. The more he tried to clear his mind, the more baffled and powerless he felt. 'All this problem weighs very heavily on me,' he said to Sutton on the second day of the new year; 'I feel absolutely without hope.'[1]

When Larkin told Sutton that he prayed the lord his mother would be superior in him, he knew there was a danger that her ascendancy would deepen his inertia: he understood that she had dealt with Sydney's increasing impatience by becoming more and more acquiescent. In later life he would often make out that passivity was valuable, since it allowed him to solve problems by the simple expedient of evading them. Now he roused himself. 'Something crops up and life goes on,'[2] he ended his 'hopeless' letter to Sutton, then packed his bags for Oxford again. As far as Larkin was concerned, the main business of the new term was to organize himself for his Finals six months away in July, and to worry about what would happen after that. 'I wonder what sort of job I could get,' he wrote to his parents. 'I contemplate them all dismally – teaching? No! Civil Service? – requires a good degree, and anyway . . . What else? Well there's probably a million jobs handy if I knew how to find them. The only thing is, I must do something fairly important, or I'm told I might get thrown into a factory and [have] a spanner put in my hand.'[3]

Within a matter of weeks he was preoccupied by his other, more personal life. Late in February the poet Vernon Watkins visited the English Club to talk about the poetry of W. B. Yeats. Before the meeting, Larkin had no detailed knowledge of Watkins's work – what he had read, including the newly published *Ballad of the Mari Lwyd*, seemed to him too full of symbols, too arty, too removed from the recognizably modern world described by Auden. During the talk, though, he was powerfully impressed by Watkins. Slighter and shorter than Larkin, with a thin nervous face and greying hair swept straight back from his forehead, he gave a 'sonorous reading', which lasted 'past coffee time, past discussion time',[4] then distributed among the audience the volumes of Yeats's poems that he had brought with him before disappearing 'exalted, into the blackout'.[5]

Larkin immediately set about arranging to see Watkins again. 'In the following weeks,' he said later, 'I made it my business to collect up [Watkins's editions of Yeats's poems] . . . – many of them were Cuala Press limited editions, and later Yeats was scarce at that time – and take them to him.'[6] He also began to discover a little more about his new hero. Watkins was 'nearly forty . . . stationed near Bletchley [to the north of Oxford] . . . and [a Flight Sergeant] in the RAF. He is also an intimate friend of Dylan Thomas . . . He's Welsh.'[7] Even if Larkin had been able to devote more time to researching the facts of Watkins's life, he wouldn't have been able to add much more: Watkins was (as yet) unmarried, he lived quietly, and in peace-time he worked as a clerk in Lloyds Bank in Swansea.

This uneventfulness impressed Larkin. It suggested a life from which all distractions had been removed, so that it could be devoted to literature. Appropriately, the word 'devotion' is conspicuous in all Larkin's memories of Watkins. 'In Vernon's presence,' he said in an obituary he wrote when Watkins died in 1967, 'poetry seemed like a living stream, in which one had only to dip the vessel of one's devotion.'[8] And again: Watkins's 'devotion to poetry' was 'quite unaffected by ambition: he had waited until what then seemed to me the farthest brink of middle age before publishing his first book . . . [He was] a genuinely modest, genuinely dedicated person, who had chosen, in Yeats's phraseology, perfection of the work rather than of the life. To anyone who, like myself, was on the edge of the world of employment his example was significant. Indeed, it was almost encouraging.'[9]

'Almost.' In later life Larkin was careful to measure the distance between Watkins's bardic, poetic manner and his own plain-speaking one – but in the weeks following their first meeting he was giddy with admiration. He devoured Yeats's poems as well as Watkins's own, announcing to Amis that 'a more charming man [than Watkins] I have never met',[10] and visiting him in Bradwell where 'he was staying with some people called Blackburn who kept a goat'.[11] At this second meeting he was again impressed by Watkins's mixture of commitment to his craft and personal modesty. 'He was sitting in a back room playing drafts with an Insurance Agent,' he told his parents. 'After he had finished his game we went out on a long walk in the sun over very nice country, and came back to tea which included a fresh egg.'[12] The quality of Watkins's conversation on this and other visits remained vividly in Larkin's mind. 'He was absolutely certain that poetry was the most marvellous – well, not the most marvellous – the *only* marvellous thing in life,' Larkin said, 'and it was a logical development of everything one did or thought, or wanted to do, or held valuable, or anything else. There was an enormous dignity and confidence about him. It was hard and bright and certain, like a crystal.'[13]

Watkins's influence is described succinctly in the Introduction to the reissue of Larkin's first collection *The North Ship* (1966). As a result of encountering Watkins, Larkin says, 'I spent the next three years trying to write like Yeats, not because I liked his personality or understood his ideas but out of infatuation with his music (to use the word I think Vernon used).'[14] This is confirmed by the poems Larkin chose to submit for the Blackwell's anthology *Oxford Poetry 1942–1943*, which was published in June: 'A Stone Church Damaged by a Bomb', 'Mythological Introduction', and 'I dreamed of an out-thrust arm of land'. These all suggested that Watkins's first effect on Larkin had been to help create a flood of derivative work which drowned the influence of Auden beneath the influence of

Yeats – and this was certainly the version of events that Larkin liked to promote. In virtually all his reminiscences of this time he says that as soon as he met Watkins he was instantly and deeply in thrall to Yeats's 'particularly potent music, pervasive as garlic'.[15]

In fact things were a little more hesitant, and a little more complicated. Larkin's rate of production did not increase dramatically the moment he met Watkins, and the influence of Yeats, though eventually strong, took a while to permeate through his writing. Why did Larkin make this small dissimulation? Forgetfulness? Out of respect for Watkins? Because he enjoyed casting himself in the role of bewitched protégé? All these things are true in part – and judging by Larkin's later accounts it is as well that he did keep his initial reaction to Yeats to himself: his friendship with Watkins might not have survived it. Although happy to concede that Watkins's 'likes became my likes',[16] he also confessed that he 'could never quite expel from [his] mind a certain dubiety'.[17] In an appreciation of the friendship that he wrote for his own interest at the end of the spring term he was even more emphatic. 'I felt no affinity with Yeats,' he said, and reckoned that his three Blackwell's anthology poems were such disastrous failures that they marked the end, not the new beginning, of his career as a poet. 'This spring term,' his essay concludes, 'saw the end of my poetry. I am not, on the whole, sorry to see it go. My prediction in the Preface of *Chosen Poems* [the booklet he had made in 1941] had been correct: "boyish gift" has ossified, and ended up in frantic, neurotic, strained, tense imitations of Yeats. There is no freedom in Yeats's poems.'[18]

It's obvious from what Larkin says here that it in fact took several months for his 'liking'[19] of Yeats to turn into a raging 'Celtic fever'.[20] Before it did so, he entered one of the most extraordinary periods of his writing life. At KHS Larkin had regarded writing as an alternative to school work, and had broken it into two distinct parts: one socially rewarded; the other private. Now he devised a similarly protective structure. 'Work' (preparing for his Finals) was once again set in opposition to 'writing', and 'writing' was divided into two kinds. One was the acknowledged variety (printing a few poems in university anthologies and magazines); the other was secret. At school this hidden writing had consisted of diaries, stories and novels which he showed to no one; now he began to elaborate a plan he had first imagined with Amis the previous autumn, for which only one or two close friends would be the audience. He would produce a series of scurrilous texts under a pseudonym. They would be a joke, yet – unwittingly – they would perform a serious function.

The idea had begun with various 'obscene and soft porn fairy stories'[21] that Amis and Larkin had written during the early part of 1942. Although these have now disappeared, their traces survive: one, Amis remembers, was called 'The Queen Who Dreamed'; another was 'The Tale of the Jolly Prince and the Distempered Ghost' (a saga of a farting medieval ghost, of which Amis can still recall fragments: 'and then the ghost made a fart like the breaking of an apple branch under the weight of good fruit'[22]). The most adventurous, Amis says, was:

a story called 'I Would Do Anything For You' – it was about two beautiful lesbians in somewhere like Oxford. The interest was divided between jazz and lesbianism. In their digs there was a mysterious cupboard full of jazz records Philip and I had heard of but never heard. It was Mr So-and-so who had left them there and might come back for them one day. We were especially interested in Wild Bill Davison, whom we'd read about, and one of the girls – Marsha, who went in for avowals of love – found 'On A Blues Kick'. Philip admired it so much he said he'd rather she found anything but that, and wrote in the next paragraph, 'As the heavy steel needle, which they never changed, clumped into the first groove...'[23]

The 'porn' element in these stories seems to have been extremely slight – not much more than girls rolling around together, twanging elastic and straps. It originated in three things: laddish daring; cryptic homosexuality; and a wish to create straightforward heterosexual titillation. In the work that Larkin now began to produce without Amis's help, these motives appeared again, particularly the last. They drove him to write more fluently than he had ever done before. Within a matter of months he had produced two novels (one of 143 typed pages called *Trouble at Willow Gables* and one of exactly the same number of handwritten pages called *Michaelmas Term at St Bride's*), a 'sheaf' of six poems (*Sugar and Spice*), and a fragment of autobiography. All were finished by the following October, and all written under the pseudonym Brunette Coleman. (The name seems to have been adapted from a jazz band of the period – Blanche Coleman and her Girls' Band.)

As Larkin began to turn himself into Brunette, he differentiated between his mildly homosexual past and his fantastic present. 'I must say,' he told Amis, 'homosexuality has been completely replaced by lesbianism in my character at the moment – I don't know why.'[24] The answer isn't hard to find. As well as being a reaction to the seriousness of his conversations with Watkins, Brunette's work is proof that in the eighteen months or so since they had produced their convulsion of guilt, Larkin's homosexual inclinations had gradually evaporated. Bred in adolescent fear and incomprehension of women, they had turned first into an irritable dislike of all forms of sex and were now mutating into a form of comedy which, though disparaging about women, also sprang from excitement at the thought of them.

The process began in March, when Larkin started to write Brunette's autobiography, *Antemeridian*. In it, Brunette reveals herself to be the daughter of an eccentric Cornish priest, who during her childhood on the coast had acquired a large number of seaside memories. (Some of these weirdly anticipate Larkin's later poems 'Absences' and 'Livings II': 'the spray flies twenty feet into the air and the black rocks are submerged by a swell of white foam'[25].) After a mere nine pages, the account stumbles to a halt, closing with a would-be comic set piece describing drunken lifeboatmen, wrecks, and people skidding on fish-heads. Evidently the failure of this scene was reason enough for Larkin to want to abandon the autobiography. Evidently, too, the idea of starting Brunette's first novel was proving irresistible.

Larkin was encouraged by Amis from a distance, and by two other friends close by. One was Diana Gollancz, whom he was now trying to persuade himself (unconvincingly) was 'really lesbian'.[26] Part model for Brunette, part confidante, she had recently taken expensively furnished rooms in Beaumont Street, mid-way between Walton Street and St John's, and had started to run a salon for undergraduates she reckoned fashionable or talented. Larkin, who fell outside the fashionable class but into the talented one, was a regular visitor. 'I like publishers' daughters,' he was soon telling Sutton. 'Oh I *do* like publishers' daughters! The more we mix together, etc. I'd like to brush some of the dust off her myself. She is quite a good painter and dislikes the Slade intensely, very rarely going there, but painting every afternoon from two to five or six. In the mornings she works in the Ministry of Food. I'm sure I don't know why I told you this.'[27]

In later life, when Diana Gollancz had drifted away from Larkin (she married Prince Leopold von Lowenstein-Wertheim, and died in 1967), he played down the extent of his interest in her. 'We used to make fun of her in a kind way,' he said. 'She seemed boundlessly good-natured and endearingly silly: I remember her wearing a piece of antique jewellery on her light fawn jumper "to hide a wine stain" – this seemed to me highly impressive at 20.'[28] At the time, his admiration for this 'pale excitable girl of boundless cheerfulness and good nature'[29] bordered on infatuation. He wrung out of her as many memories of her Buckinghamshire schooldays as he could, adopted them as Brunette's, and thanked her by making her one of the dedicatees of *Michaelmas Term at St Bride's*.

Diana Gollancz's version of camp – her intelligent frivolity – was matched by the other important new friend that Larkin made as he began to compile Brunette's works: Bruce Montgomery. Montgomery, born in 1921, had been educated at Merchant Taylors' School. Tall, curly haired, loosely built and walking with a stick (he'd suffered 'a severe congenital deformity in both feet as a child that could ... result in a joint going "out" without warning'[30]), he had been a conspicuous figure around the university throughout his three years as an undergraduate. Not only did he look dramatic, he was strikingly and variously talented. He would soon start to make a name for himself as Edmund Crispin, the detective story writer, and as a composer of film scores – he wrote the music for the *Doctor* series. Larkin, previously too much in awe of Montgomery to consider him a possible friend, now quickly warmed to him. 'Bruce,' he wrote at the end of the summer, 'living in Wellington Square, could make a very strong impression on the unwary':

[he was not only] a good pianist, a fluent composer and the author of several unpublished books, he also seemed very rich. Under his immediate influence I suddenly revolted against all the things I'd previously worshipped – poetry, law, psychoanalysis, seriousness ... and so forth. It was like being back in the fourth form again. Bruce's irresponsibility and self-confidence were exactly what I needed at the time and our friendship flared up like a flame in oxygen ... We spent a great many evenings drinking together in the Gloucester Arms, or more often the Lord Napier in Observatory Street ... Bruce was lazy but with a far more brilliant brain than I; I was lazyish, but vaguely industrious, doing a great deal of undirected work. He was expected to get a First by nearly everyone, and the responsibility weighed on him, driving him to the bar of the Randolph but rarely to his desk and books.[31]

This picture of Montgomery as a gifted sybarite is confirmed by Amis, who associated him with the world of Brideshead that he and Larkin felt they had otherwise missed at Oxford. Montgomery's 'wavy auburn hair, silk dressing-gown in some non-primary shade, [his] walk that looked eccentric and mincing ... [his] funny-waist-coated, suede-shoed style with cigarette holders and rings' marked him out as being 'already a hotel bar man while the rest of us were still largely pub men'.[32] There was, Amis thought, something despicably showy about all this, but he couldn't help being impressed. 'There would remain,' he says, 'something formidable . . . about a man who, as Bruce apparently had, had written a book called "Romanticism and the World Crisis", possessed a grand piano and had painted a picture that was hanging on the wall of the sitting room in his lodgings.'[33]

TWELVE

Bruce Montgomery and Diana Gollancz were the perfect complement to each other in their influence on Larkin. One had a rousing intellect while the other had rousing high spirits, and the sophistication of both whetted his appetite for work directed to unorthodox ends. Montgomery, instead of revising for his Finals (he was reading Modern Languages), was writing what was to become his first and highly successful Edmund Crispin novel, *The Case of the Gilded Fly*, which Gollancz would publish early the following year. The example encouraged Larkin to skimp his own revision and turn instead to the fantasy world of Brunette Coleman's first novel, *Trouble at Willow Gables*. Montgomery's 'brisk intellectual epicureanism' was 'just the catalyst'[1] he needed.

When analysing *Trouble at Willow Gables* and its sequel *Michaelmas Term at St Bride's* it would be easy to sound too serious. The novels are essentially – vitally – frivolous things, done for private pleasure and with very limited aims. Yet their facetiousness is also a kind of unguardedness. By turns comic and silly, they allow us to see some aspects of Larkin's mind that he normally kept hidden, and others that he didn't know existed. Brunette Coleman was a disguise, an amusing mask, but nevertheless also an unwitting means of self-revelation.

The first story opens with another anticipation of late, straight Larkin – with a postman arriving (as one does at the end of 'Aubade') to deliver letters and begin the day. In this case he's delivering to a girls' school, Willow Gables near Mallerton in Wiltshire. (The postman is a 'slightly ridiculous figure in cycle clips', like the speaker of 'Church Going'.) After a quick appraisal of the school's appearance (Palladian) and social pitch (upper-middle-class), we meet the uniform-wearing girls: 'some . . . were fair with rose cheeks, others were suntanned and with dark hair. Some were as freshly beautiful as April, with glossy hair and laughing eyes, but some were solid and placid as cows.'² This tone – cliché-bound, spoofily romantic, camp – continues as we meet the central characters and are told their story. Margaret Tattenham – 'a hard, clear-cut ethereal beauty'³ – is keen on horse-racing, wants to put some money on the Oaks (due to be run in three days' time) but doesn't have the cash. When young Marie Moore is sent £5 for her birthday, it is soon diverted to meet Margaret's need – but not before Hilary Russell, a prefect and a 'big girl, with a strongly-moulded body, damp lips, and smouldering, discontented eyes',⁴ has handed it in to the headmistress, Miss Holden. Lower School girls, we gather, are allowed only £2 pocket money a term.

After a brief introduction to other characters – Marie's friend Myfanwy, who has a crush on her; Mary Beech, the captain of cricket; and Marie's sister Philippa, the head of school – we are back with Hilary Russell. Clever and exotic, she has in the past been sent flowers by girl admirers but remained indifferent: the girls 'were all so singularly repellent that [she] had made no response, beyond utilizing their cheap labour to the fullest extent'.⁵ The contents of her study, though, are indicative of her true interests. Besides possessing 'many shelves of well-known and classical authors', she also has 'a whole bottom shelf devoted, curiously enough, to popular school stories for girls, and other, less innocent productions, often the heavy binding concealing their original paper covers'.⁶

It's not long before we discover that Hilary has fallen for Mary Beech, the cricket captain, to whom she arranges to give extra French tuition after school hours. The thought makes her 'thighs as weak as water',⁷ and at their first encounter Brunette's art of titillation gets into top gear:

Hilary selected 'savoir' and 'devoir', which Mary knew, and 'mettre', which she didn't. Hilary made her repeat it three times, watching the neat, pronouncing movement of her lips, the little white mordant teeth, the tender ears, and downy skin, while, letting her eyes drift below the neck, she perceived that Mary's devotion to athletics had produced a figure that a Spartan girl might have envied. The dressing gown had fallen apart, revealing two firm legs clad in poplin pyjamas: the white ankles were bare above the slippers ... Hilary stretched her arms above her head in a tolerant yawn, her breasts forcing outwards.⁸

Once this first nocturnal encounter has been more or less innocently concluded we're thrown back into the plot. The £5 is stolen from Miss Holden's study, Marie (whose money it was) confesses to the theft, she is forced to donate it to the school gymnasium fund (Lord Amis has promised to donate £4,000 if the school can raise £1,000), and the money is put in a collection box from where it immediately disappears again. This time Marie denies that she stole it, is not believed, and is held down over Miss Holden's desk by a prefect while the headmistress beats her. The scene brings to the surface of the novel the theme of sado-masochism which is latent elsewhere:

Marie, her hair dishevelled over her pale little face, her underlip mutinously jutting out, her tunic off-shoulder and her sash also, fought like a wild thing as Ursula, out of all patience, gripped her by the neck and forced her backwards over the headmistress's desk, scattering ink and papers . . .

As Pam finally pulled Marie's tunic down over her black stockinged legs, Miss Holden, pausing only to snatch a cane from the cupboard in the wall, gripped Marie by the hair and, with a strength lent by anger, forced down her head till she was bent nearly double. Then she began thrashing her unmercifully, her face a mask of ferocity, caring little where the blows fell, as long as they found a mark somewhere on Marie's squirming body.

At last a cry was wrung from her bloodless lips, and she collapsed on the floor, twisting in agony, her face hidden by a flood of amber hair.[9]

Marie consoles herself after this assault by climbing meekly into bed with her friend Myfanwy, and the following morning (after another voyeuristic account of Myfanwy 'studying the lissom lines of her [own] brown body'[10]) schemes to run away from school. This she does with the help of a school servant, Pat, who is meant to be keeping an eye on her but submits to the idea that she should be tied up as if overpowered. It's an excuse for a little more erotic carry-on: 'Pat knelt obediently while Marie tied her wrists together with a sash, and bound her arms tightly to her body with a black stocking. Then she suffered Marie to push back her dress and unfasten her own stockings and pull them off one by one.'[11]

Elsewhere in the school, Brunette explores a less violent aspect to Larkin's fantasies. Hilary, giving Mary her second late-night tutorial, admits that 'there was nothing so beautiful in the world as a fourteen year old schoolgirl . . . How anyone could regard the version of six years later as in any way superior beat [her] to a frazzle: it was preferring a painted savage dressed in bangles and skins, chock-full of feminine wiles, dodges and other dishonesties directed to the same degrading sexual end, to a being who lived a life so simple and rounded off in its purity that it only remained for it to be shattered.'[12] Hilary, of course, is not above 'shattering purity' herself, and when Mary dozes off she kisses her, undoes her pyjamas, and lets 'her hand wander eclectically over her body'.[13]

Mary awakes and runs off, scandalized – and, meaning only to calm her, Hilary gives chase and bumps into someone (she can't see who) creeping into Miss Holden's study. More violence follows: 'Hilary hit the girl hard in the face, eliciting a sharp gasp. This she repeated several times, taking care to land the blows in the same spot every time.'[14] Brunette is under no illusions about the psychological motivations here, and in naming them Larkin identifies the feelings about women which lie at the heart of the novel, and of its real author. 'Lust,' we are told, 'had turned into anger, and anger into cruelty, and now cruelty, partly sated and partly still hungry, was turning into lust again.'[15] Hilary kisses the girl – she turns out to be Margaret Tattenham the racing fan, who had been trying to steal the £5 to put on the Oaks – then blackmails her into coming back with her to her study.

We're now two-thirds of the way through the book, and well acquainted with all aspects of its eroticism: voyeurism, sado-masochism, and a pleasure in taking advantage of those who (because they are young or servants) cannot easily defend themselves. Nothing that happens in the last third varies this diet. Marie, who has abandoned the trussed-up Pat and is blundering around in nearby woodland with 'the seat of her trousers neatly torn in a semi-circle by some unexpected barbed wire',[16] is joined by Margaret, who has escaped from Willow Gables on the school horse, with 'the wind blowing her short tunic precisely against her body'.[17] Eventually they are captured by three prefects, and the truth about the £5 – as well as the truth about Hilary – emerges. No sooner has this happened than they encounter Myfanwy swimming naked in a river, clearly in danger of drowning. Managing to take off most of their clothes in the process, the girls save her, return to the school as heroines, and are forgiven their sins.

All except Hilary. The girl who has most interested Brunette and most excited Larkin is the only one to be punished: she is expelled from the school. It's a fitting end, in its disconcerting way, to a book which for all its appearance of simple frivolity is nevertheless more interested in suppression and cruelty than anything else. Once its women have been arraigned for pleasure they are dismissed; once they have been enjoyed they are treated with indifference.

If Larkin had regarded *Trouble at Willow Gables* entirely as a joke, it's difficult to imagine him bothering to elaborate it. Yet elaborate it he did – partly because Brunette liberated him from many of the emotional constraints which had hindered him in the past. As he began work on the sequel he hoped it would provide the same release. *Michaelmas Term at St Bride's* is set, like 'I Would Do Anything For You', in 'somewhere like Oxford', and several of its characters are carried over from *Willow Gables*. Mary Birch, for instance, the former cricket captain ('Beech' in her earlier incarnation), is now a scholarship girl at the all-women St Bride's College (recognizably Somerville). To her horror, she discovers on arrival that she is sharing rooms with the amorous Hilary (formerly Russell, now Allen – the name of the undergraduate who humiliated Larkin at table tennis). To her relief, she finds that other and less dangerous friends are now also members of the college: Marie, Philippa, Myfanwy and Margaret.

The story opens with Brunette ogling Mary and Marie as they roll around on a hearthrug in Marie's room:

'Beast,' hissed Marie, making a face, and made a supreme effort to lay Mary Birch on her back. But Mary's hockey-hardened muscles resisted her successfully, and Marie collapsed exhausted in Mary's lap ... Mary slipped one arm round her shoulders, and another under her knees, and with an effort lifted her up. Marie was too *solide* to be lifted without an effort. Then she carried her chum's relaxed body into the bedroom, and dumped it down on the bed, after having pulled the clothes back with one hand.[18]

This romping is a world away from Hilary's knowing advances – which embarrass Mary when she returns to her own room and undresses for bed. ('You're an exquisite figure my dear,' Hilary tells her. 'Rather unnecessarily athletic, but beautiful all the same.'[19]) Mary falls asleep wondering how long she can endure such treatment before complaining to the authorities, but the next morning she is saved by the plot. Late for a lecture, she borrows a bicycle which turns out to belong to Mary de Putron, 'one of the ornaments at college, and the principal jewel in its athletic crown',[20] thereby jeopardizing her ambition to play in the college hockey team, of which de Putron is captain. Mary felt, Brunette tells us, 'in the position of a newly-arrived courtier who learns that the testy gentleman in the washrooms whom he elbowed away from the roller towel was the sovereign himself'.[21]

Mary duly makes a hash of her trial for the hockey team, tries to comfort herself with some 'sisterly' and 'light osculation'[22] with Marie, then returns disconsolately to her room and Hilary. Hilary, it turns out, has troubles of her own: she is being pursued by a man, known as 'the creature', who has been impressed by her skill at table tennis. She and Mary drink a bottle of brandy in order to cheer themselves up – and, we suspect, to prepare for what must inevitably follow. But once again Brunette resorts to titillation: 'At this one unexpected moment when it seemed likely that Mary would yield if pressed, [Hilary's] sentiments towards her slackened and took on a remote mawkishness.'[23] Lust immediately turns to reverence: 'I have gathered armfuls of blossoms, thought Hilary with a pardonable gentility of expression, have plunged my arms elbow-deep into the rich cascade of July, but this last flower at least shall remain unpulled.'[24] Within a page she has changed her mind and is in bed with Mary, taking advantage of her while she is still unconscious with drink. Brunette, showing less curiosity than she would have done at Willow Gables, leaves the reader unconscious too: Part One of the novel comes to an abrupt close.

Part Two plays the same sort of games. At first we follow Marie, who is attending a course of lectures by a psychologist called Barnyard (obviously a relative of Layard): 'It did not take Marie very long to psychoanalyse herself, despite Mr Barnyard's professional warning that this was a dangerous practice and only to be undertaken by trained (and paid) psychologists. She bought a large metal-edged book costing nearly a pound, which she soon filled with accounts of dreams, in her sprawling childish handwriting.'[25] Her sister Philippa, who collects belts, turns out to be a more interesting subject for analysis than she is herself, especially since investigating Philippa means rediscovering Brunette's interest in beating. Once Marie has scattered worms around Philippa's room as a form of belt-aversion therapy, she is captured:

The younger girl twisted to escape but Philippa had learnt how to deal with Marie from experience. In a very short time she was lying face down on Philippa's silken knee, with her velvet skirt folded neatly round her waist. The belt had a curious metal buckle, which Philippa rightly adjudged would add an awful sting to the lashes. Oblivious of Marie's piteous tears, cries and struggles, she thrashed till her forearms ached. Towards the end she even started to enjoy it.[26]

Mary, in her newly blossomed relationship with Hilary, has also 'started to enjoy it'. Her seduction, she says breathlessly, 'was all much nicer than I'd imagined, mainly due to you. I say, could I have your copy of *Mademoiselle de Maupin*, as a keepsake?'[27] Their happy future is soon threatened, however, when Hilary falls into the river (that strain again) and is rescued by Mary de Putron's dashing boyfriend Clive Russel-Vick, a pilot in the RAF. Hilary flirts with him to punish de Putron for victimizing Mary, only to find him a disturbingly easy catch. ' "If he's anything to go by, men are ten times easier to seduce than women," ' she tells Mary. ' "Fifty times easier than you," she added as an afterthought. Mary gave her wrist a vicious nip.'[28]

In its frivolous way, this judgement exposes the complicated feelings which underlie *Michaelmas Term at St Bride's*. While pretending its main pleasure is watching girls sex each other up, it can't conceal its male self-disgust. Men are victims of their sexual attraction to women, the novel wants us to believe – and to be powerless in the grip of desire is contemptible. It's a theme which is elaborated in Larkin's two straight novels and many of his later poems – but here it is raised only to be dropped. Part Two of *St Bride's* dwindles into predictions about the outcome of the forthcoming Oxford and Cambridge hockey match.

The third part of the novel wanders even further from the concerns which are Brunette's own. It's as if Larkin, having reached his muted conclusion about the difficulties of desire, has lost interest in his story. To round it off, he spins a silly, heavily autobiographical yarn centred on a new character, Diana (Diana Gollancz), a former student of the university and a notorious trouble-maker, who returns to Oxford for a party. She meets Hilary (and greets her with a copy of *The Case of the Gilded Fly* which Hilary thinks is by Lord David Cecil or Lord Berners) but nothing comes of their meeting. Nothing much happens, either, to Marie and Philippa, who now appear again. Philippa has been traumatized by her encounter with the worms, and 'can't see a belt without feeling queer'.[29] Marie cheers her up by taking her out to get drunk, and Larkin tries to rally his own flagging interest by going in for a show of modernist self-consciousness. In one of the pubs they visit, Marie sees Pat – the woman she had tied up in order to escape from the punishment room in Willow Gables:

'Pat's story's over now, Miss Marie,' she [said]. 'Willow Gables doesn't exist any more.'

'Story?'

'Yes, Miss Marie. You tied me up, don't you remember?'

'Yes, of course, Pat, of course I remember. I'm sorry about that.'

'That's alright, Miss Marie. It was in the plot, so of course we had to do it. It wasn't your fault, Miss Marie.'

'And whose fault was it, Pat?' enquired Marie, stumbling over the brass rail at their feet.

'The woman that writes all these books. Haven't you ever met her, Miss Marie? I saw her once. She used to come in here and drink. Very tall she was, and beautifully dressed.'[30]

When Marie wonders 'Are we still in a story?', Pat tells her 'You are, Miss Marie, but I'm not'[31] – and as proof of the Lewis Carroll-like divisions between their two existences, Pat then points through a door to show the 'real' Bruce Montgomery drinking in another bar. 'If this was reality,' Marie decides, 'she would rather keep in the story,'[32] but by this stage the narrative has nowhere else to turn. It sputters into a page of notes about how the plot might be resolved (Hilary eventually drops Clive and 'the creature' and joins Diana), and Brunette's days as a novelist are done.

The main reason why *St Bride's* fails to reach a conclusion is that it loses its erotic impetus. Larkin neither maintains Brunette's interest in titillation, nor converts it into something more candidly pornographic. Beneath the surface of both stories runs a strong current of angry sexuality, but the surfaces themselves are too bashful, too giggly or too keen on the approval (the social reward) of their small audience to exploit their potential. As a result, neither novel is more than a fascinating curiosity.

As far as Larkin himself was concerned, they were necessary and valuable. He produced them quickly, full of fun, and in the teeth of demands that he revise for his exams, persevere with Watkins's ideas, and worry about the future. They allowed him to create a private imaginative world when the real world was threatening to overwhelm him; they let him rediscover the fluency he had known at school; and they enabled him to explore in secret the obstacles that had grown up between his feelings and his writing. He had known for years that these obstacles were comprised largely of his confused attitudes to sex. With Brunette shielding him and guiding his hand, he could see that his attraction to men was a thing of the past, and that his attraction to women was sincere but severely complicated. By the time the second novel was abandoned, Brunette had persuaded him that these complications – rather than inhibiting him – should become his subject. She had freed him by showing him how tightly he was restrained.

THIRTEEN

As with Brunette's novels, so – nearly – with her poems. Larkin finally abandoned *St Bride's* in October 1943, soon after leaving Oxford, and at the same time he also sewed into a booklet (in an edition of two copies, one of which he kept and one of which he gave to Montgomery) the 'sheaf' of Brunette poems he had written during the previous two months. This collection, *Sugar and Spice*, contains eight poems, only two of which are included in the *Collected Poems* ('Femmes Damnées' and 'The School in August'), and opens with a brief Foreword:

These poems were all written in the August and September of this year, and I make no apology for presenting a collection of what may seem 'trivia' in these disturbed times. I feel that now more than ever a firm grasp of the essentials of life is needed.

The two poems with titles in the French Language ['Femmes Damnées' and 'Ballade des Dames du Temps Jadis'] are suggested, of course, by their namesakes François Villon and Charles Baudelaire, but they are not, of course, 'renderings' in any sense. In my opinion they are improvements.

Finally, I dedicate this slim volume to all my sister-writers, with the exception of Margaret Kennedy, who wrote in *The Constant Nymph*: 'English schoolgirls are not interesting.'[1]

The camp tone of voice persists in much of what follows. Mixing Angela Brazil and Richmal Crompton with John Betjeman and Auden, Larkin takes us through a world of comfortless jealousies, breathless bike-rides, and deathless crushes. 'It's no good standing there and looking haughty,' begins 'The False Friend':

> I'm very cross: I think you've been a beast,
> An utter crawling worm, for nearly all the term –
> I think you might apologize at least.

Another poem, the Villon-derivative 'Ballade des Dames du Temps Jadis', treats the flip-side of this mood. It shows us sentimental nostalgia rather than foot-stamping impatience, and comes complete with instructions in the margin which advise how it should be read. Originally we are told to approach 'with something of "the monstrous crying of wind" – Yeats, of course'. Here we are 'Rising to, and falling from, an ecstasy of nostalgia':

> Now the ponies are all dead,
> The summer frocks have been outgrown,
> The books changed, beside the bed,
> And all the stitches that were sewn
> Have been unpicked, and in disgust
> The diaries have been thrown away,
> And hockey sticks are thick with dust –
> Those summer terms have flown away.
>
> Ah, tell me, in what fairy-land
> Can I meet Jacqueline or June,
> Eat lemon-caley from my hand –
> But no: it has all gone too soon,
> And Christine, Barbara, and Madge,
> Elspeth, Elizabeth, Esme
> Are with my blazer and my badge,
> So many summer terms away.

For all their absurdity, these fluently swerving feelings have as 'seriously' important an aspect as Brunette's novels. They release Larkin from the self-conscious, would-be-transcendent world of his straight poems into one where ordinary objects can be easily assimilated, and enjoyment regarded as its own reward. Generally speaking, his enjoyment does not (as it did in the novels) involve sorting out complex personal feelings. Nevertheless, in the best of Brunette's poems, such as 'Femmes Damnées', we are given a miniaturized version of the mingled desire and self-disgust we recognize in the prose.

Larkin published 'Femmes Damnées' in his lifetime – thirty-five years after it was written – with John Fuller's Oxford-based Sycamore Press. 'The piece is evidence,' he told Fuller, 'that I once read at least one "foreign poem", though I can't remember how far, if at all, my verses are based on the original.'[2] As soon as it was printed, a number of Larkin-watchers seized on the poem as evidence of his debt to French Symbolist writers, a debt that Larkin always denied, saying he knew and cared nothing about 'foreign poetry'.[3] (In 1964, when he was asked whether he read foreign poetry, he 'instinctively shuddered'[4] and replied as if appalled by the thought: '*Foreign* poetry? *No!*'[5]) His vehemence was misleading. One of the most characteristic features of his later poems is the way they introduce a demotic, street-wise language ('When I see a couple of kids/And guess he's fucking her . . .') to a more rarefied and poetic one ('immediately,/ Rather than words, comes the thought of high windows . . .'). The two languages embody Larkin's conflicting attitudes to experience, one reflecting his commitment to the here-and-now, the other registering his longing to rise above it. This second language is the one so deeply yet so subtly affected by the Symbolist writers he later decried – and the Symbolist-influenced ones he also scorned, notably Eliot – and it is this second language that Brunette helped to develop. She would be interested in Baudelaire, Villon and Mallarmé, wouldn't she? It is essential to her chic, continental personality that she should drop their names and adopt their styles. In 'Femmes Damnées' she translates Baudelaire's poem of the same title ('A la pâle clarté de lampes languissantes', from the original edition of *Les fleurs du mal*), stirs in a little Eliot, and passes it off as an improvement. Baudelaire has in his fourth stanza:

> Etendu à ses pieds, calme et pleine de joie,
> Delphine la couvait avec des yeux ardents,
> Comme un animal fort qui surveille une proie
> Après l'avoir d'abord marquée avec les dents.

In Brunette's rendering the poem ends:

> Stretched out before her, Rachel curls and curves,
> Eyelids and lips apart, her glances filled
> With satisfied ferocity; she smiles,
> As beasts smile on the prey they have just killed.
>
> The marble clock has stopped. The curtained sun
> Burns on: the room grows hot. There, it appears,
> A vase of flowers has spilt, and soaked away.
> The only sound heard is the sound of tears.

If we read 'Femmes Damnées' as being by Larkin we accept it as authentic (as people did when they first read it in 1978 and then later in the *Collected Poems*) – partly because of the detail of the vase (taken up later in 'Home is so sad'), more generally because of the hushed but pervasive melancholy. If we read the poem as being by Brunette, however, we can't ignore the way it switches from its original camp into something more straightforward in these two final verses. As it does so, it illustrates

Brunette's value to Larkin. He may have invented her as a joke, but her openness to foreign influence allowed him to find his own, mature voice. She helped him become himself by allowing him to seem entirely different. She let him see himself plainly, albeit briefly, in a distorting mirror.

Before abandoning Brunette, and in order to make sure that every form had been touched by her influence, Larkin got her to produce an essay on writing: 'What We Are Writing For'. It begins with a mention of George Orwell's famous essay 'Boys' Weeklies' (collected in *Inside the Whale*, 1940), which Jacinth – Brunette's secretary – has recently finished reading. Then it blossoms into a homily, delivered by Brunette herself, on how and how not to write for children. The speaker's voice unquestionably belongs to the author of *Sugar and Spice*, but the emphases here are more practical, more 'English'. 'The best writers,' we learn, 'tend not to have a heroine but a group of heroines' – and we also discover that 'Writers seem afraid to draw a character of any wickedness whatever.'[6] Greed, Brunette tells us, is an especially neglected vice, except in the case of Nancy Breary, who uses it 'as a kind of substitute for sentimental eroticism'. (A quotation from Breary's work is given to illustrate this point; its mention of 'Three kinds of sandwiches, and bananas, and cream buns, and chocolate cake'[7] reminds us of the way in which food is made to perform a covertly erotic function in *Jill*.)

Minor characters, Brunette thinks, also suffer at the hands of children's writers. The only exception she can remember 'is the beautiful, easy-going Dora Aubrey, from *Niece of the Headmistress* by Dorothy Vickery ... Dora, the chum of the tempestuous and wholly fascinating Una Vickers, has a soft, sluggish, sensitive, intelligent character, easily accepted without comment, and yet subtly repellent, until even Una Vickers turns on her and maltreats her in a lonely cloakroom.' And so on. Throughout the essay Larkin uses Brunette as a means of giving determinedly facetious opinions about writing. Yet as the advice accumulates – now not merely mentioning but parodying Orwell – it squashes Brunette's French sympathies, and anticipates many opinions that he would later put more simply and claim as his own:

I have a prejudice against foreigners which extends into literature, and I regard the introduction of Austrian new girls or trips into the Alps as unwarranted attempts to rush the reader off his or her feet with the 'glamour' that is supposed to hang around foreign countries. How stupid it is! To my mind, there is nowhere so glamorous as England, with its public parks, its daffodils, young girls taking out dogs, old copies of the *Tatler*, riding schools exercising under beeches, Somerville,

The Times on the breakfast table with the sausages and liver, and dances at the tennis club in small county towns. As soon as I find a story with words like 'kopje' or 'veldt' or 'Iyana' in it, or references to monkeys or native porters or chamois, I put it firmly back on the shelf. We must construct a closed, single-sexed world, which Mr Orwell would doubtless call a womb replica, or something equally coarse.[8]

'What We Are Writing For' was Brunette's last gasp. By the end of October she had disappeared from Larkin's life, to be mentioned only fleetingly in later accounts of his university life, and silently cannibalized in *Jill*. Very occasionally, her name cropped up in private. In 1947, for instance, when Larkin was at Leicester, he briefly revisited her in a letter to Amis. 'Blanche Coleman is Brunette's sister,' he wrote, referring to Blanche Coleman and her Girls' Band: ' – a natural ash blonde. In contrast with this her skin is slightly sunburnt; her bush is almost like a seeding thistle against her biscuit-coloured belly . . . Why are you plucking at the front of your trousers like that, eh?'[9]

It's only a passing crack, but this reference shows how Larkin's view of Brunette Coleman changed when he stopped using her voice. She ended up as an occasional comic reminder of lost youth. To start with she was a different kind of joke – purely frivolous as far as her small audience was concerned, yet also a way of exploring complex sexual feelings. Then, when her role as a cryptic counsellor had been played out, she became a means of investigating the various idioms and voices which would best release those feelings to a larger and more serious audience. In 'Femmes Damnées' she scored her most notable success. In the remainder of her work she demonstrated a robustly ironical attitude to art which Larkin's next few years, dominated by his reading of Yeats, would test severely.

FOURTEEN

'Thirds are given,' Larkin told Sutton early in 1943; 'I may get one.'[1] It was a gloomily defensive assessment of his chances in his forthcoming exams, but also an attempt to scare himself into working hard. He returned to Oxford on 12 May, before the official start of the summer term, and spent each day revising in the Bodleian Library from the moment it opened until late in the evening. (As if to prove his new commitment, he also ordered a bookplate. It showed a Star of David above a couplet from Blake's 'Marriage of Heaven and Hell': 'How do you know but ev'ry bird that cuts the airy way,/Is an immense world of delight, clos'd by your senses five.') Hour by hour he convinced himself that he would never catch up; week by week he became more anxious about the future. His father's well-intentioned offer to send him to the Slade made him 'howl with laughter';[2] the thought that he might join Sutton and 'set up . . . as [a] builder after the war' was 'rather fun' but 'completely mad';[3] and Montgomery's suggestion that he should (like Montgomery) become a teacher was brushed aside. How could he, with his stammer?

Struggling to maintain his new routines in the library, Larkin went to see his 'moral tutor' in St John's to ask his advice – but he was no use either. 'He was as helpful as a gatepost,' Larkin told his parents. 'Next step is to see the Appointments Board. My ideas are so desperately unclarified that I expect little success: all I can think of is publishing and of course publishers' staffs are shorter now there's nothing for them to publish, so they don't need new people. The other thing is the Civil Service. I understand the trouble with any job [there] at present is that it's temporary.'[4]

By the end of May he had reluctantly taken his decision. 'Did I tell you?' he asked Sutton in a letter decorated with a drawing of someone goose-stepping through a door with 'Civil Service' written on it, 'I'd made steps towards the CS? Gawd fuck. I hate the idea.'[5] A fortnight later he hated it even more, telling Sutton:

I have put my name down as a temporary assistant principal [the exam was due to take place in August]. I don't know what it entails and I don't much care. I don't want to 'do' anything. It seems to me, in Lawrence's words, there's nothing to be 'done'. The job will probably be loathsome, but it's only for the duration and has no prospects at all. In the meantime I am going to try and write some proper short stories that I've thought of during the past year. Trouble is, I know too well what great art entails – or even small art. Art is a release or generation of delight in life. Art is a richness.[6]

At least there was some chance of retaining that richness while he remained at Oxford. No matter how hard he worked, there was still drink, and there was still jazz. Montgomery, who found jazz 'exciting' but who in playing it made it 'absolutely dead',[7] was always willing to join him. So were Philip Brown and Diana Gollancz. So too was a new arrival at the college, John Wain. Wain was three years younger than Larkin, and had strong views and a pungent personality. Born and brought up in Stoke-on-Trent, he was proud of his Midlands good sense, obsessed by jazz and fascinated by modern poetry. Down-to-earth yet cerebral, he was especially devoted to Auden and Empson, whose writing strongly influenced his own. It was a range of interests, and a mixture of qualities, that strongly appealed to Larkin, even though their first meeting included 'a brief bitter exchange'[8] about a jazz player whose worth they disputed. To Larkin, Wain seemed bluff but clever; to Wain, Larkin seemed impressive but daunting: he was, after all, a Finalist and a published poet. His 'literary self-training', Wain wrote later, 'combined with his quietness, his slight stammer, and (perhaps) the impression of giant intelligence produced by the fact of his having a large dome-like head and wearing very thick glasses, all helped to make him "the college writer" '.[9]

Larkin hardly had time to get to know Wain before his revision overwhelmed him. 'I have collapsed miserably into the desert of work,' he had told his parents in the first week of April. 'There is *too* much to do.'[10] A few days later he had written to Sutton, 'The life of a pre-BA is very sinful. It consists in working whether you want to or not . . . and the exam is just crazy. I'll get a Third, at most a Second. I was not meant to study, but to be studied.'[11] On 17 June, when the exams started, he walked through the rain to the Sheldonian Theatre wearing his sub-fusc, convinced that 'a steady B indicated my level'.[12] Over the next few days his hopes sank steadily. 'Oh dear, oh dear, oh dear,' he moaned to his parents after another week. 'Having gently prepared you for my getting a Second, I feel I shall have to prepare you for a Third or lower.'[13] By the time the 'welter of white ties and papers, ink and sweat'[14] was over, he had made up his mind that the only result he could expect was a complete failure.

When Larkin handed in his last paper, he immediately felt more confident. Many years later, in an account written for his own private interest, he explained why:

I can still recall the sense I had of having committed myself irretrievably, and the inimitable lighthearted apprehension that accompanies this feeling. I walked the length of the street, still dressed in my uncomfortable examination suit, gown and white tie, and went into the nearest cinema to see George Sanders in *The Moon and Sixpence*. This was a conscious act of independence. My fellow examinees were probably having tea together, fearfully comparing notes . . .

And there was another element in my action: the film – and also, curiously enough, the book by Somerset Maugham on which the film was based – was about a man who throws up everything to become a painter. By walking from the examination hall into the one and ninepennies, therefore, I was symbolically rejecting the life of scholarship and putting my money on the life of the creative imagination.[15]

When he had merely been dreading disaster, Larkin felt crushed; now that he was embracing it he became defiant. Academic disgrace didn't matter, he told himself, it would only have led him into a cul-de-sac, studying for a research degree or applying for a job he knew he 'should never really have been happy doing'.[16] He decided that it was a relief to have escaped all this – it meant being an artist, instead. Without delay, he returned to Coten End and began writing, completing *Michaelmas Term at St Bride's* and Brunette's other works while his mother coddled him and his father sympathetically delayed asking about possible careers. The Ministry of Labour – for the time being – left him alone.

Then the three weeks of grace ended and Larkin returned to Oxford. His results were posted in the Sheldonian Theatre, and as soon as he had seen them he telephoned his mother. It was mid-morning and Sydney was chairing a meeting in the City Hall, where Eva knew he hated being contacted. The deputy City Treasurer, Dr Marshall, took the call, and interrupted the meeting with the news: Larkin had got a First. 'Well I'm damned,' Sydney said, and the meeting continued. 'But I could see,' Dr Marshall remembers, 'that he was jolly pleased with and proud of Philip in a detached Larkin sort of way.'[17] Larkin himself was unashamedly delighted. Returning to Warwick, he told Sutton:

My dear Jim, In whatever state this reaches you, at peace or at war (for I hear the Eighth Army is engaged in Sicily), asleep or awake, in sorrow or in joy, I simply must dance my little dance and tell you that I have got a *FIRST* in my Schools!! Oh, how clever I am! Oh, how infinite and wise in my faculties! A star descends onto my forehead! It is all the more remarkable because I made numerous blunders and know sweet bugger all about my subject. That means I was so clever and pene-trating and witty that my superior mind shone incandescently above all the ather-ather-ather wurr-wurr-marook!! (surprised belch.)[18]

Larkin's tutors, more soberly, agreed that he was lucky to have done so well. This made him wonder, briefly, whether standards had been lower than usual because of the war, but he quickly rejected the idea. At the end of his life he still felt that his First had given him more pleasure than most other things he had done, and when he took his BA (on 24 July) in the Sheldonian under the admiring gaze of his parents and sister, then went out to lunch with his family, Diana Gollancz, Philip Brown and Bruce

Montgomery, he said he felt 'like a millionaire'.[19]

Anti-climax swiftly followed. Although it was 'pleasant'[20] to be spoilt and admired by his parents at home, Coten End suffocated him, and he spent as much time out of the house as he could. It wasn't always an effective solution. Whenever he went back to Oxford – which was most weekends – he realized that his past had disappeared. Diana Gollancz had moved to London; Montgomery had taken a job teaching French at Shrewsbury School; his remaining undergraduate friends had dispersed for the summer – even Philip Brown, who would be staying in Oxford for another year. He knew, anyway, that in its latter stages his friendship with Brown had dwindled into amicable blandness, and he made no effort to rekindle it. The melancholy of the empty university lapped at him. 'I have left Oxford,' he wrote to Sutton. 'I have "gone down": I have "been to Oxford": my youth – school and university – is irrevocably ended (in theory) and shades of the prison-house begin to close about the grown boy. Ah me! It seems no more substantial now than an afternoon on the river.'[21]

In years to come he would take a sterner line, such as suited his more melancholy adult personality. While his memories of friendships dimmed, and the excitement of his youth faded, he gradually found his pleasure in Oxford evaporating. He admired it, but could not stay there easily for long. Fifteen years after going down he said, in a way which gravely undervalues the effect and achievement of his time as an undergraduate, 'I didn't approve of Oxford and I don't want to go back there. It crushes the spirit in a more subtle way than I had imagined possible. I hardly wrote a line during my stay there, except in vacations, although I acquired a certain first-hand knowledge of people and what it is like to be implicated with them.'[22] Fifteen years later still, in 'Poem about Oxford', his 'blacked-out and butterless days' were treated a little less harshly. He at least allowed the possibility that the city might have 'stuck' in his mind 'as a touchstone / Of learning and *la politesse*'.

Larkin's success in his exams did nothing to help him decide about the future. He cowered in his attic-study pretending to be Brunette, waiting for fate to intercede and make his decisions for him, suffering the boredom of family life. 'These days are unbearably dull,' he told Amis. '. . . I haven't attempted any work recently . . . Even jazz seems incongruous. I don't fuckin' drink, I don't fuckin' smoke (except a pipe) – aaooh! – I don't fuckin' fuck women – I might as well be fuckin' dead.'[23] Confronting his diary every evening, Larkin wondered again what Oxford had given him.

He added up the friendships formed, the books read, the things written, the exams passed, the self-esteem gained; then he subtracted the lingering shyness, the absence of women, the lack of creative fluency, the failure to set his life in a particular direction. He felt blocked and inert. For three years he had been able to claim that he had shaped his days to suit his devotion to art. Now the appeal seemed a hollow one. He simply hadn't written enough, or well enough. What was the point of being 'a genius' if he couldn't prove it? A life of compromise stretched ahead, threatening to douse the special gifts he knew still flickered inside him.

On 9 August his failure seemed more convincing than ever. It was his twenty-first birthday, the day he should have been celebrating his independence. Instead he was in London, being interviewed for the Civil Service. It was 'a bit flustering', he told Sutton afterwards. 'They asked me what I really wanted to do, and I said "be a novelist". I had to stick to it too – but if you'd known how presumptuous it sounded . . . Aaahhaa!! (expressing disgust.) Particularly as I have been trying to write a proper story this week, and failing miserably.'[24] Leaving the interview, he felt that he was bound to be disappointed whatever happened. If he was accepted by Whitehall it would mark the end of his ambitions as an artist; if he was rejected it would prove he was incompetent to deal with the world. If he set up as a solitary writer he wouldn't be able to make ends meet; if he stayed with his parents he would be driven half crazy. Only by turning in on himself could he avoid choosing between so many evils. He had no confidence to predict what the results might be.

FIFTEEN

Before he left Oxford, Larkin had decided that if he was going to write anything good, he would only do it by living quietly. The next three years proved him wrong. It was a time of great turmoil for him, in which he wrote faster and better than ever before. 'As far as my writing was concerned,' he said later, 'leaving Oxford was like taking a cork out of a bottle. Writing flooded out of me.'[1]

The change began almost as soon as his Civil Service interview was over. Filling in time before he heard whether he had got the job, he pressed on with Brunette's work and began more 'serious' prose as well. While revising for his Finals he had entertained various ideas for short stories without having the time to develop them; now he was free to look at them more closely he decided they were all 'negro's cock'[2] except for one. 'It could lengthen into a novel,' he told Sutton, 'if I could ever do it. It concerns a very poor young man who goes to Oxford who is exceptionally nervous and rather feminine, who is forced to share a room with his exact antithesis.'[3] This first reference to the novel that became *Jill* makes no secret of wanting to exploit the social dislocation Larkin had felt when he first arrived at university. During his time there he found ways of earning the respect of his companions; now, in the security of home and without any responsibilities to the wider world, he re-created his original shyness and linked it to various other forms of uncertainty – particularly uncertainties about sex and women. He decided that his hero, John Kemp, would have to do without the social talents he had acquired himself (he would not, in other words, quickly form a close circle of friends who shared his interests and enthusiasms). This meant painting a very partial self-portrait, yet continuing by more self-aware means the process of self-examination that Brunette had begun. He told Sutton:

As a result of adverse conditions, and also of telling his room-mate that he had a sister a year younger than himself (or two or three years) – which is untrue – [Kemp] begins to construct a complicated sexless daydream about an imaginary sister, who serves as a nucleus for a dream-life. Then he meets a girl who is exactly like this imaginary sister (the sister-aspect having by now changed into rather a more emotional relationship) and the rest of the story . . . serves to disillusion him completely. It's a jolly good story, whatever it sounds like this badly expressed, and interests me greatly – BUT I CAN'T WRITE IT![4]

No sooner had Larkin sketched his novel than it seemed he would have to abandon it. After a brief family holiday in Torquay he heard that the Civil Service had rejected him, and although he made light of his failure, he knew that it meant he might have to find less congenial employment. 'Did I tell you my Civil Service job fell through?' he asked Sutton. "Sfact. They can't have liked my cheerful determination to be a writah and to use the CS merely as a means of livelihood. I am now perilously near being dragged into the Foreign Office as a hack clerk. I suppose it means something to do with codes – it does not entice me. I must say, I expected it would be easier to get a job. What will happen in peacetime fuck alone knows.'[5]

This new possibility – the Foreign Office – was none of Larkin's doing. The Civil Service had simply passed his name along to the code-breaking outfit at Bletchley Park, outside Oxford, when they knew they weren't going to employ him themselves. Larkin was duly interviewed in Oxford on 14 September by a panel made up of officers from the Admiralty, then slunk unhappily back to Warwick. He needn't have worried. Bletchley rejected him too. 'At interviews,' he told Amis, 'I must obviously show that I don't give a zebra's turd for any kind of job.'[6] A week later he wrote again: 'How I detest being inspected and weighed up and classed as unfit for this imbecile job or fit for that imbecile job or suitable for such and such lunatic task. I boil and spit fury.'[7]

Laziness, selfishness, fear and hurt pride all raised in Larkin a formidable barrier to the idea that work could have any value for him. In a couple of years' time he would change his mind – 'Work is a good thing,' he would tell Sutton, 'in small doses. It canalizes one's energy and stops one from starving.'[8] At this stage he resented it as something which distracted him from *Jill*. His days slowed into a series of small panics, his ambitions struggled to keep their shape. Sometimes, he admitted to Sutton, he 'longed for friends to talk to – you and Kingsley and Nick [Russel], Philip Brown or Bruce Montgomery or Diana Gollancz';[9] other times he did no more than 'piss around spending money, doing housework, tossing myself off (to put it crudely) and listening to those awful blaring jazz things'.[10] Any variation on this routine, any progress with his writing, was reported cautiously and with great reluctance.

Yet progress was made. On 30 September, only a few days after telling Sutton 'I CAN'T WRITE IT', he revealed that he had been writing fast, then quickly mocked what he had done. 'I have been hacking at a novel,' he said:

Yes, the same one. I've done about ninety pages of it, which is roughly a third – a little under. This is the second draft – I abandoned the first because the construction was all wrong. Sometimes I sit back and light a pipe and leer out of the window and say, 'I'll make a writer they'll attend to': then perhaps I pick up what I have written and then a strange sensation spreads over me; I lay my pipe down, and go and stand in the open air for a bit, then come back and read a few more lines till I become stronger and the desire to retch slowly abates ... Oh, it's so infuriating to be dealing in shades of least bad when I want to write *well* ... All the time I'm hearing a voice saying 'Novel about Oxford? Oh yes, usual stuff. Ten a penny. Young hero. Intelligent, sensitive, bit of a poet. Cheap introspection. Patches of sheer beauty. First love, local colour – scraps of "varsity life", homosexuality, rags, and the rest of it. Disappears into the luminous future. Oh yes, we've all done it. Good fun. Valueless of course.' *Figures Under Glass* (its present title) is not really like that, but near enough to be mistaken for it.[11]

Larkin kept writing through October, knowing his seclusion would not last for long. He was right. In the first week of November a letter arrived from the Ministry of Labour, pointing out that his rejection by the Civil Service and the Foreign Office didn't mean he should stop applying for other jobs. What were his plans? 'I could have answered,' he said later:

that, having finished with the university and English literature, I was living at home writing a novel, but I rightly adjudged the enquiry to be a warning that I had better start doing something. Picking up the day's *Birmingham Post* (the paper we took in those days), I soon discovered an advertisement by a small urban district council for a librarian [in Wellington, Shropshire, fifty miles north-west of Warwick]. The salary was £175 per annum (plus cost-of-living bonus, Whitley scale, of £45.10s for men, £36.8s for women), and the duties included 'those usual to the operation of a Lending Library (open access) and Reading Room supervision'.[12]

Judging by Larkin's treatment of books in St John's, he didn't have much affection for libraries. However beautiful or useful they might be, and although librarianship had been his mother's first choice as a career, they were contaminated by their connection with 'literature' and with rules. It had no more occurred to him that he might become a librarian than it had ever seemed possible he would end up in Whitehall or Bletchley. If he got the job, he thought, it would be an expedient – that was all; a way of avoiding trouble with the authorities. Yet the longer he pondered the advertisement, the more advantages occurred to him. The work didn't sound too onerous: perhaps he would be able to persevere with his novel? The place, too, didn't seem likely to distract or irritate him. He had never been to Wellington, but it was small (a population of around 5,000), unpretentious, and he liked the idea of remaining in the same band of middle England that he had always regarded as home. Insofar as the town had any associations at all for him, they were attractive ones: it was crouched at the foot of the Wrekin, a large, tree-covered hill mentioned in Housman's *A Shropshire Lad*. Better still, he would be a short train-ride away from Bruce Montgomery in Shrewsbury. Reckoning this was 'a good omen',[13] he decided to apply.

Sydney helped Larkin complete his application, and also recommended how he might prepare for the interview. He presented him with a copy of a report that had been published the previous year entitled *The Public*

Library System of Great Britain and told him to find out how Coventry library worked. 'A friendly senior assistant,' Larkin recalled later, 'was kind enough to spend a morning showing me how books were ordered, accessioned and catalogued, and then given little pockets with individual tickets in them that were slipped into borrowers' cards when the book was lent.'[14] The orderliness of these procedures suited Larkin, though when he told Sutton what he was up to, he was careful to sound disaffected. He had been, he said, 'insane'[15] to apply to Wellington:

(a) I am too brilliant (you should see my testimonials! Jesus Christ, man!)
(b) I know sweet fuck all about librarianship. ('Ah, yes, you want *The Mortal Storm* by Phyllis Arse do you – pardon me, I mean Bottome, yes, of course . . . well do you, do you? Then permit me to inform you that you are the son of a whore . . .') See, I obviously shouldn't stop there very long. Still, nothing like trying. The job does not repel me on sight as many do. I should enjoy introducing lots of Lawrence and Isherwood into the placid shelves.[16]

On 13 November Larkin travelled through heavy rain to Wellington for his interview, clutching his green-bound copy of *The Public Library System of Great Britain*. Three days later, back in Warwick, he received a letter addressed to 'Mr Larking' from the Chief Clerk to the Urban District Council, Mr Astley-Jones (later to reappear as the ratchet-voiced head librarian in *A Girl in Winter*), telling him that he had got the job. Larkin wrote back pointing out the correct spelling of his name, querying the salary, and saying that he wasn't prepared to give a definite undertaking to stay in Wellington for a fixed period. When he heard from Astley-Jones a second time he accepted: he would begin work on 1 December.

Larkin reacted to the news with a mixture of pleasure, trepidation, and irritation at having to set aside his novel. He made a few preliminary visits to Wellington to look for lodgings, staying overnight in bed-and-breakfast places, and as he tramped the town he became more and more depressed. It was hideously split into two parts by a railway line. Only a handful of distinguished buildings (one a porticoed eighteenth-century church) stood out among its acres of Georgian and Victorian red brick. The central market area thickened into an ugly huddle. The Wrekin, covered in undergrowth, rose above the rooftops like a promise of romance which had long been betrayed. The chance of finding creative solitude turned into the prospect of blank loneliness. The hopes of finding a cosy flat dwindled into cold discomfort. When Larkin complained about these things to Bruce Montgomery, Montgomery told him to pull himself together:

Is this Orwellian grumble about sharing a bed literally *true*? If it is, I must say you rather alarm me. *Surely* you can get a *bedroom* by yourself? I don't think you push and agitate enough. You set out with the idea the whole thing's going to be beastly, become resigned, and not unnaturally discover that it *is* beastly. It's the same with your literary work. You set out with a conviction that anything you write will be a minute thing, nugatory and immature, and the human mind on the whole being an obedient instrument, of course it turns out like that. More willpower, Philip! More determination, you scaggot![17]

In later life Larkin was slightly ashamed of the timidity he showed when arriving in Wellington. He knew other people would think he made too much fuss about little things and wonder why he didn't take a flat of his own. His parents would have helped him – they had his best interests at heart. But that, he knew, was the point. His parents had his interests too much at heart, and were partly to blame for his incompetence. In Oxford the routines of college life had spared him from having to fend much for himself, even when he was living in Walton Street. At home he had been deeply and systematically spoiled. He had never cooked a meal, never washed his own clothes, never had to pay a bill. When he went to Wellington he looked older than his years: thin-faced, already beginning to go bald, his eyes severely shielded behind thick wire-framed glasses. In practical terms, though, he was in a state of almost child-like ignorance about the ordinary things of life. 'I simply attempted to find lodgings and lived in them,' he said later. 'The idea of getting a flat for myself was, you know, beyond my imagination.'[18]

When Larkin eventually screwed up his courage – or rather, exploited his lack of it – he settled on a 'tiny'[19] place in Alexander House (40 New Church Road), a gaunt Victorian pile on the east side of town, surrounded by evergreens. It was only a five-minute walk from the library, but utterly cheerless: a small chilly bedroom, and a sitting-room, kitchen and bath-room he shared with two other lodgers. Larkin told his parents miserably in his first letter home that his landlady, Miss Jones, wouldn't allow him to play his jazz records and had 'rigged [him] up ... with a radiator that doesn't work yet but "one of the men will fix it" '.[20] He was only to stay at this address for a couple of months, but its gloom helped to create an impression of Wellington which never entirely left him. What might have been his first exciting step towards independent adult life was a frightened shuffle.

Before Larkin had a chance to visit the very few family acquaintances who lived in the region, he started work. His predecessor, the antique 'librarian-caretaker'[21] Mr Bennett, who had been appointed in 1902, showed him round the library. He was 'a courtly old gentleman of at least seventy', Larkin said later, 'who wore a hat indoors and uttered from time to time an absent-minded blowing noise, like a distant trombone'.[22] Although Larkin knew virtually nothing about libraries, it was immediately clear that he had joined a one-horse institution in a one-horse town. The library building itself was a small, two-storey affair standing a little outside the central market area; it had a reading room on the ground floor, and a lending library and office-cum-reference room upstairs. Opened to commemorate the coronation of Edward VII in 1902 (and announcing this fact on its pediment), it was covered outside with grime-darkened rusticated stone, and filled inside with shelving of 'a heavy Edwardian type about eight foot high'.[23] The atmosphere was stuffy and faintly intimidating (borrowers had to ask at a window for the books they required), the stock poor (four thousand titles, of which three thousand were fiction), and the expectations of readers were low. Larkin had known from the outset that he would be working alone, but soon discovered that this involved him in responsibilities he would gladly have done without. As well as issuing and cataloguing books, dealing with readers and borrowers, and arguing with the Urban District Council about the need for improvements, he also had to stoke the boiler every morning, and contend with the gas lights which 'had to be illuminated with long tapers that dropped wax over the floors, and even on myself until I learned how to handle them'.[24] And one other thing. 'The real thorn in his flesh,' a friend remembers, 'was the reading room. It was ... open from 9 in the morning to 8.30 at night and offering as it did not only newspapers and periodicals but also free warmth and seating, it exercised a magnetic attraction for the tramps of the area. Once in, they were difficult to dislodge, and as the lending library and librarian's office were on the floor above, undesirables could arrive with little chance of being seen and interrupted.'[25]

Larkin quailed, torn between dread and contempt. '[I] spend most of my time handing out tripey novels to morons,' he told Sutton. 'I feel it is not at all a suitable occupation for a man of acute sensibility and genius ... The books in the library are mostly very poor, but there is a copy of *Aaron's Rod*, *Bliss*, *The Garden Party* and *Crome Yellow*, all of which make me feel at home. I can't imagine how they got there. There's no poetry later than Housman.'[26] It was not just the materials he had to deal with, but the monotony of his work that depressed him. He arrived at 9 each morning, sorted out the previous day's tickets until 11, then returned to Alexander

House 'for lunch and meditation'.[27] After lunch he worked in the library again from 3 to 5 before 'going off to a slatternly café full of soldiers for coffee and spam sandwiches',[28] then returned to the library for another stint from 6 until 8 before finally 'lounging' in his digs after supper 'until 10.30 or 11 when I go to bed'.[29]

After his first few days Larkin was convinced that he had made a mistake in accepting the job. After a month he started to change his mind. He missed home less and valued his escape from his parents – and the war – more; he began to accept his new routines; he even started to feel forgiving towards some of the 'morons' he served – the male ones, anyway.

There are some very decent men in the library – working men, you know, not labourers exactly (though there is one enormous Irish fellow called Clancy who is a perpetual delight to me) but quiet men in cloth caps who take out books of a rather serious kind with a serious expression on their face, as if they are seriously trying to get a grasp on things . . . They talk very gingerly and diffidently, as if they are afraid I shall laugh at them. It's the women that are the stupid sods. I hate women when it comes to choosing books.[30]

Larkin kept his 'hatred' well hidden. In the reminiscences of those who knew him in the library, there are as many accounts by women as there are by men praising his helpfulness and lack of condescension. Margaret Bell, who was thirteen years old when Larkin arrived and already a keen reader, is typical. 'I remember him being tall, shy and quietly spoken,' she says. 'He seemed older than he was, but he never talked down . . . I was then at a stage when I was leaving Arthur Ransome behind and moving on to adult books. The choice was not great, but I remember clearly going to have some books stamped and him saying, "You don't really want to waste your time on that, do you?"'[31]

In later life, when called upon to explain his success as a librarian, Larkin said, 'A librarian can be one of a number of things. He can be almost a pure scholar or he can be a technician . . . or he can be a pure administrator, or he . . . can be just a nice chap to have around which is the role I vaguely thought I filled.'[32] It was a typically self-effacing judgement. In all the libraries which employed him, Larkin combined the roles of scholar, technician and administrator, and increasingly regarded these things as more important than the requirement to be 'nice'. At Wellington, undeterred by his lack of experience, he quickly shook the place into a new sense of itself. He changed most of the systems used by his predecessor, and 'very soon there was hardly a trace left'[33] of Mr Bennett's forty-year reign. He lobbied at the bi-monthly Library Committee meetings of the Urban District Council; he improved stock and inter-library lending facilities; he did what he could to brighten the interior of the building; and he set about making himself of more use to the borrowers by beginning a correspondence course which would eventually qualify him as a member of the Library Association.

Needless to say, not all the pleasures of working in the library were to do with library business. Larkin's school and Oxford self – the self which enjoyed pursuing strictly personal interests behind a socially respectable front – made sure of that. After the 'hideous crescendo' of 'rushing down to the library' with the newspapers every morning, and the opening of post and inter-library loan work which took him through until lunch, he was able to retreat into his office and lead an alternative life. He kept it more or less secret at the time, but later openly admitted that 'from 11 until 3, when you were supposed to open to readers to lend books, your time was more or less your own, and I wrote in the library behind closed doors or went back to my lodgings after lunch and wrote there'.[34]

Before the year ended, Larkin also found more sociable ways of spending his time. He joined the local branch of the YMCA so that he could use their snooker table. One of the family acquaintances who lived nearby took him out to dinner and introduced him to a fellow-librarian in Shrewsbury called Adams. He met a local schoolteacher called Rosalind Musselthwaite and walked up the Wrekin with her (it left him, he said, 'feeling like a piece of chewed string'[35]). He went out once or twice with a telephone operator from Birmingham called Margaret Sutton. He wrote frequently and copiously to his friends, especially to Amis and Jim Sutton. More appealing, and more important, were his meetings with Montgomery. There was a regular train service across the twelve miles which separated Wellington from Shrewsbury,[36] and their get-togethers became the high spot of most weeks, even though it pained Larkin to see how much less comfortably off he was than Montgomery. After the first visit to Shrewsbury he admitted to his parents that he 'wept at the contrast: the enormous beautiful school, set among avenues of rich houses, the regal view of the town from the hill, the classrooms and the bellowing voices from them – and the house [Montgomery] lives in! Sumptuous ain't the word ... He is one of the rich in spirit who will always have a happy lot.'[37]

As Larkin got used to Wellington, his friendship with Montgomery recovered its balance – or deliberate lack of it. One of the main purposes of their weekly encounters was to get drunk. 'You somewhat alarmed me by suddenly falling over a wall like that,' Montgomery wrote after one session, 'and I sincerely hope you're all right. You recovered your equanimity with remarkable speed, but write and reassure me. There's nothing like a good evening's drinking, is there!'³⁸ After another, during which Larkin had put away eight pints, he admitted to Sutton that he had 'tried to break into a shop'.³⁹ After yet another, as Amis later discovered, there were even more disastrous consequences:

In those days, before he started making real money, Bruce had been a beer drinker, a fanatical one by Philip's account, setting a cruel pace and insisting on being closely followed. After a prolonged session, the pair had the hardihood to attend a meeting of the school literary society [in Shrewsbury School]. Philip found himself in the chair furthest from the door with hundreds of boys, many sitting on the floor, between him and any exit. Quite soon after everybody was settled a tremendous desire to urinate came upon him. Finding he could not face causing the upheaval that must have attended his leaving the room, and reasoning, if that is the word, that he was wearing a lot of clothes, including, in those days of fuel rationing, a heavy overcoat, he decided to rely on their absorbent qualities and intentionally pissed himself. It turned out that he had miscalculated.⁴⁰

As well as drinking, Montgomery and Larkin spent a great deal of time talking about their respective novels. By the time he reached Shrewsbury, Montgomery was at work on his second, and Larkin reported to him regularly on his own progress with *Jill*. They chivvied and encouraged each other, with Montgomery trying to quench in Larkin the tendency to anticipate failure, and Larkin urging Montgomery to write more carefully. When Larkin began producing poems again early in the new year, Montgomery also tried to control the influence of Yeats which (thanks to Watkins) was now pervasive. 'Now and then I do a poem,' Larkin told Sutton, 'which Bruce reads dolefully and says, "It won't do, you know, it's not as good as the others." This tends to annoy me but he is probably right.'⁴¹ Just how much he agreed can be judged from a series of twelve cartoon sketches Larkin sent to Montgomery: 'Life with Phairy Phantasy, a Morality in Pictures. Drawn by Mr P.A.L.' In these cartoons, 'the fairy of poetic inspiration is shown leading a young poet . . . away from his former pleasant life of gin, cigarettes and novels, and into a mystical world of occultism and Oxo-drinking', in which the poet shows 'distressing sartorial affinities with Mr W. B. Yeats' and an 'aptitude with time to float away utterly'.⁴² More briskly, in the Introduction to *The North Ship*,

Larkin remembers Montgomery 'snapping, as I droned for the third or fourth time that evening, "When such as I cast out remorse,/So great a sweetness flows into the breast . . .", It's not his job to cast out remorse, but to earn forgiveness.'[43]

Because Montgomery's reputation has declined since his death in 1978, and because the early promise of his career was never fulfilled, the ways in which he helped to form Larkin have disappeared from view. They have been submerged beneath accounts of the more celebrated literary friendship between Larkin and Amis. There is, though, no doubt that during Larkin's isolation in Wellington, and especially during his first year there, it was Montgomery who encouraged and directed him with more purpose than anyone else. By combining a devoted commitment to writing with a huge appetite for drinking and fooling around, he gave Larkin a model of the ways in which art could avoid pretension. Not surprisingly, this encouraged similarities in the local details of their work as well as its general intentions. A character called Warner appears in both their first novels; Larkin provided the idea for the plot of Montgomery's best book, *The Moving Toyshop* (1946), and also 'wrote the shaming pages about poetry';[44] Larkin is thanked for making 'valuable suggestions' in the preface to *Holy Disorders* (1945); and Montgomery's hero Gervase Fen (in spite of his fancy name) steadily combines intellect and 'anti-intellectualism'[45] in a way The Seven would have recognized and applauded.

In the early 1950s, when critics and journalists began to describe characteristics they associated with The Movement, Montgomery was no longer visible enough in Larkin's life for them to credit him as a decisive influence. But Larkin himself never disguised it. His response to the dedication 'To Philip Larkin, in Friendship and Esteem' which opens *The Moving Toyshop* was to dedicate the first poem in *The North Ship* to Montgomery, and also his second and last complete novel, *A Girl in Winter*. When he presented Montgomery with a copy of *The North Ship* he wrote in the front 'To Bruce Montgomery, for his kindness about these poems'. When he finished *Jill* he sent a copy 'with love and sincere thanks for encouraging this book'. When he gave Montgomery his dedicatee's copy of *A Girl in Winter* he inscribed it, 'To Bruce, whose consistent critical enthusiasms and encouragements resulted in this book'.[46]

SIXTEEN

To-ing and fro-ing between Wellington and Shrewsbury, toiling in the grim library and his grimmer lodgings, Larkin soon felt his new life was settling into a pattern. Then everything changed. For the first time, he fell in love.

Ruth Bowman was a sixteen-year-old schoolgirl at the local high school and a regular borrower from the library. Although schoolgirls had featured a good deal in Larkin's half-lustful, half-facetious conversations at Oxford about sex, and although they were in their different ways the main fascination of Brunette's novels as well as *Jill*, Ruth was unlike everything he had imagined. Where the most interesting characters in *Willow Gables* **and** *St Bride's* had been purely knowing and the embryo Jill purely unobtainable, Ruth was neither quite one thing nor the other. She was innocent but she was real. Her tender age put her beyond his reach, but it also made her malleable. Larkin could turn her into whatever he wanted – if he could only decide what that was.

It wasn't just Ruth's age which made her impressionable. She was also startlingly unacquainted with the world – 'a prim little small town girl', as she says herself, 'with a Methodist background'.[1] Her father, who had worked as a radio officer for Cunard, had died when she was eleven, and her mother had brought her up – an only child – in 'straitened circumstances'[2] in Herbert Avenue, a respectable road in a residential area of Wellington, close to the foot of the Wrekin. The modest house, with its half-timbering over the garage door, and tree-fenced trim front garden, was owned by her mother's parents; it had filled her with ambitions to escape to a wider world, as had Wellington itself. 'It was a town almost entirely without character,' she remembers. 'Depressing, empty, old-fashioned – especially during the war.' It offered very little by way of culture.'[3]

In such a desert the library was an oasis, and although Larkin's predecessor had seemed to 'loathe children'[4] ,and kept only two shelves of books for them, with 'nothing more recent than *Tom Brown*',[5] Ruth had nevertheless managed to read widely enough to know that she wanted to study English at university. Her mother encouraged her, and so did her grandparents (her grandfather had been sub-editor of the local paper). By the autumn of 1943 she had taken the first step towards fulfilling her hopes – successfully passing her School Certificate – and was pleased to find the new librarian eager to help her. 'To those of us who needed more reference and non-fiction books and longed for more up-to-date fiction,' she says, 'his arrival was heaven-sent.'[6]

The schoolgirl Larkin first saw was small, bespectacled, dark-haired, and with a slight adolescent plumpness. In later life Larkin would insist that she was nothing special to look at (in 'Wild Oats' she is slighted as a 'friend in specs'), partly to bolster his self-image as someone incapable of enjoying himself, partly to prove that he would have had no difficulty in doing without her. With Amis he was particularly disparaging.[7] Cruelties behind Ruth's back were matched by other, more obvious ones when she met Larkin in the company of her friend Jane Exall, who according to Amis was 'rather fine looking',[8] and appears in 'Wild Oats' as the beautiful 'bosomy English rose'. 'I would find [Jane] hard to resist if she gave me anything to resist,' Larkin told Amis, admitting that when he did once take her out 'all I got was a damp kiss on the ear. It's just not worth it. The food alone came to £3.'[9] In their discussion of both women, neither Larkin nor Amis seems to have mentioned something much more striking than who was pretty and who wasn't – namely, that Ruth looked like Larkin himself. Her apprehensive, short-sighted face mirrored his own self-doubt and potential self-disgust.

Throughout his time at Oxford, Larkin had been snubbed by girls, confused by his feelings for Brown, disappointed with himself. The nervous antagonism he had shown towards women in his first term had increased steadily until his last. Soon after taking his Final exams he had summed up his thoughts in a letter to Amis:

I personally think that going out with women is not worth it. I don't want to start a serious argument exactly, but the amount of time one has to lay out in tedious and expensive and embarrassing pursuits seems to me too much for what sketchy and problematic gains may accrue. If there were a straightforward social code that copulation could be indulged in after a couple of drinks (one of which the woman stood) then I should be more enthusiastic . . . I wrote a poem yesterday, this is it:

> I would give all I possess
> (Money keys wallet personal effects and articles of dress)
>
> To stick my tool
> Up the prettiest girl in Warwick King's High School.[10]

Larkin accepted that his attitude in this letter was 'timid' and 'unmanly'. He might have added 'mean'. 'The thought of going to bed with a woman,' he told Amis elsewhere, was 'so much trouble, almost as much trouble as standing for parliament.'[11] And elsewhere again: 'The whole business of sex annoys me. As far as I can see, all women are stupid beings. What is more, marriage is a revolting institution.'[12] In his surviving pocket diaries, he twice made the same point even more bluntly. 'Sex is too good to share with anyone else,' he jotted down in one, and in another: 'Re sexual intercourse: always disappointing and often repulsive, like asking someone else to blow your own nose for you.'[13]

Larkin's main fear was that if he got married he would end up imitating his parents' misery, trapped with 'someone who'll call me a "funny old creature"'.[14] But there were other worries as well, the main one being that marriage was incompatible with writing. In 1970, reviewing a critical biography of Edward Thomas, he said that Thomas, 'like many writers', was 'not suited' to marriage, and believed that his work suffered as a result. 'The two sides of his life were intertwined, like swimmers dragging each other down: marriage meant children, children meant more hack work, hack work meant more domesticity.'[15] Other reviews and interviews repeat the same message. 'Love collides very sharply with selfishness,' he said, 'and they're both pretty powerful things.'[16]

Clearly Larkin was only able to conceive of marriage in the most orthodox terms. It inevitably meant steadiness, faithfulness, constant companionship – and children. Children were especially threatening. He felt that if his wife were to allow him any time to himself, children would immediately invade it. The prospect horrified him, and his revulsion eventually became notorious. Reviewing *The Lore and Language of School-children* by Iona and Peter Opie in 1959, he said:

It was that verse about becoming again as a little child that caused the first sharp waning of my Christian sympathies. If the Kingdom of Heaven could be entered only by those fulfilling such a condition I knew I should be unhappy there. It was not the prospect of being deprived of money, keys, wallet, letters, books, long-playing records, drinks, the opposite sex, and other solaces of adulthood that upset me (I should have been about eleven), but having to put up indefinitely with the company of other children, their noise, their nastiness, their boasting, their back-answers, their cruelty, their silliness. Until I began to meet grown-ups on more or less equal terms I fancied myself a kind of Ishmael. The realization that it was not people I disliked but children was for me one of those celebrated moments of revelation, comparable to reading Haeckel or Ingersoll in the last century.[17]

Terrorized by sex, money, time, parental example and children, Larkin hesitated to take even the most tentative step towards anyone else, even a girl such as Ruth. Had Ruth fully understood this, she admits that she might have approached him 'more cautiously'.[18] As it was, she simply felt excited that something new had come into her life. 'He made a big contribution to the culture of the town,' she says. 'It was quite an impact. There were lots of old unwelcoming people who resisted him bringing in "unsuitable" books by Aldous Huxley, Lawrence, Joyce, but he was interested in what was taken from the shelves. I remember borrowing *Crome Yellow* and *Death of a Hero*; we began to talk about them.'[19]

Ruth was flattered to find an 'older man with inner resources'[20] confiding in her, especially when she discovered that Larkin was not as sophisticated and self-sufficient as he appeared. Beneath his forbidding manner, she found him 'starved for company', miserable in his 'comfortless digs'.[21] 'He used to stammer very badly in public then, of course,' she says, 'but in private it soon went away.'[22] When he told her that he was writing a novel, and had a friend in Shrewsbury who was about to publish one, she was 'star-struck'.[23] To meet a writer in Wellington seemed a marvel; it made her all the more anxious to become his friend, and fuelled her own ambitions.

It wasn't long before the town started gossiping. Stella Bishop, a contemporary of Ruth's at the High School, remembers: 'We often saw [them] walking up Haygate Road towards Herbert Avenue reciting poetry to each other. [Ruth's] smallness compared to his height amused my friend and I [*sic*] and we did laugh at the time, but many times since I've thought how romantic it really was; they were lost to the world. She looked at him with such adoring eyes.'[24] In due course the school authorities told Ruth to 'stop bothering the new librarian',[25] but when she passed the message on to Larkin he told her not to worry. ' "I'm so grateful," he said, "to have anyone to whom I can speak with a modicum of freedom." '[26]

Their feelings slipped from liking into infatuation and from infatuation into love. Although they didn't actually become lovers until after Ruth's eighteenth birthday (which was in May 1945), they were giving all the signs of being an established couple by early 1944. Neighbours other than Stella Bishop would see Larkin walking Ruth home in the evenings; the school accused her of becoming 'arrogant, insolent and difficult' as he encouraged her to 'be a rebel';[27] and five months after their first meeting she took him to meet her mother Ellen. The visit threw Larkin into a tizzy. Before arriving for tea, he went back from the library to his digs and had his second shave of the day. He cut himself, and spent most of the subsequent meal dabbing at his face with a blood-stained handkerchief. The room, Ruth says, was 'horribly stilled and distressing' when he left, and her mother pronounced him 'arty', 'unreliable' and 'doomed to cause heartbreak'.[28]

The young couple carried on regardless. Meeting in Larkin's office in the library, in his digs when no one else was around, or sometimes in a local pub called The Raven where he had bagged a quiet corner that other regulars regarded as 'his', he set out all his opinions for her to examine (and often to emulate). They agreed about the unavoidable tediousness of parents; they differed about religion ('he was infuriated by my sense of the numinous,'[29] Ruth says); there was no dispute about the paramount importance of writing; about the possibility of reconciling writing with marriage – well, they would see. The more they talked, the more fervently Ruth wanted to be and do whatever he needed. 'I had no other loyalty but to him,' she says. 'I adored him. He was everything to me.'[30] She even stole for him the High School's copy of Yeats's poems – the copy mentioned in the Introduction to *The North Ship*, where Larkin describes how after he had shut the library in the evenings and finished his supper, and 'before opening my large dark green manuscript book I used to limber up by turning the pages of the 1933 plum-coloured Macmillan edition, which stopped at "A Woman Young and Old" and which meant in fact that I never absorbed the harsher last poems'.[31]

After Larkin's death, Ruth wrote an account of their time together, in which she surveys these early happy Wellington days and the later, more difficult ones they feared would soon come:

What was it like being with him? In two words: never dull ... At first I was awestruck by his erudition and knowledge of modern fiction ... but as we became more friendly and our conversation more general and relaxed, his sense of humour was probably what I remember most. It ranged from devastatingly caustic when he was talking of people he disliked (and their name was legion), to gentle and charming as when he indulged me in my abiding passion for cats. (Dare I say it, but we later had a fantasy of his being a bear and me a cat: fertile ground for silly puns, etc.) Whatever his attitude he unfailingly expressed it with incisive brilliance, and he was so good at off-the-cuff, spontaneous word play. ('I see there's a sequel to *My Friend Flicka*,' I said on the subject of films we might see. 'It's called *Thunderhead, Son of Flicka*.' 'Dunderhead, Son of Thicker,' growled Philip without a second's hesitation.)

I was, as a sheltered and provincial young woman, at first often shocked by the robustness of the language in which he expressed his wit and by his outrageous sentiments, but if I found any part of his conversation distasteful and said so he might grumble at my prudishness but he would carefully avoid such expressions again. Oddly enough he had a Puritan streak which made him outraged if I attempted to reply in kind.

He was a brilliant mimic, and every train journey, every chance meeting furnished him with material for a wickedly exaggerated monologue which had me helpless with laughter. On these occasions he was the best company in the world. Our sense of the ridiculous was very much in accord and moments of tension between us could sometimes mercifully be resolved by our ability to make each other laugh.

These were the good times, but they could be followed by a mood of such profound depression that he was quite unreachable. At such a time he could say wounding, even really cruel things, usually because his blackest moods were brought about by his feeling unable to write or when what he was writing dissatisfied him, and then he resented whatever he saw as a distraction from his true vocation as a writer. This was usually me so I have reason to remember just how deep was his gloom and how total his hopelessness. After all, whatever life brought it was only a path towards death, the ultimate unescapable horror. I found this belief hard to encompass: in our healthy twenties no other friends of mine gave death a thought, certainly not as a reality for us, and yet . . . it was never far from Philip's thoughts. Over the years of our relationship I sadly came to accept that depression and melancholy were more natural to him than happiness and optimism. At such times he was a very draining companion; his despair could be infectious.

Yet he could be loving, patient and kind. His sympathy and sensitiveness to the moods and needs of others, his gentleness and consideration, were just as important a part of his character as his self-absorption, and consequently he could make me as happy as at other times he could make me desolate. He could give himself with total generosity – but only for a little while. Then he must withdraw and have equally total cut-off.[32]

Larkin was worried about what his friends would think of his new arrangements. Bruce Montgomery was comparatively easy to deal with. Larkin continued to see him a great deal, and when he took Ruth with him to Shrewsbury she found Montgomery 'charming and funny without being cruel'.[33] Amis, whom she didn't encounter until the war had ended, was another matter. 'He wanted to make Philip a "love 'em and lose 'em" type,' she felt. 'He was possessive of Philip and tried to keep me separate from him.'[34] Amis, in turn, found Ruth 'rather puritanical'. There was, he remembers Larkin telling him, 'a card in the Wellington library which said

"ENTER MARRIED WOMEN UNDER THEIR MARRIED NAME", and when Larkin joked with her about this she said, "I'm not Kingsley, you know."[35] Ruth felt Larkin behaved 'honourably'[36] in the face of these difficulties, but they made her think that he was always a little remote, always keeping something back. It wasn't just that she feared what he might say about her when she was out of earshot (even in his letters to his parents he called her 'the widow's daughter'[37]). She also suspected that he depended on his melancholy, and resisted her efforts to lift him when he was down. Proving the point, she sorrowfully remembers a train journey they once took together. Larkin suddenly interrupted their talk and sat slumped and silent. 'What's the matter?' Ruth wanted to know. 'I've just thought what it would be like to be old and have no one to look after you,' Larkin announced, evidently relishing his own unhappiness.

In her youth and gentleness, Ruth believed that these bleak moods would gradually get fewer and further between. She told herself that *Jill* would be published to acclaim. They would be able to leave Wellington. They might even be able to talk about marriage more equably.

SEVENTEEN

Larkin had always intended that Alexander House should be a temporary address. By January 1944, after spending Christmas with his parents, he thought he had found somewhere more suitable: a boarding house in King Street called Glentworth. It stood on the western edge of town opposite the Plough Inn, and was, like Alexander House, only a five-minute walk from the library – through the graveyard of All Saints Church. A rambling Victorian building, Glentworth was owned by a draper who had vainly tried to brighten its appearance by painting the window-frames dull cream and the sills dark green. Miss Tomlinson, the landlady, charged him 35s. a week for a large bedroom, as well as a kitchen, sitting-room and bathroom he had to share with three other lodgers. (The house has since been demolished and a garage built where it stood.)

Larkin moved before the end of January and was immediately disappointed. 'There is plenty to grumble about,' he told his parents. 'It is undeniably dirty: the food is scarce and occasionally badly prepared (we had an incredible kind of ray fish last week that smelt and tasted strongly of ammonia) and Miss Tomlinson is uncouth and moody.'[1] His fellow-lodgers added greatly to his discomfort – the art master at the High School, Leslie Spaull; a 'youngish, rosy, moustached, tall man, insufferably boring and pedestrian'[2] called Evans who worked for the local brewery; and a journalist called Mansley who 'sucks his teeth and belches softly'.[3] Evans, in particular, infuriated him. 'The trouble is,' Larkin told Sutton, who was still with the RASC in Italy 'he regards the natural state of two strangers in the same room as conversation. I regard it as respectful and preoccupied silence. In consequence he tries to make conversation, which I consider rude, and I try to shut him up, which no doubt he considers rude. He's one of those people who regard you as a fit target for conversation if you are reading a book. The cunt.'[4]

When the lodgers weren't driving him crazy there was always (as there would be later in 'Mr Bleaney') a 'jabbering' wireless to try his patience. 'Christ, the blasted wireless is loud,' he complained time and again to Sutton. 'No wonder Dickens and Trollope and Co. could write such enormous books, if this bastard way of rotting the mind hadn't been thought up.'[5] To make matters worse, Larkin's friendship with Montgomery suddenly and briefly went through another difficult patch. In February, when Montgomery published *The Case of the Gilded Fly*, it reinforced Larkin's own sense of failure. Although he was approaching the end of his first draft of *Jill*, he was gravely doubtful about its chances of success, and envious of his friend. 'I have seen reviews and handled copies like the Israelites picking up manna and wondering what the fuck it was,' he wrote to Sutton. 'What is more, most of the reviews have been favourable, and that surprises me, because the book is not terribly good, even when one makes allowance for the kind of book it is.'[6]

Montgomery was delighted with his success but sensitive to Larkin's feelings. He urged him to finish *Jill*, and drenched him with 'heady optimism'[7] until he finally completed work on it 'at 9.10 on Sunday May 14th'.[8] Montgomery then read it, liked it, made some suggestions about revisions to the last chapter, and offered to send it to his acquaintance Charles Williams, who was a director of Oxford University Press, intending that he should in turn pass it on to T. S. Eliot at Faber. 'This is such a tenuous and dizzy chain of impossibilities that I don't place much faith in it,'[9] Larkin told him even before finishing the book, but he was grateful. He was pleased, too, soon to continue the pattern of regular meetings with Montgomery that he had established before Christmas.

Tuesday was market day in the 'crapulous town'[10] of Shrewsbury and the pubs were open from 10.30 in the morning until 10.30 at night: it became Larkin's regular day for visiting Montgomery (it was his day off at the library). At other times of the week Montgomery would travel to Wellington to drink and talk in The Raven.

Larkin's jealousy of Montgomery quickened his tendency to excessive self-criticism. Whereas in March, as he drew near the end of *Jill*, he felt that he was 'in a period of subdued excellence',[11] and could report 'to my surprise that I've kept up an average of 700 words a day since being here',[12] a month later he was not so sure. 'I used to think I was a relatively stable person,' he told Sutton, 'but these days I'm up in the air and down in the shit non-stop.'[13] A month later still, he was even more volatile. Although work in the library left him less 'urgently discontented'[14] than he had been to start with, although a finished novel was better than no novel at all, although he had Ruth, he felt bitterly depressed and lonely. He turned to Sutton, who in combining sympathy with distance (they now hadn't seen each other for four years) made the perfect audience. His other friends, he said, were 'all right up to a point ... [But] Art has seemed to them a sort of clever competence which can be done at will ... and to a certain extent I have allowed myself to fall in with this view and be led away – *and it won't do* ... Art requires more modesty, more self-effacement, more *delicate listening* than they can begin to understand. You know that, and so I thirst for your company.'[15]

Earlier this same spring, Larkin had tried to fight his way out of his misery by analysing it. 'The strongest feeling I have these days,' he had said to Sutton in May, 'is a double one – personal sorrow and impersonal joy. Everything that my personality colours is a balls up – my own affairs and so on. But when I am being "no more, no less than two weak eyes" everything is filled with a blessed light, bells, bugles, brightness and lord knows what. It's an odd feeling, and the split – which seems to widen day by day – is alarming.'[16] For several weeks it looked as though Larkin's attempts to heal this 'split' would come to nothing. Then, in the early summer, help came from an unexpected quarter. With the fate of *Jill* undecided (Charles Williams had said he couldn't help, and Montgomery had sent the manuscript to Gollancz, who would eventually reject it), Larkin received a letter from R. A. Caton, the owner of The Fortune Press. It was nearly two years since they had last been in touch, when Charles Hamblett had inquired whether Larkin would submit work for the anthology *Poetry from Oxford in Wartime*. After the initial spurt of excitement nothing had happened. Now the idea was revived, and the contact this time was through 'some chap I dimly knew at Oxford'[17] – William Bell of Merton College. Undaunted by the dilatoriness of The Fortune Press, Larkin sent ten poems he had written since arriving in Wellington. They were all accepted.

There's very little anecdote or narrative in these ten poems. They contain nothing about arriving in a new place, nothing precise about the local landscape, nothing detailed about Ruth, nothing about Larkin's lodgings or his work. Even the poem which comes closest to telling a story, 'I see a girl dragged by the wrists', ends up substituting observed facts for symbolic speculations. Occasionally there are indications that some sort of struggle is taking place between these two things – between fancy rhetoric and everyday circumstances – but on the whole Larkin is happy to surrender his interest in the quotidian, and settle instead for the misty imaginative world he had derived from Yeats.

This world seems remote, but it reveals Larkin's state of mind very accurately. Sheltering behind the clichés and conventions of such things as an invocation to spring, running water, the moon, rivers, and 'the horns of morning', he is able to concentrate on the conflicts which had beset him since his arrival in Wellington. One set of contradictions stemmed from his sense that any impulse to '"Rejoice!"' had to accommodate the knowledge that 'A drum taps: a wintry drum'. In later poems this is worked up and elaborated into one of his major themes, but here it takes second place to another and more urgent concern: love. Some of these poems admit that love and desire are wholly exciting; others find them doubtful and even degrading – merely 'love and its commerce' – and leave him unsatisfied:

> The moon is full tonight
> And hurts the eyes,
> It is so definite and bright.
> What if it has drawn up
> All quietness and certitude of worth
> Wherewith to fill its cup,
> Or mint a second moon, a paradise? –
> For they are gone from earth.

As a way of trying to solve these tensions, Larkin strips away any realistic trappings from the object of his love – from Ruth – and turns her into an image. She becomes a fantasy figure, someone he's only really happy to meet in dreams. 'I wonder love can have already set/In dreams, when we've not met/More times than I can number on one hand', he says in 'Morning has spread again'. Similarly, the poem 'So through that unripe day' (in a passage which anticipates the imagery and subject of 'Lines on a Young Lady's Photograph Album') ends:

> Now we are safe.
> The days lose confidence, and can be faced
> Indoors. This is your last, meticulous hour,
> Cut, gummed; pastime of a provincial winter.

This transformation of Ruth makes two kinds of appeal. One, predictably, is to the self: by changing her from real to unreal Larkin secures for himself the freedom of solitude, in which he can practise whatever private dominations he chooses. The most striking passage in all ten poems (and one which again anticipates a later poem, this time 'Next, Please') is a powerful vision of separation and independence in 'Love, we must part now':

> There is regret. Always, there is regret.
> But it is better that our lives unloose,
> As two tall ships, wind-mastered, wet with light,
> Break from an estuary with their courses set,
> And waving part, and waving drop from sight.

The other appeal is more complicated. By turning Ruth into a fantasy figure Larkin conflates her role as lover with her associations as Muse, and thereby registers his need for her to be both in his life and distinct from it. In a poem eventually added to *The North Ship* several years after its first appearance, 'Waiting for breakfast' (which was written on 15 December 1947), he makes this explicit, wondering whether it's possible to be on speaking terms with the Muse ('you') and 'a real girl' ('her') at one and the same time:

> Are you jealous of her?
> Will you refuse to come till I have sent
> Her terribly away, importantly live
> Part invalid, part baby, and part saint?

In 'I see a girl dragged by the wrists' this argument appears only in embryo – but it's given a good deal of urgency because its terms are derived from worries about sex. Will the 'golden horn' of the elusive Muse be a match for the pleasures of erotic excitement in ordinary life? The poem wants us to believe the 'golden horn' gets the vote, but it can't quite manage to seem convinced:

> each dull day and each despairing act

>> Builds up the crags from which the spirit leaps
>> – The beast most innocent
>> That is so fabulous it never sleeps;
>> If I can keep against all argument
>> Such image of a snow-white unicorn,
>> Then as I pray it may for sanctuary
>> Descend at last to me,
>> And put into my hand its golden horn.

Within a few days of hearing that Bell would include him in *Poetry from Oxford in Wartime*, Larkin had a letter from Caton himself: would Larkin 'care to submit a volume of poems for consideration'?[18] He decided to delay. 'I wrote back,' he told Sutton, 'saying I should care very much but I just had not enough poems to make a satisfactory book.'[19] This was putting things too simply. In fact Larkin was happy to wait because he suspected that he would have a 'satisfactory book' before long: he had written as many poems in his first six months in Wellington as in all his time at Oxford. But he was also inclined to hesitate for other reasons. He didn't much like the idea of appearing on a list consisting largely of 'masterpieces for "students of intersex"',[20] and he was still bothered by Caton's reputation for inefficiency and his 'virtually non-existent'[21] distribution and royalties.

The longer Larkin waited to get in touch with Caton, the more uncertain he felt – especially since, when he came to look at it closely, the work he had produced during the middle part of the year seemed inferior to everything he had written at the beginning. A break in Warwick in August, during which he attended his sister Kitty's wedding, did nothing to help. (Sydney had retired as City Treasurer in April, so now he, as well as Eva, was 'there all day' at Coten End.) 'The brotherhood of man is a lot of balls,' he groused to Sutton. 'I do not give one single shag for anything but the creation of art or for anyone but actual or potential artists.'[22] In his diary he was even grumpier. 'Bloody service at St Nicholas' church, bloody reception at the Tudor House, bloody lot of people I didn't bloody well know. Couldn't get pissed. Bawd stiff.'[23] Larkin resented the wedding not just because it interrupted the rhythm of his own life, but because the sight of families on the rampage forced him to confront the future he was beginning to imagine with Ruth. Throughout his holiday in Warwick, everything seemed to justify the entry he had made in his diary on his recent birthday quoting Hugh Kingsmill's parody of A. E. Housman:

> What, still alive at twenty-two
> A clean upstanding lad like you?

I lie awake meditating suicide: Philip Larkin 1922–1944: he had outstayed his welcome. Life holds no promise of pleasure.[24]

When he returned to Wellington, Ruth could do little to reassure him. Feeling he 'must move',[25] he applied for a library job in London but was not summoned for an interview. Irritated, he debated with Sutton whether they might both leave England when the war ended, and swagger the nut-strewn roads in America. Even as he considered this, he knew he would never allow the idea to become a reality. Although his circumstances were depressing, they offered a strange sort of comfort. It suited him to feel that he had 'done'[26] with all his Oxford friends who were 'not artists', to bellyache about his lodgings, to rail against the domestic implications of love and the dreariness of Wellington, to object that his new poems were no good. These things justified the need for greater solitude and at the same time provided him with a subject.

Or rather, he thought they would provide him with a subject if he could manipulate them successfully. The problem was knowing how to prevent them overwhelming him. 'Life at present seems a series of minor irritations, humiliations, boredoms, frustrations and disgusts,' he told Sutton, 'none of which is worth bothering about at the time, but which in all produces a state of nervous rawness which quite precludes getting down to any writing.'[27] His least anxiety about these things was that they would distract him; his greatest was that they would altogether dull his curiosity about life. 'I have realized,' he said in the early autumn, as he began work on a second novel, 'that I don't care very much about the people in [the novel] and what they are doing. This is a bad thing. My poems don't seem to be able to capture the punch of the ones I wrote in the spring. Further, I don't care very much about anything. I don't care about putting literature over on the people, which is what most education, literary propagandists, booksellers, publishers, authors, librarians and other gombeen men are doing to earn a living.'[28]

Eventually this accumulating misery became the force which drove

Larkin to discover his true voice and subject as a poet. While he suffered its first onslaughts, though, it seemed merely a blight, and when Caton wrote to him again in mid-October, asking about progress with the collection, he regarded the letter as his only chance of release. Keeping his opinion of their quality to himself, he sent Caton everything he had written during the past year, under the title *The North Ship*. This meant, in addition to the ten poems already accepted for *Poetry from Oxford in Wartime*, twenty-one others, including 'Conscript' (dedicated to Sutton) and two poems ('This was your place of birth' and 'I dreamed of an out-thrust arm of land') which had been written at Oxford and published in undergraduate magazines. Such as it was, the earlier work was chosen because it conformed more or less exactly to the Yeatsian style of his later pieces. Virtually all trace of Auden was obliterated, and his 'split' poetic personality was concealed. An arty, *fin-de-siècle* manner dominated, no matter how vehemently Larkin insisted in private that 'more and more I feel [the poet] should wander unnoticed through life, colourless and unremarkable, wearing ordinary clothes, smoking a common brand of cigarette, hair parted on the left, queueing for cheap seats'.[29]

On 20 November, suspiciously soon after receiving Larkin's manuscript, Caton replied from his office in Buckingham Palace Road. '[We can] undertake publication,' he said, 'early next year, and perhaps have the book ready in February.'[30] Larkin was unimpressed by the lack of comment on his work, and wrote back asking what the details of the contract would be. A month later, on 23 December, Caton wrote again, thanking him for his letter and telling him that no agreement was necessary.[31] Reluctantly, Larkin acquiesced.

EIGHTEEN

The acceptance of *The North Ship* left Larkin with various practical worries, but it also stirred up his ambitions as a writer. When he returned to Wellington in January 1945 after visiting his parents in Warwick for Christmas, he immediately began to extend his plans. He pressed on with his new novel, now called *The Kingdom of Winter* (it would eventually become *A Girl in Winter*), and busily developed theories of his evolution as a poet. Most of his friends were too busy elsewhere to pay much attention: Amis was in Germany, Iles was 'hiding',[1] and Philip Brown was still in Oxford. More depressingly, he felt that kindred spirits closer to home couldn't give the sympathy and understanding he wanted. Montgomery, Larkin was beginning to feel, didn't 'realize that art is as near to religion as one can get',[2] and Ruth, though anxious to help him in this as everything else, didn't have the 'requisite ... interest in *style*, in *mechanics*'.[3] Only Sutton could provide the kind of audience he needed – the Sutton to whom he had written six months before, 'We must stick together both as people and as artists. There is no one like you for me: since you left [for the war] I have tried each friend carefully and plumbed them to their depths and found them wanting.'[4]

However affectionately Sutton replied to these protestations, he couldn't dispel Larkin's unhappiness. Nothing in the wider world seemed to connect with him ('I don't think there is anything to celebrate,' he said as the end of the war drew near) and nothing in Wellington cheered him either; he felt, he said, 'seven-eighths below the surface, like an iceberg'.[5] In April, when the local council agreed to grant him an assistant in the library, he still thought that he should leave as soon as possible. Threading his pursed-up way through the snow which lingered late into the spring, trapped in drab routines, counting on Ruth yet despising himself for needing her, he felt more and more doubtful of his future. He disliked *The North Ship* even before it appeared, and no one to whom he sent *Jill* wanted to publish it.

Caton kept the flame of his ambition alive – but only just. His first encouraging act had been to send, in November 1944, complimentary copies of the white-dust-jacketed anthology *Poetry from Oxford in Wartime* (which was published the following February). Larkin was not impressed. 'I have a copy,' he reported to Sutton. 'God, but it is chock full of shit. Naturally I think my poems good but really, by any standards, the rest is shit, or I should say considering the polite company we're in CRAP. *The North Ship* will be out in about three months and that will contain enough Larkin to wipe the arses of all the one-legged men in Nottingham. Throw in Derby, too.'[6]

'Three months' was hopeful. By March 1945, when proofs eventually arrived (a month later than the book itself had originally been promised), Larkin responded by asking Sutton, 'Why can't the bastards print the bastard book bastard bastard? Goddam son of a bitch a shite,'[7] and by nagging Caton angrily about the details and date of publication. When he gathered that he could expect the book at the end of July his rage subsided. He conceded that although Caton was in some ways a 'menace to young writers', he at least 'gave one the satisfaction of seeing one's work in print'.[8] The longer Larkin pondered this, the more convinced he became that he could do worse than let The Fortune Press have *Jill* as well as his poems. Before Caton had a chance to do anything else which might annoy him, he parcelled up the manuscript (on Easter Sunday) and posted it, asking Sutton whether he would 'accept [the novel] if I dedicated it to you?'[9] By the time Sutton had replied saying he would be honoured, Larkin had also heard from Caton: the Press would be happy to publish. It later transpired that Caton had taken on the book without reading it.

The Fortune Press managed to keep their word about publishing *The North Ship* in July. Copies were delivered on the 31st, dedicated to Sydney and Eva. Larkin had scattered the ten poems from *Poetry from Oxford in Wartime*, which he preferred to his more recent work, at regular intervals throughout the book, hoping to create an impression of variety and overall strength. The collection has usually been accepted in the spirit in which it was reissued by Faber twenty-one years later – as juvenilia, derivative, faintly ridiculous, a curiosity. Everyone agrees that it has recognizable Larkin features, but everyone also agrees that they are veiled and intermittent. Its only contemporary reviewer (in the *Coventry Evening Telegraph* on 26 October) warned Larkin what sort of reception to expect. 'Mr Larkin,' the reviewer said, 'has an inner vision that must be sought for with care. His recondite imagery is couched in phrases that make up in a kind of wistful hinted beauty what they lack in lucidity. Mr Larkin's readers must at present be confined to a small circle. Perhaps his work will gain wider appeal as his genius becomes more mature?'[10]

It is easy to sympathize with this general view of *The North Ship*. It is also easy to regret that so much attention has been paid to its style and so little to its themes – except the theme of mortality, which obviously anticipates a main concern of his later work. The real interest of the book, though, is its treatment not of death but of sex. Sometimes (as in 'This was your place of birth') the poems concentrate on the sorrow of unreciprocated desire. Sometimes they seek to dispense with a sexual partner and define the erotic self in punningly masturbatory terms ('Last night you came/Unbidden in a dream'). Sometimes they take refuge in sexual disgust ('carrion kisses, carrion farewells'). Sometimes – as in 'Climbing the hill within the deafening wind' – they ostentatiously set sex aside and clear the decks for Art:

> Submission is the only good;
> Let me become an instrument sharply stringed
> For all things to strike music as they please.

Larkin refuses to choose among the various options open to him. He prefers to leave the attractions and repulsions of sex in a perpetual limbo, where he can be exempt from the adult responsibilities of choice. Largely as a result of this, the world his poems describe is imprecise. Where symbols in Yeats's poems help to focus their argument, in *The North Ship* they obfuscate or dilute, throwing up their hands in repeated gestures of uncertainty. Even Ruth, who is obviously the spur for much of Larkin's emotion, is indeterminate. She is an unreal girl in an unreal place – Larkin's constant fascination is not her but his own condition. It is his 'heart' which obsesses him. It is 'cold' in poem X, 'impotent' in XVIII, 'unguessed-at' in XXII, trapped in XXIII, and in IX – most memorably – 'in its own endless silence kneeling'. 'Heart' is the word which dominates the book: its steady beat denotes not interest in others but absorption in the self. 'What do I believe would comfort me?' Larkin asked Sutton a fortnight before publication:

Not much, as I grow increasingly pessimistic. I believe that the world is composed for the most part of people so unlike me that we think each other mad and wicked. I know I can't save it or it save me, and I doubt whether it can save itself or I save myself. I believe that human beings can do nothing for one another except provide amusement, which is pleasant but does not last. By amusement I include everything from an evening at the cinema to a love affair. I believe when I am old I shall bitterly regret having wasted my life, which I may have done. This is because I shall never attain the absolute – in other words the *continual* ecstasy – because it doesn't exist. Therefore in addition to being afraid of death I shall feel cheated and angry.[11]

To distract himself from *The North Ship*, Larkin went for a few days' holiday to Brixham in Devon with Bruce Montgomery. It was a bad idea. Montgomery, who had recently finished *The Moving Toyshop*, which Larkin rightly suspected would turn out to be a popular success, made him feel 'discontented and jealous'.[12] Returning to Wellington via Oxford did little to revive him. Although he saw Iles and Brown, they only reminded him how indifferent he felt to the momentous events going on around him. He had hardly bothered to raise his eyes from his manuscript book when the war ended. On V-Day (8 May 1945), turning on the radio, he wrote to Sutton: 'I listened to Churchill blathering out of turn this afternoon, and the King this evening. But all day I have had a headache and felt despondent. The second draft of the novel ["The Kingdom of Winter"] has reached p. 22.'[13] Now he felt 'infuriated' that his friends should be 'wildly excited and even quarrelsome about the General Election'.[14] Travelling on to Coten End for a brief visit which coincided with his twenty-third birthday, he grew even more depressed. On the evening before returning to Glentworth he sat at the desk in his bedroom after his parents had gone to sleep, drawing up the account of his life:

At present I am working as chief and only librarian at Wellington (Salop) Public Library, where I have been since December 1st 1943, earning £225 + £49.10. p.a. I have two applications for jobs outstanding: one for an education administrative job in Warwick, and one for a Readership at the OUP. I hope without confidence.

I have written two novels and one book of poems. The Fortune Press are [publishing] the poems and the first novel ... The second novel ... awaits a publisher at present and is still untyped. No one has read it yet. I feel it may be a forerunner of the kind of novel I shall write: but as *Jill* was foredoomed by subject matter, [the second one] is foredoomed by construction.

So the news on the two fronts varies. I have neither a good job nor a prospect of getting one, and while I have at least continued to write I have no certainty that I am writing well, and I have not made the slightest step in the direction of achieving a reputation. This I probably shall not do. It will have to come of itself if it comes at all.

For the major part of the past year I have been filled with a sensation new to me – that of being irrevocably cut off from the rest of man. By this I don't mean I am too shy to desire a sexual partner – there's nothing novel in this – but that on the whole I am indifferent to them and do not care what they say or do. This forms the basis for [my new novel].

How do I look to the future? Not, as usual, with confidence. The news of the 'atomic bomb' makes such foresight a shade preposterous, but I can fairly say that [I] expect the following things when I am 23:

1. To write another novel.
2. To continue trying to change my job.
3. To remain in Wellington.
4. To have nothing to do with women.
5. To grow sourer and sourer.

> 'Yet be it less or more, or soon or slow,
> It shall be still in strictest measure even,
> To that same lot, however mean or low,
> Towards which time leads me, and the will of Heav'n.'[15]

Larkin's clinical tone, evaluating his life as if he were a stranger to himself, speaks of self-regard as well as unhappiness. It is a note for posterity, not just a private record, and to prove the point he returned to it a year later, writing by his numbered expectations (1) WRONG; (2) RIGHT; (3) RIGHT; (4) WRONG; (5) ?. While seeming candid, it is also an evasive account. It makes no mention of Ruth, and demotes his feelings about her to a question of desire and shyness. In doing so, it laments exclusion yet gives no plausible hope of overcoming it. When his holiday ended and he finally returned to Wellington, even Ruth's most dogged devotion could not be expected to survive such coldness. A great change in his life with her seemed inevitable.

A change occurred, but it was not the kind Larkin had anticipated. In September Ruth was accepted by King's College, London, to read English; the course would be followed by a fourth year's post-graduate training for a Teacher's Diploma. With no help from Larkin, she found lodgings in a bomb-blasted flat in Beulah Hill, Upper Norwood, and in October set off from Herbert Avenue towards the new world that Larkin had offered to show her when he had first come into her life two years previously. She was eighteen years old and – more or less – independent. Larkin assumed the separation meant the end of their relationship. In fact the difficulties of travel and distance, far from forcing Ruth out of his thoughts, drew him towards her. Within a short time they at last became lovers: it was the first time that Larkin had been to bed with anyone. 'I'm very proud of you, dear Philip, and I love you very much,' Ruth wrote to him from Norwood on 27 October. 'The fact that you like me and have made love to me is the greatest source of pride and happiness in my life.'[16] Sometimes Larkin travelled to London for the weekend, staying in the spare guest-room in Beulah Hill or lodgings nearby; sometimes Ruth came back to Wellington, where they made secret assignations in the library after closing time. It was the beginning of the second, distinct phase in their life together, which Ruth remembers as 'the years of our closest companionship':[17]

After I went to London University we met ... [in lodgings with] landladies who because of food rationing could not offer much hospitality to lodgers' friends. So we spent a great deal of time in pubs, which were the warmest places – and keeping warm was a constant battle in those days of coal rationing and power cuts – or in restaurants which served meals we should now consider uneatable – whale steak was a dreadful example.

We walked for miles and miles, both of us loving to drift round London which was still battle scarred and full of bomb sites but with an atmosphere we found incredibly romantic ... We were addicts of [the cinema] as were most people then. Our tastes differed in one respect; Philip disliked musicals and I loved them, so those we avoided, but otherwise we were pretty omnivorous, and I am constantly surprised by the number of black and white films [now] shown on TV which I remember seeing with him. In London we saw the occasional French film such as Jean Louis Barrault in *Les Enfants du Paradis* and Cocteau's *La Belle et la Bête* which wouldn't have meant much to us without the subtitles.

As we had very little money it was as well that the London theatres were more accessible than they are today. If we queued for the Upper Circle we could get in for two shillings and if we were in funds we could book quite good seats for four shillings. I remember the Old Vic production of *The Cherry Orchard* which moved Philip to unashamed tears. He not surprisingly loved Tchekov.

I would have liked us to go to classical concerts but these he firmly rejected and neither opera nor ballet attracted him, so as usual we did what he wanted and visited art exhibitions (I remember a splendid Picasso/Matisse) or wandered round the National Gallery and the Tate.

Our happiest times were our few holidays together. Perhaps because we were away from our usual backgrounds or because we were sharing common interests, Philip was relaxed and cheerful, entertaining and considerate; in short, the perfect companion. In August 1947 we spent a week in Oxford, during a summer of exceptional brilliance. Philip loved Oxford, of course, and enjoyed showing me all his favourite places, pubs and beauty spots. We punted on the Isis, went to the Playhouse, and visited Blenheim and Burford. It was one of those rare times when everything was right.

A little later we took a day or two in the D. H. Lawrence country, prowling round Eastwood, searching out Lawrence's family home, still then I think occupied as a private house, and considering possible locations for episodes in his novels. It was an unlovely area so to please me and provide a contrast we also visited Newstead Abbey as I was at that time a great admirer of Byron.

Between Christmas and the New Year at the end of 1948 we explored the Hardy country, Hardy being a writer for whom we both had the deepest admiration. The weather was, you might say, seasonable but Philip said this was a much more suitable time of year to evoke Hardy than summertime with its crowds of tourists. There were certainly none of them. After we had worshipped at the shrine of Max Gate and drunk in all the Hardy landmarks round Dorchester, Philip expressed a great desire to walk from Dorchester to Weymouth. So we set off on a bright, cold December morning feeling romantically like two Hardy characters trudging from Casterbridge to Budmouth. I suppose we expected to travel a country highway; at any rate we were outraged to find ourselves on a busy main road flanked by nasty garages and ribbon-development housing. It was the dreariest walk imaginable and the weather showed ominous change, but we set our teeth and arrived at Weymouth in driving rain and in ... a gale which dashed the waves over the sea front and had us drenched to the skin. To reward ourselves we stayed at a very fine hotel full of eighteenth-century splendour as to décor and with a tariff to match.[18]

In all her memories of their shared time, Ruth is at pains to emphasize that while she and Larkin sometimes 'could make, and did make, each other very happy', it was 'never long before the Black Dog appeared'.[19] As in Wellington, so in London: within weeks of arriving, her initial happiness had been clouded by his inability to commit himself to her. 'Remember,' she wrote to him in the first week of November, 'it matters more than anything in the world to me that we should be able to maintain some sort of relationship, however imperfect. When I read your Sunday letter I am hopeful, but then the memory of last Thursday sweeps over me like a cold wind. Well, this weekend should tell us something – but what? That it is better for us to part?'[20] If the next weekend did tell them that, they chose to ignore it – this time and many times thereafter. Advancing amorously then retreating into self-doubt, Larkin made a painfully contradictory universe for Ruth to inhabit, a universe in which she was kept in a state of permanent eagerness with no real hope of finding permanent satisfaction.

Had Ruth been aware of everything Larkin thought and said about her, she might have known better than to persevere. In the three poems he wrote between starting to sleep with her and the end of the year, the best he could do in the way of celebrating physical tenderness was to say 'Her hands intend no harm'. At the moment when love might have become his theme – or at least, sex might have remained his theme – he turned instead to the subject which was to hold his attention like no other: death. 'And death seems like long hills, a range/We ride each day towards, and never reach', he says in 'Past days of gales'; 'Mind never met/Image of death like this', he tells us in 'Who whistled for the wind'. Two months later the same set of feelings – dread overcoming desire, emptiness swallowing fulfilment, sexual anxiety converting into fear of mortality – produced 'Going', the first poem which would find its way into *The Less Deceived*, arguably his first poem of real merit:

> There is an evening coming in
> Across the fields, one never seen before,
> That lights no lamps.
>
> Silken it seems at a distance, yet
> When it is drawn up over the knees and breast
> It brings no comfort.

Where has the tree gone, that locked
Earth to the sky? What is under my hands,
That I cannot feel?

What loads my hands down?

The message for Ruth in these poems was bleak enough. Larkin's comments about her to his friends were worse. 'I feel,' he told Sutton the very month she left for London, 'as if my wings were in danger of being clipped. And it worries me also to find that I am a long way off being capable of any emotion as simple as what is called love.'[21] To Amis he was even more direct. First in letters, and then in person when Amis was demobbed in September and returned to Oxford, Larkin was scathing about love in general and Ruth in particular. At Amis's digs in St John's – where he was studying for a B.Litt. – and then in the cottage near Eynsham to which he soon moved, they quickly fell back into their familiar undergraduate ways.

In the popular mythology of their friendship, the year Larkin and Amis shared in St John's ranks as the time they were closest to each other. In fact they meant more to each other in the years immediately following the war. As before, they combined seriousness with frivolity, devotion to art with mockery of its pretensions – but now they had a greater sense of purpose and a clearer structure to their lives. Larkin showed Amis his poems, Amis discussed his own plans for writing. Sometimes they pooled their talents, writing pieces in tandem, among them a series of poems about trains in the style of various poets they knew, such as John Wain,[22] and occasionally submitting entries for the *New Statesman* weekly parody competition. (One, a spoof title for a Graham Greene novel, 'Visa to Darkness', won an honourable mention.)

Whenever Ruth was taken to meet Amis (the first time was in January 1946), the frail trust she had built with Larkin in London and Wellington seemed to vanish. Larkin, she says, only had to be in Amis's company a short while to become neglectful of her. She found Amis's views about women particularly upsetting. When Larkin tried to justify them, her sense of grievance deepened. 'Your ad lib reasons for Kingsley's liking women,' she told him, 'made me uncomfortable and unhappy and ashamed of being a woman and angry because men know so little of this really and think they know so much.'[23] For all this, the insults that Amis hurled into Larkin's world had constructive as well as disconcerting effects. They made Larkin feel that if he moaned about his life to Amis in the same way that he did to Sutton, he would receive bracing rather than merely sympathetic advice. Whereas, this autumn, he wailed to Sutton, 'I have no more determination or fire in my heart'[24], he told Amis, 'I'm rather unhappy at present due to spiritual dryness. Did you know the soul could die and the body live on? You didn't? Do you care? No, I rather thought you wouldn't do that.'[25] In the same way, Amis made Larkin take a less gloomy view of his prospects as a writer. When he arrived back in Oxford, and heard that the second draft of 'The Kingdom of Winter' had languished complete but untyped for three months, he urged Larkin to galvanize himself.

Larkin responded willingly. Although he had described the novel as 'foredoomed' on his twenty-third birthday, he had written it quickly and confidently. From September 1944, when he had started work on it, through May 1945 when Montgomery's agent (Peter Watt, of A. P. Watt) had 'expressed great willingness'[26] to handle the finished manuscript, to June the same year when he had written 'solidly, and quickly, and ecstatically',[27] he had come to believe that his 'guttering-out of personal emotion [had been] the prelude to catching that fabulous bird, universal emotion, positive objectivity'.[28] In October, when the manuscript came back from the typist (along with a bill for £5.5s.11d.), his optimism faded again. 'It seems poor stuff,' he told his parents, 'and I am altogether displeased',[29] but this didn't prevent him from sending the book to Watt. Within a few days word came back that Watt liked it, and would start offering it to publishers.

As Larkin waited for news, the Fortune Press sent him the proofs of *Jill*, restoring his sense of himself as an author about to burst upon an expectant world. Almost at once, he whizzed down the switchback of his feelings into uncertainty again. Amis, to whom he had shown 'The Kingdom of Winter', was less than wholeheartedly enthusiastic about it. So was Montgomery. So was Ruth. 'It is much more mature than *Jill*,' she told him. 'As a stylist I don't think there is anything you have to learn. The prose is extraordinarily beautiful and the handling extremely competent. But much as I hate to agree with Bruce, I feel that is both its strength and its weakness. You drug us with the perfection of your style and we are incapable of waking up sufficiently to get greatly worked up over the plot.'[30] Larkin brooded on these opinions, travelling alone to Coten End for another dreary Christmas. He asked himself once again whether he was right to sacrifice his life in order to perfect his work. The work just wasn't good enough. His friends said so; his own instincts confirmed it.

NINETEEN

When Larkin had reached his lowest ebb at Oxford in the winter of 1942, Vernon Watkins and Yeats had saved him. Now, at the bleakest moment of his time in Wellington, literature once again came to his rescue. Immediately after Christmas his landlady at Glentworth told him that she wanted his room back for her own use, so he hastily arranged to leave. On 5 January 1946 he advertised in the *Wellington and Shrewsbury Journal*: 'Single gentleman requires sitting room and bedroom with board perm.', and a fortnight later he moved into a flat in 7 Ladycroft, a street (now demolished) of two-storey red-brick houses on the northern edge of the town. It was a smaller, less gloomy place than either of his previous digs, and he told Sutton he was 'very satisfied'.[1] The bedroom, which was on the floor above the sitting room, faced east, and as the days began to lengthen he found the sun shining into his room early in the morning. Rather than struggle uselessly to go back to sleep, he decided to start reading until it was time to get up. The book with which he began his new régime was 'the little blue *Chosen Poems of Thomas Hardy*'.[2] Nothing else he read influenced him more deeply or more fruitfully.

Judging by the way Larkin came to speak of Hardy later, it seems the old man of Wessex simply toppled the old man of Ireland from his throne. This, anyway, is the impression Larkin gives in his Introduction to the reissue of *The North Ship*. Until he opened *Chosen Poems*, he says, he had known Hardy only as a novelist, and 'shared Lytton Strachey's verdict' on his verse: 'the gloom is not even relieved by a little elegance of diction'.[3] This opinion didn't last for long. 'If I were asked to date its disappearance,' he said, 'I should guess it was the morning I first read "Thoughts of Phena at News of her Death".'[4] Almost immediately the 'Celtic fever abated'[5] and his poetic universe was altered. Instead of Symbolism there was fidelity to familiar fact; instead of grand music there was the sound of a fastidious mind thinking aloud; instead of high rhetoric there was modest watchfulness; instead of a longing to transcend there was total immersion in everyday things. Justifying his late conversion, Larkin said later:

1 The Day family at Rhyl in 1906 – the year Eva Day met Sydney Larkin.

2 Eva Day with Sydney Larkin's parents, c. 1906.
3 Sydney Larkin, 1898.

4 Eva Larkin with Philip Larkin and 'Rags', c. 1926.

5 2 Poultney Road, Coventry, where Philip Larkin was born in 1922.
6 'Penvorn' (1 Manor Road, Coventry), where the Larkin family lived from 1927 until
driven out by the blitz in 1940.

7 Philip Larkin in school uniform, c. 1930.
8 Sydney Larkin on holiday shortly before the outbreak of war
(photograph by Philip Larkin).

9 King Henry VIII School, Coventry; Larkin began attending the school in 1930.
10 Colin Gunner, c. 1932.

11 Philip Larkin, on holiday in Kreuznach, Germany, 1937.

12 Philip Larkin on holiday in Jersey, 1939.

13 Philip Larkin and school contemporaries, c. 1938, on a walk during which they were only allowed to speak in French. Philip Larkin is third from right, Noel Hughes at the end (right).

14 In the garden of St John's College, Oxford, during the summer of 1941.
Left to right: Noel Hughes, Norman Iles, James Willcox, Philip Larkin, Philip Brown
(photograph by D. H. Whiffen).

15 J. B. (Jim) Sutton, c. 1946 (photograph by Philip Larkin).
16 Bruce Montgomery, c. 1944 (photograph by Philip Larkin).

17 Kingsley and Hilly Amis, July 1948, the month before they were married.

18 Philip Larkin outside Bruce Montgomery's lodgings in Wellington Square, Oxford, 1943 (photograph by Bruce Montgomery).

I don't think Hardy, as a poet, is a poet for young people. I know it sounds ridiculous to say I wasn't young [when I first read him], but at least I was beginning to find out what life was about, and that's precisely what I found in Hardy. In other words, I'm saying that what I like about him primarily is his temperament and the way he sees life. He's not a transcendental writer, he's not a Yeats, he's not an Eliot; his subjects are men, the life of men, time and the passing of time, love and the fading of love.[6]

In general terms, Larkin's readers have every reason to believe that his change of heart was immediate and absolute: the shift in his style proves it. In other respects, Larkin's account of his conversion misrepresents the poetry that he wrote for the next forty years. For all its Hardyesque devotion to the here-and-now, for all its tact and understatement, it retains many characteristics reminiscent of Yeats: the intermittent transcendence (in 'Solar', for instance), and the occasional use of images which derive from French Symbolist sources ('Absences'). Full-blooded rhetoric and Symbolist references appear beside ordinary, demotic ways of speaking, so that when we read Larkin's poems we can hear as well as see the tussle between conflicting elements in his personality. If he had abandoned Yeats as completely as he tells us he did, he would be strictly half the poet he is.

As Larkin worked through *Chosen Poems* he began to realize that what he most valued in Hardy was the importance attached to suffering. Forty years later he asked, 'What is the intensely maturing experience of which Hardy's modern man is most sensible? In my view it is suffering, or sadness, and extended consideration of the centrality of suffering in Hardy's work should be the first duty of the true critic.'[7] There were, Larkin believed, two main reasons for this. 'First he thought it was "true" ("Tragedy is true guise, comedy lies"); secondly it could be demonstrated that Hardy associated sensitivity to suffering and awareness of the causes of pain with superior spiritual character.'[8] When discussing the other poets that he particularly admired, Larkin often made the same association. Housman, for instance, was praised as 'the poet of unhappiness; no one else has reiterated his single message so plangently';[9] and Stevie Smith was credited with having 'the authority of sadness'.[10]

All these remarks could as well be applied to Larkin's own work. Hardy's greatest gift was to give him permission to confront his misery – and once this had happened, Larkin realized that his unhappiness was both all-consuming and a way of forging links with the world. 'Certainly,' he told Sutton soon after reading Hardy for the first time, 'the privilege of being able to walk about on a day like this makes nonsense temporarily of all one's hopes and fears. All that matters is that we've only got fifty years, at the outside, to look around. So let us be eager and meticulous . . . and if we should produce art, so much the better, but the only quality that makes art durable and famous is the quality of generating delight in the state of living.'[11]

This new sense of conviction had an immediate effect. Halfway through January Larkin went to London to chivvy Caton about *Jill*. It was the only time they met, and created a suitably odd impression. Although Caton's offices were in Buckingham Palace Road, the Press itself was in Belgravia Road, and Caton took Larkin to see it. 'Entrance,' Larkin said later, was 'made down the area steps and through a double-locked front door giving on to a damp front . . . hall stacked high with old newspapers, packets of unbound sheets of books considered even by Caton to be unsaleable, and string.'[12] When the tour of the premises was complete, Larkin was taken outside for a drink in the local pub, where he heard from Caton that the printers were complaining about the (actually very small) number of swear-words in *Jill*. Caton, who had once been arrested for producing obscene publications, demanded their removal. He said that 'four letter words . . . were often used casually by persons who probably failed to appreciate their full import. "You hear errand boys using the word *sod*, for instance – *do you think they know what it means?*" This not so much with a hoarse chuckle, as with an eagerness that made me profoundly uncomfortable.'[13]

Not even this encounter could dampen Larkin's spirits. Back in Wellington, he applied for a job at the University College of Southampton library in February; and in April he began a correspondence course in Library Classification, hoping that it would add some lustre to his c.v. He also stopped worrying quite so much about Ruth, whose anxieties constantly threatened to inflame his own. The longer she stayed in London, the more she resented the lack of a regular pattern in their lives. In a poem written in April, 'Deep Analysis', Larkin put these fears into the mouth of 'a woman lying on a leaf': 'Why', she asks in lines glinting with images of defence and attack:

> was all

> Your body sharpened against me, vigilant,
>   Watchful, when all I meant
> Was to make it bright, that it might stand
>   Burnished before my tent?

Larkin's friendship with Amis was still partly responsible. Every time he visited Amis, Larkin was encouraged to harden his heart against sentiment. Amis made him feel that irony was just as important as affection, and in one of Larkin's few surviving letters to Amis from this period, it's clear that his advice was readily accepted – partly so that Larkin would appear sympathetically 'manly', even if this also meant seeming misogynistic. 'Last night,' Larkin wrote after a weekend in Wellington:

I took Miss Ruth to Shrewsbury to see . . . Night Club Boom and I should say about 45 seconds of the Club Condon. This was worth the 1/8d. I paid for our admission but not the 5/2d. I paid for our railway fares or the 4/8d. for our scrambled eggs afterwards, or the 4/1d. for subsequent drink. Don't you think it's ABSOLUTELY SHAMEFUL that men have to pay for women without BEING ALLOWED TO SHAG the women afterwards AS A MATTER OF COURSE? I do: simply DISGUSTING. It makes me ANGRY. Everything about the ree-lay-shun-ship between men and women makes me *angry*. It's all a fucking balls up. It might have been planned by the army, or the Ministry of Food.[14]

Amis returned such tirades with interest, even though he had recently met Hilary (Hilly) Bardwell, whom he would marry two years later, in 1948. The moment Larkin discovered this he told Sutton about it, half resentfully and half jealously. 'Kingsley,' he said, 'is busily shagging a girl – a new girl – at every opportunity, which makes me envious: never think I dispute the desirability of women. My quarrel is that their attainment is only possible on such unwelcome terms.'[15]

Larkin soon had his consolation. At the end of the previous December (1945), full of doubts about the wisdom of the exercise, Amis had sent a collection of his poems called *Bright November* to Caton. It was accepted the following May. 'This pleases me,' Larkin told Sydney and Eva. 'If one can't get out of a mess oneself, the best thing is to drag someone else into it.'[16] At the same time, his own prospects brightened. In the week that Amis fell into Caton's clutches, Peter Watt sent 'The Kingdom of Winter' to Faber – and a month later Alan Pringle, an editor there, offered an advance of £30. Larkin was delighted. For one thing, the book had already been rejected by Chatto & Windus, Secker & Warburg, Cape and the Cresset Press. For another, Faber's reputation as the country's leading poetry publisher encouraged him to think that they might eventually take on his poems as well. When Pringle suggested that Larkin might like to come to London to discuss a few possible revisions he happily complied, and the two men met for lunch in June. Larkin did his best to behave like a model author, agreeing to do what Pringle recommended. 'After some thought,' he said, thanking Pringle some time later, 'I came to the conclusion that [the book] could be criticized on two scores: what I was trying to convey, and my occasional failure to convey it clearly.'[17] He did what he could to improve things, and returned the final text promptly.

Pringle was disappointed with the work Larkin had done, but not seriously so. 'I will not deny,' he wrote on 19 August, 'that the changes are rather less substantial than I had hoped, but if they satisfy yourself our chief hope has been fulfilled.'[18] In the same letter Pringle queried the book's title, and Larkin immediately told him, 'I have no great attachment to "The Kingdom of Winter" as a title myself: on the credit side it is a nice, mysterious, chilly phrase, expressing to a certain extent the point of the book; on the debit side it is a little pompous.'[19] Three days later he wrote to Pringle again. 'I have remembered a title I thought of soon after starting to write [the book]: *A Girl in Winter* – which, though I believe I discarded it on the grounds of sounding Mills and Boony (if you know what I mean) does conjure up a more precise image than the present one does ... Otherwise I keep thinking of things like "Frosty Answer" – which are foolish but fun.'[20] Pringle said that he liked the new title and that was that. The contract was signed, the manuscript sent off to production, and the exchange of letters between author and editor ceased until publication the following spring.

As Larkin moved calmly ahead with Faber, other elements in his life continued their erratic course. The more strenuously he tried to leave Wellington, the more agitated Ruth became about their future. Should she abandon her studies in London to be near Larkin wherever he went? Should she sever her connection with him? Should they get married? Every time this possibility was mentioned, it threw Larkin into a convulsion of dread. Dramatic action of any kind was something he felt 'cloud[ed] the mirror'[21] of his thought. Once again, he turned to Sutton for help. He knew that Sutton was shortly to be demobbed, and felt that before they met face to face – for the first time in five years – he must own up to his feelings about Ruth. Previously he had kept them to himself. Now he wrote:

What mainly worries me, if you'll excuse my speaking of my own affairs for the moment, is a strengthening suspicion that in my character there is an antipathy between 'art' and 'life'. I find that once I 'give in' to another person, as I have given in not altogether voluntarily, but almost completely, to Ruth, there is a slackening and dulling of the peculiar artistic fibres that makes it impossible to achieve that mental 'clenching' that crystallizes a pattern and keeps it still while you draw it. It's very easy to float along in a semi-submerged way, dissipating one's talent for pleasing by amusing and being affectionate to the other – easy because the returns are instant and delightful – but I find, myself, that this letting in of a second person spells death to perception and the desire to express, as well as the ability. Time and time again I feel that before I write anything else at all I must drag myself out of the water, shake myself dry and sit down on a lonely rock to contemplate glittering loneliness. Marriage, of course (since you mentioned marriage), is impossible if one wants to do this.

There are two possible answers. One is that this is an off-period for me anyway and that the wish to write will return in good time. The other is that I was never a real writer anyway, and that what little I have done was born simply from enforced loneliness and a natural way with words. In other words I am like the young ladies who become novelists instead of wives.

My reaction to all this (and probably yours too) is: it doesn't matter. If the first alternative is true, then there's nothing to worry about. If the second is true, then I should have been no good anyway. It's not much of a talent that can be overthrown by deeper contacts with other people. And of course there's nothing I dislike more than self-conscious discussion of the particular nature of one's artistic inclinations, and the suggestion that they should be in any way nursed or protected from ordinary living. Keats said once and for all that if poetry come not as naturally as leaves to a tree, it had better not come at all. I think he said 'naturally', which is better than 'easily'.[22]

Undermined by so many doubts, Larkin looked forward to having Sutton back in his life on a more regular basis. Their friendship had meant even more to him than his alliance with Amis, largely because it was collusive, not competitive. Yet when Sutton returned to Coventry to resume his career as a painter, they were wary of each other. Their remarkable correspondence meant that they knew each other's minds; what they lacked was a context in which their relationship could develop. They met, made loud protestations of affection, but said nothing about their plans to emigrate together, or share a house.

Larkin, anyway, had problems that no one could solve but himself – one of them being how to escape from Wellington. On 2 June 1946 he saw advertised a sub-librarianship at University College, Leicester – a job he had long thought would 'release me from the public library world to the student world [which] would be superb'.[23] He applied the following day, disguising the fact that he had drifted into librarianship rather than chosen it as a career, and pointing out that he was mid-way through his correspondence course for part one of the 'Registration Examination (Classification and Cataloguing)', which if he passed would take him a step closer to membership of the Library Association. In the letter accompanying his c.v. he wrote:

Though I wished to take up library work, I was at a loss to know how to begin, as the School of Librarianship was closed [because of the war], and though I applied to several libraries, including the Bodleian, I found there were no vacancies in appropriate grades for untrained persons. Wishing to gain experience, however, I applied for and was offered the post of librarian at Wellington ... This was not a good position, even if I had not been primarily interested in students' libraries, but I was attracted by the responsibility involved and the scope for individual reorganization.[24]

This elegant invention did the trick: he was summoned for interview in the last week in June, and offered the post. Even though the move would inevitably create problems with Ruth, he accepted eagerly. 'I have never felt anything but *degraded* as the librarian in this hole of toad's turds,'[25] he told Sutton, celebrating his freedom. He kept to himself, lest it be thought that he had abandoned art for bureaucracy, how much he had achieved in Wellington in spite of his boredom. He had turned a muddled and old-fashioned relic into something valuable and valued. When he arrived the library had issued an average of 300 books a month; when he left this had risen to 1,000. In the same period the number of registered borrowers had climbed from a little more than 1,000 to nearly 2,500, and the stock from 3,000 to nearly 5,500. Since the end of 1945, and the arrival of his assistant Greta Roden, the hours during which the library was open had doubled, and money had been provided by the Council to improve the furnishings. Although it wasn't until 1949, three years after he left, that the library really began to prosper (when its status was changed to County Branch Library), its transformation had already begun. It was no longer a menacing, gas-smelling, ill-lit, tramp-infested den of sloth, and when Larkin's resignation was made public he ruefully told his parents that the borrowers 'seemed quite sorry'.[26]

Before leaving, Larkin took some holiday owing to him. After a week in Churston near Paignton with Sydney and Eva, he returned to Wellington via Oxford where he saw Amis and Montgomery. Now the moment of his release had arrived, he almost feared it; he was incapable of deciding whether it meant he was splitting up with Ruth, or merely finding another way of continuing their semi-detached existence. On his final afternoon in the library he summarized his hopes and fears in a notebook:

I have exactly two and a half hours of degradation left. This gives me a strange, almost sad feeling. Like a prisoner long immured in low passages, to walk erect towards the sunlit mouth of the cave is quite an effort. Two and a half hours – and then no more books for Dad, lovers, Westerns, snot-faced children, gas lights, bothers with the idiot, bothers with the heating – just – oh . . . *freedom*! (Till the buggery starts at Leicester. Still, it'll be high class buggery.)

Kingsley wrote and said his women always paid for themselves (and Christ knows he gets the goods off them) and advised me to get Miss Bowman [Ruth] to pay for herself. This at once plunged me into the depths of despair, God's own sucker, impotent rage against all these stupid conventions that make fuck's own fool of you.

These years have destroyed my one great advantage – youth. I mean *startling* youth. When I was appointed I was 21, and I have *wasted* two and a half years.

Spent the morning typing out poems in Council time. My only regret is that I wasn't using a Council typewriter and Council paper. Nothing seems more fitting to me than that the money of oafs should be devoted to the furtherance of sensitive and imaginative work.

I find it physically impossible to feel sorry for anyone except myself.

Let me record simply that Ruth and I spent Monday in Shrewsbury, seeing *Jane Eyre*, and Tuesday afternoon (in torrential rain) at her home. I was more moved than I expected at the parting, and now feel adrift and afraid. The details will be filled in later. To the patron saint of travellers, of lodgers, of wayfarers, of wage slaves, of those who feel mourning . . . protect me. To the patron saint of artists, writers, poets, of those who swallow with silent excitement . . . inspire me.[27]

Ruth, too, was 'adrift and afraid'. The day after Larkin left, she wrote her 'beloved alaskan bear' a letter in which she claimed to believe that 'if we approach it reasonably this separation may cement rather than dissolve our feelings for each other' – but spent most of the time pitifully doubting it. 'My darling,' she told him:

this is the most difficult letter I've ever had to write to you. Whatever I say must sound nothing much more than a *cri de coeur* because it is impossible to keep my feelings under control . . . Writing to you must be my only happiness now. I still cannot wholly realize that you have gone and will never return. Now and then the impact of it hits me and it is terrible but mostly I find myself thinking how many days is it until Philip comes back? It's impossible to believe that I shall never see you in the library again . . . and that our Sunday afternoon walks and evenings at home and our coffees at Britten's and teas at Sidulies' are ultimately and finally ended. Oh Philip, my dearest, how can I battle my way through life ... without you? ...

We have had some good times together haven't we? All the days at Shrewsbury and the evenings in the front room and in the Charlton? And for me especially the evenings in the library. As you said, we are so alike and suit each other so well. We mustn't let the mere fact that we no longer live in the same town come between us irrevocably.[28]

Ruth understood why Larkin wanted to leave Wellington but she couldn't help feeling sorry that he despised the place. It was her home, whether she liked it or not. Furthermore, she knew that Larkin's sense of 'degradation' concealed a number of debts. His job had brought him obvious rewards, and his independence had provided many pleasures. He had started to establish himself as a writer. He had discovered Hardy. He had written with greater fluency than he was ever to find again (one book of poems and two novels in less than three years). More important still, in Wellington he had found reasons for being unhappy which matched for the first time his instinct for misery. Trudging through its narrow redbrick canyons, staring from the Wrekin at its dull roofs, hunched in the gas-lit library waiting for work to end and Ruth to arrive, he had discovered the authority of sadness.

TWENTY

Four-square on its hill to the south of the city, the main building of Leicester University – the Fielding Johnson Building – looks today like a requisitioned country house. In fact it's a requisitioned lunatic asylum. Built in 1837 and 'almost Prussian, a big symmetrical block of stock brick',[1] it stood for the first part of its existence in nearly forty acres of open parkland. Now it is encroached upon and overshadowed by the tower blocks and assorted faculty buildings put up since the site became the University College of Leicester, affiliated to the University of London, in 1926. Below it lie the shopping streets and red-brick residential areas of an almost entirely Victorian city. The Roman remains (part of a forum) are no more than crumbling oddments; the plan of the medieval town has disappeared. It is a busy, not a beautiful place – a centre for light industry which has lost its heart to inner ring roads and traffic.

When Larkin arrived in September 1946, the University College consisted only of the Fielding Johnson Building, and catered for a mere 200 or so students. (By 1950, when he left, there were over 700 students and all forty acres of parkland had been built on. By 1957, when the college became a university, there were 1,000 students. Today there are nearly 5,000.) Every aspect of college life was concentrated under the one roof: all academic departments, all administration, the library. 'Its main rooms,' Larkin said, 'were large and graceful, but the wings were for obvious reasons constructed on a pattern of tiny cells.'[2] Staff would gather in one of these 'main rooms' for their midday meal and sit round one table, the Vice-Chancellor himself saying grace and serving food. It was not merely an academic community but an academic family. Larkin immediately liked it. To have companionship without complicated emotional bonds suited him ideally – and he found something of the same thing beyond the university. Malcolm Bradbury, who was a student in the English Department from 1950 to 1953, described Leicester in *Eating People is Wrong* as somewhere which had 'given itself to all-comers during the industrial revolution. There were, indeed, parts ... in which one felt a real sense of place; but most of the time one felt a sense of *anywhere*.'[3]

Larkin lived in three different digs during his three years in the city. While he looked for the first he lodged in Loughborough, ten miles to the north, at his sister's house, 53 York Road, coming in to work each morning by bus. After three weeks of this he settled for the best alternative he could find: 'a bed-sitting room – an attic really – very noisy with trams and 45 shillings a week, excluding lunch'[4] at 172 London Road in Leicester itself. The noise (the trams weren't discontinued until 1949), his three fellow-lodgers and the expense irritated him, but in other respects he was content. Tucked away at the top of the plain-fronted, white-painted house, with a view across Victoria Park towards the Fielding Johnson Building, he could strike the balance he wanted. His landlady, Joan Sutcliffe, remembers him as 'always friendly and pleasant' though 'not a gregarious man'. He seemed, she says, 'older than his years. I recall his quiet unassuming manner and slight stammer; his wit and turns of phrase; his bow ties (unusual then) and his very very slight preoccupation with thinning hair. I can visualize Philip sitting in the garden with Oblomov my cat stalking him. We were never sure whether Ob was attracted by the smell of Philip's Harris tweed overcoat or the Bay Rum he used on his hair.'[5]

Larkin played down the ways in which London Road suited him. He wanted to give his family and friends the impression that he was suffering in a garret as he had been in Wellington. 'I cannot give you much of a picture of [my room],' he told Sutton. 'It is a medium-sized attic, with carpet and bed, and I sit in a basket chair by a reading lamp with an electric radiator pointed cunningly up my arse and a brown rug over my shoulders.'[6] To Amis, in a letter signed 'Handsome bum, Philip a besmirched bearer', he went for an even more romantically decrepit effect. 'I am established in an attic with a small window, a bed, an armchair, a basket chair, a carpet, a reading lamp THAT DOESN'T WORK, a small electric fire THAT DOESN'T WORK and a few books, papers, etc. "Literary men" like us count ourselves *kings of a nutshell* when we have at hand the company of "the gentle Elia" or "rare Ben", eh?'[7]

The 'papers' Larkin mentions here, almost smothered in irony so as not to seem valuable, were poems. Between leaving Wellington on 3 September and the beginning of October he had written six. Four of them ('And the wave sings', 'The Dedicated', 'Träumerei' and 'To a Very Slow Air') deal, in a language still coloured by Yeats, with the conflicting emotions he felt about leaving Ruth. He couldn't decide whether he had made a final break or a temporary separation. He didn't know whether to resign his responsibilities and allow the forces of circumstance to take his decisions for him. He was unable to sever the connection between his tender 'Eternal requirings' and his fear of death. In 'And the wave sings' (anticipating the third verse of one of his last poems, 'Aubade') he tries to dissolve his uncertainties in this larger drama:

> Death is a cloud alone in the sky with the sun.
> Our hearts, turning like fish in the green wave,
> Grow quiet in its shadow. For in the word death
> There is nothing to grasp; nothing to catch or claim;
> Nothing to adapt the skill of the heart to, skill
> In surviving, for death it cannot survive,
> Only resign the irrecoverable keys.
> The wave falters and drowns. The coulter of joy
> Breaks. The harrow of death
> Deepens. And there are thrown up waves.

The other two poems written this month dispense with Ruth by similar means. In the manner of Robert Frost's dramatic monologues, and some of Lawrence's, they tell stories which pass off their real emotional occasion as an anecdote about a third party. The earlier of the two, 'Two Guitar Pieces', opens with a description of a guitar player (he has 'a southern voice') sitting by a railroad. It then turns to an 'I' and a friend standing at a window while behind them the player 'lifts the guitar to his lap/Strikes this note, that note'. Apparently random, this music nevertheless creates art's 'accustomed harnessing of grief', consoling the speaker even as it reminds him of his isolation and social sterility. 'And now the guitar again,' the poem ends, echoing Eliot, 'Spreading me over the evening like a cloud,/ Drifting, darkening: unable to bring rain.'

In the second narrative poem, 'Wedding-Wind', which Larkin wrote ten days later, he speaks in the fictional voice of a young woman on the morning after her wedding. The final lines endeavour to annihilate his usual objections to happiness in a blaze of rhetorical questions:

> Can it be borne, this bodying-forth by wind
> Of joy my actions turn on, like a thread
> Carrying beads? Shall I be let to sleep
> Now this perpetual morning shares my bed?
> Can even death dry up
> These new delighted lakes, conclude
> Our kneeling as cattle by all-generous waters?

Five months before writing this, sitting in the library in Wellington one afternoon, Larkin had scribbled in his pocket diary: 'At 1.45 p.m. let me remember that the only married state I intimately know (i.e. that of my parents) is bloody hell. Never must it be forgotten.'[8] Now he was once again easing open the door through which Ruth might come into his life and settle down with him.

Previously there had been almost too much opportunity to brood on such things. In Leicester there was enough work and newness to distract him. Housed on the first floor of an L-shaped wing of the Fielding Johnson Building, with its entrance 'at the end of the main corridor that ran the length of the central block',[9] the library was beginning a process of expansion which would gradually accelerate throughout Larkin's time there. In 1945–6 the university's recurrent grant to the library was £12,000; Larkin's salary was £350; and the staff consisted of himself, Rhoda Bennett the librarian, and two others: Molly Bateman the senior assistant (a cheerful, dark-haired woman who wore jangling bracelets) and Maurice, a sixteen-year-old from the local secondary modern school. There was not a typewriter in the place. When Larkin left in 1950 the grant had more than doubled; the library had extended 'along another wing',[10] his salary had risen to £500, the number of staff 'both senior and junior'[11] had increased fourfold, and there was at least one typewriter (bought by Larkin himself in 1948).

His duties were only a little more focused than they had been in Wellington. As the one adult male member of staff he was expected to open packing cases, change light bulbs, climb ladders and cart around heavy objects. More orthodox responsibilities included 'issuing books to readers and answering their questions, reshelving returned books, cataloguing books and writing out library cards by hand'.[12] Within only a few days of arriving he was familiar enough with these routines to start complaining. 'I have had a tiring day today cataloguing ROTTEN OLD BOOKS,' he told Amis at the end of September:

You get BLOODY TIRED of writing the same things over and over again. For example I had a book in the Rolls Series (BOG ROLLS) containing three medieval lives of Edward the Confessor (he confessed to raping sixteen sheep in one day) edited by Jack Peebed. *Nay*, you (or rather *I* had) have to write out a full entry card under Peebed, under 942[E] (English History – sources), under Edward the Cunt-presser, under EACH life making THREE, and under ROLLS SERIES, so that anybody coming to the catalogue with even the vaguest ideas abeight it will eventually find it. This involved much MINUTE writing – about eight lines – on SEVEN cards.[13]

Larkin might soon have 'got sick'[14] of some of this work, but his colleagues found him humorous and helpful. Molly Bateman, for instance:

My own memories of Philip are very pleasant ones ... We were a very small staff then, working in conditions which would make the staff of larger libraries blench. We had to turn our hands to everything, not only skilled jobs like cataloguing and classification, but menial tasks like shelving, straightening and labelling. Relations with one's colleagues were therefore important. Philip was always fun to work with. He would lighten tasks with a keen sense of humour. He had a sardonic eye for the idiosyncrasies of the 'customers'. He reminded me in a letter he wrote soon after leaving of murmuring to me after the departure of a fussy academic a quotation from Shakespeare – 'See, it is offended. See, it stalks away.' He would tease his colleagues, too. I remember him once sending me a list of alleged overdue books I was supposed to have out. They included such gems as Plumchoker's *Foreign Policy of Boadicea*, and Garblebosh on *Undiscovered Fragments of Heraclitus*.[15]

Larkin enjoyed Leicester for leaving him to his own devices. 'I had never heard of the Association of University Teachers,' he said later; 'I never saw the minutes of the Library Committee or knew what went on in Senate.'[16] He kept his distance, too, from the teaching staff, even from those teaching English. Arthur Humphries, the Professor of English, remembers: 'He was always a private man, a capable and appreciated figure-behind-the-scenes in the library, but not much seen, an occasional unobtrusive visitor to the Senior Common Room, not much known as a writer and so not especially sought after, a frequenter of Leicestershire County Cricket matches [played at the county ground a short distance from his flat], content to sit there in his trilby.'[17] In other walks of college life Larkin was also more often a presence than a participant. He went to several departmental dances but did not dance; he played tennis without having 'any conception of how to serve',[18] he relied on the local jazz club for music, since Joan Sutcliffe wouldn't allow him to play records in his flat. Such things made for an amiable but solitary existence. Still prone to stammer, still physically unselfconfident, he lolloped quietly between his room and his work, hoping that the light ironies of his office banter would prevent his reticence from seeming abrupt.

Larkin was slow to commit himself to new friends, partly because he was still preoccupied with old ones. Sutton, Amis and Montgomery all visited him within the first few weeks of his arrival in Leicester, and he saw Ruth most weekends – either in London or, when they had found a convenient boarding house for her to stay in, near his own digs. Early in October, in a letter almost inarticulate with fear of his anger, she wrote telling him she thought she was pregnant. For several days she received no answer, then broke the silence herself by writing again to say it had been a false alarm. Judging by the two poems Larkin wrote shortly afterwards, the crisis deepened his ambivalent feelings about her, and about sex. In one of the poems, 'Many famous feet have trod', he analyses the 'double warp' of his 'mortal state', with its 'Two languages' of 'sorrow' and 'joy', then produces a strangulated gasp of praise for a life spent in the 'Perpetual study to defeat/Each slovenly grief'. In the second poem, 'At the chiming of light upon sleep', he settles the argument more convincingly. Although he had told Sutton two months before the poem was finished that 'I feel sex and death are perpetually opposed to each other',[19] in the privacy of his manuscript book he told a completely different story. He made an explicit connection between the expenditure of the self in love, and the extinction of the self in death:

> Have I been wrong, to think the breath
> That sharpens life is life itself, not death?

Never to see, if death were killed,
No desperation, perpetually unfulfilled,
Would ever go fracturing down in ecstasy?
Death quarrels, and shakes the tree,
And fears are flowers, and flowers are generation,
And the founding, foundering, beast-instructed mansion
Of love called into being by this same death
Hangs everywhere its light. Unsheath
The life you carry and die, cries the cock
On the crest of the sun: unlock
The words and seeds that drove
Adam out of his undeciduous grove.

Larkin's hopes that Leicester would help him decide what to do about Ruth had faded before he had been there a month. Late in October, the publication of *Jill* allowed him to review all the contradictions she provoked in him. Although the first draft had been completed more than two and a half years previously, in February 1944, the emotional dilemmas which prompted it were the same as those tormenting him now.

On the face of it, the novel describes the life Larkin led before he met Ruth. Its hero John Kemp – 'an undersized boy, eighteen years old, with a pale face and soft pale hair brushed childishly from left to right'[20] – is a version of his own provincial self arriving in Oxford. Larkin always pooh-poohed the idea that he resembled Kemp, and the evidence of his beer-drinking, hard-swearing, Dean-encountering undergraduate career tends to support this. But the feelings Larkin reveals in the few poems he wrote at St John's, particularly the feelings about sex, are as confused as Kemp's own.

Kemp's gaucheries are inspired by his worries about social class. His Lancashire childhood (his father is a retired policeman) has included nothing glamorous or sophisticated. When he arrives in college for his first term – a wartime autumn – and finds that he is sharing rooms with the loud-mouthed hearty Christopher Warner, he assumes that Warner is grander than he in fact proves to be. 'Lamprey School', Warner's alma mater, has been identified by the end of the novel as a shadily second-rank public school, but while some of his fellow students rely on this as a means of cutting Warner down to size, the distinction is lost on Kemp. As far as he is concerned, Warner's invasiveness (borrowing his crockery), opportunism (borrowing his money), and vulgarity (urinating, belching and vomiting 'copiously'[21]) are more than merely thoughtless. They are part of a style Kemp needs to emulate so that he can control or extinguish his feelings of exclusion. Before he has been in Oxford long, 'A dismal melancholy [had begun] to expand inside him, a great loneliness. It was the knowledge that he had nowhere to go more friendly, more intimate than this room that depressed him so, and particularly because the room was not his alone. He could not fortify himself inside it against the rest of the strangeness.'[22]

To counter these feelings Kemp invents a sister, Jill, who is three years younger than him and at school at Willow Gables in Derbyshire. One of the more remarkable (and buried) achievements of the novel is to assimilate at this point a certain amount of Brunette Coleman's material and none of her camp. Jill is a whimsical and spontaneous idea of Kemp's, but her function is serious and steady: to be an intimate in a hostile place; to be a means of impressing Warner. By inventing her, Kemp hopes to invent himself.

Kemp soon realizes that if Jill is to perform all the roles he intends for her, she has to be more than a sister. She has to become an almost-girlfriend. Accordingly, he changes her surname from Kemp to Bradley (it 'was a nice name, it was English, it was like saddle-leather and stables'[23]) and intensifies his barrage of letters to her. Rather than simply telling her the story of his daily doings in Oxford, getting their sorrows off his chest, Kemp recasts them – righting wrongs and hushing up slights. Rather than describe how Warner borrowed his crockery without permission, for instance, he tells her, 'I was able to play Lord Bountiful and unpack all my new stuff and everybody was happy and went away fed.'[24]

Writing these letters – and later, when he gives Brunette-ish details about Jill at Willow Gables to make her seem more 'independent'[25] – Kemp persuades himself that the quality which most fascinates him about her is her innocence. We hear she is 'a hallucination of innocence'[26] and elsewhere we're told, 'He thought he saw exactly what she was and how he should express it; the word was *innocent*.'[27] To an extent, Kemp is merely projecting his own personality here: because he is so inexperienced himself, an innocent character is all he can hope to create. Yet his maturing self, worked upon by the influences of Oxford, cannot hope to stay pristine for ever. As Kemp's innocence is joined or eroded by other characteristics, they too will be reflected in Jill's personality.

The invented Jill cannot contain such things, since her childhood world would be utterly destroyed by them. So Larkin changes tack, switching to real girls in real places. One afternoon Kemp sees Gillian (she's 'fifteen or sixteen years old'[28]), who perfectly embodies his sense of Jill. Perfectly but not exactly. Where Jill was static and demanded nothing more than Kemp's continuing interest in order to exist, Gillian is vivid and requires him to take decisions. Although he is slow to admit it, the thing which disturbs him most is the realization that he wants her. 'Disconcertingly,' we hear, 'the idea that [Kemp] had concocted out of the world's sight had suddenly showed itself in ordinary flesh and blood, as real, calling for real action on his part. What was he going to do?'[29]

Kemp grows increasingly alarmed as he becomes clear what 'doing' involves. The conditions of the real world are incompatible with those of his imagination; the harder he tries to get them on terms with each other, the more shaken he feels. He is revolted by his own appetites, and disgusted to see that they are shared by people around him. 'If this,' he says – meaning sex – 'was what his quest for Jill was leading him to, he would give it up without a second thought.'[30] But he cannot give it up. Once desire has been identified it leads the story forward to its conclusion. Kemp organizes a lavish tea-party for Gillian in his rooms, is prevented from entertaining her by her cousin Elizabeth, revenges himself by wrecking a fellow-undergraduate's room, then bumps into Gillian and kisses her. As a punishment he is thrown in the college fountain by Warner, and subsequently catches pneumonia before suffering the indignity of being rescued from the university by his parents. His attempt to create an independent existence has failed, at least for the time being.

While Kemp is still on his sick-bed he encompasses the novel's main themes in a series of visions. Some are purely sexual: as he remembers kissing Gillian ('everything was confined to the mouth'[31]) he is made to confront his physical frustration. Others are metaphysical, and revolve around questions of whether a fantasy life is preferable to a real one. Kemp's experience is so limited, we might think he hasn't yet acquired enough evidence to settle matters as weighty as this – but it doesn't stop him trying:

The fact that in life he had been cheated of [Gillian] was not the whole truth. Somewhere, in dreams perhaps, or on some other level, they had interlocked, and he had had his own way as completely as in life he had been denied it. And this dream showed that love died, whether fulfilled or unfulfilled. He grew confused whether she had accepted him or not, since the result was the same: and as this confusion increased, it spread to fulfilment and unfulfilment, which merged and became inseparable. The difference between them vanished.[32]

Returning to this idea a page later, Kemp wonders 'if there was no difference between love fulfilled and love unfulfilled, how could there be any difference between any other pair of opposites? Was he not freed for the rest of his life from choice?'[33] It is the novel's nearly concluding question, and the 'freedom' it recognizes is one attained only by a deep selfishness. It involves the pre-emptive refusal of all opportunities for love, excitement and difference, and binds him into a passive hopelessness.

Just when it looks as though *Jill* is going to stall in despair, it agitates itself with a couple of final questions. 'What did it matter,' Kemp asks, 'which road he took if they both led to the same place? He looked at the tree tops in the wind. What control could he hope to have over the maddened surface of things?'[34] Without much hope that it will bring him any happiness, Kemp (and Larkin) is just able here to strike a different note from the one he had sounded a moment before. Previously he had resigned his ability to make choices; now he is able to concede that control over things – which involves making choices between them – is at least desirable, even if finally impossible.

Larkin's relationship with Ruth shaped and was shaped by these questions – and by others to do with sex. He wanted it but loathed the thought of where it might lead (to marriage and children). He enjoyed it but his pleasure was hampered by self-disgust. He needed it but every time he reached out of his solitude he felt his integrity was threatened. In *Jill* these conflicts are rarely allowed into the open. Instead, they exist as speculative yearnings or as patterns of imagery, especially imagery to do with food.

In a book so concerned with the embarrassment of appetite, so conscious of wartime rationing, and so quickly brought to a crisis by a kiss (a mouth), food has to do a good deal more than simply be eaten. The first time we meet Kemp, on the train to Oxford, he is too ashamed to eat in front of strangers and gobbles his sandwiches in the lavatory. When he reaches his college (as we've seen) it is his crockery which has been appropriated by Warner, and the meal being eaten off it violates Kemp's sense of himself. Later, other characters also define themselves by reference to food – Warner by vomiting, and the Yorkshire scholar Whitbread by behaving 'like a man scouring his plate with a piece of bread'.[35] (The 'Yorkshire Scholar' was a figure of fun that he and Iles had invented at St John's to represent all kinds of academic diligence and dourness.) The conclusion, too, is precipitated by yet another meal: the seductive feast Kemp prepares for Gillian, which he is prevented from consuming. The room-wrecking which follows is an act of rape that Kemp is impelled to commit in compensation for his disappointment (in 1942 Larkin had told Sutton that a 'horrible tough is trying to ... beat me up because I helped wreck his room'[36]):

He opened the cupboard door, and, taking out the jam pot, put a large spoonful of jam on each of the open books lying on the desk. Then he snapped them shut. The rest of the jam he ladled onto the back of the fire, scraping out the pot thoroughly and licking the spoon. There was a nearly new pat of butter in the cupboard, too, and this he unwrapped from its paper and cut in half, putting each half in the toes of Whitbread's slippers. Then he filled the pockets of the jackets hanging in the bedroom with sugar and tea. In one of them was a pound note with a slip of paper bearing its numbers pinned to it, and he put that in his own pocket book. As an afterthought, he poured Whitbread's milk into the coal scuttle and lit the fire.[37]

Many people writing about *Jill* have made out that its central concerns are class difference and social awkwardness. 'An American critic,' Larkin reminds us at the beginning of his Introduction to the 1975 reissue, 'recently suggested that [it] contained the first example of the characteristic landmark of the British post-war novel, the displaced working-class hero.'[38] In fact this theme ends up being nowhere near as important in Larkin's novel as it is, say, in Amis's *Lucky Jim* or John Wain's *Hurry On Down*. It dominates the opening of the book, but becomes a part of the conflict Kemp acts out in Whitbread's room, the conflict between sexual desire and sexual abstinence. Is 'self the man' or is 'virtue social'? Should each individual obey 'your wants' or 'the world's for you'? These questions, posed throughout the remainder of Larkin's work, are evident in the novel which stands at the beginning of his career. They summarize the tensions upon which all his writing depends.

When Larkin received his first copy of *Jill* he felt let down. He was angry that it had taken so long for the book to arrive, and irritated that Caton (still fearing a second trial for obscenity) had removed 'a few mild obscenities'[39] from the text without permission. More seriously, he was disappointed by the critical response. Later he would allege that it aroused 'no public comment'[40] whatsoever. In fact it received nine reviews (one by Bruce Montgomery, writing as Edmund Crispin in the *Spectator*), all more or less respectful, but none promising the future Larkin wanted. Eventually he would make light of this, remembering, for instance, that Amis had 'enjoyed [the book] very much' and had written to tell him that he had 'seen a copy in a shop in Coventry Street [in London] between *Naked and Unashamed* and *High-Heeled Yvonne*'.[41] At the time there were no such comic compensations. 'Oh I do hope something comes of it,' he had said when the book was finished in 1944; 'I crave for tangible success.'[42] When it was published, he suspected that his career as a successful novelist was already doomed.

TWENTY-ONE

Four months after *Jill* appeared, things seemed to improve. On 21 February 1947 Faber published *A Girl in Winter*. In one sense it was as well that the two novels followed so hard on each other's heels. They had been written in quick succession, and according to Sutton were planned as the first two illustrations of Larkin's 'early theory that life consisted of three stages; the first representing innocence; the second its loss resulting in devastation; the third the struggle, after the desolation, to return to a truer and mature self: a sort of social history – his own'.[1]

Larkin's editor, Alan Pringle, had been in touch only intermittently since Faber had accepted the book the previous May. In November there had been a brief exchange of letters inquiring whether the character of Anstey, the librarian, was based on any real person and therefore libellous. 'The answer to your question,' Larkin had said, 'is as usual, yes and no. Anstey was based as far as personal manner goes on a real person [in fact Astley-Jones, who had appointed him to his job at Wellington and had been a member of the local council Library Committee]. The circumstances I placed him in were imaginary and invented to fit the book itself ... I think your first impression of the portrayal – as inoffensive – was just, because although I may not have succeeded I wished to leave a final version of good in the reader's mind. The importance of sympathizing with people like Anstey is one of the book's minor lessons!'[2]

Larkin's publishers were pacified by this explanation, and didn't contact Larkin again until shortly before publication, when they needed material to publicize the novel. He provided them with a graphic self-portrait:

[Wellington] was about the only 'adventurous' thing in my life. I was so sick of the academic atmosphere that I took this quite impossible job, replacing an aged librarian-caretaker of 76, handing out antiquated tripe to the lower levels of the general public . . . It was horrible . . .

A few visits to Germany left hardly any impression: for vivid impressions I prefer England. I am so far unmarried. The writing of novels has always been my ultimate ambition, and, if I can say so without pomposity, few days pass when I don't realize afresh how much it is my chief pleasure, task and – almost – debt. I only wish I had done more and done it better.[3]

Larkin presents himself here as someone both proud and humble, settling down to what he hoped would be a long professional relationship. It was the same when he received finished copies on 25 February. 'I find myself,' he told Pringle, 'highly delighted with the format and general production'[4] – and joked to his friends that forces other than Faber were working to promote the book. 'By God!' he wrote to Sutton. 'How are you getting on in this buggerly cold spell? The air is like the breath from the cold regions of hell, and I snuffle all day despite many jerseys and quacking patent medicines. I can only regard it as a heaven-sent advertising campaign for *A Girl in Winter* – or at least a good omen.'[5]

Later in this letter Larkin worries that the weather will 'show up my imaginings as falling short of reality'.[6] (The winter of 1947 was one of the coldest this century.) In fact every sort of description in *A Girl in Winter* – of weather and everything else – is not so much less than the truth as distanced from it. In the very first scene we are told that the landscape is 'so white and still it might have been a painting',[7] and this kind of transformation is repeated throughout the book. Where *Jill* is full of action which performs a quite unselfconscious symbolic function, *A Girl in Winter* is scattered with details which are always deliberately manipulated. *Jill* aspires to the condition of real life, *A Girl in Winter* to allegory – as Larkin himself admitted. It is what he meant when he referred to it in public as a 'Virginia Woolf–Henry Green'[8] novel, and what he said in private when he told his parents, '*A Girl in Winter* deals with less explicit feelings and so I have tried to represent them by indirect reference and allegoric incident.'[9]

These 'less explicit feelings' are concentrated on the heroine, Katherine. We're never told where she comes from (though we discover her grandfather was a silversmith), but during the first third of the novel we learn that she is an exile in England, banished from her home in middle Europe by the 'apparently meaningless disasters'[10] of the Second World War. (Like Kemp, her innate awkwardness is exacerbated by wider social upheavals.) Her isolation is evident in everything about her – even her looks mark her out: 'Her pale shield-shaped face, dark eyes and eyebrows, and high cheek bones, were not mobile or eloquent. Nor, more curiously, was her mouth, which was too wide and too full-lipped for beauty.'[11]

One might expect Katherine's displacement to make her a pathetic figure. In fact she is tough. Holding a minor position in a provincial library, and bullied by the chief librarian Anstey, she stoutly volunteers at the start of the novel to take a 'spiteful'[12] colleague, Miss Green, to the dentist. In part, her strength comes from the thought that soon she will be meeting a young man she last saw in England several years previously, before the war. This young man, Robin Fennel, is someone as much at home in the country as she is vulnerable – 'the Fennels were nothing if not English'[13] we are told – and his stability is one of the things that fortifies her. Another is the memory of the summer they spent together as adolescents in the Fennels' house outside Oxford. The holiday left her full of possibilities for happiness which haven't yet been exhausted.

The story of Katherine's summer with Robin occupies the middle section of the book, but before it begins, the plot has to beef itself up. We have to endure Miss Green's pain at the dentist (mouths, which yearned for fulfilment in *Jill*, are here punished). We glean a few more details about the Fennels (Robin's father is an auctioneer; he has a sister called Jane). We learn a detail we will need later (Katherine inadvertently swaps handbags with a Miss V. Parbury, who turns out to be Anstey's girlfriend). When the flashback to summer finally begins, it comes with reminders of both *Jill* and Brunette Coleman. Katherine and Robin first meet by writing to each other – they are pen pals – and while there's a whiff of Willow Gables about their correspondence, we realize their letters also perform a similar function to those written by Kemp to Jill Bradley. They are missives sent into the blue, designed to attract a recipient as much as to define the character of the writer. When Katherine travels to England and meets Robin for the first time, the sense of reality she has created in his absence is replaced by incredulity in his presence. It is 'unbelievable'[14] that she has crossed the Channel; she feels she has passed into 'another life';[15] she looks at him 'unbelievingly';[16] and throughout their time together she wonders when he is 'going to start behaving naturally'.[17]

The Fennels are kind to Katherine, organizing trips into Oxford, playing tennis with her, including her in family life. But the longer she stays with them, the less clearly she understands Robin's reasons for inviting her. Imagination and reality have changed places: what should be actual and exciting is remote and cool. Robin's actions 'rarely ha[ve] anything stronger than the flavour of the motive around them';[18] he is like 'a prince regent and foreign ambassador combined';[19] he is 'mechanical'[20] – so much so that the passage of time itself becomes unnatural: 'Here, with the Fennels, time had a different quality from when she was at home. She could almost feel it passing slowly, luxuriously, like thick cream pouring from a silver jug.'[21]

Robin's sister Jane contributes to this lethargy. Twenty-five years old, listless, she 'does seem prepared to be friendly, but doesn't know how to go about it'.[22] She hangs around her brother like a discontented chaperone, prompting Katherine to think that Robin might lose his 'barren perfection'[23] if they were to give Jane the slip. Precisely what might follow is unclear, but we understand that Katherine's motives, like Kemp's when he exchanges the invented Jill for the real Gillian, have something to do with sexual desire. Robin, we are told, 'treated her as he might a boy of his own age whom he wanted to impress. With him she simply could not get going. And this annoyed her because he was so attractive.'[24] Once Katherine has admitted this she becomes increasingly knowledgeable about her feelings for Robin – and about the difficulty of realizing them. 'Because Katherine was so young,' Larkin writes, anticipating the language of his poem 'Love Songs in Age', 'she had hitherto thought love a pleasant thing; the state that put order into her life, directing her thoughts and efforts towards one end.'[25] The discovery that love can be more than merely 'a pleasant thing' puts 'a curious constraint upon her'.[26] We hear that 'the desire she felt for him was cloudy and shameful',[27] it makes her feel 'guilty',[28] it is a 'burden' which might betray her 'into actions she would regret'.[29] Katherine's dilemma, once again, is very similar to Kemp's: she is prevented from happily quitting the world of innocence by realizing that the only escape route is patrolled by rampaging forces of appetite. To resist them compounds a reprehensible selfishness; to surrender to them involves recognizing a shamefully common humanity.

Eventually, in a punt on the river one evening, Robin stops being 'a figure in allegory'[30] and kisses her. It is the moment Katherine has both longed for and dreaded, the moment when desire and will, instinct and intellect, meet and cancel each other out:

He ducked his head and kissed her inexpertly with tight lips, as if dodging something that swept above their heads. It was not a bit like lovemaking, and she never thought of it as such until afterwards. He kept his face hidden against her hair. At the end of this unfathomable interval, he shivered, and the shiver changed to a short scrambling shudder, almost an abortive attempt to climb on her, then he slowly relaxed. Still he would not look her in the face. In the end he released her, carelessly.[31]

This fiasco closes the second part of the novel in much the same mood as Kemp's disastrous kiss ended *Jill*. When the third section opens, in the wintry present again, we are asked to believe that Katherine has been utterly changed by the encounter. It is the book's weakest moment but also a fascinating one. Reading it, we feel Larkin has shooed the characters off the stage of his imagination and stepped forward to speak in his own voice:

She knew – for such a break brings knowledge, but no additional strength – that her old way of living was finished. In the past she thought she had found happiness through the interplay of herself and other people. The most important thing had been to please them, to love them, to learn them so fully that their personalities were as the distinct taste of different fruits. Now this brought happiness no longer. She no longer felt that she was exalted or made more worthy if she could spin her friendships to incredible subtlety and fineness. It was something she had tired of doing. And what had replaced it? Here she was at a loss, she was not sure if anything had replaced it.

She was not sure if anything would replace it.

For the world seemed to have moved off a little, and to have lost its immediacy, as a bright pattern will fade in many washings ... She felt one of her faculties had died without her consent or knowledge, and she was less than she had been. The world that she had been so used to appraising, delighting in, and mixing with had drawn away, and she no longer felt that she was part of it.[32]

This mood is elaborated, rather than justified, on most of the novel's remaining pages. It transpires that Robin – now called up into the army and waiting to be sent overseas – is stationed nearby, and is coming to see Katherine before embarking. The excitement she had felt about this in Part One has been overwhelmed by the memories of Part Two. Now she wants to 'shut out the future';[33] she refuses 'to be surprised any more'.[34] She feels it is impossible to live a life shaped by choices, since everyone's actions are 'directed by their personality, which is not self-chosen in the first place and modifies itself quite independently of their wishes afterwards'.[35] Katherine's visit to Miss Parbury (Anstey's 'quaint, sloppy ... breathless and rather grotesque'[36] girlfriend) bears this out. Miss Parbury's life is a misery because she can't understand that an individual might have 'a duty to oneself': she says, 'It sounds so silly.'³⁷ Katherine may have cut herself off from life, but at least she has the satisfaction of feeling safe in her intransigence.

When Robin arrives, drunk, nervous and jaunty, the same point is made more despairingly. He asks to sleep with Katherine and she tells him, 'It wouldn't mean anything.' 'Damn it,' Robin replies, 'what does that matter?'³⁸ In their different ways, both remarks rephrase the conclusion of *Jill*, arguing that 'love dies, whether fulfilled or unfulfilled'. The two novels agree that the imaginary world, the world where men are characters and women fantasies, can never get on terms with the real world. This may make the imagination in some respects inferior to reality, but its role as a safe haven is secure. Within its boundaries hearts may grow cold, selfishness may become absolute, and the possibilities for joy may be savagely restricted. Outside its shelter, however, wait larger dangers – not just heartbreak, but the self-dilution involved in love and (even worse) marriage.

The last few pages of *A Girl in Winter* are preoccupied with closure and isolation, but as the novel went on sale Larkin was already looking ahead. He felt the chances of writing a third novel were all the greater now that he had a better sense of his audience. Where *Jill* had fallen on stony ground, *A Girl in Winter* benefited from the boom in fiction sales which had occurred during the war and the years immediately following, selling its 5,000-copy print run within eight months, and receiving half a dozen favourable reviews. These included one by Amis in the Oxford-based magazine *Mandrake*, one by Anthony Powell in the *Daily Telegraph*, one 'really good'³⁹ one by Michael Sadleir in the *Sunday Times*, which called the novel 'an exquisite performance and nearly faultless',⁴⁰ and one in the *Church Times* which said it was 'clever [and] sympathetic . . . in that undramatic way that can be more painful to contemplate than high tragedy'.⁴¹

The *Church Times* reviewer ended by saying, 'We look forward with eager anticipation to further work from the pen of this remarkable young writer.'⁴² Larkin cut the piece out and kept it all his life. He believed, at last, that he had written a novel which would make his name, exempt him from the drudgery of library work, and allow him to realize his ambitions as an artist. The comparative failure of *Jill* had been quickly pushed aside; Faber had replaced Caton; Kemp's cringing confusion had been transformed into Katherine's courageous self-possession.

Or so it seemed. In fact – and ominously – Katherine's fate at the end of her novel is not much less of a defeat than Kemp's at the end of *Jill*. She may have achieved a more complex version of the Pygmalion myth than he could manage (in *Jill* the best Kemp can do is create an unworkable fantasy; in *A Girl in Winter* Katherine is maker as well as made), but the price of her final independence is high. By distancing herself from Robin during their dismal seduction scene, she removes herself from the world generally. She volunteers for permanent exile in the snow-covered land-scape of her own self, preferring its low temperatures and sexual repres-sions to the risks and the possible rewards of social life. To bring her back, to forgive the world while allowing her to retain her integrity, was the work of Larkin's next several years as a novelist. It was to prove a desperate and finally a vain labour.

TWENTY-TWO

When Larkin read the reviews of *A Girl in Winter* he told his parents, 'I have been very happy receiving a certain amount of lionization from all sorts and conditions of men and one or two letters . . . I am awfully glad to think that my solitary Shropshire labour was not entirely in vain.'[1] Around the university in particular, he felt rewarded. In the space of a few days, his novel had turned him from a nondescript new recruit in the library into an object of speculation. Accordingly, he began to revise his feelings about the place. He went to the jazz club and the film club more often. Rather than returning to his lodgings whenever possible, he started to drink out occa-sionally in local pubs, or have coffee after lunch in the Tatler Café in London Road.

It was in the Tatler one lunchtime during the early spring of 1947 that he was spotted by Monica Jones, a young lecturer in the English Depart-ment. 'Who's that?' she whispered to the colleague sitting beside her. 'Philip Larkin,' she was told, 'the man in the library who's just written that book.' 'He looks like a snorer,' Monica replied.[2] It was an inauspicious start to the most important relationship of his life.

Larkin had seen Monica in the library but knew nothing about her except what he could see: that she had 'fair hair, black horn spectacles, dresse[d] rather specially and [was] quite small'.[3] She was three months older than him (born on 8 May 1922), and an only child. Her father,

Frederick James Jones, had been born in Llanelli, Carmarthen, in 1896 and apprenticed to the Welsh Tinplate and Metal Stamping Company when he was fifteen. When the war broke out he joined the Royal Army Medical Corps, serving in the Infectious Diseases Hospital in Etaples. On leave shortly before the Armistice he met Margaret Lily Peart while visiting a friend in the village of St John's Chapel, near Stanhope in Northumberland, fell in love with her, and was soon married. After the war the young couple lived in Llanelli, then in 1929, when Monica was seven, moved to a house called Ravenswood in Bewdley Road, Stourport-on-Severn, Worcestershire. The family was to stay in Stourport, where Frederick worked as an engineer, for the rest of their lives, moving from Ravenswood to 44 Summerfield Road in 1943.

When she was thirteen Monica's parents sent her to the high school nearby in Kidderminster, and although she reckoned herself to be 'a dim dull girl' she impressed her teachers. She was especially keen on English literature, but was apt to disguise her interest as mockery. Among her papers there exists a series of schoolgirl drawings called 'A Case of the Poet', in which a number of suitcases belonging to various poets are shown with their lids open and their contents spilling out. The Housman suitcase, for instance, contains a Roman relic picked up under Uricon, a pair of ear-plugs 'so not to hear when spoken to', a razor, a knife, some poison, a rope, a copy of *Oedipus Rex*, a picture of Bredon Hill, and a set of university exam papers to mark.

Any poems she wrote herself were most likely to succeed when filled with ironies. One, beginning, 'I ask no cure; I understand/How all our lives are lived alone', is much less striking than 'Songs of (Bitter) Experience':

> Dryden Dryden, hidden quite
> In the uncut leaves from sight
> What unpleasant ear or eye
> Could bare thy fearful symmetry?
> In what distant shelf or nook
> Rots thy dull and mouldering book?
> On what grounds dids't thou aspire?
> What made thee think we should admire?

In its modest way, this poem is a counterpart to Larkin's book-baiting. Like him, Monica was often facetious about the things she took most seriously, and tough on subjects which touched her deeply. It was a cast of mind which made her seem prickly when she went up to St Hugh's

College, Oxford, to read English in October 1940, the same term that Larkin arrived at St John's. Contemporaries remember her as someone whose shyness turned easily to scorn. She was scathing about merely fashionable views, prone to fits of gloomy inertia, passionate in her defence of writers she admired (particularly Crabbe and Scott) yet reluctant to broadcast her views: she never published a single academic article or book. Her idiosyncrasies were reflected in the 'rather special'[4] way she dressed. Oxford friends remember how she pushed her fair hair straight back from her fine-featured face, wore filmstar-academic's glasses, and preferred brightly coloured, hand-made, unconventional clothes. Later friends at Leicester remember her wearing tartan to lecture on *Macbeth*, and appearing wound around with a long rope of imitation pearls to talk about *Antony and Cleopatra*. With her inability to suffer fools, her slightly pouting mouth, and her abrupt speech, she contended with the world in style.

In fact her style often registered a lack of confidence. The route from Stourport to St Hugh's had been an arduous one, and much of her apparent severity was born of anxiety. Socially speaking, her undergraduate life was modest to the point of being retiring: in spite of her devotion to literature she not only failed to meet the aspiring poet Larkin, she never even came across his poems in magazines, or attended the English Club. Oxford, Larkin wrote thirty years after arriving there for the first time, was a city they 'shared without knowing'. It was a secret connection, a link which suggested discretion as well as association.

Watching her progress through the university, Monica's tutors – Ethel Seaton and Helen Gardner among them – predicted for her a brighter academic future than Larkin's expected for him. They were justified. In the same Schools that Larkin snatched his First, Monica got one too. Encouraged to think she might enter academic life, but initially doubting her ability, she taught English at Brereton Hall School not far from her parents in Stourport for a year, gathered her courage, tried and failed to get a job at King's College, London, then in 1943 applied to Leicester. She was drawn to the town, and to the university, by the same mixture of formality and family intimacy that would attract Larkin, and she stayed for the remainder of her working life. In the three years she lived there before his arrival (she had a small flat in Cross Street), she became one of the most talked-about figures on the campus. 'Monica Jones,' remembers Pamela Hanley, a part-time member of the library staff, with her 'long blond hair, black-rimmed glasses, black sweater, and brilliantly patterned dirndl skirts, attracted all the ex-servicemen who gathered round her after morning lectures. [Her] clear voice cut through the hum of provincial accents.'[5]

Monica's manner in tutorials was as striking as her performance in lectures. Bruce Woodcock, whom she taught in the 1960s, remembers her appearing in fishnet tights and a mini-skirt to hand him back the weekly essay he had written on Yeats. It had been showered with thoughts and suggestions, most of which indicate how close her own views were to Larkin's. Woodcock had quoted the well-known lines from Yeats's 'The Lake Isle of Innisfree':

> I will arise and go now, and go to Innisfree,
> And a small cabin build there, of clay and wattles made:
> Nine bean-rows will I have there, a hive for the honey-bee,
> And live alone in the bee-loud glade.

Beside these Monica had written:

I always think the 9 bean rows bit is nonsense – 9 bean rows, and *live alone*: anybody who's ever tried to keep up with even one or two bean rows in August will know that this is rubbish; better *one* bean row and 9 hives for the honey bee – honey will *keep*. This is a bit frivolous perhaps, but not altogether so. Anyway, it's something to think about; and can this *sort* of poem tell the practical truth? 9 bean rows! The liar! It's all artificial and this proves that it is.

Later in the margin of the essay, talking about 'Down by the Salley Gardens', Monica reinforces her argument, saying the poem 'does go deeper than a lot that Y. says. Who cares abt the bloody gyres? Everybody cares abt love.' At the end she returns to the fray once more, further disparaging Yeats, then asking:

in the meantime, have you read Hardy's poetry? It seems to me that at present it is rather difficult to appreciate Yeats and Hardy as it requires some catholicity to appreciate, *truly*, both Donne and Milton. 'As of today', as the Americans say, I am so strongly for Hardy that I'm probably incapable of seeing Yeats properly. I shan't change. But of course I can see a lot in Yeats to admire; he could *write* – no doubt abt that tho' his imagery is somewhat limited and there's altogether too much of the Mask and the parade . . . Sometimes I'm persuaded (I don't just mean by other people) that he's good; sometimes he seems just like a mad twinkle on the very edge of life.[6]

The resemblance between his own and Monica's sympathies explains why Larkin came to trust her. The vigour with which she expressed them shows why he at first hesitated to approach her. Compared to the few women he had known before, she seemed dauntingly intelligent. He shrank back, and for months they remained only remotely aware of each other. Gradually, though, the currents of university life drew them together. Larkin realized that Monica's looks were the outward and visible form of an inward and spiritual revolt against convention. Beneath her brave façade he discerned (like others at Leicester) 'a clever, slightly flirtatious career girl – a version of the heroine of that novel of Leicester *Scenes from Provincial Life* by William Cooper', and appreciated that 'she knew what she was doing'.[7] Monica, in turn, saw that while Larkin's looks 'certainly, were against him',[8] he was intellectually self-assured: amusing, ironical and ambitious. 'He wanted to be a great man,' she realized, 'and most of all a great novelist; he would sit around thinking about it.'[9]

Both relished each other's combination of diffidence and resilience. They had been brought up in the provinces, then been played upon by the cosmopolitan influences of Oxford; their sensibilities had evolved along similar lines. Because they were suspicious of the world they tended to dismiss it. Because they doubted other people they insisted on their independence. Because they regarded literature as a haven, they took refuge in it while insisting it should be able to survive the sarcasm of the ordinary world. Having coffee in the Tatler, chatting in the library, watching cricket together once the season started, Monica discovered that Larkin's great and receptive modesty, like her own, was founded on an iron selfishness. 'He cared,' she felt, 'a tenth as much about what happened around him as he did about what was happening inside him.'[10]

In certain obvious respects this boded ill for their future together – though for the time being nothing more than acquaintance was on offer. For one thing, Larkin had to square any interest in girls with his loyalty to Amis, and he knew from his experience with Ruth that this was virtually impossible. When Monica and Amis eventually met they didn't get on. 'There was a sort of adhesive thing about her,' Amis felt. 'Not quite predatory, but still . . .'[11] Monica, for her part, thought, 'Kingsley wasn't just making faces all the time, he was actually trying them on. He didn't know who he was.'[12]

There was another, more serious reason why Larkin didn't hurry to get to know Monica better. He didn't want to let go of the past, no matter how much Ruth might fret about their new routines. The physical distance between them was prohibitive; the distractions of his new life were becoming more than she could handle. Soon she began to question even the value of love itself. 'I place such huge importance on loving,' she told him, but 'I always find it difficult to trust in when applied to myself. It's been the same all my life, though I don't know from what queer complex it springs. When I was small if anything I ate had a peculiar flavour I immediately suspected that my mother had grown tired of me and was trying to poison me.'[13] Gradually Ruth's insecurity infected all her feelings for Larkin. Sex made her anxious because 'I always feel that *one* day we shall slip up'[14]; she felt constrained by a 'sense of sin' which exerted 'a big strain on me, bigger than I can keep on bearing'.[15]

Larkin resented Ruth's worries but couldn't help being affected by them. They disorientated him, making it difficult for him to form fresh alliances with anyone – let alone Monica. Twice, before the year was half over, he felt that moving to Leicester had been a mistake. In February he applied for a job with the British Museum; in May he tried for another at the Bodleian in Oxford. Even though he was now almost a full member of the Library Association (he passed the final exams in July), neither application was successful. Disappointment quickly turned to self-recrimination and then, as the summer vacation began, into depression. He tinkered with the beginning of his new novel; he was unable to write poems; he felt the dreariness he had known at Wellington beginning to envelop him again. 'Well,' he wrote to Sutton in June, 'life goes buggering along here like some lousy old tramp knowing he's nearly dead but all the same cadging money for beer and trying to crawl under a hedge to get into a racetrack. Meaning in plain English I suppose I am generally wasting time and money to no particular purpose, and that life is giving rather seedy returns.'[16]

Knowing it wouldn't help, Larkin went home to Coten End for August and his twenty-fifth birthday, grumpily fulfilling his family obligations by admiring his sister's baby daughter, then visiting John Wain, his near-contemporary at St John's. As undergraduates there had been no time for them to get to know each other well; now, with Wain about to start teaching English at the University of Reading, in Berkshire, there was a chance for real friendship to begin. Larkin took Ruth with him, but it was not a success, as his thank-you letter to Wain admitted. 'Ruth had been feeling rather seedy,' he explained, 'and her export-or-die feeling was being aggravated by shyness in strange company. So I thought we had better leave, though I myself would gladly have gone on talking and drinking much longer – well, you probably know me well enough for that.'[17]

When Larkin returned to Leicester at the end of August his landlady at 172 London Road, Joan Sutcliffe, announced that she wanted his room for another lodger. He hastily rented another nearby, at 6 College Street. It was an attic flat with a dormer window on the third floor of a red-brick Victorian house in a narrow street off the London Road. He moved on 7 September and hated it. 'Picture me in another garret,' he told Sutton:

– or no, garrets are supposed to be romantic; say a maid's bedroom – with a bed (of which more in a moment), a dressing-table plus drawers, a fireplace plus gas fire *plus* meter, an armchair with a disconcertingly sliding seat, a small table (three and a quarter inches by one and three-quarter inches roughly) and hard chair, large cupboard and bookcase. The bed was very hard, more like a dried-up watercourse. This morning I took the liberty of exchanging it for a better one, and got a ticking off from the landlady for my presumption. However, I kept the bed. But the row was depressing – I agree that she had to a certain extent right on her side . . . but you see she is deaf, and agrees to almost anything you ask her . . . The food is all right, really: the kitchen tends to stink foully and there is really no room to keep a bike. It is also rather a shabby house. Show me a better one and I'll go to it. But I doubt if I shall have the energy to look for one by myself.[18]

Within a few days, Larkin had redirected his anger towards his neighbours ('the worst type; they have children and wirelesses'[19]) and fellow-lodgers. He told Sutton that one of them was 'decent enough',[20] but this didn't prevent him becoming the target of furious attacks. The isolated entry in Larkin's pocket diary for 10 October, for instance, reads, 'A day marked by intense dislike of that whey-faced turd [my fellow-lodger], who wakes me up in the night, borrows my books without asking, and has not the forethought to save pennies for the meters and so has to borrow them off me who has, the stupid cunt.'[21] Because College Road posed a new threat to his solitude, it also revived his anxieties about writing. It was two years since he had finished *A Girl in Winter*, and the 'great stirring' he felt within him, 'like a blacked-out factory on the nightshift',[22] showed no sign of turning into words. For this to happen, as he had often explained to Sutton, he needed tranquillity. Because of Ruth, because of his work in the library, because of his first feelings for Monica, because of the distractions of his flat, this was impossible. 'Somewhere,' he had once told Sutton:

far down in my nature, something is uncoiling itself, stretching itself, gathering its forces for what will be at some future date, in a year or two years, a spring, a leap . . . or so I hope! I want to write a *long* book. And that means plenty of things happening. And that means equal power to balance the happenings (one needs more power to write of a death than of, say, a visit to the dentist). And that means IMAGINATIVE POWER, aha, electric force zipping through the personality and putting a gold line round everyday objects the same as whoever it was put a black line round everyday objects . . . But I am starting to write like Mary Baker Eddy.[23]

To make this 'uncoiling' more likely, Larkin decided to turn aside from prose for a while and concentrate on his poems. *The North Ship* had been sent to Caton in the autumn of 1944 and could safely be regarded as juvenilia. Three years on, he wanted to publish his first mature collection. By the end of 1947 he was ready: he selected twenty-four poems written since *The North Ship* and began typing them out to send to Alan Pringle at Faber under the title *In the Grip of Light*. It was, he told Sutton, 'a phrase which occurred to me and seems to sum up the state of being alive'.[24] If Larkin had consulted the ironical side of his mind, he would have realized the title was a mistake. Its pretentiousness, and its blend of Symbolist vagueness with a precise self-regard, make it one of his least characteristic phrases. The selection itself is similarly disappointing. While including one of the two best poems he had written recently ('Wedding-Wind'), he excluded the other ('Going'). He also omitted 'Waiting for breakfast, while she brushed her hair', completed on 15 December, preferring instead vapid neo-Yeatsian murmurings like 'Come then to prayers', and 'I put my mouth'. In 'Waiting for breakfast' Larkin pledged himself to art rather than individuals, yet *In the Grip of Light* makes very little of his commitment. The manuscript was a rare misjudgement – a proof, if proof were needed, of how desperately he wanted to build on the success of *A Girl in Winter*.

As Larkin put the collection together, he struggled to keep his gathering depression at bay. In October he bought his first camera (saying it was 'an act of madness'[25] because it cost £7; in fact photography became a favourite hobby). Shortly before Christmas he decided that more literary diversions were in order and travelled to London to meet 'a man called Arthur Ley, who was proposing to start a poetry magazine called *Canto*'.[26] The visit persuaded him that his distrust of the literary life was well placed. Ley took him, he remembered later, to

[a] poetry evening where everyone present had to write a poem on a set subject which was then transcribed in what was referred to as the Grey Book. The subject that evening was 'Up River', and I duly wrote my poem like everybody else, and I suppose it was transcribed into the Grey Book. Needless to say I have no idea of the name of my hostess (she was, as I recall, a middle-aged lady), but I remember that an absent member of the group was Kenneth Hopkins, and he was rung up in the course of the evening and made to write his poem and telephone it back. All in all it

was a terrible time: I got a little of my own back by imitating a cat mewing (a talent I inherited from my father ...), and this got my hostess out on the fire escape looking for the animal. I've never seen or heard of Arthur Ley since.[27]

Back in Leicester, looking over his manuscript for the last time, Larkin turned with new enthusiasm to a more compatible audience. In the letters he wrote to his friends between the beginning of the autumn term and the end of the year, he let fly more freely than ever before with opinions about other poets. Lawrence, he told Sutton, is 'so great that it is silly to start saying where he was wrong',[28] Eliot, he announced, was 'an old tin can';[29] Edward Thomas, he said, was preferable to Byron – and so on. The impression he creates is of someone collecting himself for an assault on life, putting his past (his poems) in order, marshalling his achievements, bracing himself for a big event. Two weeks after the new year began, he would discover that something momentous was indeed about to happen, something which for a while made him stop writing altogether.

TWENTY-THREE

Larkin spent Christmas 1947 at Coten End. Usually his visits home bored and irritated him; this time he was frightened. His father was ill, and the house hushed. Early in the new year Sydney was taken into hospital, apparently for a simple operation to remove gallstones. He failed to recover as quickly as everyone hoped. 'Whereas when he went [in],' Larkin told Sutton, 'he was in good spirits, no pain, ate well, etc., now he is much worse off having had injections to make him itch and lose appetite and not sleep and so on.'[1] Three weeks later the hospital announced that the operation had been a success, but Larkin was not convinced. Sitting at his father's bedside, he could see for himself that Sydney was depressed and exhausted. 'I fancy total recovery is by no means inevitable,' he wrote grimly to Sutton. 'The worry is of course far greater for my mother, but the dolefulness of the general situation lies very heavily on my mind.'[2]

Everyone accepted that Larkin could not stay away from work indefinitely, but when he returned to Leicester in the middle of January he felt restless. His library routines seemed dull; writing, which might have distracted him, also let him down. On 3 February he heard from Alan Pringle (via his agent Peter Watt) that Faber had decided against publishing *In the Grip of Light*. He replied that it was 'no matter',[3] but was in fact sharply disappointed and tried to bury his hurt beneath a progress report on his new novel. It 'becomes clearer to me in conception', he told Pringle, 'as time to work on it becomes shorter: the ordinary affairs of life can very easily upset the apple cart of one's plans, I'm finding.'[4]

For the next few weeks his life remained far from ordinary. Sydney became gloomier by the day and Eva more miserably agitated. In February, fussing unhappily round her kitchen, she fell and broke her wrist. Larkin considered moving back to Coten End to look after her for a while. No, she told him when he came to see her for a weekend, she didn't need him. During the same visit he learnt from the hospital that Sydney's prospects were just as bleak as everyone feared. Back in Leicester on 24 February he wrote to Sutton:

I am in bad spirits at present because of my father – I'm afraid it is all up for him, matter of weeks. Please don't tell anyone, as *he* doesn't know and we don't want it to become known in Coventry. There's little to say, of course: but in addition to sorrow I can't get used to the fact of death and am trying hard to accept it in a spirit of faith. But really, what has one any faith in? I feel that I have got to make a big mental jump – to stop being a child and become an adult – but it isn't easy for me, though I keep trying. I shall have to learn the technique right from the start.[5]

Larkin realized he was facing a crisis. Sydney had been the dominating figure in his life – a model of intellectual rigour, an audience for his writing, and an example, too, of how an independent mind might be snared in a domestic trap. The son had often been alarmed by the father's severities but had always looked up to him, and over the years they had steadily grown closer to each other. To lose him, Larkin thought, would be to lose part of himself.

On 22 March it was clear that Sydney had only a little while left. The cancer which his doctors had discovered when they operated the previous January had spread throughout his body. Eva telegraphed Larkin at the library in Leicester and told him to come quickly; four days later, on Good Friday, Sydney died. Larkin was immediately swamped by practicalities. There was the funeral to arrange. (Sydney was cremated on 31 March, his family following his instructions to adapt the service so that it made no reference to the resurrection.) There was the will to read (everything was left to Eva). There was the rest of the family to look after (Eva went to stay with Kitty at 53 York Road in Loughborough). Once all this had been dealt with,

Larkin was free to confront his own feelings. He was desolate, resisting all Ruth's efforts to comfort him. He had given her the news of Sydney's death by sending a postcard which said simply, 'My father's illness came to an end yesterday',[6] and the following morning had sent another card with nothing written on it but her address. 'I'm quite sure,' she told him, 'that together if we are patient we shall be able to lift you from that awful and quite illogical despondency you are experiencing, and make you see some point in living.'[7] Larkin made no reply. He didn't want to be reminded of the point of life; he wanted to come to terms with his sorrow by possessing it utterly and alone.

As he struggled to do so, Ruth felt Larkin was changing. It wasn't quite that he was becoming a different man, she felt, but the same man in a different key: more concentrated, more decisive about which things mattered and which didn't. Sometimes this meant that his instinct for comedy turned (as his father's had done) into sarcasm. Sometimes it meant making an unembarrassed melodramatic flourish – as when, walking one day with Ruth, he ran across a dangerously busy road in order to avoid passing a laundry which announced in the window 'DYEING DONE HERE'.[8] In these and other respects, Larkin assumed characteristics which would shape the whole of the rest of his life. Sydney's death made him feel grave yet in certain respects theatrical;[9] it strengthened his need for independence, yet increased his reliance on others; it made him his own man, yet anchored him for ever on his father's shadow. 'I felt very proud of him,' he told Sutton the day after the cremation; 'as my sister remarked afterwards, "We're nobody now: he did it all."'[10] As he cut out the obituaries from the local papers, he realized how many of Sydney's qualities had already become his own. The *Journal of Local Government Financial Officers*, for instance, said: '[Sydney Larkin] hated humbug, he hated change, and he hated circumlocution; and his directness was at all times somewhat startling . . . His approach to his work is best expressed by one of his favourite quotations from *Gulliver's Travels*: "Providence never intended to make the management of public affairs a mystery to be comprehended only by a few persons of sublime genius of which there seldom are three born in any age."'[11] The *Journal of the Institute of Municipal Treasurers and Accountants* made much the same point:

His opinions, Conservative in general, but progressive upon professional questions, were forthright, clear-cut, consistent, disconcertingly logical, and expressed in language of crystalline clarity.

Sydney Larkin hated mass opinion, sentimentality and pretence; verbosity, clichés, gush and over-emphasis, whether in speaking or in writing, were anathema to his fastidious mind. In a quarter of a century's service at Coventry he was never known to raise his voice, however provoked.

Ever able to appreciate merit in men and their work, he was unable to enthuse, let alone worship. In his own field of English literature, where, incidentally, his taste was impeccable, he had his favourites but no idols. Interested in his fellow townsman Samuel Johnson, for example, he was nevertheless in no sense of the term a Johnsonian. His interest in human affairs arose not so much from a zest for life as from a belief that human affairs were but a pageant to be enjoyed – ironically – by a cynical observer.

This preoccupation with life as a spectacle to be objectively enjoyed was akin to another of his marked characteristics – his caustic wit, his lack of a hobby other than reading, and his dislike of games and parties. To some – especially to the hearty back-slapping Englishman – Sydney Larkin was entirely incomprehensible. Others were never able to reconcile the assiduous public servant, willing to fight through a lifetime of technical progress, with the man who denied the truth of the fundamentals of democracy, disbelieved in the social services, and thought slavery the only form of human association. By the members of the Institute he will be recalled as an original fellow practitioner, conscientious, fearless, but kind, generous, sensitive and – at bottom – shy.[12]

Generally appreciative, these tributes contain awkward reminders of Sydney's ferocity and intolerance. Without actually mentioning his pro-German views or his opinions about women, they create the sense of someone hard to ignore but equally difficult to like. Larkin knew this about his father, and wasn't in the least unsettled by what he read. Sydney had made no secret of his views at home, and as his possessions were sifted and sorted nothing unexpected came to light. His pocket diaries, for instance, in which he sometimes used to record thoughts or quotations as they occurred to him, contained the sort of remarks he had just as happily made aloud: 'Women are often dull, sometimes dangerous and always dishonourable'; 'The idea that "government" should find more money for distressed areas: the sort of thing a child might say.'[13] Until Larkin's death at the same age as his father thirty-seven years later, such thoughts resonated in his own mind. He shared most of Sydney's opinions on large as well as small issues, and agreed with him about the ways in which serious and trivial matters were connected. 'I must say,' he once wrote to Monica when he was staying with Eva in 1962, 'my father in his retirement – it is a dreadful life. I remember him holding up some implement or other at the sink and saying, "That's the third time today I've washed this!" ... I wonder what he would have thought, to see me washing the same old colander, the same old saucepans, the same old cooking knives and forks – laughed, I should think. You may say there's nothing very awful about all this, but all the same I think there is – I feel it is awful anyway.'[14]

Shortly after the cremation, leaving his mother with Kitty in Loughborough, Larkin returned to College Road. He immediately wrote an elegy – one that was never published in his own lifetime – remembering how Sydney made jam every year. The thought turns his father from someone severe and dominating into someone gently and surprisingly feminine:

> An April Sunday brings the snow
> Making the blossom on the plum trees green,
> Not white. An hour or two, and it will go.
> Strange that I spend that hour moving between
>
> Cupboard and cupboard, shifting the store
> Of jam you made of fruit from these same trees:
> Five loads – a hundred pounds or more –
> More than enough for all next summer's teas,
>
> Which now you will not sit and eat.
> Behind the glass, under the cellophane,
> Remains your final summer – sweet
> And meaningless, and not to come again.

As soon as Eva became a widow, Larkin changed the tone in which he spoke to her. While Sydney had been alive Larkin had written eagerly, jokily and (except about Ruth) openly to his parents in his letters home. He had sounded like someone conscious of his youth, enjoying its freedoms and expecting to be forgiven its excesses. After his father's death, his letters to his mother become fuggy. 'Dearest Old Creature', he calls her, or 'Dearest Mop', and signs off as her 'Creature', often drawing a sketch of himself as a whiskery seal-like animal wearing a muffler. To some extent, this shift took place because Larkin knew Eva would find it consoling. It was a way of telling her their lives would always be cosy. Yet at the same time it suited him, too. It enabled him to disguise his real age (he was only twenty-five) with trivialities which were sometimes childish, sometimes like the fussy ditherings of middle or even old age. More importantly, it allowed him to maintain a relationship he knew was indispensable to his work. Although Eva was often silly, although she often drove Larkin into agonies of boredom and frenzies of rage, the ties which bound her to her son were not merely comforting but inspirational. They connected Larkin to his past, to memories of hope and excitement, and to the creative 'sense of being young'. Until the end of her life, Eva was more than a respectable excuse for dodging the frightening or complicated things in his life. She crucially influenced the accents and attitudes of his poems.

Throughout April Larkin visited his mother every weekend – first in Loughborough and then, when she returned to Warwick, in Coten End. There were papers to sort out, and her future to arrange. Should she stay on at the old house? Everyone agreed it was too big. Should she move in permanently with Kitty? Fifty-three York Road was too small. Should she leave Coten End and live alone near one or other of her children? Perhaps, she wondered, the answer was for her to sell Coten End and buy a house in Leicester where she could support herself by taking in lodgers, one of whom could be her son? Wouldn't he like that? Larkin hesitated. He was worried about Eva and he liked the prospect of being cosseted. At the same time, he didn't want to institutionalize everything his father's life had warned him against. Eva badgered him to decide, but he knew there was really no question about which way he should fall. His responsibilities lay with his mother. He would see her settled and then, as soon as he could, choose a home of his own.

Once Larkin had announced his decision, Eva asked him to handle all practical arrangements – selling the house and finding and buying another. He set about it with a bad grace, feeling he was out of his depth. 'This is a game I don't score very highly at,' he told Sutton. 'There is a house [near College Road in Leicester] going at present . . . price £2,950 or what it will fetch in an auction. I don't know whether to go to the auction and try to bid on the chance of getting it cheaper. I'm not sure how to conduct myself at an auction. In addition to which I can't help feeling that prices at present are as high as they'll ever be and that we should be faced, when we do sell, with a loss.'[15] Eventually Larkin decided to 'blow all [the] money'[16] and bought the new house privately: 12 Dixon Drive, a bow-fronted, two-storey detached 1930s house in a residential street off London Road and close to Victoria Park. It was an ugly and intensely suburban place but Eva liked it: there were three bedrooms, and Kitty's house in Loughborough was only a short bus ride to the north. Soon after the sale had gone through Larkin succeeded in disposing of Coten End – for £2,500, 'so', as he told Sutton, 'we are out of pocket, blast it'.[17] His first performance as the man of the family had not been a conspicuous success.

Even before he and Eva moved into Dixon Drive on 17 August, Larkin began to feel his mother's influence tightening round him. Telling himself that his new set-up didn't have to last for long was no consolation. He doubted whether he could stand it for even a little while. There would be no privacy once he left College Road, and therefore no chance to write. All the links he had recently started to make with the life of the university would be threatened. His relationship with Ruth would suffer. Yet if he drew closer to Ruth as a way of trying to save himself, he felt it would make things even worse. It would lead to marriage.

He decided there was a middle course. He would get engaged to Ruth, making it clear that marriage would not automatically follow. In May, soon after her twenty-first birthday, he offered her a ring which she accepted, along with his terms. 'Let's regard the ring as a symbol of the love and trust and understanding between us,'[18] she wrote to him. This is exactly what Larkin hoped she would say. Being in two minds himself, he would keep his mother and fiancée in two minds as well. By promising his life to both of them, he hoped he might be able to keep it for himself.

A few days later Larkin carefully described his motives in a letter to Sutton:

To tell you the truth I have done something rather odd . . . – got myself engaged to Ruth on Monday. You know I have known her since 1943 or 4; well, we have gone on seeing each other until the point seemed to arrive when we either had to start taking it seriously or else drop it. I can't say I welcome the thought of marriage, as it appears to me from the safe side of it, but nor do I want to desert the only girl I have met who doesn't instantly frighten me away. It has been putting me backwards and forwards through the hoops for a long time now: I still console myself with the thought that all is not yet lost. No one would imagine me to be madly in love, and indeed I'm more 'madly out of love' than in love, so much so that I suspect all my isolationist feelings as possibly harmful and certainly rather despicable. 'Are you a bloody valuable vase, man, to be kept so carefully?' The engagement, to me anyway, is to give myself a sincere chance of 'opening out' towards someone I do love a lot in a rather strangled way, and to help her take her Finals [at King's College] which she was in a fair way to buggering up . . . I don't know how it'll turn out. It's either the best thing I've done or the worst thing.[19]

Although there is no mention of it here, Sutton suspected that Sydney's death had at last freed Larkin to do what he wanted. The timing certainly made it look that way: while the censorious old man was alive, the son lived in fear of his disapproval. The truth is more complicated. Larkin's reasons for getting engaged have less to do with the assertion of independence than with the fear of losing it. The engagement to Ruth – formally linked to her but not unbreakably bound – held both the world and his loneliness at bay. It crystallized the thought that he might one day have a family of his own, and simultaneously gave him a breathing space in which to decide how he really felt about it. 'How will I be able to write,' he demanded to know when she asked about marriage proper, 'when I have to be thinking about you?'[20]

Ruth's family reacted uncertainly to the news. 'This young man is having the best years of your life,'[21] her grandfather warned her. Eva, sobbing, said much the same thing, though her main fear was that she would soon lose her son's help and company. The young couple carried on trying to be happy – and for a few weeks they succeeded, celebrating in London, then visiting friends to tell them the news. Amis continued to feel equivocal about Ruth but was in no position to quarrel since he was about to get married himself (to Hilly, in August). Sutton – at home in Coventry, painting – was more straightforwardly pleased, and in recompense Larkin offered him another honest appraisal. 'I am glad you liked Ruth,' he wrote, when he had at last introduced them to each other:

– she certainly liked you. My relation with her is curious, not at all as I imagined one's relation to one's *fiancée* (why isn't there an English word?) – we are sort of committed to each other by our characters, at least I think we are. I can't imagine, judging from the women I meet casually, that any other girl would come within a mile of my inner feelings. It's odd. Really I am not sure if I want to marry at all: but when one tries to stare into the problem to seek out its exact truth one is bemused and puzzled and can't tell true from false.[22]

In the short term these doubts could easily be hidden. While Ruth continued to work for her exams, Larkin travelled down to see her at weekends. When the exams were over they took various jaunts: to watch the Australians play cricket at Lord's, to visit the newly married Amis. At the end of the summer, when Ruth heard that she would be working at the Institute of Education in Malet Street in Bloomsbury for the next stage of her training as a teacher, she felt she had most things she wanted. She was in work and she was in love; to make her happiness complete all she needed was to believe that Larkin shared it.

For this to happen, he had to believe his social life was compatible with his writing life. It wasn't. Since finishing 'An April Sunday' he had not been able to do anything, but he could not decide why. Was it Ruth's fault or Eva's? Had his gift simply deserted him? Ten years later he admitted that 'there came a great break in about 1948 when I finished – I thought I'd finished writing. I knew I'd finished writing novels, and I thought I'd finished poetry.'[23] Although he had all the evidence to hand, he could not admit openly that his father's death was to blame. While Sydney had lived he had managed and directed Larkin's mind; in the grave, he left him feeling empty.

Slowly but surely Larkin crushed Ruth's happiness beneath his own worries, and when the new term began they were as unsure about their future as they had been before announcing their engagement. Reluctant to end it so soon, they resumed their semi-separate lives – Ruth in Malet Street, Larkin in Dixon Drive, where his self-pity soon erupted in a piece of free verse too rambling to call a poem, but too interesting for him to discard. He tore it out of his manuscript book but kept it among his other papers:

What is there in me that justifies my ignoring other people?
I used to think it was art: but at close quarters art is a fishy business . . .
To me art is a sneaking mixture of wish-fulfilment, telling the truth,
And arranging the filings of life to the magnet of my character,
And I don't like my character.
I wouldn't back it for twopence, and I don't advise anyone else to do so
    either.

They don't come any more, those moments –
Moments of Vision, as Hardy called them.
I could see astonishing pictures, splaying lines in all directions, like the
    bush
That burned and wasn't destroyed.
Now they don't come, I'm too worried.
They were really at the bottom of my writing.
So now I'm reduced to this, writing any old thing, my literary career has
    gone up the spout.
Yet I believe they would return if I were free.
So must I live alone, do nothing,
Give nothing except in writing? Oh people do harass me.
Show me someone who depends on me and I'll show you someone who
    robs me of what self-control I have
And when I look at that written down it rings like the saying of a shit
Which I suppose is what I make myself out to be.
I want to do both, write and be involved with people.
Yet always I shy off when they come too close.

It's like being too near something at best burdensome, at worst harrowing,
And it drives the power to write away from me like water scares a cat.
My great need at present is to feel my life is as good as anyone else's.

Early morning as I write this, the Jews squabbling next door,
The slanted square of sun on the wall, very bright,
And I think of the miles and miles of sunlight, the untouched downs,
    glistening with dew,
And the hundred untenanted bays where the sea comes sliding in, not
    rough,
And then I long to be in a thousand of these places at once, to have a
    thousand pairs of eyes.
To be sniffing on a bed in Leicester is not good enough.
Then, when I visit my friends at Oxford,
Their lives seem happier and more successful than mine:
Kingsley in particular seems to live at the centre of gratified desire.
But when my desire is for the past, or for immortality,
Who can gratify that?

So you see I conceive of life as a brilliantly exciting process going on all
    around me,
Only my unfortunate branch of it is dull
Only I am doomed to die without having done anything I pine to do
Because the things I want to do are essentially undoable, they belong to
    imagination –
Does nobody else see this, or am I one of a large number of hallucinated?[24]

TWENTY-FOUR

Larkin seldom hesitated to complain about whatever was bothering him to anyone who would listen, but in the months after Sydney's death he kept the extent of his wretchedness to himself. As far as his friends were concerned he was only averagely miserable. When he rebuffed a South American publisher (also in touch with Amis) who suggested writing a book about Lawrence, Larkin told Sutton that he wanted to concentrate on his new novel. When Sutton asked about the novel itself, the news was bad but not absolutely hopeless. 'My book still can't come of age,' Larkin told him. 'It remains in Chapter 2, but by gorra it will emerge or I'll know the reason why.'[1]

When Larkin spoke about his unfinished prose in later life, he usually gave the impression that he worked on only one novel after *A Girl in Winter*. In fact there were two. One he had started to plan before leaving Wellington; the other he began thinking about soon after Sydney's death. The manuscript of this latter story exists in three drafts (the longest is sixty-seven pages), has no title, and never seems more than a fragment. Nevertheless, it tells us a good deal about these unhappy months spent 'sniffing on a bed' in Leicester.

The story is a simple one, opening shortly after Easter in 1948. A twenty-five-year-old assistant lecturer in English at a provincial university, Augusta Bax, is showing her mother round the campus and wondering 'whether she had been wise'[2] to ask her colleague Dr Butterfield to have tea with them later in the day. Augusta is febrile, red-haired and jewel-wearing; Mrs Bax is tweedy and seems 'perpetually ready to sink back on a shooting stick in the enclosure of Newton Abbot races'.[3] Between them, they have a withering effect on those they meet – especially men:

Their natures fused and glowed, and everything in range was shrivelled. So much in life that they had to endure or acknowledge or pretend to believe simply for the sake of peace and quiet could be disembowelled, stunned, or strewn to the wind. A third person, a man especially, felt himself being jeered out into the open, until his exasperation swiped out at them; and then their combined retaliations landed on him like a mallet, driving his face into the mud, never, as far as they were concerned, to be entirely clean again.[4]

When Butterfield arrives for tea he seems well armoured against this sort of onslaught. He is 'an erect, spare, controlled man'[5] who has worked at the university for twenty-five years. Because his department is expanding he has an eye on a Chair, and because Augusta knows this she hopes to persuade him to make her temporary job a permanent one. As they talk, currents of personal ambition roll beneath the polite surface of their chat, leaving Mrs Bax so bored that she feels like 'someone in the early stages of mesmerism'.[6]

A few days later Augusta writes to her mother giving news of how Butterfield is preparing for his chance of promotion. As well as inching the story forward her letter takes us back into the past, with a mention of Augusta's bad-tempered father John, a 'brewery agent'. This leads to a résumé of her entire childhood – her formal upbringing (during which she learnt that 'emotion was as disgusting as the lavatory, not as necessary'[7]), her career at Oxford, her first job as tutor to the daughter of a novelist called Mellaby Vane, her arrival at the university college, her earliest teaching experiences, and her efforts to make the most of her looks:

> She had accepted the fact that to combine her red hair, her thinness, her white face into an acceptable norm, she must be prepared to look striking, and she had assembled a repertoire of coifs, buns, bangs, curls and manes; two lipsticks, and two only, for day and evening; and a growing, reliable stock of well-cut, curious-coloured clothes. In the early morning she looked washed-out, a slum brat. But when made up she achieved a precarious prettiness, light-boned, thin-wristed. Her great fear was lest her front teeth should give out: she was a calcium-deficient and the back ones were far gone already.[8]

In the first draft, Larkin runs out of steam as soon as he's finished with Augusta's past. In the second, at the top of which is written 'DO NOT SCRAP: plenty of good stuff here', he takes up the story at the moment Butterfield applies for the Chair, then spends ten pages investigating his (Butterfield's) past failures and disappointments. They are apparently inexplicable – 'The process of failure only needed starting,' we hear, 'it will endure for being so' – and have left him 'despairing, like a racehorse trained but never run, suddenly in old age brought up to the starting gate, spavined, tubed, how could he win now? It should have happened years ago.'[9]

It's easy to see the parallels with Larkin's life. The provincial university is like Leicester: it used to be a reform centre for prostitutes and the Fielding Johnson Building had been a lunatic asylum. Butterfield, although older than Larkin, describes Larkin's own feelings of failure. Augusta's 'precarious prettiness' makes her sound remarkably like Monica (bad teeth included). Mrs Bax, in seeming 'to be holding a perpetual kit inspection on life and to be finding it a disgrace',[10] conflates the characters of his parents. The resemblances help to explain the fragment's permanent sense of imminent collapse; they give it the air of something written too distinctly for private edification. Around them lie themes which Larkin tried to develop from *Jill* and *A Girl in Winter*. The hostility between men and women, for instance, which we find on the first page of the manuscript, is soon rephrased in the relationship between Augusta and her father, and then between her father and mother. Their marriage is lashed down, barely civil, seething with suppressed fury. Mrs Bax's 'tolerance and indulgence' of her husband have 'cracked right across and dropped off, leaving not quite hatred but certainly anger, and a raging unsatisfied hunger for self-gratification'.[11] Mr Bax's feelings for his wife are just as chilly. 'John Bax, knowing he was beaten, living in a flickering barrage of eye-messages and giggles and feminine defences and excuses, relapsed into black obstinacy. By sheer offensiveness he forced the two of them to regard him as head of the family: every chance he had of thwarting what they had planned he took.'[12]

In so far as the Bax fragment describes Larkin's developing feelings for Monica, it might be called sociable. Its underlying themes, shaped by distrust and dislike, are far from that. As Larkin abandoned the story he continued to keep his distance from Ruth while remaining engaged to her. Even before the end of August, when he was still taking her on outings and to meet friends, he was telling Sutton, 'I'm afraid that my engagement looks like coming to an end ... marriage doesn't attract me, except as a refuge, and it ought to be more than that.'[13] In mid-September, when he was on the point of taking a week's holiday with Ruth, he repeated the same message. 'I don't know about women and marriage. One thing I do think is that if we had known as many women as we have read books by DHL we should have a clearer idea of the situation.'[14]

As he braced himself for his first Christmas without Sydney, Larkin looked back over the previous twelve months and reckoned they were among his most eventful and least satisfactory. In trying to play his mother off against his fiancée, he had done precisely what his father had warned him against: ended up at home, feeling either nagged or smothered. 'I crave/The gift of your courage and indifference' he had written to Sydney in an unpublished poem four years previously. Now he felt the gift was beyond his reach. He was bowed down, prematurely aged and powerless to recover his youth.

TWENTY-FIVE

'Little happens: life seems to have pushed a steamroller up against the door and nailed the windows and stuffed something down the chimney. It is now dancing up and down outside the glass shouting "Live dangerously!"

I turn round and show it my bum.'[1] Larkin wrote this at the end of 1949, but it described a mood which had lasted all year. His existence in Dixon Drive was 'rather like being married/Except that there are no fucks and the pity is more piercing'.[2] His writing was jammed. His engagement was a failure. His library work boring. His self-image deteriorating ('my baldness seems to be keeping its end up well'[3]). His friends annoyingly successful or remote (in October Amis got a job teaching English at University College, Swansea). 'My great trouble,' he told Sutton:

as usual, is that I lack desires. Life is to know what you want, and to get it. But I don't feel I desire anything. I am unconvinced of the worth of literature. I don't want money or position. I find it easier to abstain from women than sustain the trouble of them and the creakings of my own monastic personality. In fact I feel as if the growing shoots of my character – though they must be more than shoots by now – had turned in on each other and were mutually neutralizing each other. Or that I had been 'doctored' in some way and my central core dripped on with acid. Shagged to buggery, that's what I be.[4]

Feeling 'unconvinced of the worth of literature' (he hadn't written a poem for a year) aggravated all his other losses – but unlike them, it didn't last for long. The following month Larkin wrote to Sutton again, telling him that the one thing he felt 'overwhelmingly' was that 'literature is a great force'.[5] He immediately proved the point by writing six poems in three months, all of which he regarded as part of a 'process of removing an endless series of false bottoms from one's personality'.[6] Every one of them describes a condition of stasis or isolation. 'None think how stalemate in you grinds away', he tells himself in 'Neurotics'; in 'I am washed upon a rock' he says, 'to think is to be dumb'; in 'Modesties' we find, 'Weeds are not supposed to grow,/But by degrees/Some achieve a flower, although/ No one sees'; and in 'Sinking like sediment through the day' he describes feeling simply 'Horror of life'.

The two remaining poems in this group, 'On Being Twenty-six' and 'To Failure', spell out the same things even more clearly. In the former, Larkin looks back to 'the slag/Of burnt-out childhood' and tells us that his original facility has been 'Quickly consumed' and succeeded by a dingy crop of 'second-best' talents. Now even these are threatening to desert him. 'I kiss, I clutch,/Like a daft mother, putrid/Infancy' he says, even though he accepts that it:

> can and will forbid
> All grist to me

> Except devaluing dichotomies:
> Nothing, and paradise.

'To Failure', written the same month, produces an equally dismal account in different terms. It is a more argumentative poem, solidly based in familiar details, and speaking in the gloomy but conversational voice Larkin used for much of his later work:

> It is these sunless afternoons, I find,
> Instal you at my elbow like a bore.
> The chestnut trees are caked with silence. I'm
> Aware the days pass quicker than before,
> Smell staler too. And once they fall behind
> They look like ruin. You have been here some time.

Larkin's spurt of faith in 'the worth of literature' soon died down again. Ruth, whose elation the previous year had meant she could absorb at least some of his worries, began to feel saturated by them. If he was so convinced that marriage was out of the question, she wondered in letters, why was she bothering to try and persuade him otherwise? The more she coaxed him, the more stubbornly he resisted. When she was loving he complained of feeling imprisoned; when she told him to brace up he felt bullied. Gradually, as the summer wore on and their weekends together became increasingly strained, she accepted the inevitable. He was beyond help, and she must decide her own future for herself. When a vacancy was advertised in the early autumn for a teaching job in Newark, Nottinghamshire, she applied for and got it. It wasn't more than an hour and a half on the train from Leicester, so Larkin could easily see her if he wanted. She told him it would be much easier for them to meet in her flat in 42 Newton Street than it had been in London.

Larkin did nothing, and Ruth soon realized that he was letting circumstances make up his mind for him, rather than trying to control them by his own actions. She made a few desultory visits to Leicester. They stopped sleeping together. By December they had turned from lovers into polite friends. At the start of January 1950 Ruth had learnt to wrap her disappointment in the language of indifference. 'I would prefer,' she wrote, 'to see you next weekend (or whenever it would suit you) rather than involve myself in extra journeying about just now ... Drop me a line and let me know if you feel like seeing me next weekend.'[7]

Larkin began the new year with no hopes of his life improving. The atmosphere in Dixon Drive was stultifying; the university, closed for the vacation, was forlorn; his friends were elsewhere. On the afternoon of 3 January he went to the cinema to try and divert himself. Before the main feature started, he watched a short film about a racehorse called Brown Jack, which had been famous before the war. 'It was,' remembered later, 'a film about, you know, "Where is Brown Jack now?" Where Brown Jack was now was at grass, quite happy, moving about, no harness, no jockey, nobody shouting the odds, simply cropping the grass and having a gallop when he felt like it.'[8] As Larkin walked home that evening he found the story of the horse had 'for some reason' impressed him 'very strongly',[9] and when he reached his room he wrote about it. The result was the poem 'At Grass', which for its filmic re-creation of actual details, its formal melancholy and its graceful swoop into familiar experience has become one of his most admired and best liked poems.

Larkin wondered why the film impressed him so much, but in the context of his feelings about himself, his mother and his fiancée, its appeal is not difficult to understand. The horses in the poem stand outside the drama of their lives – they are 'fifteen years' on from the races which turned them into legends – and if they remember anything it is success, not failure. They are secure in their achievement, enjoying a freedom which is beyond both curiosity and comment. Even the prospect of death is gentle: it is not a Grim Reaper but a groom with bridles (strictly speaking it should be halters) who comes for them at the end of their day. They:

> Have slipped their names, and stand at ease,
> Or gallop for what must be joy,
> And not a fieldglass sees them home,
> Or curious stop-watch prophesies:
> Only the groom, and the groom's boy,
> With bridles in the evening come.

Without taking its eye off the horses, 'At Grass' manages to suggest deep admiration for human lives well-lived and safely over. It is an envious poem which shows no trace of envy's corrosions. The feelings which produced it – regret, guilt, anger and disappointment – are consumed and transfigured into appreciation of 'what must be joy'.

In the next six months Larkin wrote another thirteen poems, several of which ('Deceptions', 'Coming', 'Dry Point', 'Spring', 'If, My Darling', 'Wants') were eventually to find a place in his first mature collection, *The Less Deceived*, and some of which share or comment on the mood of release in 'At Grass'. One, 'Coming', candidly describes happiness ('I ... /Feel like a child/Who comes on a scene/Of adult reconciling,/And can understand nothing/But the unusual laughter,/And starts to be happy'). And in 'Spring', although he describes himself as 'An indigestible sterility' the season has 'least use for', this allows him to see it 'best', and recognize it as 'earth's most multiple, excited daughter'.

The remainder of these thirteen poems create a sense of freedom only in the fact of their existence. What they actually describe is sexual wretchedness, veering loyalties, isolation. In 'Deceptions' it is the rapist not the victim whom Larkin insists is the more deceived when he bursts 'into fulfilment's desolate attic'. In 'Dry Point' (originally the second of 'Two Portraits of Sex') the bubble of erotic pleasure is an enveloping 'irritant' which, when popped, leaves him diminished and the prospect of marriage 'discredited'. In 'If, My Darling' he warns that if 'she' were to look inside his head she would find it full of ideas which were 'infected', 'unwholesome' and treacherous. In 'Under a splendid chestnut tree' he creates and then mutely identifies with an obsessed 'corpse-faced' under-graduate:

> Hare's eyes, staring across his prayer-locked hands,
> Saw, not a washstand-set, but mammary glands;
> All boyhood's treasure-trove; a *hortus siccus*
> Of tits and knickers,
> Baited his unused sex like tsetse flies,
> Till, maddened, it charged out without disguise
> And made the headlines.

In 'Wants', Larkin takes refuge from these torments by converting the wish which lies beyond them all, the 'wish to be alone', into something final: 'desire of oblivion'. It is the only time in his work that he makes this unqualified appeal – elsewhere death is variously whined at or withstood, never simply welcomed. Yet the directness of his statement can't avoid contradicting the meaning he intends to convey. When Larkin had written about his depression at Oxford and Wellington he had done so vaguely, transcendentally, using myths and symbols and languorous cadences. His poems stalled. In Dixon Drive his sense of failure was so acute that he had to confront its all-embracing reality. His poems prospered. Striving to succeed, he had failed; accepting failure, he had begun to triumph.

When we look at the chronology of Larkin's poems it seems as though this transformation occurred suddenly, during these early months of 1950.

As far as the actual writing of the poems is concerned, this is true enough. Produced in rapid order, they appear to bear out Larkin's own contention that as Hardy's influence replaced Yeats's, so he woke from his *fin-de-siècle* slumber and discovered his own identity. As we can see, however, the reasons for the change stretch back over many years. After he had left Oxford, the strangeness of Wellington and the early excitement of Ruth quickened the growth of *Jill* and *A Girl in Winter*. As the strangeness wore off and the affair with Ruth foundered, a tangled mass of contradictory feelings dammed the flow of his writing. When he reached Leicester, the chance that newness might once again release him was wrecked by the death of his father. He fell into inertia. He was extremely reluctant to save himself by direct action, but over the months his passive wretchedness amounted to a kind of decision. When Ruth took herself off to Newark, still hoping that her future lay with him, she opened a space in Larkin's life, allowing him to feel that he might stretch towards new opportunities if and when they arose. His prose showed no signs of reviving, but the emotions on which it had once fed flowed into poems. Where poetry had formerly been the preserve of misty high-mindedness, now it could contain ordinary talk, ordinary people, ordinary joy, anger, doubt, fear and sadness.

At the beginning of 1950, shortly after completing 'At Grass', Larkin was still repeating to Sutton the complaints of the past several months. 'My relations with women are governed by a shrinking sensitivity, a morbid sense of sin, a furtive lechery,' he wrote in January. 'Women don't just sit still and back you up. They want children: they like scenes: they want a chance of parading all the emotional haberdashery they are stocked with. Above all they like feeling they "own" you – or that you "own" them – a thing I hate.'[10] In the month following this letter Larkin adapted its message in a twelve-page play called *Round the Point*. It is not so much a drama as a Shavian dialogue – between Geraint (whom we first meet tearing up a novel he has written) and Miller (a poet who enters singing his latest poem: a version of 'Fiction and the Reading Public'). In the conversation which follows, Geraint reproduces Larkin's own difficulties as a novelist: 'My energies are ... free to devote to whatever I want. But NOTHING HAPPENS. Why not? I've done it once. Why can't I do it again? Five years: the difference between 23 and 28, between success and failure, creation and stagnation, sanity and despair.'[11] Miller, seeking to counter this, argues that 'the race is not for the swift, nor the battle for the strong'. This precipitates the main argument of the play, which concerns the relationship between the man who suffers and the man who creates. Geraint reckons they're one and the same. Miller disagrees.

Round the Point fails to reconcile these conflicts, just as Larkin had failed in the year following Sydney's death. But as his poems started to stir again, the rest of his life began to alter. At the end of February he roused himself to apply for a job in London – he didn't get it, but it reminded him that since he had qualified as a member of the Library Association his chances of leaving Leicester had improved. In the same month he also began work on his new novel, the one he had started thinking about in Wellington and had mentioned to Pringle when *In the Grip of Light* was rejected. Once again, Larkin didn't get very far with it, but it was better than nothing. He told Pringle that he had begun 'to think of the creative imagination as a fruit machine on which victories are rare and separated by much vain expense'.[12]

Three months later he had a rare drop of encouragement. The poet and critic Charles Madge wrote to compliment him on the poems in *The North Ship*, which he had recently read. Larkin told Sutton that Madge, as a contemporary of Auden and the proprietor of the small Pilot Press, seemed 'quite likely to give me a shove into some literary success. By God,' he added, 'I could do with a bit.'[13] In fact no specific help was forthcoming, but Larkin was nevertheless grateful to Madge. He visited him in Birmingham where Madge taught, invited him to Leicester, and sent him copies of thirteen new poems. Madge was left with the impression of someone 'modest and self-doubting, yet quite amazingly genuine'.[14] (They continued to correspond on and off for the next several years: in 1952 Larkin again stayed with Madge in Birmingham, and in 1955 Madge visited him in Hull.)

Other, older friendships came to life. In March Larkin visited Amis in Swansea for the first time, and in May he went as Bruce Montgomery's guest to a crime writers' dinner at the Café Royal in London, ending up 'in some unknown alley'[15] drinking orange juice with Dorothy L. Sayers. Even in Leicester things began to thaw. As he became less certain of his future with Ruth, he allowed himself to see Monica more often. Her tough independent-mindedness led him to suspect that if he drew closer to her he would not immediately re-create the life he was struggling to escape. Her stylishness attracted him. She was a clever and sympathetic companion. By the spring they were meeting 'Oh, all the time,'[16] Monica says, and by the end of the summer 'he had come to me'[17] and they had been to bed together. Eva knew things were changing, but the details were kept from her. As far as she was concerned a new flexibility had disturbed her son's routines, and a new danger darkened her horizon – the danger that he might finally assert his independence again, and leave for a job elsewhere.

Larkin realized that if such a job were to materialize, he would have to resolve his relationship with Ruth. As long as he stayed in Leicester, there was little chance of feeling either loving or hostile enough to force a crisis – Monica notwithstanding. After visiting Ruth in Newark in April he told Sutton, '[Ruth] treats me very cavalierly these days, which she has every right to, seeing how long I kept her uncertain. Only by now she has staked out a large claim in my pesky emotions and when she withdraws I feel nearly half my feeling drawn after her, as if some Friday-night poulterer were drawing my liver and lites. It's all very complicated and certainly not creditable to me, who have been piddling about like a finger-chewing curate for five years.'[18]

It is guilt, not affection or indifference, which speaks loudest in this letter – and when Larkin finally decided that he could not prevaricate any longer, it was guilt, mixed with desperation, which led him to act as he did. In late May, shortly after his failure to get the job in London, he applied for the post of sub-librarian at the Queen's University of Belfast, Northern Ireland. He knew nothing about Ireland and nothing about the university. When he took the ferry across the Irish Sea from Liverpool for his interview on 4 June he sent Eva a postcard which said merely, 'Belfast is an unattractive city. Oh dear, oh dear.'[19] He intended to console his mother by making out that life without her would be drab. He also intended to deter her from coming with him.

He got the job – largely, he claimed later, because of the 'unforeseen defection'[20] of four other candidates. His salary was to be £600 p.a., rising by annual increments of between £50 and £100 to a bar of £800. Eva panicked as soon as news of his appointment reached Dixon Drive. Who would look after her? Where would she live? With Kitty, Larkin decided, and arranged for her furniture to go into store and the house to be let while she kept up 'a great wailing'.[21] The planning and anxiety made him feel his own life was 'founded on sand',[22] and although Kitty supported his decision he wished that she would bail him out of family responsibilities altogether. He told Sutton that Kitty was 'The only person in the world I am confident that I am superior to.'[23]

Larkin was partly resentful, partly nervous. While seeking to kick away the past, he had no clear idea of who or what he should turn to instead. Northern Ireland was another country, in which he didn't know anyone.

Although he had decided during the previous year that marriage was out of the question, and although the temperature of his relationship with Ruth had dropped, he found the thought of his impending loneliness appalling. Perhaps, he asked her, they might be able to make a new start in a new place? He rolled the question round and round his mind while waiting for her answer, then described the outcome to Sutton, making no mention of the fact that one reason for his problems with Ruth was his rapidly developing affection for Monica:

I came home [from Belfast] thinking how Ruth and I could start life afresh in a far countrie (I hadn't seen her for ages), which led me when I did see her last night [17 June] to stumble along a high road of platitudes that led me to a garbled proposal of marriage. She demurred at this: but as the evening went on and we drank more and more she grew more enthusiastic, I more gloomy. Now today I cannot think what maggot was in my brain to produce such a monstrous egg. Or rather I *can* think: several maggots: – the maggot of loneliness, the maggot of romantic illusion, the maggot of sexual desire. I am not engaged, but heaven knows how I can get out of it now, decently or indecently.

You see my Trouble is that I never like what I've got. Sufficient for me to choose something to dislike it. If we part I shall be tormented by remorse at not having married. If we marry I shall spend my life mentally kicking myself for having so carelessly given up priceless liberty. Jim, your old pal is hard put to it. He is in a very narrow, very steep, very dark place. Will he come out alive? That is more than we can tell.

What a comfortable life we led when we only had bits of art to think about! Life is screwing his knuckles into my neck now all right, an unsympathetic sergeant major. And instead of being equipped with a spick and span battery of desires and the means to gratify them, I have only illusions, inhibitions, deceptions.[24]

Larkin continued to waver for several days, sometimes feeling 'sincerely in favour' of marriage, then saying 'it lowers at me like a distempered mastiff';[25] sometimes exhilarated, then convinced he was 'A BLOODY FOOL'.[26] Ruth hung on, enduring his changes of heart as the deadline of his departure for Belfast drew closer. Eventually Larkin was forced to choose. Three weeks after making the offer of marriage he withdrew it. 'I grabbed back as many of my words as I could,' he told Sutton, 'and ate them hurriedly, encountering a good deal of scorn and anger in the process, which was understandable enough. In fact I behave so badly – only I know how badly – when confronted with what Llewelyn Powys calls *matters of sex* that it is really quite extraordinary.'[27]

Even this was not the end of the matter. For his last two months on the mainland Larkin continued to 'behav[e] like a wet-legged bastard',[28] lurching between thoughts of 'matrimony', love of 'solitude and eternal wayfaring', and the wish to '"trust life" to bring ... something more decisive'.[29] By now Ruth could take no more of it. She returned the ring he had given her and refused to see him. 'I don't want a final meeting,' she wrote from Newark:

which will only serve to underline the difference between what we feel and what we once felt. Whatever our relationship has been in the past it must now be considered as something concluded and done with. Let it rest as it is. I hope that you will be happy in Ireland and that you will, in a new environment, be able to come to better terms with life and with yourself. I hope too for your own sake that you will find yourself able to write, for I know you will never rest until you do. There is really no more to say, is there?[30]

Ruth and Larkin would see each other once more, years later. Apart from this, and a brief exchange of letters towards the end of Larkin's life, when he offered her some money to help pay for a hip-replacement operation, all contact between them was broken. As they looked back on their life together they were at first able to see only the disappointments, the dissatisfactions, the lack of complete trust. In 1962, in 'Wild Oats', Larkin summarized their 'seven years' together as the time in which he:

> Wrote over four hundred letters,
> Gave a ten-guinea ring
> I got back in the end, and met
> At numerous cathedral cities
> Unknown to the clergy.

Eventually more comfortable memories would return. 'I was his first love,' Ruth says now, 'and there's something special about a first love, isn't there?'[31]

Larkin made other farewells. To Sutton, to whom he had opened his heart in recent months as never before, and whom he now called 'my only friend'.[32] To Montgomery, whom he saw 'about twice a year' and found 'too rich and successful for the likes of I'.[33] To Amis, who was 'fading away into S. Wales'.[34] To Monica, for whom his liking was still tinged by fear that he might simply re-create with her the situation he had endured with Ruth. To his mother, who, though happily settled with Kitty, mournfully reproached him for abandoning her. As a way of reassuring her, and perpetuating the fussy old-before-his-time tone of voice that she liked him to use, he compiled a list of 'Do's' and 'Don'ts' for her to keep close to hand in his absence:

FIVE DON'TS FOR OLD CREATURES
1. Don't crouch under the stairs. Walk up the garden, taking deep breaths, and see the bees at work.
2. Don't get housebound. There's no law against old creatures going for bus rides or to cinemas. Just try it.
3. Don't be chained down by housework. Do things that interest you – one a day.
4. Don't waste time worrying about *rain*. This is a wettish country. Lots of it falls. It always has done, and always will.
5. Don't fail to be on the look-out for new friends – pleasant quiet creatures who live simply.

FIVE DO'S FOR OLD CREATURES
1. Do be thankful for the fat moneybags – you might be [a drawing of a creature selling matches on a kerb].
2. Do be grateful for being alive and well. You might be [a drawing of a grave].
3. Do listen to the radio, if you can make it out. Snaps, crackles or pops are either due to faulty connections or some trouble on the circuit.
4. Do read plenty of good books – don't be afraid of rereading Hardy and other writers of merit.
5. Do write regularly to your creature in Ireland. He loves to know what's going on.[35]

As Larkin packed his few belongings, he knew another distinct period of his life was coming to an end. He reckoned it had been a 'frightful'[36] time as far as love, writing and his career were concerned. Yet it had been indispensable. His trials had taught him to speak in his own voice. In learning 'how *bad* living can be'[37] he had become one of the less deceived.

TWENTY-SIX

Early in the afternoon of Saturday, 16 September 1950, Eva waved Larkin off on the train which would take him from Leicester to Liverpool, where he would catch the night ferry to Northern Ireland. He had been bewildered by smaller dramas in the past; now he was glum but self-possessed. This was the beginning of his new life, in which he would make himself a

writer or not at all. As the *Ulster Duke* put out into the Irish Sea he sat on
deck in the moonlight and opened his notebook, writing 'Single to Belfast'
at the head of the page:

A fully-rehearsed departure: bone-dry quay,
Crimson sky-signs clambering Liverpool dark,
A lighted, stationary city: all things, except
Departure itself.

For the night boat now in fact moves down a lane of tame water,
Its corridors curved like a theatre's, its cabins once more
Allotted; the present is really stiffening to past
Right under my eyes,

And my life committing itself to the long bend
That swings me, this Saturday night, away from my midland
Emollient valley, away from the lack of questions,
Away from endearments,

Through doors left swinging, stairs and spaces and faces,
The nagging main-street night as seen from a bus,
On surface-tension of death life everywhere valid –
A voyager's visions

Whose world has boiled down to a berth, a bay, a meal,
A watch hung up to glow in the dark, voices,
The gravitational drag of loneliness:
This all was foreseen.

All was foreseen except the actual seeing:
My glum election to remain on deck,
Hearing the heave and squash of estuary water,
To watch the lights

Burn where so much lies shrugged off behind me like gravecloths,
Making a ghost of me among solid ones
Who cross from known to known, whereas I travel
To unknown from lost.

And so, long after its cue – New Brighton outdistanced,
Some gone to bed, the bar-tables almost empty –
There happens a single haemorrhage of grief
For what I abandon:

For all the familiar earths and formes of pleasure,
For all love's rare and honoured instances,
For friendship's attractive properties left to leak,
For all past good;

And, tightlier wringing, thin visitations of failure
Drily insist like a death-bed's accurate delirium:
How meanly I doled myself out, doubting and counting;
What a pensioned-off habit . . .[1]

Larkin never finished 'Single to Belfast' but its central perception ('I travel/To unknown from lost') remained with him clearly during his first few days in Belfast. Earliest impressions suggested the city was a distinct improvement on Leicester – much grander and more sophisticated. It had impressive civic buildings, a more metropolitan feel, higher aspirations and a more coherent identity. The docks, the linen industry, the opera house, the museum, the castle and beautiful countryside a short distance from the city centre: all these made it seem pleasing and complex. It was wealthy, too. While the aftermath of the war – the rationing – still meant shortages and dreariness in England, parts of Northern Ireland were comparatively prosperous. Monica, when she began making visits, looked forward to buying food she couldn't get in Leicester (especially fish), and persuaded Larkin to experiment with luxuries unknown in the dull world of his parents. 'They make custards with milk here,' he told Eva, astonished, soon after arriving. 'Quite a change from England.'[2]

The university, as well as the city, immediately attracted him. 'Queen's was very different from the small university college where I had worked before,' he said. 'The chief difference was its local character and integration. Your doctor, your dentist, your minister, your solicitor would all be Queen's men, and would probably all know each other. Queen's stood for something in the city and in the province . . . It was accepted for what it was, whereas my previous university college had been regarded, if at all, as an accidental impertinence.'[3]

Rather than leaving Larkin to find a flat for himself, the university authorities arranged for him to have a bed-sitting-room in Queen's Chambers, a tall Victorian hall of residence overlooking the main campus but divided from it by a road busy with trams. From his front door he could see the library – also Victorian, and strangely ecclesiastical in appearance – and the main body of faculty and departmental buildings. Set beyond lawns and elm trees, and approached through impressive wrought-iron gates, they evoked an academic atmosphere more like Oxford than Leicester. This comforted Larkin. He felt he had found somewhere familiar, even though in accent and character it was unlike anything he had known before.

Soon after arriving, he played down the attractions of his digs in a letter home. He told Eva that his room reminded him of 'a very cheerless very bare hotel'. He said, 'It is about the size of the Dixon Drive drawing room but not so well furnished. It contains one single bed, one wardrobe, armchair, desk, cupboard-cum-bookcase, tiny rug, bedside table, bedside lamp, radiator (with a 6d. meter), waste paper basket, steel tubing chair at the desk (horrid). This may sound a lot but in fact it leaves a great expanse of green rubber lino which appears to "flow" through the whole house, and there are no pictures on the walls.'[4] The warden of the residence was the distinguished scholar J. C. Beckett, 'a small old-maidish historian with a passion for Jane Austen and chess', Larkin said, adding, 'I think we should get on'.[5] The other lodgers included Alan Grahame (another history lecturer), Arthur Terry from the Department of Spanish, a music lecturer called Evan John, 'a classics lecturer called Bradley . . . who is very tall',[6] and the deputy warden, Jimmy Piggott, whose room was on the same floor as Larkin's.

Larkin's new colleagues were first daunted by him, then drawn to him. Piggott remembers him as shy – stammering a little but also 'using it when telling a story for timing and effect' – and soon 'becoming tremendously good value, always very good company'.[7] Alec Dalgarno, a lecturer in mathematics who did not get to know Larkin well until two years later, would feel the same. 'Philip was a warm, compassionate man,' he said, 'who could be, and with me often was, riotously funny. He could take a perfectly normal, rational situation and by small incremental modifications to its structure, each change being an entirely possible, even likely event, transform it into a wildly improbable, quite crazy scenario.'[8] Other lodgers confirm this: while Larkin appeared to be entirely conventional, he was in fact often gleefully subversive, sometimes even mocking his own tendency to fuss about little things. (Terry, for instance, recalls that as autumn approached Larkin pinned a sign for his cleaning lady on the window above his desk which read: 'Not to be opened until May or June.'[9])

It was the same around the university generally. Henry Mackle, later warden of Larkin's hall of residence, remembers that when he first saw him he seemed 'a very private, rather remote and often inscrutable person'[10] who on acquaintance turned out to have 'a good fund of mischief'.[11] Larkin realized that if he wanted to join the social life of the campus he couldn't afford simply to wait for people to discover that he was not quite as he looked and sounded. He would have to show them. Within his first few days, therefore, he began to dress as he had in Oxford. 'Flamboyant bow ties,' Piggott remembers, 'patterned sports jackets, coloured shirts, the sort of things which weren't stock in trade at the time.'[12] Another friend recalls 'pink shirts, strong white bow ties, "reverse image" shirts and coats' and an equally sharp eye (no doubt encouraged by Monica) for the way others dressed too. 'I remember having a very oversized coat which he called my "highwayman coat",' this same friend says. 'He had a theory about colours – he said, for instance, "you can't clash reds, you can wear as many reds as you like".'[13]

Larkin behaved more confidently week by week. Piggott says:

he soon built up a wide, varied circle of friends and enjoyed a beer in the evening, visiting most of our leading local hostelries. [In due course there would be] lively SCR parties, and he attended hops in the Union and the Royal Victoria Hospital as the band had pretensions to jazz ... Conversation around the staff table at dinner was the highlight of the day. J. C. Beckett and Philip were the two leading protagonists, with Alan Grahame and Evan John among others enjoying ringside seats. On Sunday lunch Larkin would frequently draw our attention to a human foible which he claimed that he had gleaned from the press that morning.[14]

Another friend, Colin Strang – whom Larkin had known slightly at St John's and who now taught philosophy at Queen's – recalls the same sort of thing. 'I mostly remember him in the SCR bar before lunch,' he says, 'both drinking our halves of plain (plain porter equals draught Guinness). He was excellent pub company, full of anecdote and malicious gossip, and a very good mimic: he did the Belfast accent to perfection. And late in the evening he would meet up with the lads in the SCR for a drink and a game of billiards.'[15] In all such accounts, it's clear that Larkin cast off the drab influence of Dixon Drive very quickly, and recovered some of his undergraduate high spirits. It's also clear that he could not repossess them entirely. For one thing, his work required him to keep a straighter face than he had done in most of his Oxford tutorials. Beckett remembers Larkin telling him that he was keen for his standing in the university to depend on his performance in the library, not on his reputation as a writer: the profession he had chosen by chance had become something in which he wanted to succeed by design.

In the year before he died, Larkin looked back on his arrival at Queen's library:

The library I came to at Queen's in 1950 was of course the old library. The first part had been opened in 1865, and resembled a large church with no transept; it had been designed by an ecclesiastical architect, and was simply a hall with rooms down either side and a gallery at the clerestory level. In the early 1900s an open competition was held for an extension, and incredibly enough it was won by the original architect (anonymously of course) so that in 1913 a second church was added to the end of the first, doubling its length.

No one had much idea of what a library ought to be like in those days ... The light was dim and religious. The lofty pitched roof of the reading room magnified the clack of rulers and tapping of heels, but seemed to absorb conversation. The stack was claustrophobic and even creepy. The galleries had a reputation for romantic assignations.

I had no room, but was given a desk from which I could see most of what was happening at the issue desk, and throughout most of the reading room. As I was in charge of what would now be called Readers' Services, this was appropriate, but it had its drawbacks. One day I woke up at my desk to find myself surrounded by a group of students I was to show round the stack ...

Eventually the reading room was divided horizontally and its tables and chairs moved upstairs to the new room so created; there was still plenty of roof space. The ground floor held a new issue desk and catalogue hall, and a private stack. I got a room and a telephone for the first time, which in some indefinable way improved my status.[16]

Larkin was to have a hand in these improvements – in 1951 he was sent on 'a short tour of the universities in the north of England [including Hull] and Scotland, studying issue desk layouts'[17] – but as a rule his duties were repetitive. He was, as he says in his reminiscence, the sub-librarian in charge of Readers' Services: his responsibilities included the issue desk, the supervision of the reading room and stacks, and the in-house book bindery and photographic department; he managed eighteen members of staff. It was a much bigger job than any he had done previously, and soon after arriving he told Eva he was 'deluged with work and feel[ing] a bit squashed'.[18]

Larkin enjoyed the library partly because he liked the people who worked in it. Initially, though, he found them disappointing. While conceding to Sutton that the Irish were 'friendly', he also thought they were 'pretty ghastly' and didn't have 'much *joie de vivre*'.[19] Before long he began to make distinctions. He found Miss Megaw, on the technical side

of cataloguing, 'rather schoolmarmy'[20] (she once reproved him for bring-
ing bottles of beer into the library in the pockets of his duffel coat).
Elizabeth Madill, on the other hand, a recent graduate, was having 'the
social time of [her] life',[21] and Larkin warmed to her. He liked Molly
Sellar, too, who ran the issue desk and had a 'strong dress sense'[22] which
he appreciated (she later married Arthur Terry, Larkin's companion in
Queen's Chambers). Winifred Arnott, another recent graduate who had
taken a job in the library for a year before deciding what to do with her
life, was even more appealing. Larkin told Terry he thought she was 'sheer
Marie Laurencin';[23] to Sutton he said that he wanted to 'fall on her like a
lion on its daily hunk of horseflesh'.[24]

With the librarian himself, J. J. (Jack) Graneek, Larkin was not so much
friendly as respectful. The son of Russian parents who had fled a pogrom,
Graneek was a 'very correct, handsome, aquiline, grey-haired man, quite
left-wing, yet also an Establishment figure';[25] he was renowned for being
'difficult'[26] though good at his job. Larkin learnt a great deal about
librarianship from him, despite the differences between their tempera-
ments. 'I'd say Graneek and Philip had nothing in common,' says Henry
Mackle – yet he realized, as did others in the university, that 'some sort of
near-paternal love'[27] developed between them. 'I get powerful sick of
work sometimes,' Larkin would say later, 'but never of Graneek.'[28]

With the shape of his weekdays dictated by the library, Larkin soon
settled into a routine: breakfast in the Students' Union (a time when
almost no students were there); lunch in the SCR or a nearby pub such as
The Eglantine ('The Egg') in the Malone Road; then a more formal dinner
at 6.30 at the university staff table, for which academic gowns were worn.
After this, he would return to his room in Queen's Chambers for a couple
of hours then go out for a last drink before closing time (11), or chat and
play cards with friends 'till one or two'.[29]

At weekends life was less predictable. Although pubs were closed on
Sundays there was a good deal of drinking done in private houses with
friends like Piggott, Strang, Mackle and a friend of Piggott's, Archie
Morrison. (The morning after one particularly heavy session Larkin
accused Morrison of spitting on him during the previous evening. 'Spit on
you?' Morrison queried. 'I never spat on you. I just cleared my throat a few
times.'[30]) There were also a good many expeditions: to The Crown in the
centre of the city and The Old Inn for snooker; to jazz concerts (with
fellow-fans such as Tom Cusack, John Loughan, Jerry McQueen and Solly
Lipshitz); to a classical music concert to hear some Mozart – Larkin

sat reading his newspaper throughout; to the countryside by bicycle along the Lagan;[31] to the Good Shepherd Laundry on the Ormeau Road, where he and Terry took their weekly wash (even though 'socks came back twice their normal length, elongated, or so we imagined, by jovial Irish nuns'[32]). It was an existence which catered to the tastes of an adult bachelor who was inclined to live as a student: it flourished within the restrictions of work, but was spared most practical worries.

Compared to Leicester, Belfast kept Larkin busy; it also allowed him to feel that he was unlikely to repeat any of the mistakes he had made with Ruth. And if his own resolve ever wavered, he knew the regulations of Queen's Chambers would defend him. When women wanted to visit rooms in his building, their names and addresses had to be registered with the warden at least two days before arrival. Once this condition had been met, they had to agree to leave by 11 p.m. – by which time they had usually discovered that the doors to all rooms had been fixed to prevent them being locked from the inside. Not surprisingly, Piggott says that 'in all the time I knew Philip I never once saw him with a woman'.[33]

It wasn't only the memory of Ruth which made Larkin settle happily in this academic fortress. He also found the intellectual life of Queen's more involving than any he had known at Leicester. In the one afternoon a week that he had off from work, he used to take out a book from the library in town, read it overnight, then swap it with something Terry had borrowed. T. F. Powys he 'read and reread'; the earliest novels in Anthony Powell's sequence A Dance to the Music of Time (which he said was 'rather like the Magnet written by Proust'); Henri de Montherlant (who 'meant a lot to him'); Cyril Connolly ('The Condemned Playground is my sacred book'); and an anthology called Nine French Poets. (He said Laforgue's 'Winter Coming On' was 'the poem I've been trying to write all my life';[34] in two poems he wrote before the end of the year, 'Absences' and the unpublished 'Verlaine', he adapted French sources.) Terry remembers Larkin enthusing about all these books, and wolfing down other favourites (William Cooper, Isherwood, Lawrence, Gladys Mitchell, John Dickson Carr) as well as new discoveries (Flann O'Brien, Conrad Aiken, John O'Hara). What impressed Terry wasn't just Larkin's eagerness, but the decisiveness of his opinions. 'Philip had no very fixed ideas as to the nature of "good literature",' he says; 'everything he considered worth reading was a matter of personal choice, just as he made one feel that any book which had earned a place on his shelves ... had helped to form what I was coming to recognize as his remarkable sensibility.'[35]

Larkin concealed from most of his friends, though not from Terry, that many evening hours were devoted not to reading but to writing. Writing his diary; writing letters; writing his new novel; writing poems. Later he was to say that Belfast gave him 'the best writing conditions I ever had . . . The first part of the evening had the second part to look forward to, and I could enjoy the second part with a clear conscience because I'd done my two hours.'[36] In his first nine weeks in Queen's Chambers he completed seven poems, of which three – 'No Road', 'Wires' and 'Absences' – were eventually included in *The Less Deceived*. Their overriding concern is with Ruth, and the struggle between love and self-preservation. 'My only crime,' he says in 'The Spirit Wooed', 'Was holding you too dear./Was that the cause/You daily came less near?' In 'No Road' he admits that their agreement 'to let the road between us/Fall to disuse' is not having 'much effect'. No matter how keenly he persuaded himself that he was right to avoid marriage, his relief was confused by regret, and by his jealousy of Ruth's independent future:

> A little longer,
> And time will be the stronger,
>
> Drafting a world where no such road will run
> From you to me;
> To watch that world come up like a cold sun,
> Rewarding others, is my liberty.
> Not to prevent it is my will's fulfilment.
> Willing it, my ailment.

'No Road', like Kipling's 'The Way Through the Woods' or Edward Thomas's 'The Green Roads', uses a conventional image of travel to create a mysterious sense of stasis. In other poems written at the same time, Larkin plays variations on this theme. In each of them, and without mentioning Belfast by name, he explores what it means to arrive in a new and strange place. In 'Wires', for instance (written 'before breakfast' on 4 November), he deals with ideas of exploration and containment; in 'Absences' it is the shapeless lanes of the sea which float him towards the exultant freedom of the final line ('Such attics cleared of me! Such absences!'); in 'Since the majority of me' he looks forward to 'unwalked ways' in his life without Ruth; and in 'Arrival' it is the 'wide-branched indifference' of the 'new city' which 'Seems a kind of innocence':

Fast enough I shall wound it:
Let me breathe till then
Its milk-aired Eden,
Till my own life impound it –
Slow-falling; grey-veil-hung; a theft,
A style of dying only.

'Arrival' ends by describing the shadow which lies over all these new poems. Although Larkin's escape from his old life has brought him to 'Eden', it hasn't entirely dispelled his longstanding fears. As he broods over them, he modulates his language from plain watchfulness (shelves, doors, windows and curtains are all seen simply and clearly) to something more imagistic and internalized. This creates a dialogue in the poem which is closely related to the one he had begun to evolve earlier, where direct Hardyesque speech was played off against echoes of Yeats. Now the debate betweeen the two styles – and the attitudes they embody – is more intense than it had been in the past. Outside his room in Queen's Chambers Larkin spent his first few weeks in Belfast eagerly making new friends; behind its lockless door, he continued to endorse the value of solitude.

TWENTY-SEVEN

Larkin returned to Loughborough for Christmas 1950 with Eva and Kitty in York Road, and came face to face with everything he had been pleased to leave behind. 'If I consider my state of permanent non-attachment,' he said to Sutton, 'my perpetual suspicion, my sexual indifferences, I should put it down to [a] mother complex if I were honest, I suppose, how irritating! And how nasty too! For I always conceive an ailment like that as resembling some . . . submarine tendrils . . . fastened onto some object and which one can't . . . release by any effort of will. What does one do about it, eh? I suppose *anything* – volunteer for the army or start a chip shop or marry a mad Irish woman – anything but loaf about introspectively, as I shall do.'[1]

There's nothing in this letter to show that Larkin had changed while he had been away in Belfast. He seems his usual introspective, mocking self.

Yet his mood had in fact begun to lighten the moment he left England, and in keeping this from Sutton he introduced a kind of deceit into their relationship. Things rapidly went from bad to worse. 'Jim is a nice old bird,' Larkin told his mother soon after meeting him early in the new year 1951, but 'fuller and fuller of windy philosophical tosh about mankind.'[2]

From his schooldays until he left Leicester, Larkin had relied on Sutton's philosophizing. He regarded it as the proof of their high-minded devotion to art: Larkin-the-writer and Sutton-the-painter were going to change the face of contemporary culture. Not even Sutton's long absence in the army had damaged their sense of kinship – this had, if anything, thrived on separation. Proximity was more difficult, especially since it allowed Larkin to watch the gradual erosion of Sutton's ambitions as an artist. The money Sutton inherited from his builder father had dwindled almost to nothing since his return from the war, and in the early 1950s he was forced to turn aside from his original course. At the end of 1951 he travelled to Belfast to see Larkin, but the visit was not a success. In the months following, their letters slowed to a trickle, then gave out. An extraordinary correspondence, in which Larkin had evolved from adolescence to maturity, was over. Sutton spent the bulk of his adult life working as a pharmacist, raising a family.

Before the Christmas holidays ended, Larkin felt the ground shift in another old friendship. He went to Swansea to see Amis, his wife Hilly, and their two young children – Philip (his godson) and Martin – and the sight of family life chilled him. 'The Amises are living even more sluttishly than usual,' he reported to Eva, 'and their children are wandering tow-haired little boys, really rather pretty, but quite squashed and timorous. Even their crying seems subdued.'[3] He realized, as he had done when meeting Sutton, that his move to Belfast had detached him from England even more decisively than he had thought. He was settling into a separate life, and his English friends were becoming cut off from him – all, that is, except one. Before Larkin finally caught the boat back to Ireland he saw Monica, and while he realized that her need for independence still matched his own, he also felt sure they were falling in love with each other. Eva thought so too. As she put her son back on the train across country to Liverpool, she moaned again about her misfortune.

As soon as Larkin was back in Belfast, he felt free to respond affectionately to his mother again. Sending Eva two letters a week, he chatted about humdrum things, giving nothing away about his deep feelings or his work. This, sent in the autumn of 1951 soon after he had moved into a hall of residence where he had a kitchen of his own, strikes a typical note of amiable banality:

My dear Mobcapped Monst-Haugh, I expect you'll occasionally be wondering how I've got on. Of course it has been very new and strange to me, and I think I've been over-extravagant on the food side for I have the sensation of having spent a fantastic amount on all kinds of food, but it has been novel and entertaining and not so far more unsuccessful than successful. One Saturday afternoon (after washing up!) I 'cleaned' the kitchen and lugged the Electrolux up three flights of stairs and went over my carpet and hearthrug. I thought very much of you and how you would run the nozzle over my slippers and up the backs of chairs and all sorts of out of the way places! In fact it is surprising how often I remember your ways of doing things and try to emulate them. This morning, for breakfast I had half a grapefruit, corn flakes, two kippers (done as you described) and bread and butter and marmalade. The Strangs were in last night and ate six sausages I'd hoped to see me through next week. Unforeseen calamity![4]

Eva's letters to Larkin, written at the same rate as his until her final illness, are similarly doting, similarly trivial. Worrying about his cooking, money and health, signing herself 'Mop', she endlessly confides such thoughts as, 'I do hope you achieved some warmth after loading all your apparel upon the bed like that. Of course you ought not to have changed those pants – remember that I thought it very unwise at the time.'[5]

Straightforward as it seems, Larkin's correspondence with Eva performs a complex function. His letters buoyed her up, and at the same time denied her an active role in his life. This did more than defeat her plans to smother him; it was also a means of keeping other women at bay. He believed that as long as he had his mother to look after he could not be expected to give himself entirely to anyone else. When he returned to Queen's Chambers in January 1951, he wondered whether his strategy wasn't working rather too well. 'I am entering,' he wrote home shortly afterwards:

– or have entered – on a very anti-Queen's phase at the present, along with sour depression and all the rest of it. Scarcity of any good companions, my own inability to do anything myself, all contribute to clay-cold depressions. When I am in I want to be out and when I am out I want to be in – last week I was out three times: once to hear Beckett read a paper about Jane Austen – that was a meeting of the Belfast Literary Society, where a man was knitting a sock in the back row all the time; once at a send-off party for Miss Webster of the library, who is going to the States for five months ... The third outing was a somewhat chronic outing to a dance with Ellen Wilson, who preserved her meek inaudibility as we shuffled backwards and forwards in front of the band which was my only reason for going. Belfast is a dull unsociable place, much worse than Leicester: they have nothing that appeals to me at all.[6]

It's the contradictions which are most striking here, not the melancholy. They imply that Larkin believed his depression would lift before long. In fact it lasted all spring. Resuming his habit of writing for two hours after dinner every day, he tried and failed to make progress with his novel, continued to keep his diary up to date, and wrote a short sequel to his play *Round the Point*. *Round Another Point*, like its predecessor, is a Shavian dialogue featuring Geraint and Miller – but whereas their previous conversation had been about writing, this one is about sex. Geraint, 'revolted by coarseness' and hating to spend money on women, admits that he wants 'sex very much indeed':

But I take leave to refuse it on the terms offered in the particular cultural pattern we have the misfortune to inhabit . . . A middle-class bachelor has four courses of action. He can go without it . . . well, he can keep it to himself, if you like that better. He can pay for it. He can pick it up as he goes along. Or he can get married. Now the first of these involves frustration, and the sense of shame [at] palpable sexual incompetence. The second involves the degradation that inhibits pleasure. The third covers a wide range of unsatisfactory circumstances and I can't go into them all now, but the most typical is the 'love affair' that starts in misunderstanding and ends in misery, with a lot of hysteria and introspection along the way. The fourth . . . is such an enormous absurdity. It's like buying a car for the sake of the mascot on the bonnet, or taking a job as a sparring partner in order to see the champ in action. It's a confession you can't get at women by other means. It's just the end of you, socially, intellectually, financially and every other way. I think the most sensible arrangement would be sort of sex clubs, rather like tennis clubs, where men and girls could meet each other with as little misunderstanding as to why they were there [–] as if they had met at the tennis club. Contraceptives would be on sale and beds available.

Miller can't think of a satisfactory counter-argument to this; he simply complains that 'what makes you so hard to argue with is your appalling selfishness, your subhuman vulgarity, your blunt-toothed ponderousness. To you sex is just sex, an unvarying spasm repeated at intervals, worthless *per se* and meaningless *per se*, the expression of nothing and the origin of nothing.' Geraint agrees with this criticism, which leaves him feeling smug but the play going nowhere. It collapses into angry intransigence. 'All I say at present,' Geraint adds before leaving the stage, 'is that so long as sex is geared to the conventions of the pre-contraception age I can have no part of it, lacking both the deceitful insensitivity necessary for promiscuous fornication and the brutish insensitivity necessary for marriage.'[7]

Miller's sterile argument with Geraint forms the background to many of the eight poems that Larkin finished during this same spring and summer. The first two are the best: 'Next, Please' (18 January) and 'Latest Face' (February). The title of the former, according to his sister Kitty, is a phrase he dreaded hearing as a child whenever he reached the head of a queue at school or in shops: it meant he would shortly have to speak, which would be embarrassing because of his stammer. But if the poem begins with a memory of shyness it ends with an image which is frankly intimidating. After rehearsing the ways in which we hope our 'sparkling armada of promises' will 'heave to and unload / All good into our lives', it says starkly 'we are wrong':

> Only one ship is seeking us, a black-
> Sailed unfamiliar, towing at her back
> A huge and birdless silence. In her wake
> No waters breed or break.

In these final lines, which sharpen the outline of 'The North Ship' and mythologize the ferry on which he now travelled regularly between Belfast and the mainland, Larkin casts a cold eye on the chance for release that Northern Ireland had initially offered him. Wherever he travels, the poem says, death's emptiness is the only reliable destination. This is, of course, something Larkin had often said in the past – yet no sooner had he done so again than he wrote another poem as a form of compensation. In 'Latest Face' he half remembers the leaping opening of 'If, My Darling' to describe 'the great arrival at my eyes' of a woman who pushes death and melancholy to the side of his mind.

In view of Larkin's feeling for Monica, it would be reasonable to think 'Latest Face' was written for her. She was, after all, the only candidate that he had mentioned to his mother and friends as a possible replacement for Ruth. In fact the impetus for the poem came from an even 'later' face than Monica's; it was written about Winifred Arnott, the young graduate working in Queen's library, whose name appears over and over again on the final page of the poem's manuscript. Larkin had kept most of his thoughts about Winifred to himself ever since first seeing her the previous winter. Recently he had begun to try and find out everything he could about her. Born in Stourbridge in 1929, she had been sent to Belfast (where her father came from) during the Blitz and had stayed when the war ended, eventually reading English at Queen's. She had decided to remain in the city for a year after taking her Finals, partly to give herself time to think about possible careers. She also wanted to work out whether she should marry her English boyfriend, who was living in London. Everyone knew her time in Belfast was limited, which gave her an appealing air of transience. It was this, combined with her brown-haired, round-faced good looks, that had drawn Larkin to her in the first place. 'I think he liked me because I was cheerful,' she says now. 'A lot of the people he knew weren't.'[8]

The more Larkin saw Winifred the more he liked her. She was open, confident and fun. To Winifred, Larkin seemed amiable but shy, and a good deal too old for her. When he first arrived in the library, however, he was – apart from Graneek and 'a fat man who tied up parcels and a little boy'[9] – the only male employee, and she therefore regarded him as 'a real asset'.[10] She learnt to enjoy his sense of humour, even while remaining a little put off by his appearance and reputation. 'You see, news of his books had preceded him,' she says; ' – he was an *author*!'[11]

It's this sense of distance and unreality that Larkin described in 'Latest Face':

> Lies grow dark around us: will
> The statue of your beauty walk?
> Must I wade behind it, till
> Something's found – or is not found –
> Far too late for turning back?
> Or, if I will not shift my ground,
> Is your power actual – can
> Denial of you duck and run,
> Stay out of sight and double round,
> Leap from the sun with mask and brand
> And murder and not understand?

The tone here is flirtatious, the manner self-deprecating, the circumstances wholly serious. Within weeks of writing the poem, Larkin realized that he felt sufficiently strongly about Winifred to start worrying again about marriage. In 'To My Wife' (19 March) he says, 'Choice of you shuts up that peacock fan/The future was', and goes on to say that marriage means exchanging 'all faces' for one face which must inevitably become the proof of 'my boredom and my failure'. In 'Best Society', which spurns any company whatsoever, he goes on to create half the argument and many of the terms of 'Vers de Société' (written twenty years later):

Viciously, then, I lock my door.
The gas-fire breathes. The wind outside
Ushers in evening rain. Once more
Uncontradicting solitude
Supports me on its giant palm;
And like a sea-anemone
Or simple snail, there cautiously
Unfolds, emerges, what I am.

In 'Marriages', he reinforces the value of this pristine singleness as he mocks partnerships created by 'old need' and 'scarecrows of chivalry'. Admitting that 'rancour' and self-hatred may seem ignoble reasons for demanding solitude, he also says they are justifiable if they manage to hold marriage at bay.

Extricating such passages from the poems Larkin wrote in 1951 makes it seem as though their concern is marriage and little else. Plagued by the sense that he had 'acted like a shite' with Ruth, unable to shake off the idea that a wife would only be 'a sort of compulsory frittering',[12] he turned the idea of weddings round and round his mind obsessively. Yet as the months wore on, other thoughts began to reassert themselves. He started to take more interest in Belfast politics (demonstrating his burgeoning Orange sympathies in 'The March Past'); he urged himself not to waste the 'prime' of his life studying the 'Step by step' advance of death (in 'I squeezed up the last stair'); and he struggled to set aside his 'clay-cold' depression by spending time with friends. Judging by the impression he created on yet another visit to Amis in Swansea during the early summer, the strategy worked. They managed to ignore the demands of the children and recapture the flamboyance of their friendship. 'I found,' Amis remembers, 'a much more relaxed, fitting-into-things Philip than I'd seen before.'[13]

He began to make the most of friends nearer to hand, as well. Alec Dalgarno drove him into the countryside at the weekends – and sometimes even further afield. Occasionally they went to Dublin for lunch on a Sunday, taking in Enniskerry and Glendalough. Once (in November 1953) they went there with Winifred among others to hear Wagner's *Tristan und Isolde*; another time (February 1955) they attended the first night of Sean O'Casey's *The Bishop's Bonfire*.

Larkin also started to see more of Colin Strang. Strang was the son of the distinguished diplomat Sir William (later Lord) Strang, who had been political adviser to the Commander-in-Chief of British forces of occupation in Germany between 1945 and 1947, and was Permanent Under-Secretary of State at the Foreign Office from 1949 to 1953. Colin Strang impressed Larkin with his dry intelligence; his wife Patricia (her friends called her Patsy, her maiden name was Avis) was more powerfully alluring. Born in 1928, the daughter of a wealthy Catholic South African shipping agent, she had spent her childhood in Johannesburg. After school at Roedean she read medicine at Somerville College, Oxford, and eighteen months after her marriage to Strang had set up house in Belfast, at 13 Kincotter Avenue, in a more sophisticated style than any Larkin was used to. She was easily bored, glamorous and generous, and her sardonic talk entertained and flattered him. She quickly came to represent the sense of freedom he had always hoped Belfast would offer, and during their evenings drinking together, or lazing through the weekends, his admiration for her grew steadily.

Judy and Ansell Egerton were less intense friends but soon just as important. Like the Strangs, their marriage was something Larkin could both envy and stand outside – creeping into its shelter for food and company (he played bridge with them regularly), but able whenever he wanted to slip back into his pensive bachelordom. Once again it was the wife, not the husband, who meant most to him. Ansell, who lectured in Economics at Queen's, was ambitious, pragmatic and a cricket-lover (years later, with Harold Pinter, he proposed Larkin for membership of the MCC). After the Egertons had left Belfast in 1956, he worked as Assistant City Editor and then City Editor of *The Times* before becoming a merchant banker; eventually he was appointed a director of Rothmans International. Judy was younger than her husband – twenty-three when she first met Larkin in 1951 – and simultaneously tough and innocent. She had been born in Australia, and as a History graduate became a tutorial Assistant at Queen's. She was striking-looking, and her shyness endeared her to Larkin; she also shared his 'passion for the *Times* crossword puzzle'.[14] As he got to know her better he discovered that she was as shrewd as her more loquacious companions. Following the Egertons' return to London, and the eventual collapse of their marriage, she worked on Paul Mellon's collection of British paintings and drawings. Subsequently she joined the Tate Gallery as a curator in 1974, organizing among other things the George Stubbs show in 1984 and the Joseph Wright of Derby exhibition in 1990. Until the end of his life, Larkin's affection for Judy never faltered; she became one of his most valued correspondents and confidantes.

With the Strangs, the Egertons, Arthur Terry, Alec Dalgarno and

Winifred Arnott at the heart of his world, and other colleagues like Jimmy
Piggott, Henry Mackle, Dennis Bradley, Elspeth and George Davie around
the edges, Larkin could easily disguise the moods that filled his poems.
Particularly the mood of sexual anxiety. In the past, his concentration on a
single woman had brought as much pain as pleasure; now his interests
were more diverse he seemed to suffer less. Terry might still detect a 'tone
of gentle ruefulness'[15] when Larkin spoke about girls, but as far as he and
everyone else were concerned Larkin was busier and happier than before.
The women in his life were either harmless sources of speculation ('marvel-
lous women library assistants'[16]), remote (Monica), or obviously barred
(Patsy). None of them could easily threaten his singleness or disturb his
equanimity.

Winifred was the person most likely to break through these defences, as
Larkin had already discovered in his poems. In certain ways she was as
safely off limits as Patsy – she was likely to get engaged to her English
admirer at any moment. Yet the more often Larkin saw her, the more
attracted he was by the very things which should have put him off. 'We
spent more and more time together,'[17] Winifred remembers:

He lent me books which I didn't know (carefully recording the loan on a card) –
and I could borrow 'anything except my unexpurgated *Lady Chatterley*'. Once
when I was in bed with 'flu he posted an enormous number of books: most of his
choices I thoroughly enjoyed, but I could never read *At Swim-Two-Birds*.

I very much regret that he didn't introduce me to jazz [but] . . . we went out to
various local functions, the QUB film society, parties and so on – and we were
quite often asked as a couple to friends' houses, where the conversation was
excellent and there was much laughter. I don't remember him *ever* being sad, and
when he expressed melancholy I think everyone took it to be a pose – after all, he
was still a young man, and young men were not allowed to be melancholy.

I think what we enjoyed most were our bicycle rides in the country, which were
usually on Saturdays. We often rode along the Lagan towpath and towards
Lisburn, where I lived with [my aunt]. I took Philip there several times and he said
it was the nicest house he had ever been in, which surprised me – it was large and
airy but shabby, as most houses were then.[18]

Occasionally their talk would hobble towards marriage, though they
never got very far. 'In my world,' Winifred says, 'people married and had
children and that was that. Philip thought it was the wrong thing to do. I
remember sitting with him in the top of a tram going down the Ormeau
Road once, and him saying that people only had children so they could be
looked after by them in old age.'[19] Although Winifred describes their time

together as 'a sort of idyll',[20] this kind of conversation bothered her. She knew she was 'conventional' in her opinions about marriage whereas he was 'unorthodox'.[21] She felt 'one ought to get twenty-four hours of enjoyment out of every day',[22] he found the idea preposterous. She valued ordinary family life, he thought it was 'very dull and destructive: he used to say that his father had been turned by his mother into the sort of closed, reserved man who would die of something internal'.[23] Such differences made it impossible to think their affection could develop far beyond kindness. 'I never did regard him as a candidate for my husband and the father of my children,' Winifred says. 'I felt our relationship was of a different sort. We never went to bed together though I cheered him up, I think. I was very fond of him.'[24]

In the past Larkin had found such differences merely irritating. With Winifred they seemed a provocation. Excited by her but free from the worries and expense of a proper affair, he could embrace questions about marriage without being suffocated by them. Partly as a result of this, Winifred also exerted a strong influence on his writing. For the first time he began to build around his poems the sort of literary theories that he had previously spurned. Most were passed off with a shrug so as not to seem pretentious. Yet his insistence that poems are a unique random blend of thought and feeling gradually elaborated into a strict code. 'I shouldn't like to arrogate a philosophy to myself,' he said. 'A poem is just a thought of the imagination – not really logical at all. In fact I should like to make it quite clear to my generation and all subsequent generations that I have no ideas about poetry at all. For me, a poem is a crossroads of my thoughts, my feelings, my imaginings, my wishes and my critical sense. Normally there are parallels, but only when all cross at one point do you get a poem.'[25] Now and later, Larkin wanted to resist analysis in order to preserve flexibility. As one of his best commentators says, he had 'no programme to fulfil, no Byzantium to seek out, no "still point of the turning world" to which all his experience must be related. Set loose from such anchorage his imagination [could] be responsive to every different, contradictory twist of his experience, every new insight, however unprecedented. None of his poems is made to fit a prepared context of meaning.'[26] In years to come, Larkin would redefine these points over and over again, always arguing that poems owe their first responsibility to his own and his readers' feelings. They were all, he said, an attempt 'to express or describe or to render or preserve emotions that people feel'.[27] In his essay 'The Pleasure Principle' (1957) he puts it more clearly than anywhere. The process of poetry, he says:

consists of three stages: the first is when a man becomes obsessed with an emo-
tional concept to such a degree that he is compelled to do something about it. What
he does is the second stage, namely, construct a verbal device that will reproduce
this emotional concept in anyone who cares to read it, anywhere, any time. The
third stage is the recurrent situation of people in different times and places setting
off the device and re-creating in themselves what the poet felt when he wrote it.[28]

For at least the first year that Larkin knew Winifred, these beliefs
evolved in step with his desire to win her good opinion. Her plain-speaking
– like Monica's and Patsy Strang's – encouraged him to tear away the last
vestiges of pomposity from his poetic manner; her appealing naturalness
was exemplary. Not that he ever gave her any credit. Poets, he believed,
should create at least the impression of distance between their own lives
and the situations described in their work. In a review of Wilfred Owen's
Collected Poems, for instance, written in 1963, he asserts:

A 'war poet' is not one who chooses to commemorate or celebrate a war but one
who reacts against having a war thrust upon him: he is chained, that is, to a
historical event, and an abnormal one at that. However well he does it, however
much we agree that the war happened and ought to be written about, there is still a
tendency for us to withhold our highest praise on the grounds that a poet's choice
of subject should seem an action, not a reaction. 'The Wreck of the Deutschland',
we feel, would have been markedly inferior if Hopkins had been a survivor from
the passenger list.[29]

Elsewhere Larkin repeatedly says the same thing less wittily, more bluntly.
'I think a poet should be judged by what he does with his subjects, not by
what his subjects are,'[30] he announced in one interview. On several other
occasions he said that his opinion of Hardy would deteriorate if he
discovered that the mood of his poems was attributable to biographical
facts.[31] In his own case, it's evident that the majority of his poems were
written in reaction to a specific set of circumstances, yet they are invariably
treated to seem like general truths. Towards the end of his life, he talked
about the most important means of achieving this transformation:

Making [an experience] seem beautiful is a little more than just prettying it up. In
fact it's something much more than that. It's trying to make it acceptable ... [and]
most truths are unpalatable. You know what a boa constrictor does if it has
something to eat that's unpalatable? It sort of covers it with the boa constrictor
equivalent of saliva until it can slide down easily. Well, I think that's really what I

214

mean by beautifying. If you have a tough truth like 'life is first boredom then fear' you've got to somehow bring the reader's mind round to the point where that is the only possible exit from this particular situation. That's what I mean by making it beautiful. It's like Shakespeare making *King Lear* beautiful. *King Lear* is beautiful but it's very painful.[32]

When Larkin had made his name as a poet and began writing reviews and articles, he rarely missed a chance to broadcast these ideas – ideas which he first formed clearly in Belfast when he started producing his own 'more vernacular kind of poem'.[33] As they emerged, he began to search for a wider audience. If he hadn't felt so crushed by the failure of *In the Grip of Light* (which had been rejected not only by Faber but by Allen Lane, Methuen, Macmillan, John Lehmann, and Dent), he would automatically have turned once more to a London publisher. As it was, his longing for recognition was matched by an equally intense desire to avoid being snubbed. Rather than risk disappointment, he decided to lower his sights. Selecting twenty poems from those he had written during the last few years (the earliest was 'Going', dating from February 1946), and excluding all those written while he had been gripped by Celtic fever, he looked round Belfast for a jobbing printer who would produce a pamphlet for him. In November 1950, he said later, 'a Mr Hennessy [of Carswells the printer] saw me about it, saying they would print it for me in ten point old face Roman on what I privately called grocer's wrapping paper'.[34] On 27 April the following year the pamphlet arrived – called simply *XX Poems*, dedicated to Amis, and looking as Larkin had ordered, except for a 'chipped "i" in the date on the cover'.[35]

In another late letter to Sutton, Larkin indicated which were his own 'favourite poems'[36] eligible for *XX Poems*. It's an interesting list, because it shows that even while Larkin was seeking to define his poetic voice more precisely, he was insisting on variety. In some of the poems – 'Afternoons', 'Wires', 'Wants' and 'At Grass' – he gives the impression of someone death-obsessed, resolutely singular. Elsewhere – in the first of his 'Two Portraits of Sex' and the conclusion of 'Next, Please' – he is open to moderating influences. Elsewhere again, in 'Latest Face', he admits that he is fascinated by society. The poems, in other words, illustrate contradictions as well as cohesion. They define a personality which is full of love as well as dread.

Although *XX Poems* contained Larkin's best work to date it was still a publishing disaster. To generate some publicity for the collection, he sent it:

off to a number of individuals, you know, the sort of queer mixture of people I thought might be interested and people I admired. They were a very queer assortment. I mean I dare say the obvious people like Cyril Connolly and John Lehmann were among them, but Wendy Hiller was among them also, whom I was greatly enamoured of in these days – you remember her *Pygmalion* and *Major Barbara* films? None of them ever took the slightest notice of this, and one of the reasons may have been that I'd sent them off in unsealed envelopes, which in those days went for a penny – at least I thought they were a penny, but in point of fact about three weeks earlier the postage had gone up to 1½d., so I suppose all those people were knocked up at about a quarter to eight in the morning and asked for a penny, which may have jaundiced their whole view of the collection.[37]

There was one exception. Charles Madge, to whom Larkin had sent a complimentary copy with thanks for past generosity, responded kindly about the poems. He drew them to the attention of another young poetry-writing friend, D. J. Enright, who wrote about them in the Catholic journal the *Month*. It was the collection's only review, and its short-term advantages were non-existent. 'I was very pleased to see a poem quoted in full,' Larkin told Enright in due course, 'and also to see a mention of *A Girl in Winter* – not that I hold it in great esteem, but if I were "a proper writer" I would be a novelist rather than a poet on the grounds that the sort of novels I should write would spring from the same roots as poems but would be of greater complexity, depths and whatnot.'[38]

In England during the summer, Larkin visited Madge in Birmingham to thank him for his intervention. The main point of returning to the mainland, though, was to visit Monica and to take his mother on her annual holiday: this year to Brixham, near where Bruce Montgomery had moved to in Devon. Duties done, he sailed back to Belfast expecting to continue with the writing he had reluctantly interrupted. But when he arrived he found his routines disturbed. The university needed his rooms in Queen's Chambers and for a while he had to stay in a flat at 7 College Park East, then for three weeks at 49 Malone Road – which he thought was 'a good ... place for anyone with the yearning to be over-charged and under-fed'.[39] More depressing still, his life with Winifred was thrown askew: early in August, while he had been away, she had left Belfast for London to study for a post-graduate diploma in librarianship at University College. Separation gave Larkin a clear view of how much she now meant to him, but in the letters he immediately started sending her there is nothing like desolation, just a great deal of flirtatiousness. The day after returning to Belfast, for instance, he wrote to thank her for some photographs she had left him, agreeing that they were 'a fairly glum collection ... *apart* from the ones of yourself, which I'm very glad to have ... You have (if I might take the liberty of saying so) a very nice class of face from any point of view.'[40] A month later he wrote in the same vein, 'Lord, I do envy you [in London]. I have a romantic fancy about London. It's so much the start of a new life! Your old one was good enough for another winter at least! The elbows were quite sound and the cuffs only the tiniest bit frayed! *Some* girls have to make one life do for as long as – well, I won't tell you.'[41]

Larkin was able to be light-hearted in these letters to 'My dear Winifred' because he never expected their relationship to develop beyond the puppyish stage. He was consoled, too, by other commitments. Not only did he feel sure of Monica in England; in Ireland he felt increasingly drawn to the food-providing, drink-pouring, dog-loving, occasionally pipe-smoking 'tall, rather gawky brunette'[42] Patsy Strang. She had done more than anyone except Judy Egerton to provide him with a home in Belfast if and when he needed it. But Patsy was more assertive than Judy – and less settled in her marriage. As autumn turned into winter, and the Strangs and Larkin spent more time together, the balance of their relationship began to change. Before the end of the year, only four months after Winifred had departed, Larkin's letters show that he knew Patsy would accept him as a lover if he asked.

Although it was widely accepted that Patsy's life with Colin was 'semi-detached',[43] Larkin's liking for her husband, and his wish to avoid causing further disruption in their marriage, made him delay. Thinking more practically, it was difficult to imagine how and where they might meet. The Strang household was always bustling – they were popular hosts, and Patsy had some years before taken in two nephews after her sister and brother-in-law had died tragically young. Larkin's own domestic arrangements were similarly inhospitable. When he moved from his flat in Malone Road to more permanent lodgings in the university residence at 30 Queen's Elms on 13 October (helped by both Colin and Patsy) he was surrounded, as he had been in the past, by prying colleagues.

Larkin felt thwarted but not cast down. Queen's Elms was too public a place in which to commit adultery, but it had other advantages. His rooms, as he preferred, were at the top of the building – a large Victorian block in Elmwood Avenue, just behind Queen's Chambers – and a week after moving in he described them to Winifred as:

romantic attics – and delightful they are. The front one is a kitchen, facing north, and the back one is the bed-sitter, facing south. Both have voracious gas fires. The kitchen has a sink and an oven – just large enough to get your head in – a table and a kitchen cabinet. The sitting-room has a bed, two armchairs, two hard chairs, wardrobe, bookcases (too few), carpet, rug and table. I've added a reading lamp and a radiogram so that my few jazz records now sound their barbaric yawp round the musty rafters, and so do some Monteverdi records borrowed from Terry.[44]

In this bachelor world Larkin was snug yet primed for adventure. 'Life turns and beckons to me like an underwater swimmer in a soundless tank,' he told Sutton the day after moving; 'beguiling, impossible'.[45] Although he made plenty of complaints about chores and expense in letters written over the next few weeks, and was occasionally gripped by the sense that everyone was having more fun than him, the pace of his life quickened perceptibly. Even his letters to Eva could not entirely conceal his pleasure. 'I'm sure I'm the best situated person in these houses,' he told her:

because my separate kitchen is so valuable. It's quite large, and has a *small* kitchen table, a kitchen cabinet, sink and oven and chair. There's blue and white check on the floor and Patsy (who is really rather taken with the place, more so than with her own house) is devoting herself to finding blue and white things to go with it. I eat my meals in there! Colin has rigged up an expanding clothesline to hang my tea-towels on. The only time I feel a bit alarmed is at the thought of providing seven meals a week for myself in the evenings. I find that all doesn't happen at once: one washes up and makes the bed and sweeps the floor, all separate actions that make up the horrible entity of 'living alone and doing for oneself', which therefore seems quite easy! No more landlady creatures![46]

What none of these letters admits, for understandable reasons, is how much Larkin's relish for his new life depended on the certainty that he was at last safe from the encroachments of his old one. In October his mother finally abandoned her half-formed plan to come and live with him in Belfast. In December she moved from Kitty's home at 53 York Road in Loughborough to a new house a few doors away at number 21. The change left Larkin as free as he would ever be.

TWENTY-EIGHT

Larkin welcomed the new year, 1952, expecting his life to blossom. He was only twenty-nine; his lodgings were the best he had known; his family was securely distant; his affections were aroused but under control; he felt full of ideas. But nothing happened. His novel sputtered and stalled; he wrote no poems all year.

In letter after letter to his friends he asked himself why. The most likely explanation seems to have been that his feelings had been mixed wrongly. In the past, long periods of silence had been produced by too much misery; now, for the only time in his life, he was fractionally too happy – and happiness, as he was fond of saying (quoting Montherlant), 'writes white'.[1] His university work was also part of the trouble. Without ever dominating his life, it became for a while more distracting than usual. The report on necessary alterations to the library (for which he had already contributed information about issue desks) had recently been accepted by the university Senate, and for the early part of the year the building was in turmoil. 'We are in the Temporary Hut Accommodation,' he told Winifred in January:

or more shortly The Huts. All else pales beside it, or them. The move was really accomplished in my absence [for Christmas] (guile again), at least as far as the R[eaders] R[equests] books and desk were concerned, but for the first week of my return I had nowhere at all to work and spent my time heavily scarved and duffel-coated talking to workmen, vaguely admonishing and mildly inveighing . . . My biggest snag is manning both stacks and Huts 9 a.m.–9 p.m. with only the same personnel. Mr Graneek calls this 'my baby'. I think an actual baby would be less trouble – though I don't know, he added hastily.[2]

Twelve weeks later, in March, Larkin was still preoccupied. The reading room of the library was strewn with girders and ankle-deep in sawdust, and windows were being let into its walls. By now, though, it was more than builders who claimed the attention he might otherwise have given to writing. At the end of the month Monica came to stay, putting up in a university student's room left empty during the vacation, before she and Larkin travelled north for a few days together to 'a lovely little town called

Glenarm on the Antrim coast above Larne'.[3] The holiday drew them even closer together. The long friendship they had shared before becoming lovers, a friendship based on similar and sympathetic views about everything from books (nothing modernist) to politics ('true blue'[4]), meant that even their most careless raptures felt real and sensible. More important still, Monica kept quiet about marriage and all that it entailed. 'I wasn't much trouble, and then I'd go and cook the supper,'[5] she says, and Larkin appreciated that. At the same time – on this visit and several others – he clung to the certainty that she loved him devotedly.

Monica's feelings were selfless to a fault, and she realized that her commitment to Larkin, coupled with her frequent and long separations from him, made it likely that she would soon get hurt. She found it 'very difficult to know exactly what was going on'[6] with Patsy, but she suspected that Larkin was on the point of starting an affair with her. On 24 June, when Patsy was away from Belfast for a few days, Larkin wrote a letter which suggests that they had already become lovers. Calling Patsy his 'Dearest Honeybear', he said, 'As always when you are out of reach I am amazed by my good fortune that you were ever within it: I'm afraid I haven't always deserved it . . . Belfast seems, if not "thoroughly small and dry" since you went, thoroughly opaque and giving off no sheen or resonance.'[7] On 18 July, again, he signs off a letter to her with paw-marks and bids her 'Goodnight, valuable Honeybird, fabulous giraffe, exquisite political prisoner', telling her, 'I reproached myself silently for being in such a gibbering funk as to have come near to spoiling such a happy weekend, such as I've never had before. Bits of it keep coming back, and it seems extraordinary that they are all part of the same forty-eight hours.'[8]

It was the same throughout the late summer and autumn. Even when they refer to the difficulties of seeing each other, Larkin's letters to Patsy are constantly passionate, constantly skittish. (In September, for instance, when she gave him some more blue and white china for his kitchen, he thanked her by saying, 'I used the eggcup this morning. If you like I will paint my eggs blue and white in hoops.'[9]) Occasionally Patsy would offer to leave her husband and 'look after Philip and do all the earning so that he could just write',[10] but such thoughts were only half serious, and interpreted as such. Occasionally too she would try to turn their conversation towards literary matters by sending him some of her poems, but it was not the sort of talk he wanted with her. 'Sorry, dear,' he told her, 'it's you I like.'[11] What Larkin valued about the affair was the fact of its being an affair. It was exciting ('I miss your generosities very much. By God, there's more to life than doing a thousand words a day!'[12]). It was enjoyably furtive (they used the false names of Mr and Mrs Crane in hotels and on letters left for collection in post offices). It was a release from the tensions of his previous lives with women ('Please don't think of me as frightfully sophisticated,' he told her, keeping quiet about the extent of his involvement with Monica; 'I'm not. You're only my second young lady, and look like being my last'[13]).

Patsy's flouting of convention was clearly an important part of her charm. She easily persuaded Larkin to break his vow never to get involved with a married woman; she dissolved his worries about sex; she even made him waive his rule that women shouldn't swear as freely as men. 'I always said at school,' he told her, 'that a foul mouth indicated among other things a readiness to push aside the accepted limits of behaviour, which I thought commendable: people who aren't foul-mouthed have yet to show their refusal to be cut to the common measure.'[14] The only time she seriously irritated him was by breaking yet another of his rules – reading his diary. When she admitted that she had done this as she waited for him in his rooms in Queen's Elms one day, he was 'outraged'[15] and made her promise never to tell anyone what she had seen. This she did as long as Larkin remained in Belfast. Eventually, though, she made one disclosure to her second husband, the poet Richard Murphy, thereby giving the only surviving report on the diaries' contents – 'a note of Philip's relief at having got rid of desire early in the day by masturbating'[16].

Apart from recording events and reactions, the diaries seem to have been a sexual log book full of masturbatory fantasies, and a repository for his rage against the world – his grimmest, sexiest, most angry thoughts, the thoughts many of his poems depended upon, cleaned up, and organized in order to produce achieved works of art. Even his most candid letters only hint at their intensity. To gauge the anger we might think of the sometimes seethingly bitter things he wrote to Sutton as a young man, then multiply them. To make conjectures about the sexual fantasies, we might speculate about the card he devised, which was discovered in his box-room after his death. It formed part of a private game which required him to write the names of women he knew along the top of a sheet of paper, and parts of the female body down the side: tits, cunt, belly etc. On the grid covering the centre of the paper he made crosses, linking the names with the nouns wherever (and by precisely what means we cannot be sure) he had scored.

Larkin's relationship with Patsy was the most happily erotic of all his affairs. Even with her, though, he insisted that there should be an element of fantasy, and said he wanted pornographic pictures to play a part in their love-making. Larkin had been keen on pornography since Oxford, when he had begun to collect whatever (modest) magazines he could get his hands on. It had been the same in Wellington and Leicester, where he continued to be quite open with his friends about his predilection. By the end of his life he had accumulated several large boxfuls of magazines, ranging from the innocuous-seeming items of his youth (girls standing around in their underwear) to the cruder pictures he collected later. He didn't go for 'hard core' material, and neither did he show an idiosyncratic sexual taste. What he liked was straightforward – pictures of women with no clothes on, and none of them taken too close up, so that he could see clearly what was what. Other women friends apart from Patsy realized how much he liked it. In letters to Monica, for instance, he reports on visits to pornographic films, sometimes complaining that bad dialogue is made 'only slightly better by the speakers having no clothes on'.[17] In due course his secretary at Hull would become aware that he kept magazines in his office. Also in Hull he once showed a woman friend 'a large cupboard full of both literary and photographic pornography' and 'when she asked him what it was *for*, he replied (somewhat embarrassed), "to wank to, or with, or at".'[18]

Had Larkin been more intrepid he might have answered this need by other means – by going to prostitutes, or at least to clubs. As it was he preferred to play things safe, alone and at home, pleased that he had avoided unnecessary expense. If friends (Amis, for example) had suggested something more adventurous in the past he had always spurned it, and by now most of those close to him knew better than to ask. As Patsy's influence took hold, however, Larkin made at least one uncharacteristically daring decision. In April 1952, when Bruce Montgomery invited him to Paris for a few days, he said yes. They left England on 25 May and booked into the Hôtel Madison at 143 boulevard Saint-Germain. Reporting back to Eva, Larkin gave the impression that what concerned him most was the traffic. 'Apart from being quick and ruthless,' he complained, 'it comes at you from the wrong side all the time, so that, bothered already, you fall into a worse confusion and onto your knees in prayer.'[19] In a letter to Patsy he gave a less cautious account, but one which nevertheless shows the limits of his desire to live dangerously. Rather than speeding off to night clubs, he settles for drinking and jazz:

My chief emotion at present is one of horror at the amount of sleep I seem to be doing without. The street is so noisy and the bed so warm I don't seem to sleep until 4 a.m. or *want to*. My heart beats in a new, queer way and I daren't lie on my left side for fear of stopping it. On Friday night we drank till late, on Saturday we saw the Monet, drank what can only have been a bottle of champagne each in the Ritz bar and saw Benjamin Britten (this, to Bruce, was like being vouchsafed a vision of Martin Luther after years of devout Roman Catholicism), went up the Eiffel Tower (never again for me!), and at night after a luxurious meal went to a night club where Bechet was reputed to be appearing. This proved fallacious in fact, but we did hear Claud Luter's band, which I knew from records and was pretty exciting at times. To balance this we intend hearing *Salome* on Monday ... always assuming we have enough money. Today we had better spend in the Louvre, which I am told does not charge on Sundays.[20]

Exotic, exhausting and – in later life, when he had hardened his image as a stay-at-home – hardly mentioned, Larkin's Paris trip was one of the last signs of a fading friendship. He and Montgomery stayed in touch until Montgomery's death in 1978, but their holiday indicated that the intimacy they had known in Wellington was long gone. This saddened Larkin, and he was relieved to return to Belfast. In July Amis tried to make things better by applying for a job in the English Department at Queen's. He didn't get it. The job went instead, Larkin told Winifred, 'to a white-faced little worm whose name sounded like something out of Bunyan: *Carnall* ("Faith," he said, "my name is *Carnall*, brother to Mr *Fleshley* of the town of *Concupisance*; my wife is Mistress *Lust-of-the-Eye*, a very fine ladye ...")'.[21]

Later the same month, as if to compensate for the disappointment, Winifred returned. Throughout her absence, Jack Graneek had been saying he wanted her to become chief cataloguer. Larkin, of course, had other motives for wanting her back, and greeted her eagerly. His excitement soon died down. During her time in London Winifred had decided to get engaged to her admirer – 'young sparks'[22] as Larkin dismissively called him (in fact his name was Bradshaw and he worked in the Ministry of Defence) – and she told Larkin they could not continue in their former, flirtatious ways. He was sorry but said he understood – and anyway knew that for all his efforts he had only managed to graduate from '"queer" to "queer but nice" in her mind'.[23] When she showed him the ring on her finger he said, 'I feel as though someone had said that a new manuscript by D. H. Lawrence had just been discovered and they'd left it on my desk and I'd said I'd look at it in the morning.'[24] Once he was alone again, he showed the full extent of his angry disappointment. Amis said later, 'He had a picture of her in his room. He came back one night full of beer and wrote to say he'd noticed more than usual how it brought out her resemblance to Stan Laurel. "In a hearty way," he said, "I let a bit of beer fall on it and now I can't get it off. I can't get the shine back."'[25]

'Think of doing that!' Amis says, remembering the letter, 'and also writing "Latest Face"!' In fact it was entirely characteristic for Larkin to combine delicacy and coarseness. With Winifred, as with the other women he valued, he was always protecting his feelings by disparaging what he admired, and passing off self-disgust as disgust with others. For the next several weeks he converted his frustration into rage against the whole world of his affections. Before he went home to his mother for five days at Christmas he wrote to her testily, 'I feel I should *pay* you for my entertainment.'[26] After he had seen Montgomery in London over the new year he said dourly, 'I'm grateful for these glimpses of high life he gave me, as long as they don't come too often.'[27]

Once the immediate effect of hearing about the engagement had worn off, Larkin began to recover his equanimity. He continued to see Winifred in the library, and wrote to her 'a great deal'.[28] He also – and without telling her what he was up to – continued to write about her. Happiness had silenced him for the previous year; now that it was disturbed he started to produce poems again. On 18 January 1953 he began 'Arrivals, Departures', finishing it a week later as he remembered his recent return from England to 'This town [which] has docks where channel boats come sidling'. Faced with the struggle (the punningly 'horny dilemmas') between conflicting desires, he could do no more in the poem than insist on the difficult necessity for choice. '*Come and choose wrong*', he imagines the 'dilemmas' calling every morning. In the evening, too, they 'sound' again, and

> we are nudged from comfort, never knowing
> How safely we may disregard their blowing,
> Or if, this night, happiness too is going.

Larkin distinguishes here between the need to make a choice and the ability to do so. In the interval between thought and action he exists in a wretched passivity – feeling, as he says in an uncollected jotting about Winifred, 'You for certain are happy,/And if I am not, there is nothing to be done about it'.[29] A week later, addressing a poem to her fiancé, 'C.G.B.', his mood changes. Inertia turns to contempt, then cools down again:

> What you did, any of us might.
> And saying so I see our difference:
> Not your aplomb (I used mine to sit tight),
> But *fancying you improve her*. Where's the sense
> In saying love, but meaning interference?
> You'll only *change* her. Still, I'm sure you're right.

This final concession suggests something like tolerance. In fact it is delivered in the same wearily unhappy voice that Larkin would use six years later in another poem about marriage, 'Self's the Man'. It occurs, too, in the novel he had been trying to write for the past several years, and which recently he had begun to work on again. He persevered with it until the middle of the summer and then abandoned it once more, this time for good. It was almost exactly six years since he had begun to write it – in August 1947 – and this was the third time he had tried to finish. (He had originally 'push[ed] on v. slowly and badly'[30] for nearly fifty pages in September 1947, then made another attempt in the autumn of 1948 when he told Sutton, 'I sit like an old ape occasionally thinking about [it],'[31] then had another go in the winter of 1950 when he said it was 'all to buggery'.[32]) Alan Pringle at Faber still occasionally inquired about progress and Larkin was only able to apologize. Sometimes friends also encouraged him to finish. 'To me it reads extremely cleverly but without the least merit,'[33] he told them.

Larkin showed his drafts to no one, but acknowledged that they existed, allowing rumours to proliferate freely. The novel only ever had a provisional title – *A New World Symphony*, which he said was a 'lovely title, I always think – of course it won't *do*, but that's its private title, its nickname'.[34] Of the three drafts which survive, one is forty-one pages long, one fifty-six pages long, and one ninety-five pages long. Each tells substantially the same story and has the same cast of characters occupying the same time-scale in the same Midlands environment. In every one of them (but with varying amounts of detail) the action opens on Christmas Eve with Sam Wagstaff about to arrive at the home of Mrs Piggott and take her daughter Stella to the local Rugby Club dance. Sam and Stella – a small, fair-haired young woman with an 'inquiring, distant, perhaps estimating'[35] expression – have known each other since they were teenagers: Sam's father and Mr Piggott (Stan) started the Eland Motor Company together twenty years previously. Now it is accepted that Sam and Stella will soon be married, though it's a prospect that neither much relishes. Stella admits to her mother that 'honestly, I can't get very excited about [him] really'.[36] Sam is similarly uncertain. He likes Stella, occasionally lusts after her, but doesn't love her. Furthermore, when he eventually turns up to collect her, he is preoccupied by someone else. Driving to the Piggott house he has knocked a girl off her bike and injured her: 'He was horrified to see a great wound, really a tear, in her left cheek: blood was streaming from it down her chin on to her collar.'[37]

The accident has a powerful effect on Sam, who has little experience of life. He lodges with his grumpy hypocritical father, 'old Sam', and has served in the air force during his National Service, but otherwise has seen nothing of the world beyond Birmingham – where he works. His confinement has made him indolent, and it's this which most affects his feelings for Stella:

For a few hours every time he came home he thought she was both damned good looking and a decent sort: it might even be that lately this period had been lasting longer. It had suited him well to come out of the Air Force and find her disengaged: it saved him the trouble of making her acquaintance, while preserving – for she had grown up since he had left home – an air of novelty. The situation had appealed to a lazy streak in Sam's nature. It allowed him familiarities which with another girl would mark a closer relation: they could visit each other without any fuss.[38]

Half of Sam wants to have 'a serious bash'[39] at Stella, half of him can't be bothered, but the source of his confusion has nothing to do with desire. It's to do with marriage. His dilemma is the one Larkin himself had been confronting ever since beginning the novel. Sam thinks that if he marries he will re-create his parents' unhappiness; if he doesn't marry he knows he will feel sexually deprived.

These thoughts drive the memory of the accident from Sam's mind when he and Stella reach the Rugby Club dance. A friend immediately hurries up to him saying, 'It's only a matter of time, isn't it – you and our Stella?' 'That's what everybody seems to be deciding,'[40] Sam tells him. Shortly afterwards, the club drunk Porky Haines is evicted by the officious MC Alex Chattaway, whereupon other members, including Sam, take off Chattaway's trousers and hand them in to the cloakroom attendant, giving the receipt to Stella. The scene is a crude parody of a sexual encounter, aggressive not erotic, denying all tenderness. Yet again, when Sam finally dances with Stella he finds that his need for her flares up, threatening to engulf his fear that it will eventually lead him to the altar: 'By holding her low down in the back he could feel the alternate shifting of her hips, which was enough to send a sudden illumination all over him, making the dance a dead skin of behaviour it was time to cast. "Let's go and see if the car's still there," he whispered, and felt he had called right when Stella replied, "Be awful if it got stolen, wouldn't it?" '[41]

Much of the business of *A New World Symphony* revolves round the trouserless Chattaway and the drunk Haines. (It's eventually resolved when Sam and the other de-baggers are reprimanded by the club secretary; Stella suspects Sam of wimpishly apologizing when no such thing was required.) The novel's interest, though – and the author's – lies elsewhere. When Sam and Stella eventually return to Sam's father's house, where they are spending Christmas together, they enact the fragment's main drama of desire and obligation. Locked in the 'sour and unwelcoming'[42] building, where nothing looks 'as if it had been put down for a few minutes and was waiting to be picked up again',[43] they crouch (almost literally) in the shadow of the miserable widower 'old Sam' who is in bed upstairs.

In the two shorter drafts Stella goes to bed alone and quickly, full of a sense of anti-climax. The narrative then turns its waning attention to the rest of the Christmas holiday – to gift-giving, to 'old Sam's ailments', to jazz, to a rugby match. In the longest draft, though, Sam keeps Stella downstairs, leading her to the sofa:

Everything went out of his mind except [Stella]; his hands moved about her as if seeking rest, but each touching was another bundle of dry hay thrown on to the central blaze. Her head being pressed back, the pearl collar became unfastened and dropped down: her hair was tousled, one shoe was scraped off. She was repaid to the exact measure of trouble she had taken to dress herself up; each accoutrement, dab of powder, and adjustment was crossed off one by one, and, these being accounted for, Sam went on to pay out each hurt gesture, attractive smile, instance of flirting . . . and covert embrace in dancing.[44]

This encounter, part seduction, part assault, leaves neither of them satisfied. Sam is guilty, frustrated, and admits to being motivated as much by anger as by attraction. Stella is described more neutrally as 'not all that eager to get married. She regarded it as equivalent to middle age, something inevitable and solid that she would gradually settle into.'[45] When the following day dawns, and the dreary routines of Christmas begin, nothing has been decided. 'The only thing' that prevents Sam from asking Stella to marry him is his feeling that 'the question seemed unreal, almost like a half-remembered dream'.[46] During lunch he evades the question, and when he turns to her again on the sofa at tea-time he once again 'did not like the thought of mentioning'[47] marriage. In fact, Larkin tells us, 'he quite forgot everything except that he must go on making love to Stella':

His free right hand slid up her bare leg till he was holding her thigh. The fact that she made no objection gave the episode an unreal quality: he caressed her more freely and undid the few buttons of her clothes, so that her body was built up from isolated patches into a warm whole. Handling this made him feel desperate to have her, far too desperate to conduct the politic negotiations to get her successfully, far too desperate too not to try. He had been kneeling by her all this time, and now offered to pull her down on to the thick carpet, where they would be reflected in the round brass belly of the coal scuttle: he dropped a cushion on to the floor for her head, and patted it. She took advantage of his leaning back to sit up and swing her feet off the sofa, pulling her skirt down over her thighs again. As she tucked at her hair, the two halves of her unbuttoned shirt hung away from her body, showing her bare breasts. Her side nearest the window was stained wine-coloured by the light through her shirt. She was not largely built.

'No, we'd better relax, Sam dear,' she said. 'Really, I mean it. No, really.'[48]

By the time Sam releases Stella for the second time, his desire has curdled into revulsion: 'There ran through him a slight shiver of pure dislike, and he felt suddenly that he could not stand any more of her, that he must at once busy himself with anything that had nothing to do with her.'[49] The rest of this longest draft tries to keep faith with his cold resolution. Instead of persevering with Stella, Larkin gives us a section describing 'old Sam', another about a boxing match, and then takes us to the same rugby match that appears in the other two versions. Then it stops. A draft plan for the remainder of the novel survives, but no detail; in so far as the plan can be decoded, it seems to suggest that Sam tries again to 'seduce or rape' Stella, is rebuffed, and then remembers the girl (Grace) he had knocked off her bike. His relationship with Grace develops against a background of turmoil in the Eland Motor Company, during which old Wagstaff dies and Sam behaves disloyally towards him. Eventually Sam leaves for America, while Grace tries to persuade him to remain in England with her. The plan ends: 'His [Sam's] whole attitude swings round to embrace [the idea]. Sincerely believes it and condemns her. (She is so alien to him, and of course it is true in a way.) . . . The flight to Southampton – he is on board, she telegraphs him "he is disgusted at this frank pursuit" . . . Does not reply. Second wire . . . Sends back wire choking her off. Immediately feels worse . . . Grace *seule* to end.'[50]

Considering how long he worked on it, *A New World Symphony* is not only disappointingly short, it is also disappointingly thin. Even in the longest draft all the characters apart from Sam and Stella are sketchy, and the narrative pace unsure. Whichever way Larkin tried to turn the story, he could not escape the suffocating gloom of Wagstaff's house, or the questions which had to be resolved there. It was his hope that this third novel would follow *Jill* and *A Girl in Winter* with an assertion of recovery and fulfilment. In fact the fragment offers little of this. Its three drafts give a picture of sexual indifference, disgust, and/or violence towards women. They show a deep and insoluble fear of marriage; they are snagged in family relations which are resentful and resented.

It would be easy to argue that these things comprised Larkin's reason for failing with the book: they were so urgently his own obsessions that he was unable to transmute them into art. Yet he was perfectly well able to perform this transmutation elsewhere in his writing – so why not here? The answer sounds simple, but its implications are complex. Larkin gave up *A New World Symphony* because none of the endings he could envisage allowed him to write about the regeneration he longed for. Whether Sam got married or not, the outcome would be equally miserable. Had Larkin been able to feel that in pushing aside the novel for the last time he was also ridding himself of the problem it described, the waste of his effort might have been more bearable. But even the controlled happiness of his affair with Patsy, the safe flirtation with Winifred, and his well-regulated to-ings and fro-ings with Monica gave him no confidence that his worries about marriage were finally over. The ruined stump of his novel was more than a reproach; it was also a warning.

TWENTY-NINE

It wasn't sorrow but rage that swept through Larkin when he abandoned his career as a novelist – rage with what he knew was a personal as well as an artistic failure. Monica, being one of the friends he would have most liked to impress by completing *A New World Symphony*, had to bear the brunt of his disappointment. In April 1953, while spending Easter with his mother, he visited her in Leicester and 'directed' his 'irritation' against her. He behaved, he admitted to Patsy, 'most unjustly, for I had two very quiet and comfortable days with her, though my guilt complex is increased rather than dispersed.'[1]

By July, when he and Monica were about to go on holiday together to the island of Skye off the west coast of Scotland, her connection with the fate of his prose had become more explicit. As he finally set his novel aside he turned briefly to the Bax fragment – only to find, 'I *can't* write this book.' He told Patsy:

If it is to be written at all it should be largely an attack on Monica, and I *can't* do that, not while we are still on friendly terms, and I'm not sure it even interests me sufficiently to go on ... I must say I don't look forward to this bloody holiday [on Skye]: if I feel in as ugly a humour as at present it may be the last we take together. There seems no point in carrying on, if it's out of pure cowardice as it mainly is. Well! This may be taking an unduly black view. We'll see. I always get these fits of depression before a meeting.[2]

A good deal of this anger was designed to make Patsy feel better. In fact Larkin's Skye holiday, like the other times he and Monica spent together, was intimate and undemanding. She suited his selfishness in virtually every respect – especially since, on their return to Loughborough, it was clear that Eva was at last prepared to admit her as a fellow guardian of his needs. When demanding to know how well Monica looked after him (meaning, for instance, that he should have chicken to eat – or 'chicking', as she pronounced it – rather than duck, which she reckoned exotic and therefore inferior), she just about managed to sound collusive. Monica resented her intrusiveness, but kept her counsel. Privately she thought 'the Larkins felt they were superior' and scoffed at them for thinking the least expenditure of effort was 'something heroic'.[3] 'Mrs Larkin's home,' she says, 'was one in which if you'd cooked lunch you had to lie down afterwards to recover.'[4]

Larkin regarded every visit to York Road as a convenient way of measuring the difficulties he could expect if he attached himself to another woman. Rubbing the point in, he said goodbye to Monica and took his mother to Weymouth for a week – and judging by the small handful of poems he wrote immediately afterwards, it was Eva and not Monica who most stirred his imagination. In July he began 'Love Songs in Age' (he didn't finish it until 1 January 1957, three and a half years later). Two other poems begun at the same time fill in the background to that poem. 'Mother, Summer, I' takes Eva's fear of thunderstorms and his own distrust of 'emblems of perfect happiness' to indicate that mother and son are both uncomfortable in their summer present and would prefer autumn. In 'At thirty-one, when some are rich' he refers to his habit of writing 'letters to women' as a way of avoiding more complicated forms of communication:

> Why write them, then? Are they in fact
> Just compromise,
> Amicable residue when each denies
> The other's want? Or are they not so nice,
> Stand-ins in each case simply for an act?
> Mushrooms of virtue? or, toadstools of vice?

At the end of the poem, Larkin tells us these two questions 'taste the same', which leaves him exactly where he was at the beginning: poised between the need for the 'much-mentioned brilliance' of love and fear of where it might lead. By the time he returned to Belfast after Weymouth, he had reminded himself once again of the advantages as well as the drawbacks of his ambivalence. All his new poems told him that he might cherish his freedom, but would have to endure loneliness.

Patsy's departure from Ireland was the first blow. Early in August her husband Colin was appointed a lecturer in the Philosophy Department at the King's College Newcastle; she decided to go with him. (In fact she spent only the weekends in Newcastle; during the week she lived in Boar's Hill outside Oxford.) 'Well, dear one,' he wrote to her:

I always thought it'd come like this – sudden as a guillotine! – and so it has, and perhaps the better for coming in a period when I'm not expecting you from day to day. My dear, do you think you'll like Newcastle any better than Belfast? ... to think of next year here gives me a curious sinking in the stomach. I'm not sure how I'll carry on without you. It's like being told that I have to go through the winter without an overcoat – all right *now*, but what about when it gets cold? So much of my content in the past two years has been due to you. You are the sort of person one can't help feeling (in a carping sort of way) *ought* to come one's way *once* in one's life – without really expecting she will – and since you did, I feel I mustn't raise a howl when circumstances withdraw you, however much I miss you – it would be ungrateful to fortune, if you see what I mean ... do you? At least, that's what I try to feel! But oh dear, oh dear! ...

You '*made*' Belfast for me: to think of returning to 1950 makes my mouth contract like a lemon-sucker's. Of course, if it's too insupportable I can always try to move back to England.[5]

By the early autumn, Larkin's 'sense of solitude' had begun to deepen into dread that he might be 'alone irrecoverably'.[6] He wondered whether he should have set up house with Patsy. Thinking rationally, he knew it was out of the question: her marriage, her flightiness, his own selfishness all made it impossible. Yet it was equally obvious that his affair with her could not continue. 'If a "wrong thing" becomes harder to do,' he told her in November, 'it seems wronger in consequence, and – well, we have our obligations. I wish I could write this without sounding priggish and unfriendly: you know there exists a particular *rapport* between us that I'm not denying, nor do I deny that if you were here perforce, or I there perforce, well . . . I'm very fond of you and very interested in all you do.'[7]

Patsy and Larkin were never to spend much time together again. They met occasionally in England, usually in London, and 'what they got up to I don't know,'[8] says Monica. A year after leaving Belfast Patsy went, alone, to study at the Sorbonne in Paris where she met the Irish poet Richard Murphy. By December 1954 they had fallen in love, and she wrote to Larkin to tell him. He regretfully wished her well, reassuring her, 'this doesn't mean that I'm breathing vengeful jealousy and determined to drop you with maximum rudeness! I reckon, on balance, you treated me better than I treated you. The only thing I hold seriously against you is reading my diary – really. You must not *tell* people if you read their diaries! Remember! – and that's not an awful crime.'[9]

After Colin Strang had begun divorce proceedings against his wife, Patsy went with Murphy to Greece for the winter of 1954. The following May they were married (a month after Colin Strang had also remarried), and started dividing their lives between London and Connemara, where Murphy rented a house. They had a daughter, Emily, in 1956, but not even the child could keep the marriage intact. Before long Patsy left Murphy and went to live in Dublin. She was, Larkin gathered, spending her father's money by drinking herself to death.

Even while telling Patsy that he 'wasn't sure how [he'd] carry on' without her, Larkin was making plans to do just that. If marriage remained out of the question, flirtation certainly did not – even (especially) if it was directed at someone out of reach. Winifred, engagement notwithstanding, swam back into his life as Patsy left. In July, when Larkin was in Skye with Monica, he discreetly wrote a letter to 'Sweet Winifred', telling her, 'Oh! How I regret this separation,' fondly remembering bicycling expeditions they had made together to Lisburn and Lough Neagh, and ending, 'I rage, I pant, I burn for a letter from you, telling me all that is happening . . . *Je t'embrasse un peu partout* (this is the only bit of French I know, but it's rather a good bit isn't it?) Your devoted Philip.'[10]

Winifred objected to being called 'sweet', but not so vehemently that

Larkin was put off trying other forms of endearment. 'Sorry ... about "sweet",' he wrote when he reached Weymouth with Eva, 'but to tell you the truth the phrase came so naturally I didn't think twice about it: and all it reminded me of was some little-known wild flower: "In these lanes the observant traveller will be cheered by many a gay clump of Ratsbane, Old Man's Slaver, Wild Oscar, and even (in the first half of June) the shy, Sweet-Winifred, loveliest and most elusive of our English etc. etc." So please think of it like this. Alternatively, you can consider yourself a small furry animal.'[11]

Larkin thought it was safe to write such letters because he was even more confident than before that Winifred wouldn't take them entirely seriously. Their mood survives in a poem he began writing for her on 17 August – 'Lines on a Young Lady's Photograph Album': he told her, '[it] can't make up its mind whether it's going to be serious or not'.[12] In the end (the poem was finished the following month) he makes a virtue of his indecision: as he pores over the 'thick black pages' of the album, feasting on their 'nutritious images', he treats desire candidly but lightly. The details of 'pigtails' and 'a reluctant cat'; the sexy, Tennysonian innuendo of 'furred yourself, a sweet girl-graduate'; the disquieting 'chaps who loll/At ease about your earlier days' are all part of an environment which is engrossing yet separate. It is a world impervious to the transforming power of high art (photography, we're told, is not an art at all), which therefore has to be rejected or accepted on its own terms: ridiculous as well as fine, ugly as well as graceful.

Once Larkin has convinced himself that the pictures show 'a real girl in a real place', and are 'In every sense empirically true', his sense of their value changes. The mood of the poem alters. Instead of lightness we get gravity; instead of mere separation we get division. 'We cry,' Larkin says, 'Not only at exclusion, but because/It leaves us free to cry'. No matter how greatly he might prize a relationship which leaves him 'free' in any sense, he can't stop his gratitude turning into melancholy when he confronts the plain fact of isolation. Looking at the photographs of Winifred allows him to possess her without becoming involved, but as time passes and the difference between them and the 'real girl' widens, their link with the present grows weaker. Eventually they seem like the stills of a fantasy.

The precise source for 'Lines on a Young Lady's Photograph Album' is easy to trace, even though Larkin altered some details. 'I mean,' says Winifred, 'there were in fact two albums not one, there's not a picture of me wearing a trilby hat (though there is one of me in a beret and moustache for Rag Week). On the other hand, I'm afraid to say, there's definitely my double chin, he got that right. And there's also one of me bathing.'[13] Behind such details, and behind the feelings which make them precious, lies another, less obvious source. By covertly admitting to the pleasure it takes in fantasy, the poem connects with the other pictures Larkin liked to gaze at: the photographs in pornographic magazines. The sex life they entail – solitary, exploitative – is a crude version of the pleasure he takes in the album. We are reminded of it, too, in other poems which contain pictures of women – the girl in the wallet in 'Wild Oats', the poster in 'Sunny Prestatyn' – and more faintly in others which render women as icons: 'The Large Cool Store', even 'An Arundel Tomb'. In all these, working unseen, Larkin transforms a masturbatory impulse and an addiction to solitude into poems of great beauty and sociable truthfulness.

At the end of 'Lines on a Young Lady's Photograph Album' Larkin tells us the cause of his melancholy is the fact that the album distils 'a past that no one now can share,/No matter whose your future'. In ordinary life, he knew precisely who would share Winifred's future – 'young sparks' – and a month after the poem was finished she left Belfast to begin it. When the moment of departure came Larkin was relieved as well as sad. He would miss her cheerfulness, her prettiness and her company on expeditions into the country, but he still had his independence. He stopped writing to her, and references to her soon became few and far between. Some were grudging ('I wish,' he told Amis, 'I had some of the money back I spent on her, *and the time*'[14]); some were wistful: when he bumped into her on holiday in 1957 he said, 'We goggled at each other in constrained fashion, then her atomic-energy husband arrived and took her away.'[15] Eventually, towards the end of his life, Larkin reviewed their friendship:

I don't know that I'm glad that nothing passed between us except a few etc. – I think in those days I thought one shouldn't look at a girl unless one intended to marry her, and anything else meant fearful conflict and heart searchings and the like, and no doubt I was right. But looking back I suppose Samuel Butler was right when he said life was a question of being spoilt in one way or the other. Do you remember saying that the trouble with me and my friends was that we never *did* anything?[16]

In his poems, Larkin was less restrained about how much he missed Winifred. 'Maiden Name' (written in January 1955, shortly after her marriage) repeats the conclusion of 'Lines on a Young Lady's Photograph Album' by resigning its interest in the present to concentrate on the past. In the earlier poem, the pictures froze Winifred in her youth and available singleness; now it is the 'five light sounds' of her maiden name which do the same thing:

> since you're past and gone,
>
> It means what we feel now about you then:
> How beautiful you were, and near, and young,
> So vivid, you might still be there among
> Those first few days, unfingermarked again.
> So your old name shelters our faithfulness,
> Instead of losing shape and meaning less
> With your depreciating luggage laden.

Larkin wrote eight poems in the three months between Winifred's departure and the end of the year, and in several of them he emphasized the sharp divisions he now felt existed between past, present and future. They're most clearly dramatized in 'Triple Time', but appear too in 'Whatever Happened?' ('At once whatever happened starts receding'), and in the strictly separated time-zones described in 'Autumn' (the only existing fragment of a sequence he planned to deal with the seasons). Winifred accentuated these divisions by making Larkin think of the present as a place he could not escape. Shut in its glass-sided vantage point, he was condemned to weigh for ever the rival claims of self and society, sexual loneliness and sexual attachment – as he does in 'Reasons for Attendance':

> Sex, yes, but what
> Is sex? Surely, to think the lion's share
> Of happiness is found by couples – sheer
>
> Inaccuracy, as far as I'm concerned.
> What calls me is that lifted, rough-tongued bell
> (Art, if you like) whose individual sound
> Insists I too am individual.

Clearly Winifred's influence on Larkin extended beyond the poems in which she appears – 'Lines on a Young Lady's Photograph Album', 'Maiden Name' and 'He Hears that his Beloved'. Exciting but separate, she helped him reaffirm his devotion to 'Art' rather than 'Life'. She also made him realize that while he continued to avoid marriage, he couldn't give his other and even greater fear the slip so easily. 'Hospital Visits' (implicitly) and 'Tops' (explicitly) – both of which he wrote within a couple of months of 'Lines' – show him glancing nervously at the 'black-/Sailed unfamiliar' of 'Next, Please' and finding it has moved closer. Previously, his reaction had been to recoil in articulate despair; now, although grieving that he was 'starting to die', he responded energetically, rousing himself to characterize the life which remained, and to emphasize that the past was well and truly 'over'. Visiting his mother and Monica for Christmas he wrote an eight-page account of his earliest days (quoted in Chapter One), and also the poem 'I Remember, I Remember', which in mocking Lawrentian and Dylan Thomas-ish ideas of childhood creates a distinct and consolingly disillusioned adult persona:

> By now I've got the whole place clearly charted.
> Our garden, first: where I did not invent
> Blinding theologies of flowers and fruits,
> And wasn't spoken to by an old hat.
> And here we have that splendid family
>
> I never ran to when I got depressed,
> The boys all biceps and the girls all chest,
> Their comic Ford, their farm where I could be
> 'Really myself'.

The defiance which gleams amidst deprivation in 'I Remember, I Remember' ('nothing, like something, happens anywhere') is burnished in the poems Larkin continued to write into the new year, 1954. It emerges in the exuberance of 'For Sidney Bechet' ('On me your voice falls as they say love should,/Like an enormous yes'); in the cautious but realistic definition of happiness in 'Born Yesterday' (written to celebrate the birth of the Amises' third child Sally on 17 January). It appears again in two of his most memorable poems, 'Poetry of Departures' (23 January) and 'Toads' (16 March), both of which recommend the virtues of caution in a voice which is robustly comic and confident. In 'Poetry of Departures' he decides that to 'swagger the nut-strewn roads,/Crouch in the fo'c'sle/Stubbly with goodness' would be 'a deliberate step backwards'; in 'Toads' he accepts that while he resents the daily grind in the library, he relies on it:

> For something sufficiently toad-like
> Squats in me, too;
> Its hunkers are heavy as hard luck,
> And cold as snow,

And will never allow me to blarney
My way to getting
The fame and the girl and the money
All at one sitting.

I don't say, one bodies the other
One's spiritual truth;
But I do say it's hard to lose either,
When you have both.

As a younger man, Larkin's feelings of exclusion had created bitter uncertainties. When he approached the middle of his life he stopped seeing the conflict as something which must be resolved, and regarded it instead as the means of self-definition. Transcendence was no good: he must accept that failure and success, misery and happiness, confinement and freedom could not be separated from each other. There remains, however, 'a rather strained element of self-consoling'[17] in this acceptance, as Blake Morrison has said. Larkin had – finally – deliberately turned away from Ruth, just as he had more recently let Winifred and Patsy go. In 'Toads', as in 'Poetry of Departures' and 'Reasons for Attendance', he addresses the elements in his personality that have allowed this to happen – the passivity and the need for solitude – and has tried to persuade himself that they are inevitable and desirable. But there is a lack of conviction in the argument. The questions remain open even while seeming to warp tight shut like doors, and he knows that he must continue to ask them. It is a solemn realization, but not one to be discussed only in solemn terms: it should be tackled openly, hilariously, argumentatively, and sometimes savagely. At the same time as he gave Winifred loving and publishable tributes, he also scribbled in his notebook:

Not love you? Dear, I'd pay ten quid for you:
Five down, and five when I got rid of you.[18]

THIRTY

When Larkin had ended his engagement to Ruth he had turned to other, less volatile friendships. Now that Patsy and Winifred were no longer in Ireland he did the same thing again. Over Christmas he reassured the long-suffering Monica about his feelings for her; on his return to Belfast he relied on the Egertons, Alec Dalgarno, Jimmy Piggott and others for their company. There were some unexpected additions, too. Early in the new year Harry Hoff visited Queen's – Harry Hoff who under the pseudonym William Cooper had written *Scenes from Provincial Life*, which Larkin called 'the great Leicester novel'.[1] Shortly afterwards, in February, he met the young poet and critic Donald Davie, who was teaching at Trinity College, Dublin, and invited Larkin to come and give 'a talk on modern poetry'. He accepted, in spite of his reluctance to speak in public ('God,' he told Patsy, 'the sweat runs down my back'[2]), and found Davie 'quite a pleasant and businesslike young man from Yorkshire'.[3] The meeting marked the beginning of a long acquaintance. In years to come their work would often be mentioned in the same breath, and in the short term Davie tried to help his fellow-writer by urging the Dublin-based Dolmen Press to publish Larkin's poems. He had no success.

In April 1954, during the Easter vacation, Larkin hurried back to England and older friendships again, staying with the Amises in Swansea for two nights after a brief holiday with Monica in Malvern. He found Amis as amusing and sympathetic as ever, yet the visit left him troubled. The reason was easy to find but hard to admit. On 25 January, three months earlier, Amis had published his first novel, *Lucky Jim*, and Larkin was jealous of its success – even though the book was dedicated to him. 'I do think that it is miraculously and intensely funny,' he told Patsy at the time of publication, 'with a kind of spontaneity that doesn't tire the reader at all. *Apart* from being funny, I think it is somewhat over-simple.'[4]

Larkin had been involved with *Lucky Jim* from the outset. When Amis had visited Leicester in 1948 Larkin had taken him into the Senior Common Room of the university college for coffee one Saturday morning and Amis had 'looked round a couple of times and said to myself: "Christ; somebody ought to do something with this." Not that it was awful – well, only a bit, it was strange and sort of *developed*, a whole mode of existence no one had got on to, like the SS in 1940, say. I [decided I] would do something with it.'[5] Ever since this moment of revelation, Larkin had kept closely in touch with Amis about the book. He had contributed jokes, commented on various sections, provided encouragement, and when he read the final draft said, 'cut this, cut that, let's have more of the other. I remember I said Let's have more "faces" – you know, his Edith Sitwell face, and so on. The wonderful thing was that Kingsley could "do" all those faces himself – "Sex Life in Ancient Rome" and so on.'[6]

During this process Larkin had inevitably seen Amis appropriate many things which they had evolved together. Some were private jokes, and harmless – such as the use of Eva's address in Dixon Drive for Jim's surname, or the inclusion of a letter from 'L. S. Caton' 'bearing a few ill-written lines in green ink'.[7] Others were more substantial – including the debt to *Jill*. The climax to both novels, for instance, comes with a bout of public drunkenness after their heroes have struggled against middle-class rivals (Warner in *Jill*, Bertrand in *Lucky Jim*). Furthermore, the main business of both books is to settle difficulties with girls.

Larkin reckoned he had suffered more than Amis in this respect, and it perturbed him to see his agonizings made public. In one respect especially. Amis had used certain expressions and characteristics of Monica's in creating the neurotic personality of Margaret. The parallels indicate that Larkin must have been astonishingly rude and indiscreet about Monica to allow Amis to suppose that he could use this diluted version. Alternatively, they suggest that Amis must have been extraordinarily thick-skinned to think he could create these resemblances and expect his friendship with Larkin to survive. Although Larkin persuaded Amis to change Margaret's surname from Beale to Peel[8] (Monica's full name is Monica Margaret Beale Jones), Monica's voice, looks and clothes are nevertheless ridiculed on page after page. 'What would she be wearing this evening,' Jim wonders early in the book. 'He could just about bring himself to praise anything but the green paisley frock in combination with the low-heeled quasi-velvet shoes.'[9] Shortly afterwards he comments on the 'tufts of hair ... overhanging the earpieces of her glasses',[10] mocks her laugh for sounding like 'the tinkling of tiny bells',[11] and scorns her for showing 'a large number of teeth, one canine flecked with lipstick. She always made up just a little too heavily.'[12] No matter how much Larkin might have been entertained by this, he also found it disconcerting – and the way Amis presented Dixon's dilemma with Margaret was even more upsettingly familiar. 'I've got tied up with [Margaret],' we hear Dixon saying, striking the apologetic note which resounds through his dealings with her, 'though I know that sounds ridiculous.'[13]

Larkin would not have found it so difficult to deal with *Lucky Jim* if he had been able to point to successes of his own. But his literary plans were few and modest. The previous November a new editor at Faber, Charles Monteith, had offered to look at drafts of his third novel, only to be told it was 'at a halt ... I've been thinking about the creative process a good deal since I last wrote to your firm,' Larkin told him; 'instead of a fruit machine (as I think I rather impudently called it then) it now seems to me to be a very delicate balance between what has happened and what one likes to think of as happening, and its function is to restore the balance after inroads have been made on one by reality.'[14]

Monteith made no mention of poems – they were left to smaller publishers. Early in the spring Larkin received an invitation from George MacBeth and Oscar Mellor, editors of the Fantasy Press, based at Swinford, near Eynsham outside Oxford, to contribute to one of their pamphlets. He knew the series, which had been running since 1952, publishing small gatherings of work mainly by undergraduates or recent graduates of Oxford, among them Elizabeth Jennings, Geoffrey Hill and, eventually, Amis. He sent them five poems, which they accepted. The result – 'Fantasy Poets, Philip Larkin, Number 21' – arrived in March, but attracted almost no attention: one of its few reviewers was depressed 'by the prospect that the best poetry in England [was being] written "by dons for dons"'.[15]

While he was corresponding with Mellor, Larkin was also in touch with an even smaller outfit: a new magazine called *Listen* which was based in Hessle, a large village on the outskirts of Hull in the East Riding of Yorkshire. The magazine was run by a twenty-one-year-old former art student and literature-lover, George Hartley, and his young wife Jean. George had most of the ideas, Jean did most of the routine work, and the operation ran on a shoestring. Their first number, published in 1953, had been so successful that for the second they were able to 'spread ourselves to 28 pages and a couple of book reviews, and asked Patrick Heron to design a cover',[16] which to their surprise he did. It was for this second issue that Larkin submitted three poems – 'Spring', 'Dry Point' and 'Toads' – which the Hartleys accepted eagerly. 'This handful,' Jean remembers, 'with their accessibility, wide range of mood and rare combination of wit, lyricism and disenchantment, excited us more than anything we'd been offered.'[17]

Larkin had sent the poems blind, knowing nothing about *Listen*'s owners or their circumstances. He had no hopes of the magazine becoming more than an occasional showcase for his work. George Hartley had other plans. Even though he had recently lost his job (in a shoe shop in Hull), even though Jean had recently had a baby, even though he had no support from benefactors, he decided during the spring of 1954 that he should diversify into book publishing. He intended to call his new venture The Marvell Press, partly in honour of Hull's best-known poet, and partly because he and Jean felt it would be a 'bloody marvel' if they got their idea off the ground. Jean, knowing that 'most of the work'[18] would fall on her, suggested that they concentrate on producing a third number of *Listen* instead. (When it appeared it included Larkin's 'Poetry of Departures'.) In the autumn, however, she relented and agreed that because they both liked Larkin's work so much, he should be the person they approached first.

Now it was Larkin's turn to hesitate. During the summer he had added several poems to those from which he might make a selection, including 'Skin' (almost a reply to Hardy's 'I look into my glass'), 'Water' ('If I were called in/To construct a religion/I should make use of water'), and a much larger secular-religious companion piece, 'Church Going'. 'Church Going', which he had begun on 24 April, abandoned at the end of the month after filling twenty-one pages with drafts, then picked up again in mid-July and finished on the 28th, has become one of his best-known poems – an elegant archetype of his tone, method, and interests. It takes the self-mocking, detail-collecting, conversational manner that he had begun to develop in Leicester and applies it to the kind of subject he would once have approached solemnly (as in 'A Stone Church Damaged by a Bomb').

Presenting himself as an interloper ('Once I am sure there's nothing going on/I step inside'), slightly goofy ('I take off/My cycle-clips in awkward reverence'), disrespectful, 'bored' and 'uninformed', the speaker begins the poem by banishing any signs of holy dread. Then he re-introduces religion on his own terms, speaking as someone without faith who is trying to recover the comfort that it used to give. There's no indication that people can fill the gap God left – people are as absent from the poem as Ruth, Winifred and Patsy were from Larkin's own life. Only structures will do, structures which become reliable with repetition: 'marriage, and birth/And death, and thoughts of these'. The glow of sanctity may have faded from such things, but the things themselves remain, depending on custom for their validity. 'It pleases me', Larkin says finally, 'to stand in silence' in an empty church:

A serious house on serious earth it is,
In whose blent air all our compulsions meet,
Are recognized, and robed as destinies.
And that much never can be obsolete,
Since someone will forever be surprising
A hunger in himself to be more serious,
And gravitating with it to this ground,
Which, he once heard, was proper to grow wise in,
If only that so many dead lie round.

Encouraged by the Hartleys, but feeling that he should create more general interest before offering them a collection, Larkin began to send out more of his work to magazines. The previous year his friend John Wain had broadcast 'If, My Darling' on *First Reading*, a Third Programme series that he was presenting; the BBC had also accepted 'Fiction and the Reading Public' for their *New Poetry* slot in March. Now he peppered the editors of journals and magazines, sometimes small operations like *Departure*, sometimes larger ones like the *Spectator* (which on receiving 'Church Going' lost the manuscript for a year). Very slowly, and at first only among the specialized poetry-reading audience, his reputation began to take hold. Then during the early autumn it suddenly blossomed – thanks, in a roundabout way, to the incompetent *Spectator*. J. D. Scott, the literary editor since 1953, had as his assistant a young would-be writer called Anthony Hartley (no relation of George), who had vaguely known Larkin, Amis and Wain at Oxford. (Wain had recently broadcast one of his short stories on *First Reading*.) On 1 October Scott published a lead article identifying a new school of writers, which for want of a better name he christened The Movement. Among its members, he said, were Amis, Wain, Elizabeth Jennings, Thom Gunn, John Holloway, Donald Davie, D. J. Enright and Iris Murdoch. He did not include Larkin, but implied that other names might be added to the list.

Critics and journalists enjoy making categories; writers aren't always happy to fit into them. In this case, the writers were asked to conform to such a loose standard that it seemed unlikely anyone would object. 'The Movement,' Scott wrote, 'as well as being anti-phoney, is anti-wet; sceptical, robust, ironic, prepared to be as comfortable as possible in a wicked, commercial, threatened world which doesn't look, anyway, as if it's going to be changed much by a couple of handfuls of young English writers.'[19] Broad as it was, even this seemed restrictive to Larkin. A few years after the article appeared he was approached by an American academic, William Van O'Connor, who proposed to study The Movement. In his reply Larkin said that he believed too much had been made of Scott's remarks:

I expect most writers you have met will vehemently deny any but the slenderest connections with The Movement, and I am no exception. I have never met Elizabeth Jennings, Thom Gunn, John Holloway or Iris Murdoch. My acquaintance with Donald Davie, though friendly, is recent and intermittent. I have known John Wain for about ten years, on and off, but can't pretend to be in very close touch with him, though we meet occasionally. In fact, my only close associate in the group is Kingsley Amis, whom I have known fairly well since 1941, though we have inevitably had less time for each other during the last five years or so. Our affinity is rather difficult to explain, since I do not think we have many artistic aims in common, but we usually agree in the things we find funny or derisible. I dare say you have noticed *Lucky Jim* is dedicated to me, which is a fair evidence of this, and commemorates a period of intense joke-swapping just after the war.[20]

O'Connor, realizing the coherence of any literary group depends on more than who knows whom, pressed for further details. All he got was a letter admitting, 'Perhaps it is true to say that while there isn't a Movement, there is *something*, which may as well be called a movement as anything else.'[21] Eventually Larkin apologized for these 'somewhat laconic replies',[22] but no one ever persuaded him to give any other kind on the subject. As late as 1978, when The Movement was acknowledged to have been a real thing in a real place, he was still arguing that it couldn't be all the critics said, because it was 'not based on common acquaintance. I have still never met Thom Gunn and I don't think I met Elizabeth Jennings until 1970.'[23]

Larkin was both right and wrong to resist an exact definition – right because the styles of The Movement's so-called members cover a very wide range; wrong because a new and distinct spirit is obvious in their books. For instance: he and Amis (and also, in their own ways, Wain, Enright and Davie) share a disaffected tone, while some of the others – Jennings and Gunn – seem less (or differently) guarded by ironies. Two years after the *Spectator* had begun to explore these common properties, they were on show again in Robert Conquest's anthology *New Lines*, which includes a substantial number of poems by Larkin. 'If anyone had briefly to characterize this poetry of the Fifties from its predecessors,' Conquest said, 'I believe the most important general point would be that it submits to no great systems of theoretical constructs nor agglomerations of unconscious commands. It is free from both mystical and logical compulsions and – like modern philosophy – is empirical in its attitude to all that comes. This reverence for the real person or event is, indeed, a part of the general intellectual ambiance . . . of our time.'[24]

Where Scott confines himself to matters of mood and voice, Conquest opposes the new generation to their modernist forebears. In the years to come this would have a profound effect on the way Larkin appeared to his readers, and for this reason alone the invention of The Movement marks one of the most important moments in his career as a poet. Right at the start of his life in the public eye, he was made to seem like a young member of an old guard. Scott and Conquest described his traditional forms and easily understood language in a way which made him seem not radical but reactionary, and they made no mention of the elements in his work which departed from The Movement's orthodoxy. Larkin himself, in spite of his initial reservations about seeming part of a group, was happy to go along with this. He was flattered suddenly to find himself a name to conjure with, and happy to leave it to others to argue about the small print of Movement membership. That, he thought, was the kind of thing academics were paid to do.

J. D. Scott's enthusiasm soon sent Larkin back to George Hartley. He wanted to know: if he sent a collection, could The Marvell Press promise it 'wouldn't cost him anything' and would they 'make a good job of it'?[25] The Hartleys reassured him and expected the poems to arrive immediately, but then came another delay. Late in September Graneek placed on Larkin's desk a copy of an advertisement for the job of librarian at the University of Hull. Larkin 'felt he had to apply'.[26] So far as he could tell, he was motivated partly by loneliness (he still missed Patsy and Winifred), partly by boredom, and partly by a lurking professional ambition. (He had been at Queen's for five years, and since the building programme of 1951 his work had become increasingly monotonous.) Yet he still felt that he had surprised himself by applying for the new post. 'Do I want it?' he asked Patsy rhetorically. 'Yes, in a way; knowing that it will mean harder work and more responsibility.'[27] It was only after he had been summoned for interview that he realized his 'audacious, purifying/Elemental move' was likely to prove even more complicated than he had first thought. Hull was a matter of five miles from Hessle, where George and Jean Hartley lived. He began to worry that the members of his interview panel might subscribe to *Listen*, and assume that his poem 'Toads' was an accurate account of his views about work. He didn't see how they could possibly appoint him.

He pressed on regardless and arrived in Hull on the morning of Tuesday 23 November, having spent the previous weekend with his mother in Loughborough. 'It's a bit chilly here and smells of fish,' he told her on a postcard before reporting to the university, then added, 'I'm going to put down the alternatives and then cross off which doesn't apply, so that I can post this quickly later in the day. Appointed./Not appointed./Don't know.'[28] He was relieved, when he reached the Registrar's Office, to see that seven other candidates were already waiting. He thought he was almost bound to be passed over.

In his application, Larkin described his responsibilities in Queen's University library, and gave Dr Marshall (his father's successor at Coventry City Hall), Rhoda Bennett (the librarian at Leicester), and Jack Graneek as his referees. Graneek told Hull that he had 'come increasingly to rely on [Larkin's] judgement', and admitted, 'I have delegated to him rather larger areas of responsibility than normally falls to the lot of a sub-librarian ... He has the ability to assess a problem, arrive at a decision and act upon it without delay, which is not too common among academic administrators.'[29] The Chairman of the interview panel was 'very impressed' by this, and also felt that Larkin was 'much the nicest of the candidates',[30] as well as the most eloquent. His fellow-interviewers agreed. Ray Brett, the Professor of English, spoke for them all when he said he found Larkin:

a tall, shy, serious-looking young man with thick-lensed glasses and a slight stammer. But all this seemed unimportant as he outlined his work in Belfast. There was a quiet authority in the way he described, of all things, the work on the issue desk in the library there. One could hardly imagine a less promising subject to impress the committee, but he made it intensely interesting, with a wealth of detail which never approached the tedious. Above all, I remember the exact and lucid sentences formed without hesitation and the incisive mind.[31]

As soon as the interviews were over Larkin was able to finish his postcard to his mother. 'Not appointed' and 'Don't know' were both crossed out; 'Appointed' was ringed.[32] Then he sailed back to Belfast. He was due to begin work in Hull in March, so there was plenty of time to bid a leisurely farewell. His poems, though, couldn't wait, and within a few days of reaching his lodgings he wrote to the Hartleys again, expressing 'nervousness about being published so near to what would become his home, his poems being "nothing if not personal"'.[33] Once again, George Hartley rightly rejected the idea that Larkin was being self-mocking, and replied as soothingly as he could, assuring him that neither he nor Jean had anything to do with academic life – indeed, he said, they were only 'dimly aware that there was a university'[34] in Hull. Larkin remained cautious. In December he sent Hartley a card which 'revealed his growing enthusiasm' for the book, and promised to send 'about twenty-five poems for inspection' before long. Once again, he stressed 'his distaste at the thought of any link between his profession as a librarian and his life as a poet'.[35]

A short while afterwards the collection finally arrived in Hessle. It included two recent poems – 'Places, Loved Ones' and 'Myxomatosis' – and was, Jean says, 'a ragbag assortment printed on different sizes of paper, some quarto typescript and others cut out of the various magazines or pamphlets in which they had first appeared'.[36] George immediately wrote to Larkin saying that he would be 'thrilled'[37] to publish. Nine months later, on 18 November 1955, when 'Church Going' was published in the *Spectator*, Charles Monteith got in touch with Larkin, asking whether he would consider a selection of his poems for Faber. He was told he was too late.

THIRTY-ONE

Even though he was soon to be living in England permanently, Larkin nevertheless travelled back from Ireland to spend the Christmas of 1954 with his mother. Afterwards (and following a weekend with Monica in the Royal Hotel, Winchester, to celebrate New Year) he visited Bruce Montgomery in Devon, only to find that their friendship seemed in worse repair than ever. 'I didn't enjoy my visit to Bruce,' he told Eva. 'Really his way of life is *not* mine.'[1] By the time he returned to Belfast, he had begun to regret his decision to leave Ireland. It meant exchanging a comparatively easy job for a demanding one, and swapping affable singleness for exposed bachelordom. Hull and Leicester were only a two-and-a-half hour train ride apart. He wondered whether he would be able to avoid sliding into a dilute version of marriage with Monica – one which had few of its regular comforts and all its constraints.

As the date of his departure drew near, he clung more appreciatively to his old life. 'I'm slowly being killed with kindness,'[2] he told Eva a week before he left. Arthur Terry (now engaged to Molly Sellar, the young woman in the library whom Larkin himself had admired) was particularly assiduous, and Larkin responded by presenting him with a potato-masher as a wedding present: the Terrys called it 'Philip's cattle gelder'.[3] Graneek, too, was sorry to see him go. 'I said,' Larkin remembered later, 'I thought he should replace me with "a good librarian". "But I don't want a good librarian," Graneek replied. "I want someone like you." '[4] More than anyone, the Egertons regretted the end of 'those few lovely years'.[5] On Larkin's final evening Judy cooked him supper and gave him enough drink to make sure he sailed the next day, 12 March, with a clanging hangover.

Larkin would always refer to his years in Ireland gratefully. Soon after arriving in England he told his former colleagues, 'It was extraordinary how at home I felt [there] . . . and how much I disliked leaving . . . Queen's is a perfect little paradise of a library.'[6] Twenty years later his feelings were the same. 'I never forget [Belfast's] individuality and humour and friendliness,'[7] he said. Hull, by contrast, seemed inhospitable, largely because of the digs the university had found for him. They were on the first floor of Holtby House, a student residence (formerly the home of Winifred Holtby's parents) in Cottingham, a large village on the northern edge of Hull. As soon as he arrived he started to howl. Holtby House, he told Judy Egerton, 'is *not* suitable: small, bare floored and noisy: I feel as if I were lying in some penurious doss-house at night, with hobos snoring and quarrelling all round me. There is a negro in the next room who would benefit enormously from a pair of bedroom slippers.'[8] A month later, things were no better. 'The inhabitants are so noisy all the time,' he told his mother. 'Oh dear, the future now seems very bleak and difficult – I really don't know what I'm doing in this job at all! Still, I shall try to bear in mind the words of Llewelyn Powys: "Nothing matters but physical pain and death: all else is experience enviable enough to those lying under the churchyard sod." '[9]

When Larkin wrote this he had to endure Holtby House for only another week before moving – but when escape came, on 20 April, he found himself somewhere even worse: 11 Outlands Road, also in Cottingham, where the landlady Mrs Dowling was 'extremely kind and thoughtful', the food 'not bad', but 'the house too small' and the family's radio 'like a nightmare'.[10] In a letter to Enright he also fulminated against the 'blasted RADIO', complaining that it 'prevents me from sitting, thinking and scribbling in the evening'.[11] In the one poem he did manage to finish soon after arriving in Hull, 'Mr Bleaney' (originally 'Mr Gridley'), it is the 'jabbering set', even more than the mean room with its short curtains and sixty-watt bulb, which makes him feel that his horrible surroundings are a reproach, not merely a misfortune. They lead him to suspect that his own life and Mr Bleaney's might be interchangeable:

> if he stood and watched the frigid wind
> Tousling the clouds, lay on the fusty bed
> Telling himself that this was home, and grinned,
> And shivered, without shaking off the dread

> That how we live measures our own nature,
> And at his age having no more to show
> Than one hired box should make him pretty sure
> He warranted no better, I don't know.

Before starting work on 21 March, Larkin decided to see whether the town could offer him anything better. He discovered a much bigger and more diffuse place than any he had known previously (in fact the tenth largest town in England). It had been founded during the reign of Edward I, starting life as a modest settlement called Kingston, concentrated where the small River Hull meets the River Humber (nearly two miles wide at this point). Its ports and docks soon prospered, relying mainly on European trade and – later – whaling, and as time passed a number of impressive buildings began to appear: the medieval church of Holy Trinity, the red-brick grammar school where the poet Andrew Marvell was a pupil (he was later MP for Hull), the river-side mansion where William Wilberforce was born (it's now 'the slave museum'), the heavy stone blocks of the City Council buildings. Until the beginning of the nineteenth century, Kingston-upon-Hull (as it became) still swarmed round the junction of its two rivers, mixing elegance and business, grand houses and warehouses. By the start of the twentieth century, though, the town had grown prodigiously, spreading across the flat hinterland 'like a great sigh out of the last century', creating mile after mile of cheaply built terraces. During the 1930s there was another surge (the town prospered from its glue-making and seed-crushing businesses, as well as its docks), so that villages like Cottingham, or Hessle where the Hartleys lived, were swallowed. The entire area was saturated with the not-so-sweet smell of its commercial success – as Jonathan Raban discovered many years later:

[The] fishy culture had settled deep into the brickwork of the city. When the wind blew from the south, one breathed dead fish. Fish got into the drawers of socks and shirts, permeated one's books, clung to the thin curtains of the bed-sitter. On hot summer afternoons the reek of cod was so thick in the air that one could have bottled it for fish-manure. No stranger, stepping off the train ... could possibly have been stupid enough to ask what Hull 'did'. Hull went fishing.[12]

The war drew the people of Hull together but smashed their town apart. It was bombed widely and deliberately in order to disrupt its port, and also wrecked haphazardly by planes returning from the west coast of England, using the Humber as a navigation aid and throwing out the bombs they hadn't dropped on Liverpool. By the time Larkin arrived, ten years after the war had ended, the first efforts to put the city back together again were under way, but it was still badly damaged. The Old Town was dispirited and run down, several of the big docks in the city centre were empty or filled in, and the commercial future was uncertain.

Amongst the ruins, people had to be grateful for small mercies. Jean Hartley, for instance, remembers 'some riches':

On the riverfront was the two-tiered wooden pier – a fine goal for family Sunday walks. Our children larked about on the superstructure, scaring themselves by peeping at the water through the cracks between the planks. It was also an excellent vantage point for looking across ... to the ferry terminal at New Holland. As a child I thought this must be a foreign country. On the left of the pier was a horse wash – still used in 1955. On the right was the ferry boat ticket office and the gangplank which led to the steamer. On some evenings in summer, local jazzbands were hired to play for a riverboat shuffle, and the voices of boozy revellers would ring out over the dark waters.[13]

What Larkin found, in other words, was a city at the end of one kind of life, waiting for another to begin. Wandering along the wooden cobbles of the deserted high street in the Old Town, past the disintegrating ware-houses and sunken boats rotting in inland docks, he felt he was in a place set on the edge of things. Isolated on the hook of land which forms the north shore of the Humber, on the way to nowhere except the North Sea, it felt particular, intriguing and remote – just as it had done to Winifred Holtby in her novel *South Riding* twenty years earlier:

[The] wide Dutch landscape, haunted by larks and seabirds, roofed by immense pavilions of windy cloud: the miles of brownish-purple shining mud, pocked and hummocked by water and fringed by heath-like herbs; the indented banks where the high tides sucked and gurgled: the great ships gliding up ..., seen from low-lying windows as though they had moved across the fields; the brave infrequent flowers, the reluctant springs, the loneliness, the silence ...[14]

Six and a half years after arriving in Hull, Larkin celebrated these qualities in his poem 'Here'. Sweeping like a camera in a helicopter over the 'widening river's slow presence' towards the 'surprise of a large town', he lingers over the clutter of civic detail before veering on again to the country between Hull and the coast, where he plunges into the solitude of one of the least visited, least known-about places in England. If Larkin wrote anything which gave the lie to his statement (made before leaving Belfast, in 'Places, Loved Ones') that 'I have never found / The place where I could say / *This is my proper ground / Here I shall stay*', 'Here' is it:

> Swerving east, from rich industrial shadows
> And traffic all night north; swerving through fields
> Too thin and thistled to be called meadows,
> And now and then a harsh-named halt, that shields
> Workmen at dawn; swerving to solitude
> Of skies and scarecrows, haystacks, hares and pheasants,
> And the widening river's slow presence,
> The piled gold clouds, the shining gull-marked mud,
>
> Gathers to the surprise of a large town:
> Here domes and statues, spires and cranes cluster
> Beside grain-scattered streets, barge-crowded water,
> And residents from raw estates, brought down
> The dead straight miles by stealing flat-faced trolleys,
> Push through plate-glass swing doors to their desires –
> Cheap suits, red kitchen-ware, sharp shoes, iced lollies,
> Electric mixers, toasters, washers, driers –
>
> A cut-price crowd, urban yet simple, dwelling
> Where only salesmen and relations come
> Within a terminate and fishy-smelling
> Pastoral of ships up streets, the slave museum,
> Tattoo-shops, consulates, grim head-scarfed wives . . .

Such rapt identification with a place, such sensuous understanding of its values, obviously takes time to form – and is, anyway, unlikely to begin within the confines of a 'hired box'. Yet once the initial trauma of his move from Ireland was over, Larkin settled into the habit of praising Hull – not least for its remoteness. Sometimes he put it simply ('I like it because it's so far away from everywhere else'[15]); sometimes comically ('I love all the Americans getting on to the train at King's Cross and thinking they're going to come and bother me, and then looking at the connections and deciding they'll go to Newcastle and bother Basil Bunting instead'[16]); sometimes romantically: 'you get some very fine effects of light, particularly in the evenings when you have the sunsets building up westwards down the river, with magnificent pilings up of cloud, all golden and rose and so forth. That, again, is not the sort of thing you'd see in the average mid-England provincial town, and that's the sort of reason I like being in Hull.'[17]

To start with, Larkin had little chance to enjoy it. As if Holtby Hall and Outlands Road weren't enough to contend with, there was the university library, which was about to undergo the biggest upheaval in its history. The university college at Hull – like Leicester, an extension of London University – had been founded in 1926 when the Lord Mayor T. R. Ferens, a philanthropic industrialist, volunteered a large endowment. This had led to the purchase of three fields flanking the road between Hull and Cottingham, and teaching had started in 1928 when the university college, comprising a mere two buildings, had opened. For many years it remained – again, like Leicester – a small operation. When the Barlow Committee reported in December 1945 on the needs for education in Britain after the war, it recorded that the number of full-time students at Hull was only 174. As the university college campaigned to be upgraded to a full, independent university it anticipated a rapid increase in numbers, but when the Charter was finally granted, in September 1954, no one foresaw just how dramatic the expansion would be. In its first year as a university Hull had 727 students; twelve months later, when Larkin arrived, it had 858; by 1960 it had 1,660, and in 1980 just over 5,000.

This growth involved making extensive alterations to the Cottingham Road site generally, and to the library in particular. When the university college was founded, a grant of £100 had been given to each teaching department to initiate its own library, but in March 1929 these collections were centralized on the ground floor of the Science and Refectory Building: the librarian was Agnes Cuming, previously librarian at the University College of Wales. A grant of £30,000 provided for a substantial initial collection, and in the following three years 50,000 more books were added. This set a precedent within the university college for treating the library generously, and once the lean years of the war had ended, growth continued quickly. Brynmor Jones, the Vice-Chancellor of the university appointed a few months after Larkin became librarian, was largely responsible. Between 1955 when Brynmor Jones took over and 1979 the library binding and purchase grant increased from £4,500 to £284,148.

As the library's holdings had increased, so the need to rehouse them had become more acute. At first it was intended that the still largely empty three-field site should accommodate a separate and central library, but when plans were drawn up in 1932 they were judged too expensive and dropped. Nothing further had happened by the time the Charter was granted twenty years later, when it was assumed that a library would soon be built with a capacity of 500 working places and a million books. Miss Cuming regarded this as sufficient provision for 2,000 students, and in due course schemes were proposed, sub-committees set up, and experts consulted in order to discover precisely what was wanted. In 1954 the plans and the money to execute them were all in place.

Then Agnes Cuming retired, Larkin arrived, and everything was thrown into confusion again. Would he settle for plans drawn up by others? How adaptable were the plans? They needed to be flexible since the university was steadily increasing its prediction of how large it would become in the future. On Larkin's first morning in his new office (he overlapped with Miss Cuming by ten days), he realized that, with only a matter of months to go before work on the new library was due to start, he had to become a master of more aspects of his job than he had previously known existed.

The situation he found was this: a book stock of 124,000 volumes; eleven members of staff (nine women and two men – their average age was twenty-one); an obstinate-looking deputy librarian called Arthur Wood; and accommodation consisting of 'a series of badly designed, ill-lit, sometimes unheated and frequently unrelated areas'.[18] Evidently the library's needs were urgent: Larkin's first task was:

[to] finalize plans for a new building and to secure their acceptance by Building Committee. Although the need for a proper library had been canvassed for years, it had never been made the university's main building priority: many [teaching] departments still existed in prefabricated huts, and the university's residential policy could always justify the provision of another hall of residence. The librarian therefore had to choose between accepting the sketch plans more or less as they stood, or undertaking their substantial revision with the attendant risk that meanwhile another building would be allowed precedence.[19]

Larkin's choice sounds easy but was in fact complicated. The existing plans consisted of two stages – Stage 1 and Stage 2 – the first of which envisaged a central administrative three-storey block with a two-storey wing of the same height joined to it on the south side. The second proposed a stack tower large enough to hold a million volumes, which would at some later stage be built to the north of the central block, and have transferred to it all the books and shelving from Stage 1. As Larkin examined these proposals he could hardly help noticing one disadvantage: when the two stages were complete, readers and books would be separated from each other by the central administrative block.

'The library they are planning looks at present like a rejected design for a cinema,' he told Judy Egerton; 'if it is put up, it will be the laughing stock of the British Isles.'[20] He was similarly forthright with his new colleagues at the university. Ray Brett, the Professor of English, remembers 'the discussions we had about the new library revealed a mind concerned with the particular and the concrete. He had little taste for theorizing and a dislike of abstract speculation.'[21] What he proposed (in consultation with the Buildings Officer Donald Campbell, the Vice-Chancellor and the university architects W. A. Forsyth and Partners, represented by L. R. Foreman) was a rationalization of the existing plans to bring readers and books together in what would eventually become the east wing of the building.

Donald Campbell, while recognizing that Larkin exploited his own innocence of matters architectural in order to get what he wanted, was 'astonished' by the amount of expert knowledge he quickly acquired. 'For the briefing of the architects,' he says, 'Larkin did a stupendous amount of research and wrote treatises on the requirements – and indeed oversaw everything throughout the design and building period.'[22] A young member of the library staff, Maeve Brennan, was similarly impressed, especially since Hull was one of the first post-war libraries to be built in England, and therefore had to be created without the benefit of existing examples. While Larkin was working out his solutions, she remembers:

[he] closeted himself in a hermit-like cell, far removed from library staff, readers and the telephone. This small hide-out, at the extremity of the top floor of the building in which the library was then accommodated, had bare sloping shelves designed for studying maps and bound volumes of newspapers. There he spread out the plans for the new building and worked on them most afternoons. We had strict instructions that his whereabouts were not to be revealed nor was he to be interrupted except on matters of urgency.[23]

Larkin's revised plans were presented to the university in the autumn and accepted by the end of the year: work was scheduled to begin in January 1958. This meant that for the next two years all his other work had to be done at the same time as he prepared for the new building. No detail was too small for him: he even chose which colours would be painted on the end of the stacks to denote their subjects, and watched the construction, Maeve Brennan says, 'with all the pride and anxiety of a mother for her first-born'.[24] He was determined that the completed library should be his, stamped everywhere with his personality.

In Wellington, Leicester and Belfast Larkin had worked ably but unremarkably, and had skived whenever he could. Now he turned himself into his father's son: thorough, incisive and autocratic. As work with the architects moved ahead, he also inspected and overhauled the library's existing systems, and busied himself with other functions of the university. Over the years these grew to a daunting number. From the outset, he took the minutes for the Library Committee, which met five times a year. ('The minute as an art form,' he said, 'has its limitations.'[25]) From 1958 until 1980 he was secretary of the Hull University Press, and during that time steered more than a hundred books, lectures and articles through publication. He chaired monthly library staff meetings, which discussed everything from major library matters to the provision of soap in the lavatories. He set up the Bookshop Committee, which acted as a means of registering and endorsing students' book-buying needs. He inaugurated a parking committee (which some thought existed largely to guarantee that he could park his car where he wanted: by the back door to the library). He sat on Senate at its twice-termly meetings. He was a member of the Fine Art Committee. And he helped to set up the committee which administered the Audio-Visual Centre. In all these things he struck his colleagues as fair-minded but brisk, devising various ways of accelerating a meeting towards the conclusion he wanted it to reach. He often used his stammer for theatrical effect, and when in later years he started to go deaf he turned off his hearing-aid if there were things he didn't want to know. If he began to lose patience he would take out his pocket-watch (attached to a leather strap which had belonged to his father), and consult it 'in the palm of his hand as if he [were] holding a treasured irritant, a small mammal which might bite not him but you if you waffle[d] on much longer'.[26]

In all his university dealings, Larkin made the needs of the library paramount. His colleagues admired him for this and the Vice-Chancellor continually supported him, not only to the extent of endorsing his building proposals, but in sharing his view that the library should be rich in specific collections, as well as generally well stocked. In the years to come these special collections would cover a wide range, a range which included several areas of interest outside Larkin's own. The most significant was the

Labour Archive, centred on the acquisition of the Fabian Society Library. Others were the archive relating to the Union of Democratic Control and the National Council for Civil Liberties; the archive of the literary magazines *Wave* and *Phoenix*; a library of poets reading their own work on record; manuscripts by a number of contemporary writers including Stevie Smith, Gavin Ewart and Douglas Dunn; and the collection relating to the university's photographic service, which was run by the university's photographer, Alan Marshall.

Many of these things were only possible because Larkin began working in the library as he meant to continue: by making it the heart of the university. As we contemplate the extent of his achievements, it's tempting to think that within a few weeks of leaving Belfast he had changed decisively and absolutely. Decisively but not absolutely would be nearer the mark. As Larkin took up his new responsibilities, he became more confident than he had been before, but nothing could break the web of anxieties, or shatter the delicate feelings which held his personality together. His young staff were quick to sense this, and while they felt it made him reserved, they took to him at once – especially the women. 'I feel,' says Mary Judd, who began working on the issue desk the year Larkin arrived, 'that in spite of his having some long-standing male friends, most women liked him more than most men did. Possibly this was because, if he put himself out to do so, he could talk to a woman and make her feel entirely unique and valuable.'[27] Peter Sheldon, who joined the library in 1959 as a sub-librarian in charge of Readers' Services, confirms this; although he admired Larkin's 'analytical mind, his ability to stick to the point, and his gifts as a tremendous administrator', he felt the chances to create other links, man to man, were few. It was a feeling keenly shared by Arthur Wood, the deputy librarian. A small, plump, ex-naval Glaswegian, and an admirer of fine bindings and rare editions (as Larkin never was), Wood turned over the years into a source of irritation and an object of ridicule. In 1958, for instance, Larkin wrote to Eva, 'Mr Wood's driving lessons continue and there is no sign of his being killed – I think he drives too carefully. I must tell him a good driver is a *fast driver*.'[28] In August 1962 he reported again: 'Mr Wood, the sawn-off little rocking horse of stupidity, has gone off on a three-week holiday to Scotland. Hope the Loch Ness Monster gets him.'[29] Seven years later he was still at it: 'Mr Wood has been off for a week with flu. People say he looks old, but to me he is the same grinning subnormal gnome that has plagued me for fourteen years.'[30]

Like most of her women colleagues, Maeve Brennan, who at this stage was 'a sort of superior dogsbody who did a bit of everything',[31] and eventually took charge of Periodicals, reckoned her new boss was rather austere – yet as she watched him settle into his job, rumours travelling round the university told her that he was the model for the hero of *Lucky Jim*. At first she found them hard to credit. Larkin, she says, 'was a staid figure who appeared at Senate and Faculty boards wearing a dark suit, with a pocket watch ... which he consulted frequently and in doing so conferred on himself a gravity that could not be questioned.'[32] As the weeks passed, however, and he was glimpsed in town wearing 'a bow tie and a highly-coloured shirt', or 'cycling ... on an old-fashioned machine into the neighbouring countryside to visit parish churches', or heard deploying 'his devastating gift for mimicry',[33] her first impressions began to change. He was, she discovered, someone whose sense of form made him behave sedately when on duty, but also someone who was capable of hilarity in private – and, very occasionally, in public. For a few years after Stage 1 had been completed, for instance, he encouraged the idea of an annual Christmas party in the library. 'Since the whole building was at our disposal,' Maeve remembers, 'there was greater scope for all the presentation of party fare, dancing, competitions, films ... and other entertainment ... One vivid recollection is of him emerging from the stack area behind the leader of the conga in which everyone had joined.'[34]

Larkin's library was intended to provide the students at Hull with an unrivalled service. Yet even as he began work there, his determination to meet his readers' every need was matched by distrust and even dislike of them. In September he welcomed the new intake with a heart-felt talk – which his shyness made a great trial to him – and at the same time suspected them of being devious, lazy and stupid. By the end of his life, many students' respect for the library would be overshadowed by their sense of his remoteness. For most of the 1970s, an electric fuse-box high on the wall in one of the library's lavatories bore the legend: 'Knock three times and ask for Philip Larkin.'

THIRTY-TWO

When Larkin arrived in Hull in March 1955 his salary was £1,550, nearly double what it had been in Ireland. (Ten years later it had risen to nearly £4,000; twenty years later it was just over £9,000, and when he died it was over £22,000.[1]) For the first time since leaving Oxford he could afford to decorate his life a little, yet he shrank from doing so. He was too busy in the library; Outlands Road was 'dreary as hell',[2] and 'a frightful dump';[3] he was usually alone, poring over plans in the library, stewing in his digs in the evenings, taking solitary bike rides at the weekends. 'I usually pedal miles and miles,' he told Judy Egerton, 'always winding up in the Beverley Arms [the main hotel in a pretty market town five miles north of Hull] for tea, not because it's good tea, but because I never know where else to go.'[4]

Within the university, he relied on the library staff for his social life. As they got to know him better, their sense deepened of his being two people – one formal and reserved, the other spontaneous. Maeve Brennan detected this division in the very look of him. Grave-faced, slender, old for his years, almost completely bald and with bleak wire-framed glasses, he seemed at first like an archetypal librarian. At second glance his exceptional qualities were apparent: his expression of guarded amusement, his evidently delicate sensibility. In her account of his early days in Hull, she remembers the staff 'saw a lot of each other outside working hours . . . and we openly called him "Sir", an epithet we picked up from a book called *To Sir with Love*, that caught his and our imagination'. At the same time, she understood that his humour was stretched over a deep melancholy. 'He was often somewhat at a loss,' she says moderately. 'At times lonely, not a great socializer.'[5]

Outside the university, Eva and Monica provided most of his company – though with his mother, proximity created as many problems as it solved. Promising to visit her every month, he worried that she would soon re-create the stifling atmosphere he had endured in Leicester. (Larkin continued to visit his mother once a month until the last few years of her life, when he doubled his rate to once a fortnight instead.) The most obvious danger was that Eva would want to move to Hull and set up house with him. Less extreme but nevertheless wearisome were the demands she made every time he visited her. She had little talent for amusing herself (she was, Monica says, 'only a bit of a reader and she never got used to the television'⁶), and she was shy of the slightest responsibilities. Even shopping was a trial. Not surprisingly, she soon produced in her son the first of a long series of explosions and apologies.

Often Larkin buried his irritation with Eva in self-recrimination. In October, for instance, after ending a visit early, he wrote grovellingly, 'I feel *bitterly ashamed* of leaving my breakfast – if it were here I would eat it ten times over . . . Really it is *not* easy to leave home with equanimity when I know what I am coming back to, not that it's very terrible, I suppose. You were goldenly good to me and I'm very grateful.'⁷ Six months later, he wrote after another visit, 'Home safely, and am about to go to bed, but I must say how bitterly I regret my inexplicable irritability. *Please* forgive me. You do everything to make my visits enjoyable and then I have to go and upset everything. I love you very dearly and you mustn't worry about me. I'm sure I'll get better eventually.'⁸ In fact there was very little chance of Larkin's 'getting better'. Behind the tight-fitting mask of politeness in his letters to Eva, the strangled cry of anger is plainly audible. Anger with her interference, anger at her helpless pettiness, anger at the emotional legacy he believed that she had bequeathed him, and anger with himself for needing her in spite of everything. To understand the heart-shrivelling tedium of her manner, and to catch the unignorable plangency of its appeal, we have only to dip into the hundreds of letters she wrote him over the next twenty-odd years. This, to her 'very dear creature' from his 'old creature', is typical: 'Here we seem to have a succession of gloomy evenings. It looks as though it will rain again, like it did last night. Kitty and Walter are going to see *Look Back in Anger* at the Stratford Theatre this evening. Connie and Ivor are staying with Rosemary this time. Have at last heard from Kenneth. He has written such a long and interesting letter thanking me for the handkerchiefs. I have written to thank him.'⁹

Eva's effect on Larkin would have been much greater had he not been able to combine seeing her with visiting Monica in Leicester a short distance away. His return to England had done nothing to alter their view that they were best off as they had always been – loving but unmarried – and in the letters they exchanged between their fortnightly visits they were careful not to threaten each other's independence. Where they might have been adoring they were sentimental. Just as Larkin was 'a creature' for Eva and had been 'bear' for Ruth and Patsy, so Monica was 'Bun' (short for

Bunny Rabbit) to him. They transposed their tenderness into the language of Beatrix Potter (whose books they both admired), and among their correspondence are sprinkled many postcards showing pictures of rabbits making daisy-chains, walking through snow in muffs, or playing bows and arrows. Some are signed from 'the Directors, Peter Brotherhood, Ltd', others are from 'G. F. Pussy'. Soppy as they were, these terms of endearment had their serious side. Monica suited Larkin: she was convenient and she was fun – as well as his most stimulating intellectual companion.

His feelings about Amis survived the move back to England less comfortably. As far as the wide world was concerned (and especially after Larkin himself became famous) their friendship never tarnished; both men went to some lengths to publicize it as a way of consolidating their literary reputations. Yet it was not quite the simple mixture of conviviality and respect that they made out. The reasons were almost entirely to do with Larkin's continuing annoyance at Amis's success with *Lucky Jim* (and possibly with its portrayal of Monica). In 1957, describing the first occasion for ten years on which he and Amis had been together with Bruce Montgomery, he complained, 'Kingsley has less and less conception of talking *to* you: you are simply an audience ... Bruce seemed curiously modest and gentlemanly beside him.'[10] Six months later, reacting to some jazz programmes Amis had introduced on the radio, Larkin pictured himself as 'a corpse eaten out with envy, impotence, failure, envy, boredom, sloth, snobbery, envy, incompetence, inefficiency, laziness, lechery, envy, fear, baldness, bad circulation, bitterness, bittiness, envy, sycophancy, deceit, nostalgia *etc.*'.[11] Six months later still, commenting on an article that Amis's wife Hilly had written about her husband for a newspaper, Larkin groused to Judy Egerton that 'Kingsley's "very good degree" was a "shortened" one, designed to rush ex-Servicemen through in 1948. First Class, admittedly, but *only in five papers*. Sometimes I think I'm preparing for a huge splenetic autobiography, denigrating everyone I've ever known: it would have to be left to the nation in large brass-bound boxes, to be printed when all of us are dead.'[12] Although he continued to write to Amis, and although they met regularly and happily in London, Larkin was reluctant to let Amis see how and with whom he lived on his home patch. He only once asked Amis to visit him in Hull. Amis said yes, then cancelled at the last minute. The invitation was not repeated.

Larkin's envy of Amis was part of a broad distrust of London 'literary life'. Hull literary life was another matter, and within a month of arriving in Cottingham Larkin had pedalled out to 253 Hull Road, Hessle, where

George and Jean Hartley lived. They had warned him not to expect much in the way of sophistication at their house; even so he was taken aback. It was, he told Judy in March, 'frightful ... with papered ceiling, yellow paint and so on'[13] – or, as Jean herself admitted, 'a tiny two-up and two-down, hundred-and-fifty years old, jerry-built workman's cottage on the main road from Hull, with an outside lavatory, no bathroom, a cold-water tap in the kitchen, a shallow yellow stone sink and indoor slugs'.[14] The Hartleys were 'self-conscious'[15] about their home and half expected Larkin to suppose it implied all kinds of inefficiencies in their business operation. His appearance did nothing to reassure them: ten years older than they were, repeatedly giving 'white rabbit' glances at his pocket-watch, he seemed 'a dignified gent, slim, with dark hair (receding), very formally-suited, serious and quite unsmiling ... With his chin tucked well in he paced up and down our small living room, his tall body bowed to avoid a head-on collision with the light bulb.'[16]

In fact Larkin was pleased by what he saw: like Hull itself, the Hartleys made up for their lack of polish by seeming entirely without pretension. They replaced the flatteries and lunches a more established publisher might have offered with simple admiration for his work. Had they known more about the practicalities of the task they had set themselves, they might never have set about book publishing in the first place. As it was, they were borne along on a strong current of enthusiasm – and Larkin respected them. In George he saw someone less concerned with the daily grind than with ambitious schemes and noble ventures. In Jean he recognized a steadier, no-nonsense temperament, someone able to deal with a young child in addition to the day-to-day running of *Listen*. For the time being, at least, they complemented each other well.

For the time being, too, Larkin was grateful for their company as well as their patronage. Jean realized that he was 'very lonely'[17] in Hull and encouraged him to become a 'regular visitor'.[18] As his initial shyness wore off she found it easier to relate the unyielding man they had first met to the sometimes witty, sometimes fierce, sometimes melancholy one they already knew from the poems. He made trips out of Hull at weekends, or on other days would 'come bowling along on his enormous bike' to their front door with a 'huge haversack'[19] on his back full of washing he had collected from the laundry, or of food he had bought from Hammond's Food Basement. Soon their professional connection began to turn into real friendship. 'Philip's visits,' says Jean, 'were pleasant islands of civility'[20] in her exhausting life; for him they were a chance to unburden himself of anxieties both great and small. 'One day,' Jean remembers, 'a woman in front of him accidentally knocked over and smashed half a dozen jars of jam, and Philip worried about what he would have done had it been he who had knocked them over. Anxiousness came easily to him, and fear of death was a subject which featured frequently in his conversation, but his unpretentiousness and self-mockery stopped him from ever seeming morbid or self-dramatizing.'[21]

Larkin was lastingly grateful to the Hartleys for making his name after many other publishers had failed him. 'It is rather nice,' he said on one occasion, 'to have a publisher who publishes your poems because he likes them, and not because you're somebody's aunt and may one day write a novel.[22] Even before his book appeared, however, he began to worry about the Hartleys' lack of experience. On the one hand there was a contract (eventually signed on 12 January 1956, two months after publication) which worked in his favour by stating: 'The publisher undertakes to pay the author, after the cost of production has been covered, an equal share of the profit.' On the other hand, the Society of Authors – which Larkin approached the following February – judged 'the agreement ... much too loosely drafted[;] we would suggest that on another occasion you send us any agreement offered to you by a publisher for our comments before it is signed.'[23]

In the years ahead, the disadvantages of being published by a small press steadily overtook the advantages. By the spring of 1956, when a second printing of Larkin's book was required, he was saying, 'George Hartley goes a long way towards proving Oscar Wilde's first law of economics: *Wherever there exists a demand there is no supply.* Poor chap, it isn't his fault, though I do wish now [that he] represented some influential firm rather than his own enthusiasm.'[24] As the book's life continued, and Hartley's methods of passing on Larkin's dues began to vary, such understanding weakened. In December 1959, for instance, Larkin reported that he had been given £60 in notes 'to cheat the tax man'.[25] By the mid-1960s his patience had snapped. References to 'that ponce of Hessle ... sod him'[26] come thick and fast in his letters, and when he later compared the treatment he got from Hartley with that he received from Faber he regretted having ever had anything to do with him. Hartley, Larkin told Charles Monteith at Faber, 'brought death into the world and all our woe'.[27]

To start with, everything moved ahead smoothly. Hartley chivvied him about the order of the poems in the collection, and argued for its title to be changed from *Various Poems* (which Larkin feebly told his mother hadn't 'been used lately'[28]) to something more arresting. By mid-summer Larkin had decided to retitle one of the poems 'Deceptions', and use its original title for the entire book: *The Less Deceived*. (The phrase stands on its head Ophelia's remark in *Hamlet* that she is 'more deceived' than the Prince: even if readers didn't pick up the reference, Larkin intended that his adaptation should summarize the book's mood of restrained self-awareness and 'sad-eyed and clear-eyed realism'.[29])

Hartley also urged Larkin to write a blurb for the book – something Larkin failed to complete, but which in draft gives a glimpse of how he intended the poems to strike his readers. More than anything, he wanted people to find them emotional, even though when he said so in a version written on 27 May he immediately scribbled 'cock and balls' across the page and added drawings of men with erections and women wearing funny underwear. 'For some years now,' he then wrote, persevering, 'the poems of Philip Larkin have been increasingly well-known for their unusual combination of deep personal feeling and exact, almost sophisticated choice of words. This volume, the first collection of his work since 1945, contains poems previously unpublished together with others that have already helped to establish their author as one who, while no less witty and intelligent than his contemporaries, deals with emotion more simply and intensely than is common today.'[30]

Once all production matters had been sorted out, Hartley turned to the larger problem of distribution. Rather than risk expense and complication by venturing into the world as a salesman as well as a publisher, he invited the world to come to him. He decided to revive 'an eighteenth-century practice and publish *The Less Deceived* by subscription, sending out forms to possible subscribers and printing their names as a roll of honour at the back of the first edition. This would give us some cash in hand to pay part of the printer's bill and [to cover] the frightening lull between the book being reviewed, bookshops placing orders and the money actually rolling in.'[31] By advertising the book to *Listen* subscribers and asking Larkin to provide the names of friends likely to buy a copy, they attracted 120 'suckers' (as Larkin called them). The first to reply was a young man teaching the WEA course at Hull, Richard Hoggart; some, like Amis, Wain and Montgomery, were friends from Oxford; others, like the Egertons and Arthur Terry, were comparatively recent connections; still more were people he only half knew (Enright, Hoff) or didn't know at all but who had admired his work in magazines (young poets like A. Alvarez, Alan Brownjohn and Anthony Thwaite). By June everything was agreed:

the Hartleys would publish in November and print 500 copies. Larkin thought this was 'handsome'.[32] In the event, flushed with 'last minute optimism',[33] they printed 700 copies and bound up 400. They were dedicated to the person who, while appearing only fleetingly in individual poems, had done more than anyone to create the mixture of stability and strangeness which had brought them into being: 'Miss Monica Jones'.

THIRTY-THREE

Seven months before *The Less Deceived* came out, George Hartley had to hand over day-to-day responsibility for the book to his wife; he was sent to London on a training course by the Hull branch of Austin Reed, the 'Men's Outfitters', with whom he had taken a job. Larkin knew that his poems were safe with Jean, but nevertheless felt restless as publication approached. Outlands Road was proving more than he could bear, and although he detested the bother of moving he decided in June to uproot himself again.

Within days he realized that his new address – 200 Hallgate, only a short distance away – wasn't much of an improvement. His landlady Mrs Squire was 'a nice old thing'[1] who played her radio quietly, but the place itself was 'not very spacious or cheerful'.[2] It reminded him how '*comfortable*' he had been in Belfast, and left him defenceless against all that was unfamiliar in his new life. 'I think,' he told Eva in June 1955:

it should be laid down that the wretchedness of moving is not really related to where one moves to or from. Of course it is *in a way*, but not so much as you might expect. The wretchedness of moving is like losing a skin – one is in fact losing a whole set of circumstances and things one takes for granted, all very simple, but by their immediate relation to the way you live very influential – bed, food, noises, warmth and so on. Deprived of these at a blow and thrust into another set, one feels as if skinned and clad in a coarse shirt. Of course this new shirt of circumstances becomes one's skin in time. But until it has one feels, as I say, wretched, and I don't intend to minimize this![3]

Isolated in the present, hungry for the past, anxious about the future: once again Larkin felt divided between distinct time zones, and once again the sense of dispersal led him to his desk. Previously the result had been 'Triple Time'; now it was 'Long Sight in Age', and 'The Importance of Elsewhere', in which he decided that his happiness in Belfast had depended on his feeling the place was 'not home' at all. In Ireland, he says, he was always a stranger, with a stranger's right to be considered 'separate'. In Hull this right had gone. After five years of self-imposed exile, his sense of nationality and nationhood began to sharpen:

> Living in England has no such excuse:
> These are my customs and establishments
> It would be much more serious to refuse.
> Here no elsewhere underwrites my existence.

This theme gathered strength during the August holidays, when he spent a few days with his mother. Soon after arriving in York Road he suffered a bad bout of hay fever and tried to cheer himself up by listening to some of the jazz records Mrs Squire wouldn't let him play in Hallgate. When he put on Oliver's 'Riverside Blues' it triggered yet another reaction to the problem of 'triple time' – a reaction he soon described in 'Reference Back'. As the music in the poem travels from 'I' in 'an unsatisfactory room' to 'you' (Eva) in the 'unsatisfactory hall', it links his 'unsatisfactory prime' to her 'unsatisfactory age':

> Truly, though our element is time,
> We are not suited to the long perspectives
> Open at each instant of our lives.
> They link us to our losses: worse,
> They show us what we have as it once was,
> Blindingly undiminished, just as though
> By acting differently we could have kept it so.

However unsatisfactory this visit to York Road might have been, it was at least self-contained: even Eva could now see that her son's life in Hull was too resolutely independent for her to consider moving in with him. To make sure, he planned various expeditions during the summer which took him out of her orbit. In June he went to his old college, St John's, for its Founder's Day celebrations and met John Wain and Noel Hughes ('my old room mate, with an irritatingly attractive wife'[4]); in August he went to watch the Test Match at Lord's; and in September he and Monica set off together for their annual holiday. They had booked into the Dixcart Hotel on the Channel Island of Sark: it had been recommended to them by

Monica's mother and was, they gathered, peaceful (there were no cars) and idiosyncratic. Furthermore, it would take them to the extreme edge of the British Isles without actually depositing them abroad.

Before pleasure, though, came business. On their way to Southampton (to catch the Sark ferry which went via Guernsey), they stayed at the Strand Palace Hotel in London, where Larkin had arranged to meet the young historian and poet Robert Conquest. Conquest had recently contacted him in Hull, proposing to include a selection of his poems in his anthology *New Lines*, and suggesting they meet to discuss the final choice. It was a meeting which, in the course of a few hours, turned a professional connection into a friendship. Older than Larkin by five years, clever (he was educated at Winchester and Magdalen College, Oxford), and widely experienced (he had served in the army for seven years and was now working for the Foreign Office), Conquest seemed both sensitive and worldly-wise. He was about to publish his own first collection of poems and shared many of Larkin's opinions about the value of formal structures and plain language. He was, however, more willing than Larkin to frame his beliefs as theories. Developing the argument of Scott's *Spectator* article, he came closer than anyone to defining the common aims and purposes of The Movement. When Larkin heard what he intended to say in the Introduction to *New Lines* he replied that he would have 'preferred it milder' and told him:

I think you are quite right in stressing the poor quality of poetry during the war – a period which can laud the poetry of Keyes is no period for me – and perhaps this was a product of the hysterias and insincerities associated with the time. On the other hand, I am not quite so happy when you suggest that 'we' have returned to 'the principle that poetry is written by and for the whole man'; I don't think 'our' poetry stands up for a single second, in this respect, alongside poets who I should say did adopt that principle – Owen, Hopkins, Hardy, Edward Thomas – and I should be chary of suggesting that it does. One reason for this is that much of it seems so 'literary' in inspiration . . . For my part I feel we have got the method right – plain language, absence of posturings, sense of proportion, humour, abandonment of the dithyrambic ideal – and are waiting for the matter: a fuller and more sensitive response to life as it appears from day to day, and not only on Mediterranean holidays financed by the British Council.[5]

When Conquest revealed which poems he wanted to include in *New Lines* Larkin was delighted; he thought they illustrated his range as well as his main strengths. (The poems were 'Maiden Name', 'Church Going', 'I

Remember, I Remember', 'Skin', 'Born Yesterday', 'Triple Time', 'Toads', and 'Lines on a Young Lady's Photograph Album'.) The following January, when the anthology was published, he thought its 'sluggish start'[6] was undeserved. (It eventually sold 2,000 copies in its first two years.)

By this time, Larkin didn't value Conquest only as a literary ally. During the course of their dealings with the anthology he had discovered the sort of irreverence that he always looked for in his closest men friends. Treading in the footprints of Gunner and Amis, Conquest seemed simultaneously respectable and subversive. He especially endeared himself to Larkin by sharing his interest in pornography, soon raising it to a new pitch by posting magazines from London or overseas when he was travelling abroad. (Larkin's taste, Conquest felt, 'was really very unchallenging. Perhaps a bit of spanking, that's all, but nothing violent.'[7]) At first Larkin was not always happy with the material he was sent. 'How kind of you,' he wrote in July 1956, 'to send the goods, so carefully and amusingly wrapped! No, it's not worth £3, or anything like it – about 10/6 would be a fair price – but then what *is* worth three quid? Doubt if anything in life is.'[8] In 1960, however, when Conquest started to send *Swish* (formerly *Helios*) he was more enthusiastic. 'Jolly good stuff, *Swish*,' Larkin said in response to one consignment. 'I thought the author of Miss Hobson's Choice deserved the Maugham Award ... I regretted that rather prudish clean-up of pics in the second vol., but there you are. Also I wanted to know if the head master stuck his cock up her bum or up her cunt but no doubt I shall go to the grave unsatisfied.'[9]

Over the years of their friendship Larkin and Conquest diversified their postal business. 'It has occurred to me,' Larkin told him once, 'that practically all social activity is either for chaps to get their hands on girls, or for chaps to get away from their wives,'[10] but he might have added that a good many un- or anti-social activities were also devoted to the same ends. On his trips to London, Larkin would join Conquest and hurry to pornography shops in Soho, usually opting for 'legit' places, and 'funking'[11] specialist ones. Once, hesitating outside a shop in just such a funk, Larkin was approached by the owner who discreetly asked, 'Was it bondage, sir?' Another time, Conquest preyed on his fear of discovery more cruelly. He wrote to Larkin pretending to be a member of the Vice Squad who had found Larkin's name on the subscription list of a pornographic publisher: he intended taking proceedings against publisher and subscribers. Larkin panicked and went to see his solicitor, convinced he would lose his job and reputation, before Conquest relented. Larkin was remarkably tolerant in his relief. 'The experience', he told Conquest, 'has left a frightful scar on my sensibility, which will probably mean that nude pics will act as a detumescent in future, not that I shall ever have the courage to buy any. You've probably turned me homo, come to think of it. Perhaps you'll be the first to suffer the fearful consequences of this. What?'[12]

Encouraged by Conquest's example, Larkin became increasingly open about his liking for pornography, and increasingly dependent on it. This was no surprise to his old friends. Amis had known for years that he was 'a great man for the mags' and 'an assiduous shopper',[13] and Larkin had often swapped pictures with Montgomery ('Would you like them back after I've sucked them dry?'[14] Montgomery once asked him). Comparatively recent friends like the Egertons and the Hartleys found it more unsettling, even when they understood it as the outward form of the inner conflict which dictated Larkin's feelings about women generally. He enjoyed pornography, they eventually realized, because he believed it was both cynical and romantic – cynical in obvious exploitative ways, romantic in so far as it implied (he thought) that sex was 'too good' for the tainted real world.

Larkin did not simply deploy in his daily life the attitudes which governed his private fantasies; he translated them into gruffly comic terms which most people tolerated, enjoyed, or took to be characterful. Jean Hartley, for instance, remembers:

most weeks Philip would have a good moan about the aridity of his sex life ... I think he was too polite, diffident and gentlemanly to have the sort of rakish success he thought he wanted, and also, I imagine, too fastidious. A typical complaint would start thus: 'Sex is so difficult. You ought to be able to get it and pay for it monthly like the laundry bill. I'm pissed off with the effort that has to be put in for so little return. You meet a girl and she seems to fancy you so you invite her round to your flat. The lights are low and you've spent lots of money on caviare and poured expensive champagne into her. Then, just as you are about to move in for the big seduction scene, she starts talking about this bloke she's engaged to.'[15]

The voice Jean Hartley catches here – a kind of sexually disappointed Eeyore – would become more and more characteristic during Larkin's years in Hull, and it conforms to the one he often used in his poems. (That autumn alone he wrote two, 'Ignorance' and 'Counting', which agree that 'counting up to two/Is harder to do;/For one must be denied/Before it's tried'.) Yet it disguises his actual circumstances. Thanks to Monica, he was easily able to find something other than 'aridity' as the alternative to 'rakish success': self-possessed yet accommodating, she was willing to go to bed with him whenever he wanted. Although (or because) their affair was always conducted at long distance, it was also exciting. 'I lay thinking how nice it would be to have you beside (or under!) me,' he told her in one letter, 'just gathering your great smooth hips under me and shoving into you as I felt inclined.'[16]

In saying that his love life was virtually non-existent, Larkin concealed the extent to which he chose his deprivation. Monica understood this, and knew there was a danger that in due course his self-absorption would become complete. She also realized that holidays, by allowing them more time together than usual, offered the best chance of reminding him how much he enjoyed her. This seems improbable, in view of Larkin's well-known opinion that holidays were 'a wholly feminine conception, based on an impotent dislike of everyday life and a romantic notion that it will all be better at Frinton or Venice',[17] but once he had overcome his initial reluctance he invariably came round to her way of thinking. In Sark, after his business with Conquest had been settled, Larkin didn't need much persuading. He told his mother after he and Monica had settled into the Dixcart Hotel that it immediately brought back the happiness he had known as a child on holiday at Caton Bay. 'The island,' he said, 'is about three miles by one and a half miles and is traversed by small lanes, wide enough to be used by horses and traps and farm tractors (the only kind of transport on the island). There are also many footpaths. Here and there are houses and farms, but there's [sic] only a few shops and it's not easy to find them. All we do (if it's fine) is walk to some point up the coast and sit there till lunch or tea. Evenings are spent sitting or mopping up drinks.'[18]

Larkin knew that when he returned to Hull he would be busier than ever with plans for the library. As soon as he arrived in Hallgate, however, it was his own affairs and not the university's which preoccupied him: his landlady announced that she was ill and would have to ask all her lodgers to leave. Larkin rushed round the Cottingham estate agents in a panic, drew a blank, then bumped into his neighbour Mrs Drinkwater (her husband Ronald worked at the university) and complained to her about his plight. She took pity on him and offered to lease him the flat at the top of her own house, 192 Hallgate. It wasn't self-contained, and the Drinkwaters' young child was noisily evident, but it spared Larkin the trouble of continuing his search. He gladly accepted.

He had a particular reason for wanting to feel settled: *The Less Deceived* was due to appear late in November, a month after his move.

19 Ruth Bowman photographed by Philip Larkin, c. 1947.

20 Philip Larkin in Wellington, c. 1946.

21 Sydney Larkin, shortly before his death in 1948 (photograph by Philip Larkin).
22 Coten End, Warwick, as it looks today; the Larkin family lived here from 1941 until Sydney's death.

23 Eva Larkin, the widow, c. 1950 (photograph by Philip Larkin).

24 Dixon Drive, Leicester, as it looks today. Eva Larkin lived here from 1948 until 1951; Philip Larkin lodged here from 1948 until he left for Belfast in 1950.

25 University College, Leicester, as it looked when Philip Larkin arrived in 1948.

26 Monica Jones, c. 1947 (photograph by Philip Larkin).

27 Monica Jones in the garden of her flat in Leicester, c. 1950
(photograph by Philip Larkin).

28 Queen's Chambers, Belfast (now demolished) where Philip Larkin lodged from 1950 until 1951 (photograph by Philip Larkin).
29 Arthur Terry, c. 1950.

30 The male Library staff at Queen's University, Belfast, 1951. Left to right: J. J. Graneek (Librarian), Philip Larkin, Harry Pedlow and, in front, Ernest the stack boy.

31 Ansell and Judy Egerton, after their return from Belfast to London, c. 1962.

32 Winifred Arnott, the 'sweet girl', graduating from Queen's University, Belfast, 1950.
33 Winifred Arnott, c. 1951. Philip Larkin refers to this picture in 'Lines on a Young
Lady's Photograph Album' when he wonders 'if you'd spot the theft /
Of this one of you bathing'.

34 Patsy Strang, in Belfast, c. 1952 (photograph by Philip Larkin).

'My book is binding at the moment,' he wrote to Judy Egerton in October. 'I don't know if I told you I was quarrelling with G. Hartley about the contract – well, we've settled it after a fashion, so I suppose everything is hunky-whatever-it-is. I'm not completely happy, but perhaps when I see the olive-green binding in the old rose dust jacket financial considerations will fly out of the window. We had a meeting on Thursday night in an aura of goodwill, but I left feeling as if I had been skinned somewhat. Oh well.'[19] When the book came out these resentments were set aside (even though Larkin refused to give Hartley the option on his next book) as publisher and author waited for a reaction. 'I don't think I've ever offended anyone except John H[eath]-S[tubbs],' Larkin wrote apprehensively to Conquest, 'but no doubt I shall come in for a good deal of anti-Movement sniping.'[20] For days nothing happened. Perhaps, he wondered, the book would suffer the same fate as his previous collections, and get no public attention at all? Friends, he thought gloomily, were one thing (Montgomery had recently written to say, 'you are almost the only contemporary I know of who takes naturally, and of strong personal volition, to the traditional subject matter of poetry'[21]); reviewers were another. With only a week to go until Christmas, there had still not been one mention of the book in a newspaper.

Then, on 22 December, *The Times* changed everything; it included *The Less Deceived* in its round-up of the year's outstanding books, and orders began to rain down on 253 Hessle Road. Some, Jean remembers, were more hopeful than accurate; she fielded requests for *Alas! Deceived*, *A Lass Deceived*, *The Less Received*, *The Kiss Deceived*, *The Less Desired*, *The Ilex Deceived*, and *The Gay Deceivers*, by Carkin, Lartin, Lackin, Laikin and Lock.[22] Other reviews quickly followed. The *Times Literary Supplement* was anonymously cautious but encouraging; the *New Statesman* was enthusiastic; and Donald Davie, Anne Ridler and Roy Fuller, among others, produced praising pieces later in the spring. For the rest of 1956 and into the following year, articles and appreciations followed at regular intervals. Most of them concentrated, as Larkin hoped they would, on the book's emotional impact and its sophisticated, witty language – and the poetry-buying public soon took notice. So did the academic community, especially after F. W. Bateson, the English Fellow at Corpus Christi College, Oxford, had written about the book in *Essays in Criticism*, urging people to 'Come buy!'[23] The first 400 copies were sold within weeks, and the 300 sheets had been bound and dispatched by the end of April. When the Hartleys set about ordering a reprint they found that the printer had broken up the type. Undaunted, they had the book reset and published a paperback edition of 1,300 copies in August. Within a year, a further 1,500 copies were needed for a third impression; a fourth and fifth soon followed. The first book from The Marvell Press was a best-seller. Publishing poetry, the Hartleys thought, was as easy as falling off a log.

THIRTY-FOUR

The publication of *The Less Deceived* in November 1955 marked the decisive turning point in Larkin's career. Previously he had been almost no one, now he was someone; previously small presses had humiliated him, now one of them made him special; previously he had suffered his failures in solitude, now he was able to dramatize them for an audience. All the faces, voices, attitudes, beliefs, jokes and opinions that had evolved during his growth to maturity were suddenly enshrined in the personality which his public decided was 'him'. Like the characteristics he later described in 'Dockery and Son', they hardened into all he'd got.

There were obvious advantages: because Larkin knew that his gifts had been recognized ('I am a genius'), he felt justified in seeking to perfect the work rather than the life. But there were drawbacks, too. Fame endangered his poems by threatening the delicate balance between a desire for private rumination and a longing for a public hearing. He wondered how he could continue to 'be himself' if his self depended on remoteness and disappointment, neither of which he could truly be said to possess any more.

Inevitably, he was tempted to freeze his life in postures of continuing unhappiness. As far as his work was concerned, this meant making things out to be worse than they actually were, and at the same time denying that there was anything redemptively strange or unique involved in writing about them. The effects were immediately apparent. As soon as a wide audience began approaching Larkin for his opinions, he evolved a way of responding which was at once polite and uncommunicative. Questions about how he wrote were met with answers which cut the whole business down to a size not worth sophisticated investigation (it was 'like knitting', or 'like laying an egg', or 'like having a crap'[1]). Questions about interpretation got similarly short shrift: 'My poems are so self-explanatory that any words of commentary seem superfluous. They all derive from things I have seen or done or thought, and I doubt if there is anything unusual about their subjects.'[2] It was a line he had taken before, but now pursued with more vigour. 'My point,' he insisted, 'is that because what one writes depends so much on one's character and environment – either one writes about them or to escape from them – then it follows that basically one no more chooses what one writes than one chooses the character one has or the environment one has. And further, one no more likes what one writes than the character one has or the environment one has.'[3]

Simple as they seem, these opinions are as contradictory as those Larkin had started to formulate in Belfast five years earlier – and for the same reason. While feeling in his guts that poetry was a convulsive response to whatever experience life threw at him, he also stressed that a writer must 'act', not merely 'react'. He made the point best in a letter written in 1978 to Virginia Peace, wife of the then Professor of Russian at Hull. At Larkin's request Virginia Peace had shown him a novel she had written based on her experience of losing her son, who had recently been killed in a tragic accident. He replied:

If I had known that it was based on that dreadfully unhappy experience in your life I shouldn't have asked to read it – this for at least two reasons: first, because in such circumstances adverse criticism can't help seeming cruelly unsympathetic, and secondly because I guess it would be virtually impossible to write a good novel about such a thing, or about such a thing only. And I think this is really my principal criticism: you have done amazingly well to describe what happened in so dispassionate and calm a way, but for you this is enough, the events speak for themselves. Unfortunately for the reader it isn't: the reader wants that impure thing, literature – plot, suspense, characters, ups, downs, laughter, tears, all the rest of it. Your narrative isn't a story, it's a frieze of misery; your characters are numb with unhappiness; there is no relief, no contrast. Now I can quite see that to 'play about' with the kind of subject matter you have taken would seem heartless, frivolous, even untrue, an offence against decency or decent feelings, something you couldn't do, and yet in literature it somehow has to be done – one might almost say that it's the mixture of truth and untruth that makes literature.[4]

The more celebrated Larkin became, the more reluctant he was to comment on what was 'truth' and 'untruth' (or what was 'active' and 'reactive') in his own work. 'There's not much to say about my few poems,' he insisted time and time again, 'without venturing into the region

of psychiatric analysis. And I don't want to do that!'⁵ Even more dis-
agreeable was the thought of reading in public. He received invitations to
do so, particularly during the last part of his life, at the rate of several a
week, and by the mid-1960s his secretary in the library had taken it upon
herself to compile a dossier of various forms of rejection, catalogued
from type 'A' to type 'F'. It was not, he explained to one beseecher, just
shyness which made him refuse. 'I really think,' he said, 'the number of
writers who enhance their reputations by public appearances is *very
small indeed*, and I am quite sure this is one of the cases when I am in the
majority.'⁶ Sometimes he was forthright in his refusal ('Many poets are
paranoiac bores, and those impure assemblages known as poetry read-
ings are a wonderful new way of being paranoiacally boring'⁷); some-
times subtle ('the reason I don't like it is that I don't like going about
pretending to be myself'⁸). Nowhere, though, is he elaborately theoreti-
cal. Public reading was out because it was vain and foolish. If poems
themselves couldn't quite get away with seeming simple, at least his
methods of separating himself from his audience could remain straight-
forward.

Straightforward, but not absolute. Briskly and often brusquely spur-
ning invitations, Larkin acquired after 1955 a reputation for being a
hermit that he did not entirely deserve. While keeping himself to himself
he also went out of his way to tell his readers a great deal about his life.
Scarcely a year went by without him outlining his beliefs, habits and
opinions – in reviews (he began writing about modern poetry regularly
for the *Guardian* in April 1956), articles and chunks of autobiography,
let alone poems. He may not always have named names (friends like
Amis were one thing, lovers and family another), and he may not have
appeared much in public outside Hull, but after *The Less Deceived* came
out he put almost as much effort into explaining himself to the world as
he did into keeping it at bay.

He started doing so almost exactly as the book was published. D. J.
Enright, with whom Larkin had corresponded when *XX Poems*
appeared, was now teaching in Japan and planning an anthology of
British poetry which would complement Conquest's *New Lines*.
Although Enright's title – *Poets of the 1950s* – was less combative than
Conquest's, both men shared the sense of living in a distinctly new lit-
erary climate. Rather than risk his neck in an Introduction, as Conquest
did, Enright asked the contributors themselves for their views. Larkin
replied in a letter written shortly before Christmas:

I write poems to preserve things I have seen/thought/felt (if I may so indicate a composite and complex experience) both for myself and for others, though I feel that my prime responsibility is to the experience itself, which I am trying to keep from oblivion for its own sake. Why I should do this I have no idea, but I think the impulse to preserve lies at the bottom of all art. Generally my poems are related, therefore, to my personal life, but by no means always, since I can imagine horses I have never seen [in 'At Grass'] or the emotions of a bride [in 'Wedding Wind'] without ever having been a woman or married.

As a guiding principle I believe that every poem must be its own sole freshly created universe, and therefore have no belief in 'tradition' or a common myth-kitty or casual allusions in poems to other poems or poets, which last I find unpleasantly like the talk of literary understrappers letting you see they know the right people.[9]

Larkin later claimed that this letter was written quickly and with no thought that it might be published. When Enright printed it as the preface to Larkin's work in the anthology (which was published on 14 January 1956), reviewers saw it as an expression of the anti-modernist feelings which lay at the heart of The Movement. Larkin may have been startled to see the extract from his letter in the book, but he had no reason to regret what he had written, or the way in which he had written it.

A more familiar form of self-defence, his gloom, returned as soon as *The Less Deceived* was safely launched. Arriving in Loughborough for Christmas he found his mother ill with a complaint her doctor could not identify, and early in the new year she was taken into Carlton Hayes Hospital at Narborough for tests. She stayed there nearly a month, making Larkin 'terribly sorry for her and worried about her'.[10] Torn between fears for her recovery and anxiety about the threat her frailty posed to his independence, Larkin himself fell ill as soon as Eva showed signs of improvement. He consulted the doctor at the University Health Centre in Hull, who suspected a stomach ulcer and sent him to Kingston General Hospital for tests which included a barium meal and X-rays of his throat, chest and stomach. 'To anyone used to downing Guinness,' he told Judy Egerton a short while afterwards, 'the barium meal presented no difficulties, but I expect anyone who didn't make a habit of downing pints would find it pretty hard going. I don't know what the X-rays showed. I kept thinking of Auden's "We seldom see a sarcoma/As far advanced as this . . ." No doubt I shall be told in due course.'[11] He was. There was nothing to worry about, the doctor said – he should put his hypochondriacal fears out of his mind.

Before going back to work in January, Larkin and Monica took a short holiday on the south coast. When they reached Chichester they visited the cathedral and saw a beautiful 'pre-baroque' monument to the Earl of Arundel and his wife, which shows their two figures lying side by side in state, holding hands. (Larkin subsequently discovered that the joined hands were a later addition – in fact the work of Edward Richardson (1812–68) who reworked the sculpture in the 1840s to repair damage it had suffered during the Reformation and the Civil War.) Soon after returning to Hull he revisited the monument in 'An Arundel Tomb', which he finished on 20 February, using the detail of the hands as the focus for one of his most moving evocations of the struggle between time and human tenderness. In its covert way, the poem is a form of thanks for his recovery. Recently his worries about his own and Eva's health had led him to brood on mortality even more deeply than usual; now he celebrated survival and the possibility of certain kinds of immortality as he surveyed the 'faithfulness in effigy' of the earl and countess. No matter how 'blurred', 'vague' and 'plain' the couple look, no matter how merely 'commissioned' was their hand-holding, and no matter how 'changed' and 'damaged' is the world into which they have passed, they have 'Persisted, linked':

> Now, helpless in the hollow of
> An unarmorial age, a trough
> Of smoke in slow suspended skeins
> Above their scrap of history,
> Only an attitude remains:
>
> Time has transfigured them into
> Untruth. The stone fidelity
> They hardly meant has come to be
> Their final blazon, and to prove
> Our almost-instinct almost true:
> What will survive of us is love.

At the end of the manuscript draft of 'An Arundel Tomb' Larkin wrote, 'Love isn't stronger than death just because statues hold hands for 600 years.' It's a remark which reinforced, privately, the sense of futility that hovers around the poem's conclusion in words like 'helpless', 'scrap', 'attitude', 'Untruth' and 'almost' (and it typifies his habit of writing cynical graffiti on his own most monumental lines). Publicly, the rhetoric of the final line takes charge and establishes it as a separate truth: an Augustan wisdom arising from a part-medieval, part nineteenth-century monument.

In Larkin's personal life things were just as equivocal. During his first year in Hull he had confirmed that regular meetings and holidays were all he wanted with Monica. It was a relationship based not on passionate intensity but on comfortable familiarity – so much so that now he could even write with her in the same room: she provided the word 'blazon' for 'An Arundel Tomb' when he called out to her that he needed 'something meaning a sign, two syllables'.[12] But at the same time as the poem celebrates their continuing life together, it also shows Larkin's doubts about the value – let alone the possibility – of long-lasting relationships in general and marriages in particular. Monica might have helped him finish the poem, yet behind the tender triumphalism of its ending lies an assumption that no living couple could ever be truly happy and remain permanently in love. Even as it acknowledges Larkin's need for loving partnership, 'An Arundel Tomb' doubts that such a thing is possible.

The success of *The Less Deceived* strengthened his resolve to live alone. Never mind that his rate of production was so low (only two poems in 1956) – he now regarded every development in his career as proof that he was right to behave as he did. Enright's and Conquest's anthologies were two cases in point; a third was the chance to read some of his poems on the BBC radio programme *New Poetry* on 24 April. 'Is that plum-voiced pansy, gobblingly unsure even of his sudden baying mongrel vowels, really me?'[13] he asked Conquest self-mockingly, but he was pleased nevertheless. Two months later he was pleased again, when he was included in the series 'Four Young Poets' published in the *Times Educational Supplement*. He found something to grumble about (he said the piece made him sound like 'a book drunk'[14]) but he approved the general approach, which confirmed his credentials as an accessible anti-modernist:

As native as a Whitstable oyster, as sharp an expression of contemporary thought and experience as anything written in our time, as immediate in its appeal as the lyric poetry of an earlier day, it may well be regarded by posterity as a poetic monument that marks the triumph of clarity over the formless mystifications of the last twenty years. With Larkin poetry is on its way back to the middlebrow public.[15]

While such judgements helped Larkin justify his solitude, they didn't necessarily help him defend it. Throughout the summer, with his landlady's child squawking through the house below his flat, he found life at 192a Hallgate increasingly unattractive. 'I'm beginning to realize how much noise the little girl here makes,' he complained to Judy, 'and how much I dislike it. Silence, silence, silence. Where shall I find you, outside the grave?'[16] Monica, realizing that he was bound to move again soon, couldn't help wondering whether she would at last be included in his plans. When the university authorities told him an unfurnished flat would soon be available, she realized that his decision to take it was 'a declaration of eternal independence'. He wrote to her awkwardly, writhing on the hook of his conscience:

I'm sure if I say I'm sorry it will sound hypocritical. But I *am* sorry, and like all my so-called actions it was forced on me till I couldn't in all reason refuse it, hardly a decision at all . . . I'm sure you'd have behaved just the same. One isn't being called on to decide any more than whether or not all one's bleating complaints about one's present condition are sincere or not – it was almost a challenge that had to be answered. This will sound lame, I know. I suppose in a sense it might be a step nearer domesticity – to think of myself owning furniture gives me a sort of sinking feeling. Paying rates. Practically a *householder*. I'll probably have to get all the stuff *insured*. I'm being woven into the fabric of society so fast my head is spinning. But I feel extremely sad when I think of you 'creeping to hide away in your hole' – when I know what kind of hole it is. And oh dear, I do despise these bachelors such as I am qualified to be classed among – uneasy jovial selfish mum-loving compensated crew.[17]

The flat Larkin had accepted, and moved into at the end of October, was in 32 Pearson Park. He stayed eighteen years, and the place became more nearly his home than anywhere else he lived. It's still easy to see why it suited him so well. Pearson Park itself, which was built by Zachariah Pearson, a rich shipowner, in 1862, lies to the north of the centre of Hull: a five-acre expanse of grass, flowerbeds and chestnut trees, dotted with statues of Queen Victoria and local worthies, and embracing a bowling green and a small conservatory. It is charming, slightly tatty, bracing in winter, jolly in summer. John Kenyon, who was appointed Professor of History at Hull in 1962, remembers it as 'a rather impressive relic of ambitious Victorian town planning; comfortably classless now, it lies between the westward spokes of the Avenues, lower middle class with a whiff of the bohemian, and a rather sordid working-class area abutting on to the lower end of the Beverley Road. It is preserved from further decline by a number of small private hotels catering for commercial travellers.'[18]

Number 32 is one of the more modest houses overlooking the Park, in spite of having once been used as the American Consulate. It stands in the south-west corner – three-storied, red-brick, with a view through (or in high summer into) a clump of chestnuts. Larkin's flat, once again, was on the top floor: a decent-sized front room overlooking the Park, one bed-room, a cramped kitchen and a bathroom. Kenyon says it had 'something of the atmosphere, if not the spaciousness, of a set of rooms at Oxford or Cambridge; or more accurately, the apartments in similar houses in north Oxford in which J. I. M. Stewart places some of his elderly dons.'[19]

Larkin would have preferred artistic to donnish. Although he had no previous experience of doing up a flat, he set about buying 'comfortable and chintzy'[20] armchairs, a wide old-fashioned metal-frame bed and a carpet 'like autumn leaves'.[21] He didn't like the colour scheme that he inherited (green ceiling in the hall, and elsewhere pale creams, greys and blues), but did his best to minimize its 'rather chilling' effect by hanging a 'few pictures'[22] and creating in the bathroom a montage 'juxtaposing Blake's "Vision of Body and Soul" with a Punch-type cartoon of the front and back legs of a pantomime horse pulling in opposite directions against one another and captioned "Ah, at last I've found you".'[23] Twice a week a cleaning lady came to tidy for him – Mrs Noakes to start with, then Mrs Oates, who found him 'a very humorous man and a good employer. He used to leave little notes for me, telling me what to do. He was no trouble, but I found his windows difficult. They were very high, and because they had no sash they were difficult to clean on the outside.'[24] With his books and records carefully shelved, his Pye 'Black Box' record-player, and his binoculars for gazing down into the Park, he was both snug and defended. The flat was a place of retreat and of surveillance.

He thought it was continually under siege. The worst problem was the noise of other tenants on the two floors below. Bill and Janet Duffin, for instance (Bill worked in the Physics Department), who occupied the second-floor flat during the late 1950s, endured his trudging up and down stairs with heavy knapsacks of washing, and 'capering'[25] round his sitting-room listening to jazz, only to find that he stigmatized one of their daughters as 'Squeaker', and reviled their own mild habits. 'The Duffins are making a fearful noise downstairs,' he complains in a typically explo-sive letter to Eva. 'I should like to go down and lay about me with a cudgel. The squealing of the little girls, the deeper imbecilities of Duffin himself, all mingled with stamping of little feet, crashes and explosions ... I should like to hurl teargas bombs down the chimney.'[26]

The Duffins' eventual replacements were no better, and Larkin's letters of the next eighteen years regularly describe how he has spent evenings 'pounding on the floor in a frenzy'. He knew it was 'scarcely dignified'[27] to behave in such a way, but he made no effort to restrain himself. The flat may have been rented but its peace was the only peace he had, and he defended it ruthlessly. Soon even visits from friends seemed a threat. Amis, as we've seen, offered to come, cancelled, and wasn't invited again. ('He *is* a wretched type,'[28] Larkin growled to Eva at the time.) Monica, at least for the first few years of his tenancy, slept in one of the nearby hotels when she visited for the weekend, to keep up the appearance of respectability. University colleagues and friends such as the Hartleys were only occasionally admitted for a drink and/or lettuce sandwiches (a speciality). Otherwise he insisted on solitude even if it meant courting loneliness. It was a more emphatic way of being alone than he had known in Ireland, where the camaraderie of the campus had infiltrated his life in lodgings. At Hull the society of work was kept separate from the tree-muffled eyrie of Pearson Park. In the library and staff bar he was a shy but convivial colleague, at home he felt 'really himself'.

Over the years this division had a powerful effect on his personality, and on the way others saw him. Whereas he had once mixed gravity with levity in the world at large, now he became increasingly restrained. Judy Egerton, when she moved to London at the end of 1956 as her husband took up the Assistant City Editorship of *The Times*, noticed a marked difference between the Larkin of Pearson Park and the Larkin of Belfast. 'I could feel he was more sombre,' she says, 'wearing more sombre clothes, darker suits and so on. It had something to do with becoming "respectable", but something to do with sadness, too.'[29]

THIRTY-FIVE

'Something to do with sadness.' As far as worldly ambitions were concerned, Larkin didn't have much cause for complaint. He was performing well in a difficult and senior job, and *The Less Deceived* had securely established him as one of the best poets of his generation. Yet he was not often able to begin – still less finish – a poem. The library was partly to blame; it kept him distractingly busy. A larger and more nebulous difficulty was the fact that his life only rarely attained the right emotional temperature for writing. Pearson Park gave him space for concentration, but this alone was not enough. There had also to be intensity, 'a knife as well as a fork',[1] for a poem to suggest itself. As the year ended, he wondered whether he had stripped his life bare instead of stripping it for action. 'Absolutely no news here,' he wrote to Conquest early in the new year 1957, 'except that I have a sodding cold and feel as if the end is near. The prospect of the start of term makes it all much worse. Feel as if I shall never write another *poem*, or fuck another *girl*, or drink another *pint*, or even read another good *book*, before they cart me off to the bone yard – you know the feeling, I expect. Hull is like a backdrop for a ballet about industrialism crushing the natural goodness of man: a good swingeing, Left-wing ballet.'[2]

Four days before writing this, Larkin might reasonably have thought it was unjustified: he completed 'Love Songs in Age'. The conclusion of the poem, like the opening, had been prompted by a Christmas visit to his mother – a visit which provoked the usual mixture of worries and frustrations. 'Christmas really bore little relation to any festival of the same name experienced by anyone else,' he told Judy. 'I stayed in, like the sun, for a whole week, and nonetheless seemed to return with an incipient cold which flowered exotically in my unmarried bed (like snuggling into a grave) which is why I now have an electric blanket of some seven days' standing. Soon I shall be the only unmarried man in the western hemisphere. I feel like some ancient enemy of youth and spirit – how *can* they? What do they *gain* by it?'[3]

As soon as he left Loughborough, he had began lacing these questions through another memory of his time there: the song-books Eva used to play on the piano in her youth (one had even been 'coloured' by the infant Kitty). Originally these songs had suggested hopefulness; now they seemed to describe a world of delightful but impossible illusions. 'The unfailing sense of being young' and 'even more,/The glare of that much-mentioned brilliance, love' had promised a future which was both excited and organized. At the end of the poem Larkin sorrowfully understands that this kind of balance is out of the question.

> To pile them back, to cry,
> Was hard, without lamely admitting how
> It had not done so then, and could not now.

The observer is here observed: the lessons Larkin draws from his mother's experience are the same as those he derives from his own. Love, which is extraordinary (a 'bright incipience') and natural ('like a spring-woken tree'), might be able to redeem him from his unsatisfactory prime, but the

terms on which he is prepared to let it exist are bound to limit its effects –
if not crush them altogether.

Three months after finishing 'Love Songs in Age' Larkin began another,
longer poem which would repeat this theme: 'The Whitsun Weddings'. He
didn't finish it until October 1958, eighteen months later, and his struggle
to do so formed the backdrop to his life throughout this period. It was a
low-key, low-spirited time – burrowing into his flat, digging into his job,
feeling alternately bothered and lonely, actively frustrated, dozily feeble.
More often than before, he turned to Judy Egerton for the comfort of
complaining. Because she was in London and married she was no threat,
because she was attractive and fond of him he felt galvanized by her. 'You
are often in my mind,' he told her during the spring, grumbling about his
inertia:

I could only explain [it] by giving a long and probably not over-convincing account
of a kind of lingering spring cold, of the kind that turns one's bones to outmoded
lead piping, and some plaguey reviewing that looks nothing when done but of
which my slow brain makes very heavy weather. I am a lazy incompetent person
and spend far too much time staring at the treetops out of the window while
another LP clicks discreetly into place and an over-loud piano intro knells the
death of thought for the next twenty minutes. And then one gets into bad habits:
Kingsley never writes, and my last letter from Bruce began 'Mr Montgomery is
frantically busy on a new picture, but has asked me to tell you ...' One begins to
equate non-writing with success. But you wouldn't be interested in these shuffling
excuses ...

This institution totters along, a cloister of mediocrities isolated by the bleak
reaches of the East Riding, doomed to remain a small cottage-university of arts-
and-science while the rest of the world zooms into the Age of Technology. The
corn waves, the sun shines on faded dusty streets, the level-crossings clank, bills
are made out for 1957 under billheads designed in 1926, and the adjacent water
shifts and glitters, hinting at Scandinavia ... that's a nice piece of evocation for
you.[4]

Genuinely melancholy but also playing the part of a Parnassian Ron
Glum, Larkin clearly illustrates in this letter the paradoxes which now
ruled his life. It shows him as someone increasingly self-dramatizing and
also as someone more concerned to describe an interior landscape than to
record the flow of things happening. This was partly done for the sake of
politeness – he didn't want to bore friends with accounts of things that
might not interest them. Yet his attitude has the effect of disconnecting his
moods from at least some of their sources, and concealing their origins.

This letter to Judy, for instance, makes no mention of two important events which occurred around the time it was written. The first helps to explain his feelings of exclusion. The poet Charles Tomlinson, writing in the journal *Essays in Criticism* in April, had attacked Larkin's 'tenderly nursed sense of defeat'[5] in an article headed 'The Middlebrow Muse'. It was the first serious sign of a backlash against The Movement, and Larkin had been forced to realize that his new eminence would bring him enemies as well as friends. He retaliated in a letter to Conquest, angrily concealing his earlier interest in 'foreign poetry' – and especially in Laforgue: 'Why can't these chaps emulate Yeats and say simply "It may be a way, but it is not my way"? And why [does Tomlinson] assume I haven't read *Tradition and the* etc.? I have, and think it piss. If he wants to take his tone from bookish young Yanks, let him, but I prefer my own taste in these things. And if that chap Laforgue wants me to read his things, he'd better write them in English.'[6] In previous remarks about his poems, Larkin had always been defiantly no-nonsense. Here it is evident that since the publication of *The Less Deceived* he had taken to couching his beliefs in overtly reactionary terms.

The other change Larkin didn't mention to Judy was one that he might more easily be forgiven for thinking parochial. In fact it introduced him to someone who would soon become one of the most important people in his life. On 20 May he took on a new secretary in his office, Betty Mackereth. She was a Hull woman born and bred. After attending Newland High School and the Commercial College she had been called up soon after the outbreak of war and sent to the government training centre in Leeds where she worked as a quality-control inspector. (Her course included learning how to do welding.) For part of the war she had worked in Gloucester, then in 1945 she returned to Hull, taking up a post with the city's Transport Department which she held for twelve years. On her bicycle ride into work she sometimes accompanied Hilary Penwill, the secretary whom Larkin inherited from his predecessor, Miss Cuming, and when Betty gathered that this secretary was retiring, she decided to apply for her job.

Larkin immediately recognized Betty's combination of tact and directness, tolerance and strictness. Although she still lived with her parents, she was experienced and unflappable. Her war work, Larkin knew, had thrown her 'into a pretty rough world, and I sometimes suspect nothing since has ever made much impression on her'.[7] This (not to mention her golf handicap) set her apart from the other women in Larkin's life, and made him feel relaxed and trusting. She was a handsome, tall woman, but he was able to speak to her as plainly as he would to a man. Betty realized that her job was twofold: to oil Larkin's work as a librarian and to shield him as a writer. At the same time as he explained her professional duties, he told her 'to keep his readers at bay. He even gave me a set of questions to ask people when they rang up, and although I made some mistakes to start with, and let some people through, I soon became more self-assured. He saw being a librarian and writing as two very different things, you see, and he didn't want people bothering him. At work, unless he was writing to someone he knew, he even signed his letters "P. A. Larkin". Keep them all off – you see – that was the thing.'[8]

Within a short time Larkin saw that Betty wasn't only practical and efficient. 'She's an odd person,' he would one day tell Eva, 'under, or alongside her stern secretary manner is a completely frivolous, almost skittish person, a kind of schoolgirl that giggles at the back of the class.'[9] Larkin liked this, not least because it allowed him to show his own lightheartedness without fear of seeming boorish or trite. She indulged his habit of keeping a tortoiseshell spy-glass on the window-sill of his office so that he could examine pretty students as they passed by; she forbore to mention the red socks that he sometimes wore with his dark suit, even though she privately 'used to wonder whether he wasn't a bit homosexy – those colours he wore'.[10] The longer they worked together, the more they found to enjoy in each other. Betty, more deeply than anyone, understood his need to develop the library, while also sympathizing with the personal cost it sometimes involved – his hands 'damp' with dread every time he had to make any sort of public address. He, in turn, rewarded her with his confidence, to the point at which she realized, 'I was like a wife, really. I knew everything a wife knows, more than some wives know, probably.'[11] For the twenty-seven years that Betty worked for him she was, he knew, 'my mainstay ... [She has] boundless energy, [is] always cheerful and tolerant, and if she doesn't do half my work she sort of chews it up to make it easier for me to swallow. I'd be lost without her.'[12] He might also have said that without her he would have withdrawn more quickly into himself. Fiercely as Betty protected him, her candour and practicality linked him to the world.

THIRTY-SIX

Shortly before Betty started working with Larkin, the Queen paid an official visit to the university in her capacity as Visitor. The librarian was not reckoned to be worth presenting. 'Ah well,' he told his mother, 'one day I shall meet her as Philip Larkin and not as the paltry librarian.'[1] Once Betty was installed she learnt not to take this kind of remark too seriously, and discovered how devoted he was to his work. When he returned from his summer holidays (with Monica on the west coast of Ireland where they visited Richard Murphy and Patsy, then to Portmeirion for a week with Eva) she helped him prepare for the annual conference of SCONUL (the Standing Conference of National and University Librarians, held this year in Glasgow), and for the beginning of building work on Stage 1 of the library.

Then came another and stranger interruption. Alec Dalgarno, his friend from Belfast, wrote to say he was getting married in October 1957: would Larkin act as best man? Barbara, the bride-to-be, was a former student at Queen's and knew enough about Larkin to realize that he would find it difficult to assist others in a service he dreaded for himself. In the end his liking for Dalgarno won the day and he agreed to co-operate. He sailed to Belfast, arrived for the service at St George's Church in the centre of the city, was alarmed to hear the priest's name was St John Puke but gratified to discover the congregation was small (just the two families), went to the party afterwards, gave the happy couple some rare American jazz records, then bolted back to England grateful that he was still single. Judy Egerton, who knew most of those involved, was the first to hear the story:

Alec preserved his icy demeanour to the last, and appeared capable of running not only his own wedding but anybody else's who happened to be around. I must say I admired him for this, also for his lack of impatience with the parson, who came as near to spoiling the wedding breakfast as he could by getting tight and attempting unsuccessfully to convert it into a routine anthropological debauch by singing songs, introducing smutty innuendos, proposing toasts and speeches, and leaping to his feet every so often to shower on some poor victim a stream of sentimental verbiage so nauseating as to be laughable ... At times I wondered if as best man I ought to knock him out, but he had apparently played rugger for Ireland in his day and was built on the general lines of Spencer Tracy and Tom Teevan (both of whom he strongly resembled) so I decided against so doing, perhaps wisely.[2]

Normally this episode would have made Larkin agonize about his 'indigestible' bachelor existence. This time he was diverted. Library plans swamped him as soon as he returned to Hull, and as the year ended he rushed south to Loughborough for Christmas. In compensation, he took Monica to London to see *The Boy Friend*, which he enjoyed for its 'gay energy and really tuneful tunes',[3] before apprehensively returning to work. Building started in January and he knew that until it was completed (in August 1959, if everything went according to schedule) it would take most of his time and attention. Checking with architects, providing adjustments to his original specifications, and ensuring that readers were well provided for at the existing site, he watched the shell of the new building gradually materialize. It was engrossing but frustrating – almost everything to do with the library was his idea, yet he had to trust others to carry out his wishes. Often he erupted angrily, chafing at slow work and castigating the architects as 'doltish',[4] but he always went out of his way to make things easier and more enjoyable for his staff. Some of the photographs of him touring the site show him extravagantly mopping his brow as he inspects the manual for a cooling system. To Maeve Brennan, a Catholic, he wondered about the function of the 'RC girder'.

Larkin also made time for his second, literary, self. In February 1958 he read another selection of his poems on the Third Programme. Although this meant ignoring his own strictures about performing in public, he decided, 'I don't like professional readers . . . What finally gets me down is the *inhumanity* of their voices, the sort of absence of any . . . inflexion or attractiveness.'[5] Eva reported that he sounded 'strong and clear'[6] when the programme was broadcast. Five months later the BBC approached him again, and this time it was a more personal contact. Anthony Thwaite, who had admired Larkin's poems ever since first reading them in the early 1950s, invited him to contribute to a series he was compiling for the European Service called 'Younger British Poets of Today'. (The other writers he approached were Elizabeth Jennings, Christopher Logue, Dom Moraes and Donald Davie.) On 2 July Thwaite and Larkin met and discussed the programme at Durrants Hotel in London (where Larkin was staying), and Larkin agreed to read 'Skin', 'An Arundel Tomb' and 'Church Going'. They were rehearsed and recorded on 20 August, again at Durrants, and Larkin provided a defensive introduction, worrying as ever about the relationship between his poems and his own experience:

I have never claimed to know fully how or why I write poetry: it seems to me a skill easily damaged by self-consciousness, and poetic theory is not much good if it hinders the poet. If I must account for it, I think it would be best described as the only possible reaction to a particular kind of experience, a feeling that you are the only one to have noticed something, something especially beautiful or sad or significant.

Does this mean my poetry is over-personal, in the sense of being narrow or shallow? Certainly the poems I write are bound up with the life I lead and the kind of person I am. But I don't think this makes them superficial; I think it improves them. If I avoid abstractions such as are found in politics and religion it's because they have never affected me strongly enough to become part of my personal life, and so cease being abstractions.[7]

Anthony Thwaite, the producer of 'Younger British Poets', soon became more important to Larkin than the programme. After leaving Oxford in 1955 when he was twenty-five, Thwaite had taught in Japan for two years with his wife Ann, returning to England to join the BBC as a trainee radio producer. He had worked hard to promote contemporary writing, and his own reputation as a poet had flourished. The Marvell Press had published his first collection, *Home Truths*, in 1957, and Larkin had liked the formal skill of the poems, and their elegantly explicatory structures. It was this, as well as Thwaite's personality, which drew the two men together. 'From an early stage,' Thwaite says, 'we got on extremely well. I was a colossal admirer, but when we first met he wasn't so famous that I felt in awe of him.'[8]

Over the years their friendship deepened steadily. Larkin enjoyed staying with the Thwaites in Richmond (and later in Norfolk, where they bought a converted millhouse in 1971), and referred admiringly to their four daughters as 'the chorus line'. He also valued Thwaite's literary judgement and the publishing opportunities he offered when he left the BBC in 1962. From 1962 to 1965 Thwaite was literary editor of the *Listener*, from 1968 to 1972 he was literary editor of the *New Statesman*, and from 1973 to 1985 he was co-editor of *Encounter*: thanks to him Larkin published many reviews and poems in these journals. Furthermore, Thwaite in due course mooted, collected and edited material for *Larkin at Sixty*, assisted Larkin with the *Oxford Book of Twentieth Century English Verse*, and helped with the selection of pieces for *Required Writing* (which is dedicated to him). 'I was,' Thwaite says, 'his editor – that was my place in his life. Even though there were of course a number of areas in which we couldn't meet, such as jazz and cricket, there were plenty where we could. He loved me to retail literary gossip; he liked me to give him the taste of literary London and spare him the trouble of having much to do with it. That's it: I was his editor and I became his friend. We all did, all the family.'[9]

By the time 'Younger British Poets' was broadcast Larkin was embroiled in yet another and more time-consuming literary business. Towards the end of the previous year the London-based PEN Committee had asked him, for a fee of twenty-five guineas, to edit with Bonamy Dobrée and Louis MacNeice the seventh annual anthology of *PEN New Poems*. He had accepted without a clear idea of how much time the book would take up, and now found (due largely to MacNeice's not answering letters) that most of the work devolved on to him and Dobrée. 'Why should MacNeice do less for his money than we?'[10] he complained to PEN, only to be told by the organization's secretary that there was nothing she could do. 'My husband saw [MacNeice] the other day in the Tavern at Lord's,' she informed him, 'but I'm afraid I don't feel up to taking advantage of this opportunity.'[11]

The selection was made and the short Introduction drafted without MacNeice's help at the end of August. By the time it was finished Larkin felt the book had become a chore, one which deterred him from undertaking such tasks lightly in the future, and which confirmed his suspicions about the laziness and unreliability of most literary types. Most but not all. Almost exactly as the manuscript was delivered Amis invited Larkin to lunch at the Ivy Restaurant off St Martin's Lane in central London to meet Anthony Powell, whose novels Larkin had enjoyed since first reading them in Leicester. The lunch was a success, even though Larkin was later careful not to seem too impressed. 'Powell is about Kingsley's size,' he reported to Judy, 'and very "charming" and funny, at least he never says anything *really* funny, but he's full of droll anecdotes and laughs a lot, so one imagines he's funny. He dresses in country style and has a big red spotted handkerchief to wipe the tears of laughter away with.'[12]

Back in Hull, Larkin turned to less glamorous but more productive aspects of literary life. George Hartley had been badgering him for some time to co-operate with the latest Marvell Press scheme – to make recordings on disc of selected authors. Because Larkin had been cheered by the reaction to his recent radio broadcasts he agreed to go along with the idea, and on 24 October he and Hartley set off for HMV Studios where they imagined they would 'get a perfect recording'.[13] What they ended up with was characterful rather than immaculate. In the background of the record it's possible to make out some distant noises, which Larkin claimed were a poltergeist, and the murmur of a flushing lavatory. In the reading itself, the remains of Larkin's stammer are evident – 'a sort of clenched-palate, tongue-sucking sound, a bit like a bushman's click'[14] – and also the surviving traces of his Coventry accent, a slightly nasal Midlands whine overlaid by the round vowels of 'standard' pronunciation. Only half mockingly, he claimed that the sleeve (which shows him sitting amongst the overgrown graves at Springbank Cemetery in Hull) was 'the best part'[15] of the whole enterprise, but when the record was released the following year the critics didn't agree. As it accomplishes the 'little miracle'[16] of speaking without hesitation, Larkin's voice allows the sense and emotional weight of his poems to emerge in a way which is dramatic yet intimate. There are no grand vocal gestures, no flourishes, just the cadenced plainness of a well-organized mind thinking aloud. Only very rarely is there a surprise; in 'Lines on a Young Lady's Photograph Album', for instance, he emphasizes the word 'art' in the line 'But o, photography! as no art is . . .' so that we understand him to be saying he doesn't reckon photography an art, rather than stressing 'is' and denigrating art generally.

Larkin's recording of *The Less Deceived* catches the true voice of ambivalent feeling. So do the notes printed on the back of the sleeve, which take the form of a question-and-answer interview but were in fact written entirely by Larkin himself. Self-confidence and self-mockery exist in equal parts, though in the end confidence gets the upper hand. While making the recording he had good and particular reasons for thinking it should: his poem 'The Whitsun Weddings', which he had begun nearly two years earlier, had finally been completed on 18 October after almost thirty pages of drafts. 'There's hardly anything of me in it at all,' he once said. 'It's just life as it happened.'[17] In fact there is everything of him in it – the yearning for love as well as the standing-off.

The poem had first begun to take shape during a journey from Hull to London on Whit Saturday, 1955. On that day, Larkin said, he caught

a very slow train that stopped at every station and I hadn't realized that, of course, this was the train that all the wedding couples would get on and go to London for their honeymoon[;] it was an eye-opener to me. Every part was different but the same somehow. They all looked different but they were all doing the same things and sort of feeling the same things. I suppose the train stopped at about four, five, six stations between Hull and London and there was a sense of gathering emotional momentum. Every time you stopped fresh emotion climbed aboard. And finally between Peterborough and London when you hurtle on, you felt the whole thing was being aimed like a bullet – at the heart of things, you know. All this fresh, open life. Incredible experience. I've never forgotten it.[18]

During its three-year gestation 'The Whitsun Weddings' became an archetype of many of Larkin's manners and methods – the poem which illustrates his achievement better than any other. It combines a discursive, novel-ish spread with the emotional intensity of a lyric. It strews the path to its extraordinary climax with deliberately ordinary sights and sounds (hot carriage-cloth, industrial froth, dismantled cars). It achieves a tone which is both awe-struck and sharply conscious of absurdity ('fathers had never known/Success so huge and wholly farcical'). It is bound to the here-and-now while longing for transcendent release:

> There we were aimed. And as we raced across
>   Bright knots of rail
> Past standing Pullmans, walls of blackened moss
> Came close, and it was nearly done, this frail
> Travelling coincidence; and what it held
> Stood ready to be loosed with all the power
> That being changed can give. We slowed again,
> And as the tightened brakes took hold, there swelled
> A sense of falling, like an arrow-shower
> Sent out of sight, somewhere becoming rain.

All the paradoxes of the poem, and all those which govern Larkin's thoughts about love, are collected here in an image adapted from a film he had seen as a young man during the war. It was, he told Jean Hartley, the arrows fired by the English bowmen in Laurence Olivier's film of *Henry V* which gave him the idea for the last verse. Dipped in the blood of patriotic fervour, Larkin's arrows serve Cupid's purpose, not Mars'. But while he admires the train-load of just-married couples, he knows he cannot join them. Alone in his carriage, sealed behind his window, he is conscious of loss but appreciative of his singleness. As he prepares to watch them disappear, he reminds himself that the arrow-shower of love wounds as well as inspires.

Larkin wrote another poem three weeks later, 'Self's the Man', which makes a similar point in a different voice. Its immediate impetus was the wish to deride his deputy librarian Arthur Wood (transformed in the poem into 'Arnold'), who on 29 September returned from his summer holiday 'with his Glasgow bookie's suit on', making Larkin wish he could 'drive a horse and cart over him'.[19] In truth, Wood had done nothing in the library to deserve Larkin's wrath, which was always expressed in terms so hilariously extreme as to appear deliberately unreasonable. Neither did Wood's marriage deserve to be turned into a grim paradigm. Yet where 'The Whitsun Weddings' rises from ordinary detail to exalted tenderness, this new poem maintains a steady note of cynicism. It concentrates on the woe that is in marriage rather than the exhilaration that is in weddings. It is a comic but completely serious vision of the life awaiting the couples when they step off the train at King's Cross:

> Oh, no one can deny
> That Arnold is less selfish than I.
> He married a woman to stop her getting away
> Now she's there all day,
>
> And the money he gets for wasting his life on work
> She takes as her perk
> To pay for the kiddies' clobber and the drier
> And the electric fire . . .

No sooner has Larkin set out the differences between himself and Arnold than he begins to question them. Is there, he wonders, really 'such a contrast' between their lives? Aren't they both as selfish as each other? More precisely, aren't they both as trapped as each other? It's the disappointments of life, Larkin insists, that make up the common human lot; the one thing which distinguishes him is that he decided – or he supposed he decided, anyway – what he could and couldn't stand years ago, whereas the likes of Arnold are surprised to find themselves so put upon.

Larkin ends 'Self's the Man' by affirming the value of being less deceived. Within a matter of weeks he was doubting it again. 'What an awful time of year this is!' he wrote to Judy:

Just as one is feeling that one can just hold on, if it just won't get any worse, then all this Christmas idiocy bursts upon one like a slavering Niagara of nonsense and *completely wrecks* one's entire *frame*. This means, in terms of *my* life, making a point of buying about six simple inexpensive presents when there are rather more people about than usual . . . No doubt in terms of yours it means seeing your house given over to hoards of mannerless middle-class brats and your good food and drink vanishing into the quacking tooth-equipped jaws of their alleged parents. Yours is the harder course, I can see. On the other hand, mine is happening to me.[20]

As in 'Self's the Man', Larkin here angrily acknowledges his selfishness, hoping that by admitting it he will be forgiven. In the event, it wasn't anger he felt when he arrived to see his mother in Loughborough but sadness – the feeling he distilled in 'Home is so Sad', which he finished on New Year's Eve after he had returned to Pearson Park. The poem stands as a coda to 'The Whitsun Weddings' and 'Self's the Man': in the former he sees love at its most enviable; in the latter he reminds himself of its realities. Now he explains where his sense of the realities comes from: his parents. His mother's house preserves all the odds and ends ('the pictures and the cutlery./The music in the piano stool. That vase') which represent the original good intentions of a couple making a home together. But all that remains of their 'joyous shot at how things ought to be' is faded hope. What will survive of us, the poem says, is not love but the wish to love – and indelible signs of how the wish has been frustrated.

With the holidays over, Larkin turned gratefully back to his work, in the library and at home. It didn't let him down: 1959, he said, 'is the busiest year of my life'[21] both because the completion of Stage 1 required his careful supervision and because his poems continued to flow steadily after the recent drought. In February he produced the short star-gazing lyric 'Far Out', in March he had his first inkling of 'The Building' (which he would eventually finish thirteen years later), and in September he wrote 'Afternoons' and began 'Talking in Bed'. In these last two poems he continued to elaborate the thoughts in and around 'The Whitsun Weddings': people who seem to exist at a 'unique distance from isolation' (young couples, young mothers and two people in bed) can only expect to possess their happiness briefly if at all. In 'Afternoons', 'something is pushing' the women 'To the side of their own lives'; in one of the few poems he wrote about himself and Monica, 'Talking in Bed', the 'emblem of two people being honest' turns out to show how:

> It becomes still more difficult to find
> Words at once true and kind,
> Or not untrue and not unkind.

There is nothing 'told-you-so' in the way Larkin reaches this conclusion. Each time he decides that 'love dies whether fulfilled or unfulfilled' he does so with a fresh sense of loss. Instead of crowing he grieves; instead of abandoning the pursuit of happiness he sets off on its trail once more. In his lifetime it was generally thought that the focus of his interest was death, and that what bound his poems together were themes of mortality. Reading his poems in chronological sequence, it's clear that his obsession with death is inextricable from his fascination with love and marriage. Even in 1959, when the emotional claims being made on him were comparatively few, feelings of guilt and anxiety about his relationships with women continued to gnaw at him.

The actual writing of poems could hardly be blamed for making him feel at his 'busiest'. As in Belfast, they belonged to the two hours between the end of his work in the university and the drink he rewarded himself with before going to bed. Publishing was another matter, and as the reputation of *The Less Deceived* continued to spread, so the demands on his time increased. In January, Charles Monteith at Faber invited him to London to discuss plans for a second collection. Larkin went to see him before the start of the spring term, and while he was in the offices in Russell Square he met T. S. Eliot. It was their only meeting, though Eliot had already seen *The Less Deceived* and told Monteith, 'Yes – [Larkin] often makes words do what he wants.'[22] When Larkin described the encounter to his mother he tried – as usual – to appear casual but couldn't help sounding excited. 'London seems much as ever,' he told her breezily. 'I spent some time on Thursday talking to a friend of mine in Faber's, who eventually startled me by saying, "Have you ever met Eliot, I'll just see if he's next door," and to my alarm reappeared leading an aged but spry Eliot who said he was sorry he couldn't talk to me but he had a visitor himself, but he was "pleased to see me in this office" – meaning, I suppose, that they'd like to publish me!'[23]

Back in Hull, Larkin found himself in the role of promoter rather than promoted. Among the latest batch of poetry books he had undertaken to review for Hartley's magazine *Listen* was the *Collected Poems* of John Betjeman, a book he had already written about for the *Guardian* the previous December. Ever since reading Betjeman's work at Oxford he (like Amis) had praised its formal variety and idiosyncratic tone, believing that it embodied old-fashioned virtues which made a nonsense of the modernists' experiments. Now he wanted to spread the word, even if it meant taking on extra work. 'All day I am struggling with memoranda and committees,' he told Judy, 'and all night with articles about John Betjeman.'[24] Before long Betjeman was to return the compliment, and over succeeding years their friendship became a matter of public knowledge and interest. Most people assumed they grew very close to each other – reasonably enough, in view of the number of times they were photographed together, appeared on film together (two of Larkin's three TV appearances were made with Betjeman), and scratched each other's backs. In fact they met only a couple of dozen times, and wrote to each other admiringly but occasionally. It was an affectionate but not an intimate friendship. In Larkin's case, there was something self-protective as well as proselytizing about his enthusiasm: by extolling Betjeman's virtues he helped to create the taste by which he wished his own work to be judged.

By mid-summer Larkin had run out of time for reviews. He could see that. when the hard work of building Stage 1 was complete, moving in would be harder still. To brace himself, he took Monica away for a fortnight's holiday, this time to the Shetland Islands. In a letter to his mother he reported that they were 'very pretty and full of birds and sheep . . . The grub is very much like the university hall of residence and there is not a specially noticeable atmosphere of comfort.'[25] Even allowing for the fact that he wanted to prevent his mother feeling jealous, the tone of his letter suggests the holiday was only a partial success. The explanation is simple. Out walking one day on a lonely hillside, Monica told Larkin how beautiful she thought the larks sounded, singing high overhead. Larkin stopped, listened, but couldn't hear them. He realized for the first time that he had started to go deaf. It was the latest in a series of minor disabilities, all of which cut him off from the world. As a child and young man his stammer had made ordinary life complicated. His weak eyesight had made school lessons difficult, then separated him from his contemporaries during the war. Now, with his stammer considerably improved and his eyesight showing only slight signs of further deterioration, he was again at a disadvantage.

As his hearing grew weaker in the years ahead he felt more and more isolated, trapped in an incompetent body, foolish and pathetic. Work in the library became awkward, talking in public places (bars, for instance) a trial, even listening to jazz at home – one of his greatest pleasures – was a strain by the mid-1970s. Colleagues grew used to seeing his face remain blank as they spoke to him, or to watching him fiddle with first one and eventually two hearing-aids. (Often these produced a high-pitched whine disconcerting to friends but inaudible to Larkin himself.) In a more temperate person this would have been bad enough; in Larkin it fuelled powerful feelings of self-disgust and resentment. His deafness steadily darkened his melancholy.

If he anticipated these problems on his return from Shetland in late July, he gave no sign. At the start of his holiday he had left workmen 'trying to fill' the shell of the new building 'with pipes, cables and whatnot',[26] and now he applied himself to the final stages with the kind of enthusiasm he had never shown at work before. He was intolerant of anything slipshod (once reprimanding the architect '[who sees] nothing amiss in leaving a façade like a broken brick'[27]) but 'excited' by things like choosing 'wall-paper, lino, and coloured stacks and panels'.[28] He enjoyed working, too, with the sculptor Willi Soukup, who had been commissioned to carve a relief owl ('emblem of wisdom'[29]) on the south wall. 'Willi,' he told Judy, 'has the charm and instinctive tolerant agreeableness of the refugee, and intense blue eyes. I quite like his owl. I wish I felt as sure about his Genius of Light, an abstract figure bearing a torch that is already scrawled in rough over the front door.'[30]

By September everything was ready, and when Larkin showed his staff round the empty building they were impressed. 'We were enchanted,' Maeve Brennan cooed, 'by the brightly coloured end panels of the book stacks (colour denoted subject), the attractive tungsten lighting between each bay, the bright, light airiness and space of the catalogue hall and main reading room, the natural polished wood used for many of the fixtures, and the large oriel window, with seats around the base at the western end of the catalogue hall.'[31] Like the other seventeen members of the library staff, Maeve bent willingly to the huge task of moving the books to their new shelves. For the first fortnight of September, 'sustained by a wonderful spirit of camaraderie and glorious weather'[32] (and by a dinner Larkin gave them in Beverley), they filled the book-boxes, loaded them on to a furniture van which trundled between the old and the new accommodation, then unloaded them again. (The staff were divided into four teams, two taking the books off the shelves in the old building, and two putting them on other shelves in the new.) The local press took pictures; a television camera appeared; Larkin hovered and guided, feeling the whole operation was 'like Passchendaele':

Although I am not needed as long as things go right, there is rarely half an hour without some crisis questions such as 'We've filled the space you left for BX and it's still coming.' 'Blue team has taken our empty boxes.' 'Where shall we fix this fire extinguisher?' 'Don't you think Bridget ought to rest?' 'Are they going to lift another load before half past five?' 'Where are the clean dusters?' and so on. Everyone is working terribly hard, shifting ten to fifteen thousand books a day, and only doing so by maintaining a kind of wartime hysteria, reminiscent of amber warnings, strong tea, and small newspapers.[33]

By 18 September it was done: 250 tons of books had been moved ('and since each [book] has to be lifted five times before it reaches its new home,' Larkin explained, 'this means [we've been] employed in shifting 1,250 tons'[34]). There were still 'a few electricians and french polishers'[35] hanging about, but the furniture was in place and the systems ready for service. 'My room is so beautiful I can hardly believe it,' Larkin told his mother. 'Just you wait till you see it! I'm afraid it will make everyone so green with jealousy that I shall be the most hated person in Hull.'[36] From the way he wrote, Eva might have thought he was describing somewhere he lived, rather than somewhere he worked. At every point in the design, Larkin had demanded that the merely functional be softened by his instinct for the homely, so that a place for study also became a place of pleasure. 'Everyone looks at the wallpaper I've chosen,' he told Judy, 'and scoffs "domestic", or more specifically "bedroom".'[37]

The completion of Stage 1 at Hull banished the dreary ghost of Larkin's original 'single-handed and untrained' life as a librarian. He had begun his career in a gas-lit one-up-and-one-down, now he was lord of a building which was set to become one of the most distinguished regional libraries in the country, and had a desk which he was proud to boast was 'larger than that of President Kennedy'.[38] He had started out half-heartedly, now he was willing to acknowledge, 'librarianship suits me – I love the feel of libraries – it has just the right blend of academic interest and administration'.[39] (To prove the point: this year, 1959, was the first that he appeared in Who's Who; he gave his occupation as 'librarian' rather than 'novelist and poet', in the belief that 'a man is what he is paid for'.[40] He gave his hobby as 'resting'.) Spurred on by a sense of achievement, he was able to pass off his occasional irritations as no more than the sort of thing that all work is heir to. When he sat in his new office for the first time, he put on his desk a photograph of Guy the Gorilla where one might normally expect to see a snap of a spouse and children. It was the finishing touch to a world in which Larkin could be his own kind of public man: confident but contained; proud but protected.

Larkin knew that while the new building had 'many desirable features' it remained 'far from perfect. The enormous first-floor reading room was not conducive to concentration and the large ground-floor windows ... showed the two-tiered stack rather awkwardly. The reference bay that opened off the catalogue hall was much too small.'[41] These things meant that as soon as Stage 1 had been opened, he had to begin lobbying for funds for Stage 2. (It was three years before he began talking to architects again in earnest.) He knew he could count on the support of the Vice-Chancellor, Brynmor Jones, and appreciated that he had to let Stage 2 wait its turn in the university's building programme. In the meantime, it was agreed at a Senate meeting in December that the Queen Mother should be asked officially to open Stage 1. She accepted, but said she wouldn't be able to do the deed until the following June. Larkin didn't mind waiting. As the Duchess of York, the Queen Mother had been present at the laying of the university college's foundation stone by the Duke in 1928. The sense of continuity appealed to him.

THIRTY-SEVEN

Larkin's working life had never been so secure; his private life was about to be shaken to its foundations. On 12 October 1959 Monica sent him a telegram to say that her mother had died – of a heart attack at her home in Stourport-on-Severn – and she was going to stay with her father until the funeral. Larkin wrote to her soon afterwards: 'Really I can hardly believe it is all true, and wish it weren't. It shows, or seems to show to me, how thin the surface of life is that we scuttle over like water beetles. I thought of you yesterday, and deeply hoped you were not being simultaneously ravaged and numbed by it all. I think it is affecting me by making me peevish and unwilling to undertake cheerfully the increased bothers of the new term. Of course I might have been peevish anyway. More than likely!'[1]

Sympathy is here diluted by cold drops of self-interest. No doubt this is partly because Larkin couldn't help being reminded of his own mortality as he contemplated someone else's – yet there is also something more scheming in his letter. He knew Monica's friends were few and far between, and understood that her life with him, together but separate, prevented her from easily forming other attachments. Without her mother, there was a danger that Monica might rely on him more than she had done in the past. He suspected that she might want to move in with him. She might even re-open the question of marriage.

Two months later his fears increased. Monica's father, who had been ill with cancer for some time, also died. When Monica returned to Leicester early in the new year, worn down by grief and the gruesome labour of dealing with her parents' house and possessions, she had only Larkin to turn to. But turn to for what? He had already kept her at arm's length in letters, and had never once visited her in Stourport or offered any practical help. 'It never dawned on him to do that,' she says. 'That's what the Larkins were like.'² All the time she had been away – taking leave from the university, making lightning visits to her flat in Leicester to make sure all was well – he had been sympathetic but distant. The intimacy they had shared for fourteen years almost might not have existed.

As she began work in Leicester again, Monica rehearsed the reasons why Larkin had failed her. He was paralysed by his fear of death; he was busy in the library; above all, he was nervous of committing himself to her more deeply. Sometimes she added another reason, though it was one she found difficult to formulate: namely, that Larkin's feelings about women were so often polarized around either romantic or cynical attitudes that he was incapable of recognizing the middle ground she now needed him to occupy. Although she didn't know it, Larkin had been addressing this problem in a poem he had written while she was burying her father, a poem called 'Letter to a Friend about Girls'.

Ever since this 'Letter' first appeared in the *Collected Poems* in 1988, Amis has usually been taken to be the 'friend'. In fact it's more likely to be a familiar compound (Amis, Conquest, pals from Oxford and Belfast), if only because the sense of sexual inferiority that Larkin describes is something he derived from a wide variety of sources. The premise is a simple one: where the friend enjoys 'staggering skirmishes' with girls 'In train, tutorial and telephone booth', the speaker (who signs himself 'Horatio') is perpetually out of luck. His girls:

> have their world, not much compared with yours,
> But where they work, and age, and put off men
> By being unattractive, or too shy,
> Or having morals – anyhow, none give in:
> Some of them go quite rigid with disgust
> At anything but marriage: that's all lust
> And so not worth considering; they begin
> Fetching your hat, so that you have to lie
>
> Till everything's confused . . .

These lines help us to see why Larkin was cold to Monica when she needed him most. He was too self-absorbed to respond to her grief, and his obsession with his independence made him emotionally stingy. His defence of his actions could not disguise their cruelty. Although he begins the poem by saying that he thinks all the girls are 'the same', he ends by realizing it is he who makes them so. Discussing the poem with Anthony Thwaite he said:

What it was *meant* to do was to postulate a situation where, in the eyes of the author, his friends got all the straightforward easy girls and he got all the neurotic difficult ones, leaving the reader to see that in fact girls were all the same and simply responded to the way they were treated. In other words, the difference was in the friend and not in the girls. The last line originally ran – 'One of those "more things", could it be, Horatio?' – making it a letter from Hamlet to Horatio: to make it a letter from Horatio to Hamlet may make better or worse sense, according to whether you think Horatio was a nicer chap than Hamlet or not.[3]

Monica thought that if she did nothing Larkin would come back to her; her passivity, after all, had won him round in the past. But there was one aspect to this new situation which she hadn't anticipated, an aspect which, in the early months of 1960, she couldn't see clearly. During the weeks that Monica had been in Stourport nursing her father, Larkin had begun to take an increasing interest in Maeve Brennan, his 'superior dogsbody' in the library. He and Maeve had known each other for nearly five years (she had already been working in the library when he arrived in Hull), and hitherto their relationship had been friendly but professional. Now it began to shift. By turning to Maeve when he did, Larkin ensured that Monica could not become too dependent on him.

Because he was the librarian and Maeve was a member of his staff, Larkin realized that he must be discreet. During the early spring he announced that he would 'take in hand'[4] those colleagues who wanted to improve their career prospects by passing the Library Association exam, and started to give a series of lunch-time 'tutorials'. (The first part of the exam was due to take place in December 1960, the second part in June 1961.) Maeve was one of the half-dozen who signed up, and found Larkin 'very strict'[5] in his new role as teacher. 'He set and marked weekly homework,' she says, 'and his encouragement gave [us] a much needed stimulus to complete [our] courses.'[6] One thing, as Larkin hoped it would, led to another. After hours and occasionally at weekends, they began to see each other to discuss the course, and in the process Larkin learnt Maeve's story. She had been born in Beverley on 27 September 1929, the eldest of three children; her mother was from Beverley, and her Irish father was a dental surgeon in Hull (his family were originally from Kilkenny in

Ireland). After school at St Mary's in Hull she had attended the university college (as it then still was) and took 'a general degree – French, History, English'[7] before starting to work in the Hull Public Library. In 1953 she moved to the university library, beginning and then abandoning the Library Association course that Larkin was now helping her to complete.

It took several months for Larkin to reveal his feelings to Maeve. While coaching her for the first part of her exam in the autumn of 1960 he was encouraging but restrained – anxious to preserve a proper professional distance. Maeve looked for nothing else, and accepted that Larkin, her boss, was merely trying to be helpful. Anyway, she had little appetite for a more complicated relationship: she had recently broken off her engagement to another man (also called Philip). She was, she says, 'very reserved in those days, diffident, unassuming and certainly entertained no notion whatsoever that Philip L. regarded me with more interest than any of the rest of the female staff who surrounded him'.[8]

Week by week, tutorial by tutorial, Larkin's feelings began to develop. Eventually he would tell Maeve that she 'reminded him of Maud Gonne'[9] – not meaning that there was a physical resemblance between the two women, but that Maeve aroused all his most romantic feelings. Small, with a good figure, short brown wavy hair, an eager face and unusually hairy forearms and legs (which Larkin found 'very exciting'[10]), Maeve was unsophisticated, conservative, cautious and capable of behaving coquettishly. She was more trim than glamorous, more emotionally canny than intellectually able. It was for her intense enthusiasms that Larkin began to love her – and for not frightening him, for being cosy, for recognizing he was special, and for being – he thought – someone he could easily control and pamper. Monica, who was his 'Bun', admired him but was never in awe of him. Maeve, who became his 'Mouse' and would in due course be inundated with gifts of little furry creatures (a mouse in a chorister's costume, for instance), always looked up to him. If Larkin thought this meant she would do his every bidding, he was soon proved wrong. Maeve was quick-witted and highly principled. She was also devoutly Catholic.

Even before she began to study for her exam, Maeve had liked what she had been able to discover about Larkin's character. He was, she understood:

full of contradictions. A compassionate man, his observations were often keenly acerbic. A modest man, he did not suffer fools gladly. A man of remarkable intellect, he loved the commonplace. He took refuge in solitude, but was dependent on close friends. He appeared detached, yet sought warmth and reassurance. Public speaking

298

filled him with dread yet his delivery was confident, urbane, witty and extremely polished. The cricket enthusiast and the jazz fanatic was a passionate devotee of boxing and Gregorian plain chant.[11]

To start with, these ambiguities seemed entirely good and interesting, and Larkin and Maeve straightforwardly enjoyed each other's company. They walked in the overgrown Springbank Cemetery 'which held great fascination for him'.[12] They had tea in local cafés or at Maeve's home in Beverley High Road, Hull. Two or three times a week – sometimes more often – Larkin invited her to Pearson Park. 'The highlight for us,' she says, 'was tea at his place with Gentleman's Relish and Earl Grey tea, served in his primrose decorated china tea service which was brought out especially on these occasions.'[13]

Maeve realized that she couldn't expect things to be simple for long, and by the end of the year she already felt that the 'innocent charm and fun' of their meetings was fading, and everything was becoming 'more complex and sophisticated'.[14] She learnt more about his other commitments, he discovered more about her naturally anxious temperament. (When the time came for her to take her exams, for instance, she 'retired to bed with a species of breakdown',[15] and on their excursions she sometimes interrupted their journey to return home 'to see if she ha[d] switched fires off etc.'[16]) In so far as such traits made Larkin feel dominant they were fine; because they represented another assault on his independence they worried him. He tried to steady himself by concentrating on his work.

Larkin had called 1959 his 'busiest' year; 1960 was busier still. He kept up a steady flow of short lyrics – in January an aphoristic paean to selfishness (it's 'like listening to good jazz/With drinks for further orders and a huge fire'); in February an equally concise and more resonant *memento mori* 'As Bad as a Mile', and in August finished 'Talking in Bed' and wrote 'Take One Home for the Kiddies' and 'A Study of Reading Habits'. This last one has become famous for its final line – 'books are a load of crap' – a sentiment which seems hilariously at odds with Larkin's career. In fact the route by which he arrives at the line is one he had taken many times before. What once seemed exciting about books, he says at the beginning of the poem, was their ability (like pornography) to fool the sexually insecure reader into thinking he was adventurous and successful: 'The women I clubbed with sex!/I broke them up like meringues'. Now, jaded by failure in the real world, he can see in books only the reflection of his own incompetence:

> the dude
> Who lets the girl down before
> The hero arrives, the chap
> Who's yellow and keeps the store,
> Seem far too familiar.

Like its companion pieces, 'A Study of Reading Habits' aspires to the condition of epigram. This aspect of his writing, which often leads him to sound terse or even brutal, also survives among the gentler rhythms and more flowing shapes of his longer poems. Two such were also written this year: 'Faith Healing' (begun on 19 March and finished on 10 May) and 'MCMXIV' (begun on 7 November 1958, finished eighteen months later on 17 May). In the former, an evocation of women filing forward to be blessed by a faith healer (which Larkin had seen on a film in the cinema[17]), he rises through details of dress, voice and behaviour to a climax which links successive ringing statements:

> In everyone there sleeps
> A sense of life lived according to love.
> To some it means the difference they could make
> By loving others, but across most it sweeps
> As all they might have done had they been loved.
> That nothing cures. An immense slackening ache,
> As when, thawing, the rigid landscape weeps,
> Spreads slowly through them – that, and the voice above
> Saying *Dear child*, and all time has disproved.

In 'MCMXIV' the dramatic movement of the poem is more complicated, its escalation from local and familiar things (like 'Faith Healing' it begins with 'lines' standing patiently) to rhetorical drama is quickened by a vain search for a main verb. When the conclusion arrives, it does so with epigrammatic emphasis:

> Never such innocence,
> Never before or since,
> As changed itself to past
> Without a word – the men
> Leaving the gardens tidy,
> The thousands of marriages
> Lasting a little while longer:
> Never such innocence again.

Fluid yet contained, modest yet eager for grandeur, nostalgic yet involved with the drama of the present: these are the balances Larkin managed to create in his poems at precisely the moment Maeve started to 'strike at his control'. Far from destroying the tensions on which his writing depended, falling in love with her intensified them. Far from making him take refuge from the world, she spurred him into making closer imaginative contact with it. All experience, no matter what its nature, became charged and alluring because of his feelings about her: a faith healer, an Edwardian summer, books. There is no mention of Maeve by name in any of these poems – not even a 'she' or a 'her' – but the fact of her existence helped to bring them into being. She was his secret sharer. Monica, his more public sharer, had the benefit of being acknowledged as his friend, but also had the pain of hearing (as he says in 'Talking in Bed') 'more and more time [passing] silently'.

It wasn't only by immersing himself in his writing that Larkin hoped to prevent the crisis he knew was looming. As before, he also relied on the library. It was the beginning of a historic decade for the university: student numbers were still increasing rapidly (1,660 in 1960–61, 4,000 by 1970), and to cater for their needs the library boosted its acquisitions by 95 per cent between 1960 and 1963. The number of Larkin's staff rose from twenty in 1960 to over ninety by the mid-1970s; the book stock trebled; and the overall grant increased sixfold. By as early as 1962, according to the reckonings of the University Grants Committee, Hull had the highest percentage figure for library expenditure of any university in the country. The 'pony' that Larkin had inherited was well on its way to becoming 'a Grand National Winner'.[18]

As existing subjects were reinforced, sections dealing with new subjects were inaugurated and ancillary services developed. These included some obvious necessities (the Photographic Department), and some more surprising developments. Larkin arranged, for instance, for the purchase of a complete run of *Picture Post* (1938–57); he bought a large number of Trollope first editions; and he acquired the manuscript of *Novel on Yellow Paper* by Stevie Smith – a writer he liked, who had been born in Hull. He also gave office space in the library to the journal *Critical Quarterly*, which had been started in 1959 by a young lecturer in the English Department, C. B. (Brian) Cox. Larkin admired the initiative, but spoke of Cox's doings in typically plaintive terms. 'We have *Critical Q*. in our building now,' he told Judy soon after the office had been set up. 'Cox's secretary gave me a practical criticism quiz that is to be presented at the coming

Scarborough weekend. I spotted seven authors out of nineteen ... Cox is slowly moving into the library, I fancy. He uses our lavatory constantly – I tell him I'm glad he finds the library such an essential institution.'[19]

In all this work, Larkin continued to count on the support of the Vice-Chancellor, Brynmor Jones. 'We were never close friends,' Brynmor Jones said after Larkin's death, 'but I did find him very charming while at the same time thinking he was totally uncommunicative. He would never talk about himself. I think people who have written about him have made too much of his poems and not enough of him as a librarian. He used to come to me and say: "Do you think you could raise another £20,000?" and I'd pretend to complain, and tell him I gave him a librarian's salary to write poems. We got on very well.'[20] When the Queen Mother arrived on 20 June to open Stage 1, Brynmor Jones made sure that she didn't ignore the librarian as her daughter had been instructed to do three years previously. He arranged for Larkin to accompany her on a tour of the book stacks, and for a photograph of her beaming beside him as she signed the visitors' book. 'I look pretty oily don't I,' Larkin said to Judy afterwards; 'I fancy my back stud is showing. I need a haircut too. And a shave.'[21] Jean Hartley also remembers him as simultaneously self-satisfied and self-mocking: 'He mimicked beautifully the Vice-Chancellor's lilting Welsh accent, "This is Mr Larkin, our poet-librarian," and the Queen Mother's piping reply: "Oh, what a lovely thing to be." '[22]

Larkin had every reason to feel his work in Hull was a success. Yet in the late spring 1960 he applied for the post of librarian at the University of Reading. As far as his colleagues and his mother were concerned, the move would be made purely for professional reasons. It would also, he knew, mean that he could avoid the approaching crisis in his feelings for Maeve and Monica. He was duly summoned for an interview and travelled south, spending the night *en route* with Bruce Montgomery, who was staying near the university. He arrived in Reading early the next day, looked around the town, toured the university and inspected the library – and abruptly scuttled back to Hull without attending the interview. The Reading authorities were astonished, and Larkin himself, when he recovered his composure, admitted that his behaviour had been strange. 'They said,' he told Eva, playing down the drama so as not to alarm her, 'that only once before – or was it never before? – had anyone declined a job before being interviewed.'[23]

Publicly (and more or less acceptably) Larkin gave the reason for his sudden about-turn as disappointment with 'the librarian's room, a hideous little den, dark and bare, not above twice the size of my present desk. I thought it was *impossible* for me to work there.'²⁴ Privately he realized that the very things which had driven him to consider the job in the first place were those which prevented him from taking it. Moving to another town would not free him from the two women in his life but force him to choose between them. He didn't want to leave Maeve, and he felt he couldn't abandon Monica. Before applying to Reading it was already obvious that his fears about the effect of Monica's bereavement were well founded. In March he had told Eva that she was 'very depressed and low. I sometimes wonder if she will ever get over all this: her work seems to weigh her down so much and she feels so alone in the world.'²⁵ In July he took her back to Sark for a holiday (after taking his mother to Minehead in Somerset for a week), but what should have been peaceful was dull:

We usually go for a walk in the morning – the island is so small you can walk anywhere – ending up in the village paper shop: the papers come in about noon. Then we have a drink and brood over the papers. Then we have lunch. After lunch if it is fine we go and sit on the beach and perhaps bathe, but it hasn't been the week for that kind of thing. Then we return to the hotel, change, and drink again. Tea is included in the bill, but it is just rotten tea, and accompanied only by biscuits, so we don't bother to have it, and eat dinner. After dinner we sit and read, or play Scrabble until ten, when we walk up the road to the Dixcart bar, at the hotel where we stayed in '55.²⁶

Once they were back on the mainland, Monica forced herself to finish the dreary and upsetting business of sorting out her parents' effects. Her sadness and her need of Larkin deepened, even though she knew she couldn't rely on him for practical help. 'Don't feel too badly about the red-eyed scavengers who come roaming round,' he told her:

The things are only things, and not parts of your parents now; and don't reproach yourself for letting them go, or not extorting enough – do you think I should like you more if you jewed and chaffered over everything? All through the animal kingdom the small are being robbed by the large and the weak by the strong. Just think as each thing goes 'One more load off my back!' All the same, I think a funeral pyre would be a great thing. Not only would it be more dignified: it would annoy people so! Clothes, hardly worn! A sheepskin rug! A lovely shawl! Wouldn't they squirm!²⁷

The tone here is meant to be heartening, as it more obviously becomes later in the same letter, when Larkin invents a number of mock pubs in which they might drown their sorrows: 'The Lecturer and Increment', 'Hoggart Himself' and 'The Light Meal'. As the bleak summer wore on, though, he became more and more defensive, guarding himself against Monica's sense of being 'so alone'. In one rare attempt to address her condition directly, he told her, 'From my point of view I don't resent you being near – not as you thought, anyway. It will be a pleasure to me to know you are comfortably settled no matter where it was, but easy access would be nicer. My only reservation I suppose is what you would think if I wanted to move. To people like me life is only bearable if they think they might move. Oh dear, this all sounds callous: it is so, perhaps. You mustn't think this is all I think about it.'[28]

As Monica's spirits foundered, he fussed in letter after letter about how he might fulfil his obligations without putting himself out. 'Monica is very keen on my visiting whenever I can,' he told his mother, 'since she is so low and unhappy and lonely, but I don't want to come at an inconvenient time for you. I could I suppose just go and stay at Leicester and not see you, but this means coming again to see you! And then I shouldn't be happy about returning without seeing Monica, as she really does seem so near giving up, or perhaps paralysis would be a better word.'[29]

Eva encouraged Larkin in such ditherings, since she didn't want to lose him to another woman. His hesitations were also fuelled by his feelings for Maeve. In December she took the first part of her Library Association exams; he had already admitted that he was 'much concerned'[30] for her success. After taking the exams, he took the first decisive step to turn friendship into courtship. He invited Maeve out to dinner 'as a reward', she says, 'for the hard work I'd put in. I had more to drink than I was used to – but that wasn't much! As we prepared to go home, he proposed calling a taxi to drop me off first and I exclaimed, "Heavens! I can't go home yet; I'm drunk." So the taxi was directed to Pearson Park where Philip sobered me up with coffee and I then left, promising that *if* I passed the exam I would return the compliment and take P. out to dinner.'[31]

On 7 February the following year, when Maeve had duly passed the exam, the second dinner took place. This time she and Larkin mixed innocence with experience even more seductively. 'It was a bitterly cold, bright night,' Maeve remembers:

and we went to the Beverley Arms [in Beverley]. On leaving, for some inexplicable reason, Philip did not get the hotel to call a taxi and we walked the half mile or so to Wednesday Market to pick up a car. Because it was so frosty underfoot, Philip took my arm which he did not release when we got into the taxi. Once at Pearson Park and from then onwards the course of our relationship was set . . . However, I was fully prepared for the memory of this evening to have been blotted out by the following day. This was by no means so and a few days later, after a brief trip to London, Philip gave me, with immense shyness and embarrassment, a bottle of Elizabeth Arden's *Mémoire Chérie.*[32]

'Set' as it now was, the relationship never became simple. Firstly, and urgently, there were difficulties about sex. Maeve says that because of her religion, Larkin felt he could not ask her to sleep with him:

My religion has always guided my behaviour: this is the very essence of Catholicism. This, in addition to my romanticism, meant that my attitude to sex was high-principled, idealistic and not to be indulged in outside marriage. Home upbringing, education and the time I was born all reinforced this, plus the fact that I'd led a sheltered life in this and other respects. Catholicism always did and still does mean a lot to me and I wasn't prepared to cut myself off from the sacraments. Philip knew how I felt on this score from the start – it is something I always make clear in the early stages of a relationship – and he never tried to coerce me. I think he respected my views.[33]

Maeve emphasizes that within these limits her relationship with Larkin was 'extremely sensual'.[34] Nevertheless, it was also bound to prove frustrating – and although Larkin never tried to force himself on Maeve during the seventeen years of their life together, he did make regular wistful appeals for sympathy. 'I found it hard to resist temptation,' he told her in March 1961 when hoping he hadn't 'embarrass[ed]' her 'by demonstrations of affection'.[35] Later in the same year he told her 'regretfully' that 'We haven't been very villainous.'[36] And in 1964 he wrote, 'Sometimes I want to write *very* passionate things, out of frustration I suppose, but they'd no doubt end up sounding embarrassing, like bad sexy novels. So you'll just have to imagine them – you know my general line of thought!'[37]

Dismaying as they were in some respects, the obstacles that Maeve built round her relationship with Larkin also suited him. He knew that by remaining inviolate Maeve preserved her romantic appeal. This had more than merely sentimental or moral effects; it also had poetic consequences. By keeping him in a state of erotic expectation, Maeve produced in Larkin a state of sensual eagerness which, combined with his wish to woo and please her, created the mental and emotional climate in which he was most likely to write. (He once told her that because of his erotic make-up, he was in a constant state of appreciation of her.[38]) Furthermore, her denial also comforted him in certain practical respects. He realized that as long as he obeyed Maeve's rules she would not 'hold the threat of marriage'[39] over him. Insisting on her independence might make him feel thwarted or jealous, but it was also a guarantee of his own continuing freedom. In defending herself, either by restraint or by cultivating a 'rather flirtatious façade',[40] Maeve was also protecting Larkin. She told herself that she 'wanted him to feel free to cut adrift from me if necessary';[41] she insisted on taking intrepid annual holidays – to Grenoble, to Bruges, to Freiburg – which Larkin regarded with 'admiration and romantic envy';[42] she heeded her mother's warning that she 'could not build her own happiness on Monica's unhappiness';[43] and she never stopped asking herself why, if 'Philip was not prepared to commit himself to me to the extent of forsaking Monica ... should I surrender my independence to him?'[44] In the process, and often causing herself much personal unhappiness, she gave the middle part of Larkin's life much of its intensity and interest.

Most of the evidence for Maeve's effect on Larkin lies in their correspondence. Many dozens of letters from her to him survive: affectionate, tender, enthusiastic and gossipy. Larkin regularly told her how much he enjoyed receiving them, especially those written in bed, which had 'an added fascination'.[45] Even when he was away on holiday with Monica he urged Maeve to stay in touch – sometimes with awkward consequences.

His letters to her – there are more than 200 of them – are as remarkable for what they leave out as for what they contain. His love for his 'Maeve, dear' is evident on every page, but the candour and intellectual companionship of his letters to Monica is absent. There is one practical explanation for this: because Larkin and Maeve were together in the library most days, he usually wrote to her only when on holiday with Monica – and therefore feeling hampered – or when staying with his mother in York Road – distracted, 'tense and full of suppressed rage', and 'irritated ... beyond words'.[46] But there is another reason for their restraint, as well. As he said at the outset of their relationship, Larkin 'always [felt] romantic'[47] about Maeve, and this meant that when speaking to her he habitually checked the more rumbustious side of his personality. There is no 'bad' language in his letters, very little anger (except occasionally towards his family), no meanness, no wailing, no sour politics, no broad gesturing or gesticulating. Their control is so strict that when Maeve eventually discovered 'the contrast in the values he showed to me (which accorded with mine) and the different values I discovered he revealed to others (in conduct and conversation as well as letters)', she felt that he had 'concealed' from her 'much of his true self'.[48] 'I wonder whether I really knew him at all,' she says. 'He had feet of clay, didn't he? Huge feet of clay.'[49] As far as she was concerned, during his lifetime, he was

a wonderfully chivalrous, even courtly lover . . . Throughout our entire friendship – i.e. the whole thirty years I knew him – he concealed the grosser side of his mind from me. When, after his death, I learnt about the pornography collection . . . I was astounded and upset: *I* felt degraded by the knowledge. I saw his cruel side, of course, but he learnt to moderate his invective if it concerned friends of mine or if I thought he was going too far.[50]

Occasionally the modesty of Larkin's letters to Maeve makes them seem – in their well-meaning way – deceitful. At the same time, they show him at his least selfish, least self-absorbed. Showered with 'dears', dotted with kisses, signed 'affectionately yours', and decorated with drawings of mice, they are smooth with confidences and well stocked with familiarities: library gossip, university news, chit-chat about colleagues. As the correspondence unfolds, it shows Larkin associating Maeve not just with romance but with kindness. In 1961 he refers to 'Dear, kind Maeve' as a 'kindhearted companion',[51] and in a copy of the New English Bible that he once gave her for a birthday he wrote, ' "Love is patient, love is kind and envies no one" because, he said, that summed me up'.[52] 'Kind' was a word which, in 'Talking in Bed', he had recently (in August 1960) struggled to reconcile with the truth of his feelings about Monica, reaching for 'Words at once true and kind,/Or not untrue and not unkind'. Near the end of his life, in 'The Mower', he would plaintively insist 'we should be kind/While there is still time'. By combining charity with excitement, Maeve linked her role in Larkin's ordinary daily life to her function as a 'fantasy figure'.[53] While developing her 'power over him'[54] she still allowed him to feel: 'self's the man'.

THIRTY-EIGHT

As Larkin complicated his private life he diversified his public responsibilities. Since becoming the regular poetry reviewer for the *Guardian* in 1956, he had written nearly fifty pieces of journalism. At the beginning of

1961 he augmented his literary criticism with another kind. Peter Coveney, warden of one of the university halls of residence, introduced him to the young music critic Donald Mitchell, who was spending a weekend in Hull; Mitchell, who worked for the *Daily Telegraph*, immediately suggested that Larkin become the newspaper's regular jazz critic. Within weeks it was fixed: on 11 February the first of Larkin's monthly jazz reviews was printed; he would continue producing them for the next decade. The result – as his collected pieces, *All What Jazz*, would make clear when it came out in 1970 – was both a pungently idiosyncratic view of the contemporary music scene and a means of defining his aesthetic opinions generally.

Although Larkin sometimes complained about the way journalism filled the time he might otherwise have spent on poems, he welcomed it as a way of occupying the evenings on which poems showed no signs of appearing. 'He took it very seriously,' Monica says; ' – you know, sitting up night after night, working really hard.'[1] One such labour now rewarded Larkin by bringing him a new and important friendship. For several years he and Monica had admired the work of a middle-aged novelist much favoured by the library market: Barbara Pym. Larkin's sister Kitty had first recommended Pym's books to him – 'the only clever thing to do with books she did in her life',[2] according to Monica. In an essay published in 1971, Larkin summarized Pym's virtues as being to do with 'conduct ... as well as love';[3] he felt that she defined a world of deep feeling made bearable by lightness of tone and exactness of eye. And 'what stays longest with the reader', he wondered, when this had 'all been acknowledged?':

Partly it is the underlying loneliness of life, the sense of *vulnerant omnes*, whatever one thinks of when turning out the light in bed ... then partly it is the virtue of enduring this, the unpretentious adherence to the Church of England, the absence of pity, the scrupulousness of one's relations with others, the small blameless comforts.[4]

It's clear from everything Larkin said about Pym that he thought her excellences were his own: a modest manner embracing large issues; infinite riches in a little room. But where he was reluctant to speak about his own work, he was keen to discuss hers. On 16 January 1961 he wrote to her, care of her publishers, 'I should like to give further consideration to an idea I had of a general essay on your books, which I might persuade the *Spectator* to publish in the form of a review of the next.'[5]

When Pym wrote back she signalled the beginning of a correspondence which would continue until her death in 1980, and draw from Larkin some of his funniest and most charming letters. They are also among his most public. Although he felt a genuine warmth towards Pym (genuine in spite and because of the fact that they didn't meet until 1975), he nevertheless addressed her as if he knew an audience was listening. He projects himself more dramatically than he does in other correspondences; he is more categoric in his prejudices – racial and otherwise. Within a year, for instance, he was telling her, 'I'm afraid I always feel London is very unhealthy – I can hear fat Caribbean germs pattering after me in the Underground.'[6] A year later still he was claiming, 'I have a great shrinking from publicity – think of me as A. E. Housman without the talent or the scholarship, or the soft job, or the curious private life.'[7]

The facets of his personality that Larkin parades for Pym are reactionary, little-Englandish, self-deprecating – and she responded in kind. Both of them hid their more acerbic and subversive natures, and neither inquired deeply into the other's circumstances. Larkin knew the obvious things about Pym. She had been born in 1913, educated at Liverpool and Oxford, had served in the Women's Royal Naval Service during the war, and in 1948 begun work for the journal *Africa*, publishing her first novel in 1950 (*Some Tame Gazelle*) and five more in the next ten years (*Excellent Women, Jane and Prudence, Less than Angels, A Glass of Blessings* and *No Fond Return of Love*). Everything else about her remained a sympathetic mystery. It was the same vice-versa: Pym was acquainted with Larkin's books and professional work but knew nothing of his personal life and never asked him about it.[8]

To the extent that Larkin ever shouldered Pym's worries, he did so knowing he would never be crushed by them. To the degree that he flirted with her, he did so confident that he would never have to worry about the consequences. With Maeve, as he had always suspected, it was turning out to be different matter. Throughout 1960 they had inclined towards each other almost imperceptibly, never speaking openly, never making gestures which those around them might interpret as other than merely friendly. After February 1961, and the second of their celebratory dinners, the momentum of their feelings had become irresistible. Their weeks were now shaped by the time they spent together. They went to the cinema. They drank in Pearson Park. They walked across the Wolds or travelled by train or bus to visit nearby churches or the seaside. Apprehensively, Larkin started buying more extravagant presents than the bottles of scent or little furry animals he had given in the past. (Six silver coffee spoons, for instance, a silver bon-bon dish, and a pearl pendant with the message: 'For Maeve, herself a jewel'.) Gradually, library staff learnt to leave Maeve's room when Larkin appeared, and expected him to call for her at the end of the day. University staff grew accustomed to seeing them together at public functions. Marion Shaw, for example, a lecturer in the English Department, remembers sitting near them at a poetry reading in Hull given by John Wain, at which Wain read Thomas Hardy's 'Lines to a Movement in Mozart's E-flat Symphony'. 'I saw Philip clutch Maeve's hand convulsively as the poem began,' she says. 'It's not often you see such naked emotion in public.'[9]

As the year went by, Maeve says that she started to feel 'exquisitely happy' with her new life in Hull, ' – and so did Philip. Temperamentally we complemented each other. I was outgoing, lively, and made him more sociable. He deepened my spiritual side, taught me to enjoy music more deeply, to read poetry out loud; he increased my sensual pleasure in things.'[10] Away from home, life was more complicated. Larkin rarely introduced Maeve to his friends outside the university (Conquest once glimpsed her in the back of a taxi in London, she met Judy Egerton once, and John Wain). It wasn't exactly that he was ashamed of her, though he knew she would seem like a country mouse, and realized that her looks were 'an acquired taste'.[11] Only his mother, he felt, could be relied on to appreciate her qualities properly, and he was right. As soon as she was introduced to Maeve, Eva recognized her as a woman of her own sort. Maeve in turn endeared herself to both mother and son by involving herself with Eva's life and worrying about her happiness.

Things were more difficult with Monica. 'I have built her,' Larkin told Eva at the start of 1961, 'in my own image and made her dependent on me, and now I can't abandon her.'[12] When Monica discovered his feelings for Maeve – which was almost as soon as he discovered them himself – she was 'utterly depressed'.[13] Larkin did what he could to rally her, but was hampered by his instinct for self-preservation. 'I'm terribly sorry you feel so miserable these days,' he told her in January, 'though not surprised – it is a most trying position to be in, and I should hate it and feel utterly down and out, hopeless, scared to death, just as you do.'[14] On his monthly visits to Leicester, and when she visited Hull, Monica begged Larkin to tell her exactly what was happening and yearned for reassurance. He lied to her, telling her everything was all right. 'Oh, he was a bugger,' she says now, remembering how she suffered. 'He lied to me, the bugger, but I loved him.'[15] It was the same in the letters he wrote between visits. Monica knew that if she appealed strongly for his support she was in danger of driving him away for ever. If she demanded to know what was going on she risked being branded a bore and a snooper. She tried to divert herself by making trips to the north of England to search for a place to live during the university vacations, when she didn't have to be in Leicester, but it was no good. After every excursion she was dragged south again by jealousy and anxiety.

For several weeks Larkin managed to hold his life in suspension. By balancing the rival claims of the two women he hoped to play them off against each other as he had done before (with Ruth and his mother, with Patsy and Winifred). He even, in the first two months of the year, found enough calm to write two poems – 'Ambulances' and 'Naturally the Foundation will Bear Your Expenses'. The latter is a piece of savagery aimed at an opportunistic name-dropper, an attack which relates to Larkin's immediate circumstances only in the most general terms (its speaker is a university academic). 'Ambulances' is much more elaborately connected: every imaginable pain in life, it says, is as nothing compared to the 'permanent and blank and true' fact of death. Elaborating its argument, the poem becomes a celebration of the values of consciousness. In Belfast, with less reason than now, he had admitted to a 'desire for oblivion'; in Hull, facing the greatest drama of his life, he clung to 'the unique random blend/Of families and fashions', which he realized he could not possess easily or for ever. 'All streets in time are visited' by ambulances, and all people are eventually:

> carried in and stowed,

> And sense the solving emptiness
> That lies just under all we do ...

'Ambulances', like all Larkin's best poems, modestly and devoutly collects evidence of ordinary life to create a truth which can be universally acknowledged. Within a matter of weeks it was personally experienced as well. On 5 March, without any warning, Larkin collapsed during a Library Committee meeting and was carried 'unconscious and incontinent'[16] – by ambulance – to Kingston General Hospital. He regained consciousness as he arrived, but was detained for a 'neurological investigation'. His doctor, Dr Cummings, was understandably concerned to find a precise cause, questioning Larkin about his medical history in general and his family's health in particular. Had any of them suffered from epilepsy? No, Larkin told him – but he had been experiencing some difficulty with his eyesight, and his own theory (supported by Maeve) was either that his shirt-collar had been too tight, or 'that some new glasses he had recently been prescribed were not in correct focus[;] his perseverance in wearing them had caused dizziness, followed by loss of consciousness'.[17]

Dr Cummings wasn't convinced and asked for a second opinion. When he discussed this with Larkin, he found 'the patient undecided partly because of his innate difficulty in making decisions which affect him personally, and partly because he didn't want ... any of us here to feel that he was unappreciative of what has been done for him'.[18] This was understating the case. In fact Larkin was in a panic, lying in bed writing despairing letters to his nearest and dearest. One person, he discovered in his misery, was nearer and dearer than all others: Monica. 'I still feel profoundly grim and frightened,' he told her on 12 March, shortly after she had visited him:

You can understand, can't you, that it's a very frightening time for me, this. Or it's a frightening time for a cowardly funk. I find it hard to put down anything that seems worth saying – and isn't abjectly funky. But to whom can I be frank, if not you? Though whether I shall be as anxious to be frank when I learn what's the matter with me I can't imagine. I suppose it depends what it is! ... It's not nice to wake into this world again – not a nice world at the best of times, but I should be better able to stand it if I knew I wasn't seriously ill. It's that that's undermining me at present. Is it silly of me to tell you this over and over again? At least I suppose it's a sign I *can* tell you. But to have to lie here, hour after hour, not feeling well, not knowing what's wrong, with a lot of grizzly speculation to choose from, and pretty off-putting meals every so often, yet ones which one feels one would be hungry for if one hadn't a grave disease ... And of course the knowledge that there is the X-ray to come and all that woe – oh dearest, do have patience with me.[19]

'To whom can I be frank, if not you?' Although no one asked Larkin a single question in Kingston General (or during his later tests) which might have revealed a psychological element in his illness, it nevertheless seems likely that the complications of his relationship with Maeve and Monica played an important part. He hadn't been able to deal with the drama any more; he had blacked out. Now, as he worriedly recovered, he was reminded of qualities in Monica which he had neglected in recent months. He realized how much he valued her familiarity, her companionship, her resilience. Day by day he leaned on her more heavily for support. On 13 March he wrote, 'All my symptoms are mild ones, but they don't show an inclination to lessen. Oh darling, there is so long to sit and worry and dread: I just can't keep from miserable worrying. Suppose there is something seriously wrong with my brain?'[20] Three days later he turned to her again, admitting for the first and last time that his condition might have been caused by something other than his glasses or his shirt:

I feel quite cast down and scared. All the grim devils are at my back, such as I needn't specify, and this place has begun to depress me: I feel frightfully alone and uncared for. Is all this a sort of breakdown? Should I 'try to buck up', and all that? It's not just feeling depressed: I feel depressed because my head still feels wrong: it isn't pain of any kind, but a kind of swimming giddiness that undermines everything I do, and makes it impossible for me to *enjoy* doing anything. And this in turn worries me and gives me a central apprehensiveness in the chest.[21]

A day later, still fretting, he was sent home. His mother came to collect him, taking him briefly to Pearson Park to pick up some clothes ('it seemed just completely strange,' he told Monica, 'as if I were a revenant, or someone coming back after ten years'[22]), then to recuperate in Needler Hall, the university hall of residence where his friend Peter Coveney was warden. Larkin took his time (Eva insisted on staying with him for several days), simultaneously consoled and depressed by a number of inconclusive tests. He went to Wakefield Hospital but 'the electro-encephalo boys ... found nothing amiss with my brain';[23] he had some more X-rays in Hull; then, he told Judy Egerton, 'after Easter my doctor ... arranged for me to go to Fielden House, Stepney Way, [London] EI for a tremendous going over. No doubt they'll find something in the end.'[24]

They didn't. Even though he was examined by the eminent neurosurgeon Sir Walter Russell Brain, had 'skull and chest X-rays, audiogram and ear, nose and throat examination; EEG again, another X-ray and X-rays of my stomach',[25] no obvious cause of his illness was discovered. Brain himself performed an air encephalogram, and referred in his notes on Larkin to a 'deep-seated abnormality in the left cerebral hemisphere', but could reach no firm conclusions. 'He has,' he said, 'epilepsy of late onset [Larkin was thirty-nine] with no positive evidence of an organic cause.'[26]

As before, Larkin was comforted to know that he was being properly looked after, but terrified by the thought of what might happen next. Also as before, he distracted himself by creating as much anxiety as he could in those around him. His mother and Monica took rooms in different London hotels so that they could see him regularly, and Maeve wrote him several letters to which he replied in slightly less 'frank' terms than those he used with Monica. 'One good thing,' he said valiantly, 'morally, anyway, about hospitals is that you can see so many people worse off than yourself: this makes you ashamed of any feelings of self-pity or undue self-regard.'[27] Over the next few days, as Maeve kept up a steady flow of 'sympathetic' inquiries, he came to value her kindness even more highly than he had done in the past. On 18 April he told her:

I don't connect [the letters] with flirtation or my taking advantage of you or your making yourself cheap or any other cliché of human relations: they are just one person showing kindness to and concern for another, and this is a jolly rare thing in my experience. Thank you, dear, with all my heart . . . I feel rather depressed and unwilling to resume a life which hasn't got much to recommend it – I mean it was a blind alley sort of existence, leading nowhere but THE GRAVE – of course it has become much pleasanter just recently, thanks to the indulgence of a certain kindhearted person (not an outstandingly successful description of you, but still).[28]

Other friends rallied round him too. Stephen Spender paid him a visit, and so did Kingsley and Hilly Amis. Conquest brought some cheering pornography. John Betjeman called and generously 'asked if he could help to pay the specialist's fees or any other medical expenses'.[29] It was an unorthodox place for their first meeting, but Betjeman's kindness quickened their friendship. 'He was much gentler and quieter than I expected,'[30] Larkin told Maeve.

Between them, his mother, lovers and friends managed to lift Larkin from his misery. On 24 April, a little over two weeks after arriving in Fielden House, he was discharged. Never again, until his final illness, would he suffer a fit of unconsciousness, and never again would the symptoms of his illness return. Back in normal life he continued to tell anyone who asked that the cause of his collapse had been his glasses or his shirt. 'I tried my rogue spectacles,' he told Monica when he felt fully recovered, 'the ones everyone said couldn't possibly affect me: at tea time I had a recurrence of the focus failure that prefaced my previous flop, so I hastily abandoned them.'[31] Neither he nor anyone else raised again the possibility that he might have had 'a sort of breakdown'. Neither he nor Monica nor Maeve did anything to change the circumstances which produced it. He felt as bleak as he had done after his initial collapse, when he had written to Maeve:

I'm beginning to feel I have little hold on life, or stake in life; I'm not only thinking of things like houses and wives and children, but more fundamental things like wanting things and getting them – I do believe that the happiest way to get through life is to want things and get them: now, I don't believe I've ever wanted anything in the sense of . . . a Jaguar Mark IX – I mean, although there's always been plenty of things I couldn't do with, there has never been anything I couldn't do without – and in consequence I 'have' very little . . . Perhaps I don't believe that one can 'have' things in any sense that makes it worth while putting up with them. But, whatever the reason, the result is a sensation of standing still, marking time, not getting anywhere, which wouldn't matter if time were doing the same but alas it isn't. I think I've come to the time of life now when you really feel the passage of years. At first one wants to get older in order to be grown up; then there's no difference between 25 and 26, it's just like wearing a different tie; but once past 35 it's impossible not to feel that each year is taking one further from what is desired and pleasant and nearer to what is loathed and dreaded UNLESS as I say you have wound yourself thoroughly into life by conceiving and gratifying a chain of desires.[32]

THIRTY-NINE

Larkin spent the ten days following his discharge from Fielden House with his mother in York Road. Now that one good reason for feeling gloomy was no longer available, others soon took its place. There was Eva herself, indispensable but infuriating; there was 'Sir R. B.'s bill . . . about a guinea a minute';[1] there was the prospect of having to plunge back into his complicated daily life. 'I feel intermittently depressed since being here,' he told Judy Egerton in May 1961:

The sense of approaching forty is strong upon me, and [of] having completely wasted the time of twenty to forty, when power should be greatest and relish keenest. Anything I do now will be a compromise with second or third best. I suddenly see myself as a freak and a failure, and my way of life as a farce. I suppose work normally shields one's eyes from home truths of this nature.

Or domestic ties![2]

Larkin had no more intention of creating 'domestic ties' with Monica now than he had done in the past, and no urgent wish to make them with Maeve either. During the years ahead he would sometimes confide to friends, 'There is one woman I ought to marry' (Monica) and 'one I want to marry' (Maeve; without telling Maeve, he even went so far as to buy and read a copy of the Catholic marriage service),[3] but for the time being he wanted them both in his life without being bound to either. He returned to Pearson Park intent on making his wish a reality. 'I'm feeling better now,' he told Eva in early June, 'really improved, [with] only very faint reminders of how I used to feel. So that's good.'[4]

Relief, and the kind of amorous excitement which didn't threaten his independence, immediately had their usual effect: he started to write. 'Funnily enough,' he said to Monica, 'the last poem I wrote (in January) was about *ambulances* . . . Little did I think how soon I should be in one myself. One of life's little ironies, as my favourite poet puts it.'[5] Another of Hardy's phrases, 'moments of vision', could equally well be applied to the new poems: 'The Large Cool Store', for instance, which he finished on 18 June after visiting the department store Marks and Spencer in Hull. (Maeve had recently bought a handbag there, and had described the shop in terms which appealed to Larkin.) The poem explores the differences between 'the weekday world of those/Who leave at dawn low terraced houses/Timed for factory, yard and site', and the tantalizing alternative which is summarized by the (faintly pornographic) 'stands of Modes For Night':

> To suppose
> They share that world, to think their sort is
> Matched by something in it, shows
>
> How separate and unearthly love is,
> Or women are, or what they do,
> Or in our young unreal wishes
> Seem to be: synthetic, new,
> And natureless in ecstasies.

'The Large Cool Store' struggles to reconcile commitment to himself with commitment to 'women', only to concede that they are 'out of reach'. In the next poem he finished, 'Here', this phrase appears at the end of a pastoral hymn to solitude. Arising from the continuing wrangle between his feelings for Monica and Maeve, it serenely celebrates the town- and landscapes around him. The poem is a 'swerving' journey up through England towards Hull, slowing down as it reaches the city to take in its 'cut-price crowd' and the objects and sights which define their existence, then swooping out beyond the suburbs into Holderness before stopping at the coast:

Here silence stands
Like heat. Here leaves unnoticed thicken,
Hidden weeds flower, neglected waters quicken,
Luminously-peopled air ascends;
And past the poppies bluish neutral distance
Ends the land suddenly beyond a beach
Of shapes and shingle. Here is unfenced existence:
Facing the sun, untalkative, out of reach.

In 'Here' (originally called 'Withdrawing Room') Larkin finds the kind of solitude which allows him to feel that he can belong in and around 'the surprise of a large town' while remaining 'unfenced'. Its lines are full of chariness but of commitment also. Ten days after finishing it, he swapped the exhilarating release of its flowing sentences for the confined and definite bleakness of 'Nothing To Be Said'. All activities, this new poem tells us, and all cultures 'advance':

On death equally slowly.
And saying so to some
Means nothing; others it leaves
Nothing to be said.

Where Larkin in 'Here' could rejoice in things being 'untalkative', now he is troubled by silence. In the face of death, not talking means either not thinking, or being too appalled to form any thought whatsoever. There's no doubt which sort of silence is Larkin's own, and early the following month, in the sonnet 'And now the leaves suddenly lose strength', he implied that he had been wrong ever to suppose that anyone felt differently. It is 'all men' who 'hesitate/Separately' as the year reaches its end: 'all silent, watching the winter coming on'.

Obviously this slowly darkening mood had something to do with anxiety about Monica and Maeve. Ever since returning to Pearson Park in June, he had been worried about re-creating the situation which had produced his illness, yet he had done nothing to avoid it. Maeve, who felt that while her love was 'increasing' it still didn't 'amount to any deep commitment',[6] struggled and failed to distance herself from Larkin as the year moved to its close. Monica, too, was determined to force a change. In September she ended her search for somewhere to live in her university vacations and bought a small house in Haydon Bridge, near Hexham in Northumberland. Two-up and two-down, white-painted, simple, on the main Newcastle–Carlisle road, it looked nothing at all from the front. At the back she discovered a kind of miracle: the River Tyne, seventy-five yards across at this point inland, rushing a few feet beyond the kitchen window – placid and muttering in summer, swollen and angry in winter, crashing branches against the old stone bridge which stands a short distance downstream.

Monica wanted the house because of this view, because her mother's family had originally come from nearby, because Haydon Bridge was an excellent starting-point for holidays and sight-seeing in the north of England, and because having a place of her own made her less dependent on Larkin. To start with he disapproved. He resisted such an obvious attempt to seize the initiative. He also, while pondering the journey that he would have to make in order to see her there, resented the effort, time and expense it would involve.

As soon as Monica had persuaded him to make his first visit Larkin changed his mind. 'I thought,' he wrote to her in April 1962:

your little house seemed (how fond I seem of that word) distinguished and exciting and beautiful: clever of you to have found it, bold of you to have furnished it in rabbit regency: it looks splendid, and it can never be ordinary with the Tyne going by outside. Others may have Swedish glass, or Swedish forks, or . . . theatre in the round around the corner, or a Picasso, or a stereo hi-fi, or a split level living area – you have a great English river drifting under your window, brown and muscled with current! Isn't my writing awful![7]

Haydon Bridge made Monica appear both adventurous and cosy to Larkin. She was his 'Bun' in her regency-decorated rabbit hole – someone who needed his comfort but also someone whose confidence he had to regain. He had hurt her, and she might take flight at any moment, yet because she had no one else in the world he was indispensable. Or so he had been telling himself, anyway. Soon after she had bought the house, he wasn't so sure. In their letters and conversations Monica had begun to refer affectionately to one of her research students at Leicester – a young man who was obviously also drawn to her. Larkin was in no position to feel jealous, but couldn't help himself. As he asked for reassurances, he admitted more openly than usual his need of her:

I imagine he *is* attracted to you, in that you are about two hundred times more interesting and amusing than anyone he is likely to meet, leaving aside the tremendous physical attraction you have (I say, I am piling it on, but you know what I mean – legs and body); but whether he is attracted in a straightforward way, or whether you give him the pleasure of being with a woman without the strain he would find with a girl of his own age, I don't know. I mean he would think a girl OHOA [of his own age] would expect him to make advances to her, which he might not want to do, because of being too shy and not wanting to be involved; and that you didn't expect this.[8]

For all their contradictions, such letters make several things plain. After two years of misery following her parents' death, Monica had at last begun to assert herself again, and therefore to challenge Larkin and rekindle his interest in her. Furthermore, she was able to offer him a place of exciting escape – away from the world they knew, away from Eva, away from Maeve – where they could behave as they liked. For a long time their relationship had evolved only in response to external pressures; now it could flourish naturally. In Haydon Bridge they lazed, drank, read, pottered round the village, and amused themselves with private games. Soon after the move, for instance, they began systematically defacing a copy of Iris Murdoch's novel *The Flight from the Enchanter* (1956), taking it in turns to interpolate salacious remarks and corrupt the text. Many apparently innocent sentences are merely underlined ('Today it seemed likely to be especially hard'). Many more are altered ('Her lips were parted and he had never seen her eyes so wide open' becomes 'Her legs were parted and he had never seen her cunt so wide open'). Many of the numbered chapter-headings are changed ('Ten' is assimilated into 'I Fuck My STENographer'). Even the list of books by the same author is changed to include 'UNDER THE NETher Garments'. They continued this precise but childishly naughty game for years, doodling through long evenings and wet weekends, and finally producing a bizarrely sustained performance: nearly 300 pages, every one altered to create a stream of filth, farce and clumping ironies.[9]

It would be easy to look on *The Flight from the Enchanter* (or, as it becomes, *The Shite from the Non-Enchanter*) as being purely scatological (which much of it is), or as a criticism of Murdoch's prose (which is never out of the question). It is also a window on to the most private areas of Larkin's relationship with Monica. For all the crudity and silliness of their alterations, they show a touching complicity. By sharing in Larkin's ribaldry and bawdiness, Monica offered things that he normally found only with a few male companions. Compared to her, Maeve was still a convent girl. (Twenty-five years later, when Maeve first read Larkin's poem 'Love Again', she didn't know what 'wanking' meant. If she'd read the unauthorized Murdoch she would have known that and a lot more besides.)

Yet Larkin needed Maeve's innocence. The secret thrill of Monica's dark river-fringed hideout was intense, but it couldn't release him from the bind in which he lived. Within six months of Monica's moving in to Haydon Bridge, Larkin was writing the poem 'Broadcast' for Maeve as he sat in Pearson Park listening on the radio to a concert she was attending in Hull, 'desperate to pick out/Your hands, tiny in all that air, applauding'. Two weeks later still, in 'Breadfruit', he was fighting shy of domesticity ('A mortgaged semi- with a silver birch;/Nippers; the widowed mum' and so on). By Christmas Larkin was once more confronting the fact that his own life contained a 'widowed mum' whether he married or not. A year which had begun with illness then contained a brief moment of release was ending with a reminder of the one certainty he had always known. 'I really have no sense of the future now,' he told Judy as soon as Christmas was over:

except as the approach of death: I suppose I don't really believe this or I'd be more depressed and frightened than I am, but it does seem barren of any hope in the usual directions of writing or sex or changing job. I seem to have got into a rut which, however comfortable, tends to frighten me whenever I realize how deep and narrow it is. Of course such ghastly festivals as the one we have just endured make life seem blacker and bleaker and generally more savourless. Or perhaps it is just this appalling cold, the whole hostile universe baring its teeth at one like some bald batwinged Chinese dragon.[10]

FORTY

New Year was never a time Larkin associated with new hope: after the dullness of Christmas, the best thing January 1962 could offer was the pleasure of being alone again. As the 'appalling cold' lessened, he slowly began to revive. On the 13th he finished the sonnet 'A slight relax of air' by saying 'All is not dead'. In the previous twelve months he had produced six poems; in the next twelve he wrote another seven, and also nearly twenty reviews, including important pieces on Hardy, William Barnes, Stevie Smith and Betjeman.

The first two poems to follow 'A slight relax of air' still focus on his apprehensions about women, but they do so in a way which is robust and unillusioned. 'Wild Oats' remembers his courting days in Wellington and admits that the pictures he keeps in his wallet are not just of Ruth but of her friend the 'bosomy English rose' Jane Exall. By comparing the two, Larkin lets us understand that the unattainable beauty, the untried experience, only keeps its bloom because it never becomes actual. The same point is elaborated in 'Essential Beauty'. The poem begins by extolling the world shown on advertisement hoardings (they 'face all ways/And block the ends of streets with giant loaves'), then reminds us that the 'unfocused she' they depict is impossibly perfect. Larkin can only enjoy her by ignoring the disappointments of the real world, just as he can most easily appreciate women at home by poring over their idealized pictures in magazines. Billboards, Larkin once told Thwaite, 'seem to me beautiful and in an odd way sad, like infinitely platonic essences'.[1]

As with writing so with work. After Christmas Larkin returned to the library with a greater sense of purpose than he had felt for months. In May the Project Committee began meeting to discuss Stage 2 of the building programme, and his colleagues turned to him, as they had done before, for guidance. Within a year of Stage 1 being completed in 1959 the university's Buildings Committee has asked him to prepare a statement of the library's 'ultimate spatial requirements'; now he was able to provide it. He asked for space for a million books and seats for a student population of 6,000 – a fourfold increase. It was the opening salvo in a long battle – not a battle against the Vice-Chancellor and the university, on whose support he could still rely, but against the slowness of committees, the difficulties of funding, the problem of matching his preferences to those of others. The Buildings Committee's first instinct was to drop the idea of the 'original [Stage 2] tower',[2] and to expand instead the existing building westwards into an 'enormous three-storey square'.[3] As soon as funding was secure, the young London-based firm of Castle and Park (later Castle, Park, Dean and Hook) were chosen as architects and sent the existing plans for consideration. Larkin waited apprehensively, knowing that whatever the architects suggested was likely to become his monument.

The Stage 2 Project Committee defined the shape of Larkin's working life for the next six years. It filled his days with meetings, minutes, sudden emergencies, disruptions to existing routines, panics about money, and arguments with other interested parties. Remarkably, he maintained the pausing rhythm of his writing and the more hectic negotiations of his private life throughout the whole long business. Someone less well able to divide their existence into discrete units might have short-changed one or other of their commitments. Larkin did them all justice. He was decisive about his needs for the library, determined to find time for writing, endlessly vacillating in his dealings with Monica and Maeve.

The Project Committee Chairman, Sir Basil Reckitt, agreed that the Chief Consultant Architect for the new building should be the university's regular adviser on such matters – Professor Sir Leslie Martin, about whom Larkin felt ambivalent. (Martin taught at Cambridge and had helped plan the buildings for the Festival of Britain in London.) Castle and Park turned out to be more to his taste. They had 'ghosted' work for Martin at Hull before, and although not long established had done a good deal of building for schools up and down the country. They were energetic and, as Maeve says, 'jolly'.[4] John Kenyon, who joined the Committee in 1965, called them 'chummy'.[5]

Once the appointment was officially confirmed in 1963, there began a series of monthly meetings for which Geoff Hook and Paul Castle – and, less often, Alan Park and Christopher Dean – would travel up to Hull from London for a day and a night. At all these meetings, Hook says, they were impressed by Larkin. 'He was able to by-pass obstacles by operating person to person. He knew it was a seat of the pants job, and therefore went straight to the heart of the matter, whatever it was. It was an extraordinary talent – if he'd been planning London airport it would have been the same. And he had this sane sense of humour; he didn't take the job lightly but he did realize there was something more important.'[6] While Larkin 'stuck like glue to a blanket' to the 'principle of flexibility',[7] he always moderated his demands by speaking helpfully, and in due course admiringly. At the end of each Committee meeting he usually joined Hook and Castle for a drink; on summer evenings he sometimes went with them (and, occasionally, Maeve) into the country nearby for supper in a pub. He also travelled with them on several of their visits to existing university libraries – in Birmingham, Newcastle and Sheffield – to explore alternative solutions, and was almost persuaded to visit Sweden 'to look at some flooring'. (He 'cancelled at the last minute for unconvincing business reasons'.[8]) Larkin, says Hook, was 'an ideal client – we never had disagreements, he allowed us to make mistakes, he always four-square believed in us when we got tetchy with the Buildings Office, and he never gave the impression he was going to fudge anything'.[9] Hook and company, said Larkin, were similarly co-operative. Using a typically deflationary image, he explained that the relationship he tried to create with them

was based on a card game I used to play when I was young – I've forgotten what it was called – but each player has a stopping card which can stop the game at any point. If I play the game of professional expertise, librarianship in other words, then the other two have got to say all right, let's go back to the beginning and start again. I'm not quite sure which card the architects should choose as their own – good architecture perhaps, by which I mean a strong streak of aesthetic rightness coupled with functional efficiency; and certainly the Buildings Officer has got to speak for his university on costs ... We all try to play our stoppers from time to time.[10]

When Castle, Park, Dean and Hook finally put forward a revised plan to the university, it met all Larkin's requirements. Shelving the two previous proposals, they suggested linking the proposed new building to Stage 1 at ground and first floor level; there would be no further integration. Because the site was restricted, it would not spread sideways but rise as a tower of seven storeys, each with its own band of sharply-angled windows. As the Project Committee considered this proposal, the Robbins Report on university education was published – in November 1963 – and the need for haste became obvious. Hull should spend, the Committee decided, while the going was good.

The Buildings Committee and Senate duly gave their verdict: work on Stage 2 should start in 1965 and be completed by 1968; the expenditure limit was £978,000; the architects would do the basic design and planning work, but Larkin would supply what practical help he could. It turned out to be a lot. 'Librarians need to learn a new skill,' he discovered; 'the art of drawing up a brief for an architect.' Commenting on a note of standards for air conditioning, planning modules, finishes, lighting, shelving, tables, fire prevention and other measures circulated by SCONUL, he wrote to their Secretary in 1964 asking them to publish

an ideal brief, which would include all the directions an architect requires but which a librarian might unthinkingly omit because he takes it for granted ... I make this proposal because I find myself engaged on the second major library building of my life without ever having been told how to draw up a brief or even learning what it is an architect needs to know before commencing work. If I am the only person in this predicament, then I gladly withdraw the suggestion but somehow I feel I am not.[11]

SCONUL gave Larkin what help it could, but most had to come from near at hand – from his own invention, and from his colleagues, in particular Brenda Moon, a sub-librarian he appointed in February 1962, and who later became his deputy. Born in north Staffordshire, she had read Greats at St Hilda's College, Oxford, then worked in London, Birmingham and Sheffield before arriving in Hull. Quiet, diminutive, easily overlooked in a crowd, she was nevertheless 'a little bomb'.[12] Larkin left an increasing amount of work in her care, though she insists that this was because he wanted 'to give people plenty of scope for initiative'.[13] She found him sometimes moody, sometimes 'almost cruel', sometimes 'the kindest person you could meet', sometimes expansive and sometimes shy – even now 'his stutter would sometimes return if he was going to say something important'.[14] He, in turn, found her a model of efficiency, rustling in and out of his office with a huge trolley laden with papers relating to the new designs. In the long planning stage which preceded the start of building in 1965, in the first burst of work leading up to the completion of the North Wing in 1967, and in the final stage which was completed in 1969, Brenda became his most trusted colleague in the library.

Another colleague, Maeve, was able to give a different kind of comfort, regularly having meals with him, meeting him after work, going on expeditions at the weekend when he wasn't in Leicester or Loughborough or Haydon Bridge. Monica, remembering the situation years later, is passionately fond and bitterly resentful. 'I loved him,' she says, 'but I couldn't make him love me enough.' She consoled herself by deciding that 'nobody could have succeeded'[15] where she failed, and bided her time, continuing to offer Larkin the companionship he could not find elsewhere, eager to believe him when he told her that his feelings for Maeve were fading.

Part of her reward, during the early part of this year at least, was a series of letters from Larkin in which he searched more thoroughly than before for the strengths and weaknesses in their feelings for each other. In May, for instance (the month Monica turned forty), he wrote to celebrate the sexual fulfilment he enjoyed with her and no one else:

Spring comes with your birthday, and I love to think of you as somehow linked with the tender green shoots I see on all the trees and bushes – linked in one practical way, perhaps – but also by your ever-fresh love of the real stuff of life, the beauty and comfort of it. I wish I could be with you and we could plunge into bed – I wished it yesterday *very* much. Do you remember putting on your red belt and openwork stockings? I shall remember *that*, a cataclysmic spiritual experience, like somebody's *Lear*. Ogh ogh ogh. You are really terrifically attractive.[16]

No matter how Larkin worked himself up, he couldn't forget his fears. A little later, in another letter, he told Monica:

It's curious, isn't it, the way that characters like mine and perhaps yours prove gradually to have a kind of oil and water relation to life – it isn't apparent at first, but as time goes on we assimilate nothing and adopt nothing, remaining stuck at where we started – is it that we, or I, never threw the six to get off the base, or are ordinary lives a succession of trunks and hatboxes gaily piled in on the frantic stowaway in the unlit cabin? I mean, I often think that the conventional accoutrements of house, car and kiddies must seem less like additional limbs than dreadful mistakes there is no escaping, leaving the person feeling in Hugh Kingsmill's words 'my heart's in the right place, but I am not'. But then it's 'a bit late to think of that'. I'm sure my father felt like that – it was a mistake, his own, but none the less irrevocable for that.[17]

As the weeks dragged by, Larkin searched more and more deeply for the influences governing his behaviour. His own fortieth birthday, on 9 August, provided a focus for his thoughts. 'Half life is over', he wrote in 'Send No Money' (which he finished on 21 August):

> And I meet full face on dark mornings
> The bestial visor, bent in
> By the blows of what happened to happen.
> What does it prove? Sod all.
> In this way I spent youth,
> Tracing the trite untransferable
> Truss-advertisement, truth.

In a letter to Maeve written when this poem was starting to brew – a letter which draws on other, earlier poems – Larkin makes much the same point. He tells her that the exercise of will, the ability to choose, the opportunity to direct his own life have all been denied him, not by force of present circumstances, but by something ancestral. In a sense his argument is designed to license his passivity, but this brings no comfort. It simply makes all the means by which people assert their humanity seem vain:

Looking back on my first forty years, I think what strikes me most is that hardly any of the things that are supposed to happen or be so do in fact happen or are so. What little happens or is so isn't at all expected or agreeable. And I don't feel that everything could have been different if only I'd acted differently – to have acted differently I should have needed to have *felt* differently, to have *been* different, which means going back years and years, out of my lifetime. In a way I feel I am still waiting for life to start – for all those things that are supposed to occur as a matter of course.[18]

All summer Larkin dramatized his dilemma in order to understand it more clearly. On holiday with his mother in the Lake District for a week he proved yet again that family life was 'boring, infuriating, *hell*';[19] opening the revamped Wellington library in early September he discovered that the past made him feel 'bored' and 'rather sad';[20] at a SCONUL conference in Aberystwyth he thought his future looked merely tedious. Returning to Hull in October, after spending a few days in Haydon Bridge, he regretted the greater warmth he had shown towards Monica earlier in the year: all his recent experience suggested it did neither of them any good. Perhaps, he asked her, the grinding stasis of their existence was due to some basic incompatibility? Monica replied that there were times when she thought they were 'wasting their lives' too. He was both cheered and chilled by her honesty, and wrote her another long analytical letter:

Well, of course I do understand and agree with that you say ... When I say I wish we could talk more easily about ourselves, I mean just that; I mean it seems strange not to, and I think it's something of a barrier between us, or a failure between us – it's difficult to know precisely what I mean: I don't say I want to bore you with my feelings, or be bored, so to speak, by yours, but I have a curious feeling that in some ways we are not in sympathy and this keeps off any kind of discussion that might reveal the fact. I have the continual feeling that you either know me too well or don't know me enough. Again, I suspect my own motives in 'talking': some holidays I have felt as they ended that I *must* get closer to you, that it was absurd, almost wrong, to be like this, but this time I felt it was that I simply wanted to get rid of my guilt feelings to enable me to carry on in the way I felt guilty about, which isn't fair. Anyway, I feel that you shrink from such talk, as from hens – indeed I do myself unless I can feel a sympathy in you to encourage me. But then what is the point of talking if there isn't anything in particular you want to say, or feel you can say? – By you I mean either of us of course. I can't say how badly I feel about the way we are wasting our lives: it terrifies me, and it gets worse every day.

My dear, I don't think you are incompetent, or whatever you said you were in your letter: I think you are very good at knowing what should be done, very good at not being afraid of doing it, and pretty good at doing it. Big things I mean. And little day to day things I don't know – you seem to *drag* rather, represented by your unwillingness to have the right time anywhere about, but I do realize – fully – really and truly – and lovingly and sympathetically – that you have, at Leicester anyway, *too much to do*. I understand, in a way, about not wanting people despite being lonely, but of course I behave badly about people ... I do think you dislike people more than I do, not that I like them enough to have them in the house.[21]

Supportive yet evasive, this letter was Larkin's last sustained attempt this year to try to explain his behaviour. It ends with him admitting to a 'queer disagreeable feeling' when he imagines Monica with her young Leicester admirer, and also with a promise that he is 'not, for the record, feeling attracted by Maeve again',[22] but neither of these things, nor his year-long self-examination, persuaded him to change the shape of his life. He would, he decided, stay whole by remaining divided, he would be kindest by being uncommitted, he would be as happy as possible by ensuring there were always good reasons for feeling melancholy. He had already told Monica it was a 'policy of seclusion',[23] one which would not so much remove him from the world as keep him alert on its margin.

Three poems written at the end of the year obliquely confirm these decisions. After months of revisiting his past (by means of self-analysis, by contemplating Ruth in 'Wild Oats', by returning to Wellington) he finished 'Toads Revisited' in October. It was more than eight years since he had discussed the advantages and disadvantages of work in the original 'Toads'; now (remembering 'an astounding hair-do, like a half-loaf or a leg of mutton'[24] that his secretary Betty had briefly tried the previous August) he stressed its value even more vigorously. As well as shielding him from his sense of failure, work also distracted him from graver thoughts:

> give me my in-tray,
> My loaf-haired secretary,
> My shall-I-keep-the-call-in-Sir:
> What else can I answer,
>
> When the lights come on at four
> At the end of another year?
> Give me your arm, old toad;
> Help me down Cemetery Road.

Within days of finishing 'Toads Revisited' Larkin wrote 'Sunny Prestatyn' and then, in early December, 'Love'. In the first, a girl on a poster is defaced and judged 'too good for this life'. In the second, the rival claims of self-interest and self-effacement in love are resolved into the claim 'My life is for me'. Whichever way people turn, the poems say, love lets them down: all images of perfection are unreal, all compromises are disappointments. Torn between his requirements for himself, his need for Monica, and his attraction to Maeve's romantic innocence, Larkin ensured that he possessed nothing entirely.

FORTY-ONE

Two years after he had fallen in love with Maeve, Larkin's divided feelings no longer struck him as exceptional: he was used to being in two minds, and remained so for the next several years. Sometimes there would be a crisis, sometimes one corner of the triangle would buckle, but more often than not he managed to preserve the difficult tensions and balances which gave his life its shape. It was an emotionally demanding and time-consuming business, and not one to which he had unlimited hours to give.

The reputation of *The Less Deceived* continued to spread. In 1960 it had even begun to make its mark in America, where St Martin's Press published an edition of 1,000 copies. It was respectfully but quietly reviewed, failing to catch much public support, but attracting the attention of a number of American poets. Robert Lowell, for instance, declared, 'No post-war poetry has so caught the moment, and caught it without straining after its ephemera. It's a hesitant, groping mumble, resolutely experienced, resolutely perfect in its artistic methods.'[1]

In Hull, the bald, stern-looking man who had once been able to prowl around town without attracting much attention was now a figure of curiosity. In the country at large he was becoming the subject of controversy. During the spring of 1962 the then much-respected literary critic A. Alvarez, compiling *The New Poetry* for Penguin, had attacked Larkin in his Introduction, charging him with 'gentility', neo-Georgian pastoralism, and a failure to deal with the violent extremes of contemporary life. Larkin had shrugged off the remarks more easily than he had done Charles Tomlinson's smaller-scale attack in *Essays in Criticism*. 'Al's intro,' he told Conquest contemptuously, 'is just a reprint from some crappy paper, quoting a whole ... poem of mine he hasn't paid for ... Says I'm badly dressed, too, which I take a bit hard.'[2]

Simplistic as its argument now seems, Alvarez's book was the first popular statement of 'anti-Larkin'[3] sentiments, but rather than quenching Larkin's reputation it added to his distinction. In its wake, he was even more frequently invited to give readings (he always declined), to comment on other people's poems (he invariably refused), and to introduce other writers when they visited the university (he couldn't always get out of it).

The previous November, for instance, Ted Hughes had given a reading in Hull – Ted Hughes whom Alvarez praised as he blamed Larkin in *The New Poetry*. Larkin had his revenge in private by telling Judy Egerton that Hughes's poetry 'struck me as appallingly bad read aloud' and added, 'I felt quite embarrassed for him, poor sod.'[4] (Thirteen years later Hughes returned to Hull but Larkin hadn't changed his mind. Hughes 'filled our hall', Larkin told Charles Monteith, 'and got a great reception. I was in the chair, providing a sophisticated, insincere, effete, and gold-watch-chained alternative to his primitive, forthright, virile, leather-jacketed *persona*.'[5] When Larkin later discovered the university photographer had snapped them together on the podium, looking as different as he described, he ordered a copy of the picture, framed it, and hung it in his lavatory.)

The more famous Larkin became, the more he worried about The Marvell Press. It was too slow to respond to orders. It couldn't distribute the books properly. When he remonstrated with George Hartley he disregarded the devotion he had once admired. Charles Monteith at Faber made sure this irritation never stopped bubbling. He had written to Larkin at intervals since the publication of *The Less Deceived*, met him occasionally, and encouraged him steadily. 'You remind me of a Catholic priest,' Larkin would eventually tell him, 'wondering why little ones aren't making regular appearances.'[6] Monteith was confident that when Larkin had a new collection ready, it would be offered to Faber. In April 1962 Larkin had told him, 'I should like to ... write three or four stronger poems to give the whole thing some weight';[7] when they met a year later he announced that the delivery of the manuscript was only weeks away.

It was preceded by a flurry of business. Early in 1963 Larkin told Hartley that he would be taking his new book elsewhere, as his contract allowed; Hartley was 'depressed'[8] but accepted the inevitable. In March Larkin finally severed connections with his agent Peter Watt, using as his excuse, Monteith said, the fact that 'P.W. didn't give him any practical assistance when he was making a contract with The Marvell Press ... and that the contract has turned out to be an extremely disadvantageous one from his point of view'.[9] In the same month, on the 21st, he had lunch with Monteith in London and discussed how *Jill* might be rescued from The Fortune Press. Since Larkin had never had a contract with Caton, Faber's solicitors reckoned it was 'no more than a fair business risk [for Faber] to proceed'[10] with publication themselves, which they would be especially happy to do, Monteith said, if Larkin were to write an Introduction.

Larkin went back to Hull with his publishing affairs in better shape than they had ever been. In the eighteen years since he had brought out his first book he had only once been in the care of a large well-established firm, and then for something (*A Girl in Winter*) which had ornamented but not made his reputation. Forced back on to a small press for his first mature collection of poems, cut off (to his advantage, sometimes, as well as his disadvantage) from London literary life, he had cultivated the image of a marginal or even alternative figure. Yet all the time his work had spoken in the accent of the Establishment; it was orthodox, formal, familiar and derived from middle England. By throwing in his lot with Faber, Larkin matched the manner of his publication to the idiom in which he wrote.

Larkin's lunch with Monteith marked a turning-point in their personal as well as their business relationship. Hitherto it had been amiable but restrained, conducted largely by letter, with Larkin striking the facetious note he habitually used as a way of seeming friendly while giving nothing away. (He once warned Monteith that the Greek wine retsina 'tastes of cricket bats'; on another occasion he sent him a postcard of a fox eyeing a partridge telling him it was a picture of 'a British author and HM Inspector of Taxes'.[11]) Now that he knew his writing would be inseparable from Faber, his friendship with Monteith deepened. He never, in the years to come, 'opened his heart and discussed his private life',[12] but he treated Monteith as a respected colleague and welcomed him as a companion.

In spite of significant differences between their backgrounds and characters, the two men had many things in common. Monteith had been born in Lisburn in 1921, the son of a devout Presbyterian, and had been educated at an English university – at Magdalen College, Oxford – then a rare distinction for a grammar-school boy from Belfast. He was awarded a shortened 'war degree', and in 1940 joined the Enniskillen Fusiliers before returning to Oxford when the war ended. Originally he had read English, now he switched to Law, progressing rapidly to the Bar and a Fellowship at All Souls College, but deciding after two years that 'I couldn't give Law my full attention. Whereupon I started casting around for a way to get back into books.'[13] Oxford provided it. A colleague at All Souls, Geoffrey Faber, suggested that Monteith join the family firm, which he did in 1953, becoming a director the following year and Chairman in 1976 (until 1981). By the time he first met Larkin, Monteith was already acknowledged as one of the finest publishers of his generation, traditional but enthusiastic, conservative but daring (it was he who signed up William Golding when a fistful of other publishers had turned him down; he also took on John McGahern and Seamus Heaney). His taste showed a balance of sympathies which reflected Larkin's own.

As Larkin settled down with Faber, there came an unexpected reminder of the vicissitudes he had known in the past. Barbara Pym, having sent her new novel *An Unsuitable Attachment* to her publishers Jonathan Cape in February 1963, got a letter from them in March saying they could not accept it. 'In present conditions,' she was told, 'we could not sell a sufficient number of copies to cover costs, let alone make any profit.'[14] When the response had 'sunk in',[15] she wrote to Larkin. 'I'm *astonished* at your bad news,' he replied, 'and really can hardly believe it. It seems *quite* out of character for a reputable publishing firm to turn down one of its established authors.'[16] Pym would not have been surprised if Larkin had let the matter rest there – she knew some of the other demands on his time, and she also appreciated his reluctance to get involved in arguments of any kind. In fact his initial outburst signalled the beginning of a battle for her reinstatement which lasted many years. Even as late as 1981, when Pym's star was once again in the ascendant and Larkin was writing an Introduction to the posthumous publication of *An Unsuitable Attachment*, he sent a letter to Tom Maschler at Jonathan Cape, inquiring about the precise terms of the novel's original rejection, but making it clear that no answer could possibly be satisfactory.

More immediately, he sent a stream of letters to Pym herself, reaffirming his admiration for her work. In July, for instance:

I really am puzzled about your book. Unless it is not as good as your earlier ones by some appreciable degree, I can't understand why publishers are taking this line. I have introduced several people to your work and they all like it (my sister introduced *me*): not everyone yearns to read of South Africa or Negro homosexuals or the woes of professional Rugby League players. Or not exclusively. Of course, Cape will have the sales figures, which I suppose cannot be gainsaid, but it seems a sad state of affairs if such tender, perceptive and intelligent work can't see the light, just because it won't 'go' in America, or some tasteless chump thinks it won't 'go' in paperback.[17]

It was the same a year later, when Larkin told Pym, 'I have been re-reading your novels in one fell swoop, whatever that is ... Once again I have marvelled at the richness of detail and variety of mood and setting.'[18] A year later again, when she still had no publisher in view, he tried to get Faber to take her on. 'I feel,' he told Monteith:

it is a great shame if ordinary sane novels about ordinary sane people doing ordinary sane things can't find a publisher these days. This is the tradition of Jane

Austen and Trollope and I refuse to believe that no one wants its successors today. Why should I have to choose between spy rubbish, science fiction rubbish, Negro-homosexual rubbish, or dope-taking nervous-breakdown rubbish? I like to read about people who have done nothing spectacular, who aren't beautiful or lucky, who try to behave well in the limited field of activity they command, but who can see, in little autumnal moments of vision, that the so-called 'big' experiences of life are going to miss them; and I like to read about such things presented not with self-pity or despair or romanticism, but with a realistic firmness and even humour, that is in fact what critics would call the moral tone of the book.[19]

Not even this special pleading could persuade Monteith, and Larkin wrote back to Pym dispiritedly. It seemed that all he could do, for the time being at least, was keep her reputation alive among his friends, and continue his correspondence with her. Henceforth, whenever Pym finished a new novel he would offer to read it, responding to each book honestly and – where necessary – toughly. When she sent him *An Unsuitable Attachment* in 1968, for instance, he told her that he 'found it a curious mixture of successful and unsuccessful: the characters are strong and credible ... but their destinies aren't clear, and they move briefly and jerkily, and without any sense of inevitability'.[20] Again, when she sent him the first draft of *The Sweet Dove Died* he said, 'I think it could be a strong, sad book, with fewer characters and slower movement.'[21] And when she gave him a version of the novel that became *Quartet in Autumn*, intending to call it *Four Point Turn*, he advised against, reckoning the title 'a little smart for so moving a book'.[22]

When not discussing novels with Pym, Larkin's letters to her remained as they had always been: witty, a little quaint, appealing to reactionary instincts. 'Why are *single rooms* so much worse than double ones?' he had asked her, typically, after his summer holiday with Monica in 1968. 'Fewer, further, frowstier? Damper, darker, dingier? Noisier, narrower, nastier? By the end of my time [away] I had had quite enough of cardboard partitions, brooms at 6.45 a.m., absence of bedside tables etc.'[23] In less kind and skilful hands, such droll theatricality might have led to a suspicion of insincerity – but Larkin's letters to Pym are completely genuine, even if they exhibit only one facet of his personality. Just as he divided his private life with Monica and Maeve into compartments, so as he grew older he was more inclined to show each of his correspondents the face he knew would please them most: slightly old-maidish for Pym, bloke-ish for Amis, doubly bloke-ish for Conquest, rueful for Judy Egerton, helpless yet dogged for Eva. The probity of his social existence demanded that a great deal of effort be spent making distinctions, while the integrity of his poems depended on his ability to draw on the whole range of his selves, and speak in all their voices.

In the 'three or four stronger poems' he wanted to finish before handing Monteith the manuscript of his new collection, Larkin aimed to harmonize these voices within a single structure. As things turned out he managed only to write a couple of poems before deciding the book was ready, and only one of them met this requirement. The first, 'Long Last', is a narrative of old age: in spite of its well-observed details ('Her neck was leaf-brown./ She left cake on the mantelpiece'), the poem struggles to generate the sadness and alarm upon which it must depend for its success.

The second poem, 'Dockery and Son', creates both these things, and more. Begun on 14 February and completed after fifteen pages of drafts on 28 March, it describes a visit Larkin had made to his old college at Oxford, St John's, on the way back from the funeral of Agnes Cuming, his predecessor as librarian at Hull, almost exactly a year earlier. (Agnes Cuming had died on 8 March 1962, and her funeral had taken place on the 12th.) The precise circumstances help to explain why Larkin describes himself as 'death-suited' in the poem, as well as illuminating larger questions of theme and mood. By permitting itself a great deal of novelistic detail ('Was [Dockery] that withdrawn/High-collared public-schoolboy, sharing rooms/With Cartwright who was killed?'), and a structure loose enough to give the impression of thinking aloud ('If he was younger, did he get this son/At nineteen, twenty?'), the poem makes room for nearly all Larkin's tones and techniques. It is anecdotal but lyrical, analytic but expansive, realistic ('awful pie') but metaphorical ('sand clouds'), reminiscent but locked in the present. Visiting the college does more than remind him of the divisions between past, present and future. By providing him with evidence of his youth, it forces him to look squarely at the issue which sits at the centre of his continuing debate about marriage: the issue of children.

There is no doubt in Larkin's mind about what he thinks of children. To Dockery, whose son is now at the college, they mean 'increase', whereas 'To me [they are] dilution'. Yet while the expression of the opinion is sure, the reasons for believing it are doubtful. Larkin's sense that his choices are made 'by something hidden from us' smothers the differences between his own and Dockery's life. It compels him to admit that the fears they have in common are more striking than the hopes which separate them. 'The whole passage,' Larkin once said, describing the conclusion of the poem, 'is saying that the different innate assumptions of our lives brought Dockery a son and me nothing, and that nothing patronizes me in the same way that Dockery's son no doubt patronizes him':[24]

> Why did he think adding meant increase?
> To me it was dilution. Where do these
> Innate assumptions come from? Not from what
> We think truest, or most want to do:
> Those warp tight-shut, like doors. They're more a style
> Our lives bring with them: habit for a while,
> Suddenly they harden into all we've got
>
> And how we got it; looked back on, they rear
> Like sand-clouds, thick and close, embodying
> For Dockery a son, for me nothing,
> Nothing with all a son's harsh patronage.
> Life is first boredom, then fear.
> Whether or not we use it, it goes,
> And leaves what something hidden from us chose,
> And age, and then the only end of age.

Bitterly funny and grievously melancholic, 'Dockery and Son' is a compressed autobiography. It encapsulates Larkin's views about the effect of his parents on his personality, it reports spiritedly on his undergraduate career, it grimly sketches the attitudes which dominated his adult life. Furthermore, its cunning deployment of epigrammatic wisdoms (culminating in 'Life is first boredom, then fear') ensure that the poem rises from its authenticating details to spell out general truths. For this reason alone it was a good last choice for the manuscript Larkin was preparing to send Monteith. On 11 June he made his final decision about which order the poems should appear in, gave them the overall title of *The Whitsun Weddings* and put them in the post. Two days later Monteith wrote accepting the book.

In the same letter, Monteith offered terms: an advance of £75 (it was usual at this time for Faber to offer their poets £50), and royalties of 10 per cent to 2,000 copies, 12½ per cent to 4,000 and 15 per cent thereafter. Larkin, without the support of an agent, replied that he wanted the royalty rate to rise to 17½ per cent after 7,500 copies but was told this would be impossible. He agreed, but Faber had been warned: in all their future business dealings they would find Larkin keen to drive a hard bargain. It was the same in America. In July of this year, when St Martin's Press (who had published *The Less Deceived*) offered to take 500/750 copies of *The Whitsun Weddings* and 1,500/2,000 copies of *Jill*, Larkin wrote to say he thought their terms were 'miserable'. Explaining why, he felt he was creating a 'verbal hedgehog'[25] but made no apologies. Defending his rights as an author, he was prepared to be almost infinitely prickly.

Two months after posting *The Whitsun Weddings*, and shortly before taking his summer holiday with Monica in Shropshire, Larkin sent Monteith the new Introduction to *Jill*. He had started writing it the previous April, while staying with Eva in York Road. 'My Oxford life,' he told Maeve as he began work, 'seems full of card-playing, late nights and drunkenness on two bottles of light ale. There is a pathetic note [in a diary] saying, "If I had a job in an office, I could get on with writing and go to bed early."'[26] The result of his labours, he now told Monteith, was 'not quite as serious as I originally thought. My purpose is to set up an unexplained contrast with the book.'[27] It was a purpose he achieved with spectacular success: compared to the pained and introverted world of the novel, the Introduction is rumbustious and high-spirited. Taking its lead from the reminiscence in 'Dockery and Son' about how 'Black-gowned, unbreakfasted, and still half-tight/We used to stand before that desk, to give/"Our version" of "these incidents last night"', it insists that while 'life in college was austere',[28] Larkin and his fellow-undergraduates were not. The effect is not just comic but candid – or apparently candid, anyway. While emphasizing that in Larkin's undergraduate days 'a lack of *douceur* was balanced by a lack of *bêtises*',[29] the Introduction conceals his own activities behind accounts of his friends. Norman Iles, the 'large pallid-faced stranger with a rich Bristolian accent', and Amis the imaginary-gun-toting mimic are given the largest roles, but Noel Hughes, Frank Dixon, Dick Kidner, Graham Parkes, Nick Russel, Edward du Cann, Alan Ross, Bruce Montgomery, Diana Gollancz and his tutor Gavin Bone all have cameo parts, usually one which finds them 'roughing up my general character and assumptions'.[30] In other words, we hear nothing significant about his work, nothing about Philip Brown, nothing about his difficulties with girls (and boys), nothing about his traumatic visit to Coventry after the Blitz. Providing a vivid impression of his milieu, he gives little clear idea of his role within it.

Soon after finishing the Introduction, it seemed as though Larkin might have to ask Monteith to make room for an extra poem in *The Whitsun Weddings*. It was, like many others he had written in the last couple of years, prompted by Maeve. Although he had told Monica the previous September that he was 'not, for the record, feeling attracted by Maeve', he nevertheless continued to see a good deal of her, both in the library and elsewhere. At the end of 1962, while he had been breathing life back into his relationship with Monica, Maeve had become involved with someone else. It didn't last for long, and when Maeve and Larkin turned back towards each other again, they found themselves facing familiar difficulties – difficulties about Larkin's attitude to marriage, and about Maeve's attitude to sex. She says now:

I marvel that our relationship remained so intense and yet technically so chaste for so long. Although the sixties were a time of immense sexual liberation ... *Vatican II* (1962) – and, later, *Humanae Vitae* (1968) – did not relax the Church's teaching on birth control or sexual behaviour in the slightest degree. In fact they reiterated its rulings in even harsher terms. Priests at that time were baffled by the renewed strictures of the Church in this area and were unable to help ... When I sought advice on one occasion I was unable to articulate my problem regarding even limited sexual conduct ...

It *was* a problem and weighed heavily on my conscience (I was once refused absolution in confession) and the last thing I wanted to do was to become pregnant – imagine the panic into which that would have thrown Philip.

... Thus the situation continued. I think in many ways it suited Philip not to have the guilt of sexual infidelity to Monica added to that of spiritual infidelity, and ironically at the same time he probably felt freer to indulge his romantic aspirations towards me.[31]

Larkin knew that during the most recent hiatus in his relationship with Maeve his attraction to her had been suppressed rather than dispersed, and suspected it might flame up again at any moment. The moment came in May, at the university's annual Staff Sports Club dance (encouraged, perhaps, by memories of Sam's feelings for Stella at the annual Rugby Club dance in *A New World Symphony*). It was an improbable occasion. Larkin's dislike of parties was well established, and so was his hatred of dancing. (Maeve would later try to teach him and found 'it wasn't very successful. He would just shuffle around, really rather awkwardly.'[32]) In his few later accounts of the evening, Larkin tried to make his decision to attend the party seem involuntary – a passive submission. 'On Friday Maeve magnetized me to a dance at the university,' he told his mother, 'where I felt my usual fish out of water self. However, people were fairly tolerant. I do think I ought to know how to dance and drive a car! How badly educated I was! Quite unfitted for the modern world.'[33]

Six weeks later, in June, Larkin began a poem, 'The Dance', which makes his feeling of being 'magnetized' sound more distressing than he could admit to Eva. Maeve remembers him turning up 'a bit like a spectre at the feast',[34] and in the poem Larkin is hideously trapped in himself, in a body he dislikes and attitudes he knows are politely aggressive. As he changes and sets out for the dance we hear about his 'contemptuous speech', his 'equally contemptuous glance', 'the shame of evening trousers', his 'scorn' and how he is 'lacking the poise' even 'To look about me' when he arrives.

This prologue is an excursion into self-disgust which is thinly disguised as disdain for others. When he reaches the heart of the poem he finds other forms of deception await him. 'Grinning my hopes, I stalk your chair' and then begins dancing. Immediately he discovers that his partner, like him, is acting:

> In the slug
> And snarl of music, under cover of
> A few permitted movements, you suggest
> A whole consenting language, that my chest
> Quickens and tightens at, descrying love –
> Something acutely local, me
> As I am now, and you as you are now,
> And now; something acutely transitory
> The slightest impulse could deflect to how
> We act eternally.
> Why not snatch it? Your fingers tighten, tug,
>
> Then slacken altogether.

A New World Symphony, at a similar moment, is full of sexual confidence; 'The Dance' is packed with anxieties. The speaker drifts to and from the woman, watching her dance with others, trying to make himself leave but failing, then dancing with her again. His movements are less like someone dancing than someone writhing on a spike of self-loathing, despising his own lack of experience ('It's pathetic how/So much most people half my age have learned/Consumes me'), and convinced that his awakened desire is a form of collapse – of feeling that 'something in me starts toppling'.

Within days of beginning the poem Larkin realized that he wouldn't be able to finish it in time to include in *The Whitsun Weddings*. Within

337

months he understood that he might never finish it at all. Within a year (on 12 May 1964), after forty sheets of drafts, he had abandoned it – though for some time afterwards he discussed with Maeve the possibility of working it to a conclusion, and on one occasion told her that he thought of it, in its unfinished state, as 'a great obstacle in my creative life: I shan't write anything until it's out of the way'.[35] Its five printed pages in the *Collected Poems* are a fascinating ruin, their fragmentariness powerfully reinforcing the poem's theme of incompletion. They are articulate about inarticulacy ('something snapped off short, and localized/Half-way between the gullet and the tongue'); their strong lyrical momentum describes a turbulent stasis; their glittering wealth of detail reflects two people's hidden feelings. 'Sexual intercourse began/In nineteen sixty-three', Larkin was later and famously to say in his poem 'Annus Mirabilis', which was 'just too late for me'. In fact sexual intercourse had begun with Ruth in October 1945. What happened in 1963 was that Larkin confronted, on the public stage of a Sports Club dance, clear evidence that the mutually destructive elements in his personality had hardly changed since he was a boy. Shyness and scorn nourished each other now, just as they had always done.

Larkin told Maeve that their evening together at the Sports Club dance reminded him 'how glad I always am to be with you'.[36] As well as rekindling their feelings for each other, it also showed him yet again how greatly her sexiness depended on her inaccessibility. Shortly after beginning the poem he remembered that Monica's greatly depended on her being available. In July, when they set off together for their annual holiday (this year to Sark for the third time), what soon 'started toppling' in Larkin was the resistance he usually felt to constant companionship. Writing to Judy Egerton from his room in the annexe of the Dixcart Hotel, he forgave his immediate surroundings – 'a grim shed with 15-watt lamps, jugs and basins, and coconut matting' – and praised the island as 'this jewel of the channel'.[37] It was the same when he returned to the mainland. Excited by memories of the holiday, Larkin wrote Monica a 'randy' letter, admitting that his need of her was quickened by 'visions'. He began by recording without comment that 'Kingsley is rumoured to be leaving Hilly permanently for ... E. J. Howard, as you'd put it', then mentioned the latest parcel from Conquest before turning to Monica herself:

Many thanks for your letter this morning, dear Bunny, dear one – somewhat aggravated the condition of randiness I've been in all the week, ever since getting those pictures! When you talk about hair under the arms and bare breasts and nipples and the like it makes me think of *you* in these respects and I get *colossally* excited, almost unreally really – well, really unreally, I suppose. As you once said, I dwell in my own imagination. I spend too much time on . . . visions – and honestly 95 per cent are about *you* – to be effective when I confront you in reality. I never know what you think about me – whether you think I'm loving or selfish – indifferent or what, or whether I just 'use' you, or if you think it's all rather unsatisfactory but better than nothing – I know you are always very delicate in not blaming me for the way I seem to leave you to yourself for years and years, apparently content with seeing you about once a month, and of course I'm grateful, I daresay I shouldn't like any more taxing attitude, but (I hadn't really meant to get into this sentence) I feel so *unsorted out* . . . getting kinkier every year like Dr Ward (according to the *News of the World*) and remorse [sic] for the sort of stalemate I have brought into your life – and mine! I *mean*, to put it a bit more simply, that it seems inconsistent to feel as I do about you and your lovely body (and you're quite right, you're absolutely luscious these days) and yet not get the sort of *guiding* pleasure from it that one can found one's life on, or that people do found their lives on – I don't mean in the women's magazine sense really as much as some less exalted way like having a comfortable chair or proper bedlight, at least on one level, but certainly in the sense of this is what I have been wanting and I'll put up with a good deal of minor trouble to keep it. Oh hell! I didn't really mean to start all this. It's you talking about putting elastoplast over your nipples and sending me into a sort of incapable trance all day. It's this mood that prompted the talk of Polaroid cameras – in one sense there's nothing I'd like more than photographs of you in your private clothes, or in no clothes at all, but I can't feel it's right when it seems more exciting than the reality. *L'art robuste survit la cité*, what?[38]

For all its circumlocution, this letter speaks to Monica more openly than any Larkin had sent her before. 'I am ashamed of my treatment of you and so awkward at explaining about it,'[39] he ended, without giving any indication that he intended altering his ways to admit her as a '*guiding* pleasure'. He was, in fact, both seeking to assure her that there was no one else like her in his life, and warning her that now the glow of their holiday had faded, he was returning to business as usual: the business of vacillating, Eva business, Maeve business, writing business.

There was, of course, library business, too. As he developed the special collections in his new building, he began to wonder what sort of provision other librarians were making for the preservation of literary manuscripts, particularly British literary manuscripts. In 1960, urged on by SCONUL, he had written to twenty 'leading British writers' (including T. S. Eliot, E. M. Forster and Graham Greene) to ask whether anyone had ever tried to buy their notebooks and papers. He had discovered an almost complete indifference on the part of most libraries, and when he reported his findings in a paper to SCONUL in March 1961 they were relayed to the Arts Council. The Assistant Secretary Eric Walter White had expressed an interest in establishing a national collection. Now, two years later, negotiations had ended and work was about to begin. An annual grant of £2,000 was agreed and the cumbersomely named National Manuscripts Collection of Contemporary Poets was formed. Its members were White, Larkin, C. Day-Lewis and two representatives of the British Museum. Their brief was to act as an agent buying those manuscripts they thought fit, then reselling them to the Museum. (Eventually, in 1967, their terms of reference were widened to include manuscripts of all imaginative litera-ture, and all university and all national libraries were encouraged to make known their particular interests.)

Larkin devoted himself energetically to the Manuscripts Committee. To show his good faith, he donated to the Museum in 1965 the manuscript book in which he had written most of the poems in *The North Ship*; he missed none of the thrice-yearly London meetings; he helped to assemble a collection which included material by W. H. Auden, Andrew Young, Peter Porter, Ted Hughes, Sylvia Plath, Edmund Blunden and Keith Douglas; and he wrote an introduction to a published checklist of holdings. 'All literary manuscripts have two kinds of value,' he insisted: 'what might be called the magical value and the meaningful value'[40] – and by 'manu-scripts' he didn't only mean 'the worksheets of a poem[. W]e could mean,' he said, 'the revised proofs of a novel, or even the engagement diary of a playwright. I think above all that a country's writers are one of its most precious assets, and that if British librarians resign the collection and care of their manuscripts to the librarians of other countries they are letting one of their most rewarding responsibilities slide irretrievably away.'[41]

Even when Larkin sent out his twenty letters in 1960 he knew that his plans would, if successful, have important implications for his own work. When the Manuscripts Committee first met, with the publication of *The Whitsun Weddings* only weeks away, the likely effect was clearer still. His own poems, with their sophisticated assimilation of jagged private feeling into smooth structures, would one day have their hidden workings pored over by biographers and critics. He never flinched, not until the final day of his life, when he urged Monica to destroy his diaries. The instincts of a good librarian, which he had evolved steadily through four jobs, were now solidly based and inclusive. He accepted that in seeking to save the papers of other writers he would also make it easier for his Executors, in due course, to preserve his own.

Monica, with whom his relationship had seemed steadier in recent months than for several years, told him in December that she was upset by his renewed interest in Maeve. She continued to complain of the amount she had to do in her job in Leicester, and to chide Larkin for not supporting her more enthusiastically. He was sympathetic in theory but not much help in practice. 'I do feel sad and depressed about your low state,' he told her; 'I feel I am responsible, having slowly reduced you over the years. Sort of paralysed you!'[42] To his mother he showed precisely how reluctant he was to let that feeling of responsibility turn into action. 'Monica has been very busy and [is] consequently tired,' he told her. 'I don't know why she doesn't get organized more . . . All these holidays lecturers have.'[43]

The year ended with Larkin's reasons for feeling blocked and static perfectly in place. Yet while he resented them bitterly, he still knew that his frustrations offered him a kind of protection. 'Never write anything because you think it's true,' he noted in a new manuscript book shortly after spending another 'ghastly'[44] Christmas with Eva, 'only because you think it's beautiful.'[45] In the poems which would eventually fill the book, he was as good as his word. The indecisions, lies and contradictions which often characterized his life with Monica and Maeve would be transmuted, dignified and sometimes even rarefied in virtually everything he wrote. What survives of them is love – or at least a finely judged, finely shaded attempt to love.

FORTY-TWO

Larkin complained to Judy Egerton in December 1963, 'There's a campaign afoot to make me *more like other people*, which involves much social effort.'[1] The main culprit was Maeve. Ever since he had started to 'topple' back towards her at the Sports Club dance she had occasionally lured him into other university gatherings; she also – inadvertently – encouraged him to take driving lessons: 'I am mad with jealousy when I see other men driving you to places which I would like to take you to,'[2] he told her. Maeve greeted the news about the lessons with mixed feelings.

Judging him as 'mechanically speaking . . . illiterate',[3] she appreciated that a car would increase their freedom. She also feared that it would allow him to see Monica more often and more easily.

Larkin had taken a few lessons in Belfast ten years earlier, but had given them up. Now he persevered, sometimes roping in Betty as an instructor (she was one of only three members of library staff who already had a car), and passed his test first time. He told Pym it was 'an extraordinary experience, and a quite unexpected outcome, as no one who had ever sat in a car driven by me held much opinion on my competence'.[4] Needless to say, his excitement wore off as soon as he was 'faced with the fearful onus of *buying a car*'.[5] After a good deal of bellyaching about expense he chose a Singer Gazelle with an automatic gearbox (Maeve's father had the same model), and immediately set about decrying it. 'I don't suppose I shall use it much,'[6] he told Eva, and to Monica he presented himself in letter after letter as an emasculated Mr Toad. 'Groogh,' he groaned when the Singer finally arrived:

what a day, get my first driving licence and my first car in it, six months less three days after I took my first lesson, creeping petrified round the park in low gear. Now I creep petrified along the road in no gear at all. Oogh, groogh, urrrghgh. Instead of the cross, the Singer Gazelle about his neck was hung. Oh dear, what have I done . . . I feel I ought to go out and see that I've locked the boot and that no one can steal my jack, spare tyre, etc. Oh dear! Isn't it all *untypical*! I feel as if I had somehow slipped through into a different character. Phew.[7]

Three weeks later Larkin had to deal with weightier matters. On 28 February *The Whitsun Weddings* came out, seven months before it was published by Random House in New York. In America, as had been the case with *The Less Deceived*, attention was modest and sales unspectacular (2,000 copies in two years, then a reprint of 1,500, in spite of an enthusiastic review by Christopher Ricks in the *New York Review of Books*). In England it was an immediate success: the first 4,000 copies were sold in two months, a further 3,000 in the next year, and two more reprints were ordered in the next six years.[8]

Larkin had arranged the thirty-two poems, he told Barbara Pym, 'to create a variety of mood: if you aren't enjoying one, at least the next one will be different'.[9] Yet for all their range, they describe a single and singular poetic sensibility. Compared to *The Less Deceived*, in which traces of Larkin's Yeatsian and Symbolist inheritance rub against a simpler manner, *The Whitsun Weddings* is a more uniform book. Its gaze is steadier, and it more precisely illustrates the qualities associated with The Movement, even though it appeared nearly a decade after The Movement had been identified. It tackles the big, central issues of ordinary life in the language of ordinary speech, and makes them numinous. Its details (posters, pet-shops, parents) are the details of the everyday; the truths it wrings from them are abiding. Intensely lyrical, it is nevertheless often discursive, speculative and argumentative. Deeply personal, it diversifies its origins until they become exemplary. Reviewers were quick to identify if not always to appreciate these qualities. A. Alvarez, for instance, writing in the *Observer*, felt the world Larkin described was too circumscribed and 'commonplace'. ('I'd like to know what dragon-infested world these lads live in that makes them so free with the word "commonplace",' Larkin told Monica. 'Pink elephants perhaps.'[10]) To those who felt the poems made the familiar strange (like Betjeman in the *Listener*, Enright in the *New Statesman* and Thwaite, anonymously, in the *Times Literary Supplement*), its achievement was correspondingly great. The book was the spring choice of the Poetry Book Society (the selectors were Ted Hughes and Ian Fletcher), and was awarded a prize of £250 by the Arts Council for 'the best book of original English verse by a living poet published from July 1962 to June 1965'.[11] It did more than confirm Larkin's reputation; it turned his voice into one of the means by which his country recognized itself.

Larkin felt he deserved his praise, and ordered one copy of his book to be expensively bound for him to keep on his shelves in Pearson Park. But it was those who criticized him who took most of his attention. 'People don't seem to deny that I'm good,' he told Eva, 'but oh, dear, I'm not what they want.'[12] The problem, as he had already indicated to Monica, was 'the word "commonplace"'. On the one hand Larkin was anxious to demonstrate that his poems dealt with the familiar thoughts and actions of familiar people; on the other, he insisted on his difference. In his response to his critics, therefore, we find him treading a thin line between defiant recognition of their accusations, and irritated repudiation. When people attacked him for showing excessive melancholy he protested that it was a universal condition; at the same time he agreed that he was a special case. When he was told that his world and personality were remote he both valued the information and denied it. 'Why all this remoteness?' he wondered to Monica. 'Never in my life have I lived in a town of less than 250,000 souls – except Wellington, and I suppose Oxford and Warwick. Tokyo isn't remote. California isn't remote. Majorca isn't remote. Oh no.

Just Leicester, Belfast and Hull.'¹³

A plain man, speaking plain truths about plain lives. A sophisticated man, creating beautiful and intricate artefacts to show all human complexity. These are the two versions of himself that Larkin encountered as *The Whitsun Weddings* was published. The plain version had obvious advantages. It exempted him from having to speak about his work in any elaborate or theoretical way. He told Eva that in the few interviews he gave around the time of publication he came over as 'a dull old dog'.¹⁴ The articles and reviews he continued to write reinforced this image. Providing the Poetry Book Society with a short piece to mark the 'heartening compliment' they had paid him by choosing *The Whitsun Weddings*, he wrote, 'once I have said that the poems were written in or near Hull, Yorkshire, with a succession of Royal Sovereign 2B pencils during the years 1955 to 1963, there seems little to add. I think in every instance the effect I was trying to get is clear enough.'¹⁵

In years to come Larkin would return again and again to defend this position, insisting that good poems are self-sufficient and don't need professional elucidators. To back up his argument, he intensified his campaign against anyone who felt differently, and in particular against those with modernist sympathies, who didn't agree that poetry was 'an affair of sanity, of seeing things as they are'.¹⁶ The main culprits – or 'the loonies', as he called them to Monica – were Ted Hughes ('embarrassing'), Thom Gunn ('every time some black-jacketed young sod thunders past me on a ghastly 450cc m'bike I mutter "Thom Gunn made you up, you sod, you noisy little bounder, you leper's death puke"'¹⁷), and Robert Lowell ('a Yank version of John Heath-Stubbs'¹⁸).

Originally Larkin's mature literary beliefs had been designed to resist what he reckoned were the rhetorical excesses of Yeats, Dylan Thomas and the Apocalyptic poets of the 1940s, and at the beginning of his career he had expressed them vigorously but comparatively tolerantly. Following the publication of *The Whitsun Weddings* they quickly hardened into a set of inflexible reactionary prejudices. In 1966, he said that his feeling about Yeats was '*Revulsion*', adding, 'I do side with him about poetry being natural, song-like and so on, though of course his own poems have come to seem unnatural to me.'¹⁹ By the same token, he took every opportunity to repeat in public the names of plain-speaking poets who formed his pantheon: Hardy, Edward Thomas, Betjeman (and later Stevie Smith and Gavin Ewart). 'The chief significance of Betjeman,' he had said in 'Betjeman en Bloc' (1959), summarizing the virtues of all those he admired, 'is that he is a writer of talent and intelligence for whom the modern poetic revolution might simply not have taken place.'[20] Amplifying this in a later essay, he said:

It is as obvious as it is strenuously denied that in this century English poetry went off on a loop-line that took it away from the general reader. Several factors caused this. One was the aberration of modernism, that blighted all the arts. One was the emergence of English literature as an academic subject, and the consequent demand for a kind of poetry that needed elucidation. One, I am afraid, was the culture-mongering activities of the Americans Eliot and Pound. In any case, the strong connection between poetry and the reading public that had been forged by Kipling, Housman, Brooke and *Omar Khayyam* was destroyed as a result. It is arguable that Betjeman was the writer who knocked over the 'No Road Through to Real Life' signs that this new tradition had erected, and who restored direct intelligible communication to poetry.[21]

With the years, Larkin's detractors added to their charge that his work was 'commonplace' an accusation that his opinions were old-bufferish. It isn't surprising. Throughout his life he steadily coarsened his hostility to the modernists. He meant everything he said, but he turned up the volume to the point at which his voice began to distort. He did so partly to make audible the things he valued, partly to protect himself, and partly to irritate those who automatically sneer at tradition. The appearance of *The Whitsun Weddings* confirmed that the hermit of Hull was a willing polemicist. The shy man who found it difficult to make friends was the defiant writer who was not afraid to make enemies.

A month after the book appeared, its impact was strengthened by the reissue of *Jill* (St Martin's Press published in America in August). Larkin anticipated the event with his customary hand-wringing, saying to Pym, 'one day ... the weeklies will have articles headed "From Immaturity to Decadence", "A Talent in Decline", "Gentility's Victim" etc. etc.'[22] – but in fact the novel only increased his reputation. In April he was elected a Fellow of the Royal Society of Literature, and the following year (1965) he was awarded the Queen's Gold Medal for poetry (he was disappointed that the award came through the post: he had expected to be summoned to Buckingham Palace).

Reluctantly, he accepted that his emergence as a public man would involve him in public duties. His shyness made them a burden, and he resented the amount of time they took. In March, for instance, he told his mother that he had agreed 'to conduct the meeting of the University,

College and Research group in Leeds' and found it 'awful ... Years of not speaking in public have left me rather inarticulate: I'm not afraid of stammering now, but I can't think of anything to say. It was ghastly.'[23] No matter what faces he made in private, he performed his duties with a good grace, and although he shrank from the thought that other writers might send him their work, he responded thoughtfully whenever he judged it worthwhile. In 1965, for example, he told Pamela Kitson, 'your poems are hit or miss, rather verbose affairs, remarkably articulate and at times vivid, but essentially conversation, not poems'.[24] To John Hall, over twenty years later, he wrote, 'Many thanks for sending me your poems, which I'm afraid caused tears at breakfast, some of them are so *very* moving. I loved the last lines of "Juliot" – just the sort of thing I should like to have done myself.'[25] There were other, less personal ways of helping writers, and Larkin was equally conscientious in pursuing these. While still refusing to read his own work in public (pleading, as ever, 'laziness and a feeling that one never meets an author in the flesh without perceptible disappointment'[26]), he consented to sit on the board of the Poetry Book Society, and in March 1966 agreed to join the committee dispensing the Eric Gregory Awards to young poets. Over the next several years he helped to provide funds for – among others – Paul Muldoon, James Fenton, Douglas Dunn ('a small muttering bearded Scotsman ... studying at this university'[27]) and Seamus Heaney ('both his work and his personality impressed everyone very favourably',[28] Larkin told Monteith).

Thorough and decisive, Larkin dispatched literary business with the same energy he showed in university affairs. A month after publication, however, *The Whitsun Weddings* brought another and less easily predicted demand. In mid-March, he received a letter from a young film-maker, Patrick Garland, suggesting that a TV programme be made about his work as part of the BBC's Monitor series of films about the arts. Over the past several years, first as an Oxford undergraduate and then in the early stages of his career in theatre and television, Garland had occasionally written out of the blue to Larkin, telling him how much he admired his work. Even such gentle preparation seemed unlikely to win him round now. 'Naturally,' Larkin wrote back from the library on 24 March:

I appreciate the compliment of your suggesting that I might co-operate in a film based on the poems I've written, and I should like to thank you for this further example of the kindness you have shown me over the last few years. At the same time I am very doubtful about taking up your proposal, principally for two reasons. The first is that I refuse most suggestions that I should rave, read, recite and madden round the land, on the grounds that I am very shy and very busy and so on, and I think if I were to give proof of my ability to conquer my shyness and my business it might render certain invitations (some of them very near home) virtually impossible to turn down. The other reason is I don't honestly believe that my appearance in a film such as you describe would do anything to help my reputation. I am not a particularly impressive personality, and I've always believed that it is best to leave oneself to the reader's imagination.[29]

Undaunted, Garland replied that 'impressive personalities' were neither here nor there: the film would show the same discretion about personal matters, and the same concentration on Larkin's work, as previous Monitor programmes had done about Graves, Pound, R. S. Thomas, Roy Fuller and Lawrence Durrell. Larkin began to waver. He respected Garland's commitment, liked him for his tact and enthusiasm, and was pleased to hear that if the programme went ahead his interviewer on camera would be John Betjeman. It would be like talking to a friend, Garland told him, and would certainly 'help his reputation'. Larkin realized that if he agreed to co-operate he might open the floodgates to all kinds of other and less appealing invitations, but also felt that Garland was making him an offer he couldn't refuse. By late May (with the help of the Society of Authors) he had said yes, and accepted a fee of £130.

Filming took place between 3 and 10 June. Garland was keen to catch both Larkin's gravity and his sense of the ridiculous – whether he placed him with Betjeman on the Humber ferry looking towards Hull ('Larkin's country') with Lincolnshire behind them ('Tennyson's country'), or in 32 Pearson Park, or in Springbank Cemetery, or by the side of the River Hull among the debris of a 'fishy-smelling/Pastoral', or persuading him to bicycle towards a church and take off his cycle clips 'with awkward reverence'. Betjeman, speaking a little breathily and looking like a dishevelled bishop, ably supported Garland's efforts. His admiration for Larkin is evident in everything he says – even when, sitting among the gravestones of Springbank, he misquotes a line from 'Ambulances', diluting it from 'so permanent and blank and true' to 'so permanent and black and true'. To readers who had never seen Larkin before, the bald, slim, bespectacled man in the three-quarter-length pale fawn macintosh, nervously swallowing his stammer as he allowed the camera to follow him around town and then up to his flat for tea, was fascinating but also familiar-seeming.

By the end of filming Garland had won Larkin's confidence completely –

even if, as Larkin joked to his mother, the film had begun 'to seem like a programme about Hull introduced by John Betjeman. I suggested they should call it "To Hull with John Betjeman".'³⁰ When Garland had returned to London and seen the rushes he sought to reassure Larkin. 'For your interest,' he said on 30 June, 'you stand up very strongly to Betjeman and it is very much a two man show ... As for your reserves about the walk down the library, it doesn't look absurd at all, nor is it remotely Fritz Lang and rapist, but on the contrary full of authority and rather Wellesian.'³¹

All through the summer, as they exchanged letters, their friendship grew and Larkin's pleasure in the film intensified. In early September when Garland wrote to say the finished product would be broadcast on 12 December, Larkin responded:

My dear Patrick

Many thanks for your letter giving the news about 'Son O' The Trawlers' or 'The Fleet was my Daddy' as I expect your 28 and a half minutes is called by now – clearly your imagination has been soaring, and the only question was what kind of a film could be made out of the inexplicable scraps you found you had brought back with you. I can see it taking shape: Betjeman ('Uncle Ahab') shows me my father's grave: 'I 'e woor a reet skipper, was your dad, a great seaman, a great gentleman ...' However, I take to office work (shot of office), but the sea still calls (shot of me wandering about on dock) until heredity exerts itself and after appealing to the Great Skipper for advice (shot in church) I join Uncle Ahab on his craft The Fishknife (shot of us roaring at each other in gale): 'By, you're yer dad all over again!' 'Shall I take in the top spinnaker a couple of notches, Uncle? The glass is falling like faces watching Monitor ...' I hope [the film] wins you golden opinions as I'm sure it will; the things you say about it all sound unavoidable (you make me sound rather a stuffy zombie) or encouraging (I was never quite happy about mingling New Orleans with Hull) – or perhaps this was another line: 'Hull! The New Orleans of Yorkshire! And dwelling in the Basin Street of the North-east is colourful balding book-basher Philip Larkin, who – '. Of course the prospect of seeing it terrifies me, but I look very much forward to seeing the pictorial effects.³²

Not having a television himself, Larkin and Maeve drove over to his friend John Kenyon when 12 December arrived. Kenyon's wife Angela remembers Larkin sitting tense and silent on the sofa holding hands with Maeve as the film was shown – but he need not have worried. The programme was well received and has remained widely respected. Larkin wrote to Garland with excited relief. 'Monitor was nearly the price of me,' he said. 'I had to drive about six miles into the country to see it, and get three-quarters drunk in order to withstand its impact, and then drive back in even thicker fog than had reigned earlier. All in all it is a wonder I am still alive. However, the programme seems to have been a great success with most of those who saw it, and I've heard a lot of praise for the film work as opposed to the poems or my own fleeting appearances.'[33]

Anyone reading these letters to Garland, praising him and appreciatively chiding him for his 'steely-gentle direction',[34] would get the impression of a sometimes self-deprecating but generally light and sunny personality. Their sense of the ridiculous is steadfast. Yet as Larkin was writing them he was enduring difficulties of which the film gave no sign. It was the familiar problem. While his feelings for Maeve revived, Monica's unhappiness increased. In the spring, just before work began on the film, Maeve had briefly visited France to attend a friend's wedding and had returned to England 'fired with determination' to have 'a romantic encounter'.[35] Larkin had concluded that their 'friendship' must therefore 'be coming to an end',[36] yet within a short time he had decided that the question of marriage was looming before him once more. He dreaded having to address it – even though he later told Maeve, 'I don't feel capable . . . of behaving as if I don't love you.'[37] In the past he had been able to avoid committing himself by appealing to Monica's plight. Now that Monica's independence was better established she was no longer such a good excuse. Monica understood this, and demanded that he make up his mind once and for all. She told him that if he had 'toppled' so far towards Maeve that he wanted to become her husband, then she (Monica) would be bitterly sorry but would at least have the satisfaction of knowing where she stood. If, on the other hand, he was still undecided about Maeve, didn't this mean he should therefore sever all intimate connections with her?

By July it was clear that another crisis was approaching. Monica suggested meeting Larkin in Hull, staying in a hotel so that she could occupy neutral ground. Larkin hesitated, vowing that he loved her, occasionally protesting that he was no longer 'seeing' Maeve, and usually making it 'obvious that he was lying'.[38] For as long as he could, he tried to persuade Monica to stay away:

Your various sarcasms about my inconsistencies are justified enough, but, or should it be and, I can't think of anything to say except that the thought of giving you up frightens me, like giving up one's home. The reason I didn't urge you to come here is that I think it's a pretty intense time when you do, I mean at present it would be more trying than a visit when one of us is in a hotel and there are periods when we can compose ourselves: I mean living *together* when there is a cause for disharmony is awkward and painful, or so I feel at the moment. I don't know whether it's worse than meeting under other circumstances, but I felt it might be just now.[39]

Monica had run out of patience with this kind of fencing. They must meet and talk, she insisted – if not in Hull, then in Haydon Bridge. Larkin agreed, and drove up to spend the weekend – cravenly telling Maeve, 'I shall hope to be agreeable to Monica ... and not make the visit a disappointment, but one can never be sure how one will behave.'[40] As always, the place worked its spell, and within hours he was admitting that he had been unwise ever to think he might marry Maeve. 'You mustn't apologize for crying,' he told Monica after he had returned to Pearson Park:

– cry all you need. It is not right to think you have to spare me the pain of remorse caused by my injuries of you, is it? I don't at the moment feel like going on with the subject – I'm sorry I caused you pain, especially in this half and half way. Anyway I liked the weekend, except as I said, that I feel the 'situation' hanging over our happiness rather ... But then I wonder if there *is* a 'situation' – do I *really* want an RC wedding with Maeve and a 'reception somewhere in Hull' etc. – I don't, of course, not really or even unreally. So then I begin to feel guilty about Maeve and I ought to confront her wearing a sandwich board bearing a résumé of these remarks. Anyway, dear, I wish I were with you now, especially if you are wearing your mauve dress. I really do. I hate my own behaviour these days and yet, God, it's pretty moral compared with some. I do send you kisses and would wash *your* dishes on any shift. This is a silly conclusion – perhaps I'm dizzied by the sun.[41]

Inevitably, they did 'go on with the subject' – throughout their August holiday in Westmorland, by letter during his mid-summer week away with Eva, and as a background to the editing of the Monitor film and the SCONUL conference he organized at Hull before the new term began. They fretted about it, too, while he tried to distract himself with more literary business: being interviewed by the young poet and literary critic Ian Hamilton for the *London Magazine*, and recording *The Whitsun Weddings* for George Hartley's series of Listen Records. (He spent an afternoon with Hartley making the recording, posing for a picture in a railway carriage at Hull station, and discussing what they should use as sleeve notes. In the end they decided to reprint Christopher Ricks's *New York Review of Books* piece about the collection.) By the autumn there was still no sign of a resolution. Larkin had done his best to convince Monica that the heat had gone out of his feelings for Maeve. He had tried to persuade

Maeve they could be friends, but she protested that she felt too strongly about him. 'She's very much in a mood,' Larkin told Monica, 'when if I don't hold out some hope of marriage she wants to sever all connections and advertise herself as free again. Nothing personal, I suppose! But you'll think it v. coarse. So it is compared with you.'[42]

No matter how much he flattered her, no matter how he played down his feelings for Maeve, Monica knew he was not giving her the whole truth. Were he and Maeve still in love? No, Larkin told her repeatedly – and at the same time wrote to Maeve: 'You know you are always in my thoughts, and it would be untrue to behave as if I were cheerily forgetful.'[43] The more loudly Larkin protested, the less Monica believed him. How could he prove it, she wanted to know. He told her it was impossible to prove, she would just have to trust him. Reluctantly, and very cautiously, she did so, putting her faith in a letter he wrote on 14 September:

Dear, don't, please, be miserable over this Maeve business. You've been extremely tolerant all the time and I shall be glad to have your sympathy, but I think we both feel this is the best thing at present. She is more upset than I, because it is she who has been rebuffed. I felt bound to say that I had not finished with you, nor did I seem likely to, and she just said, 'Well, that doesn't give me much alternative, does it?' and I couldn't honestly think of one. We are quite friendly, and have to see each other daily – the *real* break and dismay is yet to come, I feel. And I suppose it will come. This is like the interval between September 3rd 1939 and the first air raids . . .

I re-read ['No Road'] and thought how impossible to write anything *else* about this unpleasant affair – it's all there. Funny how one repeats one's experiences. Yet I ought to be able to say something even about the same experience, if only because I *know* it's the same experience. I'm afraid I have only to think, and I fall into a panic. All roads lead to a storm of hideous terror.[44]

For the remainder of the month and into the autumn Larkin continued to cast about for something 'to say', while keeping up the appearance of leading a calm and structured life. Work on the library continued. Committee work continued. He went to see Amis and his new wife Elizabeth Jane Howard in London. He visited Vernon Watkins at his home on the Gower Peninsula to try to persuade him to sell some Dylan Thomas manuscripts to the British Museum. (When the new term started Watkins – who was a friend of Garnet Rees, the Professor of French – paid the first of several visits to Hull. 'He came a number of times,' Larkin recalled, '. . . not every year, but often enough for our acquaintance to revive.'[45])

In November, at last, the silence broke. Larkin wrote 'Solar', the only poem he had finished since 'Dockery and Son' twenty months earlier, and one which revives the Symbolist style he associated with Watkins, and through Watkins with Yeats. It is as oblique an approach to his circumstances as 'No Road' had been direct. In the earlier poem he had explained his emotional situation, arguing about it and trying to solve it. Now he has nothing to do with the first person, and the 'you' is not a woman but a thing – the sun. The poem rises from the tangled mess of Larkin's private life to assert the pristine values of self-sufficiency:

> Coined there among
> Lonely horizontals
> You exist openly.
> Our needs hourly
> Climb and return like angels.
> Unclosing like a hand,
> You give for ever.

FORTY-THREE

As long as Monica believed him, Larkin could balance his conflicting interests. He kept up a steady flow of reassuring letters; he visited Leicester on his regular monthly journeys to see his mother in Loughborough; he maintained the long-faced humour and sighing efficiency which endeared him to his colleagues in the library. A few sharp-eyed friends noticed that as time passed his melancholy increased, but his sarcasms were often so funny, or so clearly comforting as well as cutting, that people seldom suspected how acute his unhappiness might be. He never confided in anyone apart from Monica – not Hull friends, not London friends. The difficulties of his indecision were hidden behind 'sophisticated wit', 'impersonations',[1] and bar-banter.

And behind the pretence of leading a dull life. When, in the spring of the new year 1965, John Horder questioned him about this in an interview for the *Guardian*, Larkin replied, '[Universities] are not ideal places for a poet to be, but was it Graves that said it's all right if he's just content to stoke boilers all day? I equate librarianship with stoking boilers. I lead a very simple life. I'm not the type of person who has always to be collecting theatre programmes or cooking Turkish dishes. I live overlooking a park with trees outside the windows and I've never got used to the idea that in summer I can't see across it but in winter I can.'²

If anyone pressed Larkin for further evidence of this restricted view, he was happy to provide it. He pointed out that his old friends – Amis, Montgomery, Conquest – were scattered, might write to him, but never visited him. His main London contact, Anthony Thwaite, had recently left England to work in Libya for two years. His friendship with sympathetic colleagues like Kenyon (and, formerly, Malcolm Bradbury, who had taught in Hull's Department of Adult Education from 1959 to 1961) were generally confined to the campus. The larger pattern of the university year locked tight around these routines. There were the thrice-termly Senate meetings, at which he would now sit with one hand cupped to his ear 'holding back on things which didn't concern him';³ there were the various weekly and monthly library meetings; there was the bi-annual SCONUL get-together – this year, in May, in Belfast. It was easy for Larkin to claim that nothing exceptional ever happened to him.

Or at least, to suggest that the only breaks in routine occurred in a private realm which was either of no interest to the outside world (in July, for instance, his camera was stolen – 'a disagreeable sensation',⁴ he told Pym), or off limits to journalists. One such disruption was the news, early in the year, that a report on X-rays which had been taken for reasons connected with his life insurance policy had been sent to Raines, the university Medical Officer, who had dealt with him after his collapse in 1961. Larkin wrote to Eva in a panic. 'You can imagine the fright this threw me into,' he said, 'as in the case of this X-ray "no news is good news", and probably the opposite is true also. I had a very unpleasant hour and then saw Raines who quickly put me out of my misery by saying it was just my old oesophagus again, not lungs at all. I'd been X-rayed after lunch and it was distended as usual I suppose. Needless to say I'd been dead and buried several times by then, and my grave well grassed.'⁵

When Monica received similar complaints, she was concerned but saw nothing unusual in them. Compared to the hectic letters of recent months, these outbursts of hypochondria gave every sign of normal service being resumed. Larkin's days, she believed, were reverting to their familiar mixture of work and – after a drought of nearly two years – writing. In February 1965 he siphoned off some of the pity he might have expressed for her into a poem protesting about animal experiments. It was a subject which troubled him increasingly as he grew older, as did all animal rights issues: on one occasion he even wrote to *The Times* about them and he joined the RSPCA. In the poem 'Ape Experiment Room', his feelings are dramatized by the contrast between the cartoonishly callous experimenter ('a Ph.D. with a beard/And nympho wife') and the imprisoned female monkey and her baby ('The bushy, T-shaped mask,/And below, the smaller, eared/Head like a grave nut,/And the arms folded round').

The reference here to the 'nympho wife' just about earns its place as a way of reinforcing the dichotomies of the poem, but it can't help seeming too pat for its own good. A month later its sexism, the kind in which scorn feeds off desire, was given a freer rein in 'Administration':

> Day by day your estimation clocks up
> Who deserves a smile and who a frown,
> And girls you have to tell to pull their socks up
> Are those whose pants you'd most like to pull down.

The same evening that Larkin wrote this squib, 3 March, he began another poem which mixes sexual frustration with the pretence of being able to rise above it. When composing poems, Larkin invariably worked very slowly, making many drafts. His progress was often hampered less by digressions, experiments and false trails than by the difficulties of retaining his chosen form with the sensuous reality of his original thought. His notebooks tend to show a recognizably finished product emerging in slow but steady stages: writing, he often said, was 'like laying an egg'. The new poem, which was originally called 'The Long Slide', was an exception to nearly all these general rules. It began:

> When I see a couple of kids
> And guess he's fucking her
> And she's taking pills or wearing a diaphragm
> I feel I am walking in paradise
> Where shame has dried up like dew
> And remember how all the writers
> Born eighty years ago said this is what we wanted
> And remember reading them twenty-five years back
> And lying thinking what this wonderful world would be like
> That held no one like them and no one like me
> And now it's here
> And God has wiped away all the tears from their eyes.

Three weeks later he returned to the poem, drafting its conclusion then immediately mocking it:

> Rather than words comes the thought of high windows
> The sun pouring through plain glass
> And beyond them deep blue air that shows
> Nothing, and nowhere, and is endless
>
> and fucking piss.[6]

'And fucking piss' stands at a slight distance from the last stanza, as a comment on it rather than a part of it, and yet the way it sabotages the high hopes of the preceding lines forms an important part of the poem's meaning. When it was finally completed two years later (on 17 February 1967), and its title changed to 'High Windows', Larkin trimmed his first thoughts into four quatrains, giving the impression that his sense of exclusion was not merely under control but also a kind of reward. In the drafts of the poem, however, we can clearly see what difficulties he has to master. The poem grows out of rage: the rage of unsatisfied desire, the rage of 'shame', the rage of having to persuade everyone that 'the thought of high windows' guarantees happiness. The poem's beautifully achieved shift from the empirical to the symbolic cannot disguise or subdue Larkin's appetite for what he has never had.

In November 1965, between starting and finishing 'High Windows', Larkin treated its subject in a less furiously personal way. 'How Distant' is a brief narrative of emigration, a condensed story of 'young men' who were 'keen/Simply to get away/From married villages'. They were people who – in the terms of 'Poetry of Departures' – were free to swagger the nut-strewn roads, making up their lives as they went. At the end of the poem it is their youth, their opportunity to begin their lives cleanly, which emerges as his main interest:

> This is being young,
> Assumption of the startled century
>
> Like new store clothes,
> The huge decisions printed out by feet
> Inventing where they tread,
> The random windows conjuring a street.

However longed-for, however cinematically exact Larkin made his descriptions, an air of unreality hangs over 'How Distant'. It advertises itself as an adventure locked in the past. If it happened at all, we understand, it cannot happen now – not for the author, at least. He is tied too strongly to the present; he cannot escape 'married villages'. As we grasp this point, we realize that the poem, like the others Larkin wrote during 1965, casts an angled but revealing light on his relationship with Monica and Maeve. It shows all the competing parts of his personality in a deadlock: the impulse to love and the yearning for self-sufficiency; the need for sex and the disgust at admitting it. It's hardly surprising that 'The Long Slide' toys with the idea of vanishing into a wide blue yonder. However improbable an escape into 'deep blue air' might be, it offered a temporary release from the struggle to reconcile disparate elements of the everyday.

Early in the summer, as he knew she eventually must, Monica discovered that Larkin had not been as good as his word about Maeve. She was distraught. Seizing the letter Larkin had sent her the previous year, in which he had said he wasn't seeing Maeve 'at present', she ringed 'at present' and wrote 'for five minutes' angrily in the margin. Elsewhere on the letter she added, 'Note the style, the irony slight, and no intention of doing anything like what is said. Perhaps style indicates. Both of you have my sympathy ... I was terribly upset by both of you while you were giggling together.'[7]

When Monica confronted Larkin with his betrayal he ducked and dived as best he could. He said he had always tried to persuade her he was 'no good': it was her fault if she had not believed him. Anyway, he went on, his unfaithfulness to her was more emotional than actual – it was she, Monica, who was the constant element in his life. As he struggled to explain, he was drawn into writing at far greater length, and in much greater detail than usual, eventually providing a résumé of their entire life together:

I've always tried to get you to see me as unlikeable, and now I must be getting near success. (Do you remember what must have been an early letter to you, certainly early in our affair, incoherently saying I was no good? I always feel I tried to warn you, insofar as a no-good person could.) I feel that as long as I was faithful, you could somehow accept the unsatisfactoriness of our relation – we might not be married legally, but we were different and perhaps superior – at least your sacrifice of yourself to me was superior to frog-marching me or anyone to the altar rails. But when I am unfaithful – not technically but spiritually – you can only feel duped and made light of, quite apart from the awful upsetting emotion, and you are wondering, I suppose, just how far you can put up with it, from all points of view.

Not telling you of the affair in the first place, or of its wan later resonances, was just infantile precaution – I didn't want to hurt you and I didn't want to give it up. I had in consequence more trouble with Maeve, who had to accept my departures and your arrivals, and our holidays – usually she did so resignedly, but she occasionally told me off. It could only have been accepted by someone as weak and selfish as myself.

This is beginning to sound like Middleton Murry! . . .

I don't think that letters are a good medium for this delicate exchange. I don't mind your allegations about Maeve, though I don't think they are true – they are your hated image of this 'real girl' (comparable to my envied image of the 'real man') rising up again. I think there's something unreal about my relation with her, as indeed there is with ours and mine with Ruth – in that it isn't 'serious' in the world sense of the word, i.e. leading to marriage and children. I don't say this is particularly comforting, but I think it's my fault. Oh well, I think this gloomy kind of oration is also unreal. Theorizing is flight. Rat flight at eventide. Rat's song at eventide.[8]

Larkin is apologetic in this letter but refuses to give ground. He reminds himself he isn't legally bound to Monica; he tells himself that he might no longer have the freedom of 'being young', but insists there's nothing on paper to say his life isn't his own. After posting the letter he waited for Monica to make the next move – and when she did, reassuring him that her anger hadn't hardened into all they'd got, he was welcoming but aloof. Even though every new crisis seemed worse than the one preceding it, he still refused to make a final decision in favour of either woman. 'The only good thing about today,' he replied to her ambiguously, 'except now, the house empty, the player playing, gin pouring in me, alone, alone, alone – I turn in solitude like a fish in its stream – was your very nice letter.'[9] It was a chilly sort of comfort, but one Monica was used to receiving. Trying to win him back to warmer ways, she begged him to spend a holiday in Haydon Bridge with her, even if it meant violating his wish to be 'alone, alone, alone'. He agreed to visit, acknowledging that his so-called 'private' life meant he was always turning from one woman to another – and then to his mother. Still urging him to visit, Monica teased him about this; he wrote back telling her, 'I think of myself "coming home at holiday time" just like the aimless undergraduate of twenty-five years ago – I am more aimless, really. He at least had his head full of "wanting to write".'[10]

When Larkin duly arrived in Loughborough for his 'holiday time', he once again felt cheated rather than cheered. He fell to brooding on the ways his life was shaped by other people's demands. Within a week he was furious – furious with his mother for her whining, furious with himself for not walking away. He wrote to Monica again:

Considering that my mother has wonderful health for her age and no financial worries, her constant barrage of grumbling – well, I don't know. I only know it fills me full of rage and irritation, as does and has and will my filthy family ever since we have known each other. My mother is such a bloody rambling fool that half the time I doubt her sanity. Two things she said today, for instance, were that she had 'thought of getting a job in Woolworths' and that she wanted to win the football pools so that she could 'give cocktail parties'. This sort of thing is said in the same tone of voice as all the other things, like going into a[n old people's] home and getting a carpet for the hall and being 80 next January and what the weather was like on her wedding day.[11]

Two weeks later, Larkin and Monica were on the 'lonely, surf-surrounded, bird-haunted, animal-inhabited'[12] island of Sark again, hoping it would restore their good spirits. For the first time, it disappointed them. Larkin missed Maeve and worried jealously about the attentions she might be receiving from other men in his absence. There was a more local problem, as well. 'A young layabout,' he told Maeve, 'has penetrated my anonymity and, being "himself a poet" not to mention a drunken mannerless insolent swine, makes it nearly impossible for me to go into the bar at night.'[13]

Returning to Haydon Bridge, Larkin sank gratefully into obscurity for a few days, and found once again that the place cheered him up. He returned to Hull in early October to face the new academic year with something like eagerness. His hopes were rewarded. At the library, work on the new building moved smoothly ahead; in his writing, an annoying problem was about to be resolved. The previous April, with no warning whatsoever, Caton and The Fortune Press had abruptly woken up to Larkin's growing fame and published 500 copies of an unauthorized edition of *The North Ship*. Larkin had been alarmed. He had no particular regard for the book, but nevertheless didn't want to lose the copyright. He consulted the Society of Authors and Monteith, who advised him that if Faber were to publish an edition this would sort things out. Larkin hesitated. The poems, he told Monteith, 'are such complete rubbish, for the most part, that I am just twice as unwilling to have two editions in print as I am to have one, and the only positive reasons for a second edition by you would be if this was necessary in order to secure the copyright, and to correct a few misprints.'[14] Monteith tactfully accepted Larkin's point about the quality of the poems, and suggested that he increase the interest of the book, as he had of *Jill*, by adding an Introduction and possibly one or two more poems dating from the period in which the original contents had been written. All summer Larkin delayed, then in September accepted, saying he would provide one poem ('Waiting for Breakfast') and a few remarks. Monteith sent him a contract on 13 September, offering an advance of £75, and Larkin at once set to work.

As he had done with the Introduction to *Jill*, Larkin created for *The North Ship* a context which was lightly self-deprecating. After sketching the poetic life of Oxford during his time as an undergraduate, he complained about the incompetence of The Fortune Press before focusing on the influence that Watkins and Yeats had exerted on him. Describing the way this influence was then dispersed ('If I were asked to date its disappearance, I should guess it was the morning I first read [Hardy's] "Thoughts of Phena at News of her Death"'[15]), he created a streamlined, portable version of the literary argument he had been advancing in reviews and articles ever since. He made it sound as though he had instantly swapped extravagance for good sense, vagueness for precision, imaginary worlds for real ones. His readers believed him, and have since referred to his conversion as something absolute and unchangeable. It was just what he wanted; while putting on a stylish and amusing display of candour, he managed to keep certain things hidden.

Once the Introduction was finished Larkin sent it to Vernon Watkins for checking. 'It's wonderful to look back to those days and see how you encouraged me,' Larkin told him. 'I think Yeats *was* a false fire as far as I was concerned, but he gave me great excitement at the time.'[16] To his mother he tried to sound more positive. 'Reading the poems through,' he said, 'I had a sneaking feeling that some of them weren't bad.'[17] To Monteith he was apprehensive. When he returned proofs to Faber the following January the whole enterprise seemed so dubious that he softened the tone of the Introduction in order to make Caton appear less villainous. 'When I came to read the poems,' he told Monteith, 'they seemed so abysmally *bad* to me that I felt the Introduction should have a much more apologetic tone, and indeed might well convey a sense of gratitude to The Fortune Press for having printed such rubbish in the first place.'[18] When the reissue eventually appeared on 15 September 1966, in an impression of 2,500 copies, it was lightly but respectfully reviewed. Most critics were content to see it as an interesting stage in the evolution of a poet they admired. John Carey in the *New Statesman*, Christopher Ricks in the *Sunday Times*, and Edmund Blunden in the *Daily Telegraph* were all appreciative. Elizabeth Jennings in the *Spectator* went one better by welcoming the poems themselves, as well as the information they gave about

Larkin's development. 'Few will question,' she wrote, 'the intrinsic value of *The North Ship* or the importance of its being reprinted now. It is good to know that Larkin could write so well when still so young.'[19]

As he finished the Introduction in October 1965, Larkin met one of the contemporaries he had been remembering. John Wain visited Hull to give a lecture, and Larkin held a drinks party in his honour, a party which contained enough comic incompetence to make their undergraduate days seem briefly real again. The lecture itself, which Larkin chaired, was 'very embarrassing'[20] he told Eva afterwards. It was immediately followed by a formal all-male dinner in the Senior Common Room, and while this was going on Maeve and Jean Hartley laboured in Pearson Park 'to prepare party canapés and drinks' for Larkin's and Wain's return. 'Philip,' Jean Hartley remembers, 'had gone to a good deal of unaccustomed expense to equip the sitting-room with extra bookcases and additional articles of furniture to impress John.'[21] When Larkin finally arrived he brought eight guests, but no Wain. Awkwardly, he poured drinks and showed off his furniture until at last 'the door suddenly burst open [again] and John came in, wild-eyed and haggard, leaving a trail of dead leaves and twigs. "I was sick in the park," he said, and subsided into a chair.'[22] Two days later Larkin felt strong enough to report on the evening to Eva, sparing her the details of drunkenness, and grumbling instead about expense and exhaustion. 'God don't people mop it up! All the cigarettes I put out vanished, all the bread and cheese I put out vanished, and the only reason all the drink didn't vanish was that I kept it in the kitchen and doled it out myself. One glass and one plate were broken, both belonging to Maeve, which was a pity. John got very drunk but was very nice about it. Oh dear, though, how exhausting I find such occasions.'[23]

As Jean Hartley says, it was very rare for Larkin to entertain at home, and significant that when he did so he installed Maeve as his helper. Whatever he was telling Monica, he continued to make no secret in Hull of his feelings about Maeve. He saw her regularly throughout the autumn, driving her to and from hospital in November when her mother was briefly ill, and taking her to see *My Fair Lady* in December (it was 'quite good',[24] he told Eva). As Christmas approached and he braced himself for his inevitable duties in Loughborough – duties he could at least now diversify by visiting Peter Coveney, his former Hull colleague, who was now working at the University of Nottingham – he realized that he was drifting towards yet another crisis.

In fact the new year, 1966, began with a surprise. For some time the

Oxford University Press had been discussing the possibility of commissioning a new *Oxford Book of Modern Verse* which would revise and bring up to date the anthology edited by Yeats published in 1936. Soundings had been taken among senior members of the literary establishment, and it had been generally agreed that the new volume, like its predecessor, should be edited by a distinguished poet – ideally, by one who would stamp his own personality on the selection without distorting the generally agreed shape of recent literary history. The Delegates at the Press thought that Yeats with his notorious hostility to Wilfred Owen had made his book more contentious than such an anthology should be. Their first choice as editor for the new volume had been Louis MacNeice, who had been approached in 1962 but died the following year. Then the Delegates decided that Larkin – formal, conservative – was their man. Dan Davin, who would in due course become one of the book's in-house editors, was instructed to write to him.

Larkin took the invitation as an honour. He told Davin he was 'most gratified',[25] and was reassuringly moderate in his assessment of what the anthology should contain. 'It is not the business of an Oxford book of this character to be eccentric,' he said, and indicated that his well-known feelings about modernism would be checked, and his affection for the native English tradition would issue in a fascinating display of neglected national treasures:

I am interested in the Georgians, and how far they represented an 'English tradition' that was submerged by the double impact of the Great War and the Irish-American-continental properties of Yeats and Eliot ... The major talents would be displayed, but my intention would also be to diversify the anthology with pieces from less familiar writers in whom the tone of the particular period was perhaps more distinctly heard. Searching for these might be the most interesting part of the undertaking. In general, however, my guiding principle would be to produce a collection of pieces that had delighted me, and so might be expected to delight others.[26]

The Delegates were content – almost. They worried that a 'special overtone' of 'experimentalism' lurked in Yeats's phrase 'modern poetry', and when Larkin told them he wanted 'to interpret the phrase as "Twentieth Century English Verse",' they were relieved. When this had been settled, it was Larkin's turn to pause; he warned them it would take him a long time to compile the book (in the event it wasn't published until March 1973, nearly seven years later). He had, he explained, his daily library work to do, he had the completion of Stage 2 to oversee, he had university business, and he had his own writing. Moreover, his investigation of Georgian and neo-Georgian by-ways would take time – they were presently only known on the evidence of received opinions, none of which he accepted. The Delegates replied that they understood all these things. There was no immediate hurry, they said; they were only pleased to find him so conscientious.

Pleased but not altogether surprised. As far as the outside world was concerned, Larkin's commitment to the business of poetry (not just the writing of it) was now deep and solid. He was already involved in work for the Arts Council, the Poetry Book Society, the Manuscript Committee and the Gregory awards. The compilation of the Oxford anthology seemed a logical extension of his existing interests. Yet in some sense his decision to accept the commission remains startling. For one thing, it involved a great deal of work which he, an efficient but a lazy man, was bound to resent. For another, his irritation with poems he disliked and his indifference to poems he found boring were as strong as his enthusiasm for poetry he admired. Furthermore, he knew that as he worked forward through the century he would be faced with the problem of choosing among his contemporaries: there were only a very few he could read with any enjoyment. He realized soon after signing his contract that he had taken on a job which would provide at least as much exasperation as 'delight', and which in the end would be likely to bring him as much opprobrium as praise.

Larkin alerted Anthony Thwaite, who was still teaching in Libya, and extracted a promise of help. Thwaite agreed that he would direct Larkin's attention to writers whose work he might not know, but make no final decisions about who should be included and who left out. 'I provided him,' Thwaite says, 'with views on who was definite, who was probable and who was possible. Seamus Heaney and Geoffrey Hill, I remember, were writ large. In the end, though, Philip would make up his own mind.'[27]

Larkin decided that at some stage in the future he would ask the university to give him a sabbatical so that he could have a long burst of reading to follow up his own thoughts and Thwaite's suggestions. Meanwhile he would pick off 'a few poets'[28] as and when his usual routine allowed. This turned out to be less often than he thought – and often less enjoyable, even when delving among writers he had expected to like. Month by month, year by year, the anthology turned into a labour. 'I'd always vaguely supposed that the by-ways of twentieth-century English poetry were full of good stuff hitherto suppressed by the modernist claque,' he would eventually complain to Judy Egerton. 'Now I find that *this isn't so*. Gibson, for instance – a lifetime of books, ending with the Macmillan *Collected Poems* just like Yeats or Hardy or Christina Rossetti: *never wrote a good poem in his life*, Grim thought. Endless verse plays! People like this make Rupert Brooke seem colossal.'[29]

FORTY-FOUR

As Larkin prepared for an assault on the pastoral narratives of the Georgians he produced an urban narrative of his own. In March 1966 he paid a brief visit to Eva in Loughborough, then hurried back back to Hull to meet Monica, whom he had invited for Easter. Arriving at the railway station, he discovered her train was late, and turned into the Royal Station Hotel for a drink. In the gloomy, almost-empty bar he found the image of 'a larger loneliness' than his own. Two months later, imagining the rooms upstairs, he began fabricating a miniature romance of solitude:

> In shoeless corridors, the lights burn. How
> Isolated, like a fort it is –
> The headed paper, made for writing home
> (If home existed) letters of exile: *Now*
> *Night comes on. Waves fold behind villages.*

Evoking the outlandishness and remoteness of Holderness, with its small communities dotted along the Humber, Larkin re-creates the Royal Station Hotel as somewhere that both represents the excitement of solitude and acts as a defence against it. The place embodied the ambiguity of his own feelings about loneliness, feelings he continued to keep alive in his treatment of Monica and Maeve. Since the crisis of the previous July he had managed to hold the balance of his interests steady. Now they were threatening to collapse again. He told Judy Egerton he was 'in pretty low spirits ... largely because of increasing dissatisfaction with me of Maeve and Monica'.[1] Later the same month he gave his mother an example of how he created this 'dissatisfaction' – in this case by appearing to act as Maeve's partner while telling Monica he was her innocent friend. 'Maeve is holding an Oxfam party next Saturday,' he informed Eva; 'I've promised to give a bottle of sherry as one of the prizes ... [Maeve] is on the Oxfam Committee and the object is to make money. I expect she will make a certain amount. You see how different she is from Monica – or from me, for that matter!'[2]

Did 'different' mean 'better', Monica wondered when Larkin told her about the evening? And were the links connecting them stronger than those which tied him to Maeve? Once again, Monica couldn't resist complaining and then apologizing for sounding jealous. He immediately tried to reassure her, writing to her in April:

Dearest Bun, dear, of course you don't have to apologize about Maeve. I know you're always fair, and would naturally hate the thought that you weren't being. You *say* the ironic things, though, which I suppose makes me think you think nothing else and are getting a distorted picture. I think you would be prepared to say she was nice, if you knew her, but you'd think her very dull and ordinary ... as indeed she is, some of the time. She's a mixture. She undertakes to sell Oxfam raffle tickets, then buys most of them herself because of the embarrassment of a refusal or two.[3]

As Monica struggled to contain her jealousy, it turned once more into self-doubt. She wrote to Larkin asking whether he thought she looked after him properly when they were together. She demanded to know whether he loved her as much as he had always done. She asked whether he no longer liked her 'rather special clothes'. His reassurances continued, sometimes to the point of making himself jealous. 'How many times must I tell you,' he asked, 'to the male mind *bright colours equal sexual provocation*? Before you know where you are, patrons of Pussy's pub will be talking about a "hot bit who lives at the end," then they will come and try your back door. Dear, be careful! I know it would upset you and I don't want that. Don't think I'm being nasty: I love your colours, but the general mind is crude, and a single lady is so defenceless.'[4]

Throughout the summer Larkin continued to play his double game, comforting Monica (he wrote her a poem in their amorous rabbit language, beginning 'Scratch on the scratch pad'), and at the same time clinging to Maeve. He fretted about the 'depraved lust-mad swine'[5] who surrounded Maeve at work. He apologized to her for his inconsistencies. He appealed for her indulgence. 'Sometimes,' he told her, 'I think Monica finds me as unsatisfactory as you do, and of course has more reason in *some* ways ... Of course [you and I] don't quarrel, or not without the aid of some third or fourth party.'⁶ When he went on holiday in August, he even encouraged Maeve to write to him when he was staying in Haydon Bridge. The letters disturbed Monica, who felt her private space had been invaded, and provoked another eruption of doubts. How could his feelings for Maeve have faded, she wanted to know, if they couldn't even bear to be out of touch for a fortnight? Once again Larkin protested that Maeve had told him she was fed up with waiting for him, and that at work they were 'too busy to see anything of each other even if we wanted to'.⁷ At the same time, he remained in close contact with Maeve, still flirting with the idea of marriage. He told her that she was 'the only person he'd ever met who (a) made him want to marry and (b) made him believe that marriage could work';⁸ he wrote her a letter reminding her that he 'thought a lot' of her 'though not very constructively, nor very decently for that matter. You know I'm never anything but happy to take you in my arms and enjoy that kind of kiss that seems to be your own speciality, or patent.'⁹

Monica, who knew nothing about these endearments, tried to believe the consoling lies that Larkin told her. By the end of the holiday she was convinced, even if the letter that he wrote her when he returned to Hull was rather too typically parsimonious for comfort:

The shock of parting from you ... after a fortnight's close association, is sharp, leaving me feeling rather dull and indifferent. But I feel I can tell people I had a good holiday – putting up at swagger hotels in beautiful scenery with a lovely woman eatin' and drinkin' my head off, I bet they'd envy me if they knew ... Thank you dear for all your kindness and tolerance and beautiful behaviour, like buying me mint cake and the flannel. I'm not sure you weren't a bit out of pocket on the final deal: perhaps not, as I call the petrol 5/6d. a gallon and said we got 30 miles for it, both errors in the right direction, though small ones.¹⁰

As the new academic year began, Monica's confidence continued to grow. Where Larkin's library business had once been the cause of only passing grumbles, leading her to suspect that he was being consoled by Maeve, now it loomed massive and weighty in his letters and conversation. 'I have never felt so busy before as I do now,' he told her, 'and so cast down otherwise. Well I don't know about cast down but this isn't quite the kind of life I expected ... Sometimes I wonder seriously how I can get out of it. I suppose I am trapped in my own personality, which of course is made by circumstances: I've never in my life felt I had a free will, have you? Like immortality, I could never see why anyone should

ever have imagined for a moment that it existed, except because they
wanted to. Then you see people like Kingsley!'[11]

Unable to 'clear out'[12] his days, unable to write 'one word'[13] in the
evenings, Larkin longed for something to explode in his life, changing it
utterly. At the same time, he dreaded any sort of upset. Early in October he
sent Monica another long self-analysis:

I slept very badly last night thinking about it all. I don't take any credit for this, for
really my thoughts were mostly selfish, I suppose – dread of being forced into
action. There isn't any need to make my situation any better-sounding than it is: a
self-centred person conducting an affair containing almost no responsibilities with
one girl, getting mixed up with another, heedless of the feelings of either. Well, not
heedless, but not heedful enough to do anything about it, anyway. I suppose one
reason I don't find it easy to talk about it all is that it doesn't bear talking about, if I
am to keep any self-respect. I also find it painful. The incident in July I half
mentioned [shortly before their holiday in Haydon Bridge] wasn't really epoch-
making: Maeve suddenly got very cross at my evident preoccupation with you and
said she was going to clear out for six months, and if I decided I wanted her I could
see if she was still available, and in the meantime she would do what she liked and
so on (as far as I can see she does that anyway). I didn't really respond to this, and
she found the separation so upsetting that she called it off, but it had left its mark.
Then her holiday came, then mine, then hers again, then you, then this week we
really haven't had any coincident time free. I suppose we are wondering 'how we
stand'. You may wonder why I don't end it, in my own interests as well as yours.
Partly cowardice – I dread the scene. Partly kindness – if I've encouraged her to
depend on me it seems cruel to turn her away. If she wanted to be free it would be
different. I could lose her completely easier than I could have her half-dependent.
And it's painful in a way to end something that however silly and inconsiderate did
at one time seem a different kind of experience from anything hitherto. All the
same, I think we are going in that direction. I only hope it can be done friendlily,
because we do have a lot to do with each other anyway. Never have the Gods of the
C[opybook] Headings been better exemplified: Don't Touch the Female Staff.

[Next day, Sunday]. Well, I wonder. If I send this, dear, it is because I want to
say something to you, and not seem to be trying to pretend the situation doesn't
exist. I wish it didn't now. I was ashamed on holiday when Maeve's letter or letters
came, not because there was anything especially amorous in them, but for seeming
so careless of your feelings and so bloody bad-mannered, even. It was incredibly
stupid and vulgar of me to spoil our holiday in such a way. I could quite easily have
said I didn't want any letters.

Darling, this seems far from the 'nice letter' you asked for: I am at home with
you and think you are delightful and irreplaceable: I hate it when you go, for the
dreary failure and selfishness on my part it seems to symbolize – this is nothing to

366

do with Maeve, you've always come before her: it's my own unwillingness to give myself to anyone else that's at fault – like promising to stand on one leg for the rest of one's life. And yet I never think I am doing anything but ruin your life and mine. I suppose one shouldn't be writing letters like this at 44, one ought to have got it all sorted out twenty years ago.[14]

Four days before writing this letter, Larkin had told Monica, 'I am not happy, and haven't been for a year or so, because of my situation, but we never seem able to talk about it.'[15] Monica realized this wasn't true. They were perfectly well able to talk about it, in letters at least. What they were unable to do was take action. Larkin knew this, but also hoped that by doing nothing the situation might evolve naturally. In the past, any developments had been short-lived; now he persuaded himself that there were signs of a deeper change. As he pondered the implication of telling Monica plainly that she had 'always come before' Maeve, he felt his affection for her increase. They had known each other for twenty years. They had invariably enjoyed each other's company when they were together. His letters to her became increasingly tender and concentrated. One Saturday late in October he even drove for two hours 'into the greying west' to '*see* her'[16] unannounced, before discovering that he hadn't brought enough money for petrol, and turning home. Back in Pearson Park he told her:

I feel I am landed on my 45th year as if washed up on a rock, not knowing how I got here or ever having had a chance of being anywhere else. Indeed, when I think of being in my *twenties* or my *thirties*, I can't call up any solid different image, typical and unshakeable. Twenties ... 1942–1951 ... thirties 1952–1961 ... Of course my external surroundings have changed, but inside I've been the same, trying to hold everything off in order to 'write'. Anyone would think I was Tolstoy, the value I put on it. It hasn't amounted to much. I mean, I know I've been successful in that I've made a name and got a medal and so on, but it's a very small achievement to set against all the rest. This is 'Dockery and Son' again – I shall spend the rest of my life trying to get away from that poem.[17]

Reading this, Monica believed that she and Larkin were closer now than they had been for years. No sooner had she received the letter, however, than she felt threatened from a different quarter. Early in November Patsy Murphy descended on Hull for a weekend, staying in the same hotel she had used on her previous visit. Monica feared she had succeeded in driving off Maeve only to make room for another rival, and said so to Larkin. He was offended. 'Oh hell!' he replied. 'You surely must know I'm not likely to cheat on you with Patsy.'[18] It was she, Monica, that he insisted he wanted – 'in openwork stockings, red suspenders, that shift, and the boots you won't buy . . . Delicious.'[19]

Monica's anxiety was understandable, but in fact Patsy's visit reinforced Larkin's wish to put his house in order. In Belfast Patsy had offered him fun without guilt; now, drinking and smoking heavily, she was 'somewhat depressing as a visitor, bringing with her an aura of death and madness in a general sort of way'.[20] On the Sunday evening, as she was about to leave Hull, she abruptly 'seemed unwilling to go' from Pearson Park, and created a 'fuss'. Larkin gave Monica a full account:

I couldn't make out what she was on about (I couldn't understand her very well at the best of times): she'd been blaming me for not being continental and so on: I suppose if I suggest that it was pique and depression at my not asking her to stay the night you'll hoot . . . and perhaps be right . . . No doubt she'd have liked to stay here but I didn't encourage the idea. Anyway, I got her back [to her hotel] about 2 a.m. and returned deeply depressed: it seemed a glimpse of another, more horrible world, quite a true world in a way, but one inhabited by people like Brendan Behan and not yours truly.[21]

Patsy's reproaches (accusing him of 'not being continental'), let alone her approaches, sharply reminded Larkin of how much now separated him from his earlier lives in other cities. He felt remote from his own youth and from young people in general. Patsy showed him that, at forty-five years old and after eleven years in Hull, he was acquiring the manner and expectations of an old man. She also convinced him – though it was not what she intended – that he was right to feel so prematurely vulnerable. As if her own 'aura of death' weren't sufficient proof of how fast he was toiling up 'extinction's alp', she also told him before leaving that Bruce Montgomery was now 'pretty well an alcoholic, looked after by a middle-aged secretary'.[22]

As Monica relaxed about Patsy, she promptly started to worry about Maeve again. Larkin fired off another salvo of reassurances, urging her to remember that Maeve felt so thoroughly rejected that she had taken up with someone else. 'I'm trying to keep things cool,' he said, 'without being unfriendly, but it's not easy . . . [Maeve] has had some sort of further session with the dopey married chap, through being rebuffed [by me], but I don't expect it means much. One thing about M., she's never idle. Hurt her feelings and she's soon making up to someone else, and letting you know about it. It made me feel a bit sick, but I don't know what else I can expect.'[23] (According to Maeve, Larkin was right; her new relationship didn't 'mean much'. It was purely platonic, and his jealousy excessive.) The day after writing this letter, when Monica reminded him of her own loyalty, Larkin returned the compliment lovingly, telling her, 'When I am most myself, then you are there.'[24] After they had spent a few days together in Pearson Park just before Christmas, he once again tried to assure her that their lives were at last settled. No one else, he said, combined the elements of fantasy that he enjoyed with the plain facts of being a 'real girl'. 'I never know,' he told her, 'whether we drink too much ("What? Too much? How, too much? Too much?") – We sort of immediately float off into a stylized unreality, but since that's a region I'm happiest in I don't know why I should suspect it, unless it's just for that reason.'[25]

Monica travelled up to Haydon Bridge to spend Christmas alone, and to wait for Larkin to arrive from Loughborough and celebrate New Year. She felt more secure than ever. If 'waves of sadness, fear, remorse, fear and all the rest of it wash[ed] over [him] periodically like the automatic flushing of a urinal,'[26] she told herself it was now likely to be for reasons which were nothing to do with her. It would be for reasons to do with writing, with the library, or with Eva. These things oppressed Monica but they did not exclude her. She could help Larkin deal with them in practical ways, and she could offer herself confidently as the person to whom he said everything.

She was particularly helpful about Eva. For years Larkin's relationship with his mother had been useful as a way of controlling his commitments to other women. Exasperating as she was, he needed her. Now, as she entered her eighties, she added a confused dottiness to the long list of characteristics Larkin found irritating. Within a few years it would be clear that she was suffering from Alzheimer's Disease; at this stage, though, he just accused her of being addled, and turned to Monica again and again to let off steam. 'I feel *full* of rage,' he said in one typical letter from Loughborough:

I used to spend my time here classifying [my mother's] remarks under *boasting* and *complaining*, but now there is a third kind, a kind of rambling natter, prefaced by the 'do you know what Mrs Somebody-or-other has done?' formula, which makes me writhe. She waits for a reply, which I refuse to give. This is called 'being grumpy'. I'll say it is.

People ought to get away from home as chickens get out of eggs, wholly, utterly, immediately, cleanly. What a frightful business it is! In Victorian times at least the bond was a financial one – you lived at home because you'd have to work if you didn't – you got something for your life being blighted. I suppose I shall become free at sixty, three years before cancer starts. What a bloody sodding awful life. Suicidal murder. And as I've said before, it's an irony of the whole thing that the people who *like* home get away ('I want one of these'), the people who don't are clawed in its clutch. What a bloody prospect.

I suppose I am selfish and all that, though I never feel I am except in a purely descriptive way ... What I am is irritable – a perpetual blazing bush of fury in my chest.[27]

So he was during Christmas. 'Mother up,' he wrote to Monica on Boxing Day morning, 'and my good humour vanishes as the continual monologue of boasting, complaining and threatening is resumed.'[28] By the time he reached Haydon Bridge he was nearly inconsolable with anger: slamming the door of Monica's house against the world, they drank themselves into their preferred state of 'unreality' and waited for the new term to drag them back to their responsible lives. It was a bleak interval, Monica accepted, but at least she had Larkin to herself. At least there was no Maeve waiting to entangle him when he returned to Hull.

If Monica had been able to read Larkin's diary during this time, she would have seen things differently. We can be sure of this (paradoxically) because soon after returning to Pearson Park in early January 1967 Larkin stopped keeping his diary for a while. He tells us so in the poem 'Forget What Did', which he began on 30 January (and didn't finish until 6 August 1971). The poem gives no reason for the break, but Maeve says it was because his jealousy of her new admirer was too painful to write down. He 'wanted them over', he says in the poem ('them' being the days of his distress):

> Hurried to burial
> And looked back on
>
> Like the wars and winters
> Missing behind the windows
> Of an opaque childhood.

In their place he wants placid descriptions of unruffled, natural things:

> And the empty pages?
> Should they ever be filled
> Let it be with observed
>
> Celestial recurrences,
> The day the flowers come,
> And when the birds go.

In the first part of the new year Larkin managed to keep his unhappiness to himself, or to pretend that its causes were to do with things and people other than Maeve. It was a precarious arrangement. Wishing to give Monica the impression that his life was hag-ridden by dreary chores, he struck her as being not merely busy but distant. Inevitably, she soon started to wonder whether he was seeing Maeve again. He told her to trust him and she tried to, turning over the evidence of 'ordinary life' that he provided as proof of his loyalty. Early in March he went to dinner in All Souls College, Oxford, with Charles Monteith, and found Bruce Montgomery was a fellow guest ('We resumed our conversation,' he said with relief, 'as if there hadn't been a ten years' gap'[29]). A fortnight later he had to be in Dublin – a place he found 'fascinating in its horribleness'[30] – for a SCONUL conference which was 'hell'.[31] A week later still and he was in Loughborough seeing Eva – and also Patsy, whom he had met briefly in Dublin and who now happened to be passing through the Midlands to collect one of her nephews from school at Downside. (This meeting, like their recent encounter in Hull, was 'rather depressing'.[32]) Larkin paraded all this activity in his letters to Monica, and added to it a mass of reassuring complaints about the library. At one point it exhausted and irritated him so much that he even considered applying again for the post of librarian at the University of Reading, which had once more fallen vacant. More resolutely than last time, he decided to let the chance pass by, and to concentrate instead on business already in hand. In March the North Wing of Stage 2 was completed (containing, among other things, the Poetry Room and the Rare Books Room), and at the same time a small ceremony was held to give the building its new name: the Brynmor Jones Library, in honour of the Vice-Chancellor who had done so much to fund its expansion.

If Monica still needed convincing that he hadn't the time to pursue Maeve, let alone the inclination, he could always point to his writing as a reason for keeping himself to himself in Hull. During the last five years he had finished only three poems he would judge worthy of inclusion in his next collection. Now, feeding off his suppressed rage with Eva and his withheld longing for Maeve, he completed four in five months. The first was what he would one day call his 'ultimate symbol of freedom from . . . restrictions',[33] 'High Windows', which had stalled for nearly two years and was finally revised on 12 February. The mocking sign-off which ended its earlier draft ('and fucking piss') was virtually reproduced in June, when after a couple of evenings' work he finished 'The Trees' as follows:

Yet still the unresting castles thresh
In fullgrown thickness every May.
Last year is dead, they seem to say,
Begin afresh, afresh, afresh.

2 June 1967. Birthday of T Hardy 1840. Bloody awful tripe.[34]

This afterthought, like the one added to 'High Windows', sabotages the
serenity of the lyric which precedes it. Larkin cannot let what he described
to Maeve as his 'astonished delight at the renewal of the natural world'[35]
emerge unchallenged. There has to be an acknowledgement, in the privacy
of the manuscript book, anyway, of wishful thinking. There has to be a
pre-emptive and self-protecting irony. (One of the best-known photo-
graphs of Larkin, taken by Monica at Coldstream on the England/
Scotland border during their summer holiday in 1962, does the same thing
in different terms. The picture shows Larkin sitting demurely, ankles
crossed, on the large sign which says 'ENGLAND'; immediately before
posing he had urinated copiously just behind the word.)

A fortnight later, in 'Annus Mirabilis', the ironies are all in the open:

Sexual intercourse began
In nineteen sixty-three
(Which was rather late for me) –
Between the end of the *Chatterley* ban
And the Beatles' first LP.

Like 'High Windows', this poem compares the apparent freedom of the
present with the miserable repressions of the past ('A shame that started at
sixteen/And spread to everything'). This time, though, we gather it is not
Larkin's fault that he missed out but society's: he was simply born too
early to benefit from the sexual revolution of the early 1960s, and there-
fore had no option other than to become a victim of shyness, fear and
ignorance. The first time Larkin asserts this, in the opening verse, we feel
he wants us to take him at face value. In the fifth and final verse, which
nearly but not quite mirrors the first, it's clear that he wants us to think
again. The 'So' with which it opens is weary, making it likely and desirable
that we'll disagree with what follows:

So life was never better than
In nineteen sixty-three
(Though just too late for me) –

> Between the end of the *Chatterley* ban
> And the Beatles' first LP.

In every respect, Larkin had been more fortunate in life than he says in the poem: sexual intercourse, as we have seen, began for him in 1945 not 1963, he read *Lady Chatterley's Lover* as an adolescent, and throughout his life he got as much of a kick from jazz as later generations did from the Beatles. But this is not the point. What the poem wants to know is whether a 'better' life consists in these kinds of freedom at all. While seeming to regret exclusion, Larkin in fact relishes solitude. He hankers after commitment, but also enjoys self-containment.

On the same evening that he wrote 'Annus Mirabilis', Larkin began 'This Be the Verse' (which he eventually finished four years later in the spring of 1971). There are many points of contact between the two poems. Both have titles which create ironical connections with a respectable past ('Annus Mirabilis' with periods of concentrated genius – Keats's 'annus mirabilis' for instance – and 'This Be the Verse' with Robert Louis Stevenson's sentimental elegy 'Home is the Hunter'). Both seem light but draw on his most profound preoccupations (the first sex, the second parents). They are in effect companion pieces – twin monuments to his gift for writing memorably as he describes a drama of private feeling in 'commonplace' language:

> They fuck you up, your mum and dad.
> They may not mean to, but they do.
> They fill you with the faults they had
> And add some extra, just for you.

In the final verse, the poem concentrates beliefs he had held since university, strips them of the qualifications which time and circumstances had woven round them, and serves them up so bleakly that we are more dared than invited to agree:

> Man hands on misery to man.
> It deepens like a coastal shelf.
> Get out as early as you can,
> And don't have any kids yourself.

The same conclusion appears in the background of 'Sympathy in White Major', which Larkin completed a couple of months later. Once again, the poem steps off from an existing title (this time – unexpectedly – it's Théophile Gautier's 'Symphonie en Blanc Majeur'), but where the previous two lyrics had groaned about Larkin's various shames and guilts, here he offers an ironical celebration of selfishness. He insists that the efforts he has made to be 'decent' to 'other people ... didn't work for them or me', but nevertheless feels:

> all concerned were nearer thus
> (Or so we thought) to all the fuss
> Than if we'd missed it separately.

Even the most reluctant form of human contact, the poem seems to be telling us, is better than none – and as Larkin toasts this verdict with a triple gin and tonic, he also presents himself with a small thesaurus-entry of praise: '*A decent chap, a real good sort / Straight as a die, one of the best, / A brick, a trump, a proper sport*'. Only when he has finished are we explicitly told what we suspected all along: that to be '*the whitest man I know*' (in other words, to be devoted to others) is far from being his 'favourite' ambition. Once again, we realize, self's the man, not somebody else.

On this evidence, Monica was right to doubt Larkin's good faith. The poems suggest that he might let her down at any moment. All through their summer holiday together – this time in a hotel in Ludlow, Shropshire, from which they visited (among other places) what he described to Maeve as 'the undistinguished little town'[36] of Wellington – she watched his ill-humour flicker, fade, then flare up. Again and again she asked him whether he was angry with her or something else. She wondered, specifically, whether his depression was partly to do with his hearing, which had deteriorated noticeably in the last year or so, and was now a daily irritation. Larkin agreed. When he returned to Hull he consented to have his ears tested and was told that his 'hearing [was] now at the threshold of social adequacy'.[37] By November he had been fitted with a hearing-aid – an expensive one for his right ear. He was later fitted with a National Health Service 'cheapie'[38] for his left one. His ear specialist, Raymond Cass, said it gave him only limited assistance until he was finally persuaded to buy another expensive but effective one in 1984.

As soon as the new term began, Larkin tried once more to blame the library for his bad temper. The building of Stage 2 entered its final phase and quickly proved exhausting. 'I don't think I've ever had to work as hard as I do now,' he told Eva in November 1967. 'In many ways I long for release. When I think of the way many people live – without responsibility or work – I feel I'm being an ass, particularly as I have no dependants. I should like a job opening and shutting gates, in some small stone lodge at the end of a curving avenue of trees that are green and sunlit in summer and sombre and many-coloured in autumn. However, I can't see myself getting one.'[39] It was some time since any of Larkin's letters had contained one of these skittish, nut-strewn fantasies of escape. Settling ever deeper into his solitude, he seemed to Monica at the end of the year to be more and more careworn. The little things of life loomed increasingly large, daunting him and sometimes overwhelming him. 'This is a hell of a week,' he said in one typical letter. 'Must get a haircut. Wanted to get another dark sweater from M[arks] and S[pencer], but doubt if there'll be time or if they'll have one.'[40] And again: 'I looked at some steak in Fine Fare [the supermarket] yesterday, wondering if I should buy it . . . I'm frightened of butchers, I feel they see you coming and bring out some dear old horse, just for me.'[41]

To a certain extent this darkening mood reflects Larkin's wish to protect himself by playing a role. Following his mother's example, he worked steadily to create an inept, Pooterish personality, partly for comic effect, partly to avoid his larger responsibilities. We can see him doing this in a letter he wrote soon after the end of his Shropshire holiday with Monica. 'Dearest Bun,' he says; 'A nice-ish evening, have eaten all I want of a good macaroni cheese (not too thick, not too thin), read most of the second half of *Laurels are Poison* [by Gladys Mitchell] (I think the chapter entitled 'Iddy Umpty Iddy Umpty Iddy' the most remarkable, and in a way the most creepy, in modern detective fiction) and am now awaiting the broadcast of the flyweight championship of the world (9.15 p.m.). Wonder what Ted Hughes is doing?'[42]

The more insistently Larkin played the part of a valetudinarian, the more suspicious Monica became. It was not, she thought, just the responsibilities of the library that he was trying to avoid, but those of giving more of himself to her now that he had finally turned away from Maeve. Or hadn't he renounced Maeve after all? In a letter Larkin sent to Maeve in September, it is clear that he was not so much a reformed character as a more self-tormenting liar. He wrote:

I know . . . that your main objection is to my not telling Monica that I had planned to go out with you. It's ironic in a way that you should be blaming me for this: Monica was, the Friday after we returned here. I behave openly to you, why shouldn't I behave so to her, etc. Sometimes I wonder if I should: I'm sure Monica imagines we see much more of each other than in fact is the case. On the other hand, I shrink from doing so because of the pain it would cause – you'll say, I don't seem to mind causing *you* pain, but this *isn't* a thing I do intentionally, and in any case M. is far from inclined to take a philosophical view of you: whatever you say, dear, we're not an innocent friendship no one could take exception to. It may be that she'd prefer me to have said I was going out with you, but to me it would sound more like either a deliberate slight, or a deliberate challenge ... At the same time, I hate to think of anything sounding like a deliberate slight or challenge to *you* – something you can't, in all self-respect, swallow.[43]

Not surprisingly, Maeve responded crisply to these attempts at self-justification – only to find herself receiving others, more vigorously expressed. '*I'm* often made unhappy by the situation,' he wailed at her. 'I'm *not* a philanderer, I'm *not* accustomed to keeping lots of girls on a string, I'm extremely faithful by nature. The trouble is there are lots of less laudable characteristics in me as well, I suppose.'[44] Maeve raised her eyebrows at such excuses, agreed with his self-criticism, and said nothing. Monica, too, kept quiet. As the year ended and Monica retreated to Haydon Bridge, she felt her truce with Larkin was more fragile than it had been twelve months earlier. Beneath the reassurances and promises, all the familiar anxieties were in place. She reckoned the only way to make sure they didn't surface again was to complain about them as little as possible.

FORTY-FIVE

At the end of 1967 Larkin complained once again that he was busier than ever before. In the new year a large number of extra chores – some literary, some honorific – were added to his university work. At the same time, he was preoccupied by other matters. Throughout his life he had tried to avoid becoming involved in politics, but had found it more and more difficult to do so as the 1960s went by. Now, as university campuses around the word were torn by protests, it became impossible for him to keep his distance. He viewed the student revolution with mingled fascination and contempt. On the one hand, it seemed to bear out his belief that freedom of expression had only recently become possible ('just too late for me'). On the other, it confirmed his view that most students were lazy and misdirected. The admiration he might have felt for their energy was cancelled by anger at their excesses – especially after the day on which demonstrators at Hull imprisoned him and the rest of Senate in the university Administration Building during one of their thrice-termly meetings. Once he been released he described the sit-in to Barbara Pym, confident of her sympathy. 'Well,' he told her:

we've had our . . . baptism of fire . . . It was a disagreeable experience: I suppose revolutions always are. I wish I could either describe it, or say something penetrating about it: on reflection it seemed to be not so much a *change* in our universities as forcible recognition that change had taken place some time ago, when we expanded them so suicidally. The universities must now be changed to fit the kind of people we took in: exams made easier, places made like a factory with plenty of shop-floor agitation and a real-life strike. Also disagreeable was the way the staff loved it, calling meetings and issuing press statements and wearing the 'campaign badge', and trying to climb on the bandwagon to get softer lives for themselves (nine cushions instead of eight). One hag said she hadn't been so excited since Spain![1]

The Oxford undergraduate who had shown a really remarkable lack of interest in what was happening around him'[2] had grown into a man with no developed political opinions but strong reactionary prejudices. He kept up a barrage of complaints about the demonstrating students to anyone who would listen, took no interest in their causes, and ostentatiously referred to the value of his own work. All spring and into the summer he 'read a few poets for this lingering Oxford book',[3] produced his monthly jazz column for the *Daily Telegraph*, and turned in regular pieces of literary journalism (including, this year, an essay on Rupert Brooke and yet another on Hardy).

There were, intermittently, other kinds of writing as well. In April, once more taking his title from another poem – this time Sidney's sonnet 'With how sad steps, O moon' – he finished 'Sad Steps'. Moving in his now familiar fashion from a conversational opening to a rapturous conclusion, Larkin concentrates on the chances stretching before 'the young', irritably admitting to his jealousy of their strength. For him in middle age all images of romance seem 'laughable' and 'high and preposterous and separate', but their power hasn't faded for those who come after him:

> One shivers slightly, looking up there.
> The hardness and the brightness and the plain
> Far-reaching singleness of that wide stare

377

Is a reminder of the strength and pain
Of being young; that it can't come again,
But is for others undiminished somewhere.

Two months later, in 'Posterity', Larkin's feeling of displacement, no doubt exacerbated by the student unrest, is even more acute. Where in 'Sad Steps' he is pushed to the side of his own life, in the later poem he is shoved to the end of it. He has become a subject, not a living writer – and at first sight a subject tyrannized by his biographer Jake Balokowsky. Jake thinks he's an 'old fart', a 'bastard', and all the worse for being these things unremarkably:

'What's he like?
Christ, I just told you. Oh, you know the thing,
That crummy textbook stuff from Freshman Psych,
Not out of kicks or something happening –
One of those old-type *natural* fouled-up guys.'

Protected by an adopted American accent, Larkin pleads a cause that he had already raised in many earlier poems. Jake realizes that his subject feels blighted by 'something hidden' from him – is 'washed up on a rock, not knowing how [he] got here or ever having had a chance of being anywhere else'. In turn, Larkin has drawn in the character of Jake someone who feels the same. He told Richard Murphy that Jake was 'wanting to do one thing but having to do something else'.[4]

Larkin eventually came to think 'Posterity' was 'not up to the level'[5] of the rest of his poems. He reckoned 'the construction [was] a bit shaky' and 'the American slang ... not quite right'.[6] For all this, the poem forms a memorable part of the series of sarcastic self-denigrations he produced in 1967 and 1968. Compared to the occasional outbursts of anger in *The Whitsun Weddings*, the work which was beginning to form the nucleus of his new collection was distinctly bitter, sometimes tetchily so, sometimes savagely. To friends and interviewers he continued to protest that he wasn't developing; in fact he couldn't help himself. The tight spirals of feeling into which he was bound with Monica, Maeve and his mother, the sense of exclusion prompted by recent events in the university, and the increasingly cluttered cycle of the academic year wound ever more tightly round him. He couldn't contemplate a life without them; neither could he prevent them making his poetic voice more acerbic.

'Sad Steps' and 'Posterity' are as much companion pieces as 'Annus

Mirabilis' and 'This Be the Verse'. They were the only two poems he wrote in 1968, which in a normal year would have seemed a familiarly disappointing output. At a time of so many new demands, it began to look almost healthy. His first requirement was to keep an eye on the university's recently created Compton Fellow. In the mid-1960s Joseph Compton, a literature-loving philanthropist, had left the Arts Council of Great Britain £25,000 a year for purposes 'to do with poetry'.[7] Originally the fund had been administered by Eric Walter White and the head of the Arts Council's Literature Panel, Charles Osborne. Then Osborne decided that something more broadly based was needed, and set up the Compton Fund Committee. He would be Chairman, and there would be a small handful of other members; they would meet twice a year, have lunch in the Caprice behind the Ritz, and decide how to spend the money. Larkin, already known and admired by Osborne, was co-opted for a three-year stint.

From the outset, Larkin was keen to use some of the money to install a writer for a year in a university. He suggested Hull, pointing out there was already a Poetry Room in the library, where the incumbent could meet students and discuss their own and other people's work. His own presence in the library, aloof as he was, proved that Hull had the makings of a literary environment. The Committee agreed, and Larkin began to consider possible candidates. His first choice was Betjeman, who declined, and his second was C. Day-Lewis, whom he knew from the work they had done together on the Manuscript Committee. Day-Lewis replied on 3 July. 'I do like the idea,' he said, 'and am particularly gratified because it comes from you.'[8] By the end of the year everything was in place. Day-Lewis had arranged 'to visit the university fortnightly in term, to lecture [once a term], and to meet students informally in the Poetry Room next day for a poetry seminar'.[9] His salary would be £2,000, and he would give the inaugural lecture on 17 January 1969.

Between accepting and starting work, Day-Lewis's standing dramatically altered. In the winter of 1968 he was appointed Poet Laureate in succession to John Masefield. 'It seems too good to be true,' Larkin said, writing to congratulate him, 'that we shall be able to claim that Hull is the only university *in the world* where students will have a regular opportunity of talking to the Poet Laureate.'[10] Hull's students, unfortunately, did not share Larkin's excitement. On the day after the first lecture, when Larkin accompanied Day-Lewis to the Poetry Room for the seminar, he found 'the number of [people] anxious to meet the Poet Laureate and talk about poetry with him was precisely nil'.[11] Subsequent seminars were more successful, but Larkin was nevertheless embarrassed by what he later called (in a paper given to SCONUL) 'A Faint Sense of Failure'. He felt Day-Lewis was 'very nice about it all',[12] and his affection for the new Poet Laureate grew (he called him 'a genuinely friendly soul'[13]). For the remainder of Day-Lewis's life they continued to see each other occasionally, and after Day-Lewis had left Hull, Larkin confirmed his admiration publicly by presenting him at the university degree ceremony where he was awarded an honorary D.Litt. in 1970. 'There is,' Larkin said, 'a deep appropriateness in the linkage [his office of Poet Laureate] so uniquely represents between the ancient, one might almost say the primitive, concepts of royalty and poetry. The king and the poet are fundamental roles in the history of mankind. It is fitting that their association should survive in our century.'[14]

Larkin continued to busy himself with the Compton Fellowship for the next four years, during which the visiting poets were Richard Murphy, Peter Porter, Ian Hamilton and Douglas Dunn. He acted as an occasional introducer, and tried to create a sympathetic atmosphere in the library. Porter and Hamilton ('the Kerensky of modern literary reviewing'[15]) saw least of him. Murphy, although his marriage to Patsy had ended almost ten years earlier, was a more awkward case, since he and Larkin had both loved the same woman. Furthermore, Murphy expected Larkin to take a greater interest in his writing than Larkin wanted to do. One evening, sitting beside him on a sofa, Murphy handed him a copy of a recently completed poem. Larkin gazed at it, his mind emptying. Eventually the silence broke and Murphy advised him, 'It goes on over the page.'[16]

Douglas Dunn was the Compton Fellow Larkin knew and liked best. Born in Renfrewshire, Scotland, in 1942, he had first arrived in Hull as a poetry-writing 'mature student' in October 1966, after working for a year in Renfrewshire County Library. The following summer, 'married and short of wherewithal',[17] he was given a dogsbody cataloguing job in the Brynmor Jones Library, supervised by Brenda Moon. When he graduated in 1969 he applied to Larkin again, and was given a job in the Acquisitions Department. (He stayed until 1971.) By this time he and his wife Lesley, an art historian who was working in the Ferens Art Gallery in Hull, had become good friends with Larkin, and Dunn had shown him some of his poems. Larkin was impressed, supported him in his application for a Gregory Award, and recommended him to Monteith at Faber. 'I have the impression,' he said, 'that they are pointillist poems – the aesthetics of attitude as well as observation – but they make their impact and for the most part succeed.'[18] Monteith agreed, and in 1969 published Dunn's first collection, *Terry Street*, which took its title from the (now demolished) Victorian street in Hull where the Dunns lived.

Dunn's tenure of the Compton Fellowship from 1974 to 1975 was the last that the Arts Council supported, and the post lapsed. The blame lay more with the audience than with the organizers: Larkin's faith in the scheme had been dented at the outset, but he had never entirely lost it This might seem strange, in view of his antagonism to most contemporary poets and his reluctance to discuss his own writing. Yet in fact his support for the Fellowship is consistent with his articles and reviews. He saw the post as a way of taking poetry away from academics and returning it to 'ordinary readers'. In the talk he gave to SCONUL after the position had folded, he said:

In universities both music and poetry tend to be thought of in terms of the departments that teach them . . . This seems to me quite wrong. Both are forms of art, and art is universal, not simply a subject to be taught . . . I feel this particularly in the case of poetry. During this century poetry has been increasingly the preserve of academic English teaching. It is thought to be difficult, like higher mathematics, something that can't be understood without preliminary study and teaching. Of course, some modern poetry is obscure, but to acquiesce in the notion that all poetry is obscure by setting up academic centres to explain it seemed to me the best way to ensure that it would go on being obscure, and probably get more obscure, which would be very much of a Bad Thing. To me, the only qualifications required for reading poetry [were] the understanding of the language it is written in, and a feeling heart. Poetry demanding more than this did not deserve close academic instruction: it deserved to be slapped down.[19]

As the first Compton Fellow, Day-Lewis, found his champion in Larkin, Larkin lost a champion of his own. While in Seattle on a Fulbright Fellowship for which Larkin had acted as sponsor, Vernon Watkins died. His memorial service was held in Swansea on 9 March (1968). Larkin's sadness was partly grief for a friend: they had known each other for nearly twenty-five years. He also felt the loss of an example. However widely their poetic tastes had diverged, Watkins remained for Larkin an ideal type of the dedicated poet, unostentatious but passionately committed. In the short elegiac piece he wrote for a memorial volume of essays about Watkins, Larkin puts this in terms which might equally well apply to himself.

Despite his kindness, his whimsicality, his friendliness, there was something hard and brilliant about his attachment to poetry: he never hesitated. It was something there, tangible and palpable, commanding instant and unending allegiance ... In Vernon's presence poetry seemed like a living stream, in which one had only to dip the vessel of one's devotion.[20]

The 'living stream' was continuing to bring more poetic business than poems proper. No sooner was Day-Lewis lined up to come to Hull than he asked Larkin to sit on the Advisory Committee of the Queen's Gold Medal for Poetry, which in the past had met and made the award annually. Larkin agreed to join but questioned the arrangements. To be awarded the medal, he told Day-Lewis – and his successor as Laureate, Betjeman – was 'a great honour, and in consequence should be a rare one'.[21] Over the years ahead (he 'faded'[22] from the Committee in 1977) he was as good as his word, arguing for (among others) Gavin Ewart and Norman MacCaig, and against Seamus Heaney and Charles Tomlinson, both of whom he thought 'dull'.[23]

Larkin's work for the Poetry Book Society (he had last served on its board from 1960 to 1963, was re-elected in May 1968, and became Vice-Chairman in 1972) was done in the same scrupulous spirit. He was always 'cautious but fair' says a fellow board member, Blake Morrison, 'and tended to side with the big battalions, as he called them'.[24] In the early 1970s, when he did a stint with Dannie Abse as a selector of the Society's quarterly book choices, he even made *The Way In*, a book by his old antagonist Charles Tomlinson, one of his spring nominations. 'He was a wonderful committee man,' Charles Osborne says; '*just* below the gloomy surface manner was an extraordinary humour.'[25] Other board members agree. 'You got the feeling,' says one, 'that he was an immensely private man, yet capable of seeming public. He made very successful transitions between these things. And of course though he was gentle he could be very stern; he had a strong sense of what he wanted to achieve.'[26]

It was the same on committees elsewhere. His Arts Council duties, his efforts to buy manuscripts for the British Museum, his work on the Management Committee of the Society of Authors (he became a member of the Society's council in 1975) were all performed groaningly but efficiently. Unswayed by fashion or precedent, unimpressed by popular reputation, he brought an unusual equanimity to the ego-haunted business of literary administration, and judged everyone on their own merits. Naturally conservative, he showed surprising enthusiasms (for the Liverpool poet Roger McGough, for instance), and always remained faithful to his first principles. Poetry should be honest, emotional, free of academic obscurities, various. The 'Establishment' should be egalitarian, adventurous, yet respectful of traditions. He, as the face of the 'Establishment', should be serious but smiling.

And so he was – in public, at least. But as his work-load grew heavier through the year, and unresolved tensions nagged him at home, the private man became increasingly irritable. Students, their demonstrations gathering momentum, dismayed him – 'How absurd they are,'[27] he told his mother. Institutional rewards for his work annoyed him (in May he declined an offer of the OBE, on the grounds that he deserved something better). Family life wearied him as much as ever. When Kitty's daughter Rosemary invited him to her degree ceremony at Warwick University he told Monica he thought it was 'not worth'[28] going, then sourly changed his mind. When he spent a week in Loughborough over the summer after holidaying with Monica in Scotland, it produced an eruption of rage. 'God, what hell,' he told Monica. '[Parents] *bugger you up*, then, then *hang round your neck* and stop you ever curing yourself. To escape from home is a life's work, like writing the *Decline and Fall of the Roman Empire*.'[29]

It was a familiar complaint, and one that Monica knew she had to accept as genuine while remembering that 'Philip was really very fond of his mother. Very.'[30] Although he now tended to concentrate in his letters to Monica on how exasperating he found Eva, his flashes of anger were interspersed with acts of devotion. Eva's mind wandered aimlessly for much of the time – she was happiest when recalling scenes from her distant past. For many of the hours Larkin sat with her in York Road he mulled over stories from her childhood, her courtship of Sydney, her happy early marriage, his own youth. She was, he told her, a 'splendid old creature',[31] remarkably steady (her letters were 'so long and clearly written and small yet legible in script'[32]), and still necessary to him. 'I shouldn't care much for my mild honours,' he told her in a message decorated with her mob-capped, storm-fearing, port-sipping caricature, 'if I couldn't tell them to you and Monica.'[33]

The more pathetic Eva became, the more Larkin regretted not being able to control his anger with her. After the fury provoked by his summer's visit had subsided, he immediately wrote again to Monica, analysing his feelings in the hope of dispersing them:

I wish I could avoid being so cross and irritable at home. I wish I knew what caused it. It's probably a stock psychological trait. Sometimes I wonder if I'm fond of my mother at all. Away from her I know that she's old, and hates living alone, and keeps on with it largely for my benefit; but she's extremely kind and considerate and conscientious; she never thinks badly of anyone or says anything malicious about them; that she's my mother after all, and it's my duty, yes ma dooty, to look after her if she can't look after herself. But once [I am at home I] become snappy, ungrateful, ungracious, wounding, inconsiderate and even abusive, longing only to get away, muttering obscenities because I know she can't hear them, refusing to speak clearly so that she can hear, refusing to make conversation or evince any interest in her 'news' or the things she says. All these traits are manifestations of a physical discomfort associated with intense irritation, and one caused by her: if I go upstairs to shave or do anything in my room, I find in five minutes I am humming cheerfully and full of creative thoughts. How does one explain it? I suppose she arouses in me strong alarm and hostility because she makes me feel guilty for not looking after her. Sometimes I think she, and my being at home, represent to me my own failure as a human bean [sic], too. 'Assume adult responsibilities' and all that, which makes me guilty – and angry – in a different way. Or is it just that I resent the slightest demand on my self-consciousness? There must be something in it to explain the violence of my feelings: it's not just being irritated with an old person, though of course she *is* irritating *and* boring, though not, probably, as much as countless other parents. And anyway, hasn't one a right to be boring at eighty? And if I'm so clever and superior and a jewel in the crown of my age, can't I put up with it? I don't suppose you know the answer to all this any more than I do: perhaps there are more pathological explanations that I haven't mentioned, but really my anger is a fight for emotional freedom against its enemy – you know all that. I suppose it links with my unhappiness at ties of all sorts, or not so much at them, but at having to do anything to honour them.[34]

Just as Larkin's letters to Monica about Maeve tend to make diagnosis an end in itself, so this account gives little sign of wanting to make analysis part of a process of change. If he can only hang on, the letter implies, relieving his feelings by talking to Monica, the scene is bound to shift of its own accord. And if it didn't, he kept telling himself, then at least he never had to endure Eva for very long at a stretch.

In this instance he knew that as soon as the visit to Loughborough ended he would be going on holiday to Scotland with Monica. But what seemed welcome in prospect turned out to be difficult in fact. For the past several months – the spring and early summer of 1968 – Monica had again doubted whether she could believe what Larkin was telling her about Maeve, and by the time he travelled up to join her in Haydon Bridge during the third week in August she was 'dominated by painful thoughts'. He told her they were 'mostly imaginary and not worth bothering about',[35] but she couldn't relax. Even though he was someone who liked 'to cling to pretence like the bathing steps at the deep end',[36] he assured her that he was telling the truth this time.

Once Monica's doubt had subsided they started to enjoy their holiday. To prove the point (and their complicity) they decided to keep a diary – Larkin writing most of the daily entries, Monica adding a few thoughts. (These diaries, which performed a different, lighter role than the others he kept on a more regular basis, were not included in Larkin's orders about material to be destroyed after his death.) Some of what they put down was purely informational, some reflective, and while they make no intimate revelations, everything generates a powerful sense of their personalities. Larkin is gloomily humorous, relentlessly intolerant, eager to see the potential for disaster in everything and mocking himself for doing so. Monica is sharp-eyed and unillusioned. 'Hell of a lot of bath grabbing in the morning,' Larkin complains when they reach their hotel outside Inverness on 25 August, and two days later grumbles again, 'We have to share [our table] with a couple from Chesham, Bucks, and their thighy daughter. He had his soup in a meat plate tonight, through a misapprehension.' When they moved on to the island of Skye for the first week in September things didn't improve. 'Set off to Applecross,' Larkin wrote, 'by a difficult road that climbs over 2,000 feet. At the top I pull off the road with all the expertise of the practised driver and tear off my front registration plate and find my foglamp smashed.' By the time he returned to Hull on 11 September he has pleased himself more by concentrating on the 'upon-thy-belly-shalt-thou-go atmosphere'[37] of the holiday than by trying to shake it off.

A more straightforward kind of pleasure awaited him. Since starting to write his jazz column for the *Daily Telegraph* in 1961 he had occasionally wondered whether he might collect his articles in a book. Fortified by his enjoyably miserable holiday, he felt the time was right to pursue the idea, but only on a modest and local scale. He decided to open the collection with an Introduction which would outline his views on art generally and jazz in particular. He began writing as term started, feeling that because the audience for the book would be a small one, he could afford to speak sweepingly. Once it was finished, in early November, he sent the manu-script, entitled *All What Jazz*, to Hull Printers Ltd, asking for an estimate of likely costs. As he did this he also wrote to Donald Mitchell, whose influence had got him the job with the *Telegraph* in the first place. (Mitchell was now working for Faber, commissioning and editing books on the music list):

I thought it would amuse you to know that I have been contemplating in recent months putting together a book made up of my articles. My idea is to print a small edition privately, just enough to send to the copyright libraries and distribute among friends, with perhaps some minor sales conducted personally.

The first reason I am writing is to ask your permission to dedicate it to you. I do hope you will agree: it is the least I can do to repay your kindness in the first place. This job, despite the peevishness of some of the articles, has brought me a great deal of pleasure, and I hope to go on with it.

Secondly, I thought it might amuse you to read the Introduction, which is a *jeu d'esprit* not perhaps to be taken very seriously. In fact, the whole book is not over serious, but I think it might be of interest to people who like jazz and who have heard of me.

Thirdly, it did just cross my mind to know whether Faber's (for instance) ever *distributed* books they had not actually published, and, if so, what their terms for doing so would be. I can see that this would make the publication of the book even more wildly uneconomic than it will be anyway, but it would certainly save me a lot of trouble.[38]

What sounds disingenuous in this letter was in fact perfectly sincere: Larkin had no secret hope that Faber would want to publish the book themselves. Mitchell had other ideas. In an internal memo dated 26 November he told his colleagues that he had asked Larkin to let him see the manuscript. 'His distinction between private and public publication seems very odd,' Mitchell wrote, 'particularly when the bulk of the book has already appeared in a mass-circulation newspaper.'[39] Larkin was happy to let Mitchell see the manuscript, provided he received 'an *honest* assurance it is worth publishing. I don't mean that you are usually dishonest! But when you look at the articles you will see that they are really very trivial.'[40] He retrieved the manuscript from Hull Printers, sent it to Russell Square, and within a fortnight heard that Faber wanted to publish. He received an advance of £200, arranged for Faber to retain his original plan for the jacket (a photograph 'showing part of my jazz library with part of my record collection underneath'[41]), and agreed that his Introduction should stand unchanged. 'I have a sneaking affection for [it],' he told Mitchell. 'It's about time jazz had its Enoch Powell.'[42]

Larkin was more cautious with Monteith. 'I am rather taken aback by your enthusiasm [for the Introduction],' he said after Monteith had written to congratulate him. It 'was really only a *jeu d'esprit* in the manner of Mencken or someone like that, and to pass it off seriously will earn me the biggest critical clobbering I have ever experienced.'[43] Monteith reassured him, and also told him that he need not worry about any sort of reaction for a while yet, since Faber wouldn't be publishing for at least a year. Meanwhile, wasn't it time Faber published a *Selected Larkin* – a volume that would include poems from *The Less Deceived*?

Larkin had been thinking along similar lines himself. Ever since he had first shown signs of dissatisfaction with The Marvell Press, his relationship with George Hartley had deteriorated steadily. While still admiring Hartley's pluck and his freedom from the taint of the metropolis, he resented what he saw as his attempts to rip him off. 'The ponce,' he says in one typical letter written the previous year, 'showed me a blurb for a reprint of *Listen* saying as PL said to read the list of *Listen*'s contributors is to call the roll of all that is best in etc. Where did I say that, I asked, genuinely puzzled. "In this very room," he said. The bastard!! The bastard!!'[44]

Recently Larkin's suspicions about The Marvell Press had deepened as he discovered the Hartleys' marriage was breaking up. He reckoned that without Jean's influence George would become even less efficient. This, rather than sympathy for their unhappiness, was his main concern; his other, as he told Eva when letting her know in September that Jean had finally left home, was the increase in social duties. 'A rudimentary tea was produced,' Larkin reported when he next went to see Hartley in Hessle Road, 'without milk or butter. We didn't say anything about Jean going, except that I had to say I know about it, and he just gave an embarrassed laugh. I suppose I shall have to start seeing both of them now – take double the time! Arrgh!'[45]

In business terms, everything turned out as Larkin feared. He agreed with Monteith that it was time for a *Selected Poems* and urged Faber to approach The Marvell Press. When Hartley refused to release any material from *The Less Deceived* Larkin was 'disappointed and irritated'[46] but willing to try another tack, persuading Hartley to release his rights in the volume altogether. 'Now [the Hartleys] have split up,' he told Monteith's colleague Peter du Sautoy, 'Mr Hartley is finding the actual distribution and invoicing of his books and records something of a labour.'[47] Once again Larkin left it to Faber to make the approach, and once again they were rebuffed. 'Dear Mr Monteith,' Hartley replied, 'We are not at this time interested in the proposal you outline or, indeed, any other proposal.'[48]

It seemed to be the end of the matter – an unsatisfactory end, as Larkin had predicted. It depressed him, clouding his pleasure in the acceptance of

All What Jazz. He felt that to be bound to Hartley for ever was just one more kind of trap, sprung as fiercely as all the others which imprisoned him. The trap of family, for instance, which caught him once more in December when he visited his mother. The restraint he had tried to show during the summer, the self-analysis he had undertaken, were of no avail. Within hours of arriving in Loughborough for Christmas he was as furious as ever. On Boxing Day, in a 'glum letter' to Monica, he said:

We had our usual row yesterday, and I told Mother I shouldn't come home for Christmas again. This is what priests call Avoiding the Occasion, I believe. After going through it all once more I have decided that it's the dinner that is the heart of the matter, and it's this I must avoid . . . Kitty's was just boring, as usual. Rosemary sat reading *The Hobbit* which mother had given her, while mother helped wash up. I can't think of anything to report that wouldn't sound spiteful, and indeed would be so. God! It seems a waste of life. I suppose someone some day will explain what went wrong. I can't believe I am so much more unpleasant than everyone else. How sick I am of it all . . . I long to get back to Hull and my own flat. Peace and quiet. It's all one ever wants, ever. One can do without everything else. I'm afraid this isn't very pleasant reading – I'm sorry. It's really rather comical when one's woes consist in being Christmas dinner![49]

FORTY-SIX

Larkin believed that he had 'never been didactic, never tried to make poetry do things'; he also admitted, 'I don't know anything at all about anything [political] and it's no use pretending I do.'[1] Yet ever since Harold Wilson's Labour government had been elected in 1964, the same year as *The Whitsun Weddings* came out, and especially since 1968, he had aired his political prejudices more and more freely. To colleagues on campus like John Kenyon, or in letters to friends like Monica, Amis, Conquest and Pym, he regularly complained about socialist policies and proposals, repudiating anything that challenged his 'true blue' beliefs. Immigrants and the trades unions had been his original bugbears; now they were joined by students (who had previously been merely contemptible, rather than actually menacing), and many aspects of government policy – particularly defence.

In May 1969 Larkin sent a grouchy couplet on this theme to C. B. Cox (who had once worked in the English Department at Hull and now taught in Manchester). Cox published it in *Black Paper Two: The Crisis in Education*, a collection of articles bemoaning what the contributors saw as declining educational standards:

> When the Russian tanks roll westward, what defence for you and me?
> Colonel Sloman's Essex Rifles? The Light Horse of LSE?

(Sloman was the Vice-Chancellor of the University of Essex, which like the London School of Economics – LSE – had a notoriously radical student population.) Larkin had dealt with the same issue at greater length in a poem begun in January 1968 and finished a year later. Originally called 'Homage to a Prime Minister' it was completed as 'Homage to a Government' – a wholly sarcastic title, since the poem is a form of elegy, regretting the government's decision to close the British base in Aden (now part of the Republic of Yemen). It was not the simple fact that soldiers were coming 'home' from their outpost of Empire that offended him; it was because they were being recalled 'for lack of money':

> Next year we shall be living in a country
> That brought its soldiers home for lack of money.
> The statues will be standing in the same
> Tree-muffled squares, and look nearly the same.
> Our children will not know it's a different country.
> All we can hope to leave them now is money.

Whereas British soldiers used to 'guard' foreign posts and keep them in 'order', now these places 'Must guard themselves, and keep themselves orderly./We want the money for ourselves at home/Instead of working'. This flimsy argument, with its sneering accusation that money saved on defence will automatically be wasted on people more lazy than unfortunate, is something Larkin chose not to mention when discussing the poem. He preferred to pass it off as having to do with 'history, rather than politics',[2] and backed away from explaining what he had meant into muttering about what might and might not be 'the best thing all round'. He told one interviewer:

That poem has been quoted in several books as a kind of symbol of the British withdrawal from a world role. I don't mind troops being brought home if we'd decided this was the best thing all round, but to bring them home simply because we couldn't afford to keep them there seemed a dreadful humiliation. I've always been right-wing. It's difficult to say why, but not being a political thinker I suppose I identify the Right with certain virtues and the Left with certain vices. All very unfair no doubt.[3]

Quickly out of his depth when discussing theoretical or abstract matters, Larkin knew that his work in the library was a less contentious way of keeping things tidy. And by the time he posted his Black Paper squib to Cox, library business had absorbed him once more. In March he went to Belfast for a SCONUL conference at Queen's, travelling by air for only the second time: 'except for being *up in the air*,' he said grumpily, it 'was uneventful'.[4] (A poem written in December 1953, 'Autobiography at an Air-Station', commemorates the first: a flight he took in July 1953 from Belfast to Inverness at the start of his summer holiday with Monica.) A few months later he went back to Queen's to receive an honorary D.Litt., which he felt was a 'signal honour'.[5] Rather than finding something to enjoy on either visit he only looked for excuses to grumble. 'Bar, and open till midnight, but horse-piss beer to drink,' he complained to Monica. 'Bed v. bad and only one pillow and only one blanket. Food – machine oil Chicken Maryland, but not bad brecca.'[6]

Returning to Hull he felt – briefly – that he should try to shake off his ill-humour. Stage 2, which had been scheduled for completion on 1 March, was finally ready for occupation. He told Barbara Pym it was 'an odd building with a curious glaring drabness and far too little space',[7] but in fact he was proud of it. Seven storeys high, and organized 'on a subject basis much more definitely than before',[8] its liver-and-white tiled mass rises out of the earlier brick buildings, dominating the university. It 'won praise from everyone'.[9] Shortly after it had been officially opened by the Chancellor of the university, Lord Cohen of Birkenhead, on 12 December 1970, it was awarded the Civic Trust Award; later it received the Architecture Award (Yorkshire Region) from the Royal Institute of British Architects.

Castle, Park, Dean and Hook were pleased, the university was pleased, Larkin was pleased – and soon dispirited again. Since arriving in Hull fourteen years earlier, he had seen the library extension as 'the Daysman of my thought, and hope and doing'.[10] As soon as it was finished he felt 'drained'.[11] The building programme had sapped the energy he might otherwise have devoted to his own work. Sometimes this had been an irritation; sometimes it had been welcome. Now that the builders had gone, he began to doubt whether his writing would suddenly prove more biddable. He also suspected that he had no appetite for making further improvements to the library. 'He was certainly all for the quiet life and a minimum of change,' Kenyon thought, once Stage 2 was complete. 'Arguably [it was] not the right attitude during a period of rapid advance in the techniques of information storage and retrieval; departmental heads who pressed him on such matters became strictly *persona non grata*, and for some of the more persistent he conceived a pathological hatred ... Thus the computerization of the library, a process he always affected not to understand, was belatedly carried through by his deputy, Brenda Moon.'[12]

The previous decade had seen an exhilarating expansion in Larkin's working life, but no sooner was his library finished than he began to feel embattled. By the end of the 1970s the effects of a national economic recession had severely hampered the university. So had government policy towards higher education. A few gains, Larkin was keen to point out in a résumé produced in 1978, were nevertheless made. In 1973 the library appointed a full-time archivist; in 1974 it was nominated as a European Documentation Centre; and throughout the period it continued to acquire fine books and notch up 'intellectual and imaginative landmarks'. At the same time, he knew his work was disastrously under-funded. No matter how well he got on with Stanley Dennison, who succeeded Brynmor Jones as Vice-Chancellor in 1973, no matter how doggedly he defended standards, the library grant failed to keep pace with the rising costs of books and periodicals. Between 1973 and 1977 the grant rose by $17\frac{1}{2}$ per cent while costs rose by 20–30 per cent. Inevitably, services were curtailed: 750 journals were cancelled, rooms were closed, resources amalgamated, fewer books than usual acquired, and $13\frac{1}{2}$ full-time and part-time posts suspended between 1974 and 1977. Throughout this time, the number of books issued by the library rose by 30 per cent.[13] Although Larkin couldn't predict how his library would cope during the coming decade, he knew in the early 1970s that 'the writing was on the wall for all to see';[14] by the late 1970s he felt that his work had become as disappointing as his home life.

During the early spring he had suffered painfully from hay fever, and in May he discovered that he could breathe in but not out through his right nostril. His doctor told him not to panic: it was only a polyp and could easily be removed. The operation was performed on 21 July under general anaesthetic and, in spite of everyone's reassurances, provoked a good deal of anxiety. He wrote to Maeve, 'The day men landed on the moon I landed in the Nuffield, not in v. good spirits but supported by Monica ... I had the operation about 10.15 (general anaesthetic) and spent the rest of the day bleeding and being sick. No question of being out by lunchtime! In fact I stayed in overnight, and was released during Tuesday morning with one nostril still blocked with dried blood.'[15] As Larkin recovered, he slipped quickly back into his familiar grouchy ways. Two weeks later – in time to mark his forty-seventh birthday, and driving a new car, a second-hand Vanden Plas Princess he had bought on 6 August – he was holidaying with Eva in the Maid's Head Hotel, Norwich. Holidaying, and trying to control his rage. 'Mother is very quiet and patient and a lesson to us all,' he told Monica, 'or me anyway. She finds interest in all sorts of small things – such as the people and waiters. She walks with a stick now and can't hear very well; however we keep cheerful enough ... Mother really is extra-ordinary. If we are in a room, she doesn't know which door she came in by ... She is perpetually lost in the hotel.'[16]

Larkin ferried Eva back to Loughborough then drove to Monica in Haydon Bridge. They had arranged to go to Ireland for a fortnight (in spite of the fact that he had already visited the north twice since March), and sailed by night ferry from Liverpool to Dublin on 25 August. Larkin promptly began a new holiday diary, filling it with his fears about the political situation on either side of the border. 'A week or so before we set out,' he wrote on the first page, 'riots of a particularly serious kind take place between Protestants etc. and Catholics etc. in Londonderry and Belfast, which scares me rather as I am (a) English (b) Protestant and (c) the owner of a large new-looking car just made to be stoned and tipped in the Liffey.'[17] After a couple of days they plucked up enough courage to visit the Municipal Art Gallery, where they inspected the pictures, 'notably a line-up of the original IRA leaders (who look like a bunch of taxi-drivers)',[18] and soon became even more adventurous. On 29 August they reached Drumcliffe churchyard in County Sligo and saw 'the grave of that old blatherer Yeats', where Larkin reported, 'No great crowd of Ph.Ds, but a wreath from the Japanese Yeats Society.' That evening, he had more to say about the packed lunch his hotel had prepared for them: 'very middling – one tomato between two, cheese spread'.[19]

Two days later, after visiting Achill Island, they called in unannounced on Richard Murphy at his house in Cleggan near Westport, where they found Charles Monteith was staying. Two days and one unsuccessful mackerel fishing trip later, Larkin wrote to Maeve, 'There's so much here to remind me of you – Brennans galore, and even one Maeve Brennan – I can't forget you, even if I had any inclination to, which I haven't. Accept a big kiss and some spectral maulings – are you wearing tights? Or stockings?'[20] Larkin posted the letter secretly, then drove Monica south to the more familiar holiday life of uncomfortable hotels. The Talbot, for instance, in Wexford: 'Awash with busloads of Americans and piped music. Our room not v. good (blocked washbasin), but we have usual drinks and a dinner, during which M. breaks a crossbar on her chair (unobserved). Dinner not at all good.'[21]

For Larkin to reckon a holiday successful, it had to surprise him with a few pleasures and confirm his view that leaving home was always a mistake. His Irish trip of this year struck just the right balance, and when he returned to the library in mid-September he found that he had enjoyed himself enough to regret having to resume his daily grind. For the first time in fifteen years there wasn't even any building work to distract him – though he did have to oversee alterations and refurbishments in Stage 1. He soon felt bored, and began to think of ways of entertaining himself. His first thought was to leave Hull altogether for a while, so that he could make some progress with his Oxford anthology. He discussed the idea with Charles Monteith, and Monteith recommended that Larkin apply for a visiting Fellowship at All Souls College, where Monteith was a Fellow and could propose him. Larkin at once began negotiating to take off the winter term 1970 and the spring term 1971.

At the same time, he found that the easier rhythms of his work allowed him more productive evenings. He began writing poems again. In 1968 he had written two, in 1969 two and a squib, in 1970 he finished five and in 1971 another five (including the three sections which comprise 'Livings'). The first of this new crop was 'To the Sea', a stately reminiscence of a visit he had made to the Norfolk coast with his mother during their summer holiday. Like the 'observed/Celestial recurrences' of 'Forget What Did', he regarded the expedition (at least for the benefit of the poem) as 'half an annual pleasure, half a rite'. All his contempt for holidays is pushed aside; he remembers his recent past with Eva, his own childhood visits to the same coast and 'further back' his parents meeting each other for the first time by the sea in Rhyl – 'listeners/To the same seaside quack'. Ushering in this little succession of contented images, Larkin eyes them with a kind of wonder. And when the day begins to wane, and the brightness of the detail fades, his own situation with Eva lies crystallized like a deposit at the bottom of the poem:

Like breathed-on glass
The sunlight has turned milky. If the worst
Of flawless weather is our falling short,
It may be that through habit these do best,
Coming to water clumsily undressed
Yearly; teaching their children by a sort
Of clowning; helping the old, too, as they ought.

The final clause here recognizes the tedium as well as the necessity of 'helping the old', just as 'a sort of clowning' admits to foolishness as well as fun. The poem is candid about the drag of social responsibilities, and about the extent to which they are fuelled by selfishness (we do as we wish to be done by). At the same time, it celebrates a 'miniature gaiety'. 'Habit', Larkin says, may hinder us but it also saves us – it satisfies what the short lyric 'How' (written six months later) identifies as 'Our need now for kindness'.

Clustered round these two poems are three narrative pieces. The first, 'The Explosion', was written early in the new year, 1970, and like 'To the Sea' relies on images from Larkin's early days. In 'To the Sea' the source was childhood holidays, now it is adolescent reading – Lawrence (for the descriptions of mining villages) and Longfellow (for the 'Hiawatha' metre). Larkin later claimed that he hadn't realized while writing the poem that he was using Longfellow's rhythms; in fact they are forcefully maintained until the final line, when their abandonment creates an apt sense of pathos, tilting the poem away from a world in which incident is pre-eminent to one in which emotion matters most:

> *The dead go on before us, they*
> *Are sitting in God's house in comfort,*
> *We shall see them face to face –*

> Plain as lettering in the chapels
> It was said, and for a second
> Wives saw men of the explosion

> Larger than in life they managed –
> Gold as on a coin, or walking
> Somehow from the sun towards them,

> One showing the eggs unbroken.

The trigger for his memories of Lawrence was a television documentary about the mining industry that he watched with Eva during Christmas

1969. In 'To the Sea' his mother is a precise presence; in 'The Explosion' she is unnamed yet pervasive. As Larkin evokes the pit community he enters a society which is based on families: human ('Fathers, brothers, nicknames, laughter') and creaturely ('a nest of lark's eggs'). When the community is destroyed, it is commemorated by a return to this image of the nest. It is a sign of continuity as robust as any in 'Forget What Did', or 'The Trees' or 'To the Sea', yet its strength and value depend on the surviving 'wives', just as the structure of Larkin's own life depended on Eva.

Four months later Larkin produced 'The Card-Players', a savage group portrait painted in the manner of a seventeenth-century Dutch genre piece. Its characters – Jan van Hogspeuw, Dirk Dogstoerd and Old Prijck – are at first glance comically gross: staggering, pissing, guzzling and farting. Yet in their vileness they enact a ripe drama of self-sufficiency, and Larkin closes the poem in an excited, Yeatsian cadence reminiscent of the end of 'Absences', saluting their 'lamplit cave': 'Rain, wind and fire! The secret, bestial peace!' This is a world without families, an exclusively and gloatingly male world, where mothers, wives and mistresses are not admitted. Perennial as 'the day the flowers come/And when the birds go', it is an earthy rather than a celestial recurrence.

Within a month Larkin had turned back to more polite rituals. In 'The Explosion' an accident had reaffirmed the need for continuity. In 'Dublinesque' a description of a funeral does the same thing. (The origin of the poem, he told Maeve, was 'a dream – I just woke up and described it'.[22]) Larkin detected in the procession 'an air of great friendliness' and 'of great sadness also' – partly, no doubt, because the dead person might have had his own sister's first name:

> As they wend away
> A voice is heard singing
> Of Kitty, or Katy,
> As if the name meant once
> All love, all beauty.

In this and all the other poems Larkin had written in the last few months, he set aside the political issues which had troubled him in 1968 and 1969. Instead, he concentrates on small-scale community life, family responsibilities, cyclical returns.

In articles written at the same time – on Edward Thomas, Walter de la Mare and Emily Dickinson – Larkin also stressed these things. And in *All What Jazz*. He had originally expected the book to be published late in

1969, and when he discovered that Faber had postponed it he was miffed. 'The agreement said it would be published in "Autumn 1969",' he complained to Judy Egerton, '. . . but in fact they just bloody well forgot about it until I raised mild enquiries and found they were idly scheduling it for March 1970 – God!'[23] Clearly his original diffidence about the book had evaporated, though in his dealings with Faber he continued to sound self-mocking. Conceding to the book's in-house editor, Rosemary Goad, that it had 'suddenly begun to mean a great deal to me as a personal testimony', he added:

of course, you realize it will be the end of me as a university librarian and also as a poet: five years today I shall be sidling into your office wearing an ankle-length coat and dark glasses, hoping to scrounge some of the petty cash to buy drugs with. If there's one lesson English life teaches, it is that you cannot ride two horses at once. As for the book itself, its reception will be similar to that accorded to one written by Humphrey Lyttelton on modern poetry, saying how silly Eliot is and how rotten Auden. My body will be figuratively weighted with concrete and dropped into the Thames.[24]

The Faber publicity department were given a similar line. Larkin told them to think of *All What Jazz* as 'a freak publication', and said they should not 'put it forward as a piece of jazz scholarship or even any sort of contribution to the field. Treat it like a book by T. S. Eliot on all-in wrestling.'[25] Yet when preparing a sheet of 'autobiographical particulars' Larkin said the book's 'interest' lay in 'the thesis of its Introduction . . . I don't think this has actually been said before, and, while it may not be wholly defensible, I think it is sufficiently amusing to say once.'[26] The mixture of diffidence and defiance is typical. Larkin wanted to promote his book as the work of an intelligent enthusiast, someone who was knowledgeable but not an expert, opinionated but not bogged down in jargon. He hoped that his jazz writing, like his literary criticism, would embody the qualities it praised: the music should be admired for its emotional power rather than its ingenuity, its originality rather than its assimilation of existing models. It should be unpretentious and 'an affair of seeing things as they are'.[27]

Larkin begins the Introduction by sketching his jazz education. He tells us we should only believe what we can prove on our pulses, then illustrates the point by telling us how he listened to the 'hot' numbers on the wireless in the 1930s, went to performances of dance music at the Hippodrome in Coventry, cherished an ambition to be a drummer, made jazz at Oxford 'part of the private joke of existence',[28] suffered a painful separation from his records in Wellington, then was united with them in Dixon Drive, and confirmed his addiction to jazz at the Plaza in Belfast before reaching Pearson Park. As Larkin recounts these things he affirms one priceless fact: jazz has given him 'more pleasure in life' than anything else because it has offered him a 'unique private excitement'.[29] The word 'excitement' appears again and again. The hot numbers, he says, are 'exciting', just as the Hippodrome drummer also 'excited'[30] him. Once this link has been forged between art and pleasure, Larkin is free to regard anyone who doesn't share his views as not simply perverse but a killjoy.

And so he does. When Charlie Parker, Miles Davis, and Ornette Coleman attacked and overthrew the melodic principles of Larkin's childhood heroes Armstrong, Bechet, Waller and the Condon groups, they created a world where there were 'no more tunes'. The cohesion of 'the music of the American Negro'[31] was lost and pleasure disappeared. The 'constant pressure to be different and difficult demanded greater and greater technical virtuosity, and more and more exaggerated musical non-sequiturs. It wasn't, in a word, the music of happy men.'[32] To dramatize his disappointment, Larkin casts himself as an outsider – not only outside the current of developing taste, but also outside the time in which he feels it appropriate to speak of such things. 'In the late forties battle had been joined in the correspondence columns between the beret-and-dark-glasses boys and the mouldy figs; by the early sixties [when he began writing his *Telegraph* columns], all this had died down.'[33] In some parts of Larkin's life, a sense of alienation brought him superior wisdom; here it leads only to bafflement. When he began reviewing, he tells us, he discovered that everything he had loved in jazz as a boy and young man had been turned into 'chaos, hatred and absurdity'.[34] The longer he persevered, suspecting his failure of appreciation was just another sign of 'drifting deeper into the silent shadowland of middle age',[35] the more mystified he became. When he finally understood the problem ('of course!') it turned out to be larger than he had first realized. 'The term "modern",' he says, 'when applied to art, has a more than chronological meaning: it denotes a quality of irresponsibility peculiar to this century, known sometimes as modernism, and once I had classified modern jazz under this heading I knew where I was.'[36]

As soon as personal opinion has acquired this theoretical dimension, the Introduction quickly rises to a climax of exasperation. Attacking 'the two principal themes of modernism, mystification and outrage',[37] he tells us:

397

I dislike such things not because they are new, but because they are irresponsible exploitations of technique in contradiction of human life as we know it. This is my essential criticism of modernism, whether perpetrated by Parker, Pound or Picasso: it helps us neither to enjoy nor endure. It will divert us as long as we are prepared to be mystified or outraged, but maintains its hold only by being more mystifying and more outrageous: it has no lasting power. Hence the compulsion on every modernist to wade deeper into violence and obscenity: hence the succession of Parker by Rollins and Coltrane, and of Rollins and Coltrane by Coleman, Ayler and Shepp.[38]

Once he has delivered this Johnsonian judgement, Larkin abandons polemic for evocation. Speculating about the lives and moods of his readers in a final paragraph which is both funny and considerate (they are people 'deserted by everything that once made life sweet'[39]), he repeats the point he made at the outset. The main purpose of his reviewing, he says, has been to remind people of 'the excitement of jazz'.[40] For all the sophistication (and occasional disingenuousness) of its supporting argument, it is a simple emphasis, passionately made. It is also, like the rest of the Introduction, made theatrically. When Larkin first mentioned the book to Donald Mitchell, he called the Introduction a *'jeu d'esprit*, not perhaps to be taken very seriously'. He didn't mean that he doubted his own argument; he meant to acknowledge its element of exaggeration. By his zealous disparagement ('the tawdry trappings of South America, the racket of Middle East bazaars, the cobra-coaxing cacophonies of Calcutta'[41]), and his gloomy-tender identification with those who share his views ('men whose first coronary is coming like Christmas'[42]), Larkin makes it obvious that he wrote the essay as much for display as diagnosis.

When we turn to the monthly pieces themselves, we find him more tolerant and flexible than he warned us he would be. Certain principles remain inviolate (the necessary appeal to the emotions, the repudiation of mere technique), but the roll call of virtuous names is surprisingly long: the 'brisk, eclectic'[43] Chris Barber; the 'unique' and 'hard-hitting'[44] Pee Wee Russell; the 'astonishing'[45] Bix Beiderbecke; the 'unforgettable music'[46] of New Orleans; the 'throbbing cantabile'[47] and 'authoritative vitality'[48] of Sidney Bechet; the 'commanding'[49] Fats Waller; the 'charm, intelligence and energy'[50] of Ellington – not to mention Johnny Hodges, Wild Bill Davison, Lester Young and Louis Armstrong, whose 'St Louis Blues', Larkin reckoned, was 'the hottest record ever made . . . By the third chorus the whole building seems to be moving'.[51] Alongside such trusted favourites Larkin praises less obviously sympathetic figures – Bob Dylan, John

Lee Hooker and the Beatles – and even discovers qualities in the players he slammed in his Introduction. Charlie Parker is commended for his 'prodigious'[52] invention, recognized as a 'classic'[53] and said to show 'an originality that had scarcely been hinted at before'[54]. Larkin never completely lowers his guard against 'mere' technicians – John Coltrane, for instance, is 'earnest, humourless',[55] and Miles Davis is 'the master of rebarbative boredom'[56] who leaves 'the ends of his notes hanging like Dali watches'[57] – but his rage against 'the silly, the disagreeable and the frigid'[58] aspects of modernism knows its own limitations. Time and again he presents his opinions as the products of increasing age. Jazz, like youth itself, 'is for others undiminished somewhere'.

The contradictions between the Introduction and the contents of *All What Jazz* are not its only surprise. It also contains a startling theoretical dimension. Ostentatiously, Larkin's only general thoughts concern the modernists, but month by month we find his opinions about Pound, Parker and Picasso run parallel to his thoughts about the importance to jazz of the colour of its players. Initially he says that jazz was purely and simply 'the music of the American Negro'[59] and that things started to go wrong when 'the Negro stopped wanting to entertain the white man'.[60] We hear that now, far 'from using music to entertain the white man, the Negro had moved to hating him with it'.[61] Larkin's mood as he reports this is tolerant – he understands that the roots of the early blues grew in white injustice, and doesn't blame later black jazz players for their anger. Yet at the same time he sounds as though a due pleasure has been destructively and uncharitably withdrawn. He explores these feelings most fully in a piece glumly headed 'The End of Jazz', which was written in the summer of 1963:

The American Negro is trying to take a step forward that can be compared only with the ending of slavery in the nineteenth century. And despite the dogs, the hosepipes and the burnings, advances have already been made towards giving the Negro his civil rights under the Constitution that would have been inconceivable when Louis Armstrong was a young man. These advances will doubtless continue. They will end only when the Negro is as well housed, educated and medically cared for as the white man.

There are two possible consequences in this for jazz. One is that if in the course of desegregation the enclosed, strongly-characterized pattern of Negro life is broken up, its traditional cultures such as jazz will be diluted. The Negro did not have the blues because he was naturally melancholy. He had them because he was cheated and bullied and starved. End this, and the blues may end too.

Secondly, the contemporary Negro jazz musician is caught up by two impulses: the desire to disclaim the old entertainment, down-home, give-the folks-a-great-big-smile side of his profession that seems today to have humiliating associations with slavery's Congo Square ... The Negro is in a paradoxical position: he is looking for the jazz that isn't jazz. Either he will find it, or – and I say this in all seriousness – jazz will become an extinct form of music as a ballad is an extinct form of literature, because the society that produced it has gone.[62]

To the extent that Larkin links 'the end of jazz' to black players, he blames them for it no matter how greatly he sympathizes with their motives. This leaves him, let alone them, in a paradoxical position: he seems to be insisting that the white audience for jazz must dictate its terms, because if it doesn't – as Tom Paulin says – 'modernism and black power will inevitably follow'.[63] Larkin reluctantly acknowledged this problem, and understood it meant that while the evident framework for his book was reactionary (anti-modernist), its less obvious structure was actually racist. Fifteen years after it appeared, he was to tell a fellow jazz fan at Hull that it 'now reads very anti-black, insofar as most of the people I bollock are black'. He also added, in mitigation, that 'most of the people I praise are black too'.[64] *All What Jazz*, in other words, lives dangerously. It 'wants everything to submit to the rational exercise of power', as Tom Paulin again points out, 'but the result is a desperate attraction to something which is apparently other than power'.[65]

Critical reaction to the book, when it was eventually published on 9 February 1970, ignored this fundamental conflict in favour of those raised in the Introduction. Larkin had presented himself as a lone voice complaining about modern 'gibberish'[66] ('was there no one ... who had realized what was going on, apart from me?'[67]), and while many lay and literary readers applauded him, more informed reviewers were not impressed. They denied his heroic isolation, identifying him instead as someone using the same terms and tone as magazines such as *Storyville*, *Jazz Journal* and *Jazz Monthly*, where it was quite usual to find hostility to music played after 1945. His book, they felt, was on a par with other backward-glancing tracts like *The Agony of Modern Music* by Henry Pleasants (a critic cited by Larkin), which also argued that after a period of initial exuberance, jazz had been laid waste by modernism. They doubted his assertion that a listener's ear 'will tell him instantly whether a piece of music is vital, musical, exciting, or cerebral, mock-academic, dead',[68] arguing that in music as in literature it took time to grow accustomed to originality. They derided, too, his opinion that the advent of modernism marked a decisive break with tradition. Wilfrid Mellers, in the *Musical Times*, was typical: 'It seems to me improbable, at a sober estimate, that for the past thirty years *all* jazzmen have been involved in a malignant conspiracy ... If [Larkin] believes that there is *no* affinity between Armstrong and Davis, Bechet and Coleman, I suspect his response to the great traditionalists must be partial and incomplete.'[69]

None of this antagonism daunted Larkin. (Neither, when *All What Jazz* was published by St Martin's Press in America in July, did its similar American reception.) His Introduction had courted disagreement, and any hurt he suffered was offset by the support of his friends: Amis in the *Telegraph*, and Wain in *Encounter*. When he read reviews like Charles Fox's in the *New Statesman* ('bully for Larkin the writer ... A pity he had to spoil things by trying to hold back history'[70]) his reaction was to shrug and carry on regardless. 'To hell with bad reviews'[71] was a standard response, even when telling his mother about the book's reception – and to hell with modernists remained his rallying cry.

Nevertheless, three years' more work for the *Telegraph* was as much as he could stand. While he continued to 'enjoy' writing the pieces, they seemed 'to carry a deepening sense of depression. The kind of jazz I liked was dying with its masters: George Lewis, Pee Wee Russell, Johnny Hodges, finally Armstrong himself, the great oak unrooted at last.'[72] In July 1971 he recommended to the paper that Alasdair Clayre replace him, and the following December he 'brought [his] contributions to an end'.[73] He was free to become a private listener again, an occasional concert-goer, a regular listener to records which friends discovered could still make him caper round Pearson Park with a large gin and tonic sloshing from a glass in one hand while the other mimed the drummer's part. It was jazz that most quickly put him in touch with his strong emotions. It described an unfading, unfailingly romantic universe, filled with the vanished potency of youth and coloured by the soft light of nostalgia.

All What Jazz continued to sell steadily but unspectacularly, turning with the years into something increasingly like the book he had first described: a highly personal statement, telling its readers more about Larkin than about music. In 1984, when Faber urged him to collect the pieces written between the book's first appearance and his giving up the column, publication found his literary reputation riding high, and the second edition was well received. 'It is being absurdly overpraised,'[74] Larkin told a member of Acker Bilk's band, but he was delighted. Articles that he had started to write by accident, and an Introduction he had produced as a *jeu d'esprit*, had nevertheless drawn on strongly held beliefs and ended up as a classic – something akin to Constant Lambert's *Music Ho!* (1934). In both books sentimentality and eccentricity are offset by energy and wit; in both the calm surface of prejudice is stirred by an exciting ripple of self-contradiction; and in both the question of their influence on current thinking was cancelled by the general recognition that they were a one-off. Lambert's book is an explosion of affection for the French traditions which he felt Russian and German musicians were threatening to overwhelm. Larkin's is a love song for his own youth, a prolonged argument for distinguishing the person who suffers from the person who creates, and a celebration of the all but extinct 'great coloured pioneers and their eager white disciples, and the increasingly remote world that surrounded their music, dance halls, derby hats, band buses, tuxedos, monogrammed music-stands, the shabby recording studios where they assembled, and the hanging honeycomb microphones that saved it all for us'.[75]

FORTY-SEVEN

The clamour of reviews faded and Larkin returned to his routines. He knew they would not occupy him for long: All Souls had granted his application for a visiting Fellowship and Hull had given him leave of absence during the winter term of 1970 and the spring term of 1971. All Souls said they would pay him £900 and provide bed and board, while Hull paid his salary for three of the six months he would be away. It was agreed that his deputy Brenda Moon would be left in charge of the library.

First, though, she had the comparatively familiar job of running it during his holiday. On 17 July Larkin drove to Haydon Bridge, collected Monica, and set off for a fortnight in the remote countryside of North Uist and the Western Highlands. He said in his diary that it was a trip which 'entailed a good deal of preliminary staff work'[1] but which nevertheless managed to be interesting and disconcerting in the equal parts that he required. Uist was 'bloody untidy. No sign of anything growing', and their meals were impoverished by a dock strike in England ('the idle Commie layabouts want £50 a week basic pay instead of a kick up the arse

WHICH IS WHAT I'D GIVE 'EM'). Outraged at having to endure 'no lettuce or tomatoes to freshen our salad',[2] they returned to Northumberland more confident than ever that their relationship had settled into a comfortable shape. When Larkin told Monica the main feature of his holiday had been the feeling that he was *'corpsed,* for no ascertainable reason',[3] she merely understood it to mean that he had relaxed.

She took heart, too, from Larkin's excitement at the thought of escaping to Oxford, the city of his youth. Not even a week with Eva (at the Queen's Hotel in Cheltenham) could altogether crush his enthusiasm. 'Roll on September 16,' he wrote to Monica, 'and deciding whether to give Thom [Gunn] and Ted [Hughes] a page between them, or leave them out altogether'[4] – then admitted that his mother was having her usual lowering effect. 'Have coined the epigram: "Everything in life is either irritating, embarrassing or frightening",' he said. 'This holiday is irritating and yet I hate myself for being irritated. Mother is so equable and patient and unselfish I wish I could refrain from snapping at her or refusing to repeat things and all the rest of it. I find very little for her/us to do: began to look round the abbey [in Tewkesbury] but they started to have a service and we fled. This was *embarrassing.*'[5] Oxford, when it eventually 'rolled on', was 'frightening', at least to start with. Not since 1943 had he spent more than a fortnight at a stretch away from his place of work, and in the twenty-seven years since he had left the university its mood and character had changed profoundly. His own war-dishevelled, proctor-darkened memories had disappeared under the lavishness and radicalism of the 1960s. It was not an old home to which he was returning but a strange city packed with surprising familiarities. 'It's a most extraordinary experience,' he wrote to Maeve, 'coming back like this, after 27 years. I feel I am exactly the same age – haven't changed, learned anything, done anything. The place itself has changed more: all scrubbed nice and clean for the dear American visitors.'[6]

Feeling that his departure had been – he told Maeve – 'a little like retiring',[7] he made straight for his lodgings – Beechwood House (owned by All Souls) in the village of Iffley to the south-east of the city, forming part of its suburbs. 'The house,' Larkin wrote in an account of his stay that he produced for his own amusement, 'stood at the end of a long drive which ended in a loop, and bore the date 1798 above the front door: it was reasonably graceful, but had been painted an unfortunate combination of pink and navy. Once inside, one was struck by the intense central heating, which had taken toll of the woodwork. My rooms were on the first floor front, a large sitting room and a large bedroom with a washbasin and a single bed and wardrobe.'[8]

Larkin was taken to his first dinner in college by the historian A. L. Rowse, who along with the Warden John Sparrow, Monteith, and other Fellows such as Alasdair Clayre, became a frequent – albeit much criticized – companion. As they eyed up the new arrival, one or two people found some of his habits disconcerting. Rowse, for instance, was alarmed by the amount he drank. ('It's odd that he should have been so pernickety and yet so undisciplined in that respect.'[9]) Rowse also – like several others – objected to Larkin's half-genuine, half-mocking disapproval of high art and academic manners. 'Falling over backwards to be philistine,' Rowse says; ' – it's an undergraduate attitude which he perpetuated into adult life.'[10] For all this, he liked him and sympathized with his fits of melancholy, even if he didn't understand their cause. 'What the hell was the matter with him?' he wonders. 'I mean, he hadn't much to complain about. He was *tall*.'[11]

Although Larkin often had his meals in All Souls or worked in the small room he had been allocated there, he soon found college life 'rather dull. I don't find any kindred spirits there,' he told Maeve, 'and there are one or two spirits who certainly *aren't* kindred.'[12] At the weekends he continued to visit Loughborough and Leicester to see Eva and Monica; he returned to Hull only a handful of times – once for the funeral of his much maligned library colleague Arthur Wood. In Beechwood he breakfasted slowly – 'I had four morning papers laid at my elbow'[13] – then in 'splendid, warm and sunny [weather], not a hint of autumn', walked into the city along the towpath beside the river. (In the evenings, too, he often walked back again to his 'set', 'going down to Iffley lock and enjoying the H. G. Wells atmosphere of the public house a little way along the bank'.[14]) When he reached the Bodleian he spent the morning on the fourth floor of the New Library, then after lunch in the back bar of the King's Arms he moved across to the Upper Reading Room until tea, which he took in college, before returning to Beechwood for drinks, and finally driving back into college for dinner. It was a relaxed yet busy routine – and one about which he had mixed feelings. While thinking it was '*terrific* having all one's time free to devote to a single interesting project',[15] he also felt out of sorts. He told Maeve after a few days that he missed her 'badly',[16] and was soon complaining, 'I feel I've had enough food and drink to last me for ten years! Fat hangs on me like a Roman toga. Oxford ... seems to consist of eating, drinking and toadying.'[17]

In the four and a half years since Larkin had first heard from Dan Davin about the anthology he had worked on it only scrappily. Using what little free time he had, exploring the modern collection in the Brynmor Jones Library, he had managed to do 'most' of the reading he thought would be necessary. The Bodleian, as a copyright library, gave him the chance to extend his range immensely. 'I wanted to examine their stock and read everything that looked interesting,' he explained, 'taking xerox copies of pieces I fancied as I'd done in Hull ... I began [in the mornings] with sequence E at 1900, which was by far the largest section, and worked my way through steadily, taking every book from the shelves and glancing at it to see if it looked interesting. At first they all did: later I became almost completely insensitive.'[18] In the afternoon, in the Upper Reading Room, the routine continued. After a twenty-minute sleep ('without, I presume, snoring'[19]), he munched his way steadily through the century, sending off the poems he judged worthy of inclusion to be photocopied by the library staff. At the end of every day he would carry the fruits of his labours across the road to his room in college and glue them on to sheets of paper. Evening by evening, page by page, the book began to grow, but as it did so he became increasingly apprehensive. 'As I feared,' he said to Judy Egerton, 'I am drawing English poetry in my own image, and it isn't going to make a good book. Also it makes me unable to appreciate some writers! If I were to tell you how many people are "out" you'd think I was joking. Incidently, I haven't done myself yet.'[20] As the year ended, even the qualified eagerness in which he had begun work no longer guided him. He began to feel that his usual Hull existence was too remote to comfort him. Even a visit from Maeve – she stayed at the Melville Hotel off the Iffley Road for a weekend in November – was as disturbing as it was comforting. 'You seemed extra young, beautiful, thin(!), kind and charming,'[21] he told her afterwards, then turned back glumly to his solitude. He longed for Monica's encouragement. He pined for Maeve. ('I think I'd better go to bed now,' he wrote to her in December. 'Pity I can't take you with me!'[22]) By the time he was due to drive back to Loughborough for Christmas with Eva, he was doubtful of what he had achieved and uncertain that another term in Oxford would allow him to make any significant improvements.

Eva couldn't do much to help him. Monica, however, defended his decisions: 'Of course it's a good book,'[23] she told him. Larkin thanked her by presenting her with an illustrated history of Oxford for Christmas, on the flyleaf of which he wrote her a poem – 'Poem about Oxford: for Monica'. It's an occasional piece but full of tenderness, expressing its affection in the description of a past they had 'shared without knowing'. The 'blacked-out and butterless days', undergraduate days, and the 'Dull Bodley, draught beer, and dark blue', encapsulate a world which still

> holds us, like that *Fleae* we read about
> In the depths of the Second World War.

The '*Fleae*' marks the most personal moment in this deeply personal poem. It is a reference to Donne's 'flea', in which the blood of a lover and his mistress are mingled to form a 'marriage bed, and marriage temple'. Beneath the superficial '*politesse*' of Larkin's poem, Monica was intended to see the gleam of something intense: the much-mentioned brilliance which lit his feelings for her.

Larkin was reassured by her support. He returned to Oxford on 14 January and for the next three months worked with more confidence than he had felt during the previous term. His original intention (he told Garnet Rees, the Chairman of the Library Committee in Hull) had been 'to get a gross selection by Christmas and a net selection by the time I go';[24] now he found he could keep his promise. In the early spring, after returning to Hull, finalizing the text with Monica, and showing it to Anthony Thwaite, he sent it to Dan Davin at Oxford University Press.

A long silence followed. When it was broken, it was by precisely the opinions Larkin had anticipated. The anthology was indeed 'in [his] own image', Davin told him, and the most obvious result was a number of dismaying omissions. Would he like to think again about David Jones, say, or Hugh MacDiarmid? Larkin replied:

Regarding omissions, I think I shall inevitably be charged with injustice towards someone or other. As I see it, there are three possible courses in producing an anthology of this kind: to include only the thirty or forty people who *must be in*; to include everybody; or to include the thirty or forty plus such other poems and poets as seem to me (as distinct from anybody else) worthy of it. The third is the course I chose, and in reply to your queries I can only say that I read the principal works of all of them, but found them wanting either that one striking poem that everyone knows them by, or the particular poem that seemed to me to rise above the ruck of their other work and of their contemporaries . . .

The one exception I would make is MacDiarmid. I am so averse from his work [sic] that I can hardly bring my eyes to the page, but I agree a lot of people will expect to find him there . . .

By all means let Helen Gardner see it . . . any advice she cares to offer will be gratefully received and (probably) not acted on.[25]

Davin and other editors at OUP made only a little headway: eventually five poems by MacDiarmid were included in the anthology. At the outset, the editors had tried to steer Larkin into the middle course they believed such anthologies should take, and he had seemed to understand their wishes. In the end they had been presented with something as idiosyncratic as Yeats's anthology had been. But there was nothing more to be done, nothing except hope that when the book eventually appeared in two years' time a virtue would be made of its oddity, and its popularity with 'ordinary readers' be as great as Larkin predicted.

However vigorously he defended himself, Larkin was disappointed. He knew that the Press's reaction was a foretaste of greater trouble to come. Even more demoralizing was the experience of returning to Hull. Oxford may sometimes have been 'lonely'[26] but it had been 'great fun'[27] working in the Bodleian, and occasionally moving to be surrounded with reminders of his earlier days. 'I have dreams of reliving my youth – of doing all the things I never did,'[28] he had told Pym when he first arrived, and for a while had 'tried to do all the things I said I would' such as buying 'a college scarf . . . and go[ing] to the theatre and the Bach choir'.[29] Even when this resolve 'collapsed'[30] the city kept showing him traces of the chances he had lost, roads he had not taken, and romances or adventures which had come to nothing. 'It was here,' he wrote wistfully, musing over his afternoons in the Upper Reading Room, 'that I'd been told to "sit on my chair properly", and Ruth Barbour had invited me to parley with some official concerning my request for *Lady Chatterley's Lover* non purgatus.'[31] Oxford had been a place of high hopes; Hull was where they had brought him. He contemplated his life even more miserably than before. He had secured his poetic reputation but the flow of his writing had slowed to a trickle. He had built his library but his opinion of the students using it didn't bear repeating. He was forty-nine. While half of him longed for a new beginning, half of him began to feel that his time was drawing to a close.

The staff of the Brynmor Jones did their best to make him feel welcome. 'They had a little sherry party,' he wrote to his mother. 'Brenda did one of her iced cakes with "Welcome Back to The Library" on it. I tried to be nice to everyone, though it was quite an effort. That too was followed by deep depression. It made me want to hide away in the corner and never be seen again.'[32] Part of his problem was purely professional; because his secretary Betty Mackereth had felt it necessary to call him only twice during his entire six months away, he felt superfluous. 'It is rather delicate,' he told Eva, 'coming back into an organization that's been running itself for six months: one feels rather self-conscious about starting to tell them what to do.'[33] The larger problem was personal. Larkin had managed to stay in close touch with Monica while he had been away, and when he returned to Hull their life simply picked up where it had left off. With Maeve things were more complicated. In spite of their successful meeting in Oxford before Christmas, and although their recent letters had been more intimate and excited than ever, Maeve and Larkin found it difficult to meet again on home ground. Their reunion brought them face to face with all their old disappointments and frustrations. Maeve felt at once that 'some of the old sparkle'[34] had gone from their relationship. Larkin was 'restless and depressed'[35] and found himself agreeing when Maeve told him 'it would be better for us both if I looked for someone else'.[36] He announced to Monica that his affair with Maeve was finally at an end. He told her that Maeve was planning to spend some time in Ireland, and was 'having a fling with an Irishman'.[37] Yet once he was at work in the library again, encountering Maeve every day, the familiar tensions returned. He couldn't deny his admiration for her. He couldn't prevent himself feeling jealous of the Irishman.

In the past such a conflict of feelings had always led to a crisis. Now Larkin strove to remain loyal to Monica, plunging into his work even though he doubted its value. He avoided students as much as he could: the poet Tom Paulin, for instance, who had been a student at Hull shortly before Larkin went to All Souls, found him 'remote'[38] even then. After Oxford, Larkin seemed even more isolated. By 1971, when another group of demonstrators occupied the Administration Building complaining about the university's 'South African affiliations', his contempt deepened still further: '[The] building stank for a week after the sitters-in ("activists") departed,'[39] he told Judy.

It was the same with official business. Although he was always punctilious, his heart gradually went out of his work. At the end of the 1970s he confessed to a colleague on Senate that he had read the whole of *War and Peace* during their meetings.[40] He was regularly seen turning off his hearing-aid in other meetings which bored him. He started to drink more heavily than before, drawing round him in the bar a regular and almost impenetrable set of cronies – John Kenyon, Bob Wallis, John Riggott, Bill Cockcroft. He withdrew, little by little, what small support he had once given to university associations, joining instead a private drinking club in Cottingham, and a men-only dining club in the university.

The change in his mood began to affect his behaviour outside the university as well. He became increasingly jealous of his contemporaries. While consenting to send his 'warmest congratulations'[41] to Kingsley Amis's son Martin when he gained a first-class degree at Oxford in 1971, for instance, he couldn't resist complaining to another friend at the same time that he found 'old Kingsley's' latest novel *Girl, Twenty* 'a thought *restricted*'.[42] He also became cruder and more vicious in the expression of his political opinions. 'Fuck the non-working classes,' goes a typical letter to Robert Conquest written in the early 1970s, 'fuck the students (fuck you students everywhere), fuck the Common Market e'en. Hurray for Ian Smith, Ian Paisley (fuck all branches of the IRA).'[43]

Another, less expected sympathizer was Colin Gunner. Since their days together at King Henry VIII Grammar School, and their occasional (inevitably drunken) meetings in Oxford during the early 1940s, Larkin had lost contact with his eccentric contemporary. Now Gunner wrote out of the blue, saying that he was living in a caravan outside Banbury, short of money and often of work, taking stock of his life. He added that since their last encounter he had written the story of his war experiences: would Larkin read it and advise him about publication? 'I'd love to read it,' Larkin replied, 'but can't promise help.'[44] In the event, Larkin liked the book enough to give Gunner more help than he offered any other writer apart from Barbara Pym. He produced a brief Foreword (though reserved the copyright) and recommended the manuscript to Monteith. When Faber declined, a number of other publishers were approached before Gunner gave up and had the book privately printed in an edition of twenty-four copies in 1975. (It was eventually published by Greystone Books in 1992.) By this time the focus of his relationship with Larkin had shifted away from writing on to politics. At school they had evolved a kind of brutal camp; now they spiced it with the prejudices and disappointments they had accumulated since their last meeting.

Larkin's letters to Gunner were written recklessly, as he unburdened himself of his most virulent opinions. To this extent, and because he knew how to entertain Gunner, they represent only a part of him. They are a kind of grim joke. Yet at the same time they are not a joke at all. For the past several years, and especially since 1968, Larkin had become increasingly bellicose, increasingly right wing. 'Fuck the whole lot of them, I say,' he had written to Amis about Harold Wilson's Labour government in 1969, 'the decimal-loving, nigger-mad, army-cutting, abortion-promoting, murderer-pardoning, daylight-hating ponces, to hell with them, the worst government I can remember.'[45] When a Conservative government led by

Edward Heath had been elected in 1970 one target of his rage had been removed only to leave others horribly exposed – trades unions, as usual; prisons ('How do I intimate that I believe prisoners to be fearful *swine*, that prisons ought to be *v. unpleasant places*, etc.'[45]); universities ('I want to see [them] closed down, except for Oxford and Cambridge'[46]); and 'immigrants' ('You'll be pleased to see the black folks go from the house over the way,' he had written to his mother in 1970; 'I fear your grade is going down. England is going down generally! It was shown recently that one child in eight born now is of immigrant parents. Cheerful outlook, isn't it? Another fifty years and it'll be like living in bloody India – tigers prowling about, elephants too, shouldn't wonder. We'll both be dead'[47]).

In letters to several friends, these views were turned into scraps of sour light verse.[48] To Monica, for instance, in 1970, he sent a grumpy post-imperial quatrain:

> The flag you fly for us is furled,
> Your history speaks when ours is done,
> You have not welcomed in the scum
> First of Europe, then the world.

To Anthony Thwaite, a few years later, he sent an 'unofficial' celebration of the Queen's Silver Jubilee:

> After [Denis] Healey's trading figures,
> After [Harold] Wilson's squalid crew
> And the rising tide of niggers
> What a treat to look at you!

And to Robert Conquest he sent instructions on 'How to Win the Next Election' – to be sung to the tune of Lillibullero:

> Prison for strikers,
> Bring back the cat,
> Kick out the niggers,
> What about that?
>   (Cho: niggers, niggers, etc.)
>
> Trade with the Empire,
> Ban the obscene,
> Lock up the Commies –
> God save the Queen!
>   (Cho: Commies, Commies, etc.).

As Gunner enticed Larkin into making bigger and bolder shows of prejudice, the restraints of the previous years – which had usually prevented his views from seeming wholly credible or serious – wore thin. Amis says Larkin had always been 'the last man on earth to make someone feel uncomfortable';[49] now he no longer cared so much about other people's feelings. Admittedly he confined his most virulent remarks to his private correspondence, but if they leaked outside these limits he didn't care. Like his father before him, he felt proud of his right-wing isolation.

This hardening of attitude was a development, not a complete change; it meant that he was now inclined to express one distinct aspect of his personality without subjecting it to the moderating influence of others. We can see this in his poems as well as his letters. In 'This Be the Verse', which he finally completed in April of this year, 1971, he gives free rein to his bitterest instincts. Then two months later, in the elegant lyric 'Cut Grass', he evokes 'young-leafed June', the 'chestnut flowers' and:

> White lilac bowed,
> Lost lanes of Queen Anne's lace,
> And that high-builded cloud
> Moving at summer's pace.

In a letter to Monica shortly after the poem was completed, Larkin admitted that it offered a partial view, however beautiful its effects. 'Its trouble is that it's "music", i.e. pointless crap,' he said. 'About line 6 I hear a kind of wonderful Elgar rhythm music take over, for which the words are just an excuse ... Do you see what I mean? There's a point at which the logical sense of the poem ceases to be added to, and it continues only as a succession of images. I like it all right, but for once I'm not a good judge.'[50]

Between these two poems, uniting the 'misery' of the first with the 'music' of the second, Larkin wrote a third which analysed his depression more argumentatively. 'Vers de Société' is one of his most condensed and memorable pieces, and encapsulates the beliefs which dominated the last third of his life as powerfully as 'Dockery and Son' did those of his earlier career. It is a poem which enlists two strikingly different kinds of language to support its case – one (the language of 'misery') being demotic, the other ('music') being romantic. The former clashes against the latter as the poem opens:

My wife and I have asked a crowd of craps
To come and waste their time and ours: perhaps
You'd care to join us? In a pig's arse, friend.
Day comes to an end.
The gas fire breathes, the trees are darkly swayed.
And so *Dear Warlock-Williams: I'm afraid* –

The remaining five verses of the poem struggle to resolve this tension in ordinary social terms – in the terms of party-going and amiable acquaint-ance. They are also, as Larkin implies but never openly admits, the terms of his own private life. It is an aged mother and the thought of marriage, just as much as it is the prospect of drinking 'washing sherry' and talking drivel, that threaten the time he would prefer to spend 'under a lamp, hearing the noise of wind,/And looking out to see the moon thinned/To an air-sharpened blade'. The opposition between two attitudes is perfectly obvious here. Our upbringing insists that even 'Playing at goodness' is preferable to no goodness at all, because 'It shows us what should be'. Larkin, wriggling in the grip of his argument, wants to reject this as 'Too subtle' and 'Too decent'. The only way he can resolve the conflict in favour of the world is to persuade himself that the consolations of solitude are no longer what they were. He decides that he needs company for much the same reason as he needs work – not for its intrinsic pleasures, but for what it precludes:

Only the young can be alone freely.
The time is shorter now for company,
And sitting by a lamp more often brings
Not peace, but other things.
Beyond the light stand failure and remorse
Whispering *Dear Warlock-Williams: Why, of course* –

Within two months of completing 'Vers de Société' Larkin was once again proving as good as his word: taking his mother on holiday 'as he ought'. This year they had chosen the King's Head in King's Lynn, in the hope that the East Anglian coast would stimulate more happy memories for Eva. If it did, Larkin didn't notice. 'The holiday has toiled on,' he wrote to Monica:

not very successfully. Market day in the town today which does remind me strongly of a little Hull – docks, bits of quaint old town, chopped down to make way for car parks and ugly shops, and the people very much a cut-price crowd:

35 32 Pearson Park, Hull: the top flat (on the right) where Philip Larkin lodged from 1956 until 1974.
36 105 Newland Park, Hull: the first house Larkin owned, and where he lived from 1974 until his death.

37 The University of Hull Library staff in 1957. Philip Larkin is centre, front; Maeve Brennan is on the left of the front row; Arthur Wood is next to her.
38 The University of Hull, from the Cottingham Road; the Brynmor Jones Library, completed in 1969, towers in the background.

39 Philip Larkin holidaying on Sark, 1955 (photograph by Monica Jones).
40 Philip Larkin and Monica Jones visiting London in the late 1950s. Philip Larkin sent a copy of this picture to Monica Jones with the message: 'Have you seen this pair? Sloppy Louis and Diamond Lil. Thought to be operating in British universities.'

41 Philip Larkin and Monica Jones holidaying in Paignton, Devon, in the late 1950s (photograph taken by Philip Larkin with a delayed-action camera).

42 Robert Conquest, editor of *New Lines*, 1963.
43 Kingsley Amis in London, 1958 (photograph by Philip Larkin).
44 John Wain, Philip Larkin's friend since Oxford, in 1968 (photograph by Philip Larkin).

45 Jean Hartley, who ran the Marvell Press with her husband George, 1968.
46 Philip Larkin and George Hartley at the back of 253 Hill Road, Hessle, where the Marvell Press started, c. 1960.

47 Philip Larkin and his mother Eva, c. 1970, at her house in York Road, Loughborough.
He wrote on the back of the picture: 'Happy As the Day is Long'.
48 Betty Mackereth, 'loaf-haired', c. 1965.

49 Maeve Brennan in 32 Pearson Park, 11 June 1961 (photograph by Philip Larkin).

50 Part of the draft of 'Dockery and Son', which Philip Larkin began writing on 4 February 1963, and finished fifteen pages later on 28 March 1963.

51 Charles Monteith, shortly before he retired as Chairman of Faber and Faber in 1981.
52 Philip Larkin and John Betjeman at W. H. Auden's memorial service in October 1974
(photograph by Jane Bown).
53 Philip Larkin and Monica Jones outside Buckingham Palace, April 1974.

54 Philip Larkin in the Brynmor Jones Library, July 1981
(photograph by Christopher Barker).

55 One of the last photographs taken of Philip Larkin – in October 1985. He is sitting
between Wendy Mann, the Library's chief assistant (administration) and – on the right –
Maeve Brennan. The occasion was a retirement party for a Library colleague.

virtually all the women pregnant, no *blacks*, and a great many stinking fish and chip shops. It would interest you in fine weather for 48 hours. But in fact I've hardly been able to explore it at all, as I can't really leave Mother, and she can't walk far enough to come with me. I haven't been in the church, or in the sort of guildhall place: fuck all that. I put my nose into the museum and art gallery and saw a pathetic little collection of stuffed birds and voles' skulls and so on.[52]

What Larkin also saw, and here only implies, is how much feebler his mother had suddenly become. Walking from her room to the dining-room was an effort; she was often badly confused. Monica urged him to discuss with Kitty what should be done, and reluctantly he did so. Could either of them take her in? No, Eva required too much attention. Should she go into an old people's home? Probably – and the cost was not a problem: Eva still had enough of Sydney's money to pay for it herself. But this still left difficulties. If Eva were to abandon York Road one of the main definitions of Larkin's own life would be altered. It would clear the way for Monica to insist that she should spend more time with him. As he came home from King's Lynn, he was faced with the prospect of losing his security at the same time as he lightened his responsibilities. To protect himself, he once again turned towards Maeve, writing her more affectionate letters than he had done for months, relying on her not just for her familiar romance and kindness, but for proof that Monica did not have an exclusive claim on him. 'Considering the strains of our relationship,' he said to Maeve, his 'luxury-loving mouse',[53] immediately before leaving for his holiday:

it is wonderfully harmonious! You almost never irritate me, and if you did the pressure of your lips would banish it at once. As I've said before, in some ways I think our natures very similar in sort of basic ways, the ways we pick things up or instinctively do or don't say certain things. I don't mean our opinions are the same, or what we like necessarily. Anyway, I'm very dependent on you . . . I don't mean I have as nice a nature as you, far from it: but I hope you feel, as I do, that despite all our differences there is a big area where we are alike. By differences I only mean where we aren't alike![54]

FORTY-EIGHT

Larkin and his sister inspected one or two possible homes for their mother, then made their choice. On 4 August 1971 Eva left York Road for Abbeyfield House, a small old people's home in Victoria Street, Lough-borough. She was too muddled by the upheaval to complain, and within a few days had settled into her new routine. She liked the company. She enjoyed the chat. Before he left her for the first time, Larkin promised he would visit her every fortnight and write to her every day.

Even on holiday. Within a month of the move, Larkin and Monica had set off for the Scottish islands of Islay, Jura and Mull, and started a new diary. 'On September 2,' it begins, 'drive to Islay. This is a fair setting for the wilder parts of *King Lear*, but we are cosy in our car with the wireless and books and papers.'[1] The next day, having 'failed to prevent [a] foxhound pissing against [the] car wheel',[2] they took the ferry to Jura where they were 'very content', then on 5 September to Tobermory, where they 'Awake and find NO HOT WATER. Well piss and fuck our horrible luck.' Worse still, they discovered the main street of the town had been taken over by a film company making *Madam Sin*. 'All the shits we have seen for the last 48 hours are gathered here,' Larkin declared, 'including the two pansies on the boat.'[3]

And so on, for the next week. As Larkin's temper rose so his pleasure increased, and by the time the holiday was over both he and Monica (who silently revenged herself on one disagreeable hotel by wearing her night-dress to dinner) agreed there had been 'many good things seen/done'. Larkin ended the diary with a flourish: 'Fuck the piermaster at Oban. Fuck the non-hot water at Tobermory. Fuck the gammon at Jura and the stores at Bridgend. Fuck the wine at Jura and the winelist at Tobermory. Hurray for my car, and M.'s patience, and the view from hotel rooms at both places (but especially Tobermory), and the scenery, and the sea, and the seaweed, and Glengorm Castle and our lunches, and hearing Al Read on Jura, and in general for our two selves.'[4]

It was a temporary respite. Back in Hull, Larkin sank once more into the irritable gloom which had stifled him on his return from Oxford at the beginning of the year. As invariably happened when he was suffering particular stress and unhappiness, he soon developed a minor ailment. Previously it had been his eyes, his nose, his hay-fever; now it was his neck, which early in the summer had inexplicably begun to ache. After a few days of discomfort he assumed it would 'be like this for ever',[5] and although he forgot to grumble about it on holiday, it started to hurt again as soon as he returned to Pearson Park. He wrote to Monica, sweeping all kinds of grievance into one untidy heap:

My bones ache and I don't seem to have any good will for housework things . . . Perhaps I have flu. Mild flu. Perhaps things will pick up. I wish my neck didn't hurt. Growl. Growl. Growl.

What canting nonsense all this is about a million unemployed. Why doesn't somebody say that your filthy money-grubbing unions have priced your products out of the world markets, just as we said they would, and nobody wants them. Still, good out of evil, because the threat of unemployment is necessary to keep you working, you're an idle shower.

Perhaps one source of malaise is my non-writing: I feel very much that my twenty or so poems [since *The Whitsun Weddings*] aren't very good and I need ten good ones, all of 'TWW' standing, to buck them up, only I can't get around to writing them somehow. I don't really want to write about myself, and everything else hardly seems worth bothering about. I mean I can't write poems about Brenda [Moon] or Newlove's food. As you know, every writer has a book he wants to re-write (Dylan Thomas said his was *Pilgrim's Progress*): mine is 'The Seasons'. Can't do it, though. Moan. Moan. Moan. Still there's always drink. Perhaps I ought to have some, till I've drunk myself cheerful and loving like.[6]

Within a week of admitting 'I don't really want to write about myself', Larkin tried to do just that in the short lyric 'I have started to say'. Immediately afterwards he set himself a sterner task – not quite 'The Seasons', but nevertheless a brief series of poems, 'Livings', which address lives and situations that apparently have nothing to do with his own. Between 16 October and 10 December he produced three: one set in 1929 (in a coastal town a little like Hull, a little like King's Lynn) about a grain merchant, one about a lighthouse-keeper, and one (incorporating memories of his recent six months in All Souls) about a university don. (John Norton Smith, who taught English at Hull and knew Larkin, recalled a dinner they attended together at Pembroke College, Oxford, in February 1971: 'Saville Bradbury spoke [the opening words of this third poem: "I deal with farmers, things like dips and feed"] as written. Philip said, "That would make a good first line of a poem." '[7])

Before the trilogy was first published in the *Observer* Larkin had told the literary editor Terence Kilmartin, 'If it isn't suitable then by all means drop it in the waste-paper basket.'[8] Not since 'Wedding-Wind' and 'Deceptions' had he written such seemingly self-contained narratives, or so obviously used strategies more commonly associated with novels than poems. For all the dramatic projection, however – especially in the lighthouse-keeper poem, which uses its marine imagery with precisely the vigour missing from *The North Ship* – 'Livings' can't avoid drawing on deeply personal feelings. Its three characters are all people enduring isolation for different reasons and with differing reactions. The grain merchant is 'wondering why/I think it's worth coming' to his father's old stamping-ground, knows 'it's time for change', but gives no convincing sign of escaping the life he was born into. His loneliness induces a myopic boredom. The lighthouse-keeper, on the other hand, 'cherishes' his creature-surrounded outcrop of rock, where human kind ('keep it all off!') has been reduced to voices on a radio. His isolation is ecstatic – the Yeatsian poet high in his tower, inspired and engrossed. The don, pedantic and soon sozzled as he and his colleagues ponder their learned but trivial questions, experiences another kind of loneliness. He is cut off from the primal, instinctual world which the lighthouse-keeper prizes; the 'Chaldean constellations' which 'Sparkle over crowded roofs' are things he can name but not enjoy. Like the grain merchant, the don is imprisoned in habit even while he is at large in the world. The lighthouse-keeper is removed from the world but transcendentally at liberty in his imagination. (On Christmas Day in 1966, five years earlier, Larkin had written to Maeve, 'Oh for Christmas in a lighthouse! Wouldn't it be lovely? The boom of the sea . . . the cry of the gulls . . . the wireless . . . I wonder how one gets to be a lighthouse keeper?'[9])

The contrasts in 'Livings' resemble the clash of voices in 'Vers de Société', but whereas the earlier poem ends up leaning towards 'decency', the lighthouse-keeper (like the speaker of 'Absences') can't control his exultant shout:

> Seventy feet down
> The sea explodes upwards,
> Relapsing, to slaver
> Off landing-stage steps –
> Running suds, rejoice!

Exultant, but as Larkin knew well, bound to be 'cut off'. Even as he filled his evenings imagining the 'freezing slither', he spent his days introducing new students to the library, or worrying about his neck. On 7 October, Dr Raines, the depressingly 'fit director of the [university] health centre',[10] sent him to Hull Royal Infirmary for X-rays, pushing him even deeper into unhappiness. The hospital, he told Eva, 'was very big, almost like a town: crowded with people. A great industry of illness! I had to sit in a little white waiting room, in a borrowed bathrobe. Couldn't help wondering who'd had it before me! My neck still clicks away cheerfully.'[11]

Within a week Larkin had been told the result of his tests: there was 'possibly some narrowing of the joints' in his neck, 'that might be indicative of a pre-arthritic state'.[12] He took this to mean his neck was *incurable ... because there's nothing wrong with it. Ha, ha,*' and obediently took the course of 'tiny red pills'[13] that Raines prescribed for him. While the pain duly receded the thought of hospitals – or at least of nursing homes – did not. Eva, after four months in Abbeyfield, was restless and anxious to return home. Larkin realized this would be impossible, and tried to say so tactfully. 'If you are going to stay in your house' in York Road, he told her, 'then you need more people looking in and doing things for you, paid if necessary. I think there's a lot to be said for staying in one's own house as long as possible, but equally I think we should face the fact that it will eventually not be possible, and make some plans.'[14]

Eva knew what these 'plans' would be and insisted she must return home, at least to give it a final try over the Christmas holidays. Larkin continued to protest as vigorously as he could, first saying that he didn't want to put her to any trouble, and finally bursting out that he couldn't endure Christmas in York Road anyway: 'Every year I swear I'll never endure it again, and make you promise to be sensible, and now here you are talking about duck again, just as if I'd never shouted and got drunk and broken the furniture out of sheer rage at it all. For two pins I'd stay here and have bread and cheese ... *To hell with Christmas.* Let us have peace, and not all this blasted cooking and eating (and washing up!)'[15] It was no good. A few days before the holidays were due to begin, Eva left Abbeyfield and went back to her house. Kitty helped her and so did Larkin, staying for Christmas and Boxing Day before driving up to Haydon Bridge. He continued to write to Eva every evening, sending her an excited description of the New Year celebrations at Allendale, where 'the men of the village walk in a procession carrying tubs of blazing pitch on their heads',[16] and promising he would see her again soon.

His next several visits were even more of a duty than a pleasure. Larkin knew his mother was at risk as long as she lived alone, and his loving concern for her was deep and genuine – but he couldn't help thinking she was being obstinate. This January, 1972, he was especially resentful of the time she took from his weekends. Before Christmas, prompted by his glimpse of 'the great industry of illness' in Hull Royal Infirmary, he had begun a long poem about hospitals, 'The Building', which enlarged some of the ideas he had first aired in the short lyric 'How' ('How high they build hospitals!') written nearly two years before. His visits to Eva also threatened to strangle another, commissioned, poem he had recently undertaken. The request had come from Robert Jackson, a Fellow of All Souls who was also a member of a government working party convened under the Countess of Dartmouth to report on 'The Human Habitat'. He wanted Larkin to write a poem about 'the environment', which would be included in the report. Before Larkin had committed himself he haggled about the fee, and now this had been agreed he wished he had argued about the timing as well. He didn't, he said, want to 'cut across' his hospital poem, with 'thinking about the environment'.[17]

The Countess of Dartmouth prevailed. 'Going, Going', originally called 'Prologue', feeds off the same sense of finality that he was beginning to create in 'The Building', but applies it to the ruin of villages, the wrecking of towns, pollution of the seas, social and commercial greed. The vision is apocalyptic ('For the first time I feel somehow/That it isn't going to last'), the tone a mixture of sadness and impatience:

> before I snuff it, the whole
> Boiling will be bricked in
> Except for the tourist parts –
> First slum of Europe: a role
> It won't be so hard to win,
> With a cast of crooks and tarts.

This verse is a form of cartoon, like the 'kids screaming for more' and the 'spectacled grins' on the business pages. As the poem performs its polemical function it becomes stereotypical: a little smaller than life where it means to grow larger. The same thing is true of the 'England' that is so endangered:

> The shadows, the meadows, the lanes,
> The guildhalls, the carved choirs.
> There'll be books; it will linger on
> In galleries; but all that remains
> For us will be concrete and tyres.

In 'MCMXIV' the countryside forms part of a vanished ideal, a better world than ours, marooned on the wrong side of a colossal war. In 'Going, Going' it floats free of a particular historical moment to become the landscape of a nebulous golden age. Not that this worried the Countess of Dartmouth's committee. They were more troubled by the poem's outspokenness than they were by its sentimentality.

On 24 January 1972, the day before Larkin completed the poem, Eva fell in her kitchen in York Road and cracked a bone in her leg. 'What a worry!' Larkin wrote to her as soon as he heard. 'I shan't rest till I hear you are feeling better.'[18] Nor did he. Talking to Kitty, it immediately became obvious that Eva should be taken to hospital for a check-up, and that once this was done she should be moved into a better-equipped old people's home than Abbeyfield. On 30 January he went with Kitty to meet the director of the Berrystead Nursing Home, a private establishment on the London Road between Leicester and Loughborough. Its core of Edwardian buildings and recently added wings were spacious and comfortable; the garden was large and well tended; they believed Eva would be happy there. She was in no position to argue, and arrived on 2 February, initially living in a room on the first floor, but shortly afterwards moving to another on the ground floor with a television. For the time being things seemed to be settled.

Larkin drove back to Hull and tried to reassemble his life. It was difficult. He was distressed by Eva's condition and, because he knew she would never go home again, felt alone in a new and deeper way. He was bedevilled by practical requirements, consolidating the arrangements at Berrystead and committed to making weekly visits. (These soon became fortnightly – and remained so for the rest of Eva's life.) He was bothered by library business – in April he was due to attend a SCONUL conference in Lancaster. He was more than usually irritated by students, who in February once again occupied the Administration Building. In the past, it had taken fewer distractions than this to persuade him that he had no hope of writing poems until he could 'turn in his solitude' again 'like a fish in its stream'. Now the urgency of his feelings about his mother, and the evidence of his own recent slight illness, drew him back every night into 'The Building'. On 9 February, only a week after Eva had arrived in Berrystead, the poem's nine large verses were finished.

In a letter written soon afterwards Larkin was candid and straightforward about its origins. 'The Building', he told Brian Cox, 'was "inspired" by a visit to the hospital here about a crick in the neck which they couldn't do anything about and which passed off eventually of its own accord. Funnily enough, as soon as I had written it [Larkin should more accurately have said 'started it'] my mother had a fall and had to spend some time in hospital in earnest, which led to many dreary visits.'[19] In the poem itself, a large part of the horror and anxiety we feel is due to Larkin's cunning indirection. The hospital (Hull Royal Infirmary, the 'lucent comb' of which Larkin could see from his library) is never called a hospital; it is just 'the building'. At first sight it might even be a 'hotel' with scruffy porters. We are not told that ambulances keep arriving at its entrance, only that they are 'not taxis', and bring people who then pass inside to somewhere 'Like an airport lounge'. There is, of course, never any doubt about the identity and function of the place, but by refusing to name names Larkin registers something unspeakable in the patients' distress. His reticence leaves him free to make large speculations, unhindered by precise circumstances, as he looks round him, registering all he sees with an appalled but unflinching steadiness:

> Humans, caught
> On ground curiously neutral, homes and names
> Suddenly in abeyance; some are young,
> Some old, but most at that vague age that claims
> The end of choice, the last of hope . . .

Throughout his life Larkin had measured his humanity by his freedom to make choices, even choices which appeared to keep him static. In 'The Building', as he explores the bleak difference between the outside world and the world inside the hospital, this theme begins to obsess him. Outside may seem run-down (the streets are 'Like a great sigh out of the last century') and 'old' and mean ('Traffic; a locked church; short terraced streets/Where kids chalk games and girls with hair-dos fetch/Their separates from the cleaners') but it is nevertheless the realm of 'loves' and 'chances'. However vain these might prove, however like a 'dream' made up of 'conceits and self-protecting ignorance', they are nevertheless always touching. They are the spirited elaborations of human instincts which in hospital are replaced by a simpler currency: the 'only coin' of crude distinctions between old and young, men and women. In the poem's final verse there is no more suspense or kindly evasion, only the bitter fact of what things 'mean':

> All know they are going to die.
> Not yet, perhaps not here, but in the end,

And somewhere like this. That is what it means,
This clean-sliced cliff; a struggle to transcend
The thought of dying, for unless its powers
Outbuild cathedrals nothing contravenes
The coming dark, though crowds each evening try

With wasteful, weak, propitiatory flowers.

If there is any consolation here, it lies not in the sure fact that modern medicine can provide something equivalent to orthodox religion ('cathedrals'). It consists in the perennially hopeful, perennially powerless 'crowds' who bring flowers 'each evening' (and are introduced with the same cadenced gravity as the groom at the end of 'At Grass'). Their gifts are the sign of an irrepressible secular faith – as much a witness to the longing for life as the leaves in 'The Trees', or the holiday-makers in 'To the Sea'. Their actual achievement may be desultory, but their endeavour is heartening, even noble.

In the six months after finishing 'The Building' Larkin produced two short poems, 'Heads in the Women's Ward' and 'The View', which are in effect codas to it. Both take up their stand at the end of life ('Where has it gone, the lifetime? / Search me'), and both refuse even the modified comfort of 'The Building'. The former flatly asserts 'Smiles are for youth. For old age come / Death's terror and delirium', and the latter:

What's left is drear.
Unchilded and unwifed, I'm
Able to view that clear:
So final. And so near.

It wasn't only Eva's frailty which led him to these bleak conclusions, though she certainly provided most of their supporting evidence. He was propelled, too, by nagging worries about his own health. As Eva declined he took to drinking an increasingly large amount in the evenings, and while this dulled his worries it made him put on weight very rapidly. 'I seem to have spoilt my time,' he told Judy Egerton the following year, ' . . . being either drunk or hung over.'[20] Once he even admitted to his mother, 'I seem to spend far too long sunk in a drunken stupor most evenings, I'm afraid. I'm a silly creature.'[21] (He now weighed over fifteen stone, and had become so worried about his size that he even took a set of bathroom scales with him whenever he went on holiday.)

The effect, predictably, was to make him adopt a more antiquated manner. As his fiftieth birthday approached, colleagues in the university could have been forgiven for thinking he was lumbering towards his sixtieth: heavily jowled, bald, cut off from the world by thick black-framed glasses and one – sometimes two – hearing-aids. The lean and hungry young librarian who had arrived in Hull seventeen years earlier was now seeing a dietician once a month in Kingston General Hospital and buying his clothes from 'High and Mighty', the 'outsized man's' shop. He was also, dismayingly, measuring his progress towards the grave by the speed of his mother's decline. He felt more strongly than ever that when her life ended it would be too late for his own to begin.

FORTY-NINE

Soon after Eva went into Berrystead Nursing Home her condition stabilized. Larkin's depression continued to deepen. Every way he turned he found evidence to justify his mood. In May 1972 he visited Cecil Day-Lewis (who was staying with Amis and Elizabeth Jane Howard at their house in Barnet). He had known for some time that Day-Lewis had cancer; now he realized that in a matter of days the Poet Laureate would be dead. 'He is remarkably cool and courageous,' Larkin told Judy Egerton. 'I suppose this sort of thing will happen increasingly as life goes on.'[1] At the end of the month, when Day-Lewis died, Larkin's sorrow at the loss of a friend turned into frustration with his own lack of fluency as a poet. When *The Times* interviewed him as a possible successor as Laureate he whimpered to Eva, 'I really don't think I want to be Laureate! Can creatures kneel?'[2] Elsewhere he put his feelings more simply: 'Just at present I am in the mood when I doubt if I shall ever write another poem.'[3]

In the event, the succession did no more than 'ruffl[e] the edges'[4] of Larkin's life: John Betjeman was appointed and Larkin told all and sundry that he was 'very pleased'.[5] Yet the sense that his life had 'gone' remained with him. When he went to a SCONUL conference at the University of East Anglia in June he agreed to a request from Anthony Thwaite (then writer in residence at the university) to read a few poems to an invited audience, and spoke of the event as if he were viewing it from beyond the grave. 'The awful thing,' he told Thwaite, 'is that people may be expecting too much – a combination of Rupert Brooke, Walt Whitman and T. S. Eliot, instead of which they get bald, deaf, bicycle-clipped Larkin, the Laforgue of Pearson Park.'[6] Two months later, on his fiftieth birthday, he felt even further adrift. Monica gave him some 'nice records' and he gave himself some 'nice whisky',[7] and Maeve spent the evening with him drinking champagne (she gave him a recording of *Hamlet* on LPs), while the BBC Third Programme put out 'Larkin at Fifty', a compilation of poems and interviews with critics and friends. He was grateful to contributors like Amis, who said 'all the things one hopes are true, but knows are false, about my poems',[8] but felt the programme marked an end to his poetic activity, not a stage in his development.

At the end of August, free at last from having to holiday with his mother for a week, Larkin tried to repossess his life. Endeavouring to keep his feelings for Maeve steady, but tormented by jealousy whenever she showed signs of backing away from him, he sometimes clung to her, sometimes cast her aside. Maeve, continuing her 'fling with an Irishman', felt variously flattered and jostled. 'It isn't a happy time,' Larkin wrote to her in August, 'nor a happy situation. You suffer through me, I suffer through you, but I know, dear, your hurt is the greater.'[9]

Larkin ended this letter by saying, 'Lots more could be said, but probably it's better said than written' – though it is doubtful whether he meant it. Grateful to be spared a confrontation, he travelled immediately to Monica and took her on holiday with him to Scotland. This convinced Maeve that she had been right to distance herself from him in recent months, and over the next few weeks she allowed herself to drift even further away. Within a year – during the summer of 1973 – she would decide that her relationship with 'the Irishman' was 'serious', and agreed to 'part' from Larkin – finally, as she thought. 'It was then,' she says, 'that Philip gave me a copy of "The Dance", inscribed "unfinished poem called 'The Dance' given to Maeve by Philip long afterwards with undimmed memories".'[10]

Larkin was still preoccupied by thoughts of Maeve as he drove to Scotland. For the first time in recent years, he and Monica had decided to do something 'different [by] *returning* to a place'[11] – Torridon, in Wester Ross, in the north-west. If their joint diary entry for 23 August is anything to go by, things started badly. 'Hotel,' says Larkin, 'seems much the same, and the old routine of some prick of a piper farting away as a signal for dinner is unchanged.' Monica promptly adds, 'P. in usual first day of holiday rage, and would fain repeat an earlier response to the effect that the purpose of all holidays is to reconcile one to ordinary life.' After a week things were no better. 'Set out for Carron,' Larkin writes; ' – busier, like all places, than we remember it – and buy papers and two bone mustard spoons. No melons or proper arse paper (this really is a winder, and exhibits the degeneracy of the human race more startlingly than anything else I can call to mind at the moment).'[12]

Eventually – and as usual – holiday disgruntlement became a kind of sport. Larkin rounded off the diary by writing:

> My specs are splashed with lobster.
> My lobster's splashed with snot,
> No woman makes my knob stir –
> A bloody cold I've got.[13]

In September, as he settled into Pearson Park once more, black comedy turned into bleak sadness. While Monica was preoccupied with moving house (her lease on Cross Street had expired and she found a new flat at 18 Knighton Park Road, near the university in Leicester), he heard that Patsy had been taken into the London Clinic and was being treated for alcohol poisoning. Soon afterwards he was unsettled again, when Judy wrote and told him that she and her husband Ansell were separating. 'Your letter today,' Larkin told her, 'was a great shock . . . and I write with only a not very precise notion of saying I'm sorry.'[14]

When he considered his own plight, he didn't find much to encourage him. 'In the old days,' he wrote in his manuscript book on 13 November 1972 under the heading 'Spare Time':

> I used to come home
> And settle to write
> In the famous evenings.
> Now I hit the jug
> And go out like a light,
> Waking, go to bed
> With a hangover.

Even jazz reviewing, his ten-year-old stand-by, no longer consoled him. On 11 December, as he had previously arranged, the *Telegraph* published his last column and he handed his job over to Alasdair Clayre. The change was Larkin's choice, but it left him empty-headed and heavy-hearted each evening when he came home from the library. He felt he was sitting among the ruins of his life. When, at the end of the year, Barry Bloomfield (then deputy and later Director of the India Office Library) asked him if he could compile a bibliography of Larkin's work, the request seemed the final straw. Larkin looked on it as proof of his redundancy rather than his eminence. The 'view from fifty' had been bad enough; the view from fifty and a half was almost insupportable.

Thanks largely to Bloomfield's tact, Larkin soon changed his mind. He respected Bloomfield's existing bibliographical work on Auden and was proud to be linked to his youthful hero in this way. He began to wonder whether the compilation would remind him of his identity as a writer, and after a few days he replied:

It would certainly be wonderful if you did [it], as I am always getting inquiries from enthusiastic Italian girls (in Italy, unfortunately) wanting just this sort of help. I am most honoured that you should think of it. On the debit side, there really isn't much material (perhaps an advantage from your point of view): I'm nothing like as prolific as Auden, nor as famous, and in all a good deal duller – however, this is your affair. Secondly, what are the ethics prevailing between bibliographer and bibliographee? If I know of a terrible poem tucked away in a magazine you've never heard of, am I bound in honour to reveal it? As you can guess, I should much prefer not to.[15]

In the months and years to come Bloomfield observed most of Larkin's wishes for secrecy yet appealed to his appetite for self-revelation. He was given more or less free run of Larkin's own archive (though kept away from manuscripts and diaries), and built a large and accurately detailed portrait of public achievements. After four years' research he approached Faber about publication. It was a measure of Larkin's standing that such an apparently unprofitable idea was accepted. The book came out in 1979 costing £25, and although its small print run took nearly two years to sell, it was counted 'a complete success'.[16]

When Larkin first heard about the bibliography he felt empty. As Bloomfield began work, a poem began to form. 'The Old Fools' (completed on 12 January 1973 after Larkin had spent the new year in Haydon Bridge) released the rage he had been storing for the previous several months. Larkin himself was disappointed. 'Although I took great trouble over the poem I don't think it entirely succeeded,' he told Monteith when it was first published in the *Listener*. 'There's always so much *more* to say!'[17] Others felt he succeeded all too well. One reader wrote complaining that she found the poem hard-hearted, prompting him to reply, 'It is indeed an angry poem, but the anger is ambivalent: there is an anger at the humiliation of age (which I am sure you would share), but there is also an anger at the old for reminding us of death, an anger I think is especially common today when most of us believe that death ends everything. This is of course a selfish and cruel anger, but is typical of the first generation to refuse to look after its aged. Here again you will have ample evidence of what I mean.'[18]

In certain obvious respects 'The Old Fools' is a companion piece to 'The Building'. Like that poem, it opens with questions, but where the earlier ones were almost coy (of course it's a hospital and not just any building), now they are direct. The capacious stanzas – which in poems like 'Church Going' and 'The Whitsun Weddings' are airy rooms for argument and meditation – have become storage-spaces for fear:

> What do they think has happened, the old fools,
> To make them like this? Do they somehow suppose
> It's more grown-up when your mouth hangs open and drools,
> And you keep on pissing yourself, and can't remember
> Who called this morning?

These are the sights, sounds and smells which in 'The Building' were guessed at, rather than seen. Yet the reason they seem hideous is the same in both poems: they describe a condition which marks 'the end of choice'. Previously it was the world's 'loves' and 'chances' which were 'beyond the stretch/Of any hand from here'; now 'the old fools'' worst delusion would be to suppose they could recover their happy youth 'if they only chose'. Their nearness to death means they have lost the defining human characteristic Larkin valued most.

Halfway through the poem, Larkin's voice changes and he becomes more plainly descriptive: 'At death, you break up; the bits that were you/Start speeding away from each other'. It's not a tone he can hold for long. Explaining the difference between the oblivion of being in the womb and the blankness of being in the grave, he is reminded too painfully of the 'million-petalled flower/Of being here' to keep his equanimity. The 'first signs' of death – the forms of death in life – begin to press on him too heavily. Heaviest of all, once again, is 'the power/Of choosing gone'. Larkin recoils, producing the poem's most freely imaginative section as he envisages 'being old' as 'having lighted rooms/Inside your head, and people in them, acting':

> People you know, yet can't quite name; each looms
> Like a deep loss restored, from known doors turning,
> Setting down a lamp, smiling from a stair, extracting

A known book from the shelves; or sometimes only
The rooms themselves, chairs and a fire burning,
The blown bush at the window, or the sun's
Faint friendliness on the wall some lonely
Rain-ceased midsummer evening.

In a different context this might be a paradigm of the imaginative life; it might be Larkin miming his own creative singleness. Here, though, it describes something so purely 'over' it seems asphyxiated. The divisions between past, present and future cannot be healed, and realizing this jolts him into the poem's final image, which exchanges the sourly lit interiors of the first three stanzas for 'Extinction's alp' ('This must be what keeps them quiet:/The peak that stays in view wherever we go/For them is rising ground'). As this mountain reminds Larkin of his comparative youth it prompts the final question:

Can they never tell
What is dragging them back, and how it will end? Not at night?
Not when the strangers come? Never, throughout
The whole hideous inverted childhood? Well,
We shall find out.

What the poem asks it answers. Second childhood, second oblivion, are superficially similar but profoundly different. One leads into the world of choice, one out of it, and however much Larkin felt he might have abused or neglected 'the power of choosing', he is reduced nearly to 'screaming' by the thought that it will one day be denied him.

Eva's final illness stands behind 'The Old Fools' in more than just the obvious ways. As well as forcing Larkin to confront painful facts about old age, she also compelled him to think differently about chance and choice. All his adult life he had arranged things to seem as though he was keeping his options open: he had a job, but he might change it; he had a home, but not one that tied him; he had women he loved, but had committed himself fully to no one. His purpose, as he had said time and again, was to be free to write. For nearly twelve years either Monica or Maeve had seemed to threaten his independence, and he believed that he had managed to keep himself to himself only with the greatest difficulty. The fact that he had succeeded was largely due to Eva. Hers was the condition to which everything else had to defer, and hers was the nest to which he could always fly instead of feathering his own. Now that she was altering the shape of his life in a way he could not control he found himself questioning his choices more urgently.

A little over a month later, in 'Money', Larkin tackled the same theme in different terms. Contemplating his quarterly bills, he wonders whether, if he had spent differently, he would have lived differently. Has he chosen a life he now finds reprehensible? In the past when he had asked the same question in poems like 'Reasons for Attendance' and 'Poetry of Departures' he had usually accused himself of meanness without apologizing for it. It's the same in his letters, too, where he is often and unrepentantly stingy. In the beautiful and strange final verse of 'Money' he gives a more elaborate answer:

> I listen to money singing. It's like looking down
> From long french windows at a provincial town,
> The slums, the canal, the churches ornate and mad
> In the evening sun. It is intensely sad.

Larkin's general observation, obviously, is that everyone dances to money's tune. Beneath this lies a more personal point, one which seems at first glance, typically, like a compromise. The noise of money singing is both a siren song, calling Larkin to the world of false hopes, and also a dirge bewailing the fact that the only world on offer to him is 'provincial', slum-infested and 'mad'. He implies that whatever short-term happiness money might bring, it will inevitably be destroyed by the pain and drabness of actual circumstances. Reality cannot help but be 'intensely sad'.

This explanation of the poem covers all eventualities, but it leaves Larkin himself veiled. Where does he stand in relation to the ambiguous picture he paints? What are his own choices? The answer is bleak: whatever the world might offer him, he is cut off from it, unable to make decisions or definitions. Behind the glass of his long, high windows he suffers a version of the 'baffled absence' that the old fools endure. His senses jitter synaesthetically (when he 'listens' to money singing he doesn't hear but sees); his sorrow is great but inarticulate, embedded in objects. In such a state the question of whether he might live more happily if he spent his money differently has almost no weight. The question is rather whether he has a life at all.

In precisely the workaday terms he didn't mean, the answer was: seldom more so. Although work in the library and the university was easier than it had been in the past, the amount of business thrown up by his writing continued to increase steadily. In January Charles Monteith had written to him as he was finishing 'The Old Fools', pointing out that Roy Fuller's term of office as Professor of Poetry at Oxford was drawing to an end: would Larkin stand as his successor? Monteith knew Larkin was likely to say no, but also felt he would be pleased to hear that Auden wanted to nominate him. Larkin hesitated only briefly. 'Your letter was immensely flattering,' he told Monteith:

To know that Auden and you yourself are willing to nominate me is the biggest compliment I have been paid for many years. I only wish I felt your confidence was justified, or could do something to justify it. But as you will know – and you know me a good deal better than Auden does – I have really very little interest in poetry in the abstract; I have never lectured about it, or even written about it to any extent, and I know that I could never produce anything worthy of such a distinguished office and audience. The effort of trying to do so, moreover, would make my life hell for five years and almost certainly stop me writing anything else, which would be (at least in my view) a disadvantage ... No, I am tempted – and the temptation is accompanied by day-dreams even more voluptuous than those of St Antony – but common sense must prevail. Please tell Auden how sincerely grateful I am for his offer: I am sure he will think my refusal pusillanimous. Much as I love Oxford, though, and much as the honour would delight me, to say anything different from the above would be to misjudge the situation, and the result would be disastrous.[19]

It wasn't just the thought of having to give lectures, advise undergraduates, and lead the violated life of a public man that made Larkin refuse. It was the thought of having to exist in a way which was self-consciously literary. No sooner had he declined than the literary life came to Hull: Geoffrey Moore, Professor of American Studies at the university, invited Robert Lowell to read, and made sure that Larkin didn't escape him. For Lowell, the meeting was the culmination of many years of admiration. In 1957, shortly after reading *The Less Deceived*, he had told Randall Jarrell, 'There's a new English poet called Larkin that I like better than anyone since [Dylan] Thomas. I've been reading him since the spring and really like him better than Thomas.'[20] (Jarrell's letters show that he soon echoed these sentiments.) By the time *The Whitsun Weddings* appeared, Larkin had a secure place in Lowell's modern pantheon. Writing to a friend about John Berryman's *77 Dreamsongs* Lowell confided, 'I think it's only here and there that I read [Berryman] with the all out enjoying amazement that I feel for Bishop, Plath, Larkin and much of Roethke.'[21]

Larkin struggled to return the compliments. Reviewing *Life Studies* in

1959 he had called Lowell's poems 'curious, hurried, offhand vignettes, seeming too personal to be practised, yet nonetheless accurate and original'.[22] Since then he had taken to referring to Lowell as 'simply barmy'[23] – but when Moore welcomed Lowell to Hull on 1 February 1973 Larkin was his customarily polite self. He drank with Lowell, listened to him read, then drank some more. The following day he wrote to Eva saying he was 'A creature that has talked too much, drunk too much and stayed up too late!'[24] For the time being the doubts he had about Lowell were drowned; they exchanged a few letters, and in April the following year Larkin even spent a night with Lowell and his wife Caroline Blackwood at their home in Millgate Park, near Maidstone in Kent. ('He looked older than T. S. Eliot,' Lowell told Elizabeth Bishop, knowing she was also a fan; ' – six foot one, low-spoken, bald, deaf, death-brooding, a sculptured statue of his poems. He made me feel almost an undergraduate in health, and somehow old as the hills – he is four years younger.'[25]) A year later still, Larkin sent Lowell a copy of his new collection, *High Windows*. 'I like the title poem best maybe,' Lowell replied, 'all the poetry is in the last lines, these would count for little without the others . . . I think you resemble Graves and maybe Auden at times, but the poet I most think of still is Herbert – elegance and homeliness.'[26]

Although he dreaded them, the other items of literary business that Larkin had to deal with during the early part of the year also gave him a surprising amount of pleasure. In May Faber published *The North Ship* in paperback – which he said was 'welcome, at least, for base commercial reasons', though he added, 'I am not sure how pleased I am at the prospect of further dissemination of this drivel.'[27] The same month he heard from the Society of Authors that he had been given a Cholmondeley Award worth £500. Within days of receiving it he was invited to become an honorary Fellow of his old college, St John's, and accepted 'with great pleasure'.[28] Eight weeks later he was installed as an honorary Doctor of Letters at the University of Warwick (the ceremony was held in Coventry Cathedral, adjacent to the 'old ruined'[29] one where he had been christened in September 1922). A week later still he was reading the citation at another ceremony, this time to install John Betjeman as an honorary Doctor of Letters at Hull. And before the summer was over he was reading the first full-length study of his own work, *Philip Larkin* by David Timms. The book was an expanded version of an MA thesis that Timms had written at the University of Leicester. 'It is most kind of you to occupy yourself with my all-too-few and too-feeble writings,' Larkin told Timms, 'and I only hope it will be worth your while, not so much in spiritual or intellectual currencies, as in hard cash. I feel it is a great honour to have a book written about me, and I look forward to its appearance with shameful eagerness.'[30]

In the midst of all this coming and going Larkin told Judy Egerton, 'I wish I could say that I had something to show for [my time].'[31] Even if he didn't spell out for her the details of his famous meetings, or his honours given and received, she knew better than to trust what he said. It wasn't just that she understood how often he needed to protect himself by pretending to be hopelessly inert. She also knew, simply from reading the newspapers, that the early part of 1973 had kept him unusually busy in a way which both explained and complicated all the other demands on his time. In March, two years after he had delivered it, *The Oxford Book of Twentieth Century English Verse* had been published. It had caused, as he expected, a furious storm of controversy.

Larkin hadn't set out to be contentious, but while he collected material he realized that he was bound to irritate or baffle many readers. Although he had been disappointed not to find more and better poems to prove his theory that the noise of the modernists had stifled healthy English voices, this hadn't led him to revise his opinion of the modernists themselves. Eliot is represented in the anthology by only nine poems – and although two of these are long – 'Prufrock' and 'The Waste Land' – they still do not take up enough pages to make him seem a supremely dominant figure. Only Hardy, with twenty-seven poems, could claim to be that – though even this big block of work is not the book's outstanding feature. What is remarkable is the large number of poets it contains (207) and the small number of poems culled from each. Only a handful are given more than two or three: Yeats has nineteen, Auden sixteen, Kipling thirteen, Betjeman and Lawrence twelve, Graves eleven and Edward Thomas nine. Larkin gives himself six, the same number as Rupert Brooke, Roy Campbell and Day-Lewis, but one fewer than Owen or Sassoon, and two fewer than Dylan Thomas.

Larkin's *Oxford* book, in other words, is an anthology of poems not poets. It celebrates the large emotions which can erupt in ordinary lives, and the small emotions which can combine to become something extraordinary. Truthfulness, lack of pretension, traditional formal skills, attitudes which help us both to enjoy and endure: these are the virtues he wanted to collect. Rank invention, references to other writers, technical high jinks, obscurity: these are the vices he wanted to exclude. He intended to extol modesty and quiet watchfulness, to provide an account of literary evolution rather than revolution, and to give a generous practical demonstration of the theories he had advanced in reviews and elsewhere for the last twenty-odd years.

In his short Introduction to the anthology, Larkin wrapped up these hopes and guiding principles in dull and cautious language. 'In making my selection,' he said:

I have striven to hold a balance between all the different considerations that press on anyone undertaking a book of this kind. At first I thought I would let the century choose the poets while I chose the poems, but outside two or three dozen names this did not really work. In the end I felt that my material fell into three groups: poems representing aspects of the talents of poets judged either by the age or by myself to be worthy of inclusion, poems judged by me to be worthy of inclusion without reference to their authors, and poems judged by me to carry with them something of the century in which they were written.[32]

Even as he said this, Larkin knew he was trying to pass off as fair and broad-minded something which was in fact strict and strongly opinionated. No one was fooled. When the book appeared on 29 March (in a first impression of 29,300 copies) only a few appreciative voices (Auden in the *Guardian* and Betjeman in the *Sunday Times*) were audible among the groans of protest. Donald Davie, in the *Listener*, was especially hostile, and his objections summarized most of those made elsewhere: Larkin had misrepresented the modernists; he had omitted people he should have included (such as David Jones); he had shown 'positive cynicism',[33] he had produced 'the perverse triumph of philistinism, the cult of the amateur, the wrong kind of post-modernism, the weakest kind of Englishry';[34] he had mistaken feebleness for modesty; he had denied experiment; he had made the book too much in what he considered to be (rather than what actually was) his own poetic image.

What Larkin called 'ordinary people who do not write in journals'[35] responded differently. It was Larkin's contention that he had created 'a readable book' and had 'made twentieth century poetry sound nice', which was 'quite an achievement in itself',[36] and those who shared his taste rallied to his flag. Others, who sided with Davie, took arms against them and for at least two months after publication the review pages and letters columns echoed with the clamour of dissenting voices. Initially, Larkin was daunted, but as he realized that 'at grass roots'[37] he had supporters as well as detractors, he began to enjoy the fray. 'Weekly reviews,' he confided to Judy Egerton in April, 'especially the *Listener* – were *bad*. Sundays were betwixt and between. It's funny how after it once starts one doesn't really care. One just writes off the hostile reviewers as jealous or imperceptive time-servers ... The battle is on. Perhaps the nicest thing is letters from total strangers, saying how they like it.'[38]

A month later his tentative good cheer had turned into something like glee. 'Davie does seem to be dancing up and down rather,' he wrote to Martin Bell. 'I hope he isn't going off his chump.'[39] This marked the beginning of a private campaign of Davie-mockery which lasted the rest of Larkin's life. In 1976, for instance, he sent Amis the following ditty, to be sung to the tune of 'Daisy, Daisy':

> Davie, Davie, give me a bad review,
> That's your gravy, telling chaps what to do.
> Forget about style and passion
> As long as it's the fashion –
> But let's be fair, it's got you a Chair
> Which was all it was meant to do.[40]

To other correspondents he was equally robust. Of course it wasn't an oversight that he'd left out David Jones, he told several of them; as far as he was concerned, Jones was 'Richard Aldington rewritten by Ezra Pound'.[41] Only in one area of his selection – the last thirty pages – was he prepared to admit a weakness. He felt they were 'not impressive',[42] though saying so only confirmed the argument of the preceding pages: the influence of the modernists had been a disaster. Otherwise he stood his ground, his original uncertainties receding as sales rose. Within a year of publication a second impression of 20,000 copies was required, and within the first ten years it brought him 'about £38,000 but I can't say I've noticed it. All goes in tax.'[43] He reckoned he had proved his point: 'My taste is much more akin to that of the ordinary person than it is to that of the professional student or practitioner of literature.'[44]

As well as stirring up a war of words, the *Oxford* book created a mass of practical anxieties. For one thing – and to Larkin's great regret – it soon became clear that the anthology contained a large number of misprints, among them the omission of half of William Empson's 'Aubade' and the last two verses of Thom Gunn's 'The Byrnies'. 'I can see myself joining Bowdler and Grainger,' Larkin told Thwaite: 'to *larkinize*, v.t., to omit that part of a poem printed on verso and subsequent pages, from a notorious anthology published in latter half of twentieth century.'[45]

Although the mistakes were not entirely his fault (the Press had to accept some of the blame) he felt them personally. He wrote Gunn, whose work he had often privately mocked, an apologetic letter.

More wearisome was the publicity surrounding the anthology's appearance. As it drew near, he stayed with Monica in Leicester for two nights, then went to a SCONUL conference in Southampton on the day of publication, then immediately returned to Leicester again 'so as to avoid reporters etc.'.[46] The few interviews he agreed to give (one on the radio, one with Betjeman in the *Telegraph*) convinced him that he had been right to resist the pressure to do more, and as the threat of two other duties loomed he began to feel increasingly 'unhappy associations'[47] with the book. The first, on 8 April, was an invitation to attend a party at Buckingham Palace which he felt was 'a wonderful compliment' but also alarming. The Queen 'was pleasant enough', he said afterwards, 'but I didn't have enough of her to lose my nervousness'.[48] The second, in early May, was a Foyles Literary Lunch at the Dorchester Hotel in London, at which he had to give a speech. This he also counted an honour, but couldn't enjoy it. 'You don't expect to start as a sensitive boy writing poems and end up making a speech [here],' he said, fighting his stammer and sweating heavily. 'If you do you probably weren't a very sensitive boy.'[49]

Elsewhere in his speech, Larkin posed the question which had occupied him all the time he had worked on the anthology. Why had he accepted the commission in the first place, since he jealously disliked most contemporary poets, and had no appetite for publicity? The answer gleams from his work, if not always from his life. The shy Larkin, the aloof librarian who would advance no more complicated theory about his writing than that it contained a report on whatever made him feel deeply, was also the opposite of these things. He was dogmatic Larkin, the man who sheltered in the provinces but wanted to know the news from London, the strong-minded, people-watching poet whose entire existence had been devoted to perfecting his work. Apparently unlike his predecessor Yeats, but with the same ambition, Larkin used the *Oxford* book to define and promote the taste by which he wished to be relished. A year after publication he told a colleague at Hull, 'Rumour has it that Kingsley is to revise – or re-do – the *Oxford Book of Light Verse*. We shall have stamped our taste on the age between us in the end.'[50]

FIFTY

As soon as the fuss of publication had died down, Larkin set about illustrating the argument of his *Oxford* anthology in other ways. He collected the poems he had written during the last ten years, and in June 1973 sent them to Faber under the title *High Windows*. It was a decisive step, but one that he wanted to appear tentative. 'Here,' he wrote to Monteith, 'is the text of the best collection I can now muster. I do realize it is short, and if I thought I were likely to write five more poems in the space of a few months I should hold back until I had done so. Unfortunately I don't feel this. On the other hand, please feel quite free to suggest a deferment if you think it is the best course. At this stage I am not asking for it to be published so much as sending it to you for you to look at.'[1]

Monteith knew there was genuine uncertainty in Larkin's letter, as well as an unacknowledged desire to ride in the slipstream of the *Oxford* book – though when he read the manuscript he thought Larkin's doubts were misplaced. There were more 'light' poems than in previous Larkin collections, but their intensity and memorableness easily earned them a place. The collection was 'short', but only one page less than *The Less Deceived* and four pages less than *The Whitsun Weddings*. Within a fortnight Monteith told Larkin that Faber wanted to publish the book early the following spring – and if, in the immediate future, Larkin were to write something he wanted to add, they would fit it in. 'As I said,' Larkin replied, 'if only I thought I could write a few more poems quickly, I would hold it another six months. But I fear that is beyond me.'[2]

At the same time as Monteith put *High Windows* into production he also sent a copy to the publishers Farrar, Straus and Giroux in New York. He knew that Larkin's reputation in America was almost non-existent except as a poet's poet (admired by Lowell, Jarrell, Bishop), and reckoned that his previous publishers hadn't served him particularly well. St Martin's Press, which had produced *The Less Deceived* in 1960, had let the book go out of print in 1972; Random House, which published *The Whitsun Weddings* in 1964, had also let it lapse. Monteith expected that Farrar, Straus and Giroux, who specialized in publishing poetry, would be more appreciative – even if Larkin was unlikely to change his view that 'all

American publishers are Neanderthal blockheads'.[3]

Robert Giroux replied within a month saying that he wanted to publish the book, but adding that he hoped Larkin would think again about including 'Posterity'. The American accent used in the poem struck him as awkward, and the references to 'Tel Aviv', 'Myra's folks' and making 'the money sign' seemed anti-Semitic. Monteith asked Matthew Evans, his colleague at Faber, to explain the problem to Larkin, knowing a row was in the offing. Larkin replied:

I have given some consideration to Mr Giroux's suggestion about 'Posterity'. My own opinion is that this is by no means the worst poem in the book, and that to delete it would materially weaken the collection, a view in which I am supported, I know, by one or two English friends [Monica and Thwaite among others]. If, therefore, Mr Giroux is asking me to delete it, I am afraid my reply must be a courteous negative. If, on the other hand, he is telling me to delete it, I would do so only on condition that their edition contains in the prelims the statement 'On the advice of the publisher, the poem "Posterity" has been omitted from this edition.' I have had the experience [in connection with the *Oxford* book] of being blamed for omissions made at the representation of others, and so I should like the situation to be clear.[4]

At the end of the year the disagreement was still unresolved. 'What did FSG say to my request?' Larkin wanted to know, his irritation mounting. 'I should like to make it quite clear that if they agree to neither of [my suggestions], the deal is off.'[5] Monteith had hoped that by doing nothing for a few weeks he would have tempted Larkin to change his position. Now he knew better, and said so to Giroux. Within days it had been decided that the poem should remain, leaving Larkin triumphant but a little guilty at causing a rumpus about a poem he half suspected wasn't worth it. He felt 'like George III or Lord North',[6] he later told Monteith gratefully.

The problems with *High Windows* were not over. Shortly before Christmas 1973, when the book was already in proof, Larkin finished a new poem, 'Show Saturday'. He sent it to Monteith at once, asking him to place it near the end of the collection between 'Vers de Société' and 'Money', then realized that the version he had posted was not one he entirely approved. 'I have now discovered,' he wrote embarrassedly, 'that stanza three has its rhymes all wrong, and I shall have to re-write it.'[7] Three weeks later, after brooding over the poem during the Christmas holiday, he felt it still wasn't right. 'One line,' he told Monteith, 'has six beats. Please ensure that I have a proof before the mighty presses roll.'[8]

It's easy to see why Larkin was eager to include 'Show Saturday', even awkwardly and at the last minute. The eight large stanzas provide the solidity he felt *High Windows* lacked, and its subject lovingly summarizes some of the collection's major themes. It celebrates pastoral pleasures that seem 'ordinary' but are in fact ancient and sanctioned by custom. Dogs, ponies, horses, side-shows, and people crowd the verses of a huge hymn to old England – the England that appears in 'MCMXIV' and 'Going, Going', and has its sentimental, reactionary, and self-consciously antique features braced by sturdy rhythms and details ('four brown eggs, four white eggs,/Four plain scones, four dropped scones'). These 'pure excellences', showing 'a recession of skills', embody for Larkin the same sense of community which is exemplified in 'To the Sea', hoped for in 'The Whitsun Weddings', won and lost in 'The Dance', and envied in many shorter lyrics. The poem insists on the need for continuity while implying that such a thing is unlikely to be granted. What begins as a hymn ends as a prayer:

> Let it stay hidden there like strength, below
> Sale-bills and swindling; something people do,
> Not noticing how time's rolling smithy-smoke
> Shadows much greater gestures; something they share
> That breaks ancestrally each year into
> Regenerate union. Let it always be there.

'Show Saturday' displays its contents clearly. It also has a veiled (if not quite a secret) ingredient. The actual scene described in the poem is Bellingham Show in Northumberland, which Larkin and Monica visited most years after she had moved to Haydon Bridge. (In 1973, the year the poem was written, they called in after a fortnight's holiday in Scotland.) The sights and sounds Larkin evokes are therefore not simply those one might expect to find at any such event; they are part of the enclosed world he shared with Monica. He knew, for instance, that when he showed her the poem she would recognize the 'Two young [wrestlers] in acrobats' tights' as the Harrington Brothers, who appeared at Bellingham every year. In this sense 'Show Saturday' is a love poem, speaking a private language that is also perfectly serviceable in public. In the past he had made much larger gestures to other women in other poems – to Winifred Arnott in 'Lines on a Young Lady's Photograph Album', to Maeve in 'Broadcast' and 'The Dance' – but Monica had hardly been serenaded at all. Now, in the remembered details of happiness they had shared, he passed her a coded message in the last line: 'Let it always be there'.

While Larkin was working on the poem he visited Oxford, on 27 October, to attend the memorial service for W. H. Auden in Christ Church cathedral. Although Larkin believed that Auden's genius had deserted him when he left England for America in 1939, he continued to revere his early poems, had been flattered by Auden's admiration for his own work, and had enjoyed their few meetings. (The most extended had been at dinner in Stephen Spender's house in London in 1972, when Auden had asked Larkin whether he liked living in Hull. When Larkin replied that he supposed he would be as unhappy anywhere else, Auden cackled, 'Naughty! Naughty! Mother wouldn't like it!'[9]) Initially Larkin had been 'terribly shocked'[10] by the news of Auden's death. As the memorial service approached he began to enjoy the sense of occasion. He and Monica had lunch with Monteith in All Souls before walking across to the cathedral through 'marvellous autumn weather'[11] with John Betjeman, and afterwards they all went to the wake organized by the Dean of Christ Church. Moved and excited, Larkin began a series of heady conversations. Betjeman told him that he wanted to resign the Laureateship and wondered whether Larkin would take it on. Larkin didn't reply, turning instead to Cyril Connolly, a literary hero of his schooldays, pumping his hand and blurting out, 'Sir, you formed me!'[12] (When Connolly himself died a year later Larkin said he was 'shattered ... He was one of my favourite living writers because he was so funny, and now there will be no more.'[13]) It was, as he wrote to Monteith later, 'a very memorable day ... filled with conflicting emotions and varied satisfactions'.[14]

A month later Oxford beckoned again. During the summer John Wain had been elected Professor of Poetry – Larkin had voted for him and attended the party which followed his victory. Now he was hoping to hear the inaugural lecture, but warned Wain that 'I tend to live from week to week, if not day to day, and I can't for the moment envisage how I shall be fixed.'[15] Remembering past meetings, especially Wain's shambling and nauseous performance in Hull, Larkin thought it best to give his old friend some advice. 'What a splendid occasion it will be. I do hope you will show them your "serious" face, with all your insight and humanity, and leave the comic-hat stuff for later: you *must* not only wipe the floor with your predecessor – you can do that before breakfast – but give us something that will be handed down like Bradley and Arnold.

Wain on Versifying. You're the only one of us twenties lot with the reading *and* the perception *and* the style. But do be serious!'[16]

When the time came, Larkin was disappointed not to be able to leave his work in Hull. Or at least that's what he said. In fact he was relieved. Ever since the *Oxford* book, he had been caught up in one kind of public chore or another, and as the year drew to a close he became anxious to get back to his own affairs. Some involved more pleasure than business. He wanted, for instance, to take up his membership of the MCC, which had recently been negotiated by his sponsors Ansell Egerton and Harold Pinter. (Pinter, who greatly admired Larkin's poems, had known him slightly since 1972, when they had lunched together in London; in June 1974 they met again at Lord's.) Some, predictably, involved more business than pleasure. On 19 December he had to inaugurate the 'Philip Larkin Collection' in the Brynmor Jones Library and the same month he made renewed efforts to take *The Less Deceived* away from The Marvell Press and pass it to Faber. He enlisted the help of the Society of Authors, assuring them that he still felt grateful to George Hartley for his initial support, but also condemning him for his amateurism. 'Although Mr Hartley treats me comparatively well,' he said, 'it would as you can imagine be more convenient for me if all my books were in the hands of one publisher, and I should dearly like to get this one away from him. Is there any point ... claiming that he is in breach of the contract and has therefore nullified it?'[17]

The answer, as Larkin expected, was no – but while he found Hartley's 'obdurate attitude ... irritating' he continued to 'see his point'.[18] His resentment, anyway, was soon overtaken by much more complicated matters. Shortly after Christmas the university announced that as part of a series of economies they had decided to sell several of their properties. Among them was 32 Pearson Park. Larkin was appalled. In the eighteen years he had lived there his flat had been both a haven from the world and a source for many of the images which haunted his poems. Its high windows, its views of the tree-muffled park, and its romantic isolation had allowed him to feel that his life and his writing were intertwined. Furthermore, it had proclaimed him not simply as a determined bachelor but also as a kind of grown-up student, someone unencumbered by possessions, paying rent not a mortgage, free (in theory) to leave whenever he wanted. It was a place filled with the idea of youth, which he feared he would lose for ever if he moved.

Practical difficulties, as well as this new sense of finality, began to weigh on him. He had reached the age of fifty-two with virtually no idea of how to buy or run a house (though he had helped his mother find Dixon Drive and York Road), and the prospect drove him to despair. 'I shrink from the trouble,'[19] he told Eva, beginning to consult friends and estate agents without even a vague notion of what he wanted. It was out of the question that he might buy 32 Pearson Park: he had no wish to set up as a landlord administering the other flats on floors below his own. He didn't, in fact, even know whether he wanted a flat or a house – or whether he should be in Hull or outside, in somewhere new or somewhere Victorian. George Cole, who organized the university dining club he belonged to, came to his rescue. There was a house for sale in Newland Park a few doors away from the Coles': number 105. It was a part of town Larkin already knew, but not one for which he had much affection. John Kenyon describes it as belonging to 'an exclusive, rather "posh", entirely middle-class backwater (not a park at all ... just a figure-eight-shaped *cul de sac* off the Cottingham Road [almost immediately opposite the university]). It attracts no idling pensioners or pram-pushing mothers, no loblolly men scavenging its litter baskets (it has no such thing anyway); only the occasional sibilance of a limousine, or the clatter of a delivery van, disturbs its rather sterile tranquillity. It is stiflingly bourgeois.'[20]

Larkin went to look. He found a two-storey, raw-bricked 1950s building, defended from the road by a crudely pollarded tree, its façade dominated by a large white garage door. It was remarkably ugly and also inconvenient: although well appointed inside, it had a long garden. Larkin dreaded having to look after this, but told himself there were advantages: the house was quiet, and it was handy for the library. With the university snapping at his heels, keen to repossess Pearson Park, he decided to buy.

His solicitor, Terence Wheldon of the Hull firm Gosschalks, prepared the papers. 'I have,' Larkin told Judy Egerton:

blindly, deafly and dumbly said I will buy an utterly undistinguished little modern house in Newland Park: ... the 'deal' isn't through yet, but I see no reason why it shouldn't be concluded, as the present owner wishes to be off to South Africa. Well, at any rate, it isn't the bungalow on the by-pass. But I can't say it's the kind of dwelling that is eloquent of the nobility of the human spirit. It has a huge garden – not a lovely wilderness (though it soon will be) – a long strip between wire fences – oh God, oh God – I'm 'taking over' the vendors' Qualcast [lawn mower] (sounds like a character in Henry James). I don't know when I shall get in. I want a few things doing first, and decorating done. I hope before the bloody

440

garden starts growing . . . I feel like calling it 'The Old Mill' – everyone I know lives in something called The Old Mill or The Old Forge or The Old Rectory – or 'High Windows'. 'High-priced Windows' would be more like it.[21]

The 'deal' went ahead as easily as Larkin feared. On 15 March he signed the appropriate papers in Wheldon's office – he bought the house outright – and during the following weeks, advised by Monica, arranged for carpets to be laid (dark pink, predominantly), curtains to be hung (William Morris patterns mostly), walls to be painted (dark green in the sitting room), bookshelves to be built and furniture to be ordered. He resented the trouble and loathed the expense but, as usual, managed everything efficiently. On 27 June he moved, spending the morning watching 'the men . . . loading my miserable belongings on to their van', then when they went off to lunch sitting among the remains of his past life writing to his mother. 'I think,' he told her, 'my chief impression is how old and dirty all my things are! When the bookcases were moved, the dirt of ages lay behind. When a man put some sofa cushions together, clouds of dust arose! I felt rather ashamed!'[22]

As soon as he reached 105 Newland Park his troubles multiplied. He couldn't find the key to the back door. The front door jammed, and for a while he had to creep in and out of the house through the garage. New machines perplexed him: he bought his first automatic washing-machine, for instance, and immediately mourned the 'pleasure' of 'dabbling and wringing' his socks and underwear by hand, 'then seeing them hang out to dry'.[23] He sprained his wrists carrying a box of books. The central heating broke down. The garden seemed possessed by demons but whenever he had a moment to subdue it he was 'too frightened'[24] to have a bonfire. He appreciated it was 'a time when one is easily affected',[25] but nevertheless made the most of every difficulty. By day he sulked angrily in the library; by night he crouched in the deep residential stillness, watching the long black hands of the electric clock he had installed over the gas fire in his sitting-room jolt round their circle, feeling that he was required not merely to continue his life, but to start it again.

He was troubled to think what this might mean for his writing. In his various top-floor flats he had relied on a feeling of cosy retirement. Now it seemed 'funny' even 'to go up stairs'[26] – especially since when he got there he found four bedrooms and no study. To lure himself back into his old habits he experimented for a while with the idea of converting one of the bedrooms into a writing room, lining it with bookcases and filling them with his father's books. It didn't work. His own books and records were elsewhere in the house. He felt scattered. He took to sitting downstairs, to the right of the gas fire, his back to the garden, within arm's reach of his favourite authors. The original régime of working for two hours every evening was one that he had found increasingly difficult to maintain even in Pearson Park. By the end of his time there, he told friends, he was drinking too much in the evenings to want to work, and had begun getting up at six in the morning instead. In Newland Park this proved too difficult. He merely lay in bed when he woke early, too hung-over and depressed to think it was worth trying to write. He was, he told strangers who tried to call on him, 'not really meetable';[27] he asked his solicitor Terence Wheldon to draw up his will.

Larkin knew there was something 'disproportionate' in his 'depression',[28] and said so whenever friends like Monica, who didn't fear his censure, told him things were not quite as bad as he made them out to be. The misery of his move had in fact been comparatively productive: he had written a reminiscence of his days at Leicester (the university there had given him an honorary degree in 1970) and had begun two poems. One ('Aubade', which he started in Pearson Park on 11 March with a description of 'Waking at four to soundless dark') he didn't finish for another three years. The other, 'The Life with a Hole in it', was done by 8 August. It opens with an attempt to justify himself to those who had recently accused him of making too much of his own discomfort:

> When I throw back my head and howl
> People (women mostly) say
> *But you've always done what you want,*
> *You always get your own way*
> – A perfectly vile and foul
> Inversion of all that's been.
> What the old ratbags mean
> Is I've never done what I don't.

As his resentment grows, Larkin looks back to the ideal he cherished as a young man, the ideal of making his living as a novelist, which now he can only mock. In 1961 he had told Barbara Pym, 'When I was about twenty-three [I] . . . hoped I was going to lead that wonderful five-hundred-words-a-day-on-the-Riviera life that beckons us all like an *ignis fatuus* from the age of sixteen onwards';[29] now he rounds furiously on 'the shit in the shuttered château/Who does his five hundred words/Then parts out the rest of the day/Between bathing and booze and birds'. The poem's anger, however, is compounded by guilt, and no sooner has Larkin snarled at those reprimanding him than he concedes the point he had denied in the first verse. Things might indeed be worse. He might be a 'spectacled schoolteaching sod/(Six kids, and the wife in pod,/And her parents coming to stay) . . .' In several earlier poems, Larkin's ability to see both sides of an argument had allowed him to feel 'really himself' – full of choices, his integrity undefiled. Here a wealth of choices only produces inertia:

> Life is an immobile, locked,
> Three-handed struggle between
> Your wants, the world's for you, and (worse)
> The unbeatable slow machine
> That brings what you'll get. Blocked,
> They strain round a hollow stasis
> Of havings-to, fear, faces.
> Days sift down it constantly. Years.

The 'hole' in Larkin's life, the poem tells us, *is* his life. All the activity which surrounds it is self-defeating, and convinces him of nothing except that time is running out.

As Larkin reached this conclusion he was busily accumulating evidence which he hoped might soften its impact. In January his long-standing admirer Harry Chambers had published a *Philip Larkin Special Issue* of his magazine *Phoenix*, which Larkin thought looked 'magnificent' and felt was 'a wonderful boost to the ego'.[30] In March he had heard from Howard Moss of the National Institute of Arts and Letters in America that he had been awarded the Russell Loines Award (Robert Giroux collected it on his behalf). And in May, a month before moving into Newland Park, he had received early copies of *High Windows*. He wrote to Monteith, 'I am delighted with them. As soon as I opened the package I saw that they had been bound in a grey cloth that reminds me of Auden's *Look, Stranger!* which seemed a specially good omen.'[31] Excitedly, he sent a copy to Monica. Apprehensively he also gave one to Maeve. She says, 'His inscription – "For Maeve with affectionate gratitude for so much" – puzzled me. When I queried it, he replied, "Because you have taught me more about my emotions than anyone." '[32] Clearly the 'hollow stasis' of his life was made up of many things other than 'havings-to, fear, faces', but his poetic identity depended, as it had done for the past quarter of a century, on keeping quiet about them.

Larkin could receive compliments and prizes without disturbing the rhythm of his sequestered life. Publication was another matter; it required him to venture into the world, and as always he did so reluctantly but with a good grace. At a small launch party for *High Windows* at the Garrick Club in London he paid for a 'special menu card'[33] to be printed, and in his speech of thanks he told Monteith, 'I now know what Eliot meant when he put "Il miglior fabbro" on the dedication page of *The Waste Land*: "It's better with Faber".'[34] The other guests – Monica, Betjeman and Lady Elizabeth Cavendish, Anthony and Ann Thwaite, Donald and Kathleen Mitchell, Mollie and Peter du Sautoy and Rosemary Goad from Faber – were pleased to find how much more cheerful he seemed than his poems. Betjeman wrote to Monteith afterwards, 'P. was in the top of his form. He told me that whenever he looked at his book he found it was full of indecent words. I think it is his best yet and I told him at luncheon I think it is a privilege to be on the same planet with him.'[35]

Most of the book's reviewers agreed. Whether they were friends (like Amis, writing in the *Observer*), or aficionados like Alan Brownjohn (who was soon to publish a short study of Larkin's work) in the *New Statesman*, or unaffiliated but enthusiastic critics like Clive James in *Encounter*, they were impressed by the book's mixture of impatience and fastidiousness. 'I think it is amazing,' Larkin told Thwaite, 'that such a tough egg as Clive James can find time for my old-maidish reservations, and I was much heartened by the unaffected and generous sympathy of his review.'[36] He was equally encouraged by other aspects of the book's reception. Not only was praise lavish and general, but there were very few doubts raised about his poetic self-image, or the attitudes he had shown in the *Oxford* book and elsewhere. For instance, almost no one questioned his contention that he had 'not developed' as a writer, when in fact the anger of his new book made it markedly unlike its predecessors. In so far as people remarked on this feature at all, they tended to confine themselves to remarks about 'bad' or 'foul' language. Larkin was ready for them. 'I think it can take different forms,' he told John Sparrow, the Warden of All Souls. 'It can be *meant* to be shocking (we live in an odd era, when shocking language can be used, yet still shocks – it won't last); it can be the only accurate word (the others being gentilisms etc.); or it can be funny, in that silly traditional way that such things are funny.'[37] Again, no one remarked on how the measured arguments and elegantly contained language of *The Whitsun Weddings* had been replaced by something more fidgety and various. Poem after poem in *High Windows* – as we've seen – creates a dramatic conflict between a plain idiom and something more nearly Yeatsian, Symbolist, or even Eliotic. In at least two pieces – 'High Windows' itself and 'Money' – Larkin invited his readers to dispense altogether with the idea of his verses as a verbal construct. Their final lines are offered as something 'rather than words', while remaining words all the same. They are put forward as a pure image, such as he also shows in 'Solar'.

Although the reviewers of *High Windows* tended to tidy Larkin up – denying his more risk-taking moments, his surprising openness to continental influence and his subversive twists and turns – they were right to stress the riches he crammed into his book. Obeying his own instructions to 'make [readers] laugh, make them cry and bring on the dancing girls',[38] he had drawn together the cathedral-like stanzas of 'The Building' and 'The Old Fools', the sour wit of 'Annus Mirabilis' and 'This Be the Verse', the pure lyricism of 'The Trees' and 'Cut Grass', the social comment of 'Going, Going', and the beguiling narratives of 'Livings' and 'The Explosion'. These widely differing achievements are linked by a tone of voice which is instantly recognizable and utterly distinctive. It is a voice which for all its extraordinary skills is not in the least intimidating. Readers could identify with it. The world it described was one they recognized. Larkin, though well known to be unsociable, seemed to be 'theirs'.

Sales were exceptional. The first impression of 6,000 copies disappeared within three months of publication; 7,500 copies were reprinted in September 1974, and 6,000 the following January. By this time Larkin had been given two more honorary degrees (at the universities of St Andrews and Sussex), seen his name in the papers incessantly, struggled through a flood of letters from admirers, and collected enough evidence to know that the national bosom returned an echo to his work as surely as it did to Betjeman's. But where Betjeman, as Laureate and TV personality, had become the country's poetic teddy bear, Larkin was its grouchy hermit. He was awkwardly reactionary rather than comfortably nostalgic. He harangued the Labour government (Harold Wilson had formed a minority government in April of this year, 1974). He railed against family life in general and children in particular. He sneered at social gatherings. Yet at the same time he was assuagingly funny and self-mocking. He defined the virtues of community and kindness. He celebrated the beauty and heart-healing of natural cycles. Most potently of all, he grieved over the certainty of approaching death, in a culture deprived of what had once seemed eternal verities. Part comforter, part Cassandra, he was both caught up by ordinary existence and yet outside it.

The book changed Larkin's life more decisively than any of his previous collections. *The Less Deceived* made his name; *The Whitsun Weddings* made him famous; *High Windows* turned him into a national monument. He fought to maintain his usual routines and obligations. In September he and Monica went to Scotland for a fortnight. Later in the same month he went to a SCONUL conference at the University of East Anglia and once again visited the Thwaites. In November he received copies of the forty-eight-page Poetry Society Christmas Supplement ('a sort of poor man's *Oxford* Book'[39]) he had assembled during the summer. On the evening of 22 November, while staying in All Souls, he made his one concession to novelty: he gave a reading of his own poems to a small group of post-graduates and Fellows in the Middle Common Room of St John's. Rob Watt, who organized the event, had managed to persuade Larkin by appealing to the loyalty he felt for his old college, and by assuring him that he would not be 'scragged by embryo-Leavises'.[40] The reading – and the short discussion afterwards, during which Larkin launched a heated attack on Yeats – passed fluently. 'Thank you for your kind words,' Larkin wrote to one of his audience afterwards. 'I found the reading part unexpectedly easy, but I was somewhat floored by the necessity to say something about the individual poems. Clearly, if I am to have a future as a reader, I must work out this part of it much more carefully or else buy a guitar.'[41]

When the Christmas holidays began, the clamour abruptly died down: Larkin returned to Newland Park and wallowed in his solitude. There were visits to be made to Monica, to his mother on three afternoons, but even when he was with others he continued to appraise his own life. In three months' time (on 12 March 1975) he would have been in Hull for twenty years – twenty years which had encompassed his gradual evolution as a writer, brought him the recognition he craved, seen the transformation of the library, and first created then apparently healed the division in his feelings for Monica and Maeve. Yet a sense of 'being in the doldrums these days' overwhelmed all these things. To Barbara Pym he explained that he couldn't write ('the notion of expressing sentiments in short lines having similar sounds at their ends seems as remote as mangoes on the moon'[42]). With Judy Egerton he was more candidly miserable: 'What an absurd, empty life! And the grave yawns.'[43]

Larkin had complained about these things countless times before, and knew that now he had less reason than ever for doing so. Women loved him, he had enough money, he had a good job, he had as much fame as he wanted. Yet even though he had recently completed one poem and started another, he insisted that he was finished. His mother, Monica, and the new house got most of the blame. However 'comfortable'[44] he might find Eva when he visited her in Berrystead, he could not expect her to live much longer. It was a thought which made him feel both trapped (what could he do with his own life but wait for hers to end?) and vulnerable: what might rush into the vacuum her death would create? His arrangements with Monica added to his sense of paralysis. Compared to their life in the 1960s, recent times together had been plain sailing. Monica believed that his affection for Maeve had cooled, and she had begun to accompany him to public functions such as degree ceremonies and the *High Windows* launch party. To all intents and purposes they behaved as a couple, yet still they both felt a last decision had to be taken before the situation was finally resolved.

The more apparent this became, the more reluctant Larkin was to make his choice. After fifteen months in which he had left Maeve to pursue her own independent existence, he had began to reel her in again. He had sought her out in the library. He had looked for opportunities to meet on campus. If there was a possibility that they might come across each other socially, he welcomed it. One chance had arisen early in November, when they were invited, separately, by a university colleague to a lunchtime drinks party – and after it had finished, Larkin had taken Maeve back to Newland Park. Their feelings for each other were rekindled immediately, and in the course of the following weeks and months their affair had blossomed as never before. Maeve explains, 'We resumed a companionable pattern, meeting several times a week, doing the things we had always enjoyed. I was aware that Philip felt more committed to Monica now, so marriage was not mentioned. This did not trouble me: I was just content that we had drawn so close again'.[45] Eventually, Maeve admits, she 'yielded to temptation, but only on *very* rare and isolated occasions, and at a cost of grave violation to my conscience, since I never, in principle, abandoned my stand on pre-marital sex.' During this period, Larkin made, Maeve says: 'more extravagant declarations of love and commitment than ever before ... and we embarked on the most serene phase of our relationship.'[46]

Serene, but shadowed. Although Larkin had finished a poem soon after arriving in Newland Park, by the time he had lived there for six months he was already protesting that the house was somewhere he would never be able to work. It was an unmistakable symbol of his success: how could it be a cradle for his true subjects, which were largely to do with failure? In the past, he had believed he should sacrifice his life for the benefit of his work; now, secure in his reputation, he realized that he was sacrificing his life in order to close his work down. Buying Newland Park was a form of creative suicide, one which left his achievements untarnished, his put-upon identity intact, and his need for sympathy undiminished. Inside its darkened rooms, where he kept the blinds drawn even at midday, he could both relish his success and seem not to enjoy it. He could freeze his talent to avoid the responsibility of having to live up to his reputation. He could watch his work float free from his life, waiting for his life to end.

FIFTY-ONE

Early in 1975 Arthur Terry travelled over from Queen's, Belfast, to visit Hull. He hadn't seen Larkin for twenty years, and was shocked by what he found. 'Philip was much gloomier,' he says, 'much. And much, much more reactionary. It was terrible, really. And sad. Very sad.'[1] Anyone meeting Larkin day by day in the University might easily not have noticed this deterioration. The tall heavy figure, slightly stooped, sometimes cupping an ear with one hand, was invariably courteous even if he seemed withdrawn. He would make sad or savage asides, but deliver them with such pleasure that it was hard to take them wholly seriously. There would be sighs and shrugs and despairing flaps of the hand, but these could reasonably be seen as the gestures of a man playing a part. Besides, the conversations they decorated were often extremely funny – loaded with vulgar deprecations, attacks on other writers, flights of ironical fancy. Occasionally he would lash out at the incompetence of colleagues (as when he sent a memo to the university catering officer saying he was 'revolted by what seems to me the taste of a very old Victorian steel kitchen knife on the cucumber'[2] in Staff House). More usually he was austere but accommodating – a popular boss in the library. 'Whilst the melancholy was more pronounced in his fifties,' says Maeve, 'it was rarely predominant . . . His now highly sophisticated wit enlivened formal meetings and subsequent impersonations of those present [were] brilliantly funny: he could mimic almost any accent.'[3]

448

It was the same around Hull generally. Regular drinking companions like John Kenyon were treated affably but kept at arm's length. Larkin showed them a version of himself which was a kind of sketch. Phil Bacon, for instance, who had worked in the Department of Social Administration since 1965, remembers conversations with 'no bullshit but no personal revelations. You got the impression that Philip was tremendously sensitive but at the same time robust. He was very opinionated yet also sort of impressionable. He'd have mild paroxysms, for instance, about cruelty to animals – that let you know how sensitive he was. Sometimes I'd make encouraging noises about poems and he'd say, "Well, yes, the trouble was I wrote all my poems when I was miserable." He wouldn't admit he was unhappy, you see.'[4]

At home it was a different story. Closing the door of Newland Park behind him at six, he would start drinking immediately (gin and tonic first, then wine), prepare the simplest supper ('something in a tin'[5]), talk to Monica on the telephone, then listen to jazz and write letters (and, at regular intervals, reviews) until he fell asleep in his chair. When he woke up again, late and fuddled, he would climb upstairs where another, briefer routine began: more drink, a menthol cigarette (rather than the Virginian he intermittently smoked elsewhere), then a drift into unconsciousness which would end in the small hours. He describes what happened next in the first verse of 'Aubade', which he had begun the previous March (1974):

> I work all day, and get half-drunk at night.
> Waking at four to soundless dark, I stare.
> In time the curtain-edges will grow light.
> Till then I see what's really always there:
> Unresting death, a whole day nearer now,
> Making all thought impossible but how
> And where and when I shall myself die.
> Arid interrogation: yet the dread
> Of dying, and being dead,
> Flashes afresh to hold and horrify.

In Pearson Park it had been rare for anyone other than Monica or Maeve to disturb these rituals. If they had, Larkin told himself, they would not simply have trampled over his privacy and put him to trouble, they would also have filled the space in which poems might grow. Now, in spite (and because) of the generally melancholy mood which descended as soon as he reached home, he became slightly more susceptible to the idea of company in the evenings. Anyone who made this transition from the outside world to his sitting room knew they were crossing the threshold which divided amiable conventions from more truthful ways of talking. Mike Bowen, for instance, who had arrived at the university the previous year to work in the Audio Visual Centre, and who shared many of Larkin's tastes in jazz, called in regularly to listen to records. So did Douglas Dunn. So, at scattered intervals, did a very few other acquaintances from the unviersity – though usually on a Saturday morning when Monica was staying. As deafness and depression made him feel increasingly cut off from life in general, so his reliance on a few individuals increased.

This even affected Barbara Pym, for whom Larkin's feelings had been chugging along unchanged for the last twenty-odd years. On 23 April their pen-friendship turned into real friendship when they met for the first time. Like everything else they did together, it was a little stagily prepared: they were to meet for tea in the Randolph Hotel in Oxford, Pym would work out who Larkin was by 'progressive elimination – i.e. eliminating all the progressives', and Larkin would recognize Pym because she would 'probably be wearing a beige tweed suit or a Welsh tweed cape if colder'.[6] As a way of increasing their mutual admiration it worked perfectly: they showed their good faith while conforming to expectations. Subsequently, Larkin took to letting Pym and her sister Hilary know whenever he was visiting Oxford so that he could call on them at their cottage at Finstock a short distance outside the city. On one of these visits, on 30 July 1977, Pym took him to see a memorial tablet to T. S. Eliot in the parish church and wrote in her diary afterwards, 'So two great poets and one minor novelist came for a brief moment (as it were) together. Philip took photos of us all with two cats outside the cottage. What is the point of saying (as if for posterity) what Philip is *like*. He is so utterly what he is in his letters and poems. In the best, like "Faith Healing", "Ambulances". And even "Jake Balokowsky my biographer". "Life at graduate level" as he once said about my novel *No Fond Return*.'[7]

Larkin's relationship with Pym, though valuable, remained much less remarkable than another he made at the same time. Or rather, remade. During the spring and summer of 1975 he began an affair with his secretary Betty Mackereth. 'It happened as follows,' Betty explains:

Philip persuaded the architects (Alan Park and Geoff Hook) on one of their last visits to Hull to have dinner with himself, Pauline Dennison (in charge of the issue desk) and me at South Dalton (I don't know who did the paying!). Philip took Pauline and me in his car, and drove us home, dropping Pauline off first, which vaguely crossed my mind as not being the right order, as she lived nearer to Hull. When we arrived at [my home] he asked me if I was going to invite him in for coffee. I was surprised, but said yes, and he later told me that he had arranged the whole thing in his mind. Nothing much occurred that evening, though Philip did break a saucer! But once on the slippery slope, there seemed nothing I could do to stop (nor did I want to).[8]

At first glance, Larkin's affair with Betty seems an astonishing development. In fact it is all of a piece with his previous behaviour. As Maeve finally yielded, her romantic elusiveness was destroyed and his attraction to her was bound to diminish. Furthermore, the sacrifice of her religious principles raised again the spectre of marriage – for Larkin at least, if not for Maeve herself. He felt that he had set in train a series of obligations which were likely to lead to the altar. There were other kinds of frustration as well. Because he and Maeve made love – even in their new, revitalized relationship – only on '*very* rare and isolated occasions', Larkin's sexual appetite was stirred but unsatisfied. By turning to Betty he was therefore taking for himself while giving of himself – not only gaining his pleasure but securing his independence. Betty reactivated the dramatic struggle between life and work on which his personality had always depended.

But it was a drama played out in secret – at least to start with. Betty knew all about Monica and Maeve, but was anxious that they should not know about her. 'My principal reason,' she says, 'was knowledge of the tumultuous traumatic episodes resulting from the Monica/Maeve affairs in the past, and I did not want to revive those deep feelings in *them* with *me* as the target. Also, all my working life I had deliberately avoided personal relationships with those with whom I worked as "business and pleasure don't mix". Again, the library staff knew I had the boss's ear, and I often put cases to him on behalf of people and ideas, and I felt it would undermine my integrity in the library.'[9] Larkin was happy to say nothing to anyone. He felt there was something slightly comic – even embarrassing – about suddenly starting to sleep with someone he had seen every working day for the last seventeen years. 'I'd have asked you sooner,' he told her, 'only I didn't want you to think I was T. S. Eliot – he *married* his secretary, you know.'[10]

For Larkin, Betty's great attraction lay precisely in her familiarity. Now in her early fifties, and still an attractive and forthright woman, she understood him better than virtually anyone else. She had typed all his letters in the library, and these had included many personal as well as purely business ones. She had seen the pornography in the cupboard in his office. She had watched him dozing off at his desk after lunch with the top button of his trousers undone. She had heard him lumbering round his room belching ('he was,' she says, 'a very eighteenth-century man in some ways'[11]). She had been taken into his confidence as he slithered up and down the rolling trough of his difficulties with Monica and Maeve. Nothing about him could shake or surprise her. 'I was,' she said once, 'really a sort of wife to him,' and again: 'there was a great fondness between us. I thought of myself as the Catherine Parr of his life once we had settled into a routine of my visits and our days out.'[12]

Larkin, in turn, admired Betty for being outgoing and understanding the ways of the world. During the last decade of his life she was the admired and trusted complement to everything that Monica and Maeve gave him. She might not have been his intellectual equal, but she stayed 'hidden' in his life 'like strength' when his spreading fame required him to do more and more in the world. Without her, the practical burdens which weighed him down during his final years would have been immeasurably heavier, and the silences which filled them much bleaker. He realized that she wouldn't frighten him with talk of marriage, and he counted on her as a discreet companion. Sensitive but plain-speaking, affectionate but not adhesive, she had 'boundless energy' and was 'always cheerful and tolerant'. For years Larkin had felt he would have been 'lost without her'.[13] He knew it was inevitable that Monica would rumble them in due course, but did nothing except hope that she would not feel threatened. As far as Maeve was concerned, he simply trusted that she would not notice anything different. If she happened to see him and Betty out together, or heard that Betty had called at Newland Park, he believed she would have no reason to feel suspicious. After all, the boss and his secretary were old friends. They were apparently behaving as they had always done.

With Maeve, at least, the deception worked; she continued to feel that her present time with Larkin was 'the best of all our years together in every way'.[14] Not until after Larkin's death did she discover that he and Betty had been lovers: she was deeply angered by his duplicity. In one sense this ignorance excluded Maeve from the affair. In another, it demonstrates that it could not have happened without her. In the 1960s and early 1970s, when their feelings for each other ran strongly, it was unthinkable that Larkin would look to anyone other than Maeve to arouse his most romantic feelings. As the 1970s wore on he retained a strong sense of her importance, even during their periods of separation. Yet when their affair came back to life in 1974–5 it contained – as we've seen – the agent of its own destruction. At the same time as Larkin was writing to Maeve, 'I am very close to Monica and very fond of her . . . But it's you I *love*; you're the one I want,'[15] he knew that fulfilment was likely to lead to failure. Self-sacrifice was bound to encourage self-preservation. Maeve did her best to deny this, and to concentrate on her happiness, but the more habitual Larkin's life with Monica became, and the more he appeared with her in public, the more Maeve was forced to accept that her time with him must soon draw to a close. For years she had been urging him to choose between herself and Monica, and for years he had refused – creating, instead, a painful but potent stasis. Now things had changed. Although nothing had been said – there had been no showdown – a decision had become inevitable. Monica, not Maeve, was Larkin's regular companion. Monica, not Maeve, was set to share his future.

Monica was not so easily fooled by the new affair. Larkin maintained his usual routine, visiting her in Leicester when he went to see his mother, taking her on holiday during the summer (this year to Scotland again), but she knew him too well to miss even a slight variation in his behaviour. She also understood that while he was devoted to her he needed to feel the door connecting him with a different life was still ajar. To an extent, this knowledge comforted her when she discovered what was going on with Betty. There were no rows as bad as those which had erupted when she had found he was deceiving her about Maeve, and no letters survive in which she or Larkin himself agonizes over how to resolve the situation. Hurt and envious as she was, Monica knew as clearly as Betty that there was no question of Larkin suddenly whisking off to get married. She also liked Betty as an individual, and appreciated that she could give Larkin certain things for which she (Monica) no longer had the appetite. She trusted Betty not to be hectic or over-insistent. She believed that her own routine with Larkin could continue undisturbed.

So it did. Larkin's life outside the library with Betty was made up of intermittent meetings during the week and occasional weekend trips out to the Yorkshire Wolds. In her adventurousness she satisfied his need for a permanently impending sense of difference. In her proximity she suited his laziness. Yet precisely because it was so convenient, and its course so comparatively unruffled, his new affair was bound to disappoint Larkin in one respect. It could not provide him with the creative tension he needed to produce poems. His renewed love for Maeve, on the other hand –

especially since it was now under pressure not just from his feelings about Monica, but from those he had for Betty as well – soon stirred him into action. On 7 August he wrote to Maeve, 'I miss you. Fearful boiling night was diversified by two dreams about you, both "losing" dreams – you going off with someone else.'[16] It was a letter which brought back to mind all the occasions in the past when he had been tortured by jealousy of Maeve's independent life – with the 'weed from Plant Psychology'; with 'the Irishman'. Hours after posting it, he began one of his most powerful last poems, 'Love Again', discovering that beneath the calm surface of his affair lurked feelings as turbulent as those he had known as a young man:

> Love again: wanking at ten past three
> (Surely he's taken her home by now?),
> The bedroom hot as a bakery,
> The drink gone dead, without showing how
> To meet tomorrow, and afterwards,
> And the usual pain, like dysentery.
>
> Someone else feeling her breasts and cunt,
> Someone else drowned in that lash-wide stare,
> And me supposed to be ignorant,
> Or find it funny, or not to care,
> Even . . .

Lost for words, Larkin put the poem aside, taking it up briefly in January the following year (1976), but not completing it until nearly four years later, on 20 September 1979. As he faltered, two other poems rose to take its place. The first, finished on 20 December, begins by putting a brave face on the very thing which tormented him in 'Love Again'. 'When first we faced' is a poem which Maeve saw as 'Philip thinking back to that February night in 1961 when first we kissed',[17] and which Betty believes may in fact be addressed to her, since Larkin sent her a copy ten days after finishing it.[18] The poem is apparently grateful for diverse sexual experience, not dismayed by it:

> When first we faced, and touching showed
> How well we knew the early moves,
> Behind the moonlight and the frost,
> The excitement and the gratitude,
> There stood how much our meeting owed
> To other meetings, other loves.

In the third and final stanza Larkin 'admits' that he can't preserve this façade of tolerant understanding. 'The pain' of Maeve's past and 'different life' is 'real', and his only consolation is knowing that his possessiveness is proof of his sincerity. 'When', he wonders:

> did love not try to change
> The world back to itself – no cost,
> No past, no people else at all –
> Only what meeting made us feel,
> So new, and gentle-sharp, and strange?

The third poem, 'Morning at last', was written a couple of months later and raises the same questions. Maeve remembers the circumstances which provoked it. 'As I was putting my boots on one winter evening [this year: 1975–6],' she says, 'prior to going home [from Newland Park], Philip teased me about them because they made my feet look stubby and short – my feet are actually long and slim. [They had previously appeared in 'Broadcast', wearing 'new, slightly outmoded shoes'.] The next day he remarked how on looking out of the window that morning, he'd been very moved by my vanishing footprints in the melting snow.'[19] In the poem, staring from his window at the 'small blunt footprints' in the snow outside, which show 'your life walking into mine', Larkin says:

> when they vanish with the rain
> What morning woke to will remain,
> Whether as happiness or pain.

In 'Love Again' the pain of jealousy had been 'like dysentery'. In 'When first we faced' it had declined into something merely 'real'. Here it has dwindled still further. It is a progression which contains important evidence about Larkin's changing attitude to Maeve in the final stages of their relationship. Rekindled passionately, it soon threatened his self-control and his independence, and made him restrain his feelings even while he enjoyed them. As he came to terms with his jealousy he also began to assert his selfishness again – establishing himself at the centre of a triangle where he was apparently vulnerable but actually secure. In public, he counted on Monica's companionship and sympathy. Secretly, he was reassured by Betty's unflappable devotion. Recklessly, and knowing it was doomed, he continued his 'highly romantic and thrilling course'[20] with Maeve.

FIFTY-TWO

One of Betty's first morning duties in the library, in her narrow room immediately outside Larkin's office, was to open his letters. These were brought to her by the library steward Bill Warley, and Larkin would sometimes jokingly call out, 'Anything from the Palace, Bill?'[1] During the spring of 1975 Betty received a call from Downing Street asking for Larkin's private address, and guessed that he was going to be offered the CBE. She was right. ' "Don't mention this to anyone," he said'[2] – and the news became part of their secret life until it was publicly announced in June. The following November Larkin went to Buckingham Palace, as he told Judy Egerton:

Monica and I came up and visited the Palace with a crowd of nice ordinary-looking people who were on a similar errand. We got there at ten . . . and I had to wait for about one and a half hours . . . before the CBEs were formed up and marched off to another ante-room, from which we were led singly into the Ballroom and the royal presence. I bowed and she lassoed me with a pink silk ribbon from which depended a gold (gold-coloured, anyway) cross with some enamelling. Then she asked me if I was 'still writing' and I said I was still trying, so she grinned very nicely and shook hands and I thankfully retreated.[3]

Larkin felt that the investiture had been 'rather an ordeal, simultaneously boring and unnerving',[4] but he nevertheless recognized it as the climax to a year in which he had been laden with honours. Shortly before his holiday in Scotland the Royal Society of Literature had awarded him the Benson Medal; on 16 June Charles Osborne, Harold Pinter and Ian Hamilton had taken part in 'An Evening Without Philip Larkin' at the Mermaid Theatre in London. Late in November he heard via the Arts Council that the FVS Foundation of Hamburg had awarded him the Shakespeare Prize. (Charles Osborne, as head of the Literature Panel of the Arts Council, had lobbied for him to receive it.) Larkin knew nothing about the terms of the prize, and as he discovered them his initial pleasure leaked away. Keith Jeffrey of the Arts Council explained that he would have to take an active role in a scheme entailed in the prize, which involved establishing an exchange scholarship between Hamburg and the Univer-

sity of Hull. Worse still, he would have to fly to Germany to receive it, and
he would have to give a speech.

For Larkin, who had only once travelled further than Sark and Ireland
since he was a schoolboy, and who – for reasons to do with the war and
his father's politics – regarded Germany as an especially problematic
place, these conditions were fearsome. 'Wouldn't Daddy be pleased,'[5] he
remarked to Eva, while simultaneously telling Osborne that he dreaded
having anything to do with 'those Nazis'.[6] Replying to Jeffrey on 24
November Larkin hastily said it was 'a great honour', then went on:

Having said that (as they say), let me confirm that my initial sense of terror and
general unfitness has done nothing but escalate, as I can see for the next five or six
months I shall be living under the shadow of what will probably be the most awful
ordeal I have undergone. I hate social occasions, being deaf; I can't eat banquets
when I'm nervous; and apart from having absolutely nothing to say on the subject
of poetry (or anything else) I abhor speaking in public. Any occasion that rolls all
these things up into one (and takes place in a foreign country to boot) is the
archetypal Larkin nightmare. The whole thing will probably go down in history as
a parallel to the murder of the Archduke at Sarajevo. However, this is meant
simply as a letter of acceptance. I'm sure you'll be getting in touch with me again
when details have to be settled.[7]

As Larkin predicted, anxiety about the trip darkened every day of the
next few months, even after he decided to take Monica with him. Everyone
who congratulated him was thanked with a grimace; all his correspon-
dents were given the news with appropriate degrees of mockery – of
himself and the Germans. To Colin Gunner, for instance, he announced, 'I
have been awarded the Iron Cross, first class, and have to go to Hamburg
... to receive it. I'll try to bring you back a Mauser as a souvenir.'[8] To
Peter du Sautoy of Faber he said, 'I am consumed with dread.'[9] To John
Betjeman he moaned, 'I can't imagine what I shall spend the [prize] money
on: I can't think of anything that doesn't commit me to greater expendi-
ture in consequence – except, as you say, drink. Perhaps 365 half-bottles
of champagne, to be drunk at 11 o'clock precisely each morning for a
year? Oh, how I dread it.'[10]

After such a build-up, the expedition was bound to seem an anti-climax.
Larkin and Monica flew into Hamburg on 19 April, collected the prize the
following day, and left almost at once, seeing virtually nothing of Ger-
many or the Germans. In his speech, thanking 'Professor Dr Haas for his
more than handsome *laudatio*',[11] Larkin talked more as a librarian and/or

Arts Council representative than as a poet. Although he began by pointing out that 'the last English poet to receive this prize was John Masefield in 1938', and said he was 'delighted to be associated even in this fortuitous way with a writer whose strength and simplicity I have long admired',[12] he spent most of the time discussing the advantages and disadvantages of 'subsidizing poetry'. Much of what he said cannibalized articles he had already written. Enumerating the dangers surrounding 'the campus poet', for instance, he warned his audience that such a person 'may insensibly come to embrace what I think of as the American, or Ford-car, view of literature, which holds that every new poem somehow incorporates all poems that have gone before it and takes them a step further'.[13] He was careful to show his listeners that he appreciated the prize, but keener still to give them a dose of anti-modernist opinion and to reassert 'the funda-mental nexus between poet and audience'[14] that he had defined in 'The Pleasure Principle' nineteen years earlier.

Back in Hull, Larkin set about making the forty hours that he had been away sound as gruesome as he had anticipated. He made little mention of the FVS Foundation's hospitality (their hotel mini-bar full of half-bottles of champagne) or the excitement and pleasure which show on his and Monica's faces in photographs taken at the prize-giving. The best he could manage was a grudging admission that he had '*survived*'. He told Judy Egerton, with typical and only half-comic exaggeration, 'It's left me pretty corpsed with a Haworth-style cough and a general feeling of having been in the hands of the political police. The bells of pain are ringing in the ruined tower of my body.'[15]

Larkin recovered quickly. Within days he was complaining as vigor-ously about his 'aimless life'[16] in England as in recent months he had objected to the prospect of interrupting it. Previously he had been pan-icky, now he was just irritable. When Alan Brownjohn sent him a copy of his appreciative short study of his poems, published by the British Coun-cil, he referred to it as one of 'these things ... produced to bemuse the wogs'.[17] In the same mood, he received an invitation to introduce his choice of eight records on the radio programme 'Desert Island Discs'. He described the recording as 'a terrible experience',[18] and when the pro-gramme was broadcast on 17 July – and repeated two days later – he declined to listen to it. His selection is an interesting one, chiefly because it shows him trying to produce a varied menu, rather than squeezing together the records he liked best. As well as four jazz records, he included a Thomas Tallis motet, the Coventry Carol, Elgar's Symphony Number 1, and Handel's 'Praise the Lord'. His 'one book' was the collected plays of one of his childhood heroes, whose dialectical structures had influenced his own so decisively: Bernard Shaw.

Larkin's anger and sense of futility kept pace with each other all summer, driving the comedy out of his extravagant opinions and clouding the pleasures that remained to him. A visit from John Wain required 'courage'.[19] The summer holidays, which included a visit to Lord's, seemed as ever both ridiculous and wearisome. His life as a letter-writer was upset by a series of missives from Helen Spalding, a mentally disturbed patient in Graylingwell Hospital in Chichester. (Eventually her sister intervened and communication ceased.) His life with Maeve and Betty continued. His love for Monica, which in early May he had celebrated in the short poem 'The little lives of earth and form', using their private language of rabbit-tenderness, burnt steadily amid this encircling gloom. 'I see', he told her, 'the rock, the clay, the chalk,/The flattened grass, the swaying stalk,/And it is you I see' – then almost at once banished the kindness from his voice in a crop of bilious letters to Gunner. Scowling at the Labour Party, which had recently elected James Callaghan its leader, Larkin said, 'there will never be another Conservative government. What there will be is a series of Labour governments that will bankrupt the country so that we are all starving, at which point the Ruskies will step in ("I am sure all members of the House will join me in extending a welcome to Mr Brezhnev") and we shall be run as a satellite Soviet state.'[20]

Over the next several years, egged on by Gunner's socialist-bashing replies, he fired off such opinions more and more readily. Imagining England as 'a sort of sub-Ireland', wailing 'God what an end to a great country',[21] he continued to warn, 'Never underestimate the left wing, motivated as it is by the powerful passions of envy, greed and idleness,'[22] even when the Labour Party had been voted out of office. To a certain extent – as had happened when he and Gunner first got back in touch with each other in the early 1970s – these outbursts were designed to entertain Gunner by presenting him with his own views. Yet he meant them sincerely. Returning from Germany to Hull in 1976 Larkin rephrased opinions about England that his father had expressed forty years earlier. Realizing this only fuelled his anger. He knew that what might sound like the barks and bites of an independent spirit were in fact the howls of a prisoner who had reached 'the end of choice'.

Not only a prisoner of the past, but a prisoner of the present. When his arrangements with Betty and Maeve had changed the previous year, 1975, they had brought more emotional colour into Larkin's days than he had known for a long time. As a direct consequence he had started one major poem and completed two other minor ones. Now that Betty's and Maeve's new roles were becoming familiar, he slipped back into the unhappiness which had suffocated him when he first arrived in Newland Park. To the world at large, he still made things out to be worse than they were. 'I haven't written anything for about two years,'[23] he told Wain in June, knowing that he had finished four poems during this time and started two more. It was the sense as well as the fact of sterility which oppressed him, and by the autumn it had grown so intense that he even tried abandoning his normally habit-bound existence and investigating something new. After a holiday with Monica in the West Country, during which they paid a visit to Anthony Powell, he told Robert Conquest, '[I have begun] slowly boiling down my diaries.'[24] Although he had briefly broken their sequence in the early 1970s during a crisis with Maeve, he had soon started writing the diaries again every week, if not every day, and had now assembled more than twenty thick A4 volumes. Once or twice in the past he had already plundered them, for instance when he was reminding himself of his time as an undergraduate in order to write the Introduction to *Jill*. Now he was planning something more comprehensive – a large canvas depicting his whole life, which would keep all his history in view and his feelings of continuity alive. It would also conceal, in the process of 'boiling down', the diaries' function as sexual log-books and a gigantic repository for bile, resentment, envy and misanthropy. He would, he told Conquest, 'burn them'[25] once he had made his selection.

By September Larkin had reached the year 1940 and was looking forward to the time when he was 'writing [his] diary one day and boiling [it] down the next'.[26] Within a few weeks, however, he had stalled. He found that the things he wanted to preserve and the things he wanted to conceal were too tightly woven together. Moreover, the editing required him to isolate and thereby inflate his 'life' rather than his 'work', and this meant overthrowing the principle which had governed his existence. It turned a process he had meant to be creative into a kind of denial, or at least into a tacit admission of failure. 'I used to believe,' he once said, putting it at its bleakest, 'that I should perfect the work and life could fuck itself. Now I'm not doing anything, all I've got is a fucked up life.'[27]

As Larkin decided he couldn't use the diaries to help himself, he was offered the chance to help someone else. Most of the assistance he had given to other writers in the past had flowed from his committee work. His efforts to relaunch Barbara Pym's career had been the exception. Since Cape had turned down *An Unsuitable Attachment* in 1960 he had spoken up for her among his friends and lobbied Faber to take her on, telling Charles Monteith, 'I do think she would fit very well into the Anglican tradition of your house.'[28] In the early winter of 1976 he found a more public place in which to speak on her behalf. The *Times Literary Supplement* wrote to him (among others) asking for the names of authors he considered over- and under-rated. After consulting Monica on the telephone he gave Pym as his candidate in the 'under-rated' category. So did Lord David Cecil, formerly a Professor of English at Oxford, and the combined weight of their recommendations did the trick. Pym was bombarded with offers from publishers – Macmillan took on her recent work and Cape soon reprinted three of her earlier novels. She sent Larkin her 'inadequate thanks'[29] for his help and he told her it was, 'Super news! I am drinking (or, come to think of it, have drunk) a half-bottle of champagne in honour of your success . . . Oh, I am so pleased; I want a real Pym year . . . I have rung up a lady to collect some *jumble* tomorrow for some "church players" – I've never done this before, so it's also in honour of you.'[30]

For the rest of her writing life, Pym's name was linked to Larkin's and their friendship became public knowledge. Larkin published a long essay on her work, 'Something to Love: The World of Barbara Pym', in the *TLS*. Her book jackets made much of his praise. 'I take a selfish pleasure in seeing my name on them,' he told her; '. . . it's so nice to think that good writing wins through in the end. I hope your books all sell like billy-o (Brewer is silent on the origin of this phrase) and that you have to register for VAT and all that.'[31] Even after Pym's death in 1980 Larkin continued to plead her cause. He produced an Introduction for *An Unsuitable Attachment* and simultaneously wrote to Tom Maschler at Cape asking why the company had dropped her nineteen years previously. Maschler reminded Larkin that two in-house readers at the time, Daniel George and the poet William Plomer, had been 'fairly negative' and 'extremely negative' respectively, but Larkin would not let the matter rest. 'I remember,' he wrote back, 'meeting William Plomer at a luncheon and saying, "Why have you turned down Barbara Pym?" to which he replied, "Don't blame me, I can't help it, it's nothing to do with me." I'm afraid I took this to mean that Cape was, so to speak, cutting out marginal authors in favour of big names such as Kingsley Amis and Len Deighton; this is certainly what

Miss Pym thought herself.'[32] This time Maschler replied a little more pointedly. Although he appreciated that Larkin had championed Pym in public since naming her in the *TLS* in 1976 he was, he said, 'curious why, given your enthusiasm for her work to appear, you have remained silent for [the previous] fourteen years'.[33]

Larkin responded at once. 'I now wish I had written and tried to publish an article about B.P.'s work,' he said:

I suppose the reason I didn't was the idea was so firmly wedded in my mind to the appearance of her next book. She never gave up writing, as you know, and the next book seemed only a matter of time. I wrote to several publishers on her behalf, stressing that I was willing to do such an article, either as an Introduction or to appear simultaneously, but it never seemed to cut much ice, and this led me to think that without publication of a new book it would stand even less chance of acceptance. Perhaps I was being unduly pessimistic. It would anyway have been something of a new departure for me: I've never, so far as I can remember, written any criticism without its being commissioned.[34]

Larkin sounds defensive here, yet he had little reason. For nearly twenty years he broke the pattern of his personality on Pym's behalf: encouraging her, exploring his few literary contacts, taking a stand. To some extent he felt able to do this because he did not regard her as competition; to some extent he did so because in praising her he was also defining his own qualities. Yet the sincerity of his admiration bulks much larger than either of these things. He simply, warmly and steadily wanted to 'help' her – 'as he ought'.

In the spring of 1977 Larkin also involved himself in other, more local causes. The *Hull Daily Mail* launched a poetry competition to find 'The Bard of Humberside', and he agreed to act as one of the two judges. The following autumn he lent his support to a (successful) campaign to save Hull's Springbank Cemetery, where he had been photographed for the sleeve of the recording of *The Less Deceived*, and in which he had been filmed with Betjeman for the Monitor programme. Overgrown and romantic, it was one of the places in Hull he most enjoyed walking in, as he showed in a letter he wrote to the City Council: 'To remove the graves, the trees or even the undergrowth in an attempt to impose on it a municipal respectability would be a disaster. The place is a natural cathedral, an inimitable blend of nature and humanity for over a century, something that no other town could create whatever its resources.'[35] In a more sociable life, such small acts of kindness might seem negligible. In Larkin's life they combine to show that as time passed his sense of social responsibility increased a little. Honours continued to rain down on him (this year, on 10 February, he received the Coventry Award of Merit in the Guildhall, Coventry), but his good deeds weren't performed with any expectation of reward. He accepted that his fame required him to do such things, and although they often produced agonies of apprehension or torrents of scorn he always concealed in public what he felt in private. ('Don't they understand,' he said behind the closed door of Newland Park, 'there already *is* a fucking Bard of Humberside?'[36])

His duties as Chairman of the Booker Prize Committee, which he also took up in the spring of 1977, were the most trying case in point. When invited to do the job, on 14 February, Monica remembers him 'squirming'[37] at the thought of having to read all the submissions (about fifty novels), turning up his nose at his fellow judges (Beryl Bainbridge, Brendan Gill, David Hughes and Robin Ray), dreading having to give a speech at the prize-giving dinner, and complaining about his fee. Eventually he suppressed all his doubts except those relating to payment. 'When a Chairman is appointed rather than elected primus inter pares,' he told the organizers of the prize, 'I should half expect the Chairman to receive more than the others, in token of the fact that he has an additional responsibility.'[38] His fee was duly raised from £500 to £650.

By November, after a long summer's reading, a holiday in Scotland 'laden with novels',[39] and two meetings of the Committee (which were 'characterized by the greatest good humour'[40]), Larkin had drawn up his own short-list: *The Road to Lichfield* by Penelope Lively, *Staying On* by Paul Scott, *Quartet in Autumn* by Barbara Pym, *Before the Crying Ends* by John L. Hughes, *Johnny I Hardly Knew You* by Edna O'Brien, and *An Ideal Friend* by Madeleine Riley. (Lively, Scott and Pym made it to the short-list agreed with the other judges; the remaining three short-listed titles were by Paul Bailey, Caroline Blackwood and Jennifer Johnston.) At the final meeting in November, when still 'nobody raised their voice or thumped the table',[41] *Staying On* was chosen as the winner (his own choice had been Pym's *Quartet in Autumn*[42]), and later that evening Larkin gave his speech. Citing Auden at the beginning and the end, he kept the idea of good poems as vividly before his audience as the idea of good prose. His intention was to draw parallels and to explore differences, and in doing so he gave some of the reasons why he had turned from prose to poems thirty years earlier:

I think it is harder to write a good novel than a good poem. The poem, or the kind of poem we write nowadays, is a single emotional spear-point, a concentrated effect that is achieved by leaving everything out but the emotion itself. But the novel can't do this. In the novel, the emotion has to be attached to a human being, and the human being has to be attached to a particular time and a particular place, and has to do with other human beings and be involved with them . . . Whereas the poet relies on the intensity with which he can say it, the novelist relies on the persuasiveness with which he can show it.[43]

These were the traditional distinctions that Larkin's listeners would have expected him to make. More striking was his admission that novelists require 'a wider and more detailed knowledge' than poets 'of life as it is lived'.[44] In arguing this while insisting on his own identity as a poet, Larkin risked disqualifying himself from his job as judge even as he performed it. Politely but firmly, he repeated the doubts he had felt when first asked to be Chairman. As soon as the dinner was over he gratefully reverted to speaking about them in his other, private voice. 'I got through the Booker marathon eventually,' he told Conquest, 'making a speech at Claridge's and all that. Caroline Blackwood was there, pissed as arseholes. So was Barbara Pym. The winner, Paul Scott, couldn't come because he is seriously ill in Yankland, poor bugger. I hadn't the faintest idea who was who: one character turned out to be Lennox Berkeley. I got within spitting distance of being pissed as arseholes myself. Felt terrible next day.'[45]

As ever, Larkin's irritation with the world was produced partly by disappointment with himself. Late in the previous year Michael Kustow – then Associate Director at the National Theatre in London – had prepared 'Larkinland', an arrangement of Larkin's poems and favourite pieces of jazz for 'Platform Performance' in the Lyttleton Theatre on the South Bank in London. When Larkin went to a performance with Amis in February he felt the programme was 'far from unpleasant'[46] but described something which belonged to the past. 'It no longer seemed like my life,' he said, 'or not exclusively my life, but something I could look at along with the rest of the audience without being personally responsible for it.'[47] Amusing, touching, and put together by people who were evidently 'fond of the poems', 'Larkinland' gave a theatrical dimension to the world-view which had been honoured almost continuously since the publication of *High Windows*. Yet as Larkin himself realized, its effect was paradoxical. Larkin the public man was famously private, hailed as a hermit. Beneath this paradox lurked another – namely, that praise for his work was increasing as he became more and more convinced that his imaginative life had ended. 'Larkinland' was the landscape of the past, which the subject could no longer enter. He was 'becoming his admirers'. He was haunted by his own ghost.

Worse still, he was becoming a ghost surrounded by other ghosts. In May Maeve's mother died, and Maeve naturally turned to him for sympathy. In the summer a host of petty chores jostled for his attention, making him more certain than ever that 'Poetry, that rare bird, has flown out of the window and now sings on some alien shore.'[48] On 1 September Patsy Murphy died. Larkin heard the news in a telegram from her daughter Emily and a letter from Monteith which he found waiting for him in Newland Park when he returned from Scotland with Monica. He replied at once. '[It] came as a dreadful shock,' he said to Monteith, 'all the more so because I had received one of her rare letters early in August (we used to write about every other year), which apart from mentioning severe neuralgia seemed quite normal, suggesting I came over and so on. I honestly can't remember when we last met, but it was years ago, and I expect her health had deteriorated much more than I realized. It is all very sad.'[49]

It was in fact almost ten years since they had met, years in which Larkin had received intermittent reports of her long slide into alcoholism. When the end came he was also in touch with another friend from his Belfast days, Winifred Bradshaw (née Arnott). She had recently written to tell him that her marriage to 'young sparks', which had left Larkin so bereft, had broken down. A sporadic correspondence had started, into which Larkin now worked the 'very shocking and saddening' story of Patsy. She had, he said, 'become a tiresome alcoholic in Dublin – cured, but then relapsed, with fatal consequences'.[50] To Amis he wrote more bleakly still: 'Did you know Patsy was dead? I forget if I told you on the phone. Found literally dead drunk, it seems – empty Cointreau bottle, half empty Benedictine bottle. Fascinating mixture, what. Been warned, of course. Got off it then went back on to it. I don't mind telling you I felt a bit queasy when I heard . . . "The last to set out was the first to arrive", and all that bop.'[51] Larkin thought his years with Patsy in Belfast were too far off in Larkinland to form part of his present, and her recent contact had been too occasional to make him feel he had been deprived of an intimate. Yet her loss pressed on him heavily. Someone he had associated with fun and sex now became part of his obsession with death.

More bad news soon followed. On 13 September, a fortnight after Patsy, Robert Lowell died, and his widow Caroline Blackwood and Jonathan Raban (whom Larkin had met a few times when Raban was a student at Hull in the 1960s) invited him to speak at the memorial service. The request brought Larkin's feelings as a friend awkwardly into conflict with his opinions as a reader. He was, he told Caroline Blackwood, 'honoured' that she and Raban should have thought of asking him, but admitted, 'though I am an admirer of Robert's poems, it is a somewhat uncomprehending admiration: no one could fail to recognize and envy their vivid fertility, and comprehensive many-mindedness, but not being a lecturer on poetry and having by now fallen into a different and more meagre tradition, I am sure I could not produce the full celebration that the occasion will demand'.[52]

Two months later still came the death which made these others insignificant, yet reinforced their effect. On 17 November, in the Berrystead Nursing Home outside Leicester, Eva died in her sleep. She was ninety-one – the same age, Larkin noted ruefully, as Thomas Hardy's mother. Larkin had expected the news virtually every day since she had arrived in the nursing home five years previously. Her body had been frail and her mind rambled; for the last several years she had been virtually immobile. 'Mother seems unable to move about unassisted now,' Larkin had told Judy Egerton in October 1975, 'and just sits, but is remarkably patient and placid.'[53] Since then, he had usually kept her company watching the television (Basil Brush, a fox puppet with a ridiculous barking laugh, was the highlight of Eva's week), or speaking to her about trivial things and long-gone days. It was the same in his brief daily letters: rather than confuse her with information about books (he never mentioned *High Windows*) or honorary doctorates and Awards of Merit, or the reading he was doing for the Booker Prize, he told her about 'Froggy' (a fluffy toy she had given him and which he kept on a windowsill in Newland Park), or about domestic trials such as the 'awful experience'[54] of leaving two dishcloths boiling in a pan on the stove, falling asleep, then being awoken by the stink of them burning.

The day after Eva died Larkin had planned to be at All Souls, where he had invited Anthony Thwaite to be his guest. Insisting that 'life must go on', he kept the appointment, turning to Thwaite after dinner and asking, ' "Will you come to college prayers with me in the morning? I think my mother would have liked that." '[55] (At Larkin's request the college chaplain read Psalm 39, which had also been read at Sydney's cremation in 1948.) Back in Loughborough shortly afterwards, he helped Kitty arrange the cremation, then returned to Hull and the task of replying to letters of condolence. He kept his feelings guarded, persuading himself that his loss was sad but not a tragedy. 'I try to think,' he told his university colleague Garnet Rees, 'that my mother had had a long life and there was nothing really left for her.'[56] To Ray Brett, the Professor of English, he wrote, 'It's just the thought of someone being wiped out of existence for ever that is so hard to comprehend. My thoughts keep turning to an empty space. But she had a longer life than most people, and was well cared-for up to the end.'[57]

Elsewhere, he was testy rather than elegiac. 'The funeral bill turned up today,' he complained in early December, 'and I noticed with some bitterness that the Rector cost £7 – I mean, even the doctor gets £14 for signing the certificate.'[58] It was the same a week later, when he and Kitty travelled to St Michael's Church in Lichfield to see Eva's ashes placed beside Sydney's in the churchyard overlooking the city. 'The rector said [the service] would be the last burial in the Old Churchyard,' he told Winifred, 'which would now be handed over to the council to be "landscaped" into a vandals' playground, or some such nonsense.'[59]

These remarks are as much a way of disguising one kind of feeling as they are of ventilating another (Kitty remembers that as Eva's ashes were interred beside Sydney's, Larkin 'remarked that now his parents were together again, with "glowing eyes" '[60]). Larkin didn't want his friends to think that Eva's death had taken him unawares or gored him painfully. Neither did he want to show how much he missed her. In truth, though, he knew that he had lost the person who had shaped his life more decisively than anyone else. Often he had felt her influence was stifling. During his childhood she had presented him with a model of timidity which later encouraged a wide range of adult apprehensions and hypochondrias. During his adolescence and early manhood she had contributed enormously to his difficulties with girls. During his middle age she had blighted his life with her wheedling and whining. Every Christmas she had reduced him to a frenzy of frustration. Frequently he had lost his temper and blamed her for stunting his life. Increasingly he had felt that her death, whenever it came, would be too late for him to start again without her.

Yet in spite of his resentment he needed her. Her demands on his time may have damaged his relationships with other women, but in so far as they ensured he stayed single and free to write he welcomed them. The example of his parents' marriage may have driven him into selfishness, but because this guaranteed his independence he was grateful. Difficult and limiting as she was, his mother produced the mental weather in which his poems prospered, and many of his best were either triggered by her or actually about her: 'Love Songs in Age', 'Reference Back', 'To the Sea', 'The

Building', 'The Old Fools'. Eva, more than Monica and Maeve, was his muse – not a beauty to be won like Maud Gonne, but a misery which had to be both resisted and accepted. Moaning and wringing her hands, she preceded her son through his life, loading him down with examples of the constraints he dreaded but also embraced. Her tenacious clinging to routines made him feel that the smallest departure from normal practice was alarming. In the process, it made him look upon the ordinary as something potentially extraordinary. Her conviction that 'the Larkins were superior',[61] and her insistence that their vision of the world was adequate, led him to his version of the egotistical sublime.

Her parting gift was to lead him to finish another poem. The first three verses of 'Aubade' had been written more than three years ago in April 1974, and in them Larkin had already imagined the 'empty space' to which he now told Ray Brett his 'thoughts kept turning'. '[T]his is what we fear', he had written in the poem:

> no sight, no sound,
> No touch or taste or smell, nothing to think with,
> Nothing to love or link with,
> The anaesthetic from which none come round.

On 27 November, having abandoned the poem at a point when 'Courage' had been dismissed as 'no good' because 'Death is no different whined at than withstood', he added a final verse which is stoic where the previous three had been terrified, and packed it with ordinary objects rather than general assertions:

> Slowly light strengthens, and the room takes shape.
> It stands plain as a wardrobe, what we know,
> Have always known, know that we can't escape,
> Yet can't accept. One side will have to go.
> Meanwhile telephones crouch, getting ready to ring
> In locked-up offices, and all the uncaring
> Intricate rented world begins to rouse.
> The sky is white as clay, with no sun.
> Work has to be done.
> Postmen like doctors go from house to house.

As Larkin finished the poem he 'unfolded'[62] it to both Monica and Maeve, then sent it to the *Times Literary Supplement*, which printed it on 23 December 1977. 'I remember reading it,' says one of his colleagues at the university, 'and it upset me so much it nearly ruined my holiday. A lot of us felt like that.'[63] It was, as the poem's many immediate admirers knew, the culmination of a lifetime's dread: the 'black-/Sailed unfamiliar' that he had described twenty-six years earlier in 'Next, Please' was not simply 'seeking' him now; it had sighted him. He shut himself up in Newland Park. He had never before spent Christmas without his mother.

FIFTY-THREE

Complaining about Eva in 1967, a decade before she died, Larkin had written to Monica, 'I suppose I shall become free at sixty, three years before cancer starts.'[1] In fact he gained his freedom at fifty-five, seven years before his cancer started, but this extra time wasn't long enough for him to change the pattern of his feelings. He needed the comforting familiarity of his constraints: he relied too heavily on dissatisfactions to give him his idea of himself. All he could do in the aftermath of his mother's death was wait for his own. 'Most people know more as they get older', he said in 'The Winter Palace', the only uncommissioned poem he wrote during the next twelve months. 'I give all that the cold shoulder.' The 'empty space' he grieved over, the dire drabness he had created in Newland Park, and his relationships with Monica, Maeve and Betty, all left his mind blank. So did his mother's absence. None of these things, taken singly, can entirely explain why he virtually stopped writing poems for the remainder of his life. When they were combined, however, they formed an unassailable barrier. They cut him off from his past. They sealed him in a drink-sodden depression. They slackened the tensions in his life – tensions he had often complained about, but which had made the world tingle. Without them, as he said at the end of 'The Winter Palace', 'My mind will fold into itself, like fields, like snow.'

Honours and invitations to 'madden round the land' continued to pour in regardless. In July 1978, at the Royal Society of Literature's head-quarters in London, he was made a Companion of Literature. Shortly afterwards he was asked to act as a literary advisor to the revision of the New English Bible, but gave up after offering only a few suggestions. His reasons for turning down this and many other requests were partly to do with modesty and laziness, as they always had been. They were also, specifically, connected to his feeling that his poetry was a thing of the past. Of the eleven short lyrics written between Eva's death and his own, more than half were commissioned, and while all are well turned, there's nothing excited or surprising about them. The earliest is a case in point. It is a quatrain requested by Charles Monteith on behalf of the Trustees of the Queen Square Garden, and engraved on a stone near the Faber offices to commemorate the Queen's Silver Jubilee. Although, after 'three nights' thought',[2] Larkin happily publicized his admiration for the monarchy as an emblem of stability, he did so in the voice of a latter-day Alfred Austin:

> In times when nothing stood
> but worsened, or grew strange,
> there was one constant good:
> she did not change.

When he sent Monteith the quatrain, Larkin said he was 'no good at this lapidary lark',[3] meaning that while he realized his poem would do, it belonged too entirely to the 'social reward' aspect of writing. To console himself, he also sent Monteith four lines which purported to be written by Ted Hughes – whom Monteith had also approached for a contribution: 'The sky split apart in malice,/The stars rattled like pans on a shelf,/Crow shat on Buckingham Palace,/God pissed himself.'[4]

Writing poems, or at least the possibility of writing them, had in the past always been able to lift Larkin's spirits. Commissioned pieces couldn't do this. If they were poems they disappointed him. If they were prose – reviews or longer essays such as the one on Andrew Marvell that he produced in the spring of 1978 to mark the tercentenary of the poet's death – they seemed too purely like work. As friends commiserated with him, they assumed they were consoling a son who was missing his mother. In fact he was not only that but a man in mourning for his own life. As he sorted out Eva's house in York Road ('I didn't take much, except books and bookcases and "archives" – photographs and letters'[5]) it wasn't the loss of her love and company – or even relief – which overwhelmed him. It was the certainty of his extinction as a poet. 'I'm so finished,' he told Judy. 'It's awful to have lost whatever talent one may have had. I could no more write a poem than achieve levitation.'[6]

All through the late winter and into the spring Larkin remained wretched, blocked, passive. He wrote almost nothing. He kept to his routines. Trivial domestic things oppressed him. As time passed, however, his inertia brought him to the brink of at least one important decision almost without his realizing it. For the past twenty years his journeys to Loughborough had been combined (in term-time, at least) with visits to Monica in Leicester. Would he decide not to see her so much, now these journeys were no longer necessary? Larkin wasn't sure, and neither was Monica. Maeve interpreted things differently. Still ignorant about Betty, she could gauge the quality of her relationship with Larkin only by reference to Monica – and as far as she could see, Monica had never had it so good. For all the intimacies that Maeve had shared with Larkin over the last three years, and in spite of all the protestations of love that he had made, it was Monica he turned to most often as he picked through his mother's house. Maeve had been heartened by his support while she had grieved for her mother the previous spring, and again when she and her father moved house shortly afterwards. (Larkin had even changed the plugs on all her electrical appliances.[7]) She had been grateful again as she prepared to go into hospital to have an operation in August: he told her that he was so concerned for her well-being he 'wouldn't take a holiday with Monica this summer'. Almost immediately, she was reminded of the limits to his kindliness. 'On the eve of admission to hospital' she discovered 'that the resolve was only to see me through the worst and he had made plans to go away with Monica in September. I was deeply hurt.'[8] Even though they drew together again later in the year as he discussed 'Aubade' with her, Maeve realized by the end of the year that their relationship was foundering. She would never have Larkin to herself. Eva's death was likely to create new complications, and Maeve feared a crisis was pending.

It came the following spring, 1978, on the evening of 16 March. 'Larkinland', following its successful London run, was put on in Hull, in the university's Middleton Hall, with Richard Johnson and Philip Stone as the readers. Larkin went to see it with Maeve, and afterwards was invited to a formal reception in Staff House. Maeve expected to go to the party too, but as they left the performance Larkin said she could not. It was the flashpoint they had both been anticipating and dreading. Ever since they had restarted their relationship in November 1974 Maeve had realized that its intensity might one day challenge Larkin's need for independence. Following the death of her mother – which had left her with the responsibility of caring for an elderly father – the danger had grown worse. Larkin was bound to fight shy of a situation which threatened to repeat the pattern he had endured with Eva. Now, outside the Middleton Hall, Maeve told him he had made a choice about his life without acknowledging it. He had decided that Monica was his companion, not her. Larkin did not disagree, and they went their separate ways – Larkin turning in to the celebration of his work while Maeve, angry and distressed, drove home with another university colleague.

The next evening, fearing that her seventeen-year relationship with Larkin really was over at last, she was 'very sharp-tongued . . . as Philip did not make any attempt to come and apologize'.[9] That night he wrote to her, addressing her merely as 'Dear Maeve' for the first time since 1958:

I write . . . to repeat my regret at Thursday's débâcle and to apologize for it . . . The whole thing was a fitting climax to a day of – a week of – increasing discomfort about it all. I am deeply sorry that you should have suffered through it. Please believe me when I say that none of it is intentional. Not that that excuses me. I realize that you are very hurt, and that this explains the angry home truths . . . I know most of these are justified (not quite all), but they leave their sting. Perhaps when we feel better we can meet again. I don't say this vindictively: I am extremely sad about it all.[10]

Sad Larkin may have been; Maeve was 'desolate'.[11] Yet when he went to visit her three days later at her home, she still agreed that 'because of Monica' it was 'best to part'.[12] For the next six years of Larkin's life – until his last few months – they saw each other regularly at work and around the university, and learnt to disguise their sorrow. Gradually they evolved what Maeve calls 'a distant but friendly relationship'[13] – one which allowed her to feel she was 'still in his confidence',[14] but which was nevertheless constrained. In truth, her whole previous life with Larkin had been restricted in one way or another. Even though 'everyone in Hull'[15] knew about their relationship, they had to avoid scandal. They also had to avoid upsetting Monica. They could not easily go anywhere outside Hull because Larkin wanted to keep her from his other friends. In some respects he was embarrassed by her: she was not conventionally beautiful, she was not his intellectual equal, and she was provincial. In some respects she irritated him. In others she threatened to suffocate him. Yet at the same time she gave him unique pleasures. She was, as she says, his 'sweetheart'.[16] Her innocence made him protective. Her restraint made him eager. Her vulnerability awoke his romantic tenderness. For as long as they loved each other she kept alive for him the sense that his life might be other than it was – he might be married, he might be a family man, he might try to perfect something other than his writing.

By the time Eva died it was too late for Larkin to believe this might be so. Henceforth there would be nothing but courtesy linking him to Maeve – that and the poems he had written for her. In some – 'Broadcast' and 'The Dance' – she appears as herself. The much larger effect of her influence spreads throughout his work, existing in everything that was a foil to his feelings for Monica. Maeve had made him hopeful where Monica appealed to his realism. Maeve was capricious where Monica had been fixed. Maeve had made his 'almost-instinct' about the resilience of love seem 'almost-true', while Monica had sympathetically doubted it. In spurning her now, Larkin was doing more than simply tidying up his life, concentrating his affection on Monica and – to a lesser extent – on Betty. He was dousing what remained of his spirit of optimism.

The decision hurt Maeve more badly than Larkin. She was still six years off retirement from the library, and still living at home looking after her elderly father. She had given the middle part of her life to Larkin and he had taken from it what he wanted, then handed it back. While she struggled to begin again, he simply settled into the existence he had decreed: the rituals of work at home and in the library, the complementing attentions of two women. Grieving in solitude, Maeve felt at a loss. Brooding over his mother, Larkin knew where he was: well tended in private, widely honoured in public.

Larkin's lack of remorse about Maeve is partly explained by his sense of dislocation after Eva's death. This deepened later in the year when Bruce Montgomery died on 15 September, a short while before Larkin was due to make one of his occasional (usually bi-annual) visits. Montgomery the glamorously successful contemporary at Oxford, whose 'unsuspected depths of frivolity' and 'brisk intellectual epicureanism' had been 'just the catalyst [Larkin] needed'[17] at the beginning of his career, was a creature of the past. The advice and healthy competition they had once given each other had long been replaced by remote friendliness or actual indifference. Montgomery had continued to admire Larkin's work, but Larkin thought less and less of Montgomery's – and was impatient, too, with his requests for money. In 1976, when Montgomery was about to get married, Larkin had hoped that it might indicate a change of luck, and volunteered some financial help – though he was only prepared to give it in small, reluctant handfuls; On 1 April, for instance, he had lent Montgomery £250, on the understanding that it would be repaid at the rate of 1½ per cent interest per month. On other occasions, when Montgomery telephoned the library, Larkin had asked Betty to say that he was out.

'Yes,' Larkin wrote to Barry Bloomfield when the news of Montgomery's death came through, it's 'very sad about Bruce . . . But I gather his health had deteriorated very badly over the last two years, and he could hardly get about.'[18] To Amis he was more confiding: 'I wish I'd seen more of Bruce when he was still on top of things. Whatever one thought of his books, and his sense (sometimes) of what was funny or desirable, he was an original and nobody else was the least like, don't you think? And he gave us a lot of laughs, as well as introducing us to things like Dickson Carr and *At Swim-Two-Birds*. I feel rather wretched about it, not least because I don't think I've ever seen a *Times* obit for a really close friend before, and it makes it all sort of realler bumhow comehow.'[19] Larkin aired the same sorrowful but self-interested feelings in a letter to Robert Conquest. 'Funeral was today,' he reported. 'All very sad, and makes the world seem very temporary.'[20] A few months later, when he drove down to High Week in Devon to see Montgomery's widow Ann and 'to look at Bruce's papers', his 'inevitable sadness' was under tighter control. 'Ann was v. kind and generous,' he told Amis, 'and gave me Bruce's cigarette lighter, which is a bit like inheriting Bix's cornet or St Francis of Assisi's bird table.'[21]

Larkin's friends knew him well enough to understand that remarks like this, which once seemed purely ebullient, now also sounded a note of desolation. Judy Egerton found him 'more and more serious'[22] and Amis himself, though still treated to some bitterly funny letters, was given candid accounts of misery as well. Earlier this year, for instance, a blast against the lack of pornography on television ('it's like this permissive society they talk about: never permitted me anything as far as I can recall'[23]) had rapidly been followed by one which admitted to feeling 'sodding awful . . . as if I'd reached some kind of am-pass . . . when I can't be alone, can't stand company, can't work, can't do nothing, can't think of the present, past or future, and am crucified every ten minutes or so by hideous memories – nothing serious, just making a fool of myself. Feel my mind's NOT ON MY SIDE any more. Do you think I'm going batty?'[24]

It was the same in the library. He tried to be conciliatory, but the impatience and ironies which had always lurked below the surface now threatened to break out more obviously. Alan Fowlie, the university's Assistant Registrar since 1972, felt that Larkin 'began gradually to drift off. He'd confine himself to the top 5 per cent of policy – which he'd do very well – but he went on finding it very hard at public occasions and so on, and his deafness made it very difficult of course, and the library cuts depressed him.'[25] Betty confirms this. As the first anniversary of Eva's death came round she felt that he had responded to the 'threat of stagnation' by embracing it rather than stirring himself to seek new choices and chances. 'We were always having "the worst day of his life",' she says:

for one reason or another. He was very nervous about addressing people, for example; his hands were always wet with tension. He'd say 'Feel my hands' and they were wet, not just damp. That's how nervous he was on public occasions. All the same, I think he did slow down a bit, you know, as if he couldn't see the point of anything. He'd always get his work done, the library would always be very efficiently run, but he'd often have a bit of a nap after lunch. Sometimes I'd look at him to make sure he was still breathing, and when he woke up I'd tell him he ought to get on with things – do something – but oh no, he never would.[26]

Almost never, at any rate. Although the twelve months following Eva's death had been empty even by his standards, the new year, 1979, began with a burst of activity. In February he wrote an eight-line poem commemorating the fiftieth anniversary of the library; the same month (as if to produce for himself what he had just spent in a commission for others) he wrote another eight-liner, 'The daily things we do'. Its observation that 'the circumstance we cause/In time gives rise to us,/Becomes our memory' boils down the argument he had made sixteen years earlier in 'Dockery and Son', when he had said that the 'style' and habits 'Our lives bring with them' will 'Suddenly . . . harden into all we've got'. What had originally been a warning is now an admission of failure. A few weeks later, cast down by his inability to turn 'the daily things we do' into more than a jotting, he was jolted into trying again. He ran over and killed a hedgehog while mowing the lawn, and the death gave him a sharper grief than several of the larger losses which had recently blighted him. 'When it happened,' Monica says, 'he came in from the garden howling. He was very upset. He'd been feeding the hedgehog, you see – he looked out for it in the mornings. He started writing about it soon afterwards.'[27] The four short verses draw on his affection for animals generally. In the past he had proved this by writing letters to the press complaining about vivisection, and by producing poems like 'At Grass', 'Myxomatosis' and 'Ape Experiment Room'. Now in 'The Mower' he concentrates on the hedgehog and his own unwilling role as Grim Reaper. In the first two verses he describes how he 'mauled [the animal's] unobtrusive world/Unmendably', and in the last two he tries to defend himself against sentimentality by reporting his distress in clipped, factual phrases:

> Next morning I got up and it did not.
> The first day after a death, the new absence
> Is always the same; we should be careful
>
> Of each other, we should be kind
> While there is still time.

Larkin realized 'The Mower' was only a qualified success: worth publishing, but not worth presenting on a national stage. He let it appear in the Hull Literary Club magazine *Humberside*. Much of the fondness he felt for the poem came from its human rather than its animal associations – specifically, as the final lines make clear, from its associations with Eva. Not only had she shared his liking for all creatures great and (especially) small, she had also, in 'To the Sea', moved Larkin to a conclusion which anticipates the end of this shorter poem. In these muted ways, and in its sorrow for 'empty space', 'The Mower' acts as an elegy for his mother. Even from the grave, her influence continued to exert itself on the very few poems for which he now had any significant ambitions.

As the summer ended Larkin's memories of Eva again goaded him into finishing one of the two unqualified successes of his last decade (the other being 'Aubade'). On 20 September he took up the manuscript of 'Love Again', a poem he had started in August 1975 at the beginning of his rekindled affair with Maeve, struggled with briefly in February 1976, and now completed by turning his thoughts away from the 'splendid and neglected subject'[28] of sexual jealousy towards childhood and parents. The stuffy bedroom in which he lies alone wanking, the pain 'like dysentery', the lacerating thought of 'Someone else feeling her breasts and cunt', the uncertainty about his own permitted response ('And me supposed to be ignorant,/Or find it funny, or not to care') – all these things are shoved aside while he searches instead for the motives and influences which govern his life. The process, as it did in 'High Windows', makes him lose his faith in the poem as a purely verbal device. Previously 'the thought of high windows' had come 'rather than words'; now, reviewing the ashen landscape of his jealousy, he wonders:

> but why put it into words?
> Isolate rather this element
>
> That spreads through other lives like a tree
> And sways them on in a sort of sense
> And say why it never worked for me.

>Something to do with violence
>A long way back, and wrong rewards,
>And arrogant eternity.

Self-mortifying yet also defiant, 'Love Again' summarizes the conflicts between 'life' and 'art' that had shaped Larkin's whole existence. Reverting to the image of the tree that he had used a number of times before (most memorably in one of his commemorations of Eva, 'Love Songs in Age', where the 'sense of being young' spreads out 'like a spring-woken tree'), he gives three reasons why love 'never worked for me'. The 'wrong rewards' are familiar enough – in many earlier poems he had complained about the disparity between 'Your wants' and 'the world's for you'. So too is 'arrogant eternity' – it resounds to the imperious demands of art, which Larkin had obeyed rather than seeking to perfect his life. 'Violence/a long way back' seems more obscure. The phrase does not mean that his parents inflicted actual physical violence on him. It means they showed him a universe of frustration, suppressed fury and boring responsibilities which threatened him all his life, and which was indispensable to his genius. With all the candour that Eva's death allowed, he identifies the smothering nullity of his parents' marriage as the third participant in the 'three-handed struggle' which year by year, line by line, wrestled him into a 'hollow stasis'. 'Love Again', the last and most intense poem that Larkin derived from his muse-mother, summarizes his inheritance by showing that his need to accept and his longing to reject were equally matched, locked in a passionate argument, unable to settle, preferring silence to reconciliation.

FIFTY-FOUR

It was more than two years before Larkin produced another poem – a birthday greeting for Gavin Ewart in November 1981 – and after that he wrote only another four short lyrics before the end of his life. So long and final a silence makes the four poems he had completed in 1979 seem like a death-spasm – an impression which is confirmed by the essays and articles Larkin also wrote this year. In the past he had made clear distinctions in his prose between obviously autobiographical pieces such as the Introduction to *Jill*, and more self-effacing, analytical appreciations of other writers. In these his opinions had always been supported by personal evidence, but only of an anecdotal kind (like a reminiscence about Kensitas cigarettes at the beginning of his essay on Stevie Smith). Now, as he struggled to come back to life as a poet, his prose became more obviously self-referring.

A review of *The Second Mrs Hardy* by Robert Gittings and Jo Manton in *Encounter* started the process. Behind his account of 'a young woman who is infatuated with literature'[1] lurk his memories of Ruth, just as his quoting of Hardy's characteristics from the Index has the half-amused, half-alarmed look of self-recognition: 'Hypochondria, self-absorption, stinginess, luxuriating in misery, selfishness, inhospitality, susceptibility to young women, mother-fixation'.[2] Later in the year, and for similarly self-serving reasons, he seized on the chance to write about Henri de Montherlant's misogynist tetralogy, *The Girls*. Describing Montherlant's 'colossal barrage' against women as 'naturally inferior, haters of reality', who 'cling and make a virtue of suffering' and 'get everything second-hand', he airs his own opinions while reporting the author's: 'Marriage is absolutely contrary to nature, both because man cannot help desiring many women and because women in any case become undesirable at twenty-six.'[3]

As he reaches the end of this article Larkin sidles away from such baldly antagonistic views, but only slowly. First he quotes a remark in a letter from the hero Costals to one of his girlfriends, Solange Dandillot ('All the misfortune came from the fact that there were moments when I preferred you to myself'), then insists, 'This is the heart of the book, one that is likely to go on beating as long as human beings are in association at all.'[4] Having spoken so plainly in his own voice, Larkin hurries to make his views seem part of a larger and more ambivalent argument. *The Girls*, he ends, 'is both maddening and exhilarating, preposterous and acute, a celebration of the egotistical sublime and a mockery of it, a satire on women that is also an exposure of men, with a hero who, even as we reject him as make-believe, settles ever deeper into our consciousness.'[5]

Reviewing Montherlant allowed Larkin to explore feelings he had nurtured in poems like 'Letter to a Friend about Girls' and 'The Life with a Hole in it', but as his conclusion made clear, he never wanted to give the impression that they constituted his whole view of women. In yet another article written this same year, on A. E. Housman, he elaborated the same point. After praising Housman as 'the poet of unhappiness' and asserting that 'no one else has reiterated his single message so plangently',[6] he begins wondering what 'the key to [his] unhappiness was'. He decides that the answer is Moses Jackson, Housman's absent, unreciprocating friend, then ends, 'It would be tempting to call this neurosis, but there is a shorter word. For as Housman himself said, anyone who thinks he has loved more than one person has simply never really loved at all.'[7] This opinion, delivered as if it were a general truth, lies on the page expecting to be universally acknowledged. In fact it is highly contentious, and certainly not true for Larkin himself. He had loved several people, often simultaneously. What is true, though, is that at least four people – Ruth, Monica, Maeve and Eva – had loved him more than they loved anyone else, and one of them – Monica – had always loved him as her one person. The Housman review, like the other pieces Larkin wrote this year, is littered with messages about its author's own life.

The more willingly Larkin accepted Monica as his regular partner, the deeper he sank into the fixed pattern of his life and opinions. Early in the summer, when Margaret Thatcher's Conservative government was elected to office, he praised her to anyone who would listen. Ever since Thatcher had become leader of the party in 1975 he had admired her, for her looks as much as her policies. 'She has a pretty face, hasn't she,' he had written excitedly to Eva; 'I expect she's pretty tough.'[8] Now he was more vehement. Her 'great virtue', he told one journalist, 'is saying that two and two makes four, which is as unpopular nowadays as it always has been'.[9] To an interviewer, later in the year, he was even more emphatic. 'I adore Mrs Thatcher,' he said. 'At last politics makes sense to me, which it hasn't done since Stafford Cripps (I was very fond of him too). Recognizing that if you haven't got the money for something you can't have it – this is a concept that's vanished for many years.'[10] For all their newly public expression, these remarks endorsed the sentiments he had always held: they are narrowly defensive and nationalistic.

It was the same in other parts of his life. On his summer holiday with Monica, for instance, this year touring the north of England, they rehearsed their usual funny-sour reactions to everything that came within range. ('Another bottle of Fleurie – three-sodding-ninety-fucking-five'; 'Have our own lunch in lane, utterly lonely except when P. goes to piss behind waist-high wall, when rain redoubles and cars full of well-born women flash rapidly past with raised eyebrows.'[11]) Back in Hull the process continued, with Larkin both welcoming and resisting his final transformation into a public man holding predictable views. In a talk given to SCONUL in King's College, London, on the need to preserve literary manuscripts, he did his duty as a librarian. For a drawing by Howard Morgan to be presented to the university he showed his conventionally lugubrious face. And in two interviews recorded at the end of the year (one in November with Miriam Gross for the *Observer*, one in December with John Haffenden for the *London Magazine*), he was winningly modest yet at the same time cartoonishly self-defining and aphoristic. ('Deprivation is for me what daffodils were for Wordsworth'; 'I see life more as an affair of solitude diversified by company than an affair of company diversified by solitude.'[12]) All his characteristics are on display in both interviews, and all are made part of a dramatic performance, partly to entertain readers, partly to shield subtler or more painful thoughts. We see him being funny, sad, withdrawn and dedicated to his art, and we hear about his parents (a bit), childhood, education, places of work, ideas and ideals, but we feel that intimacy is always more implied than actual. Larkin is sufficiently confiding to create a rapport with his audience, flattering enough to make people feel they have been given a treat, opinionated enough to seem candid, yet by dint of being always a little larger than life he allows himself to give a little less than the whole story. The only begetters of many of his poems – Monica, Maeve and Eva among them – are not mentioned. The interviews, like Hardy's autobiography, are fascinatingly endearing but strictly guarded.

Gross and Haffenden were both 'charmed'[13] by Larkin, but as soon as they left Hull he began snarling again. 'I don't know which [interview] was worse,' he told Barry Bloomfield. 'Mrs Gross wanted to know why I hadn't got married and what my unhappy childhood was like and why I was so gloomy, and Dr Haffenden had simply saved up all the criticisms his students had ever made and asked me to answer them, one by one.'[14] The complaint was likely to make Bloomfield wince, since it came hard on the heels of publication of the bibliography that he had been compiling since 1972. As Larkin had said at the outset, he was 'naturally honoured'[15] by the book, but also daunted by its implications. It confirmed the separation between himself and the writer he had once been. Even in his Introduction to the book Larkin couldn't resist making this point. He said 'The most lasting reflection' it prompted was 'that looking back at one's work is rather like looking back at one's life: it had not really turned out as one intended, little of it is worth mentioning, and much remains that will now never be done.'[16]

Early in the new year, 1980, these feelings intensified still further. He recovered from the trials of the Christmas holiday (his car 'shortcircuited and scorched a large area of metal and carpet (and rubber mat) under the pedals'[17]) only to receive news that Barbara Pym had died on 11 January. He had known for several months that she was ill with cancer, but when he drove south to see her buried in Finstock he nevertheless 'regret[ted] her death very much ... Even at her funeral,' he told Anthony Thwaite, 'I found myself looking forward to getting a letter from her describing it all.'[18] As this suggests, Larkin's feelings for Pym had depended more on words than meetings, more on the idea of her than on detailed knowledge. He had comforted her, he had helped to spread her reputation, and Pym was apt to think that all she had given in return was gratitude. In fact Larkin's debt was larger and more complicated. Although he was a much more varied and intense writer than her, he built his opportunities for surprising and diversifying himself on Pym-like qualities of good sense, clear vision and unostentatious elegance, all delivered with 'the authority of sadness'. (She had written what Robert Smith has described as 'good books for bad days'.[19]) In their correspondence Pym and Larkin had relied on each other to understand that darkness and dread lay beneath the comedy and (sometimes) quaintness of their polite manners. Three years after Pym's death, when her friend and biographer Hazel Holt published a collection of Pym's letters and diaries as *A Very Private Eye*, Larkin insisted that he had known 'her books very much better than [he had known] her', and wondered whether Holt hadn't made out that he 'played a much larger part in [Pym's] life than I actually did'.[20] It was a typically self-deprecating judgement. He knew, and Monica confirms, that he valued her friendship separately from her work. Self-conscious and circumscribed their relationship might have been, but Larkin could always 'turn to'[21] it for the comfort of knowing he would be understood. Without her, his loneliness increased.

In the past, he would have expected the library to provide him with an antidote. The toad work, lending him its arm, had guided him past more deeply felt deaths and more protracted disappointments. No longer. Within a few weeks of returning from Pym's funeral he reached the twenty-fifth anniversary of his arrival in Hull, and instead of seizing it as an opportunity to mark his achievements in the university he set up a howl about the chances he had missed. 'Twenny-fivve yeares ago, my little bro: in Xt,' he wrote to Amis, 'I took up my present position STARING DOWN THE LAVATORY BOWL. A quarter of a sodding century in fact.'²² For the first time, and tentatively, he contemplated taking early retirement, but when he suggested this to the recently appointed Vice-Chancellor, Roy Marshall, he was told he was 'of material advantage to the university'.²³ He was chagrined but relieved. 'In theory,' he told Judy Egerton, 'it would be nice to "write", but I don't suppose my departed inspiration would return along with time to exercise it. And the loneliness would be dreadful.'²⁴ There seemed to be no option but to begin his second quarter-century with as much stoicism as he could muster, take comfort from his salary (£17,435 in October 1980, £22,080 four years later), and conceal his private anxieties behind a professional mask.

Although Larkin's anniversary coincided with renewed attacks on the university's funding, there was still room for expansion and improvement in a few areas. In 1980 a GEAC computer system had arrived, enabling the library to replace its existing two-slip issuing system with an automatic one. Research into which kind of computer to buy had largely been done by Larkin's deputy, Brenda Moon, but before the machinery had been installed she left Hull to become librarian at the University of Edinburgh. Larkin was pleased for her but sorry for himself. 'I am worked to death,' he told Bloomfield in July, 'and see no prospect of respite. Computerization proceeds apace, resembling a kind of lunatic professional hari-kiri: I've never knowingly destroyed a library before. It's a curious sensation: half-exhilarating, half-frightening.'²⁵

The 'destruction' Larkin mentions consisted not only of job losses following the computer's arrival, but also of further cuts in the library's funding. 'The great god GEAC'²⁶ was an exception to what had become during the 1970s a general rule of retrenchment. In 1976 Larkin had told a colleague, 'If the U[niversity] of H[ull] lasts my time I shall be agreeably surprised,'²⁷ and throughout the early 1980s these fears seemed justified. Between 1981 and 1984 the average government grant to universities in Great Britain was reduced by between 14 per cent and 16 per cent; in Hull the cuts were 20 per cent. This meant that in the library, by 1983–4, the expenditure on books was reduced by £40,000, on periodicals by £30,000, and the number of staff had fallen by twenty-five, despite substantial increases in readers and issues. To make matters worse, the cost of books rose sharply during the same period. Larkin felt 'like the captain of a liner steaming straight for an iceberg with the steering wheel immovable'.²⁸

Although professing to 'adore' Mrs Thatcher, whose government was responsible for the cuts, and in spite of continuing to make disparaging remarks about 'mediocre degree-factories such as I inhabit',²⁹ Larkin fought loyally for his colleagues, his readers, and the ideals he had tried to embody in the construction of Stage 1 and Stage 2. He scorned the 'ratlike minds' of university officers who seemed keen to 'butcher the staff [and] keep taking the journals that no one reads';[30] he saved as many jobs as he could by waiting for people to become voluntarily redundant; and in Senate meetings he spoke up for the library as and when he could. Some students and lecturers, realizing the difference between his beliefs and his actions, continued to regard him distrustfully. One campus magazine had described him in the mid-1970s as someone who 'judged it prudent/Never to speak to any student'. In the early 1980s he told Amis that one morning when he arrived for work he had found written on the walls of the lift: 'FUCK OFF LARKIN YOU CUNT'. 'By evening,' he said, 'the last two words had been erased by some reader of more delicate mind who still agreed with the main thesis. Felt like writing underneath YOU FUCK OFF TOO – LARKIN.'[31] In a letter to Colin Gunner, he spoke just as freely. 'You'll be glad to know,' he snarled, 'that four young swine have been "rusticated" for a year for disrupting Senate here – Socialist Workers Student Organization – unfortunately "rusticated" doesn't mean flogged with rhinoceros hide whips dipped in brine, but supported by you and me through taxes.'[32]

It's difficult to find more persuasive evidence for Larkin's contention that he was 'not a political thinker'. Even allowing for the fact that his frustration as a writer had by now affected all his judgements, making them coarser and more peremptory, these letters still seem extraordinarily self-defeating. By trashing those who used the Brynmor Jones Library he found another way of expressing his self-disgust – his rage had as much to do with his own sense of failure as it did with 'identifying the Right with certain virtues and the Left with certain vices'.[33] The partial dismantling of the library seemed a public reflection of what he had already begun to feel at home. His moment had passed; his life was ending.

But still his rewards continued to accumulate – some, as ever, like burdens, some like honours. On 7 May he opened an exhibition organized by the University of Nottingham to commemorate the fiftieth anniversary of the death of D. H. Lawrence. ('No writer of this century aimed himself more at the world,' Larkin said nostalgically in his address; 'no writer took it on more completely, its countries and continents, its peoples and philosophies, everything down to its smallest birds, beasts and flowers.'[34] Before leaving Nottingham he bought a T-shirt on which a portrait of Lawrence had been printed; he later wore it when mowing the lawn at

Newland Park.) In April he once more joined the Literature Panel of the Arts Council. (He was required to attend four meetings a year in London; before leaving the Panel on 31 March two years later he counted its most significant achievement to have been a successful campaign, strongly supported by Betjeman, to keep the manuscript of Tennyson's *In Memoriam* in England.) In June his membership of the Common Room of All Souls was extended for another year. In September he was elected an honorary Fellow of the Library Association, the ceremony taking place in Sheffield City Hall. It meant, he told Judy Egerton, 'I am now a FLA instead of an ALA; the latter designation always suggested unoriginality (à la).'[35] And in December he joined Ted Hughes, Seamus Heaney and Charles Causley for a weekend in Todmorden, Yorkshire, to pick the winning poems in the first Arvon/*Observer* Poetry competition. He had accepted the invitation with extreme reluctance, said he would only read the short-listed poems, found the work as drear as he feared – 'hundreds of Yank poems, all meaning nothing'[36] – and disliked the poem to which his fellow judges wanted to give first prize.[37] 'Poems,' he told Ted Hughes, 'don't of course [have to] appeal to the reason but they have to satisfy it, and this one doesn't.'[38] He was over-ruled. Glowering, he drove to Haydon Bridge for Christmas, miserably sure that he wouldn't be spending any time there writing poems of his own.

FIFTY-FIVE

Larkin felt exhausted by his new obligations. He thought they probably blocked his poems; he knew they interfered with his correspondence. The more oppressed he became, the more eagerly he turned to his friends, drawing them closer whenever he could. 'Dear Judy,' he had written to Judy Egerton in mid-summer 1980, 'you are generosity and ferocity combined, and have all my admiring affection.'[1] He confided to Barry Bloomfield that he was perturbed by news that 'Eliz Jane [Howard] had left Kingsley ... [but] since *he* hasn't told me I don't like to write.'[2] And shortly before Christmas, when he was visiting All Souls and met there for the first time the young novelist A. N. Wilson, he immediately set about binding him into his life. In the following January, 1981, when compiling an entry on Barbara Pym for the *Dictionary of National Biography*, he wrote to Wilson asking permission to quote from an article Wilson had published in the *Spectator*, and in February, on a brief return visit to All Souls, he arranged to meet him again.

Wilson, who in the autumn of 1981 would become Literary Editor of the *Spectator*, valued Larkin for his literary reputation as well as his friendship. He persuaded him to write several pieces, the most interesting of which was an appreciation of *The Senior Commoner* by Julian Hall. (This was the public school novel Larkin had admired at Oxford for its 'brittle plangency' and 'studied circumstantial irrelevancy'.[3]) 'I've done my best,' Larkin told Wilson as he delivered the article, 'to bring out the oddness (not to mention the queerness) of it, but really only reading it right through can do that.'[4]

Books weren't the only cause of their friendship. Larkin was also intrigued by Wilson's religious faith, which at that time was stronger and more elaborate than any he had encountered. Ever since childhood Larkin had followed his father's advice – 'Never believe in God!'[5] – without the slightest hesitation or guilt, while at the same time retaining an interest in the value of ritual. 'I'm an agnostic I suppose,' he habitually said to anyone who asked, 'but an Anglican agnostic, of course.'[6] Wilson made no evangelical effort to turn Larkin towards God, but as their friendship developed, his beliefs prompted Larkin to review his own lack of them. In July 1983 Larkin bought for £120 a large Oxford University Press Bible and 'set [it] up in my bedroom on a hideous office lectern to remind me of matters spiritual'.[7] He read a few pages every day while shaving, beginning at the beginning and working steadily through. He also began to toy with the idea of going to church – or at least of going to the nearby St Stephen's in Hull, where the 'extreme Anglo-Catholic'[8] priest, Father Bown, was a friend of Wilson's.

Larkin and Bown liked each other, even though Bown thought 'there was something adolescent about Larkin's attitude to religion, in the sense that adolescents need a brick wall to butt their heads against,'[9] and Larkin thought 'he couldn't ask [Bown] to lunch in the university in case people thought he'd "got God"'.[10] Early in October 1983 Larkin finally attended Evensong and Benediction at St Stephen's with Monica. 'I'm far from being a church-taster,' he reported to Wilson, 'so I suppose it was just curiosity. However we were much impressed! Congregation numbered 7, but the service was as splendid as if there had been 70. Of course I was pretty lost – no churchgoer he – but I tried to be devout, and really quite enjoyed it.'[11] The experiment was not repeated, and the possibility that Larkin would 'get God' came to nothing. All that had been achieved, Bown thought, was 'a reaffirmation of [Larkin's] profound interest in the externals of religion'.[12] It was a fair assessment. As Larkin moved towards the end of his life he continued to hope that religious rituals, like the secular ones he had celebrated in 'Show Saturday', would 'always be there', embodying formal values and enshrining time-honoured traditions. He was too resolutely less deceived, too certain of extinction to expect more. 'It's absolutely bloody amazing,' he said soon after he had finished reading the Bible in his bedroom, 'to think that anyone ever believed any of that. Really, it's absolute balls. Beautiful, of course. But balls.'[13]

As Larkin was getting to know Wilson he confronted a loss which tragically strengthened this certainty of 'total emptiness for ever'. Lesley Dunn, the young wife of his friend and former colleague in the library Douglas Dunn, died of cancer. She had been ill for months, then seemed to recover, but by January 1981, Larkin told Judy Egerton, had fallen 'ill again, mortally so'.[14] Apprehensively, he asked to see her and soon after-wards wrote to Judy again. 'The visit', he said, 'dreaded in advance and harrowing in retrospect, was quite cheerful in fact, owing to Lesley's incredible composure and courage.'[15] Three weeks later, when Lesley Dunn died, Larkin repeated the phrase (remembering, perhaps, how he had said in 'Aubade' that 'Courage' in the face of death 'means not scaring others'). He wrote to Douglas Dunn after the service and cremation (which he had attended with Maeve):

Let me just say three things. First, like everyone else I am still shocked and saddened at Lesley's illness and death, and can only guess at how dreadful it must have been for her and for you. Like everyone else again, my thoughts were and are with you, useless though they were and are. Secondly, thank you for letting me visit Lesley in her illness. I shall always remember her composure and courage, and even the gaiety with which she made it, incredibly, a happy occasion. Thirdly, what a memorable day Tuesday was, a single-minded expression of admiration for Lesley and a celebration of her. It quite transcended the wretchedness that was inevitably there too. For this we must thank you.[16]

In the aftermath of the service his 'wretchedness' increased. Larkin had not lost an intimate friend, yet he had liked and admired Lesley, who with her husband had entertained him to dinner many times since first meeting him in 1968: he felt her loss grievously. It reminded him all too flagrantly of life's injustices, and brought death uncomfortably close. More than ever, he felt it was waiting for him, 'stalking'[17] neighbouring streets as he tried to distract himself with work. He undertook reviews (of John Gardner's 'pseudo-Bond'[18] novel *Licence Renewed*, of Gladys Mitchell's *Here Lies Gloria Mundy*); he wrote an Introduction to the sixth edition of the Catalogue of the Arts Council's Poetry Library (calling the library 'one of the occasional pure flowerings of imagination for which the English are seldom given credit'[19]); and he traded tiresome letters with the curator of the Poetry Room at Harvard about a recording of twenty-five poems he had made the previous February, which for copyright reasons Harvard had not been able to publish on cassette as they had originally intended.

More rewardingly, in April, he had proof that his work as a poet was not entirely confined to administration and adjudication. On the evening of the 11th a cantata written by the university's Reader in Composition, Anthony Hedges, was performed in Hull's City Hall to mark the opening of the Humber Bridge. (This linked the north and south banks of the Humber at Hessle; previously travellers had either taken the ferry or driven round.) When Larkin had first been approached about writing 'the words'[20] for the cantata in the mid-1970s, he had been chary. At his first meeting with Hedges – organized by Sidney Hainsworth of Fenners, one of Hull's main employers and the initiator of the commission – he said 'he felt more like writing a threnody for the things he loved about the region which the bridge would put an end to'.[21] Undeterred, Hedges followed up this first meeting by telling Larkin what he wanted: 'something colourful, visual, not too self-sufficient, and 250 lines long, to last forty minutes as Hainsworth required'. As Larkin set to work he found that he could meet almost none of these requirements. 'Eventually,' Hedges says, 'I got something forty lines long with no title. I told Philip it was half-length and he said there was nothing more he could do, so I produced a long slow introduction and lots of repetition. When I finished I wrote "A Humberside Cantata" on the score but the title "A Bridge for the Living" was pressed on us by our commissioners. Philip told me he thought it made it sound like a card game Instruction Manual for adults.'[22]

Larkin had started writing the poem in June 1975 ('I get up at 6 a.m. to do this,' he told Amis, 'it's the only time I'm not drunk'[23]), and finished it the following December as his relationships with Maeve and Betty both blossomed. Yet it is not union but 'essential loneliness'[24] that he commemorates in the first six verses of the poem. Hull is an 'isolate city', only 'Half-turned to Europe', and beyond it lies the even more 'remote' Plain of Holderness, then beyond that again is the North Sea, where:

> scattered on steep seas, ice-crusted ships
> Like errant birds carry her loneliness,
> A lighted memory no miles eclipse,
> A harbour for the heart against distress.

In form and imagery this opening section cannibalizes and slightly senti-
mentalizes Larkin's previous evocations of Holderness. The iconography
of 'Here' is redeployed throughout, the 'water/daughter' rhyme (from
'Spring') reappears in the first verse, the 'hazed over' luxuriance of
'MCMXIV' and 'The Trees' softens the central passage, and the heroic
singularity of 'Livings II' (the lighthouse keeper) dominates the conclusion.
Part self-definition, part Betjeman ('Tall church-towers parley, airily aud-
ible'), the cantata opens by summarizing all Larkin's reasons for believing
that Hull is his 'proper place'.

In the four verses of the second section he struggles to convince himself
that he doesn't mind his solitude being violated. He concedes that the
bridge's 'stride into our solitude' might be beautiful ('A swallow-fall and
rise of one plain line') but can't help implying that its function is deplor-
able – however much he might try and pretend otherwise in the final four
lines:

> Reaching for the world, as our lives do,
> As all lives do, reaching that we may give
> The best of what we are and hold as true:
> Always it is by bridges that we live.

Larkin aspires here to the same ideal of kindness that he describes in 'To
the Sea' and 'The Mower', and the same kind of resonance he achieves at
the end of 'An Arundel Tomb', but the lines' lack of conviction means that
they (like the 'local lives' mentioned elsewhere) 'fall short where they
began'. Their axiom in philosophy is not one that Larkin can prove on his
pulse. Beneath them all lies yet more proof that he felt the 'unique random
blend' of his life in Hull was coming to an end.

After the cantata had been performed to a packed City Hall, Larkin
gently tried to distance himself from the project. 'I want to congratulate
you,' he wrote to Hedges:

on what seemed to me a great personal success for you. I look forward to listening
to the music when I am not frozen by embarrassment (and also when I am in
control of the volume!), and I hear from my secretary there are plans for further
performances, which I know it richly deserves. For my part, I owe you deep

gratitude for the way you handled my 'words' – I was afraid they were too much of a formal 'poem', that is the only thing I have had any experience of writing. It was splendid the way you transmuted the formality into an emotional statement.[25]

Larkin was pleased that Hedges had reacted single-mindedly to the commission, but did not see the cantata as the sort of venture he might repeat in order to goad himself into writing poems again. Once the Hull performances had finished he went back to his familiar life, weighing his need for solitude against his responsibilities in the world.

Such as those he felt he owed to the Poetry Book Society. At the Annual General Meeting of the PBS in May 1981, a month after the first performance of 'Bridge for the Living', he was elected Chairman and immediately set about developing a recently launched scheme to increase membership. Throughout the 1970s this had hovered between 700 and 900. Now Larkin raised again the idea that the Society should become a simultaneous Book Club, offering titles at reduced rates. It would entail more work for Society officers, which in turn might mean the Society had to cut loose from the Arts Council, but if the membership increased wouldn't it be worth it? Larkin set up and chaired a sub-committee which the following November made four proposals: that an 'introductory bargain offer' be made to new members, that additional Alternative Choices be made available every quarter, that publishers be canvassed about the possibility of offering a 50 per cent discount, and that a substantial amount be spent on advertising.

When Larkin retired as Chairman of the PBS in February 1984 (he was elected Honorary President the following October), the Society was poised to implement all these proposals – even though Larkin had sometimes doubted their good sense. 'I really don't know what kind of a mess we are getting ourselves into,' he told the Society's secretary Jonathan Barker at one point, 'but it seems to be taking shape. But then so did the Spectre of the Brocken.'[26] His fears were unfounded. In the next five years membership rose from 871 to 2,000 and the Society became affiliated to the Poetry Society rather than the Arts Council. Blake Morrison, who succeeded Larkin as Chairman, says:

this was all Philip's doing – he was the motivation behind the changes. It's the sort of thing that people don't know he did. He was very energetic for poetry, in spite of what he thought about most contemporary poets, and very good on committees. Very concise, very effective, very funny. I remember, when the vote came to leave the Arts Council and go with the Poetry Society, and he was the only one of twelve who voted to stay, he said, 'Well gentlemen, as Maurice Bowra once said, we seem to have a stalemate.'[27]

Larkin's success in sorting out the Poetry Book Society, like the gratitude he received for 'Bridge for the Living', did nothing to prevent him feeling separate from the world. By mid-summer, when the university term ended and he could possess his solitude again, he was unable to enjoy it. His health started to let him down, and the relief of not 'working all fucking day'[28] was negligible when compared to the anxiety of suddenly starting to feel giddy and agoraphobic when walking out of doors. Was it, he wondered, a recurrence of the illness he had suffered twenty years earlier? Dr Wilf Richardson, the recently appointed university Medical Officer, and a robust character whose previous posting had made him used to dealing with brawny Hull fishermen, didn't believe so. Larkin told Morrison that Richardson 'clearly thought me a malingering neurotic',[29] though he continued to complain that he was set 'on the way to study a long silence'.[30]

He became even more anxious to withdraw. In letters to the 'femme supérieure' Judy Egerton, for instance, we see him cramming his time with domestic tasks. 'This has been a busy day,' he tells her one typical Saturday; '– changing of the bed (rather like changing the guards), laundry, sister on the telephone, mow front lawn, Monica on the telephone, lunch, mow three back lawns and make with the Weedol and moss killer . . . *And* scrub large potato to put in oven . . .'[31] He shrank into his shell in the library, too, reviving the idea that he might take early retirement. The Vice-Chancellor told him he was still 'of material value', and confirmed it in 1982 by making him an honorary professor. As before, Larkin was torn between disappointment and relief. Even though he kept open the possibility of retiring – and sometimes thought of retiring to live in Oxford[32] – he knew that having more time to himself would create as many problems as it solved. 'I have a notion,' he told Amis, 'that it would be absolutely marvellous for about two days, then Christ the *boredom*, the *depression*. Listening to the Morning Service on the BBC. Counting the minutes till drink time. Going out to the shops and realizing you're just one silly sod among thousands. Not being able to afford more than one bottle of spirits a week. "Home made wine" bum. Choral evensong bum. "Dear Philip, it is good to know you are writing again, and kind of you to send me a selection, but frankly" bum. Your own high standards bum.'[33]

Half wanting and half fearing more quiet, Larkin began the new year,

1982, by 'extricating myself from the Arts Council Literature Advisory Panel – not my cup of piss'.[34] But as soon as he gained time for himself in one way he lost it in others. Editors badgered him for reviews (of, among other things, Sylvia Plath's *Collected Poems*, which he called 'to the highest degree original' but from which he could only 'turn with shock and sorrow'[35]); friends of friends commissioned him (for 'doggerel'[36] to mark Charles Causley's sixty-fifth birthday); practicalities wearied him (in January his central heating system erupted while he was away and covered the house 'with a sort of oily film'[37]); and interviewers nagged him to give them an audience.

He gave in to one of them, Robert Phillips from the *Paris Review*, but only on his own terms. He demanded to be paid (he got $250 – the only other interviewee to have done this was Nabokov), and he insisted that he be sent the questions by post. 'It has taken a long time,' he wrote to Phillips when returning his answers, 'because to my surprise I found writing it suffocatingly boring. I'm afraid this may have made some of my answers rather brief and uninformative.'[38] In fact they are not so much uninformative as unsurprising, repeating the substance of previous interviews and articles. Once again he sketches the outline of his life ('The best writing conditions I ever had were in Belfast'[39]), and the intentions of his work ('the duty is to the original experience'[40]). There are a few Wildean sallies (Q: 'How did you arrive upon the image of a toad for work or labour?' A: 'Sheer genius'[41]), and a few attempts to correct false impressions ('I've never been a recluse, contrary to reports'[42]). The abiding sense, however, is of someone struggling to find himself interesting. For all their courtesy, helpfulness and flashes of wit, Larkin's answers apply familiar phrases to a familiar history.

As he typed up the interview Larkin had stronger reasons than ever for feeling apprehensive. In August of this year, 1982, he would be sixty, and a deluge of good wishes was about to descend on him. However well meant, and however much he enjoyed seeing his work praised, he knew they would weigh heavily. The main burden would be *Larkin at Sixty*, a collection of biographical and critical essays which Anthony Thwaite was editing for Faber. Thwaite had first contacted Larkin about the book as long ago as November 1979, and had reported to Monteith that 'Philip was [initially] both moved and discouraging, or self-disparaging'.[43] As Thwaite pressed ahead, Larkin continued to object that he was 'over-exposed', that his birthday was bound to coincide with a reaction against his work, and that the book would only serve to remind him of how little life he had left. Thwaite was not deterred. He approached friends (Noel Hughes and Amis), colleagues (Monteith for publishing, Bloomfield for librarianship), critics (Clive James, Christopher Ricks) and fellow-poets (Betjeman, Heaney, Ewart and Porter). As soon as they had delivered their copy, early in 1981, Thwaite sent it to Hull for approval.

In most cases Larkin was relieved to find that people had respected his privacy as much as his work. To Amis, for instance, he wrote:

Well, dalling, I cried at the end, 'cos that's just how I feel about you and your letters; the obsessively neatly typed address and Hampstead postmark sets me chuckling in advance ... It was a strange experience, reading [your essay]. A bit like looking at yourself in a distorting mirror. My principal impression is that the character you have described is more like you than me! Surely you hated literature more than I did? How about 'I have gathered up six slender basketfuls OF HORSEPISS'? 'I hop alwey behinde' TRYING TO BUGGER HIM, EH? Still, I'm not the chap to quibble about little things. I deny that I was going bald at Oxford, or that my nose is big.⁴⁴

Only one essay excited his fears. Noel Hughes, reminiscing about Larkin's childhood, wrote that Sydney had been a member of The Link – the neo-Fascist organization; he reported that he had pinched girls' bottoms in the City Treasury; and he described the atmosphere in Manor Road as 'joyless'.⁴⁵ Larkin had reserved the right to read all contributions to the book, and told Thwaite that he particularly objected to the first two of these assertions. Thwaite deleted them, letting Hughes know that he had done so. Hughes believed this was the end of the matter, but soon afterwards Larkin complained again. He wished, he said, to insert a statement about Sydney's German associations (to which Hughes refused to append his name), and added that the longer he brooded on Hughes's piece, the less he liked it. Hughes wrote a letter of apology, to which Larkin replied:

While not a hatchet job, [the essay] reads like a deflation job. Much of what you said made me seem silly or dislikeable, and wasn't balanced by anything on the other side ... [It] read like a posthumous article, to be published when I was no longer around to mind ... A writer becomes used to hostile reviews and snide aspersions ... [But] to use my 60th birthday as an opportunity to publish derogatory gossip about [my father], and to characterize [my home] by one derogatory adjective, seemed to me then as it does now very much uncalled-for.⁴⁶

Faced with this response, Hughes offered to withdraw his essay altogether. He was dissuaded, and efforts were made to calm Larkin's feelings: in the end, five small cuts were made – including the reference to Manor Road as 'joyless'. Meanwhile, Hughes says, 'the German problem had festered on, unresolved. Eventually [I] became distraught, wrote a couple of fresh sentences and declared them "non-negotiable". That really was the end.'[47] The following Christmas, Larkin sent a conciliatory card to Hughes – though he told Gunner that even in its final form he 'didn't much care for [Noel's] contribution'.[48]

As *Larkin at Sixty* went into production Larkin's fears about the contents of the book were replaced by worries about its reception. 'I'm afraid,' he told Judy Egerton, adapting a phrase he had used to Noel Hughes, 'the reviews will take the opportunity to cut me down, in a sort of private *Odessa Steps* sequence.'[49] To Monteith, when early copies arrived in late February, he wrote, 'I like the jacket ... very much, though it reminds me not so much of Reynolds Stone [the engraver] as his lesser-known but equally talented brother Tomb.'[50] On 30 March, when he went to stay with the Thwaites in Norfolk to discuss final details and hear about plans for the party that Faber had offered to hold at their offices in Queen Square, he seemed 'keen for it all to be over'.[51] Ann Thwaite noticed (as Judy had recently done) that domestic matters, which he usually found simply boring or irritating, now seemed a welcome distraction. (On one of the nights of his visit, Ann Thwaite recorded in her diary that Larkin had spoken about the extravagance of sending his shirts to a laundry in Hull – they cost 48p each to clean – and how he had explained that 'he can make a macaroni cheese in twenty minutes and then drink two gins and tonics while it cooks. Sometimes he makes too much and then has it next night as well.'[52]) To Anthony Thwaite this kind of chat seemed a sign of nerves. The essays, Larkin told him – and later told Monteith – 'would fill me with satisfaction if only I could believe them'.[53] Beyond their publication, he pointed out apprehensively, lay other and equally difficult birthday presents: an hour-long South Bank Show devoted to his work, and a half-hour programme on the BBC devised by the Labour Shadow Cabinet member Roy Hattersley.

Larkin returned to Hull and dug in, waiting for the storm to pass. The first ordeal was the South Bank Show. Melvyn Bragg had first approached Larkin about the programme in December 1977 and been told, 'your suspicion that I might decline is, I'm afraid, all too well founded. I won't bore you here with all my reasons ... except to say that, as I haven't published a poem since 1974 I am increasingly chary of making public appearances that suggest I thought I still had some standing in that medium.'[54] Three years later, in January 1980, Bragg's colleague Andrew Snell tried again, and this time Larkin said that he wanted to know more about the proposal, since he understood he would not necessarily have to appear on camera. Bragg and Snell scented victory; they went to see Larkin in Hull on 6 September, drank a good deal of Fleurie, and were given permission to go ahead. They agreed a fee of £2,000, and Bragg interviewed Larkin (on a tape-recorder, not on film) during the morning and afternoon of 16 April 1981. 'I shudder in retrospect,' Larkin wrote to Snell a few days later, 'at all the drivel I gabbled ... Melvyn seemed awfully interested in my first twenty-one years, which I should have thought were the least interesting ones; I hope he isn't planning some kind of "Rosebud" climax.'[55]

Despite Larkin's doubts ('It will probably end up as a five-minute commercial for British Rail: "Are *you* getting married this Whitsun?"'[56]), the programme was well received when it was broadcast in June 1982. By refusing to appear – partly, he confessed, out of 'shyness' and partly out of 'vanity'[57] – Larkin both confirmed and popularized his reputation as a hermit. His own view of the film was less generous than its reviewers'; he thought it was 'inoffensive' but 'lacked subtlety and intelligence' and concentrated 'rather too much [on] four-letter Larkin for my liking. "They fuck you up" will clearly be my Lake Isle of Innisfree. I fully expect to hear it recited by a thousand Girl Guides before I die.'[58] His reaction to Hattersley's half-hour, which was broadcast the same week as the South Bank Show, makes these reservations seem insignificant. Because Hattersley's political opinions were at odds with Larkin's, he spent almost as much of his programme denouncing Larkin's beliefs as he did praising his poems. It 'seemed to me', Larkin said afterwards, 'more like a combination of a public prosecutor in action and a family solicitor reading the will than any form of entertainment'.[59] To Judy Egerton he complained, 'It gave me some idea of what being a writer in Russia must be like: arraigned in public for bourgeois formalism, counter-revolutionary determination and anti-working-class deviation. That great bloated unsmiling accuser and his silent audience was the most depressing thing I've had to endure for a long time.'[60]

Larkin at Sixty helped to compensate for these things. But while he appreciated that the book was offered 'with warmth – and, indeed, love'[61] he nevertheless longed for 'Larkin fortnight'[62] to be over. He spent the spring and early summer clamouring to 'sink back into age and obscurity'[63] and 'resume my steady progress towards the grave'.[64] Throughout the rest of the year, as smaller celebrations bubbled up around him, he paid them no heed. (At the summer festival at Ilkley in Yorkshire, for instance, a programme akin to 'Larkinland' called 'Philip Larkin's Blues and other colours' was put on: he didn't go to see it.) Every word of praise told him that his work was a thing of the past. Every mention of his birthday was a reminder of mortality.

FIFTY-SIX

As Larkin's name filled the arts pages of papers in the spring and summer of 1982, the Falklands War filled their news pages. It gave him a chance to comfort himself by rehearsing his prejudices, and he took it eagerly. When not fretting about parties and programmes organized in his honour, he egged on Mrs Thatcher, complaining that England was no longer reliable. 'Well,' he wrote to Colin Gunner when it was all over, 'so we have the Argies on the run. Thank God we didn't cock it up.'[1] He turned back to his routines. The familiar pattern of his life reappeared. The library purred. He saw almost no one apart from Monica, Betty and his usual circle of university cronies.

Soon his defences were challenged again – this time in a way which he initially found disconcerting and finally endearing. The American critic Dale Salwak, an admirer of his writing (who would later edit a collection of essays, *Philip Larkin: The Man and his Work*, 1989), visited Hull in July to stay with Eddie Dawes, the Professor of Biochemistry. Like Dawes, Salwak was an amateur magician, and suggested to Larkin that he come to Dawes's house for a brief private performance. Larkin shied away from the thought that he would have to discuss his poems, but Dawes (who was then Chairman of the Library Committee) reassured him. He accepted, and after dinner saw a succession of tricks – including the three-card trick, which he took part in himself. The longer he watched, the more he relaxed, and eventually left feeling that the evening had made up for many of the discomforts he had suffered in the recent past. 'He was kind enough to refer to it,' Dawes said later, as 'one of the most remarkable he could recall.'[2]

More remarkable still, in view of his certainty that poetry had deserted him, was the fact that soon after Salwak had left Hull Larkin wrote a short poem – a lyric in the manner of 'Solar':

> Long lion days
> Start with white haze.
> By midday you meet
> A hammer of heat –
> Whatever was sown
> Now fully grown,
> Whatever conceived
> Now fully leaved,
> Abounding, ablaze –
> O long lion days!

No matter how unassuming the poem appears, it reminds us that while Larkin grumbled about his sixtieth birthday he kept faith with his work, recognizing and enjoying the fulfilment of his talent: it was 'fully grown' and 'fully leaved'.

As the (exceptionally hot) summer ended, literary business resumed. An anthology of work by local Hull poets, *A Rumoured City*, for which Larkin had written a brief Introduction, was published by Bloodaxe Books of Newcastle. Willing to endorse the book in print, he was privately sceptical about its merits. At the launch party in Hull he urged one of the contributors, Frank Redpath, 'for God's sake come and talk to me ... Yours are the only poems in the book I would have been glad to have written.'[3] Later in the autumn, when the *Penguin Book of Contemporary British Poetry* was published, he was similarly sceptical, and similarly reluctant to ignore it altogether. To start with, he said, he was 'looking forward to seeing who [the editors] can possibly pretend is worth a finch's fart',[4] then he declined the chance to review the book in the *Observer*, then he changed his mind and turned in a predictably lukewarm piece. He admitted to Blake Morrison, 'I knew ... that my sympathy with your contributors was certain to be limited. I suppose deep down I wanted to be associated with the book somehow nevertheless, with a kind of Spenderian vanity. The mind is a strange place. Console yourself with the thought that it will probably bang back on me, showing my senile taste as irretrievably ossified, and attracting to myself some if not all of the obloquy that would have come to you.'[5]

If Larkin's hostility had been directed only to younger writers, there would be no difficulty in calling him jealous. In fact he was by now quick to criticize anyone that crossed his path, becoming increasingly defensive as he became more and more withdrawn. At the end of October he proved that even the most exalted could not expect to be spared. Hugh Thomas, the head of the Conservative government's Centre for Policy Studies, invited him to dinner to meet Mrs Thatcher. Larkin had already been introduced to her once – at a reception in Downing Street on 12 May 1980. He liked to tell the story that as she welcomed him she had said, 'Oh, Dr Larkin, I am a great admirer of your poems.' 'Quote me a line, then,' he had replied. '"All afternoon her mind lay open like a drawer of knives", she recited'.[6] (Larkin gave a slightly more plausible version of the encounter in a letter to Julian Barnes, whom he never met but whose novels he greatly admired. 'Mrs T.,' he said, ' . . . told me she liked my wonderful poem about a girl. My face must have expressed incomprehension. "You know," she said, "Her mind was full of knives." I took *that* as a great compliment – I thought if it weren't spontaneous, she'd have got it right. But I am a child in these things. I also thought that she might think a mind full of knives rather along her own lines, not that I don't kiss the ground she treads.'[7]) When Larkin arrived at Hugh Thomas's house in Ladbroke Grove for his second encounter he immediately felt dismayed. 'I found I was surrounded by *intellectuals!*'[8] he said later – among them Stephen Spender, V S. Pritchett, J. H. Plumb, Tom Stoppard, Mario Vargas Llosa, Anthony Powell, Dan Jacobson and Isaiah Berlin. He was determined not to be outfaced, yet sat in silence for most of the meal, 'unable to think of a thing to say, and not hearing much',[9] until the conversation turned to Germany. 'Mrs Thatcher complained about the Berlin Wall,' Isaiah Berlin remembers. '"Surely," Larkin suddenly said, "you don't want to see a united Germany?" "Well, no," Mrs Thatcher answered, "perhaps not." "Well, then," Larkin asked her, "what's all this hypocrisy about wanting the wall down then?"'[10]

The Prime Minister was 'pleasant enough', Larkin said to friends when he returned to Hull, 'but what a blade of steel!'[11] If this suggests their meeting had qualified his 'adoration' (which cooled still more when she prepared to sign the Anglo-Irish Agreement and, he reckoned, 'sold Ulster down the river'[12]), it did nothing to make him shift his political allegiances. The following spring, when a general election was called, he woefully doubted whether 'the country has the courage and strength of character to return [Mrs Thatcher] a second time'.[13] The fact that he was wrong brought little consolation. Although his melancholy had lifted in the immediate aftermath of 'Larkin fortnight' it had soon descended again, and surprises like the Hugh Thomas dinner, or a Conservative victory at the polls, could only penetrate it briefly. Now when he looked back at his birthday it seemed less and less like a cause for celebration, more and more like a reason for remembering how much time had 'flown/Straight into nothingness'. His letters to friends continued to perform their entertaining arabesques, but more darkly; he began talking to his solicitor about appointing literary executors who would look after his estate in the event of his death.

But it was Monica, not Larkin, who became ill. In the autumn of 1981 she had arranged with the University of Leicester to take early retirement (she was fifty-nine) – though in fact she continued to teach her special subject, the Romantics, until the following summer, when she was sixty. In October 1982, alone in Haydon Bridge, she had fallen and cut her head, and been taken to Hexham General Hospital. '*Poor Bun*,' Larkin had written, agitated by her 'pain and distress'.[14] Now something more serious threatened. In March 1983, while they were spending Easter together in Haydon Bridge, Monica developed shingles (herpes zoster ophthalmicus), which gave her catastrophic headaches and seriously affected her eyesight. She was admitted to the local cottage hospital, but within a few days it was obvious she needed more sophisticated attention. She and Larkin hastily closed the house and drove south to Hull, where he left her in the Royal Infirmary suffering from 'a sort of double vision' and 'intense pain' which was 'extremely debilitating'.[15] When she had seen an eye specialist and been told she could go home, she was evidently too weak and confused to fend for herself. (To make matters worse, she was due to move from her Leicester flat in June and had yet to find another.) Larkin was extremely anxious about her, thinking she might be about to die and breaking down as he confided his worries to Maeve. He told Monica that when she recovered she must come and live with him in Newland Park.

He insisted it was a temporary arrangement: when she had recovered they would return to their normal lives. In fact they never separated again, and the relationship which both had so scrupulously avoided turning into a marriage at last became a marriage in all but name. For thirty years Larkin had defended his need to live alone and write, and since his writing had more or less dried up he had still insisted on solitude, saying it was all he knew. Now he realized he would have to give way. Monica had no one to turn to but him. She had been faithful to him for thirty-five years: it was his turn to give the devotion he had always professed but had not always shown.

He began his new régime grumpily. He told Judy Egerton on 1 May that it was 'very demoralizing' having Monica in the house 'as an invalid, getting up for a few hours daily'. More demoralizing for him than her, he meant. 'I really feel,' he went on, 'at present that life has taken a major and permanent turn for the worse, arousing a pretty fair panic in me at times. I needn't detail it all, I'm sure. Some alternatives are of course very much worse than others, but none is anything but gloomy. And there's no reason why we should have seen the worst yet – but I won't indulge my own fears.'[16] A few days later – days in which Monica 'degenerated' to 'the feeblest I've ever seen her' and he did 'a lot of washing for her' and prepared 'simple, unenterprising tray meals'[17] – he reported that their doctor, Dr Richardson, was taking 'a hard line',[18] urging her to assume more responsibility for herself. Larkin pronounced this 'ludicrous. If I didn't do things for her,' he said, defending his role as her cook and caretaker, 'she wouldn't do them: this is how she behaves when alone, all day in bed on a tomato sandwich (not literally).'[19] For several weeks Larkin continued to take 'a gloomy view of things',[20] slogging to and fro between Newland Park and the library. In early June he told Judy that Monica was still 'suffer[ing] pain, and consumes Veganins [pain-killers] as well as my three meals a day (well, it is sometimes only two), and is ... very lethargic and bed-ridden. I see no end to it, but I suppose there will be an end some time.'[21] The following month things were no better. He told Barry Bloomfield, 'The present, and the future, are ... pretty gloomy. I can't remember the past.'[22]

By the time he wrote this, Larkin in fact had grounds for feeling a little more optimistic. Monica's pain had lessened, and although she was still afflicted with double vision her regular visits to hospital for check-ups were reassuring. She would recover, her consultant told her, eventually. While the crisis had lasted, Larkin had cancelled all his commitments outside the library; now he began to venture out into the world a little once more. On 9 July he judged Monica well enough for him to leave her alone for a couple of days while he flew to Coleraine in Northern Ireland to receive an honorary D.Litt. from the New University of Ulster. For his own sake, if not hers, he regretted the trip profoundly. He told Colin Gunner he was 'shit-scared of driving over some trip-wire intended for the military patrol in ten minutes' time'.[23] Less sensationally, he was simply 'exhausted' by the journey, which he found 'a fearsome experience',[24] and by the ceremony itself. It took place during 'what really must have been the hottest week in Northern Ireland for a very long time',[25] and although he 'liked the photograph ... [taken] in a D.Sc. hood, quite a rarity', he returned to Hull vowing, 'I shan't accept any more honorary degrees.'[26]

Not for the first time, a slump in Larkin's health encouraged Monica to recover her own. In August, with a comic suddenness that pleased them both, she sneezed and her double vision disappeared. This left her considerably better able to deal with the world, but not 'much better energywise', so she and Larkin decided to postpone any idea of taking a holiday and hunkered down in Hull instead, the summer dragging past while they 'read endless Agatha Christies'.[27]

Larkin wasn't just recuperating, he was bracing himself. He knew that autumn would mean he had to face the new academic year, and the task of writing an eightieth birthday greeting for Sir Brynmor Jones. (The result was the quatrain 'By day, a lifted study-storehouse', which the library printed on its Imperial Albion hand press.) More alarming still, he would have to endure another dose of publicity palaver in November, when Faber published his *Required Writing: Miscellaneous Pieces 1955–1982*,[28] The idea for the book had first been mooted in 1974,[28] when Anthony Thwaite had tried to persuade Larkin to collect his prose. Early in the 1980s Blake Morrison had the same idea, even offering to act as an editorial assistant. 'You are not the first person to suggest that I gather up my scraps of hack journalism,' Larkin told him, 'and I think I might well propose it to Charles Monteith when I see him next. Personally, I think it is a case where the parts would be greater than the whole, but it might be worth looking at.'[29]

Larkin sounds cautious here, but he set to work at once. Within four days of answering Morrison he was in touch with Monteith, then with Betty's help (and often using Bloomfield's bibliography) he began 'convert[ing] a wilderness of press cuttings into something resembling an ordered text'.[30] Faber, who were anxious to get a third opinion about the finished manuscript, sent it to Morrison for a report, which was duly copied to Larkin. Apart from suggesting a few minor additions (a review of Graves, an obituary of MacNeice, an article about the Georgians), Morrison's main recommendation was that Larkin should include the essay about his childhood, 'Not the Place's Fault', which had originally appeared in the obscure Coventry-based magazine *Umbrella* in 1959. Larkin replied gratefully but insisted, 'I have rather a mental block about "Not the Place's Fault". In construction it is written as a kind of commentary on the original poem ['I Remember, I Remember'], but this does not come through and in consequence it seems rather rambling. In addition, I think I said just a little more about myself than I really want known. These are reasons why I should prefer it to remain in obscurity.'[31] He was equally adamant to Thwaite and Monteith. 'I feel,' he told Monteith in November, 'in some curious way that [the essay] exposes more of me than I want exposed, although heaven knows there is nothing scandalous in it.'[32]

Larkin's decision shows what care he took, when preparing *Required Writing*, to maintain the image of himself that he had created over the years. He was a candidly emotional and autobiographical writer who always disguised his self-revelations or passed them off as general truths. He was notorious for insisting that our mums and dads fuck us up, yet virtually denied the existence of his own childhood. If he had opened his book with 'Not the Place's Fault' he would have raised false expectations about the essays which followed. Whether addressing himself or others, these cleverly play concealment against confession. They show readers round the rooms of his mind without opening any secret compartments. They say a good deal about his jobs, places of work, politics, views on art and ethics, but nothing about his muses.

These silences are most noticeable in the first two sections of the book – 'Recollections', which reprints items like the Introduction to *Jill* and *The North Ship*, and 'Interviews', which contains the conversations he had with the *Observer* and the *Paris Review*, but not those with Ian Hamilton or John Haffenden. The remaining three sections concentrate on 'Writing in General' (which includes essays such as 'The Pleasure Principle'), on 'Writing in Particular' (thirty-two reviews and articles selected from those he had written between 1959 and 1982), and finally on 'All What Jazz' (the famous Introduction and ten pieces written for the *Telegraph* between 1968 and 1972).

In most of his dealings with literary editors Larkin seemed resentful of the time it took him to write reviews. He was least grudging when writing for Hartley's magazine *Listen* and for Bill Webb at the *Guardian*. At that early stage in his career, reviewing formed an important part of his evolution as a writer, focusing his interests and forcing him to consider his readers as he did so. His need to seem disaffected grew with his fame, and eventually he evolved a critical personality which matched the undeceived character of his poems. A letter written to Thwaite in 1967, for instance, referring to the literary editor Karl Miller, says, 'Miller once thought he could make a journalist out of me: he certainly once gave me a good lunch and tried to get me under contract, besides being a pest in many other ways (whenever one agreed to do an article for him, he kept sending further books along to be "added in", then when you delivered the copy he would ring you up no matter where you were – I was once hauled out of a conference in Aberystwyth in order to go through it, Leavis-wise).'³³ Fifteen years later, in 1972, he was making similarly disgruntled noises to Terry Kilmartin of the *Observer*: 'My attitude to reviewing, put bluntly, is that I'd sooner have the time it takes than the money, and the enemies, it brings.'³⁴ Another ten years on, after compiling *Required Writing*, he was still at it. When Blake Morrison tried to lure him into signing a contract with the *Observer*, Morrison felt, 'I might just as well have tried to persuade him to get married.'³⁵

Required Writing is introduced in much the same terms. 'The pieces here,' Larkin says in a Foreword, confirming the impression given by his title, 'were with one exception produced on request'³⁶ and lack 'coherence'.³⁷ He goes on: 'Although I rarely accepted a literary assignment without a sinking of the heart, nor finished it without an inordinate sense of relief, to undertake such commissions no doubt exercised part of my mind that would otherwise have remained dormant, and to this extent they probably did no harm.'³⁸ Larkin wants us to imagine him lying supine and bored behind this prickly hedge of disclaimers, rousing himself only to keep nagging editors quiet, not to enjoy himself or get something off his chest. It's a tactic which is designed to impress readers at the same time as it lowers their expectations.

The reviewers Larkin had most admired as a young man were Shaw, Orwell and Connolly (the writer he said had 'formed' him, and to whose collection of essays *The Condemned Playground* he wrote an Introduction in the last year of his life). He tried to emulate their combination of wit and clarity, taking 'enormous pains',³⁹ Monica says, with the slightest piece. His various editors agree. 'He was very fussy,' Morrison says. 'He'd usually do three drafts, and was always very punctilious about proofs. But he never let you down; he was never late.'⁴⁰ His reward was never to seem laborious. The dramatic instinct which brightens his 'Recollections' and 'Interviews' appears throughout his journalism – in general pieces (such as the child-hating review of Iona and Peter Opie's *The Lore and Language of Schoolchildren*), and in one-offs (the lecture he gave to mark the tercentenary of Andrew Marvell's death).

Taken as a whole, the essays described a much more precise interest than his Foreword implies. Like the jazz pieces which end the book, they concentrate on the period which saw the rise of modernism and its assimilation – or not – into the native English tradition. More vigorously and entertainingly than the *Oxford* anthology, *Required Writing* defends what is local, well-made, modest and accessible. Early Auden, Hardy, William Barnes, Edward Thomas, Housman, Owen, Betjeman and Pym are praised, Eliot and Pound derided. A few idiosyncratic individuals (Francis Thompson, Stevie Smith) are brought in to vary the argument, but they always reinforce it – as do his examples of popular taste, Gladys Mitchell and (via John Gardner) Ian Fleming. (Dick Francis, whom he admired but doesn't mention in the book, would be another example.) At every turn the English line is proclaimed as more resilient and various than its detractors admit: more entertaining, and more likely to produce work which is beautiful or true or both.

Required Writing was published on 7 November to universal acclaim, was much mentioned as a 'Book of the Year' in the Christmas round-ups, and in mid-January was given the W. H. Smith Award (worth £4,000). Larkin had remained mockingly glum about the book's real quality, and inscribed copies for friends with remarks like 'Crumbs from a poor man's table'.[41] Now he was only a little cheered. The prize money pleased him, the presentation (by William Rees-Mogg) unnerved him, and his health, as well as Monica's, continued to worry him. 'Naturally,' he told Monteith, '[I] am writing ... a nice letter saying how pleased I am [about the award]. In fact the future is slightly clouded by pain in my left leg, which is also somewhat swollen; I hope it will cure itself, but if it doesn't I don't know what will happen. All in all this is being a rather odd year so far, awards and miseries. Really, at times I wish they would cancel each other out.'[42]

FIFTY-SEVEN

The success of *Required Writing* inevitably meant that Larkin was once again in demand – to talk, read, be televised and have his photograph taken. Given what he felt about his appearance, he was remarkably tolerant of photographers. With his own camera he continued to take pictures of himself and his friends, pasting the results carefully into his albums, and when publishers approached him with requests for publicity shots he usually co-operated. Pictures might be 'disappointing' because they were 'faithful', but they were a way of showing himself to his readers while remaining sealed from them.

The most recent photograph of Larkin in *Larkin at Sixty* had been taken by Fay Godwin in 1974, when he was fifty-two. It shows him seated on Hull Corporation Pier against a background of the Humber ferry (on which he had appeared with Betjeman during the Monitor film). Half-smiling, wearing black-rimmed glasses, he looks kindly and apprehensive – 'an intellectual Eric Morecambe' rather than a 'bald, pregnant salmon'.[1] Eight years later, on the jacket of *Required Writing* in a picture taken by Phil Sayer, the glasses are squarer, his sideboards greyer, the face flabbier. It was not, he told Monteith, 'the particular version of my magical countenance' that had been his 'first choice, but [was] sufficiently like C. S. Lewis to inspire confidence'.[2] As he wrote this, Fay Godwin asked to take a further set of photographs and he replied, 'I now have three conditions that photographers must promise to observe in what they print (I am not bald, I have only one chin, my waist is concave), and this means that about the only picture of me now available is full-faced head and shoulders, chin up, in dark shade.'[3] (One of the last and most successful photo-portraits taken of him, by Christopher Barker in 1981, ignores all these strictures. It shows him sitting slumped and heavy in the library, sucking his cheek impatiently.)

Behind the mockery of these letters lay feelings of self-disgust which had grown steadily with the years. The boy embarrassed by his 'long back and short legs', the young man ashamed of his baldness, short-sightedness and stammer, had turned into the deaf sixty-one-year-old who hated himself for sweating so much and feeling gargantuan. (He now weighed over sixteen stone.) At least one of his friends, affectionately remembering the nervously thin and eager young man she had known in Belfast, now felt he had become 'pudgy and sort of clay-like. Sometimes you felt if you poked him with your finger it might sink in.'[4] When Fay Godwin eventually took her second set of pictures he struggled to be his usual self-mocking self, but only succeeded in sounding horrified, bewailing his 'sagging face, an egg sculpted in lard, with goggles on – depressing, depressing, depressing'.[5]

Looming bulkily over Monica, who in her illness had become bowed and brittle-looking, Larkin endured Christmas and then succumbed to another minor ailment. It was, he told Monteith early in the new year, 1984, 'what used to be called flu but which I gather is now called "virus infection". Anyway, it's certainly different in so far as it didn't yield to going to bed with hot lemon, aspirins etc., and in the end I had to call in the MO who prescribed antibiotics with the result that I'm back at the treadmill now, albeit with a fearful cough.'[6]

The treadmill meant literary business as well as library business: in January he published the short poem 'Party Politics' in the *Poetry Review*. The magazine's editors Tracey Warr and Mick Imlah had commissioned it to appear in a special issue on 'Poetry and Drink', and the weariness of Larkin's response shows in his (effective) flat tone and the (not so effective) re-creation of sentence-structures he had used at the end of 'The Life with a Hole in it':

> Some people say, best show an empty glass:
> Someone will fill it. Well, I've tried that too.
> You may get drunk, or dry half-hours may pass.
> It seems to turn on where you are. Or who.

These were the last lines of poetry Larkin wrote, and as they were printed he painfully reminded himself of how far he had declined from his earlier poems when he recorded a selection for a series of Faber Poetry Cassettes. Larkin filled one side of a tape and Douglas Dunn the other. 'I think the contrast between myself and Douglas Dunn is quite something,' he told Christopher Ricks; 'he makes me sound like Donald Wolfit. It was recorded under appalling conditions, and a friend of mine here who runs the Audio Visual Centre [Mike Bowen] is highly critical of the technical detail. Wrong kind of microphone (should have been a ribbon), room too small, cutting amateurish. There certainly seems to be a lot of heavy breathing on it!'[7]

Larkin's work in the library continued to add to his frustrations. Ever since the University Grants Committee had announced the 20 per cent reduction of its annual grant to Hull in the late 1970s, he had been pruning services to meet the deadline – 1984 – when the cuts were due to come into effect. Now the deadline had arrived he discovered that still more reductions were needed: more staff to go, more facilities reduced. He told Barry Bloomfield that in the new year alone 'over three hundred journals' would have to be cancelled 'in an effort to reduce expenditure . . . by £30,000 or so', adding that 'unless our grant goes up as fast as the cost of what's left we shall have to do it all over again next year'.[8]

It was now twenty-nine years since Larkin had arrived in Hull, and in that time the library had altered beyond all recognition. The buildings were transformed, the stock had risen from 124,000 titles to half a million, the staff from twelve to nearly a hundred, and the number of students from 700 to 5,000. Yet for the last decade or so it had been embattled, and Larkin's mood had become increasingly 'recessive'.[9] Now new cuts threatened more damage than ever, his deputy librarian Tom Graham was on the point of taking up a job at York, and both Betty and Maeve were approaching retirement. (Maeve took hers early, when she was fifty-five.) He had never felt so strongly that the injuries to the library were injuries to himself. He was 'scared', he told Bloomfield, 'scared about age and illness and other things too numerous to mention'.[10]

He made a few modest attempts to enjoy himself at intervals throughout the coming year. He bought a new car – a second-hand Audi ('I like the name because it reminds me of Auden'[11]). In a second edition of *All What Jazz* he endorsed the 'light-heartedly aggressive tone'[12] he had adopted in younger and more vigorous days. At a concert held in Hull in May to mark the tenth anniversary of Duke Ellington's death he discovered an oasis in the 'jazz desert'[13] surrounding him. When the Hull painter and magazine editor Ted Tarling gave him two of his street scenes he was 'at a loss for words to say how much'[14] he liked them. And the summer Test Match at Lord's seemed, as ever, 'half an annual pleasure, half a rite', even though, as he told Monteith, 'I couldn't face the heat of a London hotel room and in consequence we watched the match on television daily, opening a bottle of champagne at noon.'[15]

These things apart, Larkin's days were filled with Monica – with worrying about her health and his ability to look after her properly. The painful leg he had complained about soon after Christmas 1983 still troubled him, making it difficult for him to fetch and carry. In February 1984, when he went to see his doctor, Dr Richardson, and was passed on to a physician in Hull Royal Infirmary, he was diagnosed as having a superficial phlebitic thrombosis and told to rest at home for a week. He was happy to do so, since it meant avoiding other kinds of surgery in the library, but he distrusted his doctor's cheerfulness. 'He is,' he said slightingly, 'a somewhat optimistic character who assures me that my last state will be better than my first, though if it isn't then I suspect he may want to get his knife into me.'[16]

By the end of the month Larkin was back at work. After another month Monica announced that she had recovered too – if not quite fully, then at least enough to try looking after herself in Haydon Bridge. She disliked the thought of leaving Larkin, but she wanted to feel there was an alternative to the situation which had been thrust upon them. Larkin didn't want her to go either; after a lifetime spent insisting on the need for solitude he had got used to having her in the house. He found that he needed her as much as she needed him. 'Our walking sticks,' he said, 'hang side by side in the hall.'[17]

Larkin drove Monica up to Haydon Bridge for 'a few freezing days' at the end of March and reluctantly 'installed her for a fortnight, to see how she manages. The cottage is rather grim after a year's vacancy – spiders, and the telephone cut off.'[18] Alone in Hull once more, he fretted anxiously, surprised by how lonely he felt. 'I have thought of you constantly,' he wrote after their first day apart, speaking in the same caring tone of voice he had once used with his mother, 'wondering how you are feeling and doing. Did you have your bath? I hope you did and feel more rested and relaxed. Indeed I can't imagine you'll be any less *feeble*, but I hope you'll find some satisfaction in being among your own things, and your own boss again. Be careful, dear, of *stairs*, and road crossings, and be sensible about eating and drinking.'[19] The following day he wrote again. 'Of course I have missed you,' he said, replying to her fond inquiry. 'Found myself putting the butter out for your breakfast! I do hope you have felt a little more at home and able to do things. I look forward to hearing what you feel like: it's awful being cut off like this, quite the last straw. Even now I can't quite understand how it happened.'[20] This was the note of uncomplicated affection Monica wanted to hear. It told her that if she returned to Newland Park Larkin would willingingly shoulder whatever burdens she laid on him. Within a few days – when the telephone was reconnected – she rang for him and he happily brought her back: his comforter at home and his companion in public.

He needed her support almost at once. Although he had promised on his return from Coleraine that he would accept no more honorary doctorates, when the University of Oxford offered him one he changed his mind. Of all the many accolades he had received he felt this was 'the big one',[21] and when news of it first reached him, Monica says, 'he actually ran upstairs to tell me'.[22] As the occasion drew near his enthusiasm waned. 'Oh dear,' he wrote to Monteith, 'I hope I can endure it. Coleraine really shook my confidence in being able to stand up and be talked about – I swore, no more! I wonder if I could carry a stick, or have someone to lean on. My secretary says it's all in my mind and I must practise positive thinking. I say if I'm getting it for anything it's for negative thinking. Oh dear.'[23]

When he and Monica arrived in Oxford for the ceremony itself, on 27 June, Larkin had worked himself into a lather. He wore the forty-four-year-old mortarboard he had owned as an undergraduate, but felt that the new suit he had ordered looked like 'a walrus maternity garment'.[24]

Throughout the ceremony he looked round anxiously for Monica, and swayed 'giddily'[25] as he was introduced in the Sheldonian Theatre. 'People were very kind,' he told John Wain afterwards, trying to sound less worried than he had been, 'though the citation was a bit like a review in *Poetry Tyneside* – i.e. singularly failing to make clear why I should be so honoured.'[26]

Back in Hull he had to face a very different kind of public occasion, and one to which Monica could not easily go with him. On 27 June, the same day that he received his D.Litt. in Oxford, Betty reached her sixtieth birthday and retired from the library. She had worked for Larkin since May 1957, and at a small party held in her honour he gave a 'fulsome speech'.[27] He said he was relieved to know that she would be 'coming in a few hours a week to knock off my literary letters'[28] and felt that her replacement, Margaret Elliott, was 'wonderfully efficient'.[29] He didn't so much as hint at their secret relationship, which had anyway had to adapt since Monica had arrived in Newland Park. 'It was all right,' says Betty, 'because I wasn't besotted with him. He had treated me like a wife all those years, telling me everything. I wasn't suddenly going to stop seeing him when I retired, was I?'[30]

Monica said nothing. Betty was the one subject she couldn't easily raise in Newland Park, and she turned a blind eye to Larkin's occasional meetings elsewhere with his 'old flame'.[31] In every other respect she felt completely involved in Larkin's life, sharing his worries, advising him in practical things. At the same time as she steered him through the ordeal of his Oxford D.Litt., she helped him cope with something closer to home. Should he have his portrait painted for the National Portrait Gallery? The idea had first been suggested by the director of the gallery, John Hayes, in 1979, when they had asked Howard Morgan to make his charcoal drawing of Larkin. Because Larkin had thought the result made him look like 'the young Mussolini'[32] he had decided not to allow Morgan to paint a full portrait. Now that five years had elapsed, the gallery thought they might try him with another artist.

They suggested Humphrey Ocean, who had recently won the Imperial Tobacco Portrait Award and the John Player Portrait Award, and in 1983 had been commissioned by the gallery to paint the ex-Beatle Paul McCartney. 'I think that's partly why Larkin said he'd meet me,' Ocean says. 'He wanted to hear about McCartney. He welcomed me into his office in the library [in April] by holding up a glass of Tio Pepe and saying "will you join me? This is how I've been earning my living all morning."'[33] By the end of lunch, during which Larkin was appalled to discover that McCartney had never once offered Ocean a drink, they decided they could 'do business',[34] and began searching for a location. They toured the university, found nowhere suitable, then went back to Newland Park. 'My first impression of the house,' says Ocean, 'was that everything was very dull. My second was that everything had been very carefully chosen. And of course I met Monica.'[35] When Ocean returned to London that evening Monica confirmed Larkin's own impressions. 'I told him,' she says, 'we had fallen on our feet with that young man. I told him he should go ahead.'[36]

Ocean came back to Newland Park for one day in June, to make a preliminary sketch. He sat Larkin upstairs in 'the bookroom' where Sydney's library was kept, at the front of the house overlooking the half-timbered 1930s mansion opposite. Larkin immediately fell asleep. When sittings proper began, on 17 July, he frequently fell asleep again, even though the head and shoulders of the finished portrait show him looking watchful. His eyes are bright and concentrated by his black-framed glasses, his lips are slightly compressed as if he were in mid-thought, his light suit and grey-blue shirt look slightly crumpled and create a sense of action recently suspended. Against the brown armchair and dark wall, and with the right side of his face lit by cold (but not deep) blue air from the window, he looks pensive but impatient, part of the respectable suburban world but detached from it.

During the month it took Ocean to finish the portrait – he worked from ten to six for the first two weeks, then had a week off, then returned for three consecutive days – Monica was 'a wonderful catalyst'.[37] She brought coffee and biscuits at elevenses, tea and cakes at four o'clock. Larkin, when not dozing, was silent or self-mocking. 'I know what they'll say,' he told Ocean at the outset. 'Once again Larkin turns his back to the world.'[38] When he saw the finished picture he was more complimentary. Although he said to one friend it looked like a portrait of '[Alfred] Hitchcock at Eighty',[39] and another 'it looks very *brown* to me',[40] he agreed with Monica that there was 'a likeness', and that Ocean himself had been 'very good company'. When the canvas was carried downstairs on 10 August, the day after Larkin's sixty-second birthday, they had three 'vast'[41] gins and tonics in celebration, and Larkin read a passage from Connolly's *The Condemned Playground* that he thought Ocean would enjoy.[42] Then he gave him the book.

Before saying goodbye, Ocean turned the conversation to 'John Betjeman and the laureate business'.[43] On 19 May, shortly after Ocean had first visited Hull, Betjeman had died at his home in Trebetherick in Cornwall.

Larkin was saddened but not surprised. He had known for many months that Betjeman was ill with Parkinson's disease; at one of their last meetings – a televised encounter to celebrate Betjeman's birthday – this had been plain for all the world to see. Even before the funeral was over, the press began speculating about who might succeed him. The last time the Laureate question had been raised, when Betjeman was appointed, it had merely alarmed him. Since then it had started to terrify him. 'Oh, Christ,' he had told Amis in 1976, 'that's in my lap, I've no hope of getting out of that bugger.'[44] He realized now that compared to the other candidates (Amis, Ted Hughes, Gavin Ewart, Patricia Beer and Roy Fuller) he was bound to become the popular choice.

Speculation reached a peak after Betjeman's memorial service at Westminster Abbey in July. Emerging into the summer crowds with Monica on his arm, then heading back for lunch in the flat belonging to Betjeman's friend Gerald Irvine, Larkin was 'harassed' by TV people and photographers. Next day, he told Judy, 'the *Guardian* printed [on the front page] myself and M. resembling "Soho Lil stops Foxy Freddie from leaving without paying". I didn't see the TV but I gather there was something. Whole business took me as near to the Laureateship as I want to get. Phew.'[45]

It was partly shyness which made Larkin long to be passed over, partly the conviction that his poetry had deserted him. 'It's not clear what the Laureate is or does,' he said once, but – as we've seen – he believed that 'poetry and sovereignty are very primitive things' and liked 'to think of their being united in this way'.[46] He knew that he could come up with lines to order – he had done so for the Humber Bridge and for Charles Causley's and Gavin Ewart's birthdays – but he believed the Laureate should produce more than merely required writing about 'bloody [royal] babies'.[47] There were other reasons for hesitating, as well. He felt that he was 'rather a cut-price Betjeman to the general reader', and thought it would be sensible to appoint 'a completely *different* poet'.[48] He had sympathized with the difficulties Betjeman had suffered doing the job, and thought his own would be greater. 'I never thought John was happy with it,' he said, 'and this reinforced my own feelings on the subject.'[49] Furthermore, he felt dismayed by the amount of time and money it would involve. He told Colin Gunner, 'I just couldn't face the fifty letters a day, TV show, representing-British-poetry-in-the-"Poetry-Conference-at-Belgrade" side of it all.'[50] To other friends he said simply, 'Think of the stamps! Think of the stamps!'[51]

Several people tried to get him to change his mind. Amis, for instance, 'kept telling him he must take it if offered, even though I felt a fucking fool for saying so, like Gosse writing to Bridges'.[52] At the Arts Council, Charles Osborne also did what he could. When, as the head of the Literature Panel, he was asked for a short-list of candidates by the Prime Minister's office, he replied, 'I'd have thought Larkin, wouldn't you?'[53]

In December the offer was duly made. Larkin didn't reply immediately, even though he had decided what to do. When he eventually declined, his sense of relief made him feel briefly exhilarated. He cheerfully told Gunner he was 'sorry to disappoint',[54] but was happy that 'Mrs Thatcher [had been] very nice and understanding about it all'.[55] If he had any second thoughts, he confined them to feeling 'sorry about letting Ted [Hughes] in'[56] instead. 'I agree,' he told Amis, '[that] the thought of being the cause of Ted's being buried in Westminster Abbey is hard to live with. "There is regret. Always, there is regret." Smoking can damage your bum.'[57]

FIFTY-EIGHT

The elation faded almost at once. Larkin knew he had made the right choice, but it confirmed his feelings that he had no remaining role or purpose. He and the world had become incompatible. Overweight, 'terribly deaf',[1] and drinking more than ever (including 'some port in the morning' but making sure he kept the bottle downstairs 'so I have to get out of bed'[2]), he shrank into himself more and more angrily. National politics filled him with 'horrified fascination'. The trades union leaders, he told Gunner, 'can't lose: either they get what they are asking for, or they reduce the country to chaos, at which point their friends the Russkis come marching in'.[3] Local matters were no better. A neighbour's Great Dane barked loudly enough for him to feel invaded; children pedalled their bikes up and down the road outside his house, irritating him by their very presence. 'I had the pleasure of seeing one fall off his new tricycle ... and set up a howl,' he told Gunner soon after Christmas. 'Instead of cuffing him about the ears the father walked him up and down in his arms. Grrr.'[4]

There were occasional pleasures – such as a trip to London to see an exhibition of paintings by George Stubbs, which Judy Egerton had selected

and catalogued at the Tate Gallery, and which he thought 'very strange
and wonderful' for their 'static, theatrical quality as well as their super-fine
finish'.[5] The memory soon withered when he returned to Hull. Monica
was still frail. He felt apprehensive about her, let alone himself. Reviewing
began to fill him with self-doubt – he told Amis he couldn't 'think of
anything to say'.[6] Celebrations of his work embarrassed him. When
Patrick Garland, who had made the Monitor film in 1964, asked him in
January 1985 about the possibility of mounting what Larkin called 'a
one-man "entertainment" on the subject of myself', he said:

I question very much whether you can construct anything entertaining from my
recessive personality. That, I know, is your problem, but it leads on to the second
reservation, which I suppose might be best expressed by saying that you say only
what the show *won't* try to do – it won't be a chap pretending to be Larkin, it
won't be Larkin in a cloth cap and a Hull Kingston Rovers scarf – but you don't
say what kind of portrait it *will* draw. For such a project to be successful, some
kind of coherent portrait must be painted, which means you must have it in mind
already, and I am a little curious to know what it is. I could be presented in a
number of ways, none of them at all flattering, and while I have faith in your good
will, a temptation to be funny about me, or make me be funny about myself, will be
strong. Do you think you could enlarge on this point a little – Larkin as what?[7]

Eventually Garland pacified Larkin and the show was done by Alan Bates
at the Harrogate Festival, and later at Chichester.[8] Larkin's doubts about
it seemed justified when he heard that at Chichester 'every time Hull was
mentioned it produced a roar of laughter'. He told Judy Egerton it made
him feel as though 'I've wasted my life'.[9] It was the same wherever he
turned. His few close friends were almost the only means by which he
could purge himself of his misery. Everything else which had once enter-
tained or diverted him had dried up. Jazz. Poems. The countryside. Work.

Work was the last to go. Even when the university cuts hurt him most,
Larkin still clung to the idea that the library sustained him. As recently as
Christmas 1984, when complaining in a letter to Amis that he was 'pretty
depressed about my whole mental and phyusical [*sic*] condition', he said,
'My sodding job is the only thing that keeps me going.'[10] Early in the new
year even this faint and intermittent support seemed about to be finally
removed. Sir William Taylor, the Vice-Chancellor designate of the univer-
sity, who was seeking ways to save £250,000 in his first year,[11] proposed
shrinking the library by hiving off some of its rooms for other purposes.
Larkin didn't know any details of the plans but dreaded their unveiling,

and when his deputy David Baker was appointed to the University of East Anglia later in the year he felt even more vulnerable. His library was now a 'creaking old ship',[12] he told Bloomfield, and the university itself not much better. 'This place,' he wrote to Gunner in April, 'has no future, to my mind, without being combined with the "College of Higher Education" next door, thus releasing into our hallowed portals hundreds of even lower-grade characters than infest it at present, if you can believe that possible.'[13]

A month before writing this letter, when he met his new Vice-Chancellor for the first time and felt him 'weighing me up for the drop',[14] Larkin's health began to deteriorate. At first he seemed to be suffering from not much more than a combination of all his usual minor ailments: he had piles, he was constipated, he was anxious and drinking heavily, his liver was enlarged, he slept only four or five hours a night. The university Medical Officer, Dr Richardson, recommended that he have a barium enema (which he did on 7 March) and see a cardiologist, Dr Clive Aber, at the Hull Nuffield Hospital. Since Larkin had complained of occasional 'cardio-spasms' it seemed a sensible idea. Aber, who saw Larkin on 16 March, thought so too – and while he confirmed the existence of the spasms, he also agreed with Richardson that Larkin was suffering from acute depression and hypochondria. 'He had,' he noted, 'a cancer phobia and fear of dying.'[15]

Because Larkin complained that his appetite was poor, that his tongue felt 'like an autumn leaf',[16] and that he had some difficulty in swallowing, Aber arranged for him to have a barium meal. While waiting for his appointment, Larkin wrote to Judy Egerton apologizing for his recent silence. 'I have been in a sort of flap about my health,' he said, 'which has occasioned various excursions into the world of X-rays and blood tests and consultants and so on, and have in consequence shrunk back into my shell in silent, and often not so silent, terror. I hasten to say that so far nothing has been diagnosed, and the only thing that has been indicated is that my liver is not happy. To my mind the most likely explanation of this is drink.'[17]

'Likely' but not entirely accurate. The barium meal revealed to John Bennett, who examined Larkin in 'The Building' – Hull Royal Infirmary – a polypoid tumour in his oesophagus, which would have to be surgically removed. Larkin was 'terrified'.[18] He reduced his drinking and began to lose weight, but this only cleared his mind so that he could concentrate on his unhappiness more steadily. He was not consoled by knowing that his oesophagus had troubled him before – in 1956 – and had since seemed to cure itself. (Before eating a meal he always drank large glasses of water to force open his oesophagus.) Neither was he cheered by considering the medical history of his family. His mother had lived a long and healthy life, but his father had died at sixty-three, which Larkin would be in August. He had said for years that he would die at the same age as his father; now the idea began to obsess him.

Larkin told Charles Monteith that it would have been 'something to say in recompense' if 'Monica was better, but she isn't; I don't say she's notably worse, but one rather offhand medico suggested "early Parkinson's" after virtually *no* examination'.[19] Their long days together dragged by, soaked in misery. 'I should say,' Larkin told Judy Egerton in May, 'M. is the worse off of us, going downhill physically',[20] but he knew he was not far behind, and would soon overtake her. 'I have suffered a great loss of self-confidence,' he warned Monteith later the same month, 'and am in general a shadow of my former self.'[21]

Larkin meant that he was haunting his former self, as well as merely weaker than he had been. Even before his illness had taken hold, he had become increasingly 'capricious'[22] in his behaviour towards Maeve when they met in the library. Some days he was aloof from her. On others he sought her out for a chat before going home. Once, at the library Christmas party in 1984, he had even veered towards their old ways and 'talked with seeming regret about "what might have been"'.[23]

As the operation to remove his oesophagus drew closer, Larkin became more and more anxious for Maeve's support. The night before he went into hospital he waited until Monica was in the kitchen, then telephoned Maeve – as well as Betty, Michael Bowen and Virginia Peace (the wife of the Professor of Russian, whose autobiographical novel he had read) – to 'take his farewell'. Maeve says:

It was harrowing, especially as he put our relationship into mini-perspective, asking me to forgive all the hurt he had caused me and to remember 'the many, many happy times we had had' and how much happiness I had given him. To my astonishment, he also asked me to join the very select few (Betty, Mike Bowen, Virginia) to form a rota to ferry Monica [who had never learnt to drive] to hospital to visit him. This was a very public way of bringing me back into his circle. He also stressed that he had asked Monica to ring me after the operation before anyone else, and that he wanted me to be his first visitor after Monica and Mike, who alone would be able to see him in the immediate post-operative stage.[24]

Once Larkin had made these plans he beckoned Monica back into the sitting-room from the kitchen and sat her down opposite him, so that they were either side of the gas fire. He forced himself to confront what he most feared. Monica remembers him saying, '"Suppose I've got cancer?" Then he said. "Supposing I've got this? How long would you give me?" Well, I couldn't lie to him then. I said, "Six months," and he said, "Oh, is that all?"'[25]

'Six months' was a guess. Soon Monica knew it was an accurate prediction. After Larkin's oesophagus had been removed by Dr Royston in Hull Royal Infirmary on the morning of 11 June, the doctors told her it was cancerous, and contained 'a great deal of unpleasant stagnant material'.[26] Another cancerous tumour was discovered in his throat, too well-advanced for surgery. Even without his oesophagus, Monica realized, cancerous secondaries were bound to kill Larkin before long. She decided that he should not be told.

He was taken back to his ward, Ward 6, and the following day was transferred to the Intensive Care Unit of the Nuffield Hospital. He made good progress, and Monica was driven to see him. Within a few days he was even able to make a few telephone calls – the first one being to Maeve. He encouraged her to visit, and she told him she would as soon as possible, showing the ready kindness for which he had always valued her. Before she was allowed to see him, another person's attempt at kindness had nearly fatal results. 'Someone,' Richardson says, 'we don't know who',[27] brought Larkin a bottle of whisky. On 19 June, only eight days after his operation, Larkin drank most of it, vomited, and flooded his lungs. He fell deeply unconscious. Dr B. C. Hovell, a consultant anaesthetist who happened to be nearby, realized that he was in imminent danger of dying, but drained and massaged him before he was rushed back to the Intensive Care Unit at Hull Royal Infirmary, where he remained unconscious for some time. When he eventually came round the hospital told him that he was lucky to be alive.

News of his collapse – but not the cause – soon reached the press, making the front page of the *Guardian*. For several days the hospital gave regular bulletins, then stopped when the crisis passed and Larkin was transferred to an ordinary side ward. On 28 June Maeve was at last able to see him. When she arrived, she remembers:

he was having something done or checked and the curtains were drawn round the bed, but he knew I was there and his big hand came round the curtain and waved in

such a droll manner. He seemed delighted to see me, there were no gloom
moments, the room was full of sunlight, we held hands very tightly; the atmos
phere was very emotionally charged and everything began to topple again. I think
he was thinking of a similar scene in 1961 when I visited him in another hospital at
the start of our affair.[28]

On her next visit, a few days later, Larkin was 'in very bad form' and
'reprimanded' her for being 'over-anxious and phoning Monica'.[29] Dis
tressed, Maeve settled once more for seeming simply well-meaning, not
lover-like. 'I think,' she says, 'that seeing me may have upset him emo
tionally on the first occasion, reminding him of happier, headier days. He
wasn't in a state to have his emotions torn apart any more.'[30]

Messages from unknown admirers came to the hospital by every post
and continued to arrive when Larkin was moved back to the Nuffield in
early July. Many people from outside Hull asked if they might visit him,
but several, even those closest to him, were turned away. Amis, for
instance, who understood the refusal 'was like "Aubade", you know, "I"
means not scaring others."'[31] Friends from closer to hand were restricted
to the 'circle' he had created before going into hospital: Monica, Maeve,
Betty, Virginia Peace and Michael Bowen. However much Monica, Maeve
and Betty wanted to avoid upsetting him, they couldn't help it. The first
time Maeve gave Monica a lift to the hospital was the first time they had
ever met, and when they arrived Maeve sat in a waiting room for three
quarters of an hour while Monica was with Larkin, then joined them for
ten minutes. As the two women 'made to go', Maeve says, 'Philip, ill as he
was, reached out to kiss me. I froze with horror – I could not possibly
respond with Monica watching from the opposite side of the bed.'[32]
Maeve found the 'whole ordeal very harrowing', and so did Monica. On
another, later occasion, Monica was embarrassed again to see Betty giving
Larkin a kiss which she felt sure 'he wouldn't have wanted then'.[33]

The awkwardness and anxiety continued for at least another fortnight,
and as the days trailed by Larkin became implacably depressed. Pitifully
thin, forcing himself to walk round the apple-tree-dotted lawn outside his
room once a day, leaning on his stick and the arm of whoever was visiting,
he insisted that he had nothing to live for. He gazed at the small television
in the corner of his room, and for hour after hour watched the Test Match
and the Wimbledon tennis tournament. The Men's Singles pleased him: he
thought that the winner, Boris Becker, looked 'just like the young
Auden'.[34]

On 17 July Larkin asked his solicitor, Terence Wheldon, to visit him and amend his will. He was in no doubt about where to leave the bulk of his estate. He kept his existing will, which he had made ten years earlier, before him as a model, making changes which reflected the pattern of his life since then. A bequest to Maeve was cancelled. Monica, the Society of Authors and the Royal Society for the Prevention of Cruelty to Animals remained his main beneficiaries. (He was to leave, after probate, £286,360.) Two days later, relieved to have set his affairs in order but still 'intensely depressed',[35] he was driven back to Newland Park by Michael Bowen.

FIFTY-NINE

Larkin's surgeon, Christopher Royston, paid him regular visits at home and soon found him 'physically better', and 'drinking 2½ to 3 pints of beer at lunch without any ill effects'.[1] Larkin remained unchangeably pessimistic. 'It's been a shattering time,' he told Bloomfield, 'and has left me much reduced mentally as well as physically.'[2] To Judy Egerton he wrote, 'It has all left me feeling (a) very weak – can't get out of a bath, that sort of thing – (b) very depressed – never be the same again, old age here, death round the corner etc. I daresay I needn't elaborate. I haven't asked what was wrong with my oesophagus and I haven't been told; felt I had enough to worry about.'[3]

Monica, as ever, did what she could to help. Larkin told John Kenyon that she was being 'absolutely marvellous', but since she was 'never well herself' they had to enlist other friends such as Mike Bowen and Virginia Peace to help do their shopping. 'It's all rather like a play by Harold Pinter or some other merchant of cheerfulness,' Larkin said valiantly, 'but of course it could be worse.'[4] Soon it was worse. Although he had recovered enough nerve to drive short distances by late summer (once scraping his car as he tried to negotiate the entrance to the station car-park – '£150 or I'm a Dutchman'[5]), he still felt pathetically weak and 'bloody depressed'.[6] On 10 August, one day after his sixty-third birthday, he told John Wain that he was torn between anxiety about Monica, who seemed 'to be slowly degenerating physically', and fear for himself. 'I feel,' he said, 'I have at one step passed into the end of life, which of course is always in my mind, but is now real and here, and fills me with dread.'[7]

His mood stayed the same through September. 'It's hard to say "How I am",' he wrote to Judy Egerton on the 6th:

Things weren't improved by falling downstairs *backwards* a week ago, which left me 'bruised and shaken', as the phrase goes, but no bones broken. It happened because halfway up the stairs I negligently took hold of some curtains that were over the bannisters waiting to be taken up, and they were heavier than I expected. Silly of me. But my chief worry is 'a funny feeling in my throat' which lasted about a week, and which of course I fear the worst about. It makes me v. bad company. I daren't go to the doctor (anyway my GP is away for this month) because I dread another cycle of X-rays and all the rest. All this adds up to a substantial loss of nerve – I couldn't 'go to London' – though I potter about the shops, and drive, and go to the dentist . . . All my clothes are far too big, but I shrink (absurd word) from buying smaller ones. No appetite: can't eat hardly at all. Drink like a fish. My doctors are quite happy about me (they don't know about the throat or falling downstairs). I signed off 'work' till the end of October. At the moment I don't think I shall ever work again.[8]

In fact, when the new term started, Larkin experimented with the idea of going into his office for only part of a day's work. He soon found it impossible and asked his colleagues to continue covering for him. At home he also did less and less. He occasionally spoke to Maeve. He wrote a few letters. He re-read *A Dance to the Music of Time*, telling Anthony Powell he was 'simply racing through it, and my only regret is that it is so short'.[9] He lived on a diet of cheap red wine and Complan, while Monica made do with tomato sandwiches and gin. Reviews, like poems, were now entirely out of the question, though the possibility of returning to work continued to plague him. He told Monteith on 1 October that he didn't 'perceive any striking signs of recovery',[10] yet he knew that now the new Vice-Chancellor was installed the threats to the library were greater than ever. He felt he should be there to defend the world he had created. His doctors told him to try to relax.

Partly to test himself, partly out of a sense of duty, and partly because he felt death's hand on his shoulder, he gathered his strength for one last piece of sustained writing. It was an obituary of Eric Walter White, his former colleague on the Arts Council. 'Eric was my first introduction to metropolitan culture,' Larkin wrote, looking back over the level field of both their lives, 'and I am afraid I always found him slightly comical, but was consoled by the belief that he was perfectly well aware of this, and it amused him to startle my provincial attitudes. In retrospect I think he was both tough and kind, a rare combination in any man.'[11] As soon as the obituary was done, Larkin considered reviewing a book which might have made him seem tough but unkind: Dylan Thomas's *Collected Letters*. While Larkin's own life had been spent writing letters which constantly recognized the need to entertain their recipients, Thomas had filled his with 'abject whining and crawling'. Larkin told a friend, 'they divide into begging, apologizing, promising and business. Then there are the ones to Caitlin. They are extraordinary. They don't sound as if they knew each other at all.'[12]

Deciding not to write about the book, Larkin gave illness as his excuse, not incompatibility. No one doubted that he was telling the truth. By November his doctors were asking him to come into hospital for tests once and sometimes twice a week. 'They are just tests,' he tried to reassure friends, 'but clearly they are looking for something.' As the visits continued he complained of feeling 'lower than at any time I can remember':[13] despairing, exhausted and – when he imagined what was happening in the library – guilty. He was unable to attend the interviews to choose a replacement for his deputy David Baker, and no appointment was made. He cancelled a meeting with the new Vice-Chancellor at which he would have had to hear for the first time precisely what further cuts were proposed. He sent apologies to a meeting of the university Library Committee. And on 21 November he had to excuse himself from Maeve's retirement party, arranging for Eddie Dawes to read for him the short speech he had written.

Larkin was sorry but also relieved to miss the celebrations. Although – as is clear from the text of his speech – he would have welcomed the chance to pay tribute to Maeve's career as a librarian, he was glad to avoid a direct and probably painful confrontation with the past. 'I really do feel wretched and incapable,' he wrote to her apologetically, '[but] as you know I was rather dreading this occasion.'[14] Maeve regretted his decision but respected it: her own feelings were similarly mixed. While continuing to admire him, she had come to doubt the depth of his affections. She regretted his selfishness. She felt he had taken 'the best years' of her life and 'given little in return'.[15] In time to come, when she discovered the full extent of his duplicity, her disillusionment would grow still deeper. She says now:

I think Philip wanted me to believe even at the end that I had played a special part in his life, but he wasn't in a position to demonstrate this without upsetting too many other people, and especially himself. Nevertheless when I think of all the anguish he has caused me, Byron's 'When We Two Parted', rather than anything Philip wrote, sums up my feelings now. Were I to meet him again, that's how I should greet him, 'with silence and tears'.[16]

There was one more disappointment, too, to complicate Larkin's final days – a disappointment of a different kind. Mrs Thatcher, who as Larkin appreciated had been 'very understanding' about the Laureateship, nevertheless wanted to honour him in some other way. As the summer ended he heard that he was to be made a Companion of Honour; the investiture was due to take place on 25 November at Buckingham Palace. Larkin delayed until the early autumn, then let it be known he was too ill to go. In due course the official notification and regalia were sent to him through the post. He was put out, as he had been twenty-odd years earlier when the postman had delivered his Queen's Gold Medal for Poetry. Yet at the same time he was satisfied; he thought it suited him to receive the highest accolades by the lowliest means. It was in keeping with the spirit of his poems.

When Larkin should have been travelling to and from Buckingham Palace, he was at home, dazzled by fear and pain. The prospect of death, acknowledged but unnamed, raged out at him, concentrating the terrors he had kept before him all his life. In his twenties, thirties and forties he had sometimes tried to 'talk [him]self into regarding death as a merciful oblivion', but had always worried that 'the moment of death . . . must be a little choppy, a fribbling as the currents of life fray against the currents of death'.[17] In his fifties, the dread of oblivion darkened everything. Death, he said, 'remains a sort of Bluebeard's Chamber in the mind, something one is *always* afraid of'.[18] As he entered his sixties his fears grew rapidly. Reviewing D. J. Enright's *Oxford Book of Death* in 1983 he said, 'Man's most remarkable talent is for ignoring death. For once the certainty of permanent extinction is realized, only a more immediate calamity can dislodge it from the mind, and then only temporarily.'[19] Two years later, immediately before he fell ill, he told John Wain, 'I don't think about death *all* the time, though I don't see why one shouldn't, just as you might expect a man in a condemned cell to think about the drop all the time. Why aren't I screaming?'[20] Now he told Monica he was 'spiralling down towards extinction'. It was, she says, 'one of those lugubrious, melodramatic remarks he used to make, but this time I knew it was true. He said it with a fascinated horror, looking as though he was about to burst into tears. I can see him now, sitting there by the fire, saying it.'[21]

November came to an end. On Thursday 28th Virginia Peace rang Newland Park to arrange to do some shopping and found Larkin's voice 'very slurred'. He wanted her to take his cash card to the bank and collect some money, but when she did so 'the machine ate it'. She paid for the shopping herself, then took it back to the house where Larkin wrote her a cheque. 'He made it out to Mrs Virginia Peace,' she says, 'punctilious to the last, though the writing was very weak and spidery, not like his usual writing at all, which had been so beautiful. And he looked deathly thin. Really, it was terrible.'[22]

As Friday wore on Larkin grew steadily weaker. In the evening, trying to get into his chair in the sitting-room, he fell to the ground and picked himself up with difficulty. Monica, not strong enough to help him herself, rang for a neighbour. Later Larkin collapsed again in the downstairs lavatory, jamming the door shut with his feet. Monica was unable to force the door open. She couldn't even make him hear her – he had left his hearing-aid behind – but she could hear him. 'Hot! Hot!' he was whispering pitifully. He had fallen with his face pressed to one of the central heating pipes that ran round the lavatory wall.

The next-door neighbour was called again, the door was opened, and Larkin was carried into the kitchen. He asked for some Complan, and while Monica prepared this she also rang for an ambulance to take him to the Nuffield. When the ambulance arrived he looked up at her wildly, begging her to destroy his diaries, then was taken out of the house on a stretcher. 'I'll see you tomorrow, Bun,' he said as he was borne away.

The next day, Saturday, Betty took Monica to see Larkin, but he was too heavily sedated to make sense. 'He looked at the TV,' Betty says, '(not watching it), as though he was seeing beyond the bounds of the material world.'[23] On Saturday Michael Bowen ferried Monica to and from the hospital. 'If Philip hadn't been drugged,' Bowen says, 'he would have been raving. He was that frightened.'[24] It was the same on Sunday. They sat by Larkin's bed in silence, and when visiting hour was over Bowen returned Monica to Newland Park. He left her sitting by the telephone, waiting. It rang in the early hours of Monday. Larkin had died at 1.24 a.m., turning to the nurse who was with him, squeezing her hand, and saying faintly: 'I am going to the inevitable.'[25]

SIXTY

During his last few hours in Newland Park Larkin had several times urged Monica to destroy his diaries after his death. He hadn't strength to do so himself. Neither had she. As soon as she was able, she rang Betty and asked her to help. Some weeks later, Betty took the thirty-odd thick A4 notebooks into the librarian's office in the Brynmor Jones Library at lunchtime, asked for the university's paper shredder, placed it on his desk, and fed the pages into its jaws. It took all afternoon, and when she had finished she sent the remains to the university boiler house, where they were incinerated.

She kept the covers, and later transcribed the various quotations and newspaper cuttings which Larkin had pasted on to them over the years. They give a miniature, fragmented history of his beliefs, ranging from the sympathetic melancholy of Edward Thomas ('How dreary-swift, with naught to travel to,/Is time') to more robust items such as the 'motto' of the Oxford and Bucks Light Infantry ('Faint heart never fucked the pig'); from writers known to be associated with him (Hardy, Christina Rossetti) to others who demonstrate the true range of his reading (Joyce, Proust, Blake). 'I'm not sure I was right to keep the covers,' Betty says, 'but they're interesting, aren't they? About the diaries themselves I'm in no doubt. I must have done the right thing, because it was what Philip wanted. He was quite clear about it; he wanted them destroyed. I didn't read them as I put them into the machine, but I couldn't help seeing little bits and pieces. They were very unhappy. Desperate really.'[1]

Maeve's and Betty's own unhappiness was great too. Even though they had known Larkin was dying they were deeply shocked when the news broke, as was the whole tightly knit community of the university and the wider world of Larkin's friends and readers. The obituaries generally agreed that he had been 'the greatest living poet in our language',[2] the writer who spoke most intimately to an enormous range of people, and the personality who for all his reticence 'cared most about what we all care about'.[3] Within days his reputation had begun to acquire the fascination of a legend. Reporters quoted him incessantly, making his remoteness synonymous with his integrity. The *Evening Standard* was one of many papers to call him 'the Hermit of Hull', and *The Times* said he was 'the Simeon Stylites *de nos jours*'.[4] (Even the Communist daily paper the *Morning Star* reported his death, in a piece headlined 'Best-Selling Poet Dies in Private Hospital'.) The extent to which Larkin had revealed the details of his life was temporarily forgotten. His utterances were turned into general truths, his poems into founts of wisdom. By writing memorably about familiar disappointments, and lyrically about the endless struggle of the human spirit to rejoice, he had produced poems that spoke exactly as he – and Samuel Johnson – believed art should: helping people endure life, as well as enjoy it.

This was a cold comfort to Monica. Isolated in Newland Park, ill, virtually unknown to the outside world and a stranger even to the university, she felt her life disintegrate. She had no existence without Larkin. She was a widow without even the consolation of that title. She had all Larkin's possessions around her – his tweed jacket was still draped over the back of his chair – but they only reminded her of all she had lost. Drinking heavily, not bothering to change out of her nightdress and dressing-gown during the day, she surrendered to her sorrow.

At Larkin's funeral, on 9 December, a week after his death, almost no one noticed that Monica wasn't there. The mourners were led through the foggy early afternoon into the university church of St Mary the Virgin in Cottingham by Larkin's sister Kitty, by his niece, by Charles Monteith, by Kingsley Amis and his first wife Hilly. While the Rev. Terence Grigg, the rector of St Mary's, who conducted the service, and Father Bown, who read some prayers, tried to reconcile Larkin's 'Anglican agnosticism' to the Christian faith, Amis concentrated on secular matters in his address. Remembering how Larkin had once thanked him for a whole adult lifetime 'of undiminished affection and admiration', he repeated sentiments he had already expressed in print: 'We take seriously what he left us. We are lucky enough to have known him; thousands who didn't and more thousands in the future will be able to share his poems with us.'[5]

When the congregation dispersed a handful of people followed the hearse from St Mary's to the graveyard a short distance away in Cottingham: his sister and niece again, Amis and Monteith, Betty and Maeve. Bouquets of flowers were laid out in the shape of a ragged 'S' on the grass in front of the grave – there was one from Anthony and Ann Thwaite, who in April 1985 had gone to work for a year in Japan and had heard the news of his death in Tokyo; the one from the Brynmor Jones Library was made up to look like an open book. Within a few months a plain white gravestone would be erected, inscribed as Monica ordered:

Philip Larkin
1922–1985
Writer

'I think that's right,' Monica said later. 'Don't you? *Writer*, not poet. He wasn't just a poet. He lived a *writer's* life.'[6]

Before the stone was delivered, a more public commemoration took place. Charles Monteith, supported by several of Larkin's other friends, arranged for a memorial service to be held at Westminster Abbey early in the new year. The Dean agreed that jazz should be played as well as religious music, and Mike Bowen arranged it. He hired a rhythm section which included John Barnes on saxophone and Alan Elsdon on trumpet. They played Sidney Bechet's 'Blue Horizon' and Bix Beiderbecke's 'Davenport Blues'; the Poet Laureate Ted Hughes read 'Let us now praise famous men'; and C. Day-Lewis's widow Jill Balcon read 'Love Songs in Age', 'Church Going' and 'An Arundel Tomb'.

When the service ended Alan Elsdon climbed the wooden steps into the organ loft and trumpeted 'A Closer Walk with Thee' over the bowed heads filling the abbey. As the last notes faded a slow procession began down the aisle. Monica, tiny-looking and leaning on a stick, went first. Behind her, the huge congregation delayed a moment. Some felt the service had drawn Larkin too easily into the Christian fold. Some thought the ceremony suited a man who so evidently loved tradition. Some pondered a deep personal loss. Some marvelled that a poet they had never met could have spoken to them so intimately. Some remembered whole poems. Some thought of individual lines: 'the one about mum and dad',[7] 'Nothing, like something, happens anywhere', 'What will survive of us is love'. The procession thickened, flooding out into the cold, blustery afternoon. It was Valentine's Day.

NOTES

ABBREVIATIONS

Philip Larkin is referred to throughout these notes by his initials: PAL. His letters to James Ballard Sutton, now in the Brynmor Jones Library at the University of Hull (MS DP/174/2, nos. 1–219) are referred to by initial and date, thus: PAL to JBS, 26 October 1952.

In quoting from these and other letters I have silently expanded contractions such as '&' and 'wd'.

I have also referred to Larkin's other correspondents, and to my most-mentioned interviewees, by their initials. These are:

KA	Kingsley Amis	EL	Eva Larkin
BCB	B. C. Bloomfield	SL	Sydney Larkin
MB	Maeve Brennan	CM	Charles Monteith
RC	Robert Conquest	BP	Barbara Pym
WD	Winifred Dawson (née Arnott)	JBS	James Ballard Sutton
JE	Judy Egerton	RS	Ruth Siverns (née Bowman)
CG	Colin Gunner	PS	Patsy Strang
MJ	Monica Jones	AT	Anthony Thwaite

The dates following references to these and other people in the book indicate either a letter or an interview, as the context suggests.

Other abbreviations are as follows:

AGIW: *A Girl in Winter* (Faber, 1947; Overlook, 1976)

ANWS: unfinished drafts of novel provisionally entitled *A New World Symphony*, deposited in the Philip Larkin Archive of the BJL

AWJ: *All What Jazz* (Faber, 1970, 1984)

Bax: untitled, unfinished story novel about a family called Bax, deposited in the Philip Larkin Archive at the BJL

BJL: The Philip Larkin Archive in the Brynmor Jones Library at the University of Hull. Material is still being deposited in the Archive, and many of the extracts quoted in this book refer to material which is so far unsorted, and therefore has no catalogue number. I have described the material in the Archive as and when I first quote from it. Most references are self-explanatory; a few referring to 'autobiographical essays' and 'autobiographical fragments' indicate the various diary-like pieces that Larkin wrote occasionally throughout his life (when leaving Wellington, for example), which he preserved among his loose papers.

CP: *Collected Poems*, ed. Anthony Thwaite (The Marvell Press and Faber, 1988; Farrar, Straus & Giroux, New York, 1988, 1989)

J: *Jill* (first Faber edition, 1964; Overlook, 1976)

L at 60: *Larkin at Sixty*, ed. Anthony Thwaite (Faber, 1982)

MB & PAL: unpublished autobiographical essay by Maeve Brennan.

MTASB: *Michaelmas Term at St Bride's* (unpublished novel, 1943, deposited in the Philip Larkin Archive at the BJL)

OBTCEV: *The Oxford Book of Twentieth Century English Verse*, ed. Philip Larkin (Oxford, 1973)

RW: *Required Writing: Miscellaneous Pieces 1955–1982* (Faber, 1983)
SBS: the unpublished text of an interview with Philip Larkin by Melvyn Bragg for the LWT South Bank Show; interview conducted 16 April 1981
TAWG: *Trouble at Willow Gables* (unpublished novel, 1943, deposited in the Philip Larkin Archive at the BJL)

Where I have quoted from unpublished material contained in Larkin's notebooks – the eight surviving folio notebooks in which he drafted his poems – I have referred to them by their number in sequence, thus: Notebook 5. Details of these notebooks are given in CP, p. xvii.

During the ten years that I knew Larkin I never recorded his conversation in any systematic way. Nevertheless, when I was writing this book I remembered many things he had said to me, and wherever appropriate I have used them, citing them thus: PAL to author. Where I have quoted from his letters to me, I have dated them thus: PAL to author, 26 October 1982 (letter).

Since I began work on this book in 1986 I have spent many hours, on many different days, talking to Monica Jones. I have judged the dates of our meetings to be of very limited interest to readers, and have simply given references to my quotations from her thus: MJ to author.

INTRODUCTION

1 RW, p. 82.
2 My first wife, Joanna Motion, during this time was working as Information Officer at the University of Hull.
3 PAL to author.
4 'Lines Drawn in the Battle of Larkin's Will', Neil Lyndon, *Independent on Sunday* (2 November 1990).
5 RW, p. 99.
6 PAL speaking on the Monitor film made about him by Patrick Garland in 1964. (Hereafter known as Monitor.)
7 JBS to author, 26 November 1986.
8 Quoted in Michael Holroyd, 'Shaw and Biography', *Essays by Divers Hands*, vol. xliii, p. 90.
9 J, p. 12.
10 SBS.
11 *Viewpoints: Poets in Conversation with John Haffenden* (Faber, 1981), p. 114. (Hereafter known as *Viewpoints*.)
12 PAL to Richard Murphy, 19 August 1977.

ONE

1 I'm grateful to Seamus Heaney and Tom Paulin for telling me this.
2 *Springtime* [no. one], ed. G. S. Fraser and Iain Fletcher (Peter Owen, London, 1953).
3 BJL, text of Honorary Degree citation.
4 PAL to EL, 30 June 1946.
5 Ibid., 20 January 1952.
6 Ibid., 15 March 1957.
7 BJL, notebook belonging to SL, preserved by PAL.
8 See the sleeve of *Philip Larkin reading The Less Deceived*, Listen LPV 1, Hessle, The Marvell Press, 1959.
9 PAL to CM, 30 November 1984.
10 PAL to author.
11 BJL, Notebook 5, untitled autobiographical essay.
12 Ibid.
13 Ibid.
14 Ibid.
15 Ibid.
16 Catherine Hewitt to author, 26 November 1986.
17 Ibid., and 1 June 1992.
18 PAL to MB, 12 August 1963.
19 SBS.
20 PAL to author.
21 PAL to Bohdan Buciak, 21 February 1984.
22 Ibid.
23 *Viewpoints*, p. 114.
24 BJL, unpublished fragment.
25 *Viewpoints*, p. 114.

TWO

1 SBS.
2 Ibid.
3 JBS to author, 15 July 1986.
4 Alan Marshall to author, 28 June 1989.
5 Noel Hughes to author, 5 May 1987.
6 Elsie Harris to author, 4 June 1987.
7 Ibid.
8 BJL, Notebook 5.
9 Elsie Harris to author, 4 June 1987.
10 Ibid.
11 SBS.
12 John Kenyon, unpublished essay 'Larkin at Hull', in possession of author.
13 Ibid.
14 Richard Griffiths, *Fellow Travellers of the Right* (Oxford, 1983), p. 277.
15 Ibid.
16 John Kenyon, 'Larkin at Hull'.
17 Noel Hughes to author, 5 May 1987.
18 SBS.
19 Frank Smith to author, 28 August 1987.
20 John Kenyon, 'Larkin at Hull'.
21 Alan Marshall to author, 28 June 1989.
22 SBS.
23 BJL, Notebook 5.
24 Ibid.
25 PAL to author.
26 PAL to JBS, 6 September 1939.
27 BJL, Notebook 5.

THREE

1 Catherine Hewitt to author, 26 November 1986.
2 Ibid.
3 RW, pp. 47–8.
4 PAL to editor of the *Coventrian*, 12 November 1979.
5 'Not the Place's Fault', *Umbrella*, vol. i, no. 3 (spring, 1959).
6 SBS.
7 L at 60, p. 17.
8 Noel Hughes to author, 19 September 1986.
9 Brian Taylor to author, 8 October 1987.
10 Arthur Tattersall to author, 28 August 1986.
11 I'm grateful to Noel Hughes for explaining this system.

12 Noel Hughes to author, 19 September 1986.
13 L. W. Kingsland to author, 1 December 1988.
14 Arthur Tattersall to author, 28 August 1986.
15 E. J. Liddiard to author, 9 August 1986.
16 JBS to author, 15 July 1986.
17 Colin Gunner to author, 11 August 1980.
18 Bill Ryder to author, 18 August 1989.
19 Noel Hughes to author, 19 September 1986.
20 Ibid.
21 Ibid.
22 Ibid.
23 PAL to KA, 14 July 1942.
24 'Not the Place's Fault'.
25 Ibid.
26 Ibid.
27 JBS to author, 15 July 1986.
28 Ibid.
29 Ibid.
30 Ibid.
31 Ibid.
32 Ibid.
33 AWJ, p. 16.
34 Ibid., p. 257.
35 'Not the Place's Fault'.
36 PAL to JBS, 4 August 1939.
37 PAL to editor of the *Coventrian*, 12 November 1979.
38 RW, p. 50.
39 Frank Smith to author, 28 August 1987.
40 BJL, Notebook 5.
41 Noel Hughes to author, 19 September 1986.
42 Ibid.
43 Ibid.
44 Foreword to Colin Gunner, *Adventures with the Irish Brigade* (privately printed, 1975).
45 CG to author, 11 August 1980.
46 Ibid.
47 PAL to MJ, 16 September 1971.
48 Noel Hughes to author, 19 September 1986.
49 L at 60, pp. 17–18.
50 Noel Hughes to author, 19 September 1986.
51 Ibid.

52 Philip Antrobus to author, 8 September 1987.
53 *Coventrian* (December 1938), p. 570.
54 BJL, PAL's pocket diary for 1936.

FOUR

1 BJL, PAL's pocket diary for 1936.
2 SBS.
3 KA to author, 3 August 1987.
4 RW, p. 47.
5 Ibid., p. 55.
6 *Coventrian* (September 1939), p. 633.
7 'Not the Place's Fault'.
8 PAL, 'Books for the People', *New Statesman* (May 1977).
9 'Not the Place's Fault'.
10 Arthur Tattersall to author, 28 August 1986.
11 L. W. Kingsland to author, 1 February 1986.
12 BJL, Notebook 5.
13 Quoted in CP, p. xvi.
14 BJL, Notebook 5.
15 Ibid.
16 BJL.
17 BJL, Notebook 5.
18 Quoted in CP, p. xviii.
19 Quoted in CP, p. xix.
20 Brian Taylor to author, 8 November 1987.
21 PAL to JBS, 6 November 1939.
22 Ibid., 6 September 1939.
23 Ibid., 1 April 1942.
24 Ibid.
25 Ibid., 9 February 1945.
26 Ibid.
27 Noel Hughes to author, 19 September 1986.
28 BJL, foreword to booklet *Poems* (August 1940).
29 Ibid.
30 SBS.

FIVE

1 RW, p. 40.
2 St John's College, Oxford, Junior Common Room Suggestions Book, 1940.
3 Nick Russel, 'Larkin about at St John's', *Philip Larkin: A Tribute*, ed. George Hartley (The Marvell Press, 1988), p. 84. (Hereafter known as *Tribute*.)
4 'Not the Place's Fault'.
5 JBS to author, 17 October 1989.
6 David Whiffen, 'A Note on Larkin at Oxford', *Tribute*, p. 89.
7 PAL to JBS, 21 May 1941.
8 PAL to SL, 26 January 1941.
9 PAL to JBS, 16 January 1941.
10 BJL, autobiographical essay, 1943.
11 PAL to CM, 19 April 1963.
12 PAL to EL and SL, 20 October 1940.
13 PAL to SL, 1 November 1940.
14 JBS to author, 15 July 1986.
15 PAL to JBS, 9 December 1940.
16 PAL to SL, 11 October 1940.
17 Nick Russel, *Tribute*, p. 84.
18 J, p. 12.
19 Ibid.
20 Ibid.
21 Ibid.
22 Ibid.
23 PAL to JBS, 9 February 1945.
24 Bill Ryder to author, 18 August 1989.
25 PAL to EL and SL, 22 October 1940.
26 KA to author, 24 January 1986.
27 J, p. 13.
28 KA to author, 24 January 1986.
29 KA, *Memoirs* (Penguin, 1992), p. 55.
30 J, p. 14.
31 Blake Morrison, *The Movement* (Oxford, 1986), p. 12.
32 I am grateful to Judith Priestman for this information, which is contained in her article 'Philip Larkin and the Bodleian Library', Bodleian Library Record, vol. xiv, no. 1 (October 1991).
33 RW, p. 64.
34 PAL to JBS, 16 September 1941.
35 Ibid., 6 July 1942.
36 Ibid.
37 Ibid., 23 November 1941.
38 Ibid., 10 August 1943.
39 Ibid., 16 September 1941.
40 RW, p. 123.
41 BJL, autobiographical essay (1943).
42 PAL to JBS, 12 August 1943.

SIX

1 Monitor.
2 KA, *Memoirs*, p. 55.
3 PAL to author.
4 SBS.
5 PAL to Peter Dickinson, 21 December 1983.
6 SBS.
7 Mervyn Brown to author, 22 February 1988.
8 Nick Russel, *Tribute*, p. 85.
9 Edward du Cann to author, 23 February 1988.
10 PAL to EL and SL, (no date) / November 1941.
11 AWJ, p. 17.
12 Nick Russel, *Tribute*, p. 83.
13 J, pp. 16–17.
14 PAL to JBS, 9 September 1939.
15 KA, *Memoirs*, p. 52.
16 PAL to JBS, 26 March 1941.
17 PAL to EL and SL, (no date)/November 1940.
18 J, p. 212.
19 Ibid., p. 214.
20 Noel Hughes, 'Going Home with Larkin', *London Magazine*, vol. xxix, nos. 1 & 2 (April/May 1989), p. 117.
21 Ibid.
22 PAL to SL, 18 November 1940.
23 PAL to JBS, 16 November 1940.
24 Ibid., 16 April 1941.
25 PAL to WD, 20 January 1952.
26 PAL to JBS, 9 December 1940.
27 Ibid., 28 December 1940.
28 Ibid.
29 Ibid., 16 December 1940.
30 Ibid., 9 December 1940.

SEVEN

1 BJL, autobiographical essay (1943).
2 PAL to EL and SL, 24 November 1941.
3 PAL to JBS, 21 April 1941.
4 Ibid., (no date)/1941.
5 Ibid., 22 February 1941.
6 Ibid., 9 October 1942.
7 Ibid., 26 March 1941.
8 Ibid.
9 Ibid., 10 April 1941.

10 J, pp. 14–15.
11 KA, speaking on *Kingsley Amis*, a BBC Bookmark film produced by Daisy Goodwin (1991).
12 KA to author, 3 August 1987.
13 KA, *Memoirs*, p. 38.
14 BJL, autobiographical essay (1943).
15 KA to author, 3 August 1987.
16 J, p. 16.
17 Monitor.
18 KA to author, 3 August 1987.
19 J, p. 16.
20 MJ to author.
21 SBS.
22 BJL, Foreword to *Chosen Poems* (1941).
23 SBS.
24 PAL to JBS, 5 March 1942.
25 KA to author, 24 November 1986.
26 Ibid.
27 PAL to JBS, 28 February 1943.
28 BJL.
29 Ibid.

EIGHT

1 KA, *Memoirs*, p. 54.
2 PAL to JBS, 4 December 1941.
3 KA, *Memoirs*, p. 54.
4 KA to author, 24 November 1986.
5 Ibid.
6 Ibid.
7 Humphrey Carpenter, *W. H. Auden: A Biography* (George Allen & Unwin, 1981), p. 89.
8 Ibid., p. 87.
9 KA to author, 24 November 1986.
10 Ibid.
11 PAL to JBS, 16 June 1941.
12 Philip Brown to author, 17 October 1991.
13 PAL to JBS, 20 November 1941.
14 Philip Brown to author, 17 October 1991.
15 KA to author, 24 November 1986.
16 PAL to JBS, 23 June 1941.
17 Ibid., 20 February 1941.
18 KA to author, 24 January 1986.
19 RW, p. 274.
20 Ibid.
21 Roger Sharrock to author, 18 August 1989.

22 L at 60, p. 20.
23 BJL, all quotations from untitled short story.
24 Ibid.
25 KA to author, 24 November 1986.
26 Philip Brown to author, 17 October 1991.
27 PAL to Jon Stallworthy, 29 January 1975.

NINE

1 PAL to JBS, 9 July 1941.
2 Ibid.
3 PAL to Norman Iles, 23 July 1941.
4 Ibid., 22 September 1941.
5 PAL to JBS, in various letters during the summer, 1941.
6 PAL to Norman Iles, 24 July 1941.
7 BJL, autobiographical essay (1943).
8 PAL to JBS, 28 December 1941.
9 Ibid., 20 November 1941.
10 MJ to author.
11 PAL to JBS, 10 November 1941.
12 Ibid., 6 July 1942.
13 Ibid., 12 October 1941.
14 Ibid., 16 October 1941.
15 PAL to EL and SL, 31 October 1941.
16 BJL, autobiographical essay (1943).
17 KA to author, 24 November 1986.
18 SBS.
19 PAL to JBS, 20 October 1941.
20 Ibid., 15 December 1941.
21 Ibid., 20 November 1941.
22 Ibid., 1 November 1941.
23 BJL, autobiographical essay (1943).
24 PAL to EL and SL, 16 December 1941.
25 BJL, autobiographical essay (1943).
26 Ibid.
27 PAL to JBS, 20 November 1941.
28 Ibid., 15 March 1942.
29 Ibid.
30 PAL to EL and SL, 12 November 1941.
31 PAL to JBS, 28 December 1941.
32 Ibid.
33 31 December 1941.

TEN

1 SBS.
2 Roger Sharrock to author, 12 March 1990.

3 PAL to EL and SL, 2–15 May 1942.
4 Ibid., 21 February 1942.
5 Philip Brown to author, 17 October 1991.
6 BJL, autobiographical essay (1943).
7 PAL to JBS, 22 January 1942.
8 BJL, autobiographical essay (1943)
9 PAL to JBS, 1 April 1942
10 Ibid., 11 April 1942.
11 PAL to EL and SL, 10 May 1942.
12 Alun Lewis, Letters to My Wife, ed. Gwen Lewis (Seren Books, Bridgend, 1989), p. 131.
13 Timothy d'Arch Smith, R. A. Caton and the Fortune Press (Bertram Rota Publishing, 1983), p. 12.
14 Julian Symons to PAL, 16 July 1981.
15 A. J. Tolley, 'The Fortune Press and the Poetry of the 1940s', p. 94.
16 Ibid.
17 PAL to JBS, 25 March 1943.
18 PAL to Norman Iles, 30 December 1942.
19 Philip Brown to author, 17 October 1991.
20 BJL, uncollected fragment.
21 PAL to JBS, 5 August 1942.
22 Ibid., 22 April 1942.
23 Ibid., 5 August 1942.
24 Ibid., 29 August 1942.
25 Ibid.
26 Ibid.
27 Ibid.
28 BJL, autobiographical fragment (1943).
29 Ibid.
30 Livia Gollancz to author, 26 October 1990.
31 Ibid.
32 Ibid.
33 PAL to JBS, 28 December 1942.
34 PAL to EL and SL, 18 October 1942.
35 Minutes of the Essay Society of St John's College, Oxford (1942).
36 BJL, autobiographical essay (1943).
37 BJL, PAL's unpublished account of dreams, written winter/spring 1942–3. This extract dated 26 October 1942.
38 Ibid.
39 Ibid., 15 December 1942.
40 PAL to JBS, 2 January 1943.
41 Ibid., 12 April 1943.

ELEVEN

1 PAL to JBS, 2 January 1943.
2 Ibid.
3 PAL to EL and SL, 4 April 1943.
4 RW, p. 40.
5 Ibid., p. 29.
6 Ibid.
7 PAL to JBS, 16 March 1943.
8 RW, p. 43.
9 Ibid., p. 42.
10 PAL to KA, 21 March 1943.
11 RW, p. 29.
12 PAL to EL and SL, 15 March 1943.
13 SBS.
14 RW, p. 29.
15 Ibid.
16 Ibid., p. 41.
17 Ibid.
18 BJL, autobiographical essay (1943).
19 Ibid.
20 RW, p. 30.
21 KA to author, 3 August 1987.
22 Ibid.
23 Ibid.
24 PAL to KA, 7 September 1943.
25 BJL, *Antemeridian*
26 PAL to JBS 28 July 1943.
27 Ibid., 6 July 1943.
28 PAL to Michael Sharp, 9 April 1967.
29 BJL, autobiographical essay (1943).
30 KA, *Memoirs*, p. 71.
31 BJL, autobiographical essay (1943).
32 KA to author, 3 August 1987.
33 KA, *Memoirs*, p. 72.

TWELVE

1 J, p. 19.
2 BJL, TAWG, p. 5.
3 Ibid., p. 6.
4 Ibid., p. 8.
5 Ibid., p. 15.
6 Ibid., p. 13.
7 Ibid., p. 17.
8 Ibid., pp. 24–5.
9 Ibid., p. 43.
10 Ibid., p. 87.
11 Ibid., p. 89.
12 Ibid., p. 91.
13 Ibid., p. 94.

14 Ibid., p. 96.
15 Ibid., pp. 97–8.
16 Ibid., p. 109.
17 Ibid., p. 116.
18 BJL, MTASB, p. 30.
19 Ibid., p. 31.
20 Ibid., p. 37.
21 Ibid., p. 42.
22 Ibid., pp. 47–8.
23 Ibid., p. 65.
24 Ibid., p. 66.
25 Ibid., p. 74.
26 Ibid., p. 89.
27 Ibid., p. 92.
28 Ibid., p. 106.
29 Ibid., p. 127.
30 Ibid., pp. 140–1.
31 Ibid., p. 141.
32 Ibid., p. 143.

THIRTEEN

1 BJL, *Sugar and Spice*, collection of poems by PAL written under pseudonym 'Brunette Coleman' (1943).
2 PAL, 'Femmes Damnées', printed by John Fuller at the Sycamore Press, 4 Benson Place, Oxford (summer, 1978).
3 'Four Conversations: Philip Larkin' (interviewer Ian Hamilton), *London Magazine*, vol. iv, no. 8 (November 1964), p. 73.
4 Ian Hamilton to author, 29 January 1992.
5 'Four Conversations', p. 73.
6 BJL, 'What We Are Writing For', essay by PAL written under pseudonym Brunette Coleman (1943).
7 Ibid.
8 Ibid.
9 PAL to KA, 11 January 1947.

FOURTEEN

1 PAL to JBS, 7 January 1943.
2 Ibid.
3 Ibid., 21 December 1942.
4 PAL to EL and SL, 9 May 1943.
5 PAL to JBS, 23 May 1943.
6 Ibid., 15 June 1943.

7 SBS.
8 J, p. 8.
9 John Wain, *Sprightly Running* (Macmillan, 1962), p. 100.
10 PAL to EL and SL, 4 April 1943.
11 PAL to JBS, 12 April 1943.
12 Ibid., 24 June 1943.
13 PAL to EL and SL, 24 June 1943.
14 Ibid.
15 BJL, autobiographical essay (1958).
16 SBS.
17 Alan Marshall to author, 28 June 1989.
18 PAL to JBS, 18 July 1943.
19 Ibid., 28 July 1943.
20 Ibid., 6 August 1943.
21 Ibid.
22 BJL, autobiographical essay (1958).
23 PAL to KA, 13 August 1943.
24 PAL to JBS, 10 August 1943.

FIFTEEN

1 PAL to author.
2 PAL to KA, 13 August 1943.
3 PAL to JBS, 10 August 1943.
4 Ibid.
5 Ibid., 4 September 1943.
6 PAL to KA, 1 September 1943.
7 Ibid., 7 September 1943.
8 PAL to JBS, 3 April 1945.
9 Ibid., 30 September 1943.
10 PAL to KA, 13 August 1943.
11 PAL to JBS, 30 September 1943.
12 RW, p. 31.
13 Ibid.
14 Ibid.
15 PAL to JBS, 10 November 1943.
16 Ibid.
17 Bruce Montgomery to PAL, 27 November 1943.
18 SBS.
19 PAL to SL, 30 November 1943.
20 Ibid.
21 RW, p. 32.
22 Ibid.
23 R. Haynes to author, 12 October 1987.
24 RW, p. 32.
25 RS to author, 27 November 1986.
26 PAL to JBS, 13 December 1943.
27 PAL to EL and SL, 5 December 1943.
28 Ibid.

29 Ibid.
30 PAL to JBS, 22 March 1944.
31 Margaret Bell to author, 17 November 1989.
32 SBS.
33 BJL, 'Cross Him Out', autobiographical essay (?1946).
34 SBS.
35 PAL to EL and SL, 18 December 1943.
36 PAL to JBS, 13 December 1943.
37 PAL to EL and SL, 5 December 1943.
38 Bruce Montgomery to PAL, 20 October 1944.
39 PAL to JBS, 3 April 1945.
40 KA, *Memoirs*, p. 59.
41 PAL to JBS, 29 October 1944.
42 BJL.
43 RW, p. 29.
44 Quoted in Hazel Holt, *A Lot to Ask: A Life of Barbara Pym* (Macmillan, 1990), p. 234.
45 Blake Morrison, *The Movement* (Oxford, 1986), p. 14.
46 This information comes from the June 1990 Catalogue of Batstone Books, 24 Gloucester St, Malmesbury, Wiltshire.

SIXTEEN

1 RS to author, 27 November 1986.
2 Ibid.
3 Ibid.
4 Ibid.
5 Ibid.
6 Ibid.
7 KA, *Memoirs*, p. 61.
8 KA to author, 24 November 1986.
9 Ibid.
10 PAL to KA, 8 October 1943.
11 KA to author, 24 November 1986.
12 BJL, PAL's pocket diary for 1949.
13 BJL, PAL's pocket diary for 1950.
14 PAL to KA, 20 August 1943.
15 RW, p. 189.
16 Ibid., p. 54.
17 Ibid., p. 111.
18 RS to author, 27 November 1986.
19 Ibid.
20 Ibid.
21 Ibid.

22 Ibid.
23 Ibid.
24 Stella Bishop to author, 27 August 1987.
25 RS to author, 27 November 1986.
26 Ibid.
27 Ibid.
28 Ibid.
29 Ibid.
30 Ibid.
31 RW, p. 29.
32 RS to author, 13 February 1991.
33 RS to author, 27 November 1986.
34 Ibid.
35 KA to author, 3 August 1987.
36 RS to author, 27 November 1986.
37 PAL to EL and SL, 14 January 1945.

SEVENTEEN

1 PAL to SL, 27 February 1944.
2 PAL to JBS, 22 February 1944.
3 Ibid.
4 Ibid., 20 October 1944.
5 Ibid., 8 October 1944.
6 Ibid., 26 February 1944.
7 Ibid., 22 March 1944.
8 Ibid., 24 May 1944.
9 Ibid., 26 February 1944.
10 Ibid., 21 July 1944.
11 Ibid., 22 March 1944.
12 Ibid.
13 Ibid., 27 April 1944.
14 Ibid., 2 April 1944.
15 Ibid., 5 July 1944.
16 Ibid., 24 May 1944.
17 SBS.
18 PAL to JBS, 15 August 1944.
19 Ibid.
20 PAL to KA, 19 September 1942.
21 PAL to CM, 5 November 1965.
22 PAL to JBS, 20 August 1944.
23 BJL, autobiographical fragment (August 1944).
24 Ibid.
25 PAL to JBS, 20 August 1944.
26 BJL, autobiographical fragment (April 1944).
27 PAL to JBS, 4 October 1944.
28 Ibid., 26 October 1944.
29 Ibid., 20 November 1944.

30 RW, p. 27.
31 Ibid.

EIGHTEEN

1 PAL to JBS, 3 April 1945.
2 Ibid., 5 June 1944.
3 BJL, undated autobiographical fragment.
4 PAL to JBS, 5 June 1944.
5 Ibid., 8 May 1945.
6 Ibid., 9 December 1944.
7 Ibid., 9 March 1945.
8 PAL to S. L. Powsey, 3 June 1983.
9 PAL to JBS, 11 April 1945.
10 BJL, cutting from *Coventry Evening Telegraph* (26 October 1945).
11 PAL to JBS, 14 July 1945.
12 PAL to EL and SL, 22 August 1945.
13 PAL to JBS, 8 May 1945.
14 PAL to KA, 9 August 1945.
15 BJL, autobiographical fragment (summer 1945).
16 RS to PAL, 27 October 1945.
17 RS to author, 13 February 1991.
18 Ibid.
19 Ibid.
20 RS to PAL, 6 November 1945.
21 PAL to JBS, 31 October 1945.
22 KA to author, 20 January 1987.
23 RS to PAL, 20 January 1946.
24 PAL to JBS, 28 November 1945.
25 PAL to KA, 13 September 1945.
26 PAL to EL and SL, 6 May 1945.
27 PAL to JBS, 1 June 1945.
28 BJL, autobiographical fragment (summer 1945).
29 PAL to EL and SL, 14 October 1945.
30 RS to PAL, 27 October 1945.

NINETEEN

1 PAL to JBS, 27 January 1946.
2 RW, p. 29.
3 Ibid.
4 Ibid., pp. 29–30.
5 Ibid., p. 30.
6 Ibid., p. 175.
7 Ibid., p. 172.
8 Ibid.
9 Ibid., p. 264.

10 Ibid., p. 158.
11 PAL to JBS, 10 March 1946.
12 PAL to Julian Symons, communicated to author 13 September 1989.
13 Ibid.
14 PAL to KA, 1946.
15 PAL to JBS, 16 June 1946.
16 PAL to EL and SL, 5 May 1946.
17 PAL to Alan Pringle, 11 August 1946.
18 Alan Pringle to PAL, 19 August 1946.
19 PAL to Alan Pringle, 20 August 1946.
20 Ibid., 23 August 1946.
21 PAL to JBS, 31 October 1945.
22 Ibid., 7 April 1946.
23 PAL to EL and SL, 4 February 1945.
24 Leicester University Library files (PAL's job application, 3 June 1946).
25 PAL to JBS, 26 June 1946.
26 PAL to EL and SL, 7 July 1946.
27 BJL, autobiographical fragment (3 September 1946).
28 RS to PAL, 4 September 1946.

TWENTY

1 Nicholas Pevsner, *Leicestershire and Rutland* (Penguin, 1984), p. 257.
2 RW, p. 36.
3 Malcolm Bradbury, *Eating People is Wrong* (Arrow, 1978), p. 23.
4 PAL to JBS, 15 September 1946.
5 Joan Sutcliffe to author, 23 October 1987.
6 PAL to JBS, 30 September 1946.
7 PAL to KA, 30 September 1946.
8 BJL, PAL's pocket diary, 9 April 1946.
9 RW, p. 36.
10 Ibid., p. 39.
11 Ibid.
12 L at 60, p. 49.
13 PAL to KA, 24 September 1946.
14 Ibid.
15 Molly Bateman to author, 28 August 1986.
16 RW, p. 38.
17 Arthur Humphries to author, 10 August 1986.
18 PAL to JBS, 14 June 1946.
19 Ibid., 29 September 1946.
20 J, p. 21.
21 Ibid., p. 49.

22 Ibid., p. 37.
23 Ibid., p. 131.
24 Ibid., p. 132.
25 Ibid., p. 132.
26 Ibid., p. 135.
27 Ibid., p. 152.
28 Ibid., p. 160.
29 Ibid., p. 158.
30 Ibid., p. 170.
31 Ibid., p. 241.
32 Ibid., p. 242.
33 Ibid., p. 243.
34 Ibid.
35 Ibid., p. 53.
36 PAL to JBS, 7 March 1942.
37 J, p. 230.
38 Ibid., p. 11.
39 Ibid., p. 19.
40 Ibid.
41 Ibid.
42 PAL to JBS, 21 May 1944.

TWENTY-ONE

1 Maeve Brennan, 'Philip Larkin: A Biographical Sketch', *The Modern Academic Library* (The Library Association, 1989), p. 6. (Hereafter known as 'Philip Larkin'.)
2 PAL to Alan Pringle, 25 November 1946.
3 Ibid., 4 March 1947.
4 Ibid., 25 February 1947.
5 PAL to JBS, 19 February 1947.
6 Ibid.
7 AGIW, p. 11.
8 *Viewpoints*, p. 116.
9 PAL to EL and SL, 11 November 1946.
10 AGIW, p. 185.
11 Ibid., p. 15.
12 Ibid., p. 28.
13 Ibid., p. 22.
14 Ibid., p. 70.
15 Ibid., p. 72.
16 Ibid., p. 77.
17 Ibid., p. 90.
18 Ibid., p. 87.
19 Ibid., p. 90.
20 Ibid., p. 100.
21 Ibid., p. 101.
22 Ibid., p. 103.

23 Ibid., p. 109.
24 Ibid., p. 117.
25 Ibid., p. 127.
26 Ibid.
27 Ibid.
28 Ibid., p. 128.
29 Ibid., p. 129.
30 Ibid., p. 172.
31 Ibid., p. 173.
32 Ibid., pp. 183–4.
33 Ibid., p. 184.
34 Ibid., p. 185.
35 Ibid.
36 Ibid., p. 190.
37 Ibid., p. 201.
38 Ibid., p. 242.
39 SBS.
40 BJL, cutting from *Sunday Times* (2 March 1947).
41 BJL, cutting from *Church Times* (7 March 1947).
42 Ibid.

TWENTY-TWO

1 PAL to EL and SL, 3 March 1947.
2 PAL to JE, 22 February 1957.
3 PAL to JE, 20 February 1957.
4 PAL to JE, 22 February 1957.
5 Pamela Hanley to author, 29 March 1987.
6 Quoted in James Booth, *Philip Larkin: Writer* (Harvester, 1992), pp. 26–7.
7 Malcolm Bradbury to author, 27 June 1988.
8 MJ to author.
9 Ibid.
10 Ibid.
11 KA to author, 24 November 1986.
12 MJ to author.
13 RS to PAL, 12 April 1947.
14 Ibid., 1 June 1947.
15 Ibid.
16 PAL to JBS, 16 June 1947.
17 PAL to John Wain, 20 August 1947.
18 PAL to JBS, 14 September 1947.
19 PAL to EL and SL, 16 September 1947.
20 PAL to JBS, 11 October 1947.
21 BJL, PAL's pocket diary, 10 October 1947.
22 PAL to JBS, 11 October 1947.
23 Ibid., 28 June 1946.

24 Ibid., 28 January 1948.
25 Ibid., 28 October 1947.
26 BJL, PAL correspondence file, 6 December 1976.
27 Ibid.
28 PAL to JBS, 28 October 1947.
29 Ibid.

TWENTY-THREE

1 PAL to JBS, 3 January 1948.
2 Ibid., 28 January 1948.
3 PAL to Alan Pringle, 8 February 1948.
4 Ibid.
5 PAL to JBS, 24 February 1948.
6 RS to author, 27 November 1986.
7 RS to PAL, 31 March 1948.
8 RS to author, 27 November 1986.
9 See PAL's remark: poetry is 'emotional in nature and theatrical in operation', RW, p. 80.
10 PAL to JBS, 1 April 1948.
11 BJL, PAL's cutting from *Journal of Local Government Financial Officers* (July 1948).
12 BJL, PAL's cutting from *Journal of the Institute of Municipal Treasurers and Accountants*, vol. iii, no. 5 (May 1948).
13 BJL, notebook belonging to SL, preserved by PAL.
14 PAL to MJ, 12 August 1962.
15 PAL to JBS, 18 June 1948.
16 Ibid.
17 Ibid., 11 August 1948.
18 RS to PAL, 17 August 1948.
19 PAL to JBS, 18 May 1948.
20 RS to author, 27 November 1986.
21 Ibid.
22 PAL to JBS, 18 June 1948.
23 SBS.
24 BJL, Notebook 5.

TWENTY-FOUR

1 PAL to JBS, 3 October 1948.
2 BJL, unpublished fragment, here known as Bax, first draft, p. 1.
3 Ibid., p. 2.
4 Ibid., p. 4.
5 Ibid., p. 13.
6 Ibid., p. 21.

7 Ibid., p. 42.
8 Ibid., p. 45.
9 BJL, Bax second draft, p. 28.
10 Ibid., p. 1.
11 Ibid., p. 39.
12 Ibid., p. 44.
13 PAL to JBS, 11 August 1948.
14 Ibid., 15 September 1948.

TWENTY-FIVE

1 PAL to JBS, 3 October 1949.
2 BJL, unfinished poem written 26 January 1949.
3 PAL to JBS, 24 March 1949.
4 Ibid.
5 Ibid., April 1949.
6 Ibid.
7 RS to PAL, 5 January 1950.
8 SBS.
9 Ibid.
10 PAL to JBS, 26 January 1950.
11 BJL, unpublished short play, *Round the Point.*
12 PAL to Alan Pringle, 26 February 1950.
13 PAL to JBS, 4 May 1950.
14 Charles Madge to author, 30 October 1987.
15 PAL to JBS, 20 May 1950.
16 MJ to author.
17 Ibid.
18 PAL to JBS, 20 May 1950.
19 PAL to EL, 4 June 1950.
20 PAL to JBS, 18 June 1950.
21 Ibid., 13 May 1950.
22 Ibid.
23 Ibid., 3 July 1950.
24 Ibid., 18 June 1950.
25 Ibid., 20 June 1950.
26 Ibid.
27 Ibid., 3 July 1950.
28 Ibid.
29 Ibid.
30 RS to PAL, 22 September 1950.
31 RS to author, 27 November 1986.
32 PAL to JBS, 30 July 1950.
33 Ibid.
34 Ibid.
35 BJL.
36 PAL to JBS, 4 May 1950.
37 Ibid., 30 July 1950.

TWENTY-SIX

1 BJL, Notebook 5.
2 PAL to EL, 8 October 1950.
3 PAL, 'The Library I Came To', *Gown* (Queen's University magazine, 1984).
4 PAL to EL, 1 October 1950.
5 Ibid.
6 Ibid., 8 October 1950.
7 Jimmy Piggott to author, 27 November 1988.
8 Alec Dalgarno to author, 12 March 1989.
9 Arthur Terry to author, 14 June 1986.
10 Henry Mackle to author, 28 November 1988.
11 Ibid.
12 Jimmy Piggott to author, 27 November 1988.
13 WD to author, 25 November 1986.
14 Obituary of PAL by Jimmy Piggott, Queen's University Newsletter (spring 1986).
15 Colin Strang to author, 7 November 1987.
16 PAL, 'The Library I Came To'.
17 Ibid.
18 PAL to EL, 15 October 1950.
19 PAL to JBS, 5 November 1950.
20 Elizabeth Madill to author, 28 November 1988.
21 Ibid.
22 Ibid.
23 Arthur Terry, 'Larkin in Belfast', *Tribute*, p. 95.
24 PAL to JBS, 25 April 1951.
25 Elizabeth Madill to author, 28 November 1988
26 Ibid.
27 Henry Mackle to author, 28 November 1988.
28 PAL to WD, 10 April 1952.
29 RW, p. 58.
30 Jimmy Piggott to author, 27 November 1988.
31 WD to author, 25 November 1986.
32 Arthur Terry to author, 14 June 1986.
33 Jimmy Piggott to author, 27 November 1988.
34 Arthur Terry to author, 27 November 1988.

35 Arthur Terry, 'Larkin in Belfast', *Tribute*, p. 92.
36 RW, p. 58.

TWENTY-SEVEN

1 PAL to JBS, 5 January 1951.
2 PAL to EL, 29 April 1951.
3 Ibid., 18 January 1951.
4 Ibid., 21 October 1951.
5 EL to PAL, 29 March 1951.
6 PAL to EL, 11 March 1951.
7 BJL, unpublished short play, *Round Another Point* (1951).
8 WD to author, 25 November 1986.
9 Ibid.
10 Ibid.
11 Ibid.
12 PAL to JBS, 2 January 1951.
13 KA to author, 24 November 1986.
14 JE to author, 4 November 1992.
15 Arthur Terry, *Tribute*, p. 94.
16 Ibid., p. 97.
17 WD to author, 25 November 1986.
18 Ibid., 22 August 1991.
19 Ibid., 25 November 1986.
20 Ibid., 22 August 1991.
21 Ibid., 25 November 1986.
22 Ibid.
23 Ibid.
24 Ibid.
25 PAL to JBS, 10 July 1951.
26 James Booth, *Philip Larkin: Writer*, p. 78.
27 SBS.
28 RW, p. 80.
29 Ibid., p. 159.
30 Ibid., p. 74.
31 MJ to author.
32 SBS.
33 Ibid.
34 PAL to BCB, 2 December 1977.
35 Ibid.
36 PAL to JBS, 8 August 1951.
37 SBS.
38 PAL to D. J. Enright, 31 August 1951.
39 PAL to WD, 22 October 1951.
40 Ibid., 13 August 1951.
41 Ibid., 25 September 1951.
42 Arthur Terry to author, 14 June 1986.
43 Ibid.

44 PAL to WD, 22 October 1951.
45 PAL to JBS, 14 October 1951.
46 PAL to EL, 14 October 1951.

TWENTY-EIGHT

1 PAL to author.
2 PAL to WD, 20 January 1952.
3 PAL to EL, 19 March 1952.
4 MJ to author.
5 Ibid.
6 Ibid.
7 PAL to PS, 24 June 1952.
8 Ibid., 18 July 1952.
9 Ibid., 2 September 1952.
10 MJ to author.
11 PAL to PS, 13 March 1953.
12 Ibid., 1953.
13 Ibid., 1952.
14 Ibid., 1953.
15 Richard Murphy to author, 18 September 1987.
16 Ibid., 12 December 1992.
17 PAL to MJ, 18 January 1962.
18 Jean Hartley to James Booth (communicated to author 8 July 1991).
19 PAL to EL, 26 May 1952.
20 PAL to PS, 26 May 1952.
21 PAL to WD, 2 August 1952.
22 Ibid., 11 November 1952.
23 PAL to PS and Colin Strang, autumn 1953.
24 WD to author, 25 November 1986.
25 KA to author, 24 November 1986.
26 PAL to EL, 29 November 1952.
27 Ibid., 4 January 1953.
28 WD to author, 25 November 1986.
29 BJL, Notebook 3.
30 PAL to JBS, 14 September 1947.
31 Ibid., 6 October 1948.
32 Ibid., 26 January 1950.
33 PAL to PS, 3 April 1953.
34 Ibid.
35 BJL, unfinished novel, known here as *A New World Symphony*, first draft, p. 1.
36 Ibid., p. 3.
37 Ibid., second draft, p. 23.
38 Ibid., first draft, p. 4.
39 Ibid.
40 Ibid., p. 16.
41 Ibid., p. 22.

42 Ibid., p. 35.
43 Ibid.
44 Ibid., second draft, p. 34.
45 Ibid., p. 41.
46 Ibid., p. 50.
47 Ibid., p. 65.
48 Ibid., p. 67.
49 Ibid.
50 Ibid. (unnumbered loose pages).

TWENTY-NINE

1 PAL to PS, 3 April 1953.
2 Ibid., 6 July 1953.
3 MJ to author.
4 Ibid.
5 PAL to PS, 6 August 1953.
6 Ibid., 5 October 1953.
7 Ibid., 1 November 1953.
8 MJ to author.
9 PAL to PS, 7 December 1954.
10 PAL to WD, 20 July 1953.
11 Ibid., 26 July 1953.
12 Ibid., 17 August 1953.
13 WD to author, 26 November 1986.
14 PAL to KA, 3 February 1954.
15 PAL to RC, 12 July 1957.
16 PAL to WD, 26 March 1979.
17 Blake Morrison to author, 17 March 1992.
18 Quoted in CP, p. xxi.

THIRTY

1 Arthur Terry, Tribute, p. 96.
2 PAL to PS, 3 February 1954.
3 Ibid., 6 March 1954.
4 Ibid., 23 January 1954.
5 L at 60, pp. 28–9.
6 RW, p. 59.
7 KA to author, 24 November 1986.
8 See KA, Lucky Jim (Penguin, 1961).
9 Ibid., p. 11.
10 Ibid., p. 20.
11 Ibid., p. 23.
12 Ibid., p. 43.
13 Ibid., p. 200.
14 PAL to CM, 8 November 1953.
15 Quoted in Harry Ritchie, Success Stories (Faber, 1988), p. 16.
16 Jean Hartley, Philip Larkin, The

Marvell Press and Me (Carcanet, 1989), p. 58. (Hereafter known as Larkin.)
17 Ibid., p. 62.
18 Ibid.
19 Spectator (1 October 1954), p. 400.
20 PAL to William Van O'Connor, 2 April 1958.
21 Ibid., 11 April 1958.
22 Ibid., 24 March 1964.
23 PAL to Blake Morrison, 21 June 1978.
24 Robert Conquest, New Lines (Macmillan, 1956), pp xiv–xv.
25 Jean Hartley, Larkin, p. 62.
26 Blake Morrison to author, 17 March 1992.
27 PAL to PS, 28 October 1954.
28 PAL to EL, 23 November 1954.
29 Papers in the University of Hull personnel files.
30 Ibid.
31 Ray Brett, 'Philip Larkin in Hull', Tribute, p. 101.
32 PAL to EL, 23 November 1954.
33 Jean Hartley, Larkin, p.62.
34 Ibid., p. 63.
35 Ibid.
36 Ibid.
37 Ibid., pp. 63–4.

THIRTY-ONE

1 PAL to EL, 1 January 1955.
2 Ibid., 6 March 1955.
3 Arthur Terry to author, 14 June 1986.
4 BJL, autobiographical fragment.
5 PAL to JE, 30 April 1962.
6 PAL to Elizabeth Madill, 20 March 1955.
7 PAL to Jill and Basil McIvor, 3 July 1975.
8 PAL to JE, 24 March 1955.
9 PAL to EL, 17 April 1955.
10 Ibid., 24 April 1955.
11 PAL to D. J. Enright, 26 April 1955.
12 Jonathan Raban, Coasting (Picador, 1987), p. 254. (In this book Raban also gives a startlingly life-like portrait of Larkin; see pp. 261–8.)
13 Jean Hartley, Larkin, p. 65.
14 Winifred Holtby, South Riding (Virago, 1988), p. 127. Also quoted in D. J.

Spooner's essay, 'Philip Larkin's "Here"', *Geography*, Vol. 77, Part 2 (1992).
15 RW, p. 54.
16 Ibid.
17 SBS.
18 Maeve Brennan, 'Philip Larkin', p. 8.
19 Ibid., p. 9.
20 PAL to JE, 31 May 1955.
21 Ray Brett, 'Philip Larkin in Hull', *Tribute*, p. 103.
22 Donald Campbell to author, 12 November 1988.
23 Maeve Brennan, 'I Remember, I Remember', *Philip Larkin: The Man and his Work*, ed. Dale Salwak (Macmillan, 1989), p. 30.
24 Ibid.
25 Monitor.
26 Maeve Brennan, 'I Remember, I Remember', p. 26.
27 Mary Judd to author, 12 April 1988.
28 PAL to EL, 19 October 1958.
29 Ibid., 19 May 1962.
30 Ibid., 23 March 1969.
31 MB to author, 27 February 1992.
32 Ibid.
33 Ibid.
34 Maeve Brennan, 'I Remember, I Remember', p. 3.

THIRTY-TWO

1 Figures from University of Hull personnel files.
2 PAL to JE, 26 June 1955.
3 PAL to EL, 24 June 1955.
4 PAL to JE, 26 July 1955.
5 Maeve Brennan, 'I Remember, I Remember', p. 28.
6 MJ to author.
7 PAL to EL, 17 October 1955.
8 Ibid., 6 May 1956.
9 EL to PAL, 10 September 1957.
10 PAL to PS, 4 August 1957.
11 Ibid., 16 January 1958.
12 PAL to JE, 7 March 1958.
13 Ibid., 24 March 1958.
14 Jean Hartley, *Larkin*, p. 56.
15 Ibid., p. 71.
16 Ibid., p. 72

17 Ibid.
18 Ibid., p. 71.
19 Ibid., p. 72.
20 Ibid., p. 77.
21 Ibid., p. 72.
22 PAL, 'On Publishing *The Less Deceived*', *Tribute*, p. 53.
23 Society of Authors to PAL, 21 February 1956.
24 PAL to CM, 24 February 1956.
25 PAL to EL, 6 December 1959.
26 PAL to MJ, 17 August 1965.
27 PAL to CM, 24 February 1981.
28 PAL to EL, 16 January 1955.
29 Jean Hartley, *Larkin*, p. 82.
30 BJL, Notebook 4.
31 Jean Hartley, *Larkin*, p. 73.
32 Ibid., p. 86.
33 Ibid.

THIRTY-THREE

1 PAL to EL, 5 June 1955.
2 Ibid., 1 July 1955.
3 Ibid., 5 June 1955.
4 Ibid., 26 June 1955.
5 PAL to RC, 28 May 1955.
6 Ibid., 5 January 1956.
7 RC to author, 27 August 1988.
8 PAL to RC, 19 July 1956.
9 Ibid., 4 November 1961.
10 Ibid., 1 January 1956.
11 Ibid., 2 February 1959.
12 Ibid., 9 September 1958.
13 KA to author, 24 November 1986.
14 Bruce Mongomery to PAL, 24 April 1960.
15 Jean Hartley, *Larkin*, p. 95.
16 PAL to MJ, 5 August 1964.
17 PAL, 'Not the Place's Fault'.
18 PAL to EL, 18 September 1955.
19 PAL to JE, 29 October 1955.
20 PAL to RC, 9 July 1955.
21 Bruce Montgomery to PAL, 9 January 1955.
22 Jean Hartley, *Larkin*, p. 53.
23 F. W. Bateson, review of *The Less Deceived*, in *Essays in Criticism* (January 1957), p. 80.

THIRTY-FOUR

1 PAL to author.
2 PAL to Jill Balcon, when she read some of his poems in December 1967.
3 PAL on 'The Living Poet', produced by AT and Hugh Dickson, 3 July 1964.
4 PAL to Virginia Peace, 23 December 1978.
5 PAL to Richard Murphy, 27 March 1963.
6 PAL to Patrick Garland, 27 March 1963.
7 RW, pp. 136–7.
8 PAL to author.
9 PAL, *Poets of the 1950s*, ed D. J. Enright (Kenkyusha, Tokyo, 1956), p. 79.
10 PAL to JE, 10 February 1956.
11 Ibid.
12 MJ to author.
13 PAL to RC, 26 April 1956.
14 Sebastian Shakespeare, younger son of the author of the article, John Shakespeare, to author, autumn 1989.
15 'Four Young Poets: 1', *TES* (13 June 1956).
16 PAL to JE, 3 June 1956.
17 PAL to MJ, 18 September 1956.
18 John Kenyon, 'Larkin at Hull', unpublished essay in possession of author.
19 Ibid.
20 Jean Hartley, *Larkin*, p. 123.
21 MJ to author.
22 Ibid.
23 Harry Chambers, L at 60, p. 62.
24 V. Oates to author, 27 September 1990.
25 Janet Duffin to author, 26 September 1990.
26 PAL to EL, 8 June 1958.
27 Ibid., 26 August 1962.
28 Ibid., November 1956.
29 JE to author, 2 August 1990.

THIRTY-FIVE

1 PAL to author.
2 PAL to RC, 5 January 1957.
3 PAL to JE, 15 January 1957.
4 Ibid., 28 May 1957.

5 Charles Tomlinson, 'The Middlebrow Muse', *Essays in Criticism*, vol. vii, no. 2 (April 1956).
6 PAL to RC, 7 May 1957.
7 PAL to EL, 14 June 1964.
8 Betty Mackereth to author, 27 November 1987.
9 PAL to EL, 5 October 1969.
10 Betty Mackereth to author, 27 November 1987.
11 Ibid.
12 PAL to EL, 5 October 1969.

THIRTY-SIX

1 PAL to EL, 19 May 1957.
2 PAL to JE, 3 November 1957.
3 When this production of *The Boy Friend* came to Hull in 1959, PAL gave a copy of the book to every member of his staff who went to a performance.
4 PAL to EL, 5 May 1958.
5 PAL to JE, 7 March 1958.
6 EL to PAL, 9 February 1958.
7 PAL, script for 'Younger British Poets of Today' (BBC radio, 20 August 1958).
8 AT to author, 13 August 1991.
9 Ibid.
10 PAL to M. Kilroe, 1 August 1958.
11 M. Kilroe to PAL, 3 August 1958.
12 PAL to JE, 24 August 1958.
13 Jean Hartley, *Larkin*, p. 100.
14 Ibid.
15 Ibid.
16 Ibid.
17 SBS.
18 Ibid.
19 PAL to MJ, 29 September 1958.
20 PAL to JE, 17 December 1958.
21 PAL to EL, 4 January 1959.
22 L at 60, p. 40.
23 PAL to EL, 4 January 1959.
24 PAL to JE, 20 February 1959.
25 PAL to EL, 15 July 1959.
26 PAL to JE, 20 February 1959.
27 Ibid., 5 May 1959.
28 Ibid., 13 July 1959.
29 Ibid.
30 Ibid.
31 Maeve Brennan, 'Philip Larkin', p. 31.

32 Ibid.
33 PAL to JE, 2 September 1959.
34 PAL to EL, 5 September 1959.
35 Ibid.
36 Ibid., 10 September 1959.
37 PAL to JE, 13 August 1959.
38 Betty Mackereth to author, 27 February 1992.
39 RW, p. 51.
40 PAL to F. W. Ratcliffe, 8 July 1975.
41 Maeve Brennan, 'Philip Larkin', p. 8.

THIRTY-SEVEN

1 PAL to MJ, 13 October 1959.
2 MJ to author.
3 PAL to AT, 19 March 1970.
4 MB to author, 9 August 1987.
5 Ibid.
6 MB, 'Philip Larkin', p. 6.
7 MB to author, 9 August 1987.
8 MB & PAL, p. 5.
9 MB to author, 9 August 1987.
10 PAL to author.
11 MB, 'Philip Larkin', p. 30.
12 MB, 'I Remember, I Remember', p. 36.
13 Ibid.
14 MB to author, 9 July 1987.
15 PAL to EL, 26 December 1960.
16 Ibid., 13 April 1961.
17 According to AT, it was an Italian documentary film.
18 'A Sharp-Edged View' (interviewer Francis Hill), TES (19 May 1972), p. 19.
19 PAL to JE, 11 April 62.
20 Sir Brynmor Jones to author, 26 November 1987.
21 PAL to JE, 16 August 1962.
22 Jean Hartley, Larkin, p. 113.
23 PAL to EL, 20 March 1960.
24 Ibid., 13 March 1960.
25 Ibid., 20 March 1960.
26 Ibid., July 1960.
27 PAL to MJ, 11 August 1960.
28 Ibid., 15 August 1960.
29 PAL to EL, 6 November 1960.
30 Ibid., 3 September 1960.
31 MB & PAL, pp. 5–6.
32 Ibid.
33 Ibid., pp. 1–2.
34 Ibid., p. 3.

35 PAL to MB, 12 March 1961.
36 Ibid., 16 August 1961.
37 Ibid., 5 August 1964.
38 MB to author, 20 October 1992.
39 MB & PAL, p. 2.
40 Ibid., p. 3.
41 Ibid., p. 4.
42 PAL to MB, 19 June 1964.
43 MB & PAL, p. 4.
44 Ibid.
45 PAL to MB, 6 August 1966.
46 Ibid., 1960; 1966.
47 MB to author, 28 February 1992.
48 MB to author, 27 April 1992.
49 Ibid., 28 February 1992.
50 MB & PAL, p. 11.
51 PAL to MB, 24 April 1961.
52 MB & PAL, p. 1.
53 MB to author, 28 February 1992.
54 MB & PAL, p. 1.

THIRTY-EIGHT

1 MJ to author.
2 Ibid.
3 RW, p. 243.
4 Ibid., pp. 243–4.
5 PAL to BP, 16 January 1961.
6 Ibid., 26 January 1962.
7 Ibid., 8 April 1963.
8 One of their nearest approaches to intimacy came in 1968, when PAL sent BP a photograph of the new library extension.
9 Marion Shaw to author, 27 September 1990.
10 MB & PAL, pp. 15–16.
11 PAL to author.
12 PAL to EL, 1 January 1961.
13 Ibid.
14 PAL to MJ, 1 January 1961.
15 MJ to author.
16 Wilf Richardson to author, 10 August 1987.
17 MB to author, 5 April 1990.
18 PAL's medical notes.
19 PAL to MJ, 12 March 1961.
20 Ibid., 13 March 1961.
21 Ibid., 16 March 1961.
22 Ibid., 17 March 1961.
23 Ibid., 13 April 1961.

24 PAL to JE, 29 March 1961.
25 Ibid.
26 PAL's medical notes.
27 PAL to MB, 10 April 1961.
28 Ibid., 18 April 1961.
29 MB to author, 27 February 1992.
30 PAL to MB, 18 April 1961.
31 PAL to MJ, 7 May 1961.
32 PAL to MB, 8 April 1961.

THIRTY-NINE

1 PAL to MJ, 1 April 1961.
2 PAL to JE, 1 May 1961.
3 BJL; copy is preserved among PAL's papers.
4 PAL to EL, 10 June 1961.
5 PAL to MJ, 7 April 1961.
6 MB & PAL, p. 3.
7 PAL to MJ, 7 April 1962.
8 Ibid., 23 January 1962.
9 The copy is now in the BJL.
10 PAL to JE, 28 December 1961.

FORTY

1 PAL to AT, introducing 'Essential Beauty' on BBC radio, 3 July 1960.
2 MB, 'Philip Larkin', p.14.
3 Ibid.
4 MB, 'I Remember, I Remember', p. 34.
5 John Kenyon, 'Larkin at Hull'.
6 Geoff Hook to author, 15 March 1990.
7 Ibid.
8 Ibid.
9 Ibid.
10 Brenda Moon, 'Building a New Library', *Essays in Memory of Philip Larkin*, pp. 23–4.
11 Ibid., pp. 21–2.
12 Sir Brynmor Jones to author, 26 November 1987.
13 Brenda Moon to author, 13 August 1988.
14 Ibid.
15 MJ to author.
16 PAL to MJ, 6 May 1962.
17 Ibid., 12 August 1962.
18 PAL to MB, 7 August 1962.
19 Ibid.
20 PAL to EL, 14 September 1962.
21 PAL to MJ, 29 September 1962.

22 Ibid.
23 Ibid., 11 February 1962.
24 Ibid., 12 August 1962.

FORTY-ONE

1 See Ian Hamilton, *Robert Lowell: A Biography* (Faber, 1983), pp. 234–5.
2 PAL to RC, 20 February 1962.
3 Ibid.
4 PAL to JE, 20 December 1961.
5 PAL to CM, 2 June 1975.
6 L at 60, p. 38.
7 PAL to CM, 11 April 1962.
8 PAL to EL, 2 February 1963.
9 Faber archive, memo from CM, 22 March 1963.
10 Ibid.
11 L at 60, p. 41.
12 CM to author, 15 May 1987.
13 Ibid.
14 Hazel Holt, *A Lot to Ask*, p. 196.
15 Ibid., p. 192.
16 PAL to BP, 20 May 1963.
17 Ibid., 15 July 1963.
18 Ibid., 14 July 1964.
19 PAL to CM, 15 August 1965.
20 PAL to BP, 17 October 1968.
21 Hazel Holt, *A Lot to Ask*, p. 216.
22 Ibid., p. 248.
23 PAL to BP, 11 September 1968.
24 PAL replying to reader's letter, 24 October 1977.
25 PAL to CM, 9 July 1963.
26 PAL to MB, 16 April 1963.
27 PAL to CM, 3 August 1963.
28 J, p. 11.
29 Ibid., p. 12.
30 Ibid.
31 MB & PAL, pp. 12–13.
32 Ibid., pp. 11–13.
33 PAL to EL, 12 May 1963.
34 MB to author, 9 August 1987.
35 PAL to MB, 27 December 1963.
36 Ibid., 11 July 1963.
37 PAL to JE, 17 July 1963.
38 PAL to MJ, 17 August 1963.
39 Ibid.
40 RW, pp. 101–2.
41 PAL at SCONUL Conference, 1979.
42 PAL to MJ, 25 February 1964.

43 PAL to EL, 18 January 1964.
44 PAL to MJ, 26 December 1964.
45 BJL, Notebook 6.

FORTY-TWO

1 PAL to JE, 17 December 1963.
2 PAL to MB, 2 February 1964.
3 MB & PAL, p. 14.
4 PAL to BP, 20 February 1964.
5 Ibid.
6 PAL to EL, 5 March 1964.
7 PAL to MJ, 3 March 1964.
8 See *Philip Larkin: A Bibliography*, pp. 41–4.
9 PAL to BP, 20 February 1964.
10 PAL to MJ, 3 March 1964.
11 Announced in *The Times* (6 September 1965).
12 PAL to EL, 10 May 1964.
13 PAL to MJ, 11 May 1964.
14 PAL to EL, 10 May 1964.
15 RW, p. 83.
16 Ibid., p. 197.
17 PAL to RC, 1 May 1962.
18 PAL to MJ, 14 March 1967.
19 PAL to Vernon Watkins, 24 January 1966.
20 PAL, 'Betjeman en Bloc', *Listen*, vol. iii, no. 2 (spring 1959).
21 RW, pp. 216–17.
22 PAL to BP, 8 April 1964.
23 PAL to EL, 15 March 1964.
24 PAL to Pamela Kitson, 12 March 1965.
25 PAL to John Hall, 19 September 1985.
26 PAL to Peter du Sautoy, 11 March 1963.
27 PAL to CM, 2 April 1968.
28 Ibid., 29 March 1966.
29 PAL to Patrick Garland, 24 March 1964.
30 PAL to EL, 10 June 1964.
31 Patrick Garland to PAL, 30 June 1964.
32 PAL to Patrick Garland, 7 September 1964.
33 Ibid., 17 December 1964.
34 Patrick Garland to author, 12 August 1989.
35 PAL to EL, 26 April 1964.
36 Ibid.
37 PAL to MB, 1 October 1964.

38 MJ to author.
39 PAL to MJ, 14 June 1964.
40 PAL to MB, 21 June 1964.
41 PAL to MJ, 10 August 1964.
42 Ibid., 14–15 September 1964.
43 PAL to MB, 2 September 1964.
44 PAL to MJ, 14–15 September 1964.
45 RW, p. 43.

FORTY-THREE

1 MB, 'Philip Larkin', p. 14.
2 PAL, interview with John Horder, *Manchester Guardian* (27 May 1965).
3 Alan Fowlie to author, 26 September 1990.
4 PAL to BP, 30 August 1965.
5 PAL to EL, 13 March 1965.
6 BJL, Notebook 7.
7 (added to) PAL to MJ, 14 September 1964.
8 PAL to MJ, 20 August 1965.
9 PAL to MJ, 31 August 1965.
10 Ibid., 18 August 1965.
11 Ibid., 30 August 1965.
12 PAL to MB, 1 August 1961.
13 Ibid., 16 September 1965.
14 PAL to CM, 17 January 1965.
15 RW, pp. 29–30.
16 PAL to Vernon Watkins, 12 October 1965.
17 PAL to EL, 24 October 1965.
18 PAL to CM, 17 January 1966.
19 Elizabeth Jennings, *Spectator* (23 September 1966).
20 PAL to EL, 10 October 1965.
21 Jean Hartley, *Philip Larkin*, p. 125.
22 Ibid.
23 PAL to EL, 10 October 1965.
24 Ibid., 7 December 1965.
25 PAL to Dan Davin, 20 January 1966.
26 Ibid.
27 AT to author, 13 August 1991.
28 PAL to JE, 19 April 1968.
29 Ibid.

FORTY-FOUR

1 PAL to JE, 5 March 1966.
2 PAL to EL, 13 March 1966.
3 PAL to MJ, 5 April 1966.

4 Ibid.
5 PAL to MB, 17 June 1966.
6 Ibid., 1 August 1966.
7 PAL to MJ, 13 October 1966.
8 MB & PAL, p. 1.
9 PAL to MB, 6 August 1966.
10 PAL to MJ, 6 September 1966.
11 Ibid., 18 September 1966.
12 Ibid., 24 October 1966.
13 Ibid.
14 Ibid., 8 October 1966.
15 Ibid., 4 October 1966.
16 Ibid., 30 October 1966.
17 Ibid.
18 Ibid., 15 November 1966.
19 Ibid., 19 November 1966.
20 Ibid., 15 November 1966.
21 Ibid.
22 Ibid., 16 November 1966.
23 Ibid., 20 November 1966.
24 Ibid., 21 November 1966.
25 Ibid., 20 December 1966.
26 Ibid., 27 March 1967.
27 Ibid.
28 Ibid., 26 December 1966.
29 PAL to CM, 13 March 1967.
30 PAL to MJ, 29 March 1967.
31 Ibid.
32 Ibid., 2 April 1967.
33 Ibid., 11 February 1981.
34 BJL, Notebook 7.
35 PAL to MB, 4 April 1961.
36 Ibid., 3 August 1967.
37 PAL, medical notes.
38 Raymond Cass to author, 24 September 1991.
39 PAL to EL, 12 November 1967.
40 PAL to MJ, 15 June 1966.
41 Ibid., 20 September 1967.
42 Ibid., 19 September 1967.
43 PAL to MB, 16 September 1967.
44 Ibid., 20 August 1967.

FORTY-FIVE

1 PAL to BP, quoted in A Lot to Ask, Hazel Holt (1990), p. 226.
2 Philip Brown to author, 17 October 1991.
3 PAL to JE, 14 April 1969.
4 PAL to Richard Murphy, 19 August 1977.

5 PAL to CM, 15 January 1974.
6 Ibid.
7 Charles Osborne to author, 6 September 1987.
8 C. Day-Lewis to PAL, 3 July 1967.
9 PAL, 'A Faint Sense of Failure', lecture given to SCONUL in Hull in 1980.
10 PAL to C. Day-Lewis, 2 January 1969.
11 PAL, 'A Faint Sense of Failure'.
12 Ibid.
13 PAL to EL, 2 June 1968.
14 PAL, text of speech given at Hull degree ceremony, 2 May 1970.
15 PAL to John Betjeman, 5 June 1977.
16 PAL to author.
17 L at 60, p. 53.
18 PAL to CM, 1 April 1969.
19 PAL, 'A Faint Sense of Failure'.
20 RW, p. 43.
21 PAL to John Betjeman, 5 May 1977.
22 PAL to Alan Ross, 19 October 1977.
23 Ibid.
24 Blake Morrison to author, 9 October 1987.
25 Charles Osborne to author, 6 September 1987.
26 Jonathan Barker to author, 3 September 1986.
27 PAL to EL, 9 June 1968.
28 PAL to MJ, 12 May 1968.
29 Ibid., 10 August 1968.
30 MJ to author, 19 May 1991.
31 PAL to EL, 21 January 1968.
32 Ibid.
33 Ibid., 8 December 1968.
34 PAL to MJ, 4 August, 1968.
35 Ibid.
36 BJL, Holiday Diary for 1968.
37 Ibid.
38 PAL to Donald Mitchell, 20 November 1968.
39 Faber archive, memo from Donald Mitchell, 26 November 1968.
40 PAL to Donald Mitchell, 28 November 1968.
41 Ibid., 9 December 1968.
42 Ibid.
43 PAL to CM, 27 November 1968.
44 PAL to MJ, 23 August 1968.
45 PAL to EL, 22 September 1968.
46 PAL to Peter du Sautoy, 18 February

1969.
7 Ibid.
8 George Hartley to CM, 2 March 1969.
9 PAL to MJ, 26 December 1968.

FORTY-SIX

1 RW, p. 74.
2 Ibid., p. 52.
3 Ibid.
4 PAL to MJ, 26 March 1969.
5 PAL to the Vice-Chancellor of Queen's University, Belfast, 28 November 1968.
6 PAL to MJ, 26 March 1969.
7 PAL to BP, 18 March 1969.
8 MB, 'Philip Larkin', p. 17.
9 Ibid.
10 PAL to BP, 3 October 1967.
11 John Kenyon, 'Larkin at Hull'.
12 Ibid.
13 PAL, Quinquennial Report for the Library Committee, 1978.
14 Ibid.
15 PAL to MB, 23 July 1969.
16 PAL to MJ, 7 August 1969.
17 BJL, Holiday Diary for 1969.
18 Ibid.
19 Ibid.
20 PAL to MB, 4 September 1969.
21 BJL, Holiday Diary for 1969.
22 PAL to MB, 16 October 1970.
23 PAL to JE, 15 November 1969.
24 PAL to Rosemary Goad, 11 January 1970.
25 L at 60, pp. 44–5.
26 Faber archive.
27 RW, p. 197.
28 AWJ, p. 15.
29 Ibid.
30 Ibid., p. 16.
31 Ibid., p. 19.
32 Ibid., p. 20.
33 Ibid., p. 21.
34 Ibid.
35 Ibid., p. 22.
36 Ibid., p. 23.
37 Ibid.
38 Ibid., p. 27.
39 Ibid., p. 29.
40 Ibid.
41 Ibid., p. 19

42 Ibid., pp. 28–9.
43 Ibid., p. 36.
44 Ibid., p. 156.
45 Ibid., p. 51.
46 Ibid., p. 54.
47 Ibid., p. 62.
48 Ibid., p. 139.
49 Ibid., p. 85.
50 Ibid., p. 176.
51 Ibid., p. 200.
52 Ibid., p. 41.
53 Ibid., p. 58.
54 Ibid., p. 62.
55 Ibid., p. 96.
56 Ibid., p. 126.
57 Ibid., p. 97.
58 Ibid., p. 112.
59 Ibid., p. 19.
60 Ibid., p. 24.
61 Ibid.
62 Ibid., p. 87.
63 Tom Paulin, *Minotaur* (Faber, 1992), p. 243.
64 John White, *Philip Larkin: The Man and his Work*, p. 41.
65 Tom Paulin, *Minotaur*, p. 243.
66 AWJ, p. 23.
67 Ibid., p. 21.
68 Ibid., p. 156.
69 Review by Wilfrid Mellers, *Musical Times* (May 1970).
70 Review by Charles Fox, *New Statesman* (13 February 1970).
71 PAL to EL, 20 February 1970.
72 AWJ, Second Edition (1984) p. 29.
73 Ibid.
74 PAL to Campbell Burnap, 29 December 1984.
75 AWJ, p. 31.

FORTY-SEVEN

1 BJL, Holiday Diary for 1970.
2 Ibid.
3 Ibid.
4 PAL to MJ, 22 August 1970.
5 Ibid.
6 PAL to MB, 17 September 1970.
7 Ibid.
8 BJL, unpublished essay about Oxford, hereafter known as 'Oxford'.

9 A. L. Rowse to author, 4 February
 1988.
10 Ibid.
11 Ibid.
12 PAL to MB, 30 October 1970.
13 BJL, 'Oxford'.
14 Ibid.
15 PAL to MB, 19 October 1970.
16 Ibid., 18 September 1970.
17 Ibid., 11 October 1970.
18 BJL, 'Oxford'.
19 Ibid.
20 PAL to JE, 16 January 1971.
21 PAL to MB, 19 November 1971.
22 Ibid., 5 December 1971.
23 MJ to author.
24 PAL to Garnet Rees, 9 November 1970.
25 PAL to Dan Davin, 2 April 1971.
26 RW, p. 73.
27 PAL to BP, 3 February 1970.
28 Ibid., 29 May 1971.
29 Ibid.
30 PAL to MJ, 3 August 1971.
31 PAL to JE, 25 September 1971.
32 PAL to EL, 28 March 1971.
33 Ibid.
34 MB & PAL, p. 18.
35 Ibid.
36 Ibid.
37 MB to author, 26 February 1992.
38 Tom Paulin to author, 14 August 1990.
39 PAL to JE, 22 September 1971.
40 Don Roy to author, 27 May 1990.
41 PAL to MJ, 3 August 1971.
42 PAL to JE, 25 September 1971.
43 PAL to RC, 16 March 1971.
44 PAL to Colin Gunner, 6 September
 1971.
45 PAL to KA, 8 April 1969.
46 PAL to JE, 12 May 1970.
47 PAL to C. B. Cox, 23 February 1972.
48 PAL to EL, 22 March 1970.
49 Sources for light verses: to AT 9
 February 1977; RC 19 June 1970; to
 MJ 3 November 1970.
50 KA to author, 3 August 1987.
51 PAL to MJ, 1 August 1971.
52 Ibid., 20 July 1971.
53 PAL to MB, 16 January 1971.
54 Ibid., 21 July 1971.

FORTY-EIGHT

1 BJL, Holiday Diary for 1971.
2 Ibid.
3 Ibid.
4 Ibid.
5 PAL to MJ, 22 August 1971.
6 Ibid., 26 September 1971.
7 BJL, Norton Smith papers.
8 PAL to Terence Kilmartin, 7 December
 1971.
9 PAL to MB, 25 December 1966.
10 PAL to EL, 4 November 1971.
11 Ibid.
12 PAL's medical notes.
13 PAL to JE, 4 November 1971.
14 PAL to EL, 5 December 1971.
15 Ibid., 14 November 1971.
16 Ibid., 2 January 1972.
17 PAL to Robert Jackson, 1972.
18 PAL to EL, 25 January 1972.
19 PAL to C. B. Cox, 3 August 1972.
20 PAL to JE, 11 June 1973.
21 PAL to EL, 31 March 1974.

FORTY-NINE

1 PAL to JE, 11 May 1972.
2 PAL to EL, 24 May 1972.
3 PAL to P. G. Walker, 28 June 1972.
4 PAL to EL, 24 May 1972.
5 Ibid.
6 PAL to AT, 13 June 1972.
7 PAL to JE, 16 August 1972.
8 PAL to KA, 11 August 1972.
9 PAL to MB, 19 August 1972.
10 MB & PAL, pp. 19–20.
11 BJL, Holiday Diary for 1972.
12 Ibid.
13 Ibid.
14 PAL to JE, 5 December 1972.
15 PAL to BCB, 29 November 1972.
16 CM to author, 7 December 1992.
17 Ibid., 6 February 1973.
18 PAL to M. Shirley, 7 February 1973.
19 PAL to CM, 15 January 1973.
20 Robert Lowell to Randall Jarrell, 11
 October 1957. (See Ian Hamilton,
 Robert Lowell.)
21 Robert Lowell to Elizabeth Bishop,
 3 October 1957.

22 Quoted in Ian Hamilton, *Robert Lowell*.
23 MJ to author.
24 PAL to EL, 2 February 1973.
25 Robert Lowell to Elizabeth Bishop, 30 April 1973.
26 Robert Lowell to PAL, 12 June 1974.
27 PAL to CM, 10 May 1973.
28 PAL to the President of St John's College, Oxford, 8 May 1973.
29 PAL to MB, 1 July 1973.
30 PAL to David Timms, 30 January 1973.
31 PAL to JE, 11 June 1973.
32 OBTCEV, pp. v–vi.
33 John Gross, summarizing Davie, in L at 60, p. 82.
34 Ibid., p. 81.
35 PAL to A. L. Miller, 14 December 1973.
36 RW, p. 73.
37 PAL to A. L. Miller, 14 December 1973.
38 PAL to JE, 8 April 1973.
39 PAL to M. Bell, 14 May 1973.
40 PAL to KA, 1 December 1976; other versions were sent to other friends, among them RC and AT.
41 PAL to John Frazer, 26 April 1973.
42 Ibid.
43 PAL to JE, 11 June 1982.
44 PAL to A. L. Miller, 14 December 1973.
45 PAL to AT, 11 April 1973.
46 PAL to EL, 25 March 1973.
47 PAL to C. B. Cox, 5 July 1973.
48 PAL to EL, 8 April 1973.
49 BJL, text of PAL's speech at the Dorchester Hotel London, May 1973.
50 PAL to J. Norton Smith, 14 April 1974.

FIFTY

1 PAL to CM, 1 June 1973.
2 Ibid., 15 June 1973.
3 Ibid., 15 March 1982.
4 PAL to Matthew Evans, 5 October 1973.
5 Ibid., 7 December 1973.
6 PAL to CM, 7 January 1974.
7 Ibid, 28 December 1973.
8 Ibid, 7 January 1974.
9 Stephen Spender to author,

22 December 1989.
10 PAL to AT, 4 October 1973.
11 PAL to JE, 9 November 1973.
12 MJ to author.
13 PAL to AT, 27 November 1974.
14 PAL to CM, 29 October 1973.
15 PAL to JW, 8 November 1973.
16 Ibid.
17 PAL to Society of Authors, 7 December 1973.
18 PAL to Robert Giroux, 14 April 1983.
19 PAL to EL, 25 May 1974.
20 John Kenyon, 'Larkin At Hull'.
21 PAL to JE, 17 February 1974.
22 PAL to EL, 27 June 1974.
23 Jean Hartley, *Philip Larkin*, p. 172.
24 PAL to EL, 3 November 1974.
25 Ibid.
26 Ibid., 22 July 1974.
27 PAL to Henri Poulet, 25 November 1976.
28 PAL to EL, 30 June 1974.
29 PAL to BP, 18 November 1961.
30 PAL to Harry Chambers, 27 January 1974.
31 PAL to CM, 9 May 1974.
32 MB & PAL, p. 20.
33 PAL to CM, 21 February 1974.
34 PAL to author.
35 John Betjeman to CM, 5 June 1974.
36 PAL to AT, 21 May 1974.
37 PAL to John Sparrow, 6 June 1974.
38 PAL to author.
39 PAL to Charles Osborne, 29 December 1974.
40 PAL to Rob Watt, 16 October 1974.
41 PAL to Nicholas Zurbrugge, December 1974.
42 PAL to BP, 22 January 1975.
43 PAL to JE, 2 January 1975.
44 MB to author, 28 April 1992.
45 Ibid., 20 October 1992.
46 Ibid.

FIFTY-ONE

1 Arthur Terry to author, 14 June 1986.
2 PAL, memo to University of Hull catering officer, 23 December 1971.
3 MB, 'Philip Larkin', p. 14.
4 Phil Bacon to author, 3 December 1988.

5 MJ to author.
6 Hazel Holt, *A Lot to Ask*, p. 59.
7 BP, diary, 30 July 1976 (quoted in Hazel Holt, *A Lot to Ask*).
8 Betty Mackereth to author, 12 February 1992.
9 Ibid.
10 Ibid., 3 December 1988.
11 Ibid.
12 Ibid., and 1 July 1992.
13 PAL to EL, 5 October 1969.
14 MB & PAL, p. 24.
15 PAL to MB, 31 December 1975.
16 PAL to MB, 7 August 1975.
17 MB & PAL, p. 23.
18 Betty Mackereth to author, 1 July 1992.
19 MB & PAL, p. 23.
20 MB to author, 4 March 1992.

FIFTY-TWO

1 Betty Mackereth to author, 3 December 1988.
2 Ibid.
3 PAL to JE, 28 November 1975.
4 PAL to Harry Hoff, 27 November 1975.
5 PAL to EL, 21 November 1975.
6 Charles Osborne to author, 6 September 1987.
7 PAL to Keith Jeffrey, 24 November 1975.
8 PAL to Colin Gunner, 10 December 1975.
9 PAL to Peter du Sautoy, 30 March 1976.
10 PAL to John Betjeman, 24 February 1976.
11 RW, p. 87.
12 Ibid.
13 Ibid.
14 Ibid., p. 92.
15 PAL to JE, 4 May 1976.
16 Ibid.
17 PAL to George Hartley, 3 March 1976.
18 PAL to BCB, 10 July 1976.
19 PAL to JE, 22 June 1976.
20 PAL to Colin Gunner, 16 June 1974.
21 Ibid., 19 June 1984.
22 Ibid., 22 May 1984.
23 PAL to John Wain, 1 June 1976.

24 PAL to RC, 21 September 1976.
25 Ibid. See Chapter 60, note 1.
26 Ibid.
27 PAL to author.
28 PAL to CM, 2 January 1971.
29 BP to PAL, 4 March 1977.
30 PAL to BP, 22 February 1977.
31 Ibid., 20 September 1977.
32 PAL to Tom Maschler, 2 June 1981.
33 Tom Maschler to PAL, 5 June 1981.
34 PAL to Tom Maschler, 7 June 1981.
35 PAL to Chairman of Hull City Council, 11 October 1977.
36 PAL to author.
37 MJ to author.
38 PAL to Martin Goff, 21 February 1977.
39 BJL, Holiday Diary for 1977.
40 RW, p. 94.
41 Ibid.
42 Martin Goff to author, 14 March 1992.
43 RW, p. 95.
44 Ibid.
45 PAL to RC, 16 December 1977.
46 PAL to BCB, 16 February 1977.
47 BJL, autobiographical fragment.
48 PAL to JE, 24 October 1977.
49 PAL to CM, 19 September 1977.
50 PAL to WD, 13 September 1977.
51 PAL to KA, 24 October 1977.
52 PAL to Caroline Blackwood, 19 September 1977.
53 PAL to JE, 27 October 1975.
54 PAL to EL, 19 December 1971.
55 AT to author, 9 September 1990.
56 Reported by Garnet Rees to author, 11 November 1988.
57 PAL to Ray Brett, 25 November 1977.
58 PAL to J. Norton Smith, 5 December 1977.
59 PAL to WD, 13 December 1977.
60 Rosemary Parry to author, 8 July 1992.
61 MJ to author.
62 MB to author, 20 September 1991.
63 Marion Shaw to author, 5 March 1992.

FIFTY-THREE

1 PAL to MJ, 27 March 1967.
2 PAL to CM, 2 March 1978.
3 Ibid.
4 Ibid.

5 PAL to JE, 30 April 1978.
6 Ibid.
7 MB to author, 20 September 1991.
8 MB & PAL, p. 27.
9 Ibid., p. 28.
10 PAL to MB, 17 March 1978.
11 MB & PAL, p. 28.
12 Ibid.
13 Ibid.
14 Ibid., p. 29.
15 MB to author, 26 February 1992.
16 Ibid., 20 June 1991.
17 RW, pp. 23–4.
18 PAL to BCB, 20 September 1978.
19 PAL to KA, 19 September 1978.
20 PAL to RC, 21 September 1978.
21 PAL to KA, 11 April 1979.
22 PAL to JE, 10 April 1979.
23 PAL to KA, 3 March 1978.
24 Ibid., 23 September 1979.
25 Alan Fowlie to author, 20 September 1990.
26 Betty Mackereth to author, 3 December 1988.
27 MJ to author.
28 PAL to Julian Barnes, 20 April 1985.

FIFTY-FOUR

1 RW, p. 254.
2 Ibid., p. 259.
3 Ibid., p. 260.
4 Ibid., p. 262.
5 Ibid.
6 Ibid., p. 264.
7 Ibid., p. 265.
8 PAL to EL, 12 February 1975.
9 PAL to Graham Lord, 8 August 1979.
10 RW, p.52.
11 BJL, Holiday Diary for 1979.
12 RW, p. 54.
13 Miriam Gross to author, 26 October 1991.
14 PAL to BCB, 3 December 1979.
15 BCB, *Philip Larkin: A Bibliography* (Faber, 1979), p. 11.
16 Ibid., p. 12.
17 PAL to JE, 15 January 1980.
18 PAL to AT, 21 July 1980.
19 Robert Smith, *Ariel* (1971).
20 PAL to Hazel Holt, 29 April 1984.

21 PAL to Kathleen Hibbert, 21 June 1983.
22 PAL to KA, 20 March 1980.
23 PAL to author.
24 PAL to JE, 15 March 1980.
25 PAL to BCB, 16 July 1980.
26 Brenda Moon to author, 1 April 1989.
27 PAL to author.
28 PAL to J. Norton Smith, 1 June 1976.
29 PAL to BCB, 20 October 1979.
30 PAL to J. Norton Smith, 1 June 1976.
31 PAL to KA, 26 June 1980.
32 PAL to Colin Gunner, 18 March 1982.
33 RW, p. 52.
34 BJL, text of PAL's speech, delivered 7 May 1980.
35 PAL to JE, 18 September 1980.
36 PAL to BCB, 15 December 1980.
37 The prize-winning poem was 'The Letter', by Andrew Motion.
38 BJL, note to Ted Hughes, December 1980.

FIFTY-FIVE

1 PAL to JE, 18 September 1980.
2 PAL to BCB, 15 December 1980.
3 RW, p. 276.
4 PAL to A. N. Wilson, 11 December 1981.
5 MJ to author.
6 Brenda Moon to author, 1 April 1989.
7 PAL to A. N. Wilson, 10 July 1983.
8 PAL to author.
9 Father Francis Bown to author, 26 October 1989.
10 Ibid.
11 PAL to A. N. Wilson, 9 October 1983.
12 Father Francis Bown to author, 26 October 1989.
13 PAL to author.
14 PAL to JE, 15 February 1981.
15 Ibid.
16 PAL to Douglas Dunn, 19 March 1981.
17 PAL to author.
18 RW, p. 266.
19 PAL, *The Poetry Library of the Arts Council of Great Britain*, Short Catalogue (Arts Council, 1981), pp. 3–4.
20 CP, p. 203.

21 Anthony Hedges to author, 9 December 1988.
22 Ibid.
23 PAL to KA, 25 June 1975.
24 PAL to Anthony Hedges, 1 December 1981.
25 Ibid.
26 PAL to Jonathan Barker, 25 February 1983.
27 Blake Morrison to author, 12 December 1989.
28 PAL to A. N. Wilson, 1 December 1981.
29 PAL to Blake Morrison, 29 August 1981.
30 PAL to A. N. Wilson, 1 December 1981.
31 PAL to JE, 11 May 1981.
32 Barbara Everett to author, 14 August 1991.
33 PAL to KA, 18 September 1982.
34 Ibid., 23 February 1982.
35 RW, p. 281.
36 PAL to author.
37 PAL to CM, 28 January 1982.
38 PAL to Robert Phillips, 2 March 1982.
39 RW, p. 58.
40 Ibid.
41 Ibid., p. 74.
42 Ibid., p. 66.
43 AT to CM, 3 December 1979.
44 PAL to KA, 16 January 1981.
45 Noel Hughes to author, 14 August 1992.
46 PAL to Noel Hughes, 10 May 1981.
47 Noel Hughes to author, 18 August 1992.
48 PAL to Colin Gunner, 30 May 1982.
49 PAL to JE, 27 April 1982.
50 PAL to CM, 1 March 1982.
51 AT to author, 9 September 1990.
52 Ann Thwaite, diary entry, 30 March 1982.
53 PAL to CM, 6 May 1982 (letter).
54 PAL to Melvyn Bragg, 19 December 1977.
55 PAL to Andrew Snell, 28 April 1981.
56 PAL to CM, 7 April 1982.
57 PAL to Julian Barnes, 6 June 1982.
58 PAL to JE, 6 June 1982.
59 PAL to Jamie Muir, 10 June 1982.
60 PAL to JE, 6 June 1982.
61 L at 60, p. 15.
62 PAL to JE, 6 June 1982.
63 Ibid., 27 April 1982.
64 Ibid., 6 June 1982.

FIFTY-SIX

1 PAL to Colin Gunner, 15 June 1982.
2 Eddie Dawes to author, 10 September 1989.
3 Quoted in Jean Hartley, *Philip Larkin*, p. 195.
4 PAL to BCB, 26 September 1982.
5 PAL to Blake Morrison, 4 November 1982.
6 PAL to author.
7 PAL to Julian Barnes, 27 September 1985.
8 PAL to author.
9 Ibid.
10 Isaiah Berlin to author, 16 October 1989.
11 PAL to JE, 31 October 1982.
12 PAL to author.
13 PAL to author, 9 May 1983 (letter).
14 PAL to MJ, 13 October 1982.
15 PAL to BCB, 16 July 1983.
16 PAL to JE, 1 May 1983.
17 Ibid.
18 Ibid., 17 May 1983.
19 Ibid.
20 Ibid.
21 Ibid., 9 June 1983.
22 PAL to BCB, 10 July 1983.
23 PAL to Colin Gunner, 2 August 1983.
24 PAL to BCB, 10 July 1983.
25 PAL to author, 19 July 1983 (letter).
26 PAL to BCB, 10 July 1983.
27 PAL to BCB, 'Birthday of Poet Laureate'/1983.
28 CM to AT, 28 March 1974.
29 PAL to Blake Morrison, 18 February 1982.
30 RW, p. 13.
31 PAL to Blake Morrison, 22 October 1982.
32 PAL to CM, 19 November 1982.
33 PAL to AT, 11 December 1967.
34 PAL to Terence Kilmartin, 13 January 1972.

35 Blake Morrison to author, 9 March
   1990.
36 RW, p. 11.
37 Ibid.
38 Ibid., p. 12.
39 MJ to author.
40 Blake Morrison to author, 9 March
   1990.
41 In author's copy.
42 PAL to CM, 23 January 1984.

FIFTY-SEVEN

1 PAL to author.
2 PAL to CM, 7 November 1983.
3 PAL to Fay Godwin, 11 November
   1983.
4 JE to author, 9 August 1991.
5 PAL to Fay Godwin, 16 September
   1984.
6 PAL to CM, 14 January 1984.
7 PAL to Christopher Ricks, 29 March
   1984.
8 PAL to BCB, 11 March 1984.
9 Ibid., 5 June 1984.
10 Ibid.
11 PAL to author.
12 AWJ, p. 29.
13 PAL to Campbell Burnap, 29 December
   1983.
14 PAL to Ted Tarling, 7 August 1984.
15 PAL to CM, 6 September 1984.
16 PAL to JE, 1 February 1984.
17 PAL to author, 21 February 1984.
18 PAL to JE, 5 April 1984.
19 PAL to MJ, 2 April 1984.
20 Ibid., 3 April 1984.
21 PAL to author.
22 MJ to author.
23 PAL to CM, 18 November 1983.
24 PAL to author, 10 June 1984 (letter).
25 PAL to BCB, 8 July 1984.
26 PAL to John Wain, 12 October 1984.
27 PAL to BCB, 8 July 1984.
28 Ibid.
29 PAL to author.
30 Betty Mackereth to author, 3 December
   1988.
31 MJ to author.
32 Humphrey Ocean to author, 31 July
   1987.

33 Ibid.
34 Ibid.
35 Ibid.
36 MJ to author.
37 Humphrey Ocean to author, 31 July
   1987.
38 Ibid.
39 Jean Hartley, *Philip Larkin*, p. 172.
40 PAL to JE, 30 July 1984.
41 Humphrey Ocean to author, 31 July
   1987.
42 Ibid.
43 Ibid.
44 KA, *Memoirs*, p. 57.
45 PAL to JE, 2 July 1984.
46 RW, p. 75.
47 PAL to BM, 11 January 1985.
48 PAL to Harrison Boyle, 11 September
   1985.
49 PAL to Elizabeth Cavendish, 31 July
   1985.
50 PAL to Colin Gunner, 9 September
   1984.
51 PAL to author.
52 KA to AM, 24 November 1986.
53 Charles Osborne to author,
   6 September 1987.
54 PAL to Colin Gunner, 9 December
   1984.
55 Ibid.
56 PAL to KA, 27 December 1984.
57 Ibid.

FIFTY-EIGHT

1 PAL to Joan Barton, 8 January 1985.
2 PAL to KA, 3 August 1985.
3 PAL to Colin Gunner, 15 September
   1984.
4 Ibid., 26 December 1984.
5 PAL to JE, 13 January 1985.
6 PAL to KA, 27 December 1984.
7 PAL to Patrick Garland, (no date)/
   January 1985.
8 PAL to JE, 6 September 1985.
9 Ibid.
10 PAL to KA, 27 December 1984.
11 PAL to BCB, 8 July 1985.
12 Ibid., 15 August 1985.
13 PAL to Colin Gunner, 9 April 1985.
14 Ibid.

15 PAL, medical notes.
16 PAL to author.
17 PAL to JE, 15 August 1985.
18 PAL, medical notes.
19 PAL to CM, 12 April 1985.
20 PAL to JE, 12 May 1985.
21 PAL to CM, 26 May 1985.
22 MB & PAL, p. 29.
23 Ibid., p. 30.
24 Ibid., p. 31.
25 MJ to author.
26 PAL, medical notes.
27 Wilf Richardson to author, 13 August 1987.
28 MB & PAL, p. 33.
29 Ibid.
30 Ibid.
31 KA to author, 3 August 1987.
32 MB & PAL, p. 32.
33 MJ to author.
34 PAL to author.
35 PAL, medical notes.

FIFTY-NINE

1 PAL, medical notes.
2 PAL to BCB, 15 August 1985.
3 PAL to JE, 16 July 1985.
4 Ibid.
5 Ibid., 31 July 1985.
6 PAL to BCB, 21 April 1985.
7 PAL to John Wain, 10 August 1985.
8 PAL to JE, 6 September 1985.
9 PAL to Anthony Powell, 7 August 1985.
10 PAL to CM, 1 October 1985.
11 PAL, obituary for Eric Walter White, Poetry Society Bulletin (summer 1985).
12 PAL to author, 28 October 1985 (letter).

13 Ibid., 21 November 1985 (letter).
14 PAL to MB, 14 November 1985.
15 MB to author, 3 February 1992.
16 MB & PAL, p. 38.
17 PAL to PS, 10 December 1953.
18 PAL to W. G. Runciman, 26 December 1978.
19 PAL, *Observer* (24 April 1983).
20 PAL to John Wain, 10 January 1985.
21 MJ to author.
22 Virginia Peace to author, 9 August 1987.
23 Betty Mackereth to author, 9 February 1992.
24 Mike Bowen to author, 10 August 1991.
25 John Mallet to author, 12 October 1987.

SIXTY

1 Betty Mackereth to author, 9 February 1992. When 'boiling down' his diaries for possible publication in 1976, Larkin destroyed some of the earliest volumes. The thirty-odd that remained were the volumes shredded by Betty Mackereth. There is no trace of any surviving 'boiled down' material: it seems that when Larkin abandoned his plans to publish an edited diary, he destroyed this too.
2 Peter Levi, *Daily Telegraph* (18 December 1985).
3 Ibid.
4 *The Times* (16 February 1985).
5 KA, memorial address, 9 December 1985.
6 MJ to author.
7 RW, p. 48.

INDEX